HISTORY

OF THE

CITY OF BROOKLYN,

N. Y.

VOLUME I.

THE VECHTE-CORTELYOU HOUSE, AT GOWANUS.

(Fifth Avenue, near Fourth Street)

Frontispiece.

A

HISTORY

OF THE

CITY OF BROOKLYN.

INCLUDING

THE OLD TOWN AND VILLAGE OF BROOKLYN,

THE TOWN OF BUSHWICK,

AND

THE VILLAGE AND CITY OF WILLIAMSBURGH.

BY

HENRY R. STILES.

IN TWO VOLUMES.

VOL. I.

BROOKLYN, N. Y.:
PUBLISHED BY SUBSCRIPTION.
1867.

J. G. SHEA,
Stereotyper and Electrotyper

MUNSELL, ALBANY,
Printer.

J. P. DAVIS & SPEER,
Engravers.

JOHN MOONEY,
Cut-Printer.

THOMAS HOGAN,
Artist.

TO

THE CITIZENS

OF THE

CITY OF BROOKLYN,

AND TO ALL

WHOSE INTEREST IN HER PRESENT PROSPERITY MAY LEAD THEM TO LOOK WITH KINDLY FAVOR UPON THIS

RECORD OF HER PAST,

These Pages

ARE RESPECTFULLY DEDICATED.

ET PATRIBUS ET POSTERITATI.

PREFACE.

IN the year 1824, GABRIEL FURMAN, a native of the town, published a little volume which he modestly entitled "Notes on the History of Brooklyn," and which, for that day, possessed great merit as a local history. After him, in the form of occasional contributions to magazines and newspapers, came the numerous productions of that worthy citizen, Gen. JEREMIAH JOHNSON, himself a connecting link between Brooklyn's Past and Present. BENJAMIN THOMPSON, the historian of Long Island, in 1843, and the Rev. NATHANIEL S. PRIME, his successor in the same historic field, in 1845, each gave interesting but necessarily brief *résumés* of Brooklyn history; while THOS. P. TEALE'S somewhat scanty "Chronicles" in Spooner's Directory for 1848, and J. T. BAILEY'S "Historical Sketch," in 1840, close the list of what may properly be called histories of this Town and City. The Town of Bushwick and the City of Williamsburgh have had their histories outlined in a similar manner, by Thompson, Prime and Johnson; and by Mr. C. S. SCHROEDER, in the *Long Island Family Circle*, in 1852; the only work, however, which can pretend to the dignity of a volume, being the "History of Williamsburgh," published by Mr. SAMUEL REYNOLDS, in 1852, as an adjunct to the Williamsburgh Directory of that year. These were the pioneer historians of Brooklyn history, to whose efforts all honor is due.

The present history had its inception, in the Fall of 1859, in a casual suggestion of my friend Mr. JAMES S. LORING, of this city. From that time to the present, it has been prosecuted with persistency of purpose, although with frequent interruptions, and always amid circumstances least favorable to literary composition. My purpose has been to present to my fellow-citizens of Brooklyn a full and reliable history of the city of their residence, from its early humble beginnings to its present position as the third city of the American Union. Whatever was valuable in the works of my predecessors I have incorporated in these pages; and, whatever of interest could be gleaned, from sources both old and new, I have spared neither time, thought nor labor to gather for the illustration and adornment of my subject. Yet, looking over the pages of this now completed volume, I can see, as only an author can, its deficiencies, and regret that it comes so far short of my ideal of what such a history should be.

There remains, then, but the pleasant duty of acknowledging my obligations to those friends who have aided me in my self-imposed task. To John G. Shea, LL.D., of New York City, for kindness of which his modesty would forbid mention, but without which this history might never have seen the light; to Mr. J. Carson Brevoort, of Brooklyn, for his numerous and delicately rendered services, in the way of encouragement, of valuable suggestion and contribution, by pen and pencil; to Hon. Teunis G. Bergen, of Bay Ridge, L. I., whose aid—always so freely given—is indispensable to any one who undertakes to write Kings County history; to Dr. E. B. O'Callaghan, the accomplished custodian of our State archives at Albany, for the inestimable favors he has conferred by the translation of such original documents as I needed in my work, and to many others, whose names are elsewhere particularly mentioned, I return my sincere thanks. From all, indeed, to whom I have applied, either for materials or facilities of research, I have received the most uniform and flattering courtesy.

The illustrations to this volume, which have been selected with a view to preserve the fast-fading remembrance of the characteristic scenes and historic places of "Old Brooklyn," were all carefully drawn (during the summer of 1867), under my personal supervision, from the originals (where such yet exist), or from well-authenticated sketches. Their fidelity cannot be questioned, and they reflect great credit upon the artist, Mr. Thomas Hogan, a resident of this city, whose graceful pencil has gained new power from his deep interest in what has been to him, as to myself, "a labor of love."

HENRY R. STILES, M.D.

Brooklyn, N. Y., July 1st, 1867.

LIST OF ILLUSTRATIONS

TO THE FIRST VOLUME.

* From a Sketch by Miss Elizabeth Sleight, in 1808.

TABLE OF CONTENTS.

CHAPTER I.

FROM THE DISCOVERY OF MANHATTAN ISLAND TO THE INCORPORATION OF THE VILLAGE OF BREUCKELEN, 1609-1646.

CHAPTER II.

The Early Settlers and Patents of Breuckelen.

CHAPTER III.

The Civil History of Breuckelen, 1646–1664.

CHAPTER IV.

Ecclesiastical History of Breuckelen, 1628–1664.

CHAPTER V.

Civil History of Breuckelen, 1664–1674.

CHAPTER VI.

Ecclesiastical History of Breuckelen, 1664–1803.

CHAPTER VII.

CIVIL HISTORY OF BROOKLAND, 1675–1775.

CHAPTER VIII.

THE DOMESTIC HISTORY OF THE PEOPLE, FROM THE SETTLEMENT OF THE COUNTRY TO THE REVOLUTIONARY PERIOD,

CHAPTER IX.

BROOKLYN DURING THE REVOLUTION.

CHAPTER X.

FROM THE CLOSE OF THE REVOLUTION TO "THE WAR OF 1812."

CHAPTER XI.

BROOKLYN'S SHARE IN "THE WAR OF 1812."

HISTORY OF BROOKLYN.

CHAPTER I.

1609–1646.

FROM THE DISCOVERY OF MANHATTAN ISLAND TO THE INCORPORATION OF THE VILLAGE OF BROOKLYN.

THE discovery of Manhattan Island by Henry Hudson necessarily forms the initial point of this history. For, even if the "most beautiful lake" said to have been penetrated by Verazzano in 1524, and which he described in glowing colors to his Royal Master the King of France, was indeed the bay of New York, yet his visit, according to his own account, was little else than a traveller's hurried glimpse and totally unproductive of results, either in respect to exploration or occupation. But when, on the evening of the 11th of September, 1609, the "Half Moon" of Amsterdam came to anchor at the mouth of the "Great River of the Mountains," then, undoubtedly, the eyes of white men rested for the first time upon the Isle of "Mannahata," the green shores of "Scheyichbi," or New Jersey, and the forest-crowned "Ihpetonga," or "Heights" of the present city of Brooklyn. Then, all this region, now teeming with population and thrilling with the ceaseless pulse of civilized life, was wrapped in the lethargic slumber of primeval nature. The surrounding shores, where a forest of shipping pours its constantly accumulating treasures at the feet of the Empire City of the Western World, were fringed with magnificent forests gorgeous with autumnal hues. To the wondering mariners the land seemed "as pleasant with grass, and flowers, and goodly trees, as ever they had seen;"

and the savage inhabitants who thronged around in canoes curiously fashioned "from single hollowed trees," were comely in form and feature, and friendly in disposition. From its mouth to the head of tide-water, Hudson and his companions explored the noble river which stretched northward before them, spending a month of pleasant dalliance and adventure amid the varied and picturesque scenery of these virgin wilds, which they enthusiastically pronounced to be "as fine a land as the foot of man can tread upon." Though disappointed in finding that the Great River was not the long-sought and much-desired passage to the Eastern Seas, they were deeply impressed with the wonderful and apparently illimitable resources of the country which it traversed, and fully appreciated the value of their discovery to the commercial interests of their native land. The United Netherlands, whose flag they first displayed amid these solitudes, had just attained to the rank of an independent nation. Their energy and heroic persistence in waging a forty years' war with Spain had, at last, wrung from the Spanish monarch a twelve years' truce, which was in fact a recognition of their sovereignty and independence, and with which was coupled a tacit admission of their right to the free and undisturbed navigation of the seas. The treaty, signed at Antwerp, on the 9th of April, 1609, only three days after Hudson's departure on his voyage of discovery, virtually established to the States the nationality by which, according to the laws of nations, they were fully entitled to the fruits of his magnificent discoveries. These fruits comprised that vast portion of the North American continent included between the two extreme points at which he touched upon the coast; viz., Cape Cod on the north, and Cape May, at the mouth of the Delaware River, on the south. To this brave and enterprising people, suddenly relieved from the excitements of an arduous and protracted war, the discovery of so vast and rich a territory came most opportunely and gratefully. Their energies, hitherto absorbed in the defence of their rights, were now directed into the new field of commercial adventure thus suddenly opened to them by the fortunate voyage of the "Half Moon." Most alluring, among the varied treasures offered by the New World to the expanding commerce of Holland, was the inexhaustible abundance of beaver-skins and other valuable furs, procurable at a trifling cost, but commanding a most remunerative market among the northern nations of Europe. The spirit of private enterprise was stimulated to an extraordinary degree, and before the close of the next summer (1610) a vessel, laden with coarse but suitable goods for Indian traffic, was dispatched by some of the Amsterdam merchants to the Great River of the North. The "Half Moon," also, and a portion of her crew, although under another leader, revisited Manhattan and the scenes of their former adventures, to the unmistakable delight of the savages, who welcomed them as old acquaintances. During the year following, 1611, Hendrick Christiaensen made two voyages to Manhattan, the latter in company with Adriaen Block, bringing back with them to Holland two young savages, whose arrival in the civilized world fanned to a still brighter glow the already awakened mercantile curiosity and activity. In 1612 these two worthy mariners were again dispatched from Amsterdam to Manhattan, each in command of a separate vessel; and were followed, in 1613, by others, among whom was Captain Cornelis Jacobson May, afterwards honorably known in the annals of Transatlantic discovery. The mingled tide of discovery and commerce had now fairly set towards the shores of New Netherland, and its importance began to attract the attention of the States-General of the United Netherlands, which, on the 27th of March, 1614, passed a general ordinance, conferring upon the discoverers of new lands the exclusive privilege of making six voyages thither—a measure which was followed by an increased activity among the mercantile communities of Amsterdam and Hoorn.

Manhattan Island, by virtue of its admirable position, became the headquarters of the fur-trade. From thence trading-shallops and canoes penetrated into every neighboring creek, inlet or bay, and pushed their way even to the head of navigation on the rivers and larger streams. Gradually inland depots were established, where the adventurous trader, making himself comfortable among the homes and families of the natives, spent the winter months in purchasing and collecting furs and peltries, in readiness for shipment when the vessels from "the Fatherland" should arrive in the early spring. A few huts on the lower end of Manhattan Island (occupied by Block and his companions during the winter of 1613–1614, while they were engaged in building a small yacht to replace their vessel which had been destroyed by fire), were the only visible signs of occupation; while, as to cultivation of the land there was not even a commencement. Amid these untamed solitudes, secure in the good-will of the surrounding savages, and unmolested by European rivals, the plodding but honest Dutchmen pursued a lucrative traffic in peltries, sending home to Holland vessel after vessel richly freighted with furry treasures, which brought golden returns to the coffers of their owners.

By the spring of 1614, however, attention seemed to be directed towards placing affairs in the new country on a more permanent basis. Factors were appointed to reside at certain designated points in the interior and manage the growing peltry-trade; while, at Castle Island (now within the limits of the present city of Albany), was erected a small fortified warehouse, garrisoned with ten or twelve men and named "Fort Nassau." To that post resorted the Mohawks and Mohicans, and from thence went scouting parties, exploring the country in every direction, and always carefully maintaining the most amicable relations with the natives whom they met. Not less active, also, were the hardy Dutch sailors. Numerous minute explorations of the surrounding coasts were inaugurated by the captains of the various vessels which came out from Holland. Adriaen Block, in his little yacht the "Restless," which he had built at Manhattan during the preceding winter, explored the East River and the Sound, discovering the Housatonic, Thames, and Connecticut rivers, the latter of which he ascended to the head of navigation. Then crossing over to the eastern extremity of Long Island, the insular character of which he determined, he gave his name to an island near Montauk Point, and following in Verazzano's track, entered Narragansett Bay and coasted along northward as far as Boston harbor and Nahant Bay. Here meeting with his old comrade Christiaensen, he returned in the latter's vessel to Holland, leaving his own little craft in charge of Cornelis Hendricksen, who explored the coast further south. Cornelis Jacobsen May, meanwhile, was sailing along the southern shore of Long Island, passing southward to

Delaware Bay, where Capes Cornelis and May still preserve the memory of his visit.

Upon the announcement of these discoveries at home, the enterprising merchants of North Holland, under whose auspices they had been made, united themselves into a company, according to the provisions of the ordinance of March 11th, and were favored by the States-General with the grant of a special trading-licence or charter bearing date on the 11th of October, 1614. This document, in which the name "New Netherland" first appears officially in the world's annals, invested the "United New Netherland Company," as it was styled, with the exclusive right of visiting and trading in "the newly discovered lands lying in America between New France and Virginia, the seacoast whereof extends from the fortieth to the forty-fifth degrees of latitude, for four voyages, within the period of three years from the first of January next ensuing, or sooner." This specific, limited, and temporary monopoly, with which the enterprise of these associated merchants was thus rewarded, conferred upon them no political powers—their objects being simply trade and discovery, and their servants armed traders in forcible possession of an unoccupied country. As might have been expected, no attempt was made, during the term of their charter, to effect any systematic colonization of the new country. While the peltry trade increased famously, agriculture was neglected, and civilization could scarcely be said to have gained even a foothold in New Netherland. Upon the expiration of the charter, by its own limitation, January 1st, 1618, the company sought a renewal, which the government saw fit to refuse. It continued, however, to grant every facility to private trading enterprises to the North River; a new fort was erected there on Norman's Kill, in place of the former one, which had been seriously damaged by the spring freshets, and a treaty of peace and alliance was formally concluded with the famous Iroquois or "Five Nations."

The time had arrived, however, when the necessity of a permanent colonization of this distant colony became so apparent that its consideration could no longer be postponed. The States-General were meditating large and ambitious designs relative to their Western possessions, and they had already taken alarm at the pretensions which the English were beginning to assert to the same territories. The approaching termination of the Twelve Years' Truce, moreover, was prefaced by certain insulting propositions from Spain, which warned them to gird on their armor for a renewal of their long and bloody struggle with that power. As a means, therefore, of self-protection in the maintenance of their rights as an independent nation, and of aid in carrying on the threatened war with their ancient and powerful enemy, the States-General of the United Seven Provinces determined upon the creation of an armed mercantile association, on the plan of the celebrated East India Company, in which should be concentrated the entire strength of the numerous merchants now engaged in the American and West India trade. Thus originated the great DUTCH WEST INDIA COMPANY, which, supplanting all private adventurers, proposed to itself the promotion of colonization, the suppression of piracy, the humbling of Spain, and the aggrandizement of the national wealth and independence. Its charter, which was passed under the great seal of the States-General, on the 3d of June, 1621, granted to it the exclusive right of trade to the coasts of Africa, between the tropic of Cancer and the Cape of Good Hope; to the West Indies; and to the coasts of America, between Newfoundland and the Straits of Magellan. Within these limits, the company was invested with enormous powers. "In the name of the States-General, it might make contracts and alliances with the princes and natives of the countries comprehended within the limit of its charter; build forts; appoint and discharge governors, soldiers, and public officers; administer justice and promote trade. It was bound 'to advance the peopling of those fruitful and unsettled parts, and do all that the service of those countries and the profit and increase of trade shall require.' It was obliged to communicate to the States-General, from time to time, all the treaties and alliances it might make, and also detailed statements of its forts and settlements. All governors-in-chief, and the instructions proposed to be given to them, were first to be approved of by the States-General, who would then issue formal commissions; and all superior officers were held to take oaths of allegiance to their High Mightinesses, and also to the company." The company consisted of five chambers or Boards located in different cities of the Seven United Provinces; the principal one being that of *Amsterdam*, to which was confided the especial superintendence of the Province of NEW NETHERLAND. General executive powers for all purposes except of declaring war—which could not be done without the approbation of the States-General—were intrusted to a Board of NINETEEN delegates from the several chambers, and including one delegate who represented the States-General. A million of guilders and a defence "against every person, in free navigation and traffic," was promised to the company by the States-General, who were also, in case of war, to "give them for their assistance" sixteen ships of war of three hundred tons burden and four yachts of eighty tons, fully equipped. The company, however, were to man and support these vessels, besides providing an equal number of their own, the whole to be under command of an admiral appointed by the States-General.

The organization of the company was delayed by various causes for a period of two years, when its articles of internal regulation, the charter having, in the interval, been somewhat modified, were formally approved by the States-General on the 21st of June, 1623.

Meanwhile, the spirit of enterprise had not lain dormant. Amsterdam ships, under special licences, had been steadily pursuing their profitable voyages to New Netherland, and the peltry-trade had assumed larger proportions, not only on the North River, but on the Delaware, the Connecticut, along the shores of Long Island, and as far to the eastward as Narragansett and Buzzard's Bay, within twenty miles of the newly founded English settlement at New Plymouth. In Holland, the press began to teem with publications describing in glowing terms the beauties, wonders, and advantages of America, and the public mind was constantly quickened by the news of fresh discoveries, and the flattering reports brought by adventurous mariners from those far-off lands.

In England, also, public attention was at this time strongly directed towards the Western continent by the discoveries of Capt. John Smith, the plantations established in Virginia, and the charter recently granted for the settlement of New England. Maintaining, as they ever did, the right (by discovery, possession, and charters) to the entire American coast between the Spanish possessions in the south and those of France in the north, the English could not fail to feel annoyed by the active preparations of their Dutch neighbors for the occupation of so large a portion of those territories. Their apprehension found expression in an official remonstrance to the States-General against the sailing thither of the Dutch vessels, but the protest was unheeded, and after a brief diplomatic correspondence, the matter was temporarily dropped. Warned, however, by the evident and growing jealousy of the English, the West India Company lost no time, even before their final organization, in securing, in the year 1622, their title to New Netherland by taking formal possession, and by making arrangements for the building of two new forts, one on the North River, to be called "Fort Orange," and another called "Fort Nassau," on the South or Delaware River, near the present town of Gloucester, N. J. And, simultaneously with its final organization, in June, 1623, the company began to prosecute with energy the colonization of New Netherland, which was erected into a province, and invested with the armorial bearings of a count.[1] The particular management of its affairs was intrusted, as we have before remarked, to the Amsterdam Chamber, which sent out the ship "New Netherland"[2] of two-hundred and sixty tons burden, with a company of thirty families, mostly Walloons,[3] under the care of the veteran voyager

---

[1] The Provincial seal of New Netherland was a shield, bearing a beaver, proper, surmounted by a count's coronet, and encircled by the legend "Sigillum Novi Belgii."

[2] Catelina Trico's statement (see Appendix No. 1) gives the name of this vessel, in which she was a passenger, as the "Unity" (Eendragt). As, however, her deposition was made in 1688, at the age of eighty-three, concerning events which happened sixty-five years before, when she was a girl of eighteen years, we have preferred to follow Wassaneer's account, which was contemporaneous, and supported by Hol. Doc. ii. 370.

[3] "These Walloons, whose name was derived from their original 'Waalsche' or French extraction, had passed through the fire of persecution. They inhabited the Southern Belgic Provinces of Hainault, Namur, Luxemburg, Limburg, and part of the ancient Bishopric of Liege, and spoke the old French language. When the Northern provinces of the Netherlands formed their political union at Utrecht, in 1579, the Southern provinces, which were generally attached to the Romish Church, declined joining the Confederation. Many of their inhabitants, nevertheless, professed the principles of the Reformation. Against these Protestant Walloons the Spanish Government exercised the most rigid measures of inquisitorial vengeance, and the subjects of an unrelenting persecution emigrated by thousands into Holland, where they knew that strangers of every race and creed were sure of an asylum and a welcome. Carrying with them a knowledge of the arts, in which they were great proficients, they were distinguished in their new home for their tasteful and persevering industry. To

Captain Cornelis Jacobsen May, of Hoorn, who was appointed the first director of the colony. Starting from the Texel early in March, and sailing by way of the Canary Islands and the Guinea coast, the "New Netherland" arrived at the North River in the beginning of May. Eight men were landed at Manhattan Island to represent the company there, and several families, as well as sailors and single men, were dispatched to the settlements on the South River, and to the Connecticut, while the ship proceeded up the North River until she reached "Fort Orange" (the present site of Albany), where eighteen families were disembarked, and immediately commenced farming operations.

The year 1624, under May's judicious management, was a prosperous one; the industry of the pioneer colonists fulfilled the expectations of their patrons, the forts on the North and Delaware rivers were completed, and the peltry-trade was so well prosecuted that it returned to the company's treasury the handsome sum of twenty thousand guilders. Encouraged by these signs, the company dispatched to Manhattan, in the spring of 1625, a vessel well laden with "necessaries," which unfortunately fell into the hands of one of the enemy's privateers. The loss, however, was promptly made good, at the risk of one of the directors of the company, by two ships carrying a fine stock of cattle, a full equipment of seeds and farming utensils, and forty-five emigrants, among whom were six entire families. The growing colony, thus increased, now numbered over one hundred souls, and under the Directorship of William Verhulst, who had succeeded May, prospered greatly. In May, 1626, Peter Minuit arrived in New Netherland, and succeeded Verhulst as director-general of the province. His administration commenced with vigor and sagacity; Manhattan Island was purchased from the natives for the sum of sixty guilders (equivalent to

the Walloons, the Dutch were probably indebted for much of the repute which they gained as a nation in many branches of manufactures. Finding in Holland a free scope for their religious opinions, the Walloons soon introduced the public use of their church service, which, to this day, bears witness to the characteristic toleration and liberality of the Fatherland."—*Brodhead*, i. 146. These Walloons had previously applied to the English government for permission to emigrate to Virginia, but receiving no encouragement in that quarter, turned their attention to New Netherland, and were gladly accepted by the West India Company, under the sanction of the Provincial States.

about $24 of our money), and a large fort was erected at its lower end, and named "Fort Amsterdam;" while other improvements were planned and commenced.

At "Fort Orange," however, about this time, affairs took a most unfortunate turn. The commander at that post, forgetful of that neutrality which, hitherto, had been strictly observed by the Dutch in the affairs of the surrounding Indian tribes, joined a party of Mahicans on the war-path against the Mohawks, and, in the battle which ensued, was slain, together with three of his men. His folly had even a worse result, in the sense of insecurity which it threw over the settlement at Fort Orange, and, indeed, over the whole colony. And, though good feeling was finally restored with the Mohawks, yet the progress of colonization received a shock from which it did not soon recover. The Director, justly apprehensive of the danger to which the settlers at Fort Orange, Fort Nassau, and Verhulsten Island were exposed, recalled them all to Manhattan Island, in order that a concentration of householders might be made at that point where the natives "were becoming more and more accustomed to the presence of foreigners." Sixteen soldiers, only, were left at Fort Orange; the traffic to the South River was limited to the voyages of one small yacht, and every precaution was adopted by the prudent Director, which could conduce to the commercial interests of the company, as well as to the safety of its employees and colonists.

The year 1627 was marked by the establishment of friendly relations with the English settlements in New England. A special embassy was sent out from Manhattan to New Plymouth, between which colonies soon sprang up a mutually advantageous trade; the English freely exchanging their commodities for sewan or wampum, which they much needed in their dealings with the surrounding natives, and of which the Dutch—in consequence of their proximity to Long Island, the great aboriginal mint—held the almost exclusive monopoly. The annual crop of furs, also, amounting to four ship-loads, yielded 56,000 guilders; and, in the autumn of the following year, two cargoes of ship-timber from Manhattan sold at Amsterdam for 61,000 guilders. Around the fort, which was now completed with four bastions and a facing of stone, the colonists had clustered, to the number of 270 souls, subsisting chiefly by the products of their own labor, any deficiencies being supplied from the company's stores. The impression conveyed to a casual observer of that day, was, that they subsisted "in a comfortable manner" and "promised fairly both to the State and undertakers." Still, prosperous as the colony appeared, its industry was not self-supporting; and, thus far, the company's seven years' experience had neither justified their own expectations, nor fulfilled the conditions imposed upon them by their charter, in regard to the permanent agricultural colonization of the province. "Not a particle of the soil was reclaimed, save what scantily supplied the wants of those attached to the three forts, which were erected within the limits of this rich and vast country; and the only exports were the spontaneous products of the forest. Experience had demonstrated, in the interim, that no benefits had accrued to the company from this plantation, under the present system of management, except what the peltries produced; the mode of life pursued by the people was very irregular, the expenses of the establishment exceedingly high, and the results not so flattering as anticipated." These were unpalatable facts to the directors of a great mercantile corporation, whose ships under Admiral Heyn, bravest of the brave, were sweeping the Spanish navy from the seas, capturing booty which added twelve millions of guilders to their treasury, so that their dividends advanced, in one year, to fifty per cent. Flushed with the easy spoils of these glorious victories, it is not a matter of surprise that the annual returns from their far-off American colonies seemed paltry and unremunerative. They, therefore, began earnestly to consider plans for a systematic and extended colonization of the whole province—which, after a year of deliberation, resulted in the adoption of a "Charter of Freedoms and Exemptions," which was promptly approved and confirmed by the States General, on the 7th of June, 1629. In this charter, the company, with the purpose of encouraging independent colonists, offered to such the absolute property of as much land as each could "properly improve;" yet, fully aware that few or none of that class of persons possessed the requisite means, they sought to secure the co-operation of capitalists by the offer of peculiar privileges, carefully confined, however, to those who were members of the company. Any member who should plant a colony of fifty adults, in any part of New Netherland (except Manhattan Island, which the Company reserved to itself), should be acknowledged as the "patroon," or feudal chief of such colony or territory, with the high and low jurisdictions, the exclusive rights of fishing, hunting, and grinding, etc., within his own domain; to which, also, he was to have a full title of inheritance, with right of disposing of it by will, at death. Freedom of trade and of the fisheries, subject to certain limits, restrictions, and duties, were also granted to the patroons. For the space of ten years the colonists under these patroonships were to be entirely free from taxation, but were bound to the service of the patroon in an almost absolute servitude. The company, on its part, reserved to itself the fur and peltry trade, and the right of manufactures; promising, moreover, to the colonists protection and defence against all enemies; the prompt completion of the defences of Manhattan Island, and furnishing the colony with a supply of black servants. The colonists were required "to satisfy the Indians for the land they shall settle upon;" to make immediate provision for the support of a minister and schoolmaster; and each colony was to make an annual return of its condition to the local authorities at Manhattan, for transmission to the company at home. In all its provisions, the Charter of Freedoms and Exemptions carefully recognized the commercial monopoly and the political supremacy of the West India Company; and was, in fact, a transplanting to the New World of the "feudal" system so prevalent in Europe. While it cared for the rights of the aboriginal owners, and promised labor, capital, religion, and education to the young colony, it "scattered the seeds of servitude, slavery, and aristocracy." Its plan and spirit were selfish; its results most unfortunate. As might have been expected, cupidity induced some of the company's directors, even before the charter had been sanctioned, to reap the benefit of certain of its provisions, at the expense of their comrades, by appropriating to themselves some of the choicest portions of the province. Availing themselves of the privileges which it accorded to directors, patroonships were purchased, through their agents in

New Netherland, by Blommaert and Godyn on the South River; by Van Rensselaer on the North River; and by Pauw at Hoboken-Hacking and Pavonia (now Jersey City), and Staten Island. Thus, at the very outset, the selfishness which pervades all monopolies, by this sudden absorption of the most prominent positions in New Netherland, defeated and discouraged the inducements to independent emigrants which was the chief intent of the charter. So great, also, was the dissatisfaction and jealousy to which their actions gave rise, that the speculative patroons were finally obliged to share their original purchases with their fellow-directors in the company. Various partnerships were formed among them, and commercial operations commenced in New Netherland; but it was apparent, from the first, that they were far more interested in the Indian trade than in the proper colonization of the colony. And, before long, their claims came so directly in conflict with the vested rights of the company, as to necessitate a revision of the Charter of Freedoms and Exemptions, and the adoption of new articles limiting and restraining the privileges of the patroons. These quarrels finally challenged the attention of the States-General, who instituted an investigation. Shortly thereafter, Minuit, who as director had officially ratified the purchases which had created so much feeling, was recalled, and embarked for Holland in the spring of 1632. During the following summer, the company, determined to maintain its superior monopoly, and to arrest the encroachments of the patroons, dispatched commissaries to each settlement to post up their proclamation, forbidding any person, whether patroon or vassal, to deal in sewan, peltries, or maize. In the spring of 1633, the province, which had been without a head for a year past, received from Holland a new director. This was Wouter Van Twiller, a former clerk in the company's warehouse at Amsterdam, and a relative by marriage of Patroon Van Rensselaer. Singularly inexperienced, incompetent, narrow-minded, and deficient in knowledge of men, this ex-clerk came to the command of the province at a time when it was shaken with internal jealousies and threatened with aggressions from English neighbors. With him came one hundred and four soldiers, and Everardus Bogardus, the new clergyman of Manhattan. Scarcely had he assumed the duties of office, before the new director became involved in broils with English sea-captains and with the patroons, in which he displayed but little wisdom, self-respect, or courage. Yet he had, in some respects, a keen perception of what was needed for the prosperity of the company, and was ambitious to promote its interests. On the 8th of June, 1633, he purchased from the Indians a large tract of land, on the Fresh or Connecticut River, originally discovered by Block, in 1614, since which time it had been periodically and almost exclusively visited by the Dutch traders, whose purchases formed no slight portion of the annual harvest of furs and other commodities. On this spot, the site of the present beautiful city of Hartford, a trading-post was erected, fortified with two cannon, and named "The House of Good Hope." This soon brought them in conflict with the English colonists of New Plymouth, who established a fort at Windsor, a little above, and resisted a force of Dutch soldiery sent to disperse them. Meanwhile, at New Amsterdam, the fort was properly repaired, a guard-house, barracks, church, parsonage, director's house, and other improvements were in course of construction, and houses were also commenced at Fort Orange, at Pavonia, and Fort Nassau. The Indians were very troublesome this year, especially the Pequods on the Connecticut, and the Raritans of New Jersey, with the latter of whom a peace was fortunately concluded in 1634.

All this while, in "the Fatherland," there was great wrangling between the company and the patroons, and finally the questions in dispute being brought before the States-General were by them referred to a committee, before whom, in June, 1634, the patroons presented certain claims, together with a statement of their grounds of complaint against the company. After a patient hearing of the case, the States-General postponed their decision, and finally, in February, 1635, the Board of Nineteen effected a compromise of the matter by purchasing from the patroons their colonies on the South River. In that region the English, during the following summer, made an aggressive attempt to oust the Dutch, but were foiled; in the broad and beautiful valley of the Connecticut, however, during this and the succeeding year (1636), they encroached, step by step, upon the Dutch, until the latter were dispossessed of nearly all that territory, to which, by prior discovery, exploration, and occupation, they were so fairly entitled.

Amid the irregularities and dissensions which prevailed during Van Twiller's administration, neither he nor his subordinate officials neglected the advantages which they enjoyed for advancing their private interests. In June, 1636, one of these officials, Jacob Van Corlaer, purchased from the Indians a flat of land called "Castateeuw, on Sewan-hackey, or Long Island, between the Bay of the North River and the East River," *which is the earliest recorded grant, to an individual, in the present County of Kings.* On the same day, Andries Hudde and Wolfert Gerritsen purchased the flats next west to Van Corlaer's; and shortly after, the tempting level lands to the eastward of these were secured by the director himself.[1] On these purchases, amounting to some 15,000 acres, and which apparently were made without the knowledge or consent of the Amsterdam Chamber, the fortunate owners immediately commenced agricultural improvements—from which, in time, sprang the flourishing village of "New Amersfoort" now Flatlands.

In the course of the same year (1636), WILLIAM ADRIAENSE BENNET and JACQUES BENTYN purchased from the Indians a tract of 930 acres of land at "Gowanus,"[2] upon which, at some time prior to the Indian war of 1642–'45, a dwelling-house was erected—affording presumptive evidence, at least, that absolute occupation and agricultural improvement followed close upon its purchase.[3] The occupation of this farm, over a portion of which the village of Gowanus subsequently extended—and which comprised that portion of the present city lying between Twenty-seventh street and the New

---

[1] These "flats" were miniature prairies, devoid of trees, and having a dark-colored surface soil; and having undergone a certain rude culture by the Indians, were ready, without much previous toil, for the plough. On this account they were most sought for, and first purchased by the original settlers, who being natives of the low and level lands of Holland and Belgium, were inexperienced in the clearing of forests.

[2] The name of *Gowanus* is a purely Indian one, which philologists have been unable to explain. It was applied to all the land fronting on Gowanus Bay, and traversed by the creek of the same name.

[3] See description of the Bennet and Bentyn patent, in chapter on "Early Settlers and Patents."

Utrecht line—may be considered as the *first step in the settlement of the* CITY OF BROOKLYN. The *second step*, according to the best documentary evidence, was taken about a year later, by JOHN (GEORGE) JANSEN DE RAPALIE, one of the Walloon emigrants of 1623, who first settled at Fort Orange (Albany), and in 1626 removed to New Amsterdam, on Manhattan Island. On the 16th of June, 1637, Rapalie purchased from its native proprietors a piece of land called "Rennegackonk," lying on Long Island "in the bend of Marechkawieck," now better known as Wallabout Bay. This purchase, comprising about three hundred and thirty-five acres, now occupied in part by the grounds of the United States Marine Hospital, and by that portion of the city between Nostrand and Grand Avenues—although it may have been, and probably was, more or less improved as a farm by Rapalie—was not occupied by him as a residence until about 1654.[3] By that time, the gradual influx of other settlers, many of whom were Walloons, had gained for the neighborhood the appellation of the "Waal-Bogt," or "the bay of the foreigners."[4] Thus, at two isolated points—offering to the

---

[1] "*Rennegackonck*" (sometimes spelt with an *i* or a *u* in the first syllable) is a small creek or stream of water emptying into the Wallabout Bay.

[2] The Indian name of the territory of Brooklyn was *Meryckawick*, or "the sandy place;" from *me*, the article in the Algonquin dialect, *reckwa*, sand, and *ick*, locality. The name was probably applied, at first, to the bottom-land, or beach; and what is now Wallabout Bay, was formerly called "The boght of Mareckawick." O'Callaghan supposes that the Indians who inhabited that part of the present city of Brooklyn derived their tribal name from the bay; but we are inclined to the opinion that the appellation was by no means so limited, for the present name of Rockaway, in another part of the county, seems to have the same derivation.

[3] See biographical notice of Rapalie in chapter on "Early Settlers and Patents."

[4] The earliest date at which the word "Waal-bogt" (or "Wahle-Boght," now corrupted to Wallabout) appears upon the colonial records, is in 1656, by which time a considerable number of Walloons and other foreign emigrants had become located there.

In regard to the nationality of these settlers, Bergen (*Hist. Bergen Family*, 18, 19; *Hist. Mag.*, vi. 162) says: "The Montfoorts and Huybertsen may have been Walloons; the name of Cornelissen indicates that he was a Netherlander; Picet or Piquet was from Rouen, in France, which is located many miles from the frontiers; * * Peter Cæser (Alburtus), as his name indicates, was an Italian; Hans Hansen Bergen was a Norwegian; and Rapalie could not have been a Walloon by birth, if, as asserted and claimed, he was a native of Rochelle, in France, a seaport on the Bay of Biscay, several hundred miles from the frontiers of Belgium. All Huguenots in those days may, however, have been known by the general title of Walloons, and the settlement of emigrants of this class at a later period in that vicinity, may account for the name; it being customary in Holland in those days to distinguish churches in their midst, erected by French Huguenots, by the name of 'Waale Kerken,' or Walloon Churches."

settlers similar agricultural advantages and inducements[1]—were formed the *nuclei* of the present CITY OF BROOKLYN.[2]

Coincident with Rapalie's purchase at the "Waal-Bogt," the director secured for his own use the island "Pagganck," lying a little south of Fort Amsterdam, and which, from its abundance of excellent nut-trees was called by the Dutch "Nooten," or Nutten Island. From that time to the present it has been familiarly known as "the Governor's Island." One Jonas Bronck, also, became the owner of a large and valuable tract on the "mainland," in what is now Westchester County; and the West India Company secured the Indian title to the island of "Quotenis" in Narragansett Bay, and of another near the Thames River—both advantageously located for trading purposes. From Michael Pauw they purchased his rights to Pavonia (Jersey City) and Staten Island, thus ridding themselves of an enterprising patroon, whose proximity was as galling to their pride, as his success would have been injurious to

---

[1] Both around the "Bogt," and at Gowanus, were lowlands, overflowed by the sea at every tide, and covered with salt-meadow grass, coarse and hard to be cut with a common scythe, but which the cattle preferred to fresh hay or grass.

[2] The statement, so often reiterated by our local writers, and even by the historians of our State, that some of the Walloon emigrants of 1623 settled first at Staten Island (O'Callaghan, i. 101), and afterwards, as early as 1624–'5, at the "Waal-bogt," (Brodhead, i. 153, 154), is entirely unsupported by documentary or other reliable evidence. It seems to have originated in faulty traditions, and in a misapprehension of an ancient record relating to the daughter of Rapalie, the first settler in the "Bogt." (See chapter on "Early Settlers and Patents.")

Equally unreliable is the statement (Brodhead, i. 170) that the settlement was increased in 1626 by Walloon settlers, who had been recalled from Fort Orange and the South River, in consequence of Indian disturbances. It will be evident, on reflection, that, in the then unsettled state of the province, no permanent settlement would have been allowed at such a distance from the fort on Manhattan Island; and, during the succeeding ten years (until 1636), *concentration* was the necessary policy of the infant colony. Even for more than thirty years afterwards the government exercised the greatest caution in permitting the establishment of new villages where they would be exposed to hostile attack. Nor is it a reasonable supposition that agricultural settlements were made here so many years prior to the purchase of the land from the Indians, and the granting of it by patents. If, indeed, there was *any* use of land on Long Island made by the Walloons before the date of the first known settlement in 1636, it must have been temporary in its nature, and confined entirely to the most accessible and easily improved portions along the shore. If such was the case, the settlers probably cultivated their little patches by day, returning across the river at nightfall, to their families and the security of Fort Amsterdam. But this is mere conjecture, and there is no evidence of the permanent residence of any white family within the limits of our city, prior to 1636.

their interests. Their fur-trade, meanwhile, despite the loss of their traffic on the Connecticut, was steadily and largely increasing, and a new and profitable commerce had sprung up with New England and the West Indies. The constant reiteration of complaints and serious charges against Van Twiller, however, made to the West India Company, finally determined them to remove him from office. Accordingly, early in the spring of 1638, he was superseded by William Kieft, who, though "a more discreet and sober man" than his predecessor, was of an active, "inquisitive," and grasping disposition; and by no means so prudent a magistrate as the circumstances of the province demanded. He set bravely to work to correct the many abuses, both social and civil, which had grown up under Van Twiller's administration; but the people were of too mixed a character, and had been too long allowed the license of doing as they pleased, to yield readily to his proclamations, or even to the more forcible measures of restraint which he inaugurated. That he was not unmindful of the company's material interests, was evidenced by the judicious purchases of territory which he made in the neighborhood of Manhattan. On the 1st of August, 1638, he secured for the West India Company a tract of land adjoining Rapalie's plantation on Long Island, extending from "Rennegackonck" (*ante*, page 24, note) to what is now known as Newtown Creek, and from the East River to "the swamps of Mespaetches." The price paid to the native "chiefs of Keskaechquerem" for this extensive area, which comprised the *whole of the former town of Bushwick, now forming the Eastern District of the city of Brooklyn,* was eight fathoms of duffels cloth, eight fathoms of wampum, twelve kettles, eight adzes, eight axes, and some knives, corals, and awls.[1]

At "Paulus Hook" (Jersey City), at "Corlaer's Hook" (opposite Brooklyn) on Manhattan Island, and at other places in the vicinity of New Amsterdam, permanent improvements were commenced by various persons, and around the fertile region of the "Waal-bogt" began to cluster the "plantations" of active husbandmen.

Meanwhile, the prestige which the Dutch had heretofore maintained on the South River, received a severe shock. A Swedish

---

[1] The deed (the earliest recorded to the West India Company) for this important purchase, will be found, in full, as Appendix No. 2.

West India Company was formed, which sent out an expedition to establish a new colony in those parts, and its chief command was intrusted to no less a person than Peter Minuit, the former Director of New Netherland. In May, 1638, Minuit, undeterred by the protests and threats of Director Kieft, established near the site of the present city of Wilmington, Del., a trading-house and fort, which he loyally named, after the young queen of Sweden, "Fort Christina." Availing himself of the experience which he had previously gained at Manhattan, he quickly "drew all the skins towards him by his liberal gifts," so that, by midsummer, the vessels which brought him out, returned to Sweden well laden with furs.

At home, in "the Fatherland," the affairs of the province of New Netherland were again undergoing a searching investigation by the States-General, who finally directed the Amsterdam Chamber of the West India Company to take such immediate measures as should most effectually regenerate the social, political, and commercial state of the colony under their charge. Thus enjoined, the Amsterdam Chamber, by proclamation, in September, 1638, threw open New Netherland to free trade by all inhabitants of the United Provinces and of friendly nations, "in the company's ships," and subject to an import duty of fifteen per cent. and to an export duty of ten per cent. The director and council of New Netherland were directed to furnish every emigrant, "according to his condition and means, with as much land as he and his family can properly cultivate," a quit-rent of a tenth being reserved to the company, thus assuring legal estates of inheritance to the grantees. Each colonist or trader, availing himself of this proclamation, was required to sign a pledge of obedience to the officers of the company, acting in subordination to the States-General, and promising, in all questions and differences which might arise, to abide by the decision of the established colonial courts. Free passage, and other inducements, were also offered to respectable farmers who wished to emigrate to the new country.

The adoption of this liberal policy by the West India Company marked a new era in the history of the province, and gave a rapid impulse to its prosperity. Plans of colonization were formed by capitalists, and many persons of ample means came out from

Holland—as well as many from Virginia and New England. These all set about choosing favorable locations for husbandry or traffic; houses were built; vessels were sent on trading-ventures in various directions; New Amsterdam echoed with the sound of the axe and the hammer, and industry and enterprise, no longer shackled by the restrictions of a monopoly, gave to the country an appearance of thriftiness and progress. Thirty "bouweries" or plantations, "as well stocked with cattle as any in Europe," were soon under cultivation, and the numerous applications for land promised at least "a hundred more."

The increasing demand for homesteads near Fort Amsterdam induced the director and council to secure, by purchase from the native proprietors, as much as possible of the valuable land on the western end of Long Island. Accordingly, in January, 1639, Kieft effected the purchase of all the lands from Rockaway eastward to "Sicktew-hackey," or Fire Island Bay; thence northward to Martin Gerritsen's, or Cow Bay, and westward along the East River, to the "Vlaack's Kill;" thus securing to the company, in connection with his purchase of the previous year, the Indian title to nearly all the land comprised within the present County of Queens. And a few months later, the company became possessed of another large tract in what is now Westchester County. Portions of the lands thus obtained were ere long deeded by the company to enterprising settlers. In August of this year, Antony Jansen van Vaas from Saleé, obtained a grant of two hundred acres on the west end of Long Island, partly in the present towns of New Utrecht and Gravesend, of which towns he was the pioneer settler.[1] On the 28th of November following, one Thomas Bescher received a patent for "a tobacco plantation," on the beach of Long Island "hard by Saphorakan," which is supposed to have been at Gowanus, and adjoining to that of William Adriaense Bennet.[2] The next settler, in this vicinity, was Frederick Lubbertsen, who, on the 27th of

[1] Recorded in Book G. G., of Land Patents, p. 61. The house which he erected and occupied on the premises, it is supposed, was located on the New Utrecht side of the boundary line between said towns, and its remains were disturbed, some years ago, in digging for the foundations of a new building.

[2] See the discussion of the Bennet and Bentyn Patent in the chapter on "Early Settlers and Patents."

May, 1640, took out a patent for a large tract lying on the northerly side of Gowanus Cove, and having, also, an extensive water-front on the East River; comprising, with the exception of Red Hook, the largest portion of what is now known as South Brooklyn. There is abundant evidence, also, that the territory (subsequently forming the town of Bushwick, and now the Eastern District of the city of Brooklyn), purchased from the Indians, by the West India Company in 1638, had been more or less cultivated—probably, by "squatter right"—by settlers who now began to take out patents for the lands which they had thus occupied. Patents were issued in August, 1640, to ABRAHAM RYCKEN for a large plantation; and in September, 1641, to LAMBERT HUYBERTSEN (MOLL), for land on the East River previously occupied by one Cornelis Jacobsen Sille. In the same neighborhood HANS HANSEN BERGEN was already occupying a large tract adjoining that of his father-in-law Joris Rapalie, and lying partly on the "Waal-bogt" and partly within the limits of Bushwick; while along the "bend of the Marechawick,"[1] lay the farms and "tobacco plantations" of JAN and PIETER MONTFOORT, PIETER CÆSAR the Italian, and others.[2]

The West India Company, at this time, owned by purchase nearly all that portion of the western end of Long Island now embraced within the present city of Brooklyn, and the towns of Flatlands, Flatbush, and Newtown. To this was added, May 10th, 1640, the hereditary rights "of the great chief Penhawitz," the head of the Canarsee tribe, who claimed the territory forming the present county of Kings, and a part of the town of Jamaica. Thus the perfected title of all the island west of Cow Bay and comprising the present counties of Kings and Queens became vested in the company by purchase. At the eastern end of the island, during this year, Lyon Gardiner, of Saybrook, had made the first permanent English settlement within the limits of the present State of New York, on the island which still bears his name, near Montauk Point; and in the following spring, emigrants from Lynn, Mass., made an attempt, under Lord Stirling's patent, to effect a settlement at Schout's Bay, within the limits of the present Queens County. Dislodged from

---

[1] The Wallabout Bay.

[2] See chapter on "Early Settlers and Patents."

there, however, by the Dutch soldiery whom Kieft dispatched thither, they subsequently settled the town of Southampton, in the present county of Suffolk; and shortly after Southold was occupied by a company from the New Haven Colony. Both of these English colonies were allowed to pursue their way unmolested by the Dutch government at Fort Amsterdam.

While thus adding to the company's domains, Kieft also gave to the administrative affairs of the province the attention which they had so long needed; instituted various charges in subordinate officers; vigorously enforced discipline among the company's soldiers and workmen at Manhattan, and strictly forbade the selling of firearms to the Indians. This latter practice, indeed, was one of the growing evils which were now beginning seriously to disturb the friendly relations which had, heretofore, existed between the Dutch and their savage neighbors. Contrary to all existing orders, as well as to every dictate of prudence, a brisk traffic in guns and ammunition had sprung up between the Rensselaerwyck colonists and "free-traders," and the Mohawks, until the latter could number some four hundred warriors thus armed, and, of course, became more insolent and oppressive to all the other tribes. To the River Indians, who, in consequence of the strict police regulations maintained in and around Manhattan, were unable to obtain these much-coveted weapons, this seeming partiality shown to their dreaded foes by the Dutch, was a just source of annoyance and jealousy. Then, again, the colonists, in their eagerness to pursue the fur-trade, frequently neglected their farms, and their cattle straying loose often inflicted serious damage upon the unfenced cornfields of the savages, who, finding their complaints disregarded, resorted to retaliatory measures, and thus hard feelings were engendered on both sides. In their dealings with the Indians, also, too many of the traders indulged in an "excessive familiarity" with them, which naturally bred in the minds of the latter a contempt for men who, despite their apparent friendliness, did not always treat them with perfect fairness. Many of the Dutch, moreover, employed some of these savages as domestic servants, and the Indians had thus become fully informed of the numerical strength, habits, and circumstances of the colonists.

It will easily be seen, then, that but little provocation was needed to bring matters to an open rupture; nor was the occasion long wanting. Director Kieft, under the plea that the company's expenses were unusually heavy, demanded a contribution or tax of maize, furs, and sewan from the neighboring Indians. This act of meanness filled the measure of the red man's wrath to overflowing; and so sudden and imminent appeared the danger, that Kieft ordered the people to arm themselves and to be prepared against any sudden assault. Some depredations on the settlement at Staten Island occurred at this juncture, which were unjustly imputed to the Raritan Indians, and furnished an excuse for sending an expedition against them, which killed a few of them, destroyed their crops, and sowed the seeds of a long and bloody war.

By this time, under the authority of the States-General, the long-existing differences between the patroons and the company had resulted in the formation of a new "Charter of Freedoms and Exemptions, for all patroons, masters, and private persons," which, on the 19th of July, 1640, was officially approved and promulgated. The main features of this important document, which materially amended the obnoxious charter of 1629, are thus ably presented by our latest State historian.[1] "All good inhabitants of the Netherlands" were now allowed to select lands and form colonies, which, however, were to be reduced in size. Instead of four Dutch miles, they were limited to one mile along the shore of a bay or navigable river, and two miles into the country. A free right of way by land and water was reserved to all; and, in case of dispute, the director-general of New Netherland was to decide. The feudal privileges of erecting towns and appointing their officers; the high, middle, and lower jurisdiction; and the exclusive right of hunting, fishing, fowling, and grinding corn, were continued to the patroons as an estate of inheritance, with descent to females as well as males. On every such change of ownership, the company was to receive a pair of iron gauntlets and twenty guilders, within one year. Besides the patroons, another class of proprietors was now established. Whoever should convey to New Netherland five grown persons besides

---

[1] Brodhead, i. 311–313.

himself, was to be recognized as a 'master or colonist;' and could occupy two hundred acres of land, with the privilege of hunting and fishing. If settlements of such colonists should increase in numbers, towns and villages might be formed, to which municipal governments were promised. The magistrates in such towns were to be appointed by the director and council, 'from a triple nomination of the best qualified in the said towns and villages.' From these courts, and from the courts of the patroons, an appeal might lie to the director and council at Manhattan. The company guaranteed protection, in case of war, to all the colonists, but each adult male emigrant was bound to provide himself, before he left Holland, with a proper musket, or a hanger and side-arms. The commercial privileges, which the first charter had restricted to the patroons, were now extended to all 'free colonists,' and to all the stockholders in the company. Nevertheless, the company adhered to a system of onerous imposts, for its own benefit, and required a duty of ten per cent. on all goods shipped to New Netherland, and of five per cent. on all return cargoes, excepting peltries, which were to pay ten per cent. to the director at Manhattan before they could be exported. All shipments from New Netherland were to be landed at the company's warehouses in Holland. The prohibition of manufactures within the province was, however, abolished. The company renewed its pledge to send over 'as many blacks as possible,' and disclaiming any interference with the 'high, middle, and lower jurisdiction' of the patroons, reserved to itself supreme and sovereign authority over New Netherland, promising to appoint and support competent officers 'for the protection of the good, and the punishment of the wicked.' The provincial director and council were to decide all questions concerning the rights of the company, and all complaints, whether by foreigners or inhabitants of the province; to act as an Orphan's and Surrogate's Court; to judge in criminal and religious affairs, and generally to administer law and justice. No other religion save that then taught and exercised by authority, in the Reformed Church in the United Provinces, was to be publicly sanctioned in New Netherland, where the company bound itself to maintain proper preachers, schoolmasters, and comforters of the sick."

The prosperity of New Netherland was greatly quickened by this charter. New colonies were successfully founded on the North River, in the Valley of the Hackensack and on Staten Island; the municipal affairs of New Amsterdam were better regulated, and the currency of the province was reformed. This consisted, at the time, almost exclusively of sewan or wampum, of which that manufactured on Long Island and at Manhattan was esteemed the most valuable. Of this "good, splendid" variety, four beads were deemed equivalent to one stiver; but, by degrees, a large quantity of inferior wampum, loose and unstrung, had got into circulation, which had so far depreciated in the market, as to call for legislative interference. The council, therefore, ordered that thenceforth the loose kind should pass at the rate of six for a stiver; and the only reason that it was not wholly prohibited, was "because there was no other coin in circulation, and the laborers, boors, and other common people having no other money, would be great losers." Two annual fairs, one for cattle and another for swine, were also established at Manhattan, in September, 1641.

At this juncture, a sudden attack made by the Raritans upon the settlement at Staten Island, together with certain hostile demonstrations on the part of the Weckquaesgeeks, gave indication that the smouldering fires of savage resentment were about to burst forth in flames of war and destruction. The director, appalled at the imminence of the danger, was yet unwilling to take the responsibility of the initiative step of retaliation, from fear of the people, who already reproached him with folly in provoking the war, as well as with personal cowardice. He, therefore, convened all the masters and heads of families at Manhattan, on the 23d of August, and submitted to them the question of declaring war against the savages. The assembly promptly chose "Twelve Select Men," all Hollanders, to consider upon his propositions.[1] Their counsel was for preserving peace with the Indians as long as possible; or, at least, until the Dutch settlements throughout the country should be more numerous and better able to maintain and defend themselves. Dis-

[1] Among these "Twelve Men" were Jacques Bentyn, the Gowanus settler; Frederick Lubbertsen, a large landholder though not a resident, in the same vicinity; and George Rapalie, of the Wallabout.

appointed in their verdict, the director endeavored, in various ways, to secure their unconditional consent to his plan of an aggressive war; but the Twelve Men remained unshaken in their opinion, and succeeded in averting actual hostilities until the beginning of the following year. Early in January, 1641, Kieft again convened the Twelve Men, and, finally, wrung from them a consent, "conditional, specific, and limited," to the sending out of an expedition against the Weckquaesgeeks. But, while the representatives of the people unwillingly conceded this much to the director's wishes, they seized the opportunity to demand certain reforms in the colonial government: viz., that the council should be reorganized and its numbers increased to five; that, in order "to save the land from oppression," four persons, elected by the commonalty, should assist at the council, two of which four should be annually elected by the people; that judicial proceedings should be held only before a full board; that the right of free trade should be granted to all colonists, on payment of the company's imposts; that the militia should be reorganized and properly equipped; and that, to prevent the currency of the colony from being exported, its nominal value should be increased. Jealous of his own rights, which he saw to be limited by these popular demands, Kieft was aware that some concessions must be made, in order to secure their acquiescence in the war which he was so anxious to commence. He, therefore, partially granted some of the least important points demanded; and, with a significant hint that he thought they had somewhat exceeded the powers for which they had been especially convened, he dissolved the Twelve Men, thanking them for their advice, and forbidding, in future, any calling of assemblies of the people, without the express order of the director. Early in March following, the expedition against the Weckquaesgeeks set forth, and though it was partially futile, it had the effect of inducing the savages to sue for a peace, which, however, proved to be but a temporary respite.

At Manhattan, which was now becoming, more than ever, a stopping-place for transient visitors from New England and Virginia, the director built, in 1642, a "fine hotel," and also a church, both of stone; and, in consequence of the 'large number of Englishmen who were now flocking to New Netherland—rendering necessary the services of an interpreter—one George Baxter was appointed "English Secretary" with a handsome salary.

A public ferry was, by this time, permanently established between Manhattan and Long Island. The landing-place on the New Amsterdam side was at the present Peck Slip, where was a ferry-house, kept by CORNELIS DIRCKSEN (HOOGLANT) the ferryman. The landing-place on this side of the river was at the foot of the present Fulton-street, Brooklyn, near which Dircksen also owned "a house and garden." Southwardly from "*The Ferry*," along the present "Brooklyn Heights" and the East River shore, stretched the farms of CLAES CORNELISSEN VAN SCHOUW (MENTELAER), JAN MANJE, ANDRIES HUDDE, JACOB WOLPHERTSEN (VAN COUWENHOVEN), and others; while Red Hook had become the property of ex-Governor VAN TWILLER.

Religious persecution was, at this time, driving from New England, many pure-minded and gifted men, who found in New Netherland the toleration denied them by their own country and brethren. Thus, courteously treated and favored with liberal patents of land from the Dutch Government, the Rev. John Doughty, with his followers, settled at Maspeth (now Newtown) on Long Island; Throgmorton settled at Throg's Neck, Westchester County; and the celebrated Anne Hutchinson and her family, driven from New Haven, found refuge at New Rochelle.

On the South River, by the combined efforts of the Dutch and Swedes, who, in this, made common cause, the English were effectually cleared out; but, on the Connecticut, the Dutchman was sorely pressed to hold his own against the colonists of Massachusetts.

The year 1643 was to New Netherland, as to New England, "a year of blood." Indian uprisings and "rumors of wars" were on every side. Anxiety and terror hung like a cloud over Fort Amsterdam and the neighboring settlements. An Indian murder at Hackensack was followed by a descent of the dreaded Mohawks upon the River tribes, which sent the latter rushing for refuge to the vicinity of the white settlements at Vriesendael, Pavonia, and even Manhattan Island, where at "Corlaer's Bouwery" a few Rockaway Indians from Long Island, with their chief Nainde Nummerus, had already established their wigwams. Had the counsels of wisdom prevailed, these River Indians – now panting fugitives, and grateful for the shelter afforded them by the proximity of the white man's settlements—might easily have been gained over to a lasting friendship. It was, however, the old story of the dove flying to the eagle's nest for protection. At a supper at which Kieft was present, a petition was handed to him by two or three of the Twelve Men of the previous year, urging him to avenge the wrongs of the Dutch by an immediate attack upon these unsuspecting refugee Indians. Delighted with the prospect of, at last, accomplishing his darling wish, he gladly accepted the advice of the Twelve; ignoring the fact that they had been dissolved, and that he had pronounced their functions limited. In vain, Dominie Bogardus counselled peace and humanity; La Montagne begged him to wait for the arrival of the next ship from home before proceeding to extremities; and De Vries contended that no warlike step could be taken without the full consent of the people, and protested that the petition upon which he was acting, was not the expression of the Board of Twelve. The dogged director would not yield; two expeditions were secretly sent forth, on the night of the 25th of February, 1643, against Pavonia and Corlaer's Hook; and, at midnight, these poor Indians, sleeping safe, as they thought, from attack by their mortal foes, the Mohawks, were remorselessly butchered, to the number of eighty at the former place and forty at the latter. The story of that night is one of the saddest and foulest, because the meanest, upon the pages of New Netherland's history.

The success of this discreditable exploit naturally provoked emulation, and some of the settlers residing within the limits of the present city of Brooklyn sought permission from the director to attack the Marechkawiecks, who still retained some of their planting-grounds in that neighborhood.[1] Kieft, however, yielding to the counsels of Dominie Bogardus and others, refused his assent on the ground that the Marechkawiecks had always been very friendly to the Dutch, and, moreover, were "hard to conquer," and

[1] Brodhead says (i. 353): "Wolfertsen and some of his neighbors at New Amersfoort" were the actors in this outrage. The petition, however (see Appendix No. 3), is signed by five persons, *three of whom,* at least, *were, at this time, residents of territory included within the subsequent towns of Brooklyn and Bushwick.*

that it was not wise to add to the number of their declared foes. If, however, the Indians showed any signs of hostility, each colonist might adopt such measures of defence as he saw fit. The proviso was an unfortunate one; for, to those who seek a quarrel opportunity is never long wanting; and, ere long, some movements of the Marechkawiecks were conveniently construed into signs of hostility. Straightway, a secret expedition plundered two wagon-loads of corn from the Indians, three of whom were killed in the attempt to rescue their property. Up to this time, the Long Island Indians had been the constant friends of the Dutch, but this crowning act of injustice filled them with bitterest contempt and hatred. They immediately made common cause with the River Indians, who, by this time, had discovered that the midnight massacres at Pavonia and "Corlaer's" were the work of the Dutch; and war was declared against the faithless whites. From the shores of the Raritan to the valley of the Hackensack, the tomahawk was dug up and the war-paint was put on. Eleven tribes rose, as one man, and throughout the length and breadth of New Netherland, Death, Fire, and Captivity threatened unspeakable horrors to farmer and soldier, to women and children, to old and young, to rich and poor alike. From every outlying settlement the terrified colonists fled to Fort Amsterdam, and crazed by their despair and reproaches, the director hurriedly adopted such measures as he could for the common safety. He found himself obliged to take all the males into the company's service, as paid soldiers, for two months. He, also, sent a friendly message to the Long Island Indians, to which the indignant savages would not listen. Standing afar off, they derided his messenger, calling out, "Are ye our friends? Ye are merely corn-thieves." Amid the general distress, cooped up in the fort together with trembling fugitives, the victims of his own rashness, and compelled daily to hear the reproaches which his conscience told him were merited, the valiant director scarce knew which way to turn; and so, he proclaimed a day of general fasting and prayer. But, while the people humbled themselves before the Almighty, they held the director strictly responsible; and, alarmed for his own safety, he endeavored to foist the odium of the situation upon the freemen, whose advice he claimed to have followed. The indignant burghers, however, reminded him that he had dissolved the Board of Twelve and forbidden all assemblies of freemen.

"Meanwhile," says the historian,[1] "the Long Island Indians had begun to relent. Spring was at hand, and they desired to plant their corn. Three delegates from the wigwams of Penhawitz, their 'great chief,' approached Fort Amsterdam, bearing a white flag. 'Who will go to meet them?' demanded Kieft. None were willing but De Vries and Jacob Olfertsen. 'Our chief has sent us,' said the savages, 'to know why you have killed his people, who have never laid a straw in your way, nor done you aught but good? Come and speak to our chief upon the sea-coast.' Setting out with the Indian messengers, De Vries and Olfertsen, in the evening, came to 'Rechqua-aike,' or Rockaway, where they found nearly three hundred savages, and about thirty wigwams. The chief, 'who had but one eye,' invited them to pass the night in his cabin, and regaled them with oysters and fish. At break of day, the envoys from Manhattan were conducted into the woods about four hundred yards off, where they found sixteen chiefs of Long Island waiting for their coming. Placing the two Europeans in the centre, the chiefs seated themselves around in a ring, and their 'best speaker' arose, holding in his hand a bundle of small sticks. 'When you first came to our coasts,' slowly began the orator, 'you sometimes had no food; we gave you our beans and corn, and relieved you with our oysters and fish; and now, for recompense, you murder our people;' and he laid down a little stick. 'In the beginning of your voyages, you left your people here with their goods; we traded with them while your ships were away, and cherished them as the apple of our eye; we gave them our daughters for companions, who have borne children, and many Indians have sprung from the Swannekens; and now you villainously massacre your own blood.' The chief laid down another stick; many more remained in his hand; but De Vries, cutting short the reproachful catalogue, invited the chiefs to accompany him to Fort Amsterdam, where the director 'would give them presents to make

---

[1] Brodhead, i. 358, 359

a peace.' The chiefs, assenting, ended their orations, and presenting De Vries and his colleague each with ten fathoms of wampum, the party set out for their canoes, to shorten the return of the Dutch envoys. While waiting for the tide to rise, an armed Indian, who had been dispatched by a sachem twenty miles off, came running to warn the chiefs against going to Manhattan. 'Are you all crazy, to go to the fort,' said he, 'where that scoundrel lives, who has so often murdered your friends?' But De Vries assured them that 'they would find it otherwise, and come home again with large presents.' One of the chiefs replied at once: 'Upon your words we will go; for the Indians have never heard lies from you, as they have from other Swannekens.' Embarking in a large canoe, the Dutch envoys, accompanied by eighteen Indian delegates, set out from Rockaway, and reached Fort Amsterdam about three o'clock in the afternoon." A treaty was presently made with these Long Island savages, and, through their aid and influence, with the River tribes. But confidence was not fully restored; and in September following, hostilities again broke out, and the atrocities committed by the savages on the North River struck consternation to the hearts of the Dutch at Fort Amsterdam. Kieft again summoned the people to council, and they elected Eight Men to represent them in the deliberations concerning "the critical condition of the country." They advised that peace should be maintained with the Long Island Indians, and that they should be encouraged to become allies in war; but, that war should be actively prosecuted against the River Indians; and that a large force of militia should be forthwith enlisted and equipped. Before these preparations could be effected, however, the Indians fell upon the Westchester settlements, Maspeth, and Gravesend, all of which, except the latter, were laid waste. Long Island, in the language of an eye-witness, was "almost destitute of inhabitants and stock;" while from the Highlands of Neversink to the valley of Tappan, the Indian rule became more supreme. Even Manhattan Island was daily threatened; and seven allied tribes, "well supplied with musket, powder, and ball," hovered menacingly around the insufficient fort at New Amsterdam, where trembling families were closely huddled together, and the cattle were beginning to starve for lack of forage. "Fear coming more over the land," the Eight Men were again convoked, but the director adopted only one of their sensible suggestions: viz., that armed assistance should be sought from their English neighbors. The New Haven Colony, however, to whom application was made, declined, alleging among other reasons that they were not satisfied "that the Dutch war with the Indians was just;" but they offered supplies of provisions to the harassed New Netherlanders. Again, October 24th, the Eight Men met, and, for the first time, resolved to speak directly to their superiors in Holland. They sent a letter to the College of Nineteen, which, in simple and pathetic yet manly words, rehearsed the terrible situation of the province. In addition to this, on the 3d of November they addressed a remonstrance to the States-General, begging for immediate assistance, provisions, etc. While awaiting an answer from the Fatherland, the winter of 1643–44 was improved in disciplining the numbers congregated at Manhattan, and in various foraging and military expeditions against the Indians on Staten Island, and at Stamford and Westchester. Early in 1644, trouble arose between the settlers of Heemstede, a recent English colony in the present Queens County, on Long Island, and the Canarsee tribe in that neighborhood, whose chief, the one-eyed Penhawitz, was suspected of treachery. Expeditions dispatched from Fort Amsterdam against the Canarsees and against the Indians near Maspeth, both resulted in the complete discomfiture of the savages, with but slight loss to the whites. This was followed, February, 1644, by another attack upon the Connecticut Indians near Greenwich, in which the Dutch were again completely victorious. Planting season being again at hand, some of the hostile tribes began to sue for peace, which was concluded with the Long Island Indians, who had been pretty thoroughly intimidated by the affairs at Heemstede and Maspeth. The River tribes, however, remained implacable, and the settlers were kept in a constant state of alarm and incertitude, which totally prevented the progress of the settlements. Again, on the 18th of June, 1644, the director felt obliged to convene the Eight Men, whose advice he sought concerning the imposition of a tax upon wines, beer, brandy, and beaver-skin. To their better judgment, this measure seemed to be, in the impoverished state of the province, unwise, oppressive, and an overstepping of his legitimate power. Displeased with their advice, Kieft angrily reminded them that his will was yet supreme, and a few days after he issued, without their knowledge, a proclamation stating that for the purpose of carrying on the war, and "by advice of the Eight Men chosen by the commonalty," he had decided to impose the tax. This roused the ire of the Eight Men, whose sanction had been thus unwarrantably assumed, and the brewers refusing to pay the excise, their beer was confiscated and given to the soldiery. From that moment the spirit of resistance to arbitrary power became an element of the politics of New Netherland, and party spirit divided the community. The Eight Men became the representatives of the democracy, while the parasites of power espoused the cause of the director. And, although the Eight counselled active operations against the savages, and the available force at his command was strengthened by the opportune arrival of one hundred and thirty soldiers from Curaçoa, Kieft contented himself during the summer with a "masterly inactivity." The Indians finding themselves unmolested, grew more insolent than ever; so that, even at the distance of a thousand paces from Fort Amsterdam, no one dared "move a foot to fetch a stick of firewood without a strong escort." So deplorable was now the condition of public affairs, that the Eight representatives, on 28th of October, addressed a second memorial to the West India Company, stating their grievances, demanding the recall of Kieft, and the introduction into New Netherland of the municipal system of the Fatherland. This letter reached the College of Nineteen at an opportune moment, when, in obedience to a mandate of the States-General, they were in session to deliberate about the affairs of the colony. It was felt that the voice of the people could no longer be disregarded, and Kieft's recall was therefore determined upon. The College, likewise, referred all the papers in their archives relating to New Netherland to the newly organized "Chamber of Accounts," with instructions to report fully upon the condition of the province, and upon such measures as should be necessary for its advancement. Their report, communicated to the States-General a few days after, and which is one of the most important documents relating to New Netherland, fully reviewed the history of that province from its first settlement;

strongly condemned Kieft's policy; revealed the fact that the colony, instead of being a source of profit, had really cost the West India Company more than 550,000 guilders over and above all returns, and gave their decision that, inasmuch as the charter of "Freedoms and Exemptions" had promised protection and defence to the colonists, and as improvements in the management were not beyond hope, "the company could not decently or consistently abandon it." Acting upon the facts and suggestions presented in this report, the College of Nineteen, early in July, 1645, prepared a code of general instructions for the regulation of the "supreme council of New Netherland;" the expenses of the whole civil and military departments of the province being limited to 20,000 guilders per annum. Its government was vested in a "Supreme Council," composed of a Director, a Vice-director, and a Fiscal; and to this council was committed the decision of all cases involving matters of police, justice, dignity, and the rights of the company. In criminal cases, "two capable persons" were to be "adjoined from the commonalty of that district where the crime or act was perpetrated." A definite boundary was to be speedily established between the Dutch and English, and the rights of the Indians were to be strictly respected, and every endeavor made to secure their confidence. The colonists were to be encouraged to settle in towns, villages, and hamlets, "as the English are in the habit of doing;" Manhattan Island, hitherto monopolized by the company, was to be opened to immediate planting and settlements, and as many negroes were to be introduced as the patroons, colonists, and other farmers were "willing to purchase at a fair price." The fort was to be repaired and permanently garrisoned; while the colonists were required to supply themselves with arms, and to form a local militia, although without pay, which might be depended upon in case of war. The right of representation to the council at Manhattan was confirmed to the colonists "for mutual good understanding, and the common advancement and welfare of the inhabitants." Amsterdam weights and measures were made the standards in New Netherland; the Indian trade was reserved exclusively to the patroons, colonists, and free farmers; and the selling of firearms to the savages was strictly prohibited. The customs were to be rigidly enforced; and the expenses of the province, which had previously been borne exclusively by the Amsterdam Chamber, were now assumed by all the chambers of the company in common.

With the spring of 1645 came, at last, a welcome termination to the Indian war, and on the 30th of August, a general treaty of peace was ratified with all the tribes at Fort Amsterdam. But "the sting of war" remained. At Manhattan and its vicinity, scarcely one hundred men, besides traders, could be found. The church, commenced in 1642, was still unfinished. The money contributed for the erection of a common school-house had "all found its way out;" and even the poor-fund of the deaconry had been sequestered and applied to the purposes of the war. Beyond Manhattan, almost every settlement on the west side of the North River, south of the Highlands, was destroyed. The western end of Long Island was almost depopulated, and Westchester was desolated. The posts on the South River and the Rensselaerwyck Colony alone had escaped the horrors of war.

In the work of regeneration and reconstruction which was now to be commenced, Kieft's attention was first directed to securing the Indian title to lands in the vicinity of Manhattan, which had not yet become the property of the company. On the 10th of September, 1645, a tract of land on Long Island, on the bay of the North River, between Coney Island and Gowanus, and forming the present town of New Utrecht, was purchased from its native proprietors for the West India Company, thus completing their title to most of the land within the present counties of Kings and Queens. During the next month, a tract of sixteen thousand acres to the westward of Maspeth, was patented by the director to English emigrants who established there the town of Vlissingen, now known as Flushing. And Maspeth itself was soon repeopled by its former occupants, who had been driven from their homes by the desolation of war. Two months later (December, 1645), Lady Moody and her associates, who had so bravely maintained their position during these long and harassing years, received from Director Kieft a patent for their settlement on Long Island, adjoining Coney Island, now forming the town of "Gravesend."

Meanwhile, disagreements which arose among the several

Chambers of the West India Company concerning certain details of the new government of the province, delayed the recall of Kieft from the position which he filled so discreditably to himself and so disastrously to the public interests. His situation at this time was far from agreeable; the commonalty, informed of his intended recall, did not hesitate to express their satisfaction, and the director, irritated by their ill-concealed joy and reproaches, vented his spleen by fining and banishing those who were most outspoken. This was denounced as tyranny, and thereupon arose wranglings between himself and the people. Yet, amid these dissensions, which embittered the remainder of Kieft's term of office, progress was steadily made in the settlement and colonization of the country. On the east side of the North River, above Manhattan Island, in the summer of 1646, Adriaen Vander Donck established a patroonship, which is now represented by the town of Yonkers; and shortly after, Antonissen van Slyck, of Breuckelen, received from Kieft a patent for "the land of Kaatskill," on the North River, where he established a colony.

As will be seen from the preceding pages, the occupation of land within the limits of the present city of Brooklyn, commencing with the Bennet and Bentyn purchase of 1636, had steadily progressed, until now (1646) nearly the whole water-front from Newtown Creek to the southerly side of Gowanus Bay was in the possession of individuals who were engaged in its actual cultivation. Small hamlets, or neighborhoods, also, seem to have grown up at the original centres of settlement, known respectively as "*The Gowanus*,"[1] "*The Waal-bogt*,"[2] and "*The Ferry*."[3] About a mile to the south-east of this latter locality, and lying between the "Waal-bogt" plantations and those at Gowanus, was a tract, spoken of in the early patents as "Mereckawieck, on the Kil (or Creek) of Gowanus," and which was, undoubtedly, the residence of the tribe of that name. Here were the "maize lands" or planting grounds, which, in 1643 (*ante*, pages 36 and 37) were so unjustly despoiled by the covetous whites; and of which, during the war which ensued, the

[1] See page 23, and note. [2] See page 24, note; also Appendix No. 1.
[3] Identical with the present Fulton Ferry, at foot of Fulton street, Brooklyn, p. 35.

Indians were dispossessed.[1] As soon as, and even before, hostilities ceased, the choicest portions of this tract were taken up by the white settlers under patents from the Dutch West India Company. Thus, in July, 1645, JAN EVERTSE BOUT, followed in 1646 by HUYCK AERTSEN (van Rossum), JACOB STOFFELSEN, PIETER CORNELISSEN, and JORIS DIRCKSEN, and by GERRIT WOLPHERTSEN VAN COUWENHOVEN and others in 1647, established themselves in this vicinity, on either side of the road that led from Flatbush to "The Ferry." The village thus formed, and which was located on the present Fulton Avenue, in the vicinity of the junction of Hoyt and Smith streets with said avenue, and southeast of the present City Hall, was called BREUCKELEN, after the ancient village of the same name in Holland, some eighteen miles from Amsterdam.[2] Its founders were the first to avail themselves of the policy recommended by the West India Company's Chamber of Accounts, in the "Code of General Instructions" which they had prepared for the Provincial Council in the preceding autumn, viz.: "to do all in their power to induce the colonists to establish themselves on some of the most suitable places, with a certain number of inhabitants, in the manner of towns, villages, and hamlets, as the English are in the habit of doing." And their expressed wish and intention to "found a town at their own expense"[3] was promptly responded to (June, 1646) by the Colonial Council, with the following brief or commission:

"We, William Kieft, Director General, and the Council residing in New Netherland, on behalf of the High and Mighty Lords States-General of the United Netherlands, His Highness of Orange and the Honorable Directors of the General Incorporated West India Company. To all those who shall see these presents or hear them read, Greeting:

"Whereas, Jan Eversen Bout and Huyck Aertsen from Rossum, were on the 21st May last unanimously chosen by those interested

---

[1] See the discussion of the Lubbertse patent in chapter on "Early Settlers and Patents."

[2] For a most interesting account of a visit to the original Breuckelen, made by the Hon. Henry C. Murphy, of Brooklyn, while Minister to the Hague, the reader is referred to Appendix No. 4.

[3] N Y. Hist. Soc. Coll., ii., 332, and note.

of Breuckelen, situate on Long Island, as Schepens, to decide all questions which may arise, as they shall deem proper, according to the Exemptions of New Netherland granted to particular Colonies, which election is subscribed by them, with express stipulation that if any one refuse to submit in the premises aforesaid to the abovementioned Jan Evertsen and Huyck Aertsen, he shall forfeit the right he claims to land in the allotment of Breuckelen, and in order that every thing may be done with more authority, We, the Director and Council aforesaid, have therefore authorized and appointed, and do hereby authorize the said Jan Eversen and Huyck Aertsen to be schepens of Breuckelen; and in case Jan Eversen and Huyck Aertsen do hereafter find the labor too onerous, they shall be at liberty to select two more from among the inhabitants of Breuckelen to adjoin them to themselves. We charge and command every inhabitant of Breuckelen to acknowledge and respect the abovementioned Jan Eversen and Huyck Aertsen as their schepens, and if any one shall be found to exhibit contumaciousness towards them, he shall forfeit his share as above stated. Thus done in Council in Fort Amsterdam in New Netherland."[1]

This organization of the TOWN OF BREUCKELEN was further perfected, during the ensuing winter, by the appointment of a schout or constable, as appears by the following commission:

"Having seen the petition of the schepens of Breuckelen, that it is impossible for them to attend to all cases occurring there, especially criminal assaults, impounding of cattle, and other incidents which frequently attend agriculture; and in order to prevent all disorders, it would be necessary to appoint a schout there, for which office they propose the person of Jan Teunissen. Therefore we grant their request therein, and authorize, as we do hereby authorize, Jan Teunissen to act as schout, to imprison delinquents by advice of the schepens, to establish the pound, to impound cattle, to collect fines, and to perform all things that a trusty schout is bound to perform. Whereupon he hath taken his oath at the hands of us and the Fiscal, on whom he shall especially depend, as in Holland substitutes are bound to be dependent on the Upper

[1] Col. MSS., iv., 259, June 12, 1646.

Schout, Schouts on the Bailiff or Marshal. We command and charge all who are included under the jurisdiction of Breuckelen to acknowledge him, Jan Teunissen, for schout. Thus done in our council in Fort Amsterdam in New Netherland, the first December, Anno 1646."[1]

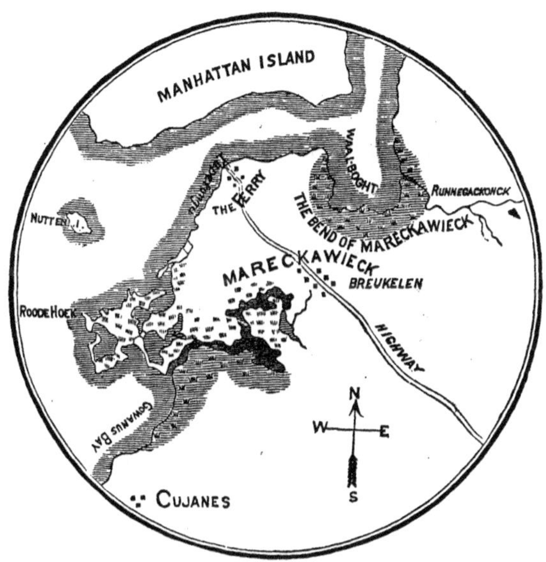

MAP SHOWING THE RELATIVE POSITIONS OF THE VILLAGE OF BREUCKELEN AND ITS ADJACENT SETTLEMENTS IN 1646.

Thus, more than two centuries ago, the TOWN of BREUCKELEN was founded upon nearly the same locality which has since become the political centre of the CITY of BROOKLYN.

---

[1] New York Col. MSS., iv., 276; O'Callaghan, i., 383; Brodhead, i., 421, 422. Teunissen appears to have been acting as schout previous to the date of his commission, as among Col. MSS. (ii., 152) are two contracts made by him with different parties for furnishing them with building materials, and dated *November* 22, 1646, in which he is called "Schout of Breuckelen."

CHAPTER II.

THE EARLY SETTLERS AND PATENTS OF BROOKLYN.*

UNLIKE the English towns at the eastern end of Long Island—which were generally settled by congregations or companies of individuals, bringing with them established religious and civil organizations—the Dutch settlements in the neighborhood of New Amsterdam mostly began as individual enterprises. The new-comers took up such tracts of land as best suited them, and commenced their cultivation. These lands were either selected from those of which the title had already been secured by the West India Company, or were purchased directly from the Indian proprietors themselves. In either case, their occupation was duly sanctioned by a patent or "ground-brief" from the Company, and confirmatory patents were also granted after the lands had been under cultivation for a certain number of years. Official transcripts of most of these patents yet exist in the office of the Secretary of State at Albany, from which, together with town and county records, we are enabled to locate the farms or "bouweries" of the early settlers with a considerable degree of accuracy. The dates of these patents mostly range from 1640 to 1646, in which latter year the period of *incubation* may be said to have terminated by the incorporation of the village of Breuckelen.

---

* NOTE.—In the preparation of this chapter we have received great assistance from Hon. TEUNIS G. BERGEN, of New Utrecht. His well-known interest in all that relates to the history and antiquities of King's County, together with an extensive fund of local information, acquired in the long practice of his profession as a surveyor, abundantly qualify him for the important services which he has so kindly rendered us in this portion of our work.

To the late J. M. GRUMMAN, City Surveyor, Messrs. SILAS LUDLAM, HENRY E. PIERREPONT, BARNET JOHNSON, NICHOLAS WYCKOFF, DANIEL RICHARDS, and others, we are also indebted for facilities for examining maps, family MSS., etc., for which we desire to return our grateful acknowledgments.

I.

In the year 1636, JACQUES BENTYN and WILLIAM ADRIAENSE BENNETT purchased from the Indians a tract of land in Brooklyn, extending from the vicinity of Twenty-eighth street, along Gowanus Cove and the bay, to the New Utrecht line,[1] as appears by the following Dutch record, being a certified copy, by Michael Hainelle, clerk, from the old records of the town of Brooklyn:

"On this 4th day of April (English style), 1677, appeared before me Michil Hainelle, acknowledged as duly installed Clerk and Secretary, certain persons, to wit: *Zeuw Kamingh*, otherwise known in his walks (or travels) as Kaus Hansen, and *Keurom*, both Indians; who, in presence of the undersigned witnesses, deposed and declared, that the limits or widest bounds of the land of Mr. Paulus Vanderbeeck, in the rear, has been or is a certain tree or stump on the Long Hill,[2] on the one side, and on the other the end of the Indian foot-path, and that it extends to the creek of the third meadows;[3] which land and ground, they further depose and declare, previous to the present time, was sold by a certain Indian, known as Chief or Sachem *Ka*, to JACQUES BENTYN and WILLIAM ARIENSEN (BENNETT), the latter formerly the husband of Marie Thomas, now the wife of Mr. Paulus Vanderbeeck; which account they both maintain to be the truth, and truly set forth in this deposition.

"In witness of the truth is the original of this with the said Indians' own hands subscribed, to wit: By *Zeuw Kamingh* or Kaus Hansen, with this mark, [mark], and by *Keurom* with this mark, [mark], in the presence of Lambert Dorlant, who by request signed his name hereto as a witness. Took place at Brookland on the day and date above written.

"Compared with the original and attested to be correct.

"MICHIL HAINELLE, Clerk."

---

[1] Ante, pages 23 and 24.

[2] The "Long Hill" referred to is the eminence now called "Ocean Hill," in Greenwood Cemetery, on the rear of the farm late of Cornelius W. Bennett and that late of Abraham Schermerhorn, and on the boundary between Brooklyn and Flatbush.

[3] The "third meadow" is the low ground, formerly meadow, between the land now of Henry A. Kent and that of Winant and Bennett; said meadow being located on the boundary between Brooklyn and New Utrecht.

In the course of a few years after this joint purchase, Bennett seems to have become the owner of the whole, or nearly the whole, of the entire tract,[1] and to have built himself a house on or near the site of the present mansion-house on the Schermerhorn farm, on Third avenue, near Twenty-eighth street, which was burned down during the Indian wars of 1643, in Governor Kieft's administration.[2] Bennett died about the same time, and probably during his children's minority, and his widow afterwards married Mr. Paulus Van-

---

[1] Dec. 26, 1639, as per deed recorded in office of Secretary of State at Albany, from JAQUES BENTIN, he sets forth: "I undersigned, Jaques Bentin, acknowledge that I have sold to William Adriansen a certain lot of land joining the land of William Adriansen, for 360 guilders;" by which he may have intended to convey his whole interest in the Indian purchase. May 25th, 1668, a confirmatory patent was granted to Thomas Fransen for "a certain parcel of land and meadow-ground upon Long Island, lying and being near unto or by Gowanes; the said parcel of land lying between the first and second meadow-ground or valley; being bounded to the north by the first, and to the south by the second valley, as by Paulus Vander Beeck it was staked out in the presence of the said Thomas Fransen and other witnesses; being also of the same breadth eastward as far as into the original ground-brief is set forth, the parcel of meadow being divided into four parts. Two of them—viz., No. 2 and No. 4—are transferred to the said Thomas Fransen, which makes the just moiety or half of the said meadow, together with a small parcel of woodland lying beyond that part of the aforesaid second valley where 'No. 4' is," as conveyed by Adriaen Willemsen (Bennett) to Paulus Vander Beeck, and, Sept. 5, 1666, conveyed by the said Paulus Vander Beeck and his wife, Maria Thomas, to the said Fransen, the quantity of land being certified by the surveyor and endorsed on the first conveyance

[2] In an affidavit, made on the 15th of February, 1663, before Walenyn Vander Veer, notary, etc., by Mary Thomas (sometimes called Badye, and widow of William Ariaense Bennett, her *second* husband; of Jacob Varden, her *first* husband; and *now* wife of Mr. Paulus Vander Beeck). it is set forth that "her houses, in the Indian wars, past about nineteen years, were burned and destroyed."

About nineteen years previous to 1663 carries back to 1643, in which the Indian wars, during Kieft's administration, took place.

This statement is further strengthened by a deed, dated January 2, 1696–7, from the Patentees and Freeholders of Brooklyn, to Adriaen Bennett, a son of the aforesaid William Ariaense Bennett (to secure his rights for what appears to be the same land covered by the patent to Mary Thomas. except that the quantity is two hundred acres), wherein it is set forth "that the said William Ariaense Bennett had formerly lawfully purchased a certain tract of land of the native proprietors, the Indians, in the year 1636, at Gowanus aforesaid, according to the boundaries and limits herein after specified; and that *by the Indian wars, and also by fire,* great part of the writings, patents, and deeds of said William Ariaense Bennett's aforesaid land is lost and destroyed, together with the records; and also that said Adriaen Bennett, the lawful heir to said William Ariaense Bennett, deceased, thereby is in danger to lose his right of inheritance," etc.

der Beeck, "surgeon and farmer." Mr. Vander Beeck, who was one of the patentees mentioned in the charter of 1667, granted by Governor Nicholls to the town of Brooklyn, and a prominent and influential citizen, died in the year 1680; and the Gowanus estate is next found in the possession of Adrian Bennett, a son of the original proprietor. During his occupancy, some dispute seems to have arisen between him and one Simon Arison (de Hart), who had become possessed of a portion of the original purchase.[1] In consequence of this controversy, and in compliance with the mandate of the Governor and Council, a new survey was ordered, as appears from the following report:[2]

"Pursuant to his Excellency's warrant, bearing date the 9th January, 1695–6:

"I have surveyed for Adriaen Bennett a certain parcel of land at the Gowanos, on the Island of Nassau, beginning at a certain small lane[3] near the house of said Adriaen Bennett,[4] and from thence it runs alongst the said lane and markt trees to a certain chesnut standing on the top of the hill,[5] marked with three notches, and thence to a black oak standing on the south side of the said hill, marked with three notches. The course from the said black oak to the first station is south 44° and 30′ easterly, distance 80 chains; and thence it runs irregularly by markt trees, said to be markt by the Indians when purchased by Willem Arianse Bennett, to a white oak[6] standing by the Indian foot-path, markt with three notches, the course 20° northerly, distance 122 chains; and thence it runs by the southwest side of Brookland Patent to the bay of the North River, and so

---

[1] Said portion being that owned by Thomas Fransen, as described in note 1, on previous page.

[2] Land papers, liber ii. 228, office Secretary of State, Albany.

[3] Probably the farm-lane between the farm late of Cornelius W. Bennett and that of Abraham Schermerhorn; said lane being near the present Twenty-first street, in the Eighth Ward.

[4] Supposed to be the present Schermerhorn house, or, at all events, the older portion of it; said house having since been modernized. (See next page.)

[5] Ocean Hill, in Greenwood Cemetery. (See note 2, p. 49.)

[6] The "white oak standing by the Indian foot-path, markt with three notches," referred to above, was a large tree with a decayed centre, which stood until some forty or fifty years ago, when it was finally prostrated by the wind. Within the remains of its stump, some twenty years since, Mr. Teunis G. Bergen, supervisor of New Utrecht, and Martenus Bergen, supervisor of the Eighth Ward, placed a stone monument, which forms the most southerly angle of the city of Brooklyn. At present all vestiges of the old tree have disappeared.

by the said bay to the place where [it] began; containing 930 acres. The bounds and limits of the land above exprest, the said Adriaen Bennett, when a day is appointed by his Excellency and council for the hearing of his evidence, doth promise to make them appear to be the bounds and limits of the land purchased by his father, Willem Ariaense Bennett, of the Indians, in the year 1636.

"AUG. GRAHAM, Sur. Genl.

"MAY 21st, 1696."

This survey was accompanied by a map, of which we give a reduced copy from the original now on file in the Surveyor-General's office at Albany.

The most easterly house on this map is undoubtedly the present mansion-house on the Schermerhorn farm, on Third avenue, near Twenty-eighth street. In course of time it has been remodelled and modernized, but the stone walls of the original house still form a part of the present building. Its site, as we have previously remarked, is identical, or nearly so, with that of the house built by Bennett and destroyed in 1643.

The house near the first meadow is the present old stone house, known as the De Hart or Bergen house, located on the shore of Gowanus Cove, west of the Third avenue, near Thirty-seventh and Thirty-eighth streets. The main portion is of stone, but the wing is of wood, and is probably a more recent erection, and has undoubtedly been several times materially altered and repaired. About fifty years ago Simon Bergen, its then owner, proposed to demolish the old building on account of its great decay, but, by the persuasion of his next neighbor, Garret Bergen (father of the Hon. Teunis G. Bergen), was induced to repair it and place a new roof upon it, and it has so remained to the present day. *Both of these houses, therefore, are older than the Cortelyou or Vechte house*, on Fifth avenue, which was erected in 1699, and hitherto has always been considered the most ancient building in Brooklyn.

The "Pond" is that since known as the "Binnen-water" (lake or marsh), located near the intersection of Fifth avenue and Thirty-ninth street.

The "Swamp" or Cripplebush, on the land of Bennett, is identical with that which formerly existed between the Third and Fifth

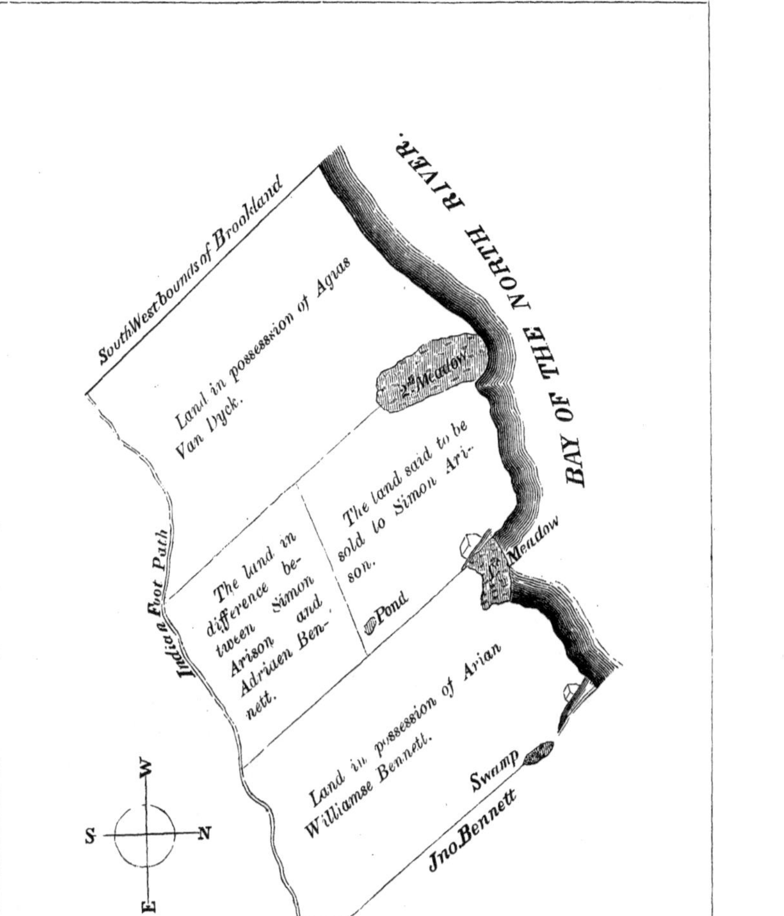

COPY OF A SURVEY made May 21st, 1696, by Augustus Graham, Surveyor-General, of the BENTON and BENNETT PURCHASE of the Indians. Containing 930 Acres.

THE SCHERMERHORN HOUSE

Page 52.

THE DE HART, OR BERGEN HOUSE.

Page 52.

avenues, in the vicinity of Twenty-eighth street, and is now mostly filled up.

The "first meadow" is located on Gowanus Cove, about Thirty-fifth, Thirty-sixth, and Thirty-seventh streets.

The "second meadow" was near the bay, in the vicinity of Forty-fifth and Forty-sixth streets and First and Second avenues.

The lands marked on the map as those "of Agias Van Dyck" were located mainly southwest of Forty-seventh street. They comprise the farms since of Henry A. Kent,[1] of Cornelius Bergen, of Theodorus Bergen, of Leffert Bergen, of Peter (afterwards Martenus) Bergen, and of the Van Pelts.

The *Cornelius Bergen* farm, between Fifty-seventh and Fifty-ninth streets, was sold, in 1760, by Hendrick Van Dyck,[2] to John Bergen, who conveyed it to his son Teunis, the father of Cornelius. It is now owned by William C. Langley and Thomas Hunt.

The *Theodorus* and *Leffert Bergen* farms, between Fifty-second and Fifty-sixth streets, together formed a tract which was originally sold by Claes Van Dyck, April 6, 1724, to Joseph Hegeman,[3] who, on May 10th, 1734, sold it to Cornelius Sandford.[4] On the 28th of August, 1744, these premises were again sold by Theodorus Van Wyck of New York and Helen his wife, the sole daughter of the above-named Sandford, "late of Brooklyn,"[5] to Hans Bergen, and was the first purchased by the Bergens of the numerous farms they afterwards settled at the Gowanus, Yellow Hook, and Bay Ridge. The estate descended to Bergen's son, Michael, who divided it between his sons Theodorus and Leffert. Leffert's portion is now owned by Thomas Hunt and M. McGrath.

The *Peter Bergen* and *Van Pelt* farms, between Forty-sixth and Fifty-second streets, were once owned by the Van Pelt family, and were divided between two brothers. The southern portion was

---

[1] The land of H. A. Kent is part of a farm since owned by Winant Bennet, and lying partly in Brooklyn and partly in New Utrecht.

[2] This property became his by conveyance, dated Oct. 6, 1708.—King's Co Convey., lib. iii. 196.

[3] Convey., King's County, lib. v. 6. Original consideration, £824.

[4] " " lib. v. 79. " " £500.

[5] Sandford's widow, Gertrude, married Joris Remsen.

conveyed by Wouter Van Pelt to Peter Bergen, who divided it between his sons Martenus and Peter.

"The land in difference between Simon Arison[1] (de Hart) and Ariaen Willemse Bennet," continued in possession of the former, who, on the 2d of November, 1696, obtained from Governor Fletcher a confirmatory patent covering "the land in difference" and the plot noted on the map as "sold to Simon Arison," which lands, a few years ago, comprised the farms of Simon Bergen and that of John S. Bergen, and are distinguished on Butts' map as lands of J. Morris, John S. Bergen, John F. Delaplaine and others.[2] They descended first to Simon, junior, a son of the first Simon; then to his son Simon, who, dying without issue, devised them to his sister Geertje, who married Simon Bergen. Simon Bergen resided on the premises prior to and in the beginning of the American Revolution, when he was accidentally shot, in 1777, "by a musket he was buying of a sailor, and died from loss of blood." The accident is said to have happened close to and in front of the old De Hart or Bergen house, described on page 52. After the death of Simon Bergen, the plantation was divided between his sons Simon, junior, and John S.; the former taking the portion (between Thirty-seventh and Fortieth streets) on which the old house is located, in which he resided for some years, until he finally built a more commodious one on the adjoining heights, after which the old one was used by tenants. After the death of Simon, junior, his daughter Leah, the wife of Jacob Morris, inherited the portion of the farm on which the old house is located, in which she resided until within a few years ago, when, in consequence of the increased value of the property, caused by the rapid strides made by the city, she was induced to dispose of it.

The lands designated on Graham's map as "in possession of

---

[1] SIMON AERTSEN (DE HART) emigrated to America in 1664, and settled at Gowanos, where he bought, probably within a short time after his arrival, a portion of the Bennet and Bentyn farm. On the death of his first wife, Geertie (Gertrude) Cornelissen, he married (June, 1691) Annatie, the widow of William Huycken of Gowanus. According to tradition, he was the builder of the De Hart or Bergen house, described on page 52, of which we find mention made as early as 1679 (see Coll. L. I. Hist. Soc., i., 122), which descended, with the plantation, to his eldest son, Simon.

[2] See note 1 on page 50, and note 1 on page 51.

Willem Ariaense Bennet" were patented, September 9, 1644, by Governor Kieft, to Mary Thomas (sometimes called Mary Badye), widow of Willem Ariaense Bennet, deceased,[1] and is the land between Twenty-eighth and Forty-first streets, designated as that of Abraham Schermerhorn, Garret G. and John G. Bergen, the heirs of Henry Pope, and that portion of Greenwood Cemetery which is taken from the rear of the Schermerhorn and Bergen farms.

II.

On the 5th of April, 1642, a patent was granted by Kieft to one CORNELIS LAMBERTSEN (COOL)[2] for lands described as

"Lying on Long Island, called *Gouwanes*, extending in length from the wagon-road between the aforesaid land and Jan Pietersen's land, lying alongside the river, till to a certain swamp (Kreppleboech), next to the land of William Adriaense (Bennet), which land was formerly occupied by Jans Van Rotterdam and Thomas Beets (Bescher), with the express condition that the roads as they now run over the above-described land shall remain as they now are. In addition to the above-described land, unto him, Cornelis Lambertsen, is granted a portion of a hay-marsh (valley) lying by the hay-marsh of Anthony Van Salee, containing six morgen."[3]

Cool's patent, extending from the northerly line of Bennet's land nearly to the head of Gowanus Cove, comprised, as near as can be ascertained, the farms designated on Butt's map of Brooklyn as of Peter Wyckoff, John Wyckoff, Henry Story, and Winant Bennet.

---

[1] Before she married Bennet, she was the widow of Jacob Vardon (or Fardon); and after Bennet's death, she married again, Mr. Paulus Vander Beeck. Alb. Rec., xxi. 41; date, 1663. See also, concerning the Bennet property, deeds of Simon Aerson to Dirck Hattum, March 7, 1677. Lib. iv. 122; also, various old deeds in possession of C. W. Bennett.

[2] Patents G. G. 46, Secretary of State's office.

[3] The Dutch *morgen* was equal to about *two* English acres. The Dutch *rod* was equal to 13 Dutch feet; or 12 feet $3\frac{62}{100}$ inches, or $18\frac{64}{100}$ links, English measure. A Dutch *foot* was equal to $11\frac{304}{1000}$ inches, English measure. The Dutch *mile* is equal to $2\frac{92}{100}$ English miles.

A deed from Thomas Bescher, above mentioned, to Cornelis Lambertsen (Cool), of May 17th, 1639, prior to the date of the patent recorded in the office of the Secretary of State at Albany, for these premises, is the earliest conveyance from one settler to another which has been found for lands in Brooklyn. In this deed Bescher conveys his right in

"A plantation before occupied by John Van Rotterdam, and afterwards by him, Thomas Bescher, situate on Long Island, by Gouwanes, in a course towards the south by a certain creek or underwood on which borders the plantation of Willem Adriaensen (Bennet) Cooper; and to the north, Claes Cornelise Smit's; reaching the woods in longitude: for all which Cornelis Lambertsen (Cool) shall pay to said Thomas Bescher 300 Carolus guilders, at 20 stuyvers the guilder."[1]

From this deed we may infer that one of the first agricultural settlements in Brooklyn was made upon these lands.

Of Claes Corneliese Smit's, afterwards Jan Pietersen's (Staats)[2] patent, above referred to, no copy has been discovered; and, in the absence of any measurements, we are only enabled to locate it as commencing about at the head of and on the southerly side of Gowanus Cove, extending some distance along the Mill Creek, or the meadows bordering thereon; including, it is believed, the land between Braxton and Ninth streets, designated on Butt's map as farms of heirs of Rachel Berry, J. Dimon, R. Berry, H. L. Clark, and A. Van Brunt.

We subjoin a few notes concerning the more modern occupation of the lands between First and Twenty-eighth streets.

From First to Fifth street, marked on our map as land of Edwin C. Litchfield, was originally the *Vechte* farm. On this farm is still standing, on the west side of Fifth avenue, near Fourth street, and on the east side of the old Gowanus road, the ancient building commonly known as "the Cortelyou house." It is constructed mainly of stone, the gable-ends, above the eaves, being of brick; the date of its erection, 1699, being indicated by iron figures secured to the

---

[1] See page 28. [2] King's Co. Convey., lib. iv. 9.

outside of the gable fronting the old road. As near as can be ascertained, Claes (or Nicholas) Adriaentse Van Vechten, an emigrant from Norch, in the province of Drenthe, Holland, owned the plantation on which the house is located, and probably erected the building. Previous to, and about the period of, the American Revolution, the property was owned by Nicholas Vechte, grandson of old Claes, the emigrant; and in 1790, Nicholas R. Cowenhoven, one of his heirs, sold the house and a portion of the farm, for the sum of £2,500, to Jacques Cortelyou,[1] who resided on the premises until 1804, when, unfortunately, having become insane, he committed suicide by hanging himself from the limb of a pear-tree in the orchard adjoining the house. He was a descendant, in the sixth generation, from Jacques Cortelyou, the surveyor, and first of the name, who emigrated to this country about 1652, and settled at New Utrecht.[2] After his death, the property was divided by his sons Adrian and Jacques, the latter taking the portion on which the old house was located, in which he resided until the enhanced value of the property, caused by the rapid spread of the city, induced him to dispose of some to parties who have divided it into city lots.

In this connection we may as well refute the popular tradition which states this house to have been the headquarters of Generals Washington and Putnam, prior to or during the battle of Long Island. The fact is, that Washington's headquarters were in New York; and although he went over to Brooklyn after the commencement of the unfortunate battle of Long Island, on the 27th of August, 1776, there is no evidence or probability that he went outside of the American lines, which extended from the Wallabout to the Gowanus Mill Creek. Putnam also had his headquarters within the lines, near to the ferry. There was undoubtedly some fighting in the vicinity of this house, as one writer says, "the British had several field-pieces stationed by a brick house, and were pouring canister and grape on the Americans crossing the creek." This building, therefore, must be the one referred to, as there was no other, answering to the description, in the vicinity.

---

[1] King's County Conveyances, liber vi., p. 434.

[2] See Coll. L. I. Hist. Soc., i. 127, 128.

The lands between Fifth and Seventh streets, designated as those of Theodore Polhemus, formerly belonged to his father.

The farm between Seventh and Ninth streets formerly belonged to Rem Adriance, whose daughter married for her first husband Cornelius Van Brunt, the father of Adriance Van Brunt.

The farm commencing on Gowanus Creek, and being between Ninth and Twelfth streets, also belonged, about 1810, to Cornelius Van Brunt, and is described in our map as divided between his son Adriance and Henry L. Clarke.

The Berry farm, on Mill Creek, extending from Twelfth to halfway between Fourteenth and Fifteenth streets, was sold, previous to the Revolution, by Cornelius Van Duyn to Walter Berry, and subsequently conveyed by Richard Berry to A. W. Benson.

From the southerly line of the above farm to the present Middle-street, was a farm which, about the year 1751, was conveyed by Christophel Scarse and Peter Van Pelt to John Bergen. He conveyed it to his brother, Dirick Bergen, who devised it to his three daughters, one of whom married Joseph Smith, another, Walter Berry, and the third, Ebenezer Carson. It is known on Butts' map as lands of J. Dimon, heirs of R. Berry, and Peter Wyckoff.

The land between Middle and Twentieth streets was originally one farm, owned by Cornelius Van Duyne,[1] and conveyed to Peter Wyckoff during the Revolutionary war. It is now owned by John Wyckoff.

The lands between Twentieth and Twenty-fifth streets originally formed one farm, owned by Jacob Fardon, and by him sold, in 1720, to one Anthony Hulsaart, of New Utrecht.[2] By him it was conveyed to Joseph Woodward and Wynant Bennet, and Woodward's portion is now known as land of Henry Story.

"*Blokje's Berg*" (pronounced, by the Dutch inhabitants, "Blucke's Barracks"), was the ancient name of a small hill on Gowanus Cove, near the intersection of the present Third avenue and Twenty-third street, the old Gowanus road passing over it. North of the

[1] This land appears to have been sold to William Huycken, in 1679, by Mr. Paulus Vanderbeeck, whose son, Conradus, in Dec., 1699, gave a confirmatory deed of the same to Cornelius Gerritse Van Duyne, who had married Huycken's eldest daughter. King's Co. Convey., lib. ii. 210.

[2] King's Co. Convey., lib. vi. 316.

hill was a ditch which drained the morass and swamp on the east into the cove, and this ditch was crossed by the road by means of a small wooden bridge. It is mainly memorable as the place where the British column, advancing by the Gowanus road, on the morning of August 27, 1776, received its first check, from an American picket-guard, on which occasion several lives were lost, being the first blood shed in that battle. Near it, on the northeast corner of Twenty-third street and Third Avenue, was the old Weynant Bennet house, which yet stands, retaining its ancient appearance, and yet bearing upon its venerable walls the marks of shot and ball received on that disastrous day.

The farms of Cornelius Bennet and Joseph Dean, between Twenty-fifth and Twenty-eighth streets, were originally one farm.[1]

Along the bay, between Twenty-fourth and Twenty-eighth streets, was the hamlet of Gowanus. It was originally laid out in village lots, and the old stone " Bennet house," which stood in the middle of Third avenue, near Twenty-seventh street, and was taken down when the avenue was opened, was probably a remnant of the original settlement.

III.

RED HOOK.

The "Roode Hoek," or Red Hook, so called from the color of its soil, has almost entirely lost its identity, in consequence of the construction of the Atlantic Docks, and the other extensive and important improvements in that part of the modern city of Brooklyn. Its original form and topographical appearance, however, has been faithfully preserved and delineated in Ratzer's map; and it may be described, in general terms, as extending from Luqueer's Mill Creek (about Hicks and Huntingdon streets), following the indentations of the shore around the cape and headland, to about the western boundary of the Atlantic Docks, on the East River; or, in general terms, as having comprised all the land west of the present Sullivan-street. Its history commences with the year

[1] Deeds of Bennett family.

1638, when Director VAN TWILLER petitioned for its use, which was granted to him on condition that he should relinquish it whenever the Company wanted it.[1] Van Twiller had previously become possessed of "Nutten" or Governor's Island, several islands in the East River, near Hell-gate, and lands at Catskill and on Long Island, amounting in all to between three thousand and three thousand seven hundred and fifty acres. These, as well as similar purchases made by other officials, were disapproved by the authorities at home,—who very justly complained that "the whole land might thus be taken up, yet be a desert,"—and finally, in 1652, were declared null and void, and the lands consequently reverted to the Company.[2]

The title of Red Hook being thus vested in the Government, was conveyed and granted to the town of Breuckelen, in 1657, by Governor Stuyvesant, and was subsequently confirmed by Governors Nicolls and Dongan.[3] It was sold, on the 10th of August, 1695, by the patentees and freeholders of the town, to Colonel Stephanus Van Cortlandt. In their deed, which recites the original grant by Stuyvesant, etc., the property is described as

> "A neck of land called Red Hook," estimated as containing fifty acres, more or less, of upland, then in possession of Peter Winants,[4] "together with all the land and meadow thereunto belonging, to the westward of Fred. Lubbertsen's patent, bounded between the Salt Water River and said patent."

To this was added, by deed from Peter Winants, "son and heir of Winants Peterson," in November following, twenty-four acres, "bounded east by the land heretofore belonging to one Frederic

[1] He afterwards (June 22, 1643) took out a patent for the same. Patents, G. G. 66, Sec'y State's office.

[2] Brodhead, i. 265, 267, 276, 536.

[3] Furman, 11.

[4] Sept. 30, 1678, Wynant Pieters had received a patent for "a piece of upland at the Red Hook, or point over against Nutten Island, within the jurisdiction or limits of Brookland on Long Island, beginning from a creek next Frederick Lubberts' land lying west from the high hook or point, and so on to the river; thence going along the river to the bay of the Gouwanes, south-southeast, and running again from the said bay easterly to Frederick Lubbertse's land. It contains about 24 acres of land." In N. Y. Col. MSS., xxviii. 165, 166, date Dec. 13, 1679, mention is made of a charge against Wynant Pieters, of having, by means of false information, obtained a patent from the Governor for *Red Hook*.

Lubbertsen ; north, by York River ; west, by Hudson's River ; and south, by Gowanus Bay." These purchases were subsequently confirmed to Colonel Van Cortlandt, by a grant from King William III., dated June 2, 1697.[1]

Van Cortlandt died Nov. 25, 1700, and on May 23d, 1712, his heirs executed a deed to Matthias Van Dyke, of property described as

"A certain messuage, mill, mill-dam, mill-house, and tract or neck of land or meadow, unto low-water mark, as far as a place called Koytes (or Kotier's) Kill (Graver's Kill),[2] lying and being upon the Island Nassau, formerly Long Island, commonly called and known by the name of the Red Hook, containing in quantity fifty acres, more or less; bounded on the east by the east side of a creek that runs by the westernmost bounds of Frederic Lubbertsen's land ; and on the south, by the Gouwanus Bay ; and on the west, by Hudson's River ; and on the north, by the East River, at low-water mark ; including the aforesaid creek, which maketh the east bounds of said lands and meadow."

The mill mentioned in this deed was undoubtedly erected during the occupancy of Van Cortlandt and prior to 1689, at which time it is referred to in an agreement between Corssen and Seabring. The mill-pond, which was formed by damming off the creeks and natural ponds in the adjoining marsh, contained in 1834 over forty-seven acres of drowned marsh, but it is long since filled up and obliterated by the march of modern improvements. The mill was located on the corner of the present Dikeman and Van Brunt streets, and the dwelling-house appertaining thereto stood about the corner of Partition and Van Brunt streets.[3] By a deed, dated Feb. 1, 1736, Matt. Van Dyke conveyed these mill premises to his son John, who is mentioned as one of his father's executors in 1749. He devised his estate to his two sons, Nicholas and Matthias, who, in 1784, divided it between them. On Ratzer's map, in 1766, these buildings are designated as of A. Van Dyke, probably Matthias, who with his son, is mentioned as residing on Red Hook, with their

[1] Also recorded, Pat., lib. vii. 132, etc., Secretary of State's office.

[2] So called from its being a convenient place to "*grave*" (from the Dutch *graaven*) or cleanse and recaulk the bottoms of boats and vessels. It was located at the "Red mills," or Cornell's mills, near junction of present Harrison and Columbia streets.

[3] Map of property belonging to heirs of Matth. Van Dyke, by R. Graves, junior, city surveyor, 1834.

respective families, during the Revolutionary war, and were described as "good staunch whigs and very clever folks."[1] At the time of the battle of Long Island a fort was erected here, named Defiance, and mounting four 18-pounders, *en barbette.*

The Nicholas Van Dyke mill, which was erected after the date of Ratzer's map, on the same pond, was located on the ground now bounded by the present Van Brunt and Richards, Van Dyck and Partition streets; the dwelling-house being on the northeast corner of Van Dyck and Van Brunt streets. This mill was called the "Ginger Mill," by which name it is yet distinctly remembered by some of our oldest citizens.

Boompties Hoek, or "tree-point," sometimes corrupted to Bombay Hook,[2] was the name applied to the southerly projection of Red Hook, and which, in common with all the natural features of this vicinity, has shared the oblivion consequent upon recent city improvements. "The Hook" originally extended from about the junction of the present Otsego and Cuba streets (where its memory is still preserved by "Bomptje's Hook Wharf") around to "Meuwee Point,[3] as it was called, at about the junction of the present Henry, Bay, and Grinnell streets.

Tradition asserts that Red Hook and Governor's Island were once connected, and that people and cattle waded across Buttermilk Channel.[4] The legend probably originated in statements made by witnesses in a trial which took place in 1741, between Israel Horsfield, plaintiff, and Hans Bergen, defendant, as to the boundaries of their respective farms.[5] The theory, sustained by some in support of this tradition, that the docks erected along the New York shore effected a change by diverting the currents of the East River towards Buttermilk Channel, is hardly tenable. Old traditions, how-

---

1 Onderdonk, Rev., Incidents Kings County, 117. In 1744 a battery of eight guns had been erected on this point. See Valentine's Manual of Common Council.

2 Benson's Memoir, p. 16.

3 Deed of Matthias Van Dyke to Nich. Van Dyke, Feb. 7, 1742, King's County Conv., lib. v. 120. "Meuwee" (from the Dutch *meeuw,* and German *mewe*) signifies "a gull;" and the Point probably derived its name from its being a common resort of sea-fowl.

4 Furman's Notes mentions it as "an established fact," and is followed by subsequent historians of Long Island. Buttermilk Channel is so called, undoubtedly, from the abundant white foam on the water, in a part of the channel where the tide of the East River, passing through the channel, meets that of the North River.

5 See Appendix, No. 5.

ever, on being compared with documentary evidence, are found to be very unreliable; for Ratzer's map of 1766, which is a remarkably careful and accurate survey by an accomplished engineer of the British army, gives *three fathoms as the least depth of that channel!* And no docks, certainly, until about the period of the trial, were built east of Wall street, which could have had the least effect in affecting the currents of the river in the manner supposed. It is well known, also, to residents on the bay of New York, that the loss by abrasion on its shores is caused mainly by the waves during storms and high tides, and very little, if any, by the ordinary currents.

IV.

We come, next, to the consideration of FREDERIC LUBBERTSEN'S[1] patent, dated May 27, 1640. His farm comprised the whole neck of land between the East River and Gowanus Creek, northeast of the meadows which formerly separated Red Hook from Brooklyn. This neck, formerly known as the "neck of Brookland" or "Lubbertsen's neck," has now lost its original appearance by the filling in of the Atlantic Docks, the grading of streets, and the various

[1] *Lubbertse*, an early emigrant to this country, seems to have been a sailor, as he held the position of chief boatswain to Governor Kieft in 1638, and was then a resident of New Amsterdam. In 1641 he was one of the Twelve Men chosen by the commonalty, and in 1643 purchased a house in Smit's Valley, which, in 1653, he sold to Albert Cornelissen, and removed to Breuckelen, which town he represented in the general convention held at New Amsterdam in December of that year. In 1653, '54, '55, '64, and 1673 he was a magistrate of Breuckelen; on the 17th April, 1657, was created a "small burgher" of New Amsterdam; and in February, 1660, was assessed in that city for repairs made to the "Heere Graght" (canal), on the north side of which he owned a lot. In February, 1662, he was an unsuccessful candidate for the office of burgomaster in the city, and in July, 1663, represented Breuckelen in the convention called to secure the co-operation of the Dutch towns in a system of armed defence. He died in 1680. In 1657 he married a second wife, Tryntie Hendricks, widow of Cornelis Petersen (Vroom), who, at the time of this marriage, had by her first husband three sons—Cornelis Corssen (Vroom), aged twelve; Peter, aged six; and Hendrick, aged three years. Lubbertse, also, had by his first wife, Styntie Hendricks (possibly a sister of his second wife) three daughters—*Elsje*, who married Jacob Hansen Bergen; *Rebecca*, who married Jacob Leendertse van der Grift; and *Aeltje*, who married Cornelis Seubring. Of the Corsens, Cornelis married in Breuckelen, and removed to Staten Island, where he became the ancestor of the Corsen family there. Hendrick married also in Breuckelen, and settled on the Raritan, where his descendants are numerous by the name of Vroom, one of whom is Governor Vroom of New Jersey. Peter Corsen remained in Breuckelen, where he married.

improvements of the modern city; and Lubbertsen's farm can only be defined, in general terms, as bounded by a line drawn between Degraw and Harrison streets west of Court street, the East River, Hamilton avenue, Gowanus Creek, and by Warren street east of Court.[1] This tract is described in the patent as land

"lying on Long Island, at Merechkawickingh,[2] near to Werpos,[3] extending in breadth from the kil and marsh coming from Gouwanus northwest by north, and from the beach on the East River with a course southeast by east 1700 paces of 3 feet to a pace; and in the length, from the end of said kil northeast by east and southwest by west[4] to the Red Hook."[5] This was accompanied with the "express condition that whenever the Indians shall be willing to part with the maize-land lying next to the aforesaid land, then Frederick Lubbertsen shall have the privilege of entering upon (*i.e.*, occupying) the same, in the breadth of the aforesaid parcel of land, and extending from that, without his being hindered by any one."

This Indian "maize-land" or cornfield was situated along the east side of Court street, somewhere between Atlantic and Baltic streets, and was probably in possession of the Indians two years later, in 1642, when it is called "Sassian's maize-land," and mentioned as one of the boundaries of Manje's patent. Three years after this, in 1645, it is mentioned in both Hudde's and Ruyter's patents as "Frederick Lubbertsen's maize-land." It is quite possible that the

---

[1] Lubbertse's patent appears to have covered (with the exception of Red Hook) a large portion of what is now familiarly known as South Brooklyn, comprising a large tract of upland, together with the adjoining salt meadows and marsh, which formerly separated Red Hook from the mainland; extending 5,100 feet along the East River, in addition to the water-front on Gowanus Cove and the Mill Creek, and including a portion of the surrounding salt meadows. These lands, afterwards owned by the Seabrings, and subsequently by the Cornells, are designated in Butt's map as lands of Luquer, Bergen, Coles, Conover, Hoyt, Cornell, Kelsey and Blake, Johnson, Heeney, and others.

[2] Or "Merechawieck," which name, although originally applied to the Waal-boght, was also used to designate the country between that bay and the head of the Gowanus Kil.

[3] Or Warpoes, from *warbase* or *warpoos*, a Dutch word signifying *a hare*. The name was applied to a place near the head of Gowanus Kil (see testimony of Peter Stryker, in case of Horsfield vs. Heirs of Hans Bergen, in Appendix, No. 5), and probably derived its significancy from the fact that the place abounded with these animals. There was a place on Manhattan Island bearing the same name. See Benson's Memoir, p. 7; Schoolcraft, in N. Y. Hist. Soc. Proceedings, 1844, p. 93; E. B. O'Callaghan, Hist. Mag., iii. 85.

[4] W. S. W. by W.

[5] Patents, Book G G. 53.

natives became dispossessed of the property during the troubles consequent upon the Indian war of 1643.

But, although thus early in possession, Lubbertsen did not take up his residence upon the land until some thirteen years after, in 1653. He received from Governor Nicolls a confirmatory patent of the above lands, dated March 28, 1667,[1] and devised them by will, Nov. 22, 1679,[2] to "his own two daughters, Aeltie, the wife of Cornelis Seubring, and Elsie, the wife of Jacob Hansen Bergen, each one a plantation as then in fence; and to his wife's two sons, Peter and Hendrick Corsen (Vroom), by her former husband, other lots."[3]

On the 17th of April, 1726, agreeable to an award of commissioners appointed to divide the property, Lubbertse's two daughters, Aeltje (then the widow of Cornelis) Seabringh, and Jacob Hansen Bergen and his wife Elsie, executed releases to one another.

Bergen's property, consisting of over two hundred acres, was given to their eldest son, Hans Jacobse Bergen, in 1732,[4] who subsequently resided upon his grandfather Lubbertse's patent, in South Brooklyn, his land extending to the head of Freeke's Mill-pond. He died before 1749, and by his will, made in 1743, a portion, if not the whole of his farm, became the property of his only son, Jacob Bergen, who occupied the old Lubbertse dwelling-house, near the junction of the present Hoyt and Warren streets. That portion (one hundred and thirty acres) of land, located in the vicinity of Court street and Gowanus Creek, and designated on Butt's map as land of Jacob Bergen and Jordan Coles, was conveyed by him to John Rapalie, in 1750, for £700;[5] "and it is probable," says Mr. T. G. Bergen, "that he sold during his lifetime, although the deeds have not been seen, other portions of his patrimonial estate, and that he purchased a portion of Gerret Wolphertse Van Couven-

---

[1] Liber iv., Patents, p. 30, office Sec. State.

[2] Liber i., Conveyances, 130, Kings County.

[3] Testimony of Abraham Lott in case of Horsfield vs. Heirs of Hans Bergen.

[4] Kings County Conveyances, lib. v. 160.

[5] Kings County Conveyances, lib. v. p. 164. Rapelje, in 1794, conveyed the main portion of this purchase to Robert Stoddard, having previously sold a portion to Jordan Coles. One hundred and ten acres of this was sold by Stoddard, in 1799, to Jacob Bergen, for $8,750.

hoven's patent (since of George Bergen, and afterwards of Horsfield), and a portion of Jan Evertse Bout's patent (since of Debevoise, and afterwards of Horsfield), said purchased lands lying between the northerly portion of his patrimonial estate and those of Van Rossum's patent (once of Michael Hanse Bergen, and late of Powers). This probability is founded on the fact, that the Van Brunts, the descendants of his daughter Sarah, owned said portions of Van Couvenhoven's and Bout's patents, and that they resided in the ancient dwelling-house located on the Bout patent, which the spirit of improvement, caused by the spread of the city, some twenty years ago, swept out of existence."[1]

That portion of the original Lubbertse estate devised to his two step-sons by his first wife, Peter and Hendrick Corssen (Vroom), finally passed into the hands of the former. In August, 1689, we find two indentures or agreements, of similar import, executed between one "John Marsh, of New Jersey," and Corssen, and Cornelis Subring, the husband of his step-sister Aeltje, concerning the erection of "a water-mill for grinding of corn," located "at the southwest side of the Graver's Kill, within the meadows belonging severally to Corssen and Sebring," over against New York. Marsh was allowed to make a dam in the said kill, near the house of Peter Wynants, and was to pay, for the privilege of building the said mill, "700 feet of good canoe wood, one half inch thick, to both Sebring and Corssen, and to grind for them corn for their own family use, free of charge, so long as the mill remained there." This was the mill designated on Ratzer's map, and subsequently known as Cornelius Sebring's Mill, and still later as Cornell's or the "Red Mill," situated south of present Harrison street, between Columbia street and Tiffany Place, and about opposite to Sedgwick street.[2] It probably passed into Sebring's hands prior to March, 1698, at which time Corssen conveyed to Sebring, land,

"in the neck of Brookland, commonly called by the name of Frederick Lubbertsen's neck, and formerly in the occupation of the said Lubbertsen; bounded east by the land of Jacob Hansen (Bergen); west, by the Red

---

[1] For various conveyances, mortgages, etc., of portions of this land, see Kings County Conveyances, lib. i. pp. 157, 180, 271.

[2] Map of property in Sixth Ward, belonging to Kelsey, Blake, and other heirs of John Cornell, deceased 1838.

Hook and Koll's Kyer Kill, so called (Graver's Kill); and north, by the lands of said Cornelius Sebring,"[1]

amounting to one hundred acres, with the meadows thereto appertaining. A bond, executed on 20th of same month,[2] binds Subering to maintain Peter Corssen, furnishing him with suitable board, clothing, etc., from which it may be inferred that Corssen's wife was at this time dead, and that he had no surviving children.

Along the shore, between the mouth of the Gowanus Creek and the place designated on Ratzer's map as I. Seabring's mill, and at about the junction of present Court and Sigourney streets, were a few sand-hills, known to the ancient Dutch as the *Roode Hoogtjs*, or "Red Heights."

This Seabring mill was built prior to 1766, the mill-pond being formed by enclosing, with a lengthy dam, a small cove and creek near the head of Gowanus Bay. The mill itself was located on the northeast corner of the present Hicks and Huntington streets, the Seabring house being on the north line of the latter street, between Hicks and Columbia streets. These mills became known, later, as the "Luquer Mills." One of the old mill-buildings, between Hicks and Columbia, Nelson and Luqueer streets, is still used as a white-lead factory, and the old dam extended from about the corner of Bush and Hicks to near the corner of Grinnell and Clinton streets.[3] On the Lubbertse patent, also, on the north side of the present Ninth street, between Smith street and Gowanus Canal, was the mill and mill-pond, built originally by John Rapelje, after 1766, and better known as "Cole's Mill." The mill-pond was an artificial work, being excavated out of the marsh, on the side of Gowanus Kil, by negro labor. Jordan Cole's house was situated on Ninth street, between Gowanus Canal and Smith street, and to the east of the latter.

On Ratzer's map may be seen, southerly from the Graver's Kill, a canal, running from the East River to Gowanus Cove, and separating Red Hook from the mainland. This canal originated in the necessity which presented itself to the residents of the Gowanus district, of avoiding the difficult and dangerous navigation around

[1] Kings County Conveyances, liber ii. 162. [2] Ib., 164.

[3] See map of property of Nicholas Luquer, sold at auction, Feb., 1833. The mill-pond is there estimated as covering 20 acres, 1 rod, 10 poles.

Red Hook, by row-boats. In May, 1664, Adam Brouwer, who had a mill on the Gowanus Creek, at the place more lately known as Denton's Mill-pond, petitioned the Governor and Council, in the name and behalf of the inhabitants of Gowanus, thus:[1]

"To the Right Hon[ble] Director-General and Council of New Netherland:

"Respectfully sheweth Adam Brouwer, in the name of the inhabitants of Gowanes and other persons at the Manhattans, that there is situate a kil at the end of Frederick Lubbertsen's land, and between (that and) the Red Hook, which might be made fit to pass through it to the Gouwanes and the Mill, without going west of the Red Hook, where the water is ordinarily shallow, inasmuch as the said kill, which now is blocked up by sand at the end, might be made, without much trouble of digging, fit and navigable for the passage of boats laden with a hundred skepels of grain, full of wood and other articles; and whereas your petitioner knows that neither he nor others, in whose name and his application is made to your Honors, can attempt or undertake to dredge or render navigable the aforesaid kill, without the special approbation and consent of your Honors, therefore the Petitioner turns to your Honors, respectfully praying, in the names as aforesaid, that your Honors would be pleased to consent and allow that the kill aforesaid, at the cost as above mentioned, may be dredged and rendered navigable, which would greatly serve to the accommodation of the inhabitants here and at Gouwanes, and to all appearanee, in time of storm, prevent accidents. Awaiting hereupon your Honors' favorable apostile, which granting, I remain, your Honors' humble servant,

"Mark of AB ADAM BROUWER.

JAN PIETERSEN.
GERRIT GERRITSE.
The mark of JANNBEUS.
JACOB TEUNISSEN KEY.
HENDRICK WILLEMSEN.
JAN GERRITSEN of Bredenhiesen.
LOUWERENS VAN DE SPIGHEL.
HENDRICK JANS VAN FEURDE.
HANCK DE FOREEST.
JOHANNES LOUWER.

WILLEM BREDENBENT.
Mark of WILLEM WILLEMSEN.
Mark of LEFFER JANNSEN.
Mark of JAN LEFFERSEN.
Mark of BARENT LEFFERSEN.
Mark THOMAS WARTONN (or NEWTOUN?)"

---

[1] N. Y. Col. MSS., x. Part iii. 225, May 29, 1664.

Frederic Lubbertsen, to whom the said marsh belonged, was also examined, and said he had no objection. So they were allowed to deepen the kil at their own expense; with reservation, however, of Fred. Lubbertsen's right in the property. The petition was granted, and the settlers were thus relieved of the necessity of going around the Hook. In August, 1751, Isaac Sebring, in consideration of £117, conveyed to Nicholas Vechte, Jurry Brouwer, and others, all Gowanus residents, the fee of a strip of meadow, "beginning at the east side of a little island where John Van Dyke's long mill-dam is bounded upon, running from thence northerly into the river," and twelve feet and a half wide. He was also to make a ditch along this strip at least six feet deep, and to allow the grantees the use of a "foot-path, two foot and a half wide, to dragg or hall up their canoes or boats." March 16, 1774, the Colonial Assembly of the State passed an act empowering the people of Gowanus to widen the canal, keep it in order, and tax those who used it. This canal was partially closed, some twenty-five years ago, by improvements at Atlantic Dock, but there are persons yet living who have frequently passed through it with their boats, in going to or returning from New York.

V.

We come next to the farm of CLAES JANSEN VAN NAERDEN, called in his neighbor Manje's patent, Claes Janse *Ruyter*. He received, September 30, 1645, from Governor Kieft, a patent of

"land, lying about south by east, a little easterly, over against the Fort, on Long Island, and bounded on the southwest and southeast sides by Frederick Lubbertsen, and on the northeast side by Jan Manje; it extends along the said Jan Manje's land from the beach, southeast one half point easterly, one hundred and eighty rods, then southeast fifty rods, south round the hill southwest by west and west southwest eighty rods; again through the woods next to the said Frederick's northwest by north one hundred and eighty rods, yet fifty rods more northwest by west, further along the beach seventy-four rods, amounting in all to twenty-one morgens, two hundred rods."[1]

[1] Kings County Conveyances, liber ii. 245, 246.

This tract was conveyed by Claes Janse, March 11, 1660, to Machiel Tuddens, and by him transported, April 3, 1666, to Michael Hayneste (probably Hainelle), from whose heirs it was subsequently purchased by Dirck Janse Woertman.

VI.

Next to Ruyter's patent, on the East River, lay that of Jan Manje, granted to him by Governor Kieft, Sept. 11, 1642, and described as

> "a piece of land, greatly (i. e., of the size of) twenty morgen, lying about southeast a little easterly, over against the fort in New Amsterdam, in Breuckelen, stretching about southeast one hundred and ninety rods inward the woods towards Sassian's maize-land, along the limits of the said maize-land fifty rods, and then again to the water-side two hundred and twenty rods, north northwest well, so northerly, and along the strand or water-side seventy rods. Which aforesaid land is lying upon Long Island, between Andries Hudde and Claes Janse Ruyter."[1]

This tract was sold, January 29, 1652, by Pieter Linde, who had married the widow of Jan Manje, to one Barent Janse.[2] On the 23d of August, 1674, Jan Barentse and Aucke Janse, together with Simon Hansen, as guardian of the minor children of Barent Janse, and his wife Styntje Pieterse, both deceased, "all living within the town of Midwout or Flackbush," appeared before Nicasius de Sille, the Secretary of the Dutch towns, and declared that they had transported the above land ("house, barn, orchard, upland, and bush-land,") to Dirck Janse Woertman.[3]

VII.

Andries Hudde, a member of Director Van Twiller's Council, in 1633, and an enterprising and prominent citizen of Nieuw Amsterdam, was the patentee of the lands adjoining Jan Manje's. Following the example of the Director, Mr. Hudde dabbled largely in real

---

[1] Kings Co. Conv., liber i. 246, and deed of Woertman to Remsen, lib. iii. 76.
[2] Kings County Conveyances, liber i. 24"
[3] Ibid., 247

estate, a pursuit for which his occupation as "town surveyor" afforded him ample facilities. In 1636 he was concerned with Wolfert Gerritsen in the purchase of several flats on Long Island, since occupied by the town of Flatlands and Flatbush. And in 1638 he became the owner of a fine plantation on Manhattan Island, near Corlaer's Hook. This property in Brooklyn was obtained by him, by patent, from Governor Kieft, September 12, 1645. It is therein described as being

"upon Long Island, over against the fort (at New Amsterdam), lying to the southwest of Jan Manje, and to the south or behind to the maize-land of Frederick Lubbertsen, and to the easterly side against Claes Cornelissen Mentelaer, stretching in front at the water or river side from the land of said Mentelaer to the land of said Manje, southwest by south 72 rod, next the land of the said Manje to the aforesaid maize-land, south southeast and betwixt south by east 245 rods, along the maize-land east by west 40 rods, and further through the woods to the land of the aforesaid Mentelaer, north by east well so northerly 145 rods, all along the land of the aforesaid Mentelaer to the first beginning due northwest 156 rods, amounting together to 37 morgen, 247 rods."[1]

Hudde never occupied this land himself, being, for several years thereafter, actively engaged as commissary at Fort Nassau, on the South River, where, in 1646, he purchased for the West India Company the site of the present flourishing city of Philadelphia.[2]

On September 10, 1650, however, Pieter Cornelissen, by virtue of a power of attorney from Hudde, dated July 27, 1650, conveyed the above patent to Lodewyck Jongh, for the sum of four hundred guilders, which conveyance was approved by the Governor and Council by an order dated January 2, 1651.[3] On the 19th of July, 1676, Harmatie Janse, the widow of Lodewyck Jongh, conveyed eight morgen and five hundred and thirty-six rods of the land mentioned in the above patent, to Jeronimus Rapalie; and February 12, 1679 (English style), she conveyed another portion, comprising twelve morgen, to Dirck Janse Woertman.[4]

On May 3d, 1685, Woertman, by order of Harmatie Janse, con-

---

[1] Conveyances, liber i. 249.

[2] Brodhead's Hist. N. Y. i. 426.

[3] Conveyances, liber i. 250.

[4] Convey., lib. i. 250.

veyed to the heirs of Joris Dirckse, "a small stroke of land lying at the east side of the highway (now Fulton street), being all they can pretend (to claim) by the aforesaid patent."[1]

The three patents of *Hudde*, *Manje*, and *Ruyter*, described in the preceding pages, comprehended, as will be seen, the whole territory afterwards occupied by the Remsen and Philip Livingston estates, Ralph Patchen, Cornelius Heeney, Parmenus Johnson, and others, The entire tract lying northeast of Lubbertse's patent, and having a river front (of two thousand six hundred and forty-six feet) extending from about Atlantic to Clarke streets, and from Court street to the East River, being at present one of the most thickly settled portions of our flourishing city, was purchased, as we have already seen, by Dirck Janse Woertman,[2] and was by him sold to his son-in-law, Joris Remsen, on the 10th of October, 1706, for the sum of £612 10s. current money of New York.[3] This deed, after reciting at length the several patents to Manje, Hudde, and Ruyter, together with the chains of conveyances vesting the same in Woertman, specifies that all these parcels, "now lie near the ferry, bound round to the Salt River, the lands of Garret van Couvenhoven and Garret Middagh, the highway leading from Brookland to the ferry, the land of the heirs of Jurian Briaz, and the lands of George Hansen (Bergen),[4] and Jacob Hansen (Bergen),[5] and Cornelius Sebring."[6] Joris Remsen, who was the second son of Rem Jansen Vanderbeeck, the ancestor of the Remsen family in this country, built a mansion near the brow of the Heights, which then presented the appearance of a rough and bold promontory of rocky cliffs, rising

---

[1] Conveyances, Kings Co., liber i. 251.

[2] There is still extant (Kings Co. Conveyances, liber i. 165) a marriage settlement between this Dirck Janse Woertman, "last man of Marrietie Theunis," and Annetie Aukes, "last wife of Wynant Pieterse," and a list of the goods and chattels she brought her husband.

[3] Conveyances, Kings County, liber iii. p. 76.

[4] He bought of Marritje Gerritse, widow of Nicholas Janse, baker, the land patented by Governor Kieft, in 1647, to Gerrit Wolphertsen (Van Couwenhoven).—Kings Co. Conveyances, liber ii. 181.

[5] Jacob Hans Bergen held the lands which his wife Elsie had inherited from her father, Frederick Lubbertsen.

[6] Sebring bought of Peter Corson, in 1698, one hundred acres "in the neck of Brookland, commonly called Frederick Lubbertsen's Neck," etc.—Kings Co. Conveyances, liber ii. 162.

from a sandy beach, and covered with a fine growth of cedar-trees, which gave to the place a remarkably picturesque appearance, as seen from the New York side. The Remsen mansion was used for hospital purposes by the British during their occupation of the town in the Revolution; was afterwards occupied by William Cutting, the partner of Robert Fulton in the steamboat business, and after his death it was sold to Fanning C. Tucker, Esq. He lived there several years, and then sold it to ex-Mayor Jonathan Trotter. From him it passed to Mr. Wm. S. Packer, and its site is now marked by Grace Church. The building itself was launched down the face of the Heights, and now stands on the site of the old Joralemon street ferry-house, on Furman near Joralemon street.

Philip Livingston, Esq., became the owner of an extensive portion of the old Remsen estate, prior to 1764, and in August of that year received from the city of New York (in whom it had been vested by the Montgomery charter of 1736), a perpetual grant (subject to an annual rent of thirty shillings currency, $3.75), of all the land fronting his property, along the whole breadth of his lot, between high and low water mark. The Livingston mansion-house stood on the east side of the present Hicks street, about four hundred feet south of Joralemon street, and, during the Revolutionary War, in consequence of Mr. Livingston's adherence to the American cause, was appropriated by the British, who then occupied Brooklyn, to the purposes of a naval hospital. After Mr. Livingston's death, the trustees appointed by Legislative Act of February 25, 1784, to sell his estate, disposed of that portion known as "the distillery property," to Daniel McCormick, in July, 1785, and on the 29th of April, 1803, they conveyed to Teunis Joralemon the property south of the distillery, and the Livingston mansion thenceforward became known as the Joralemon House. It was taken down at the opening of Hicks street.

VIII.

On the 14th of November, 1642, Claes Cornelissen (Mentelaer) van Schouw, received from Governor Kieft, a patent for land "on Long Island, over against the island of Manhattan, betwixt the ferry and the land of Andries Hudde, as the same lies thereto next, extending from Hudde's land along the river, 102 rods; into the woods southeast by south, 75 rods; and south southeast, 75 rods; south by west, 30 rods; and along the land of the said Hudde, northwest, 173 rods to the beach, amounting to 16 morgen and 175 rods."

This property, having a water-front of 1,276 feet six inches, probably extended from the north line of Hudde's patent to the ferry at the foot of the present Fulton street.

At "the Ferry" and its immediate vicinity, grants for house or building lots were made to several individuals, and by the beginning of the last century there was probably quite a hamlet at this point, having several streets and lanes, with houses clustered closely together. This is evidenced, not only by a number of deeds of lots "at Brooklyn Ferry," purchased and sold by Hans Bergen,[1] but by an interesting map, entitled, "A Draft of Israel Horsfield's Land at the Old Ferry, in the township of Brooklyn, in King's county, near the New York ferry on Nassau Island," drawn, on a scale of forty feet to the inch, by Englebert Lott, May 13, 1763. The copy, attested by Horsfield, September, 1767, which we have seen in the possession of Silas Ludlam, City Surveyor, is particularly

---

[1] March 23, 1716, Hans Bergen bought from the freeholders of Brooklyn, a lot, "bounded northeast by *highway* from Brooklyn to the ferry; southeast by *highway* between the lot and ground of Thomas Palmeter; southwest by *highway* lying between the ground of said Hans and said lot of land to the river; northwest by the river. (Kings Co. Convey., liber iv. 303, 119.) This purchase apparently covered the whole westerly front of Fulton street, from the alley known as Elizabeth street to the East River.

May 2, 1717, Hans Bergen bought Thomas Palmeter's dwelling-house and lands, at Brooklyn ferry, late of John and Sarah Coa; east, west, and north by roads, and south by land of Garret Middagh, two acres. (Kings Co. Convey., liber iv. 154.) This covers the lands fronting on Fulton street, from Elizabeth street to the Middagh property, southeast of Hicks street.

January, 1728, Hans Bergen conveyed to Israel Horsfield land at the ferry; southwest by Bergen's land; east southeast by land of Gabriel Cox; northeast by *highway;* northwest by *highway,* and partly by land of Horsfield and Middagh, beginning at a *street or highway* at east corner, now of Gabriel Cox, then by said *street* towards East River; north 60, west 226 feet, to *another street* leading to the East River side; then by said *street,* south 60, west 120 feet, to lot of I. Horsfield; then by the lot," etc., etc.

valuable, inasmuch as the original, formerly deposited in the Town Clerk's office, is now lost. A map of the Fulton street widening, and also the Village Map of 1816, by Jeremiah Lott, now in the Street Commissioner's office, need to be carefully studied, as throwing light upon the existence of this settlement at the ferry, which it is probable was mostly located on the grounds subsequently owned by John Middagh and Cary Ludlow, on the southwest side of Fulton street.

North of the Ferry, as near as can be ascertained, came, either a patent for a small parcel belonging to Cornelis Dircksen (Hooglandt), "the Ferryman," or that of Jacob Wolphertsen (van Couwenhoven).

IX.

On January 24th, 1643, Dircksen sold this property (of which we have been unable to find any recorded patent), then described as "his house and garden, with some sixteen or seventeen acres of land on Long Island," to one William Thomassen, together with his right of ferriage, provided the Director would consent, for 2,300 guilders in cash and merchandise.[1] William Thomassen we suppose to be the same individual as William Jansen, who is known to have succeeded Cornelis Dircksen as ferryman about this time. Dircksen, after retiring from the charge of the ferry, obtained from Governor Kieft, December 12, 1645,

"a piece of land, both maize and woodland, lying on Long Island, *behind the land by him heretofore taken up;* it lies betwixt the land of Herry Breser and another parcel; it extends along the said Herry's marsh till to the aforesaid parcel, and further into and through the wood and maize land to the buildings and improvements of Claes Cornelissen Mentelaer, west by north and west northwest between both, 172 rods; its breadth behind in the woods to the said Herry, northeast by east, 59 rods; further on to the maize-land, east a little south, 45 rods; further through the maize-land to the marsh, southeast by east, 109 rods; amounting in all to 12 morgen and 157 rods."

---

[1] N. Y. Col. MSS., ii. 44.

The patent for the land of Dircksen, above described, as "heretofore taken up," has not been found, but is probably covered by the land sold to Willem Thomassen, and by that described in the following conveyances.

January 4, 1652, Cornelis Dircksen, ferryman, sold to Cornelis de Potter,

"a lot of land on Long Island, near the ferry, next the lot of Breser's, granted to him by the Director-General, by deed of April 28, 1643, and now as measured in behalf of Claes Van Elfland, November 7, 1651; broad towards the north, 39 rods; then along the shore towards the woods till a marked tree to the east side, 63 rods; and to the west, 76 rods; this measured lot lays in a triangle amounting to 2 morgen."[1]

December 3d, 1652, Cornelis Dircksen (Hooglandt), of the ferry on Long Island, conveyed to Cornelis de Potter,

"certain buildings and a piece of land, containing 2 morgens and 67½ rods, extending along the wagon-road, whereof the perpendicular is 65 rods, and the base 39 rods,"

by virtue of the ground-brief given to the grantor by the Director-General and Council, April 28, 1643.[2]

August 28, 1654, a patent was granted to Egbert Van Borsum, then acting as ferryman, for

"a lot on Long Island, situate at the ferry, beginning at an oak-tree near the fence of Mr. Cornelis Potter, is broad 40 feet Rynland; from thence to the strand, broad 40 feet Rynland; further back to the oak-tree, broad 40 feet Rynland."[3]

March 12, 1666, a patent was granted to Egbert Van Borsum to confirm to him a piece of ground, with a house thereon, at the ferry in Brooklyn, on Long Island,

"beginning at a certain oak-tree near the limits of the land heretofore belonging to Cornelis de Potter, containing in breadth 40 feet; so to run down to the water-side as much; then to go along the strand, in breadth 40 feet; and from thence to strike up again to the oak-tree, as aforesaid."

---

[1] N. Y. Col. MSS., iii. 99. [2] Patents, H H, 8. [3] Patents, H H, Part ii. 19.

Also a grant to the said Egbert of "20 foot of ground more, adjoining to the former, both above and below, along the strand."

X.

The land referred to in the preceding patent as that of Herry Breser was originally granted to Jacob Wolphertsen (von Couwenhoven), by Governor Kieft, July 3, 1643. It was

"a piece of land lying on Long Island, on the East River, bounded north by west by Cornelis Dircksen (Hooglandt), ferryman's land; stretching from said ferryman's land, east by south, along the river, 56 rods; and along ditto into the woods, south by east, 132 rods; in breadth in rear in the woods, 40 rods; and on the east side, north by west till to the river, 120 rods; amounting to 10 morgen and 48 rods."

The same land, having a water-front of 686 feet, was confirmed to Herry (Henry) Breser, by Governor Kieft, September 4, 1645, and described as

"land lying at the East River, between (the river and) the land of Cornelis Dircksen (Hooglandt), ferryman; south by east from the strand (beach), 132 rods; thence 45 rods east a little southerly till to the maize-land; further on through the maize-land till to the marsh, 109 rods; through the marsh, northeast by north, 20 rods; further again to the woods, next to the land of Jan Ditten, west northwest till to the woods, and through the woods, next to the land of Frederick Lubbertsen, to the East River, north by west 120 rods; along the strand to the place of beginning, 56 rods; amounting in all to 16 morgens 468 rods."[1]

This property was conveyed by Breser, on the 29th of August, 1651, to Cornelis de Potter, for the sum of 1,125 guilders.[2]

The patents of Lubbertsen and Breser comprised the balance of the Comfort and Joshua Sands' property, as described on our map,

[1] Patents, G G, 112. In N. Y. Col. MSS., vi. 37, is a document, dated 1655, in which Harry Breser, who retired "from here during the (Indian) troubles, contrary to the Placard," solicits permission to return, and is allowed to "reside and trade here, and to bring his mercantile concerns in order, and dispose of his real property, but not to recover permanent residence."

[2] N. Y. Col. MSS., iii. 92.

up to line, probably, of Fulton street; and previous to the Revolutionary War were owned by John Rapalje, a great-great-grandson of the first settler. Mr. Rapalje was a person of considerable importance, was the owner of the largest estate in Brooklyn, had occupied, at one time, a seat in the Provincial Assembly, and enjoyed the highest confidence and respect of his fellow-citizens. Upon the breaking out of the Revolution, the family adhered to the British cause, in consequence of which a bill of attainder was passed against him, October 27, 1779, and he was banished to New Jersey. After the occupation of Long Island by the British, he returned to Brooklyn, and there remained with his family until October, 1783, when, in company with his son, his son-in-law, Colonel Lutwyche, and a grand-daughter, he removed to England, and settled at Norwich, in the County of Norfolk. All efforts to procure a reversion of his attainder, and the restoration of his confiscated estates in America, having failed, his losses were reimbursed to him by the British government, and he died at Kensington, in his seventy-fourth year, January 12, 1802. Loyalist as he was, it was often said of him by his old neighbors of Brooklyn, that "he had an honest heart, and never wronged or oppressed a Whig or other man."[1]

His lands and other property, in various parts of Brooklyn, having been confiscated to the people of the State, were sold by the Commissioners of Forfeited Estates.[2] That portion under consideration, lying between Gold and Fulton streets, was purchased, on the 13th of July, 1784, by Comfort and Joshua Sands, for the sum of £12,430, paid in State scrip.[3] Some ten or twelve years after the

[1] See genealogy Remsen family, in Riker's Hist. Newtown, 385; Holgate's American Genealogies, 20.

[2] Liber 6, Conveyances, p. 345, Kings Co.

[3] Described as "all that certain farm or parcel of land and the several dwelling-houses, buildings, barns, stables, and other improvements thereon erected, and being late the property of John Rapalje, Esq., situate, lying, and being in the township of Brooklyn, Kings County, and State of New York; bounded, southerly, partly by the highway leading from Brooklyn ferry and partly by the lots of Jacob Sharpe and others; easterly, by the land of Matthew Gleaves (the Tillary parcel on our map), and the lands now or late belonging to the estate of Barent Johnson, deceased; northerly, by the land of Rem Remsen; and westerly, by the East River; containing 160 acres," etc.—Lib. vi., Conveyances Kings Co., p. 345.

The land at this time was unfenced, the title deeds were in Rapalje's possession, and unrecorded, and the boundaries of his lands were given by the Commissioners from common report.

war, Rapalje's grand-daughter, who had married George Weldon in England, came, with her husband, to New York, with the intention of prosecuting for recovery of the estate, on the ground that its confiscation had taken place subsequent to the treaty of peace. They brought with them the original title deeds and other documents of the estate, and, it is said, the town records of Brooklyn, which Rapalje carried to England. A number of depositions were made and collected in Brooklyn, relative to the property, and Aaron Burr and other eminent counsel were consulted, whose advice was adverse to the prosecution of the suit. The Weldons, therefore, returned to England, carrying with them all the valuable records and papers which they had brought with them.[1]

No further attempt has ever been made to disturb the title, and the land was afterwards laid out in streets and lots by the Messrs. Sands.[2]

XI.

Adjoining Fiscock's patent, on the East River, was that of FREDERICK LUBBERTSEN, granted by Governor Kieft, September 4, 1645, having a water-front of nine hundred and fifty-five feet six inches, and described as extending to "Herry Breser's, formerly Jacob Wolphertsen (Van Couvenhoven's) land:"

"northwest by west, 120 rods; its breadth behind, in the woods, east by north, 59 rods; back again to the strand (beach), north and north by west, 134 rods; along the strand, west by south one-half point southerly, 78 rods: amounting in all to 15 morgens and 52 rods."[3]

---

[1] MSS. of Jeremiah Johnson, who says that these facts were concealed, and unknown until subsequent researches had been made in the public Government offices of England, for the true Records of Brooklyn.

[2] See "A Plan of Comfort and Joshua Sands' Place, by C. Th. Goerck, 1788," in possession of Silas Ludlam, City Surveyor. The streets were somewhat differently named from the present names. The present Washington street was named *State;* the present Adams street was named *Congress;* the present Pearl was *Elizabeth;* the present Jay, *Hester.* In present Water street, a little west of present Jay (then Hester), stood Sands' Powder-house Dock. On the foot of Dock street was the "Storehouse Dock." See, also, Cooper's map of Comfort Sands' property, 1806.

[3] Patents, G G, 114.

XII.

ALONG THE EAST RIVER.

The "land lying at the west corner of Marechkawieck, on the East River," was first granted to EDWARD FISCOCK, whose widow married one JAN HAES. On April 2d, 1647, Haes received from Governor Kieft a confirmation of this property, which was described as extending

"from the land of Frederick Lubbertsen, east, southeast, and southeast by east to the marsh, 80 rods; and along the valley (meadow), northeast, 126 rods, with certain out and in points; further north by east, 45 rods; west-northwest, 30 rods; west by north, 80 rods; west and west by south, 67 rods; along the land of Frederick Lubbertsen, and south and south by east, 134 rods: amounting to 38 morgens 485 rods."[1]

This tract, having a water-front of eight hundred and twenty feet and nine inches, was located at the west cape or point of Wallabout Bay, and embraced a part of the present United States Navy-yard, and a portion of the Comfort and Joshua Sands estate. The point formed by the junction of the Waale-boght with the East River was subsequently called "Martyn's Hook," probably from one Jan Martyn, who is mentioned as a proprietor in that vicinity about the year 1660.[2] At a more modern day the name became corrupted to that of "Martyr's Hook."[3] A portion of this

---

[1] Patents, G G, 206.

[2] Oct. 19, 1660, a patent was granted to Jan Martyn, for "a lot on Long Island, at the Ferry on the east side of the East River, on the west side of the land of the aforesaid Jan Martyn, on the north side of Joris ——. The north side is 15 rods 7 feet; the east side, 18 rods 4 feet; the west side, 12 rods 3 feet; the south side, 18 rods 7 feet.

July 8, 1667, Peter Meet received a confirmatory patent for two parcels, one being the above-mentioned, and the other a parcel granted, Dec. 12th, 1653, to Adriaen Hubertsen, being a lot and house-garden, "lying by the Ferry aforesaid, on the west side of the lot of Francis Poisgot, on the east side of Samuel Minge, being in breadth, on the north side, 6 rod, and on the south side the like," which piece, transferred by the said Adriaen to the said *Jan Martin*, was, together with the former, transferred by the latter to Jan Jacob de Vries, who afterwards conveyed the same parcels to Peter Meet.

[3] Also "Martense's Point," a corruption of *Martyn;* subsequently, from its successive owners, "Remsen's Point" and "Jackson's Point."

property was sold by Haes, on 4th of January, 1652, to Cornelis de Potter, who on the same day became the owner of lands in the same vicinity, previously owned by Cornelis Dircksen (Hooglandt), the ferryman (ante, pp. 75, 76).[1] The property afterwards came into possession of Aert Aertsen (Middagh), the ancestor of the Middagh family, who, in 1710, erected a mill on this Hook, where a natural pond in the marsh, requiring a short dam, afforded the necessary facilities. He sold, Feb. 9, 1713, an undivided half of the premises to Hans Jorisse Bergen, who, on the 28th January, 1722–3, conveyed to Cornelius Evertse the same, described as "one-half of the meadow, sand, creek, grist-mill, dam, beach of the old dwelling-house, bolting-mill and bolting-house (the new dwelling-house only excepted), situated in Brooklyn, at a place called *Marty's Hook*, as in fence, and as bought by the said Hans Jorisse Bergen of Aert Aertsen (Middagh)."[2] This above-mentioned mill, built by Middagh, is undoubtedly identical with that marked on Ratzer's plan as *Remsen's Mill;* and the same property in the Wallabout (now occupied by the United States Navy-yard), together with the land as far as the line of Gold street, was afterwards known as the Remsen estate. As such it belonged to Rem A. Remsen, who died in 1785,

[1] N. Y. Col. MSS., iii. 100.

[2] Conveyances, liber iv. 309, 336, Kings County Reg. office. *Aert Anthonize* (or *Teunissen*) *Middag*, the ancestor of the Middag family of Brooklyn, married Breckje (or Rebecca), second daughter of Hans Hansen Bergen and Sarah Rapalje; and on the 24th of October, 1654, together with his wife's step-father, Teunis Gysbert (Bogaert), received a patent for "a piece of land lying on Long Island, named Cripplebush," adjoining the land of Joris Rapalje, and containing 100 acres. This is supposed to be the land since owned by Folkert Rapalje, in the Wallabout, and the patent is not recorded. Middagh was an early resident of the Waal-boght, where his children were born. They were (1), *Jan*, baptized Dec. 24, 1662, who signed his name Jan Aersen, and married Adriaentje, daughter of Cornelis de Potter (mentioned on pp. 76, 77), and owned some 200 acres on the East River, west of Fulton street, since known as the Comfort and Joshua Sands property; (2), *Garret*, who married, in 1691, Cornelia Janse Cowenhoven, and had a farm of thirty acres, near the ferry, on the west side of the present Fulton, near Henry street; (3), *Dirck*, who married, and, as well as his brother, had children.

The farm of Garret Middagh, above-mentioned, may be described as bounded, on our present maps, by Fulton street, a line midway between and parallel to Henry and Hicks streets, and a line about midway between Pierrepont and Clarke streets. It descended to his son Aert, and in 1827, when the property had become valuable, on account of the expansion of the village, a lawsuit occurred in the family as to the provisions of his will. The family name is now extinct, being only commemorated by a street on the Heights. A portion of the old Middagh mansion is, however, standing on Fulton street, just below Henry street.

leaving a widow and four children, two of whom were by a former wife. The late General Jeremiah Johnson married Remsen's daughter by his first wife, who died within a year, leaving a child, who also died in infancy. Johnson, having thus become a tenant by coutesy for life, subsequently conveyed his interest to his brother-in-law, Cornelius Remsen. He failed, after two years, and the estate being sold under judgment, was purchased, for the sum of $17,000, by John Jackson, Esq., who afterwards bought the rights of the widow and remaining children, and became the owner of the whole property. Forty acres of this tract was purchased from Mr. Jackson by Francis Childs, a middle-man, who, on the 23d of February, 1801, conveyed it to the United States Government, which has ever since occupied it as a navy-yard.

XIII.

Next to the Haes patent came that granted to Hans Lodewyck, November 3d, 1645,

"containing 14 morgen and 494 rods, lying next to the land of Michael Picet, extending exactly such as the surveyor has laid it out."[1]

It is possible, however, that other lands may have been patented between those of Haes and Lodewyck, and that the latter had no river or meadow front.

XIV.

Michael Picet, a Frenchman, and referred to as owner of the farm adjoining Lodewyck's, did not remain in possession long, as, on February 19, 1646, it was granted to Willem Cornelissen.[2] It contained twenty-five morgen "in the bend of Marechkawick, with the marsh (salt meadow) of the breadth of the aforesaid land," and was probably of the same general dimensions as the adjoining farms. Cornelissen transported the property, January 22, 1654, to Paulus Leendersen Vander Grift, "for the use and behoof of" one Charles Gabrey, and it was subsequently confirmed, 1668, to the said

---

[1] Patents, G G, 127.

[2] Ibid., 135.

Vander Grift. Gabrey afterwards fled from the country, and the estate being confiscated, was again granted by the Governor, July 12, 1673, to Michael Heynall, Dirck Jansen, and Jeronimus Rapalie.[1]

XV.

Peter Cæsar Italien, elsewhere called Cæsar Alberti,[2] received from Governor Kieft, June 17, 1643, a grant of land

"for a tobacco plantation, lying in the bend of Marechkawieck, next to Peter Montfoort's on the east side, and Michael Picet on the west; extending along the marsh 57 rods, and along the land of Peter Montfoort, in a southerly direction, towards and into the woods, in the length, 270 rods: amounting to 24 morgens and 250 rods."

On May 1, 1647, he received an addition to the westerly side of his farm, two hundred and twenty rods in length and twenty-eight and a half rods in breadth, provided it could be done without prejudice to his neighbors.[3] On the 17th of May, 1647, "Jacques Cortelyou, as vendue-master and as attorney of the heirs and children of Peter Ceser Italian," and the "Deacons" of the City of New York, conveyed to John Damon the above patent, in which the premises are described as

"stretching along the middow 57 rods, and along the land of Pieter Montfoort, southward, into the woods, in the length, 270 rods; and after in the bosch (woods), broad, 57 rods; and then again to the middow, alongst Michile fransman (Frenchman, *i. e.*, Michael Picet) to the middow, 270 rod: amounting to 24 morgen 450 rod."

The heirs and children also executed a conveyance, confirming that of Cortelyou.

May 10th, 1695, the above property, with the exception of six acres previously sold to Garret Middagh, was conveyed by John Damon, and Fitie his wife, of the Wallabout, to William Huddle-

---

[1] Gen. Entries, iv. 287; Kings County Conveyances, lib. i. 89.

[2] Pieter Cæsar Alberti was the ancestor of the Alburtus family. (See Annals of Newtown.)

[3] Patents, G G, 65.

stone, of the city of New York, who also received, August 8th, 1695, from the attorney of John and William Alburtis, children of Peter Ceser, a confirmatory conveyance, in which the premises are estimated at one hundred acres. On the 2d of May, 1696, William Huddlestone, and Sarah his wife, conveyed the above patent to John Damon.

These two farms, of Peter Cæsar Italien (which had a river or meadow front of six hundred and ninety-nine feet three inches) and that of Picet, comprised the land now lying between Clermont and Hampden avenues.

XVI.

Peter Montfoort received, May 29th, 1641, from Governor Kieft, a patent for

"land on Long Island, extending from Jan Montfoort's land to Pieter the Italian's, in breadth 300 paces, (extending) with the same breadth straight into the woods."[1] On the 19th August, 1643, it was confirmed by a patent wherein it is more particularly described as "a piece of land for a tobacco plantation, lying on Long Island, in the bend of Marechkawieck, bounded by Jan Montfoort on the east, and Pieter Italien on the west, extending along the marsh into the woods, 70 rods; and 220 rods along the land of Jan Montfoort, to the woods, 70 rods; again to the marsh, in a northerly course, 227 rods, along the land of Peter the Italian: amounting to 25 morgens and 8 rods."[2]

On May 1, 1647, he received a grant of an addition to the westerly side of the above land, two hundred and twenty rods square, "provided it did not interfere with other grants." Pieter Montfoort's land had a river or meadow front of about nine hundred feet, and is now comprised between Hamilton avenue and a line a little beyond the line of Clermont avenue.[3]

XVII.

Jan Montfoort (probably a brother of Peter Montfoort) received, at the same time, May 29, 1641, a grant from Governor Kieft of a

[1] Patents, G G, 89.
[2] Patents, G G, 63; Valentine's Manual, 1851, p. 473.
[3] Designated on map as farms of John and Jeremiah Spader.

piece of land on Long Island, adjoining the farm of Rapalie on the east, and that of Peter Montfoort on the west, "in the breadth 350 paces, and so straight into the woods." In a second patent, dated December 1, 1643, the land is described as lying

> "on the bend of the Marechkawieck, betwixt the land of Jorse (George) Rapalie on the east side, ... and the land of Peter Montfoort on the west side; extending along the marsh 88 rods; and along the land of the said Jorse Rapalie, in a southerly direction, into the woods, 210 rods; and behind, in the woods, in the breadth, 88 rods; the breadth (*i. e.*, length) to (*i. e.*, from) the marsh to the marsh, 210 rods: making and amounting in all to 28 morgen."[1]

In 1647 Montfoort's widow received a grant of an addition to the rear of the above land, of the same breadth, and one hundred and ninety rods in length. The Montfoort land, which had a river or meadow front of about 1,078 feet, was identical with that now located between Hamilton and Grand avenues, and described on our map as farms late of John and Jacob Ryerson. These were sons of Martin, who originally owned the whole tract, and who was a descendant of Marten Ryerse,[2] an emigrant from Amsterdam, and first husband of Annetie, daughter of Joris Janse de Rapalie.

XVIII.

Joris (George) Jansen de Rapalie, who is supposed to have been a proscribed Huguenot, from Rochelle in France, came to this country in 1623, in the ship Unity, with Catalina Trico, his wife, and settled first at Fort Orange, near Albany, from whence he removed, in 1626, to New Amsterdam. Here, in the occupancy of a homestead on the north side of the present Pearl street, and adjoining the south side of the fort, he resided for more than

---

[1] Patents, G G, 40.

[2] Marten Ryerse was a brother of Adriaen Ryerse, of Flatbush. The patronymic, Ryerse, was retained by Marten's descendants, who are now quite numerous, and known as *Ryersons*. Adriaen had two sons, Elbert and Marten Adriaense. The first settled in Flushing, and his posterity bear the name *Adriance;* while Marten remained in Flatbush, and his descendants form the *Martence* family. See Riker, Hist. Newtown, 269, 386.

twenty-two years, and until after the birth of his youngest child, in 1650. During a portion of these years he was an innkeeper or tapster, and his name frequently occurs as such upon the books of the Burgomaster's Court until 1654. That he possessed the confidence of his fellow-citizens is evidenced by the fact, that in August, 1641, he was one of the Twelve Men representing Manhattan, Breuckelen, and Pavonia, chosen for the purpose of deliberating upon measures necessary to be adopted to punish the Indians for the murders which they had committed. About 1654,[1] he probably removed his permanent residence to his farm at the "Waal-boght;" for in 1655, '56, '57, and 1660, he was one of the magistrates of Breuckelen, with which town his whole subsequent life was identified.

The Waal-boght farm consisted of a tract of land which he had purchased on the 16th of June, 1637, from its Indian proprietors, *Kakapeteyno* and *Pewichaas*, and called "Rinnegackonck," situated on Long Island, south of the Island of Manhattan, and

"extending from a certain kill (creek) till into the woods, south and eastward, to a certain swamp (Kreuplebush), to a place where the water runs over the stones."[2] This was confirmed to him by a patent from Governor Kieft, dated June 17, 1643, wherein it is more fully described as "a piece of land, called *Rennagaconck*, formerly purchased by him from the Indians, as will appear by reference to the transport, lying on Long Island, in the bend of Marechkawieck (*i. e.*, the Wallabout Bay), east of the land of Jan Montfoort, extending along the said land, in a southerly direction, towards and into the woods, 242 rods; by the kill and marsh, easterly, up, 390 rods; at the Sweet marsh, 202 rods on a southerly direction, into the woods; and behind, into the woods, 384 rods, in a westerly direction; and certain outpoints next to the marsh: amounting in all to the contents of 167 morgens and 406 rods" (about 335 acres).[3]

On this tract, which may be described in general terms as comprising the lands now occupied by the United States Marine Hospital, and those embraced between Nostrand and Grand avenues, in

---

[1] Riker's Newtown, p. 267. The sale of his house and lot in the city, on the 22d June, 1654, probably fixes the date of his removal to the Wallabout

[2] Patents, G G, 20. [3] Ibid., 64.

the present city of Brooklyn,[1] and on the easterly side of the Waal-boght, Rapalie spent the remainder of his life, dying soon after the close of the Dutch administration, and having had eleven children. The property then passed into the hands of his eldest son, Jeronimus, a prominent citizen, being a justice of the peace, as well as a deacon of the Breuckelen church. After his death, it was occupied by his son Jeronimus, who, in 1755, sold it to his son-in-law, Martin Schenck. At the death of the latter, it was devised to his two sons, Martin, junior, and Lambert, together with their sister, the wife of Francis Skillman.[2] Lambert died unmarried, and his portion fell to his brother Martin, and his sister, Mrs. Skillman. Martin sold to the United States Government the present Marine Hospital grounds, and Mrs. Skillman sold to Samuel Jackson the Johnson farm.

The parcel designated on the map as the land of Garret Nostrand was conveyed by Joris Rapelje to Jeronimus Remsen, in 1714;[3] and by him, in 1719, to John Van Nostrand; and by him, in 1729, to Daniel Rapelje. He devised it, in 1765, to Garret Nostrand, with legacies to his sister, which, in 1770, were satisfied, and he remained in possession until his death, in 1789.[4] It then came into possession of his son John, who died intestate, in 1795, leaving no issue.

The facts stated (on pages 23, 24) concerning the Bennett and Bentyn purchase and settlement at Gowanus in 1636, completely disprove the claims which Tradition (aided by the misapprehension of our earlier historians) has set up in behalf of Rapalie as being the first actual white settler of Brooklyn. Of the similar and connected traditionary error, which has so long given to his eldest daughter, Sarah, the honor of having been the first white child born in Brooklyn, we shall speak in another place.[5] His widow, Catalyntie, died, Sept. 11, 1689, aged eighty-four.[6]

---

[1] Designated on map as lands of Gen. Johnson, J. F. and E. P. Delaplaine, Jackson, Skillman, and Teunis Cowenhoven; together with woodland in the Hills (*i. e.*, where the Penitentiary is), and some meadow-land where the City Park now is.

[2] Father of John Skillman.

[3] King's County Conveyances, lib. D. 82, 83, 84.

[4] Will in King's County Surrogate's office, lib. ii. 46.

[5] See discussion of her husband, Hans Hansen Bergen's patent.

[6] The two Labadist travellers, who visited the colony in 1679, have, fortunately for us, preserved in their journal an account of a visit which they paid to Catalina, the

XIX.

On the 30th of March, 1647, HANS HANSEN BERGEN, or "Hans the Boore,"[1] as he was sometimes familiarly called, received a patent for 200 morgens (400 acres) of land on Long Island, being a portion of the extensive purchase made by Governor Kieft, in 1638, from the Indian proprietors.[2] It is described as lying

"on the kil of Joris Rapalje," from whose house "it extends north by east till to Lambert Huybertsen's (Moll) plantation; further on (to) the kil of Jan de Sweede,[3] according to the old marks, till to the kil of Mespaechtes (Newtown Creek), to and along the Cripplebush; further to the division line of Dirck Volkertsen's land, which he purchased from Wilcox, and the division of Herry Satley."[4]

This tract of land extended from the Creek of Runnegaconck to the present Division avenue, which formerly marked the boundary between the cities of Williamsburgh and Brooklyn. Following the direction of this avenue to near its intersection with Tenth street, it there passed over it and stretched in a somewhat southeasterly

---

widow of Joris Janse de Rapalie, then in her seventy-fourth year: "Mr. De la Grange with his wife came to ask us to accompany them in their boat to the *Wale-bocht,* a place situated on Long Island, almost an hour's distance below the city, directly opposite Corlaer's Hook. He had an old aunt and other friends living there. . . . . We reached the bay in about two hours. This is a bay tolerably wide, where the water rises and falls much; and is at low water very shallow, and much of it dry. The aunt of De la Grange is an old Walloon from Valenciennes, seventy-four years old. She is worldly-minded, living with her whole heart, as well as body, among her progeny, which now number 145, and will soon reach 150. Nevertheless she lived alone by herself, a little apart from the others, having her little garden, and other conveniences, with which she helped herself." (L. I. Hist. Soc. Coll., i. 341, 342.)

Thus peacefully and pleasantly passed the later years of this "mother of New York," who, with her mission fulfilled, still active, and with habits of industry begotten by her pioneer life, now reposed contented amid the love and respectful attentions of her kindred and her descendants.

[1] Riker's Newtown, 16.

[2] See page 26, and Appendix 2.

[3] For lands of "Jan the Sweede," see chapter on "Early Settlers and Patents of Bushwick." "The Sweede's Kill," now Bushwick Creek, probably then came up as far as the bounds of the old Village of Williamsburgh.

[4] Patents, G G, 205.

direction, probably as far as the head of Newtown Creek, in the neighborhood of Vandervoort avenue and Montrose street. This patent, therefore, was situated partly in Brooklyn and partly in Bushwick, comprising lands designated on Butt's map as belonging to General Jeremiah Johnson, James Scholes, Abraham Remsen, Abraham Boerum, Abraham Meserole, McKibbin, and Nichols, Powers, Schenck, Mills, and others, including the settlement known as "Bushwick Cross Roads,"[1] and the meadows adjoining Newtown.

Hans Hansen Bergen, the common ancestor of the Bergen family of Long Island and New Jersey, was a native of Bergen, in Norway, from whence he emigrated to Holland. From thence, in 1633, he came, probably with Van Twiller, the second Director-General, to Nieuw Netherland. For several years he was a resident of Nieuw Amsterdam, where he owned a lot on the present Pearl street, abutting on the fort, and adjoining that of Joris Jansen de Rapalje, his future father-in-law. In 1638 he appears to have been engaged in a tobacco plantation, either on Andries Hudde's or the West India Company's land; and in 1639 he married Sarah, the daughter of Joris Janse de Rapalje, born, according to the family record, on the 9th of June, 1625, and who was *reputed* to be the first white child born in the colony of Nieuw Netherland.[2] From the tenor of a

---

[1] Riker also says, in his Hist. of Newtown, 18: "The farm of Hans Hansen has been already noticed as lying near Cripplebush. It comprised 400 acres, or nearly two-thirds of a square mile; and from a careful examination of the patent and those adjoining, I think it must have covered a part, and perhaps the whole, of the present settlement at the Bushwick Cross-roads."

[2] The recently discovered journal of the Labadists, who visited this country in the year 1679 (translated by Hon. Henry C. Murphy, and forming the first volume of the Collections of the Long Island Historical Society), brings forward a statement which, if true, *limits* the historic honor hitherto enjoyed by Sarah Rapalie to that of simply being the first white *female* born in the colony. These travellers (pp. 114 and 115 of the volume above mentioned) speak of conversing with the first male born of Europeans in New Netherland, named Jean Vigné. "His parents were from Valenciennes, and he was now about sixty-five years of age. He was a brewer, and a neighbor of our old people." To this Mr. Murphy adds the following note: "This is an interesting statement, which may not only be compared with that hitherto received, attributing to Sarah de Rapalje, who was born on the 9th of June, 1625, the honor of having been the first-born Christian child in New Netherland, but is to be considered in other respects. According to the data given by our travellers, who, writing in 1679, make Jean Vigné sixty-five years old at that time, he must have been born in the year 1614, eleven years before Sarah de Rapalje, and at the very earliest period compatible with the sojourn of any Hollanders upon our territory. Jean Vigné belonged to the class of

lawsuit, in 1643, relative to the sale of a shallop, it may be inferred that he was at that time engaged in the trade of a shipwright. In

---

great burghers in New Amsterdam, and was one of the schepens of the city in the years 1655, '56, '61, and '63 (O'Callaghan's Register of New Netherland, '61–3, 174). He was twice married (New York Manual, 1862). Valentine says (Hist. of New York, 73) that he died in 1691, without issue. In this statement in regard to his being the first person of European parentage born in New Netherland, there are some notable points. The first trading voyages to Hudson's River were made by the Dutch in 1613–14, and the first wintering or habitation there was in 1614–15. There must have been, therefore, one European woman, at least, in the country at that early period. Whether Jean Vigné's parents returned to Holland or remained here, during the obscure period between the time of his birth and the occupation of the country by the West India Company, it is impossible to determine. Either may have been the case. If the statement, however, be correct—and there is nothing inconsistent in it with the history of the colony, as far as known—Jean Vigné was not only the first born of European parents in New Netherland, but, as far as known, in the whole United States north of Virginia. We deem it of sufficient importance to give here the statement of our travellers in regard to him in the original language: *Wijhadden ind it geseltschap gesproken den eerst geboren mans-persoon van Europianen in Nieu Nederlant, genoemt Jean Vigné. Sijne ouders waren van Valencijn, en hij was nu ontrent* 65 *jaer out, synde ook een brouwer en buerman van onse oude luij.*"

In regard to the erroneous tradition which has given to Breuckelen the honor of being the birth-place of Sarah Rapalie, we quote the words of one of her descendants, the author of the History of the Bergen Family, who says: "The early historians of this State and locality, led astray by a petition presented by her, April 4th, 1656 (when she resided at the Walle-boght), to the Governor and Council, for some meadows, in which she states that she is the 'first born Christian child in New Netherlands,' assert that she was born at the Walle-boght. Judge Benson, in his writings, even ventures to describe the house where this took place. He says: 'On the point of land formed by the cove in Brooklyn, known as the Walle-boght, lying on its westerly side (it should have been *easterly*), was built the first house on Long Island, and inhabited by Joris Jansen de Rapalie, one of the first white settlers on the island, and in which was born Sarah Rapalie, the first white child of European parentage born in the State.' In this, if there is any truth in the depositions of Catalyn or Catalyntie Trico (daughter of Jeronomis Trico of Paris), Sarah's mother (see appendix to this History), they are clearly mistaken. According to these depositions, she and her husband, Joris Janse de Rapalie, came to this country in 1623; settled at Fort Orange, now Albany; lived there three years; came, in 1626, to New Amsterdam, 'where she lived afterwards for many years; and then came to Long Island, where she now (1688) lives.' 'Sarah, therefore, was undoubtedly born at Albany, instead of the Walle-boght, and was probably married before she removed to Long Island, there being no reason to suppose that she resided there when a single woman without her husband." Indeed, if the family record of her birth be correct, she was married between the age of fourteen and fifteen, improving somewhat, in this respect, on the example of her mother, who married before she was twenty years old.

She early became a church member in New York, and united with the Dutch Church at Breuckelen, by certificate, in 1661. She died about 1685, aged about sixty.

While, therefore, Albany claims the honor of being her birthplace, and New Amsterdam of having seen her childhood, Brooklyn surely received most profit from her; for here, in the Wallabout, she was twice married, and gave birth to fourteen children,

March, 1647, he became the patentee of the above land on Long Island, on which he seems to have resided until his death, which took place in the latter portion of 1653 or the beginning of 1654. He must, however, have been in possession of this plantation prior to the date of his patent, either by extinguishing the Indian title or otherwise; for, in Abraham Rycken's patent, dated August 8, 1640, his land is located on Long Island, opposite Rinnegackonck, bounded by Gysbert Rycken, Hans Hansen, etc.; in Cornelis Jacobsen Selle's deed to Lambert Huybertsen Mol, of 29th of July, 1641, his plantation is described as lying next that of Hans Hansen, on Long Island;[1] and in the patent of Mespât, or Newtown, given to Rev. Mr. Doughty and his associates, in March, 1642, mention is again made of the meadows belonging to Hans Hansen.[2] His widow, in April, 1656,[3] petitioned the Governor and Council for the grant of a piece of meadow-land adjoining the 200[4] morgen previously granted her at the "Waale-bocht,"[5] stating that her neighbors disturb her in the use of them, by mowing thereon, although they have meadows of their own; that she is a widow and burdened with seven children, and asks an exemption from taxes. The meadows were granted, although the exemption was refused. "Sarah, in stating in this memorial that she was a widow, neglected to state that she was again married, and the wife of Theunis Gysbert Bogaert, which must have been the case, judging from the baptismal records of New Amsterdam, wherein the birth of their first-born, Aartje, is entered as baptized December 19, 1655. She probably resided, at

---

from whom are descended the Polhemus, the Bergens, the Bogarts, and many other of the most notable families of Kings County. Few women have been more highly honored in the number and the character of their descendants than SARAH DE RAPELJE.

The first correction of this historical error is due to Mr. James Riker, the author of History of Newtown, L. I., who, in a paper read before the New York Historical Society, in May, 1857, thoroughly investigated and *exploded* the time-honored tradition which had disfigured the pages of all previous historians. Prime (Hist. L. I., 358–61) especially has collected a great mass of tradition, which is more interesting than reliable.

[1] N. Y. Col. MSS., vol. i. 251.

[2] Riker's Newtown, pp. 18, 83.

[3] N. Y. Col. MSS., vol. vi. p. 353.

[4] In the original Dutch record, 200 morgen, erroneously translated 20 by Vanderkemp.

[5] The earliest recorded use of the name "Waale-bocht." (See note 4, p. 24.)

this time, on the farm in the Waaleboght, patented to her late husband, Hans Hansen Bergen, and her petition probably alludes to those lands. No evidence exists on the Colonial records as to any grant to her, either from the government or the Indians, of 200 morgen, except her statement in the petition. "From this petition," says the family historian, "has probably arisen, with the aid of a little stretch of the imaginatien, the story of the Indians having presented her with a farm, in consideration of her having been the first-born white child in the colony."

When, upon the conquest of the colony of New Netherland, by the English, in 1664, the inhabitants were obliged to take out new patents for their farms, BOGAERT, Sarah's second husband, embraced the opportunity, as it would seem, to take out the new patent for Hans Hansen's 200 morgen in his own name, instead of that of Hans' children, who were rightfully entitled thereto. At least no record has ever been found of their possession of any portion of their father's estate, nor any evidence of any compensation made to them therefor by their step-father. It is possible, however, although not very probable, that compensation may have been made, and that the written evidence has disappeared in the lapse of time. If Bogaert defrauded the orphans, it can only be said that it was not an isolated case, the records showing that others, similarly situated at that time, took out the new and confirmatory patents in their own name. By virtue, therefore, of this confirmatory patent, which was dated April 5th, 1667, the whole property, excepting that tract known and designated on the map as the General Johnson Homestead Farm, remained in the possession of Bogart, and was divided among his heirs.

The above-mentioned "Homestead Farm" was probably purchased from Bogart by Rem Jansen Vanderbeeck, the ancestor of all the Remsens in this country,[1] who, in 1642, had married Jannetie, a daughter of Joris Janse de Rapalie.[2] He resided at Albany for

[1] Riker (Hist. Newtown, 386) says his trade was that of a "smith," and he came from Jeveren in Westphalia. A valuable and interesting genealogy of the family may be found in Riker's work. The name of Vanderbeeck seems to have been dropped in the second generation.

[2] It is of this lady that the curious tradition remains, that she was taken, when a child, across from Governor's Island to Long Island, in a tub. (See Appendix, 5.)

some years, and the period of his removal to the Waaleboght is uncertain. As a citizen and a magistrate he was highly esteemed in Brooklyn, where he died in 1681, leaving a widow, who survived him for many years, and fifteen children, all of whom, according to tradition, were present at his funeral, and all of whom were married.[1] In 1694, the widow and her children conveyed the property to two of their number, Isaac and Jeremias Remsen,[2] and in 1704 Isaac

---

[1] Riker, 386 ; Prime. 359.

[2] We have been favored by Teunis G. Bergen, Esq., with the following translation of this deed, the original of which is in the possession of Jeromus B. Johnson of Flatbush. Some portions of the document have become illegible through the ravages of time, etc.:

"m . . . . . In the . . . . . third, King . . . . . Our Lord, one thousand six hundred and ninety-four, tenth day of April ; declared . . . . of the deceased Rem Jansen, of the Walle-boght, in the aforesaid county . . . . through his children, to wit, Joris Remsen, Rem Remsen, Jacob Remsen, Jeronimus Remsen, Daniel Remsen, Abraham Remsen, Jan (Dorlant), Aris Vanderbilt, Joseph Hegeman, Gerrit Hansen, Elbert (Adriaensen), Marten Adriaense, each for himself and his heirs, to Isaac Remsen and Jeremias Remsen, and their heirs and assigns, have set over, granted, and conveyed a certain parcel of land, situated in the Walle-bocht, in the aforesaid county, on the southerly side of the land of Teunis Gysbertse ; also bounded and encompassed by the kil in the Walebocht, as set forth in the patent for the same ; also with the length, breadth, course, and number of morgens made known in said patent, with all the right and privileges in any way appertaining to said parcel of land ; also, as included with and appertaining to said land, three parcels of meadow: the 1st, held in common with Jacob Hegeman, situated in the limits of Midwout (Flatbush), over the second kil, and known as Number 10 ; the 2d, a block lot, situated on the third kil, and lying between Tomas Lambertsen and Jan Vanderbilt ; the 3rd, situated over the third kil, in the long neck in the limits of Jamaike, and held in common with Jerominus Rapalie. For the above-described land and meadow, with their appurtenances, declared the above-named parties to convey to the said Isaac Remsen and Jeremias Remsen, to be fully satisfied and paid for the same, to the first and last cent, therefore deliver (give) over said land and meadow, with the appurtenances and privileges, for themselves and their heirs, to the aforesaid Jeremiah and Isaac, clear and unencumbered, to be kept, with all their rights, by them, the said Jeremias and Isaac, and their heirs and assigns. . . . . .

the mark of
Jannetie Jorisse, by herself.
Joris Remsen.
Rem Remsen.
Jekob Remsen.
Jerominus Remsen.
Daniel Remsen.
Abram Remsen.
Jan Dorlant.
Aris Vanderbilt.
Joseph Hegeman.
Gerret Hansen.
Elbert Adriaensen.
Martin Adriaensen.

"Signed in the presence of . . . ys Hegeman, Johannes Van Eckelen, and also delivered."

sold out his share to his brother Jeremias, who thus became the sole owner of the paternal farm.[1] It was inherited, after his death, in July, 1757, by his son Jeremias, who, dying without issue, in 1777, left it to his relative, Barent Johnson.[2] This worthy citizen and patriot, deceased in 1782, and his executors in 1793, conveyed the estate to his son, the late General Jeremiah Johnson, by whom it was first laid out in streets and city lots, and by whose eldest son, Barnet Johnson, the old homestead and a portion of the original farm is now held.[3]

The history of the remaining portion of the Hans Hansen Bergen patent is briefly as follows:

The parcels since known as the *Boerum* and *Abraham A. Remsen* estates were originally comprised in a farm owned by one Teunis Bogert, who, by will, dated June 22, 1767,[4] devised it to his sons Adrian and Cornelius. Partition deeds were executed between them, April 25, 1769, whereby Adrian took possession of the northerly half, now known as the *Boerum* farm, and Cornelius of the remaining or southerly portion, being the greater portion of the *Abraham A. Remsen* estate.[5]

Adrian sold his farm, April 13, 1775, to Jacob Bloom, who devised it by will, dated March 5, 1797, as a life-estate to his son Barent.[6] His heirs, in March, 1816, conveyed it to Abraham A. Remsen,[7] who, in November of the same year, sold it to Abraham Boerum,[8] who remained in possession until his death, in 1848, and from whom it derived its name of the "Boerum farm."

Cornelius Bogert sold his portion of the paternal estate, March 8,

---

The southerly portion of the land described, in the above deed, as lands of Teunis Gysberts Bogart, is that since known as land of James Scholes.

[1 & 3] See "Deduction of Title to so much of 'the Homestead Farm,' so called, of the late Jeremiah Johnson, deceased, as is embraced within the limits of the City of Brooklyn, and as was in his possession at the time of his death. Dated Brooklyn, May, 1853. Prepared by William M. Ingraham, Brooklyn." Folio, pp. 20.

[2] Will dated 1776; proved 1782. N. Y. Wills, liber xxxv.

[4] Liber xxvi. 210, N. Y. Co. Wills.

[5] See map on file in Kings County Clerk's office, endorsed "Map showing the Farm of Teunis Bogart, deceased," as divided between his sons Adrian and Cornelius, and to be filed in Kings County Clerk's office with the old deeds not recorded.

[6] Kings Co. Wills, liber i. 227.

[7] Kings County Conveyances, liber xi. 461.

[8] Ibid., 458.

1774, to Abraham Remsen, who, in April, 1793, conveyed it to his son William, and he, in May following, transferred it to his brothers, Jeremiah and Abraham Remsen, junior. Adjoining the southerly side of this farm, and including the late Scholes tract, was a farm of 76 acres, owned and possessed, prior to 1729, by one Gysbert Bogert, and by him sold, in December of that year, to his son Gysbert Bogert, junior. By him it was conveyed, June 29, 1741, to Jeremiah Remsen, the then owner of the present Johnson farm. Mr. Remsen, on the 28th of January, 1742, conveyed it to his son Abraham, and he, on April 10th, 1795, conveyed it to his sons, Jeremiah and Abraham.[1]

The title to the farm of Cornelius Bogert, and to that of Gysbert Bogert, having thus become fully vested in the brothers Remsen, partition deeds were executed between them on the 14th of September, 1795, by which Abraham became possessed of the northerly portion, since known as the *Abraham A. Remsen* estate; and Jeremiah of the southerly portion, sold after his death, in 1831, by his executors, to James Scholes, and since known as the *Scholes* estate.[2]

Having thus completed our survey of the early patents along the water-front of Breuckelen, from the bounds of New Utrecht to those of Bushwick, we now enter upon the consideration of what may be termed

THE SECOND TIER OF PATENTS,

located between the Waale-boght and the head of Gowanus Creek, in the rear of those already discussed. These lands are all especially described as "lying at Marechkawieck, on the Gowanus Kill;" proving, beyond a doubt, that the name of "Marechkawieck," although applied primarily to the shores of the Waale-boght, was also used to designate the whole of the country between the two localities. The existence in this neighborhood, as we have seen, of "Sassian's" and other tracts of maize-land, as well as the fact that various Indian skeletons and relics have, from time to time, been exhumed in the same vicinity, incline us to the belief that this was

---

[1] Conveyances, lib. xxi. 213, Kings County Clerk's office. [2] Ibid., 209.

the locality occupied by the "Marechkawiecks," whom we know to have been the original proprietors of the soil.[1] They were undoubtedly dispossessed during the war of 1643, and on the very patents which we are about to examine, the village proper of "BREUCKELEN," as distinguished from the hamlets at the "Waale-boght," "Gowanus," and "The Ferry," was afterwards established.

XX.

March 11, 1647, GERRIT WOLPHERTSEN (VAN COUWENHOVEN)[2] received a patent for

"a certain piece of land, at the (Ma) Rechawieck, both the maize and woodland, on the marsh of the Gouwanus kil, between the land of Jacob Stoffelsen and Frederick Lubbertsen, extending from the aforesaid marsh till into the woods next the land of said Frederick, till to the land of Andries Hudde, northeast by north, a little northerly, 148 rods; behind through the woods, till to the land of the aforesaid Jacob Stoffelsen, southeast by east 80 rods next to the land of Jacob Stoffelsen aforesaid, till to the aforesaid marsh, southwest a little westerly 165 rods, along the marsh to the place of beginning 60 rods, with an oblique outpoint: amounting in all to 19 morgens, 341 rods."[3]

This plot evidently fronted on the main road leading from Flatbush, through the village of Breuckelen, which was located at this

[1] A large Indian burying-ground was located northeast of Freeke's Mill Pond, and the surrounding meadows, and in grading streets some remains have been disturbed on the Bout and Van Rossum patents, hereafter described.

The following fragment (from N. Y. Col. MSS., iv. 158), probably relates to this locality: "January 27, 1643. Deposition of Geertjen Manníncks, wife of Claes Mentelaer, said, that Roelant (Robert) Hackwaert, told at her house in the Bay, that there were seven hills of corn about a pistol-shot from the road, which he would confirm by his oath.

"Roelant Hackwaert declared that he saw the savages at Marechkawieck cover the corn-hills."

[2] In N. Y. Col. MSS., i. 234, 235, is a receipt of Wolphertsen, who is there mentioned as a "resident of Keskachquerem, on Long Island," for four cows hired by him of the deacons of New Amsterdam. From this, he would appear to have had at that time a farm at "Keskachquerem," which was, probably, the name of the original territory of Bushwick, purchased by Kieft in 1639. See ante, p. 26, and Appendix 2.

[3] Patents, G G, 172.

point, to "the Ferry," and is included in lands marked as G. Martense's on Butts' map. Wolphertsen sold this property to Nicholas Janse, baker, of New York, whose widow, Maritje Garritse, sold the same, Sept. 13th, 1698, to George Hansen (Bergen), of Broockland, for the sum of £176 11*s*. The lands were described as bounded "southeast by land of Jurian Andriese, northwest by land of Jacob Hansen (Bergen) and land of Derick Wortman, southwest by Gowanus Kil, and northwest by the King's highway, as formerly in possession of Gerrit Wolphertsen." Also, "the just and equal part of all that hook or neck of land in said township, containing 55 Dutch rods broad and 250 Dutch rods long; bounded south by land of Jacob Brower, north by land of Machiel Hansen (Bergen), west by Gowanus Kil, or Mill Creek, and east by the common woods."[1]

Martense and Gerritsen possess, through their wives, these lands of Bergen; but it is probable that Bergen, or his heirs, subsequent purchasers, added other lands to the estate, besides Wolfertsen Van Couvenhoven's patent.

XXI.

Jacob Stoffelsen, the West India Company's overseer of negroes, and engaged under Van Twiller, in 1635, in the construction of Fort Amsterdam, had a farm next to Wolphertsen's, but of which no patent is found on record. Its position, however, is clearly defined by the adjoining patent of Wolphertsen, which is described as lying between it and that of Lubbertsen; and its size is specified in Bout's patent as being of the same dimensions, viz, 28 morgens and 270 rods. Like the others, it commenced on the meadows at the head of Gowanus Creek, and ran northeasterly to the "King's Highway," *i. e.*, the old Flatbush and Breuckelen Ferry Road. On the maps of the present city, it may be described as extending along Fulton avenue, from Bond street, or thereabout, to a line between and parallel to Smith and Hoyt streets.

Stoffelsen seems not to have been a resident of Breuckelen after 1656, in which year he hired the Company's farm at Aharsimus,

[1] Kings Co. Convey., ii. 181.

which was renewed to him in 1661 and 1662. In 1663 he, with other farmers in that vicinity, was fined for working on Sunday; and in 1664, his wife petitioned for, and was granted, 8 or 10 acres additional behind the company's farm, on which latter she had received, in 1658, permission to build a house.[1]

XXII.

JAN EVERTSEN BOUT, a somewhat prominent man in the colony,[2] was the patentee of the lands adjoining Van Couwenhoven's on the west. This property was described in the deed granted to him by Gov. Kieft, July 6, 1645, as

"land at Marechkawieck, on the Kil of the Gowanus, as well the maize-land as the woodland, bounded by the most easterly end of (the land of) Huyck Aertsen (von Rossum), and by the most westerly end of (the land of) Gerrit Wolphertson (von Couwenhoven), it extends next the said land (*i. e.* of Wolphertsen); along till out of the woods, northeast a little northerly 165 rods, its breadth in the woods southeast to the land of Huyck Aertsen, 69 rods, next to the land of said Huyck Aertsen along to the maize-land 55 rods, southwest and southwest by west, further on till to the valley (marsh) southwest, a little southerly, 137 rods further on to the place of beginning, along the marsh, with certain outpoints, laid out in a parallelogram. Amount in all, both the places, as well (*i. e.* likewise) of Jan Evertsen (Bout) and Jacob Stoffelsen, 28 morgen 270 rods.[3]

February 14th, 1667, Bout received a confirmatory patent of the above premises, which covered the neck of land on which a few years ago were located Freecke's and Denton's flour-mills, and also a considerable tract east of Freecke's mill-pond, extending to the

[1] N. Y. Col. MSS., viii. 313, 1044; ix. 572; x. 40; Part ii. 294, Part iii. 21.

[2] In 1643 he had a bouwery at Pavonia; in September of same year was selected by the Eight Men to fill the vacancy in their Board, caused by the expulsion of Van Dam; in 1646, became one of the founders of Breuckelen; in 1647, was a farmer there and chosen a member of the Nine Men, who formed Stuyvesant's Council; in 1649, was one of the signers of a memorial to the Home Government, requesting certain reforms in the management of the Colony, and also of the Remonstrance which accompanied it, and of which documents he and two others were chosen to be the bearers to the Fatherland; was successful in his mission, and returned to Nieuw Netherlands in 1650. (See Col. Doc. N. Y., i. 367, 379.)

[3] Patents, G G, 108.

main road in the then village of Brooklyn. Bout gave the neck to the children of Adam Brower, the common ancestor of the Browers of this vicinity.

April 1st, 1668, a patent was granted to Jan Evertsen Bout for

"a certain Hook or corner of land . . . . . within the jurisdiction of the town of Breucklyn, ... beginning from the fence of Gerrit Croesus' land, where the marke stands, and soe goes across to the highway, being in breadth 110 rod, as also 3 or 4 rods along the said highway, and reaches in length 250 rods in the woods."

In 1674 this land, being the same as that known on Butt's map as belonging to G. Martense, was in possession of Andries Janse Jurianse, who had married Annetje Para, Bout's widow. He died before 1695, and she married Jan Janse Staats, and on the 17th March of that year she conveyed to Jurian Andriese (probably the son of her second husband) for the sum of £150, certain premises in Broockland, described as

"on the north side of the King's highway, on the east side of Michiell Hansen (Bergen), on the west side of Joras Hansen (Bergen) and Lambert Andriese, with all the meadow there annext and thereunto belonging, and that soe great and small as it always was possessed by her above said deceased husbands."

February 19th, 1707–8, Jurian Andriese conveyed to Carell Debevois, for £400, premises in Broockland,

"containing 27 morgens, or 54 acres, be it more or less, and bounded southeasterly by the land of Machiell Hansen (Bergen), westerly by the land of Joris Hansen (Bergen), and in the rear southwesterly by a certain creeke running through the meadows coming from Gowanos mill soe called, including all the meadows in the rear of the said land, and adjoining thereto between the said creek and the said land."

These deeds covered that portion of Bout's patent not included within "the Neck," and possibly may have included some additional land of Jurianse, the second husband of Annetie Para.

Upon Bout's patent was located Freeke's Mill, or the "old Gowanus Mill," probably the oldest in the town of Breukelen. As early as in 1661, it was occupied conjointly by Isaac De Forest and Adam Brower, the latter purchasing the interest of the former.[1] They were, undoubtedly, tenants of Bout, who, in 1667 (King's Co. Convey., p. 179), gave "the corn and meadows and place whereon the mill is grounded," to the children of Adam Brower. And, according to a deed, dated April 30, 1707, of Sybrant Brower to Abram and Nicholas Brower (King's Co. Convey., liber iii. p. 201) it appears that their ancestor, Adam Brower, had received from the heirs of Bout and Teunis Nuyse a conveyance of the neck of land upon which the mill was located. This mill-pond was formed by damming off the head of Gowanus Kil, and the old mill was located just north of Union, west of Nevin, and between that street and Bond.[2]

Denton's Mill, or "the Yellow Mill," in Gowanus, was also built upon Bout's patent, by Adam and Nicholas, the sons of Adam Brower, in 1709. The mill-pond was formed by the damming off a branch of the Gowanus Kil, and the mill was located on the northeast side of the present First street, about midway between Second and Third avenues. The dwelling-house, which was burned down about 1852, was in Carroll, midway between Nevins street and Third avenue.

There is some uncertainty regarding the precise limits of these three patents of Bout, Stoffelsen, and Van Couvenhoven, which together evidently cover that portion of our city included between Fulton avenue, Smith and Nevins streets, and described on our map as lands of Martense and Gerritsen.[3]

XXIII.

On the 22d of February, 1646, Huyck Aertsen (van Rossum) received from Gov. Kieft,

"a piece of land lying at the Marechkawieck, on the marsh of the Gowanus Kil, the maize-land as well as the woodland, bounded on the southeast by the land of Jan Evertse (Bout), along the marsh east 68 rods, southeast 30

---

[1] See Dr. O'Callaghan's note in Hist. Mag. for Aug., 1862.

[2] See map of land, mill and mill-pond of John C. Freeke, by J. Lott, 1833.

[3] See *ante*, pp. 96, 97, Wolphertsen's patent.

rods further up the maize-land till to the woods, northeast by east 85 rods, northeast by north 60 rods, the breadth in the woods till to the land of said Jan Evertsen (Bout) northwest eighty-seven rods, again to the maize land next the land of the aforesaid Jan Evertsen (Bout) southwest and southwest by west 55 rods, through the maize-land to the place of beginning, southwest a little southerly, 137 rods: amounting in all to 19 morgens and 105 rods."

To this was subsequently added another parcel, making in all 29 morgens.[1] This tract may be described as lying between Fulton avenue, Fourth avenue, Nevins and Douglass streets, designated on the map as belonging to Mary Powers and to Nicholas Casthalez.[2] It was confirmed by Gov. Nicholls, June 21, 1667, to Albert Cornelissen (Wantenaer),[3] who had married Trientje, the widow of Huyck Aertsen van Rossum, deceased. March 7, 1680–1, Cornelissen conveyed, by endorsement on the back of the patent from Gov. Kieft, and the confirmatory one from Gov. Nicholls, the above premises to Michael Hansen (Bergen); also, by a separate conveyance, the adjoining meadows, which he had bought of Theunis Nyssen on the 16th of May, 1656, and which had been confirmed to him by a patent from Gov. Nicholls, dated June 26, 1668.[4] The original patent to

[1] Patents, G G, 136.

[2] It, however, covered rather more than these two pieces.

[3] Or "the glove-maker." Albert Cornelissen, in June, 1643, let himself as a wheelwright to Conyn Gerritsen, for one year (N. Y. Col. MSS., ii. 61). On June 5, 1665, he was tried for killing Barent Jansen, of Brooklyn, by striking him in the side with a knife, of which wound he died the same day. As the deed was done in self-defence, the jury returned a verdict of manslaughter, and he was sentenced to be burned in the hand before the rising of the court, to forfeit all his goods and chattels, and to remain in prison for a year and a day. He was, however, pardoned on the same day by Gov. Nicholls. (Alb. Rec. Patents, vol. i. 165.)

[4] These meadows of Teunis Niessen are referred to in Holl. Doc., i. 338, in the Answer of the W. I. Co. to the Remonstrance of the New Netherlands, 1650. Jan Evertsen Bout and J. Van Cowenhoven complained, in that remonstrance, that "after the transfer had been executed of the patents to the proprietor, Kieft had added thereto a little clause which was manifestly contradictory; inasmuch as the patents included the land and valley, and the clause takes the valley (or meadows) back to the Company," &c. The reply (p. 340) says: "We are informed, and therefore say, that the petitioners will not prove the late Director, William Kieft, hath called in more than one patent; and he subjoined with his own hand, that he reserved the valley, not for the Company, but for the town of Breuckelen, in general. The reason for the revocation was because Jan Evertsen Bout, one of the petitioners, who occupies part of the valley, together with others beside him, who undertook to found or improve the town of

Van Rossum specified the amount of land as being 29 morgens; the confirmatory patent of Nicholls, with substantially the same boundaries, estimated it at 90 morgens. Bergen took possession of 90 morgens, whereupon the freeholders of Breuckelen, about 1722, brought a suit against him in Chancery, claiming that he had a right to only 29 acres, and that the balance belonged to the town. During the progress of this suit Bergen, for the sum of £800, conveyed the property in question to his son, Hans Bergen,[1] who compromised with the freeholders of Breuckelen for the sum of £40, and thus ended the suit.[2] He, by his will, dated January 18, 1731, and proved January 13, 1732,[3] devised to his oldest son, Michael, the farm on which he then resided, being 180 acres (90 morgen), which he (Hans Bergen) had purchased from his father. On the 12th April, 1748, Rachel, widow of Hans Bergen, released to her son, Michael Bergen, her right of dower in the farm in Brookland, which was devised to him by his father, said farm being bounded in the release as follows: "Southerly by land of Jacobus Debevois; northerly by land of Carell Debevois and Israel Horsfield; easterly by the King's Highway, leading from Flatbush to New York ferry; and westerly by the meadows; containing 120 acres:

Brooklyn, at their own expense, represented to the Director how prejudicial it would be to the town that one man, named Teunis Nyssen, should have too exclusive possession of so large a valley (meadow), directly contrary to the (provisions of the) Freedoms. The Director signed the report of Hudde (Surveyor-General) without then specifying the morgens. And after information had been received from said Jan Evertsen Bout (one of the petitioners) and others, the Director allowed Teunis Nyssen, agreeably to the Freedoms, as much of said valley as he should have need of, in proportion to his plantation."

January 26, 1668, a patent was granted to Albert C. Wantenaer to confirm to him a lot of ground in the town of Breuckelen, on Long Island, said lot "being on the west side of the town next to J. E. Bout, abutting on the highway, which lot being, on the 22d day of April, 1654, surveyed and measured in the presence of the then Schout and Schepens, was found to contain on the southeast side 26 rods, to the north the like, and northeast by north 5 rod 9 feet," as owned by said Albert, also "a certain parcell of valley or meadow ground, lying behind the said Albert's plough-land, stretching from the Great Kil to the entrance into the woodland," as sold by Teunis Nysse, May 26, 1656, to said Albert." These patents and conveyances are now in possession of Hon. T. G. Bergen.

[1] Conveyance dated August 21, 1723. Kings Co. Convey., liber v. 19.

[2] Conveyance (signed by 61 freeholders) dated January 7, 1723–4. Kings Co. Convey., liber E, 29.

[3] Liber ii. 311, Wills—Surrogate's office, city of New York.

also her right of dower in the meadows and woodland."[1] This Michael Bergen devised the farm, by will, to his grandson, Michael Bergen Grant, who subsequently conveyed it to George Powers.

XXIV, XXV, XXVI.

On the east side of the King's Highway (now Fulton avenue), we find that the somewhat triangular section of land, which we may describe, in general terms, as at present included between Fulton street and avenue, Raymond street, and a line drawn a little south of and parallel to Tillary street, was taken up by JORIS DIRCKSEN, PIETER CORNELISSEN and CORNELIS DIRCKSEN.

To JORIS DIRCKSEN was granted, March 23, 1646,

"a certain piece of land, woodland as well as maize-land, lying at Marechkawieck, bounded on the northwest by the land of Pieter Cornelissen, and extends next the said Peter Cornelissen till into the woods west, southwest and southwest by west, 187 rods; into and through the woods east southeast and southeast by east, between both 115 rods; further toward the valley (marsh) into and through the wood and maize-land, northeast 66 rods till to the maize-land and further, 80 rods; northeast by north till to the valley (marsh) to the place of beginning, 35 rods: amounting in all to 18 morgens, 501 rods."[2]

To this was afterwards added by purchase, in 1685, a small piece of land on the east side of the road, belonging originally to the patent of Andries Hudde,[3] on the opposite side of the highway.

February 28th, 1687–8, the heirs of Susanna Dubbles, deceased wife of Joris Dircksen, conveyed to Hendrick Sleght, "land at the northwest of the land of Peter Cornelise," as granted by ground brief of Gov. Kieft to Joris Dircksen, March 23, 1646.

Sleght's heirs, on May 1st, 1705, conveyed the same to Carell Debevois, it being described as

---

[1] See old deed in possession of T. G. Bergen, Esq.

[2] Patents, G G, 138.

[3] Deed dated September 13, 1668. Liber ii., 181, Kings Co. Convey. Consideration, £176 11s.

"bounded east by a certain creek, northerly by the land of Adryan Hoogland, westerly by the country roade that leads to the Ferry, and southerly by the land of Jacob Vandewater, with a small piece of meadow adjoining thereto, and all as it is now in fence, and formerly in the tenure and occupation of Hendrick Sleght, deceased, containing 18 morgens and 510 rods, English measure."

The parcel possessed by CORNELIS DIRCKSEN, the ferryman, has been already described on pages 75 and 76.

That of PIETER CORNELISSEN, carpenter, was a piece of land

"lying at Marechkawiech, both the maize-land and the woodland, bounded north by Cornelis Dircksen, ferryman; on the southeast by Joris (or George) Dircksen: it extends next the said ferryman's (land) from the marsh through the maize-land (and) the woods, to the division line of Claes Cornelissen, west by north and west northwest, between both, 172 rods; behind in the woods next the buildings and improvements of Andries Hudde, south by west, 138 rods; further east southeast and southeast by east, between both 31 rods; and along the said Joris's land, through the wood and maize land till to the marsh east, northeast and northeast by east, 178 rods; along the marsh 25 rods, to the place of beginning: amounting in all to 27 morgens, 119 rods."

The date of this patent was February 8, 1646.[1]

[1] Patents, G G, 133.

CHAPTER III.

THE CIVIL HISTORY OF BREUCKELEN.

1646—1664.

THE history of Breuckelen, during the period intervening between its incorporation in 1646 and the conquest of Nieuw Netherland by the English, in 1664, presents but few points of interest or importance. It is mentioned in 1649 as one of "two villages of little moment;"[1] and its course, as illustrated by the scanty records which remain to us, was simply that of an agricultural community, differing in no respect from the neighboring towns, and inferior to none (except, it may be, to Midwout, now Flatbush) in wealth or political influence.

Stuyvesant, the new Director-General, on his arrival in 1647, found Nieuw Netherland in an exceedingly "low condition." Excepting the Long Island settlements, the colony contained scarcely fifty "bouweries" under cultivation, and less than three hundred men capable of bearing arms. The commonalty were disorderly and discontented; the public revenue seriously impaired by inefficient or dishonest officials; trade ruined by smuggling; and the general safety weakened by bickerings and disputes with colonial patroons, concerning rights of jurisdiction. The savages, also, brooding over their past defeats, evidently waited only for an opportunity to avenge their losses; and jealous neighbors were secretly plotting against the Dutch rule in America. Stuyvesant, however, entered upon the task of reform with an energy peculiarly characteristic, and in less than three months, disorder was restrained, the revenues protected, and trade revived. The Indians were conciliated, and a tolerably good understanding established with the New England Colonies. The powers of government—executive, legislative, and judicial—which he assumed, were quite extensive, and

---

[1] N. Y. Col. MSS., i. 285.

often arbitrary. Directly or indirectly, he appointed and commissioned all public officers, framed all laws, and decided all important controversies. He also heard all appeals from subordinate magistrates, who were required to send such cases as were pending before them to the Council, for their decision. He directed churches to be built, installed ministers, and even ordered them when and where to preach. Assuming the sole control of the public lands, he extinguished the Indian title thereto, and allowed no purchase to be made from the natives without his sanction; and granted at pleasure, to individuals and companies, parcels of land, subject to such conditions as he saw fit to impose. In the management of these complicated affairs the Director developed a certain imperiousness of manner and impatience of restraint, due, perhaps, as much to his previous military life as to his personal character; and it is not strange that he sometimes exercised his prerogative in a capricious and arbitrary manner, and with little regard to the wishes of his people. During the whole of his predecessor's unquiet rule a constant struggle had been going on between the personal prerogative of the Executive and the inherent sentiment of popular freedom which prevailed among the commonalty, leading the latter constantly to seek for themselves the franchises and freedoms of the Fatherland, to which, as loyal subjects, they deemed themselves entitled in New Netherland. The contest was reopened soon after Stuyvesant's installation, and the firmness of both Director and people, in the maintenance of what each jealously considered their rights, gave indication of serious disturbance to the public weal. In 1647, however, the doughty Governor found himself in a predicament from which only the good people could relieve him. Trouble was brewing among the Indians, whose promised annual presents were considerably in arrears, and there existed an imperative necessity for certain repairs upon Fort Amsterdam. But the provincial treasury was bankrupt; and Stuyvesant, well knowing that the people would never submit to be taxed without their consent, found it convenient to yield his much-valued prerogative to the sentiment of the community, and, by advice of his Council, demanded a popular representation in the affairs of government. An election was therefore held, at which the inhabitants of Amsterdam, Breuckelen,

Amersfoort, and Pavonia chose eighteen of "the most notable, reasonable, honest, and respectable" among them, from whom, according to the custom of the Fatherland, the Director and Council selected NINE MEN as an advisory Council; and although their powers and duties were jealously limited and guarded by the Director's Proclamation, yet the appointment of the Nine Men was a considerable gain to the cause of popular rights. Distinctly considered as "good and faithful interlocutors and trustees of the commonalty," they were to confer with the Director and Council, "as their tribunes, on all means to promote the welfare" of the public, "as well as that of the country," and after due consultation upon the propositions of the Director and Council, might then "bring forward their advice." The Director might at any time attend their meetings and act as president. Three of their number, in rotation, were to have seats at the Council once a week, on regular court day, to act as arbitrators in civil cases; and their awards were binding, although, on payment of a special fee, appeal was permitted to the Council. Six of their number were to vacate their seats annually, whose successors were to be chosen by the Council, the Director, and "the Nine assembled;" by which means, in the first election only, the choice proceeded directly from the people. In this first popular assembly Breuckelen was represented by *Jan Evertsen Bout*, a farmer by occupation, and one of the original founders of the town.

The various measures of improvement in civil, municipal, military, religious, and educational matters, which the Director submitted to the Nine Men, were approved, and they promptly undertook to tax themselves for all, except for the expenses of finishing the fort, which they claimed the Company, by the charter of 1629, had bound themselves to do, and the Governor was obliged to waive that point.

The subsequent history of Stuyvesant's government is a record of quarrels with colonial patroons, with the English in New England, the Swedes on the South River, and last—not least—with his own people. In fact, the government was by no means well adapted to the people or adequate to protect them. The laws were very imperfect, and the Director and Council either incompetent or indisposed to remedy the serious defects which existed in the administration of civil and criminal justice. And, finally, so far did the Governor's assumption of authority exceed the patience of the commonalty, and so general was the feeling of public insecurity and discontent, that the people resolved, with great unanimity, to make a formal presentation of their grievances to the Governor, and demand redress.

Accordingly, on the 26th of November, 1653, "the most important popular convention that had ever assembled in New Netherland" met at New Amsterdam. It adjourned, however, to the 10th of December following, at which time delegates appeared from the city, Breuckelen, Flatbush, Flatlands, Gravesend, Newtown, Flushing, and Hempstead. Breuckelen was on this occasion represented by Messrs. *Frederick Lubbertsen*, *Paulus Van der Beeck*, and *William Beekman*, all men of position and ability. The Convention, after mutual consultation and discussion, adopted a remonstrance which our space will not allow of quoting in full, but which we may characterize as ably drawn and firmly but courteously expressed, and as manifesting an intelligent appreciation of their own rights, as well as a thorough acquaintance with the legitimate objects of civil government. It substantially demanded necessary reforms, and laws "resembling, as near as possible, those of the Netherlands." Stuyvesant winced under the truth which this earnest popular protest contained, and sought to weaken its effect by declaring that Breuckelen, Midwout, and Amersfoort had "no right of jurisdiction," and therefore no right to send delegates to a popular convention, and that the Convention itself was an unorganized body who had no right to address the Director, or "anybody else." Nothing daunted, the deputies, on the 13th of December, appealing to the law of Nature, which permits all men to assemble for the protection of their liberties and property, presented a second remonstrance, and declared, that if the Governor and Council would not grant them redress and protection, they would appeal to their superiors, the States-General and the West India Company. Irritated by their pertinacity and overmatched in argument, Stuyvesant fell back on his prerogative, and in an arrogant message—which declared that "We derive our authority from God and the Company, not from a few ignorant subjects, and we alone can call the inhabitants together"—he ordered the Convention to "disperse, and not to assemble again upon such business." Breuckelen, Amersfoort, and Midwout were also ordered to prohibit their delegates from attending, for the present, any meeting at New Amsterdam. The popular voice found partial expression, however, in letters addressed to the West India Company by the authorities of New Amsterdam and Gravesend, which were forwarded to Holland by an agent who was authorized to use every legitimate means to secure the reforms which the people demanded. Meanwhile, the exigencies of the times gave to the disaffected community an excellent opportunity of demonstrating that their discontent with the existing government of the colony did not arise from any lack of loyalty to the home government in the Fatherland.

The rapid increase of piracy on the Sound, and robberies on Long Island, led the magistracy, early in February, 1654, to recommend to the Director and Council that a force of forty men should be raised from the several towns, for the common defence.[1] This number was levied as follows: From the Manhattan, 8; from "Breuckelen, the Ferry, and the Walloon quarter," 4; Hempstead, 4; Rensselaerswyck, 4; Beverwyck, 4; Staten Island, 2; Middleburgh and Mespath Kill, 3; Gravesend, 3; Flushing, 3; Amersfoort, 2; Midwout, 2; Paulus Hook, 1. Letters were also addressed to the towns of Breuckelen, Amersfoort, and Midwout, requesting them "to lend their aid, at this critical juncture, to further whatever may advance the public defence." In response to this communication, the magistrates of the three towns, together with the court-martial, assembled at Breuckelen on the 7th of April, 1654, and adopted the most energetic measures for the general welfare. Every male was required to do guard-duty in his turn, "each acting schepen, at his discretion, trusting on his active and cheerful aid in times of peril." In case of invasion, "every inhabitant, of whatever station and condition," was to "unite in a general resistance," or pay a heavy fine. Every third man was

---

[1] New Amsterdam Rec., i. 378; Col. Rec., v. 213, 214. This document was signed by Frederick Lubbertsen, William Bredenbent, and Albert Cornelissen, of Breuckelen, and five others.

detailed as a minute-man, and was bound to obey any warning, "at a moment's notice." Any person who might discover an enemy at night was required to fire his gun three times, to warn his next neighbor, who was to do the same; and any firing of guns at night, except as signals, was prohibited, under strong penalties. Several military officers were also chosen.[1]

Subsequent alarms, of invasion by the English, occasioned similar calls upon the Dutch towns of Long Island, which were all responded to with the same alacrity. Of the divers troubles which now surrounded Stuyvesant's government it is needless for us to speak. Suffice it to say, that the English colonies were full of disaffection and plottings, while the Dutch were somewhat alienated by the Director's former arbitrary dealings; and, on every hand, disorganization threatened the colony. At this critical juncture came welcome news of peace between England and Holland; and shortly after, Stuyvesant, having learned wisdom from his past experience, and wishing to counterbalance the political preponderance of the English towns, determined to reward the loyalty of Breuckelen, Amersfoort, and Midwout, by enlarging their municipal privileges. Two schepens were added to the two which Breuckelen already possessed; and DAVID PROVOOST, the former commissary of Fort Hope, was appointed her first separate schout or constable. Similar additions were made to the magistracy of Amersfoort and Midwout; and a superior "district court" was also organized, of delegates from each town-court, together with the schout. To this court, which existed in this form till 1661, was intrusted authority to regulate roads, build churches, establish schools, and enact local laws. It was also, to a limited extent, a court of record.[2] By the creation of this court, these towns became entitled, under the Dutch law, to the rights of jurisdiction and representation, which had been so absolutely denied them by the Director-General in 1653, "for under the feudal law it was the fief, whether manor or town, that was entitled to be represented, and not the people; and no delegation could exist without a local court from which it could emanate."

Previously to this time, also, the Dutch inhabitants of Long Island

---

[1] Col. Rec., v. 240, 242.

[2] New Amsterdam Rec., i. 376–427.

had been without church or minister of their own, and were obliged either to attend public worship in New Amsterdam, or to avail themselves of the occasional ministrations, at private houses in the villages, of some of the metropolitan dominies. To remedy this want of a settled ministry now became the endeavor of the Director and Council; and soon (December, 1654) a small church-edifice was erected by the joint effort of the three towns, at Midwout (Flatbush), and the Reverend Johannes Theodorus Polhemus, formerly stationed at Itamarca, Brazil, was duly installed as the first Dutch pastor on Long Island. In this first Reformed Dutch Church on the island, services were held every Sabbath morning, and in the afternoon at Breuckelen and Amersfoort alternately. This arrangement continued until 1660, when Dominie Selyns was settled as the pastor of the people at Breuckelen.

In July of this year, the ferry between Manhattan and Long Island was regulated by an ordinance of the Council, which also established the rates of toll, etc. A tavern had been established at "The Ferry" some time before this.[1] The subject of the ferry, however, is of so much importance as to demand a full chapter to itself, which the reader will find in another portion of this volume.

April 8th, 1655, the magistrates of Breuckelen petitioned the Council that they might be permitted, inasmuch "as the present schepens have served their time, to send in a nomination of a double number to the High Council," from which a selection might be made to supply the places of those schepens whose time had so expired. The Council, in reply, requested the magistrates to inform them, "as far as it is in their power, of the character, manners, and expertness of the most respectable individuals of their village, and places in its vicinity under their jurisdiction;" and the schepens having done so, the Council appointed Messrs. *Frederick Lubbertsen*, *Albert Cornelissen*, and *Jacob Dircksen*, and *Joris Rapelje* in the place of Peter Cornelissen.[2]

On the 5th of May ensuing, David Provoost, "schout or temporary secretary" to the three Dutch towns, petitioned for a salary

---

[1] Mentioned in N. Y. Col. Doc., i. 425, under date of Nov. 29, 1650, as being (with exception of that at Flushing) the only one outside of Manhattan Island.

[2] N. Y. Col. MSS., vi. 27, 29.

equal to that enjoyed by Secretary Kip of New Amsterdam. It was granted to him in the form of fees, of which the following schedule may be interesting to legal gentlemen of the present day. For copying every judicial act passed by the schepens, or for each apostille, 12 stivers, and 6 stivers for each "extract from the notules." For a petition which was to be signed by the petitioner, if of a civil nature, 16 stivers; or if it related to a criminal case, injuries, etc., 20 stivers. For procuring a certificate, 24 stivers; but he was not to charge any thing for petitions or remonstrances, prepared for and by order of the schepens, and directed to the Governor and Council.[1] Provoost died in January, 1656, and was succeeded by Peter Tonneman,[2] who acted until August, 1660, when he became sheriff of New Amsterdam; and in his stead Adriaen Hegeman was appointed, who enjoyed a salary of 200 guilders[3] per annum, with half of the civil fines imposed by the courts, and one-third of the criminal fines levied by the towns, together with certain clerk's fees for entries and transcripts.

In March, 1656, the schepens of Breuckelen, in view of the fact that there were several building-lots remaining within their village, upon which no buildings had been erected, contrary, as they supposed, to the wish and order of the Director-General and Council, requested that advertisements might be posted up in the village, requiring all village lot owners to build thereon within a certain specified time, under penalty. This measure, which they considered would promote the prosperity of Breuckelen and the increase of its population, met the approval of the Council, who fixed the time at two months, with an extension of six under certain circumstances.[4]

In September following, the magistrates of the three Dutch towns requested the Director-General to make a peace with the Indians in their neighborhood, before his contemplated departure on a visit to Fort Orange, as they were apprehensive of an attack.[5]

April 11, 1657, in response to a petition of the magistrates of Breuckelen, Thursday of each week was declared a market-day in the village of Breuckelen.[6]

---

[1] N. Y. Col. MSS., vi. 37, 38.
[2] Ibid., 245.
[3] Or £33 6s. 8d. (Alb. Rec., x. 248.)
[4] N. Y. Col. MSS., vi. 344, 345
[5] Ibid., viii. 215.
[6] Ibid., 523.

November 28, 1658, the burgomasters and schepens of Nieuw Amsterdam, in a petition for an annual fair (for lean cattle, to be held during the month of May, and for fat cattle, from the 20th to the last of November), desire that no stranger in attendance shall be liable to arrest or summons; also, that the ferryman shall ferry over all cattle going to the fair, at 25 stivers per head (instead of 20 stivers), with an accompanying reservation that he shall ferry back, free, all cattle not sold at the fair. The petition was agreed to.[1]

In February, 1660, the villages of Breuckelen and New Utrecht were ordered to be immediately put into a state of defence, with palisades, etc., and the Hon. Nicasius de Sille was directed to survey and attend thereto.[2]

During the same month, several Frenchmen settled, by Stuyvesant's permission, at a place "between Mespath Kil and Norman's Kil," and laid the foundation of a village since known as Boswick, or Bushwick, now included in the Eastern District of the city of Brooklyn.

On the 1st of March, 1660, Aert Anthonissen Middagh, Teunis Gybertsen Bogart, Jean Le Clerc, Gerrit Heyndrick Backer, Philip Barchstoel, Christina Cappoens, Jacob Kip, and Joris Rapalje, all residents of the Waal-boght neighborhood, petitioned the Director for permission to form a village "on the margin of the river, between the lands of said Bogaert and Kip, so that," as they expressed it, "we may be in sight of the Manhatans, or Fort Amsterdam."[3] The position selected was, probably, the elevated point of land which jutted into the river about the foot of South Fourth street, in the present Eastern District of our city, and which was known in the ancient time as the "Keike," or "Lookout." Jacob Kip, the owner[4] of the land adjoining the Hans Hansen (Bergen) patent (described pages 88 to 97), had been secretary of Nieuw Amsterdam, and was an influential and enterprising man in the colony. It was, probably, owing to his desire to improve the value of his real estate, by securing the establishment of a village thereon, that this petition was made; and his influence with the authorities was such, that permission was granted to erect the

[1] N. Y. Col. MSS., viii. 1047. [2] Ibid., ix. 78. [3] Ibid., ix. 522.

[4] There is, however, no evidence that he ever resided on the property.

block-house, and the settlers in the vicinity were directed to remove thither.

In May following, the Governor and Council appointed Jacques Cortelyou, surveyor, Albert Cornelissen (Wantenaer), and Jan Evertse Bout, as commissioners to examine the situation and quality of the land in the neighborhood of the village of Breuckelen, and to report (with a map) how much of it remained undisposed of, how it was cultivated, and how many plantations might be advantageously laid out upon it.[1]

This year (1660) is also noticeable as the year in which the first church was organized in Breuckelen, by the installation of the Reverend Henricus Selyns, of which memorable event a full account will be found in another chapter. The town at that time had a population of thirty-one families, or 134 souls, who, being unprovided with a church, assembled, at first, in a barn for public worship.

On the 10th of February, 1661, the residents in the vicinity of the Waal-boght were notified that they must comply with the previous orders of the Council against isolated dwellings, and that they must remove to the village erected during the previous year on Kip's land (*ante*, p. 113), for greater security, before the 15th of the next month.[2]

To this they demurred, and requested permission to construct a block-house for their defence, on the point of Joris Rapelje's land—*i. e.*, on the easterly side of the Waal-boght.[3] They were ordered to "appear on the next Council-day, together with Jacob Kip and Christina Cappoens, to be heard *pro* and *con*." On the 3d of March, therefore, the same petitioners—viz., Joris Rapaille, Teunis Gysbert Bogaert, Rem Jansen Smith, Evert Dircx van As, Jan Joris Rapaille, Jean Le Clercq, Wynant Pieters, "all residents or landholders in or about the Waale-boght"—set forth in a petition that "some time ago (*i. e.*, in March, 1660), on the petition of Jacob Kip and others," it had been decreed that "a village and blockhouse should be laid out *on the height* at the end of said Kip's land,"

---

[1] N. Y. Col. MSS., ix. 197.

[2] N. Y. Col. MSS., ix. 523. The reference of this order to *Brooklyn*, in the printed Calendar of Documents, is evidently incorrect.

[3] N. Y. Col. MSS., ix. 530, date Feb. 24, 1661.

and that they had been ordered to remove thither. To this they objected, "inasmuch as the place is wholly unfit for the purpose, partly because the woodland thereabout, being stony, is not suitable for arable land," and "little or no crops can be, apparently, expected from it, as it cannot be ploughed, in consequence of the large number of rocks and hollows thereabouts; wherefore, it is impossible, even by the hardest labor, to obtain a scanty living there. Moreover, in consequence of the uncommon height of the land there, it is impossible to find good and sufficient water to make a well. Jan de Kaeper's (Jan, the sailor's) well is an example of this: it adjoins his house in the valley (meadow), and people must descend into it by means of ladders, and then scoop the water in a little bowl, which (*i. e.* the well), nevertheless, does not suffice (to supply) two families who are dwelling there at present." The streams in the neighborhood are mostly dried up in summer, and during the winter season the roads are often very "hard and pointed by the frost, or deep and muddy in heavy rains, or well-nigh impassable from snow," so that, when people wish to water their cattle, they are obliged to fetch the water in barrels from Theunis Gysbertse (Bogaert's) well, which is a most fatiguing and injurious business for farmers, both in summer and winter;" a drudgery, in fact, which the petitioners state they "daily see performed by their neighbors with a weeping eye." For these reasons the petitioners requested permission "to build a block-house on Joris Rapaille's point (hoeck)," which they considered a much preferable place for the purpose," being "by nature more defensible and stronger," the water there being "by far the richest fountain in the entire country, and the spot being conveniently "near their bouweries and plantations." They admitted the possibility of being separated from each other by occasional high floods; but they expected to lay a bridge over the Kil[1]—two or three planks broad—and to grant to each one who was willing to settle there convenient lots for houses and gardens, of which they would transfer to them their whole right and title, "so that, under God's blessing, it might soon increase to a convenient village." Their arguments prevailed with

[1] "Runnegackonck," the creek which formed the easterly boundary of Rapalie's farm, and emptied into the Wallabout Bay.

the Director and Council, and the petition of Jacob Kip and Christina Cappoens was rejected.[1]

In June, 1661, the people of Breuckelen presented a petition to the Council, through their schepens, asking that,

" *Whereas*, it pleased your Honors to allow them, for purposes of pasturage for their cattle (which now, God be praised, are increased to a considerable number), the use of certain portions of the 'valley' (or meadow), situated near the corner of Fred. Lubbertsen's (land), at the Red Hook; also, a small valley (meadow) in the Walle-bocht, located in the woods between the mountain and the underwood (Kreupelbosch); besides a portion of the valley (meadow) beyond the 3d kil, towards the seaside, extending easterly towards the 4th kil, and westerly from the sea towards the woods,"

the aforesaid tracts may be granted to them in perpetuity. This petition was granted as soon as the land could be surveyed.[2]

The tithes of Breuckelen, Gowanus, and the Waal-bocht, for this year, were sold by the Director-General and Council to Messrs. Paulus Van der Beeck and Warnaer Wessels, and the people were forbidden to remove any thing from their farms until the tithes had been collected by these purchasers.

The year 1661 will also be ever memorable in the history of Breuckelen as having furnished to the good people their first *schoolmaster*. On the 4th of July, 1661, the following petition was presented

" To the Right Hon[ble] Director-General and Council of New Netherland: The Schout and Schepens of the Court of Breuckelen respectfully represent that they found it necessary that a Court Messenger was required for the Schepens' Chamber, to be occasionally employed in the Village of Breuckelen and all around where he may be needed, as well to serve summons, as also to conduct the service of the Church, and to sing on Sundays; to take charge of the School, dig graves, etc., ring the Bell, and perform whatever else may be required: Therefore, the Petitioners, with your Honors' approbation, have thought proper to accept for so highly necessary an office a suitable person who is now come before them, one

---

[1] N. Y. Col. MSS., ix. 547. [2] Ibid., 647, 648.

Carel van Beauvois, to whom they have hereby appropriated a sum of fl. 150, besides a free dwelling; and whereas the Petitioners are apprehensive that the aforesaid C. v. Beauvois would not and cannot do the work for the sum aforesaid, and the Petitioners are not able to promise him any more, therefore the Petitioners, with all humble and proper reverence, request your Honors to be pleased to lend them a helping hand, in order thus to receive the needful assistance. Herewith, awaiting your Honors' kind and favorable answer, and commending ourselves, Honorable, wise, prudent, and most discreet Gentlemen, to your favor, we pray for your Honors God's protection, together with a happy and prosperous administration unto Salvation. Your Honors' servants and subjects, The Schout and Schepens of the Village aforesaid. By order of the same,

" (Signed) Adriaen Hegeman, Secretary."

In answer to this petition, the Director and Council were graciously pleased to say that they would "pay fifty guilders, in wampum, annually, for the support of the precentor (*voorsanger*) and schoolmaster in the village of Breuckelen."[1]

FAC-SIMILE OF THE SIGNATURE OF CAREL DE BEAUVOIS.

Carel de Beauvois, who was thus commissioned to fulfil the multifarious duties of court-messenger, bell-ringer, grave-digger, chorister, reader, and schoolmaster of Breuckelen, is described by Riker as "a highly respectable and well-educated French Protestant, who came from Leyden, in Holland. He was of a family whose name and origin were probably derived from the ancient city of Beauvais, on the river Therin, to the northwest of Paris; but there is reason to believe that he himself was a native of Leyden. He arrived at

[1] N. Y. Col. MSS., ix. 678.

Amsterdam, in the ship Otter, February 17, 1659, accompanied by his wife, Sophia Van Lodensteyn, and three children born to them in Leyden, and now aged eight, six, and three years respectively. His literary merits and acquaintance with the Dutch language soon acquired for him the situation of a teacher;" but in 1661, as we have seen, his duties were enlarged by his appointment to the office of chorister and reader. He afterwards served as public secretary or town clerk, which office he held till 1669. His descendants have ever been numbered among the most respectable citizens of Brooklyn, Bushwick, and Newtown.[1]

The arrival of Governor Winthrop at New Amsterdam, *en route* to England in July, 1661, afforded an opportunity to the inhabitants of Breuckelen to honor their distinguished guest, and their own Governor, who escorted him, with a salute, for which purpose *ten pounds* of powder were issued to them from the public stores.[2]

In this year, also (1661), Boswyck, which now numbered twenty-three families, received its official recognition as a town by the creation of a subaltern court and magistrates; but, having no Schout of its own, was, together with New Utrecht, annexed to the jurisdiction of Hegeman, the Schout of Breuckelen, Amersfoort, and Midwout,—the district being afterwards known as the "Five Dutch Towns."

In Sept., 1661, the inhabitants of Harlem, Bergen, Breuckelen, and the Dutch villages on Long Island, were notified to have their lands surveyed, and to take out patents therefor.[3]

In June, 1662, in consequence of a petition from Breuckelen, Middleburg, Mespath, and other villages, Mr. Jacques Cortelyou is directed by the Council to survey and apportion to each of those towns, shares in the meadow between the 3d and 4th kils. Breuckelen was to have 100 morgens, and Middleburgh and Mespath 80 morgens each.[4] The meadows here referred to were probably those lying on the south side of the island, within the limits of the town of Jamaica, and known as "Seller's Neck."

The year 1663 dawned over New Netherland, pregnant with im-

---

[1] See Riker's Hist. of Newtown, pp. 407, 410, for genealogy of the De Bevoise family.

[2] N. Y. Col. MSS., ii. 460.

[3] Ibid., ix. 788.

[4] Ibid., x. 149.

pending trouble to the Dutch. An earthquake, bringing terror to their hearts, was followed by a great freshet which devastated their harvests. The dreaded small-pox raged through their villages, and decimated the neighboring Indian tribes. Then ensued the horrors of savage warfare, and men's hearts failed them before the terrors of the red-man's tomahawk and firebrand. When at last comparative peace had been restored, Stuyvesant turned his attention towards making some definite settlement with the colony of Connecticut concerning their respective jurisdictions. The Connecticut authorities, however, claimed that several of the English towns of Long Island were under their rule, and even ventured to hint that they would reduce the adjoining Dutch villages also. After long and fruitless negotiations, the Dutch agents returned "with fleas in their ears" to New Amsterdam. Finding themselves powerless to resist their English and savage neighbors, the towns of Haerlem, Breuckelen, Midwout, Amersfoort, New Utrecht, Boswyck, Bergen, and the City, assembled in convention, by Stuyvesant's order, Nov. 1st, and adopted a remonstrance to the Amsterdam Chamber, wherein they attributed their troubles to the supineness of the authorities in Holland. The action of the Convention was at once prompt and loyal to the interests of the country and the Fatherland. But, even while they deliberated, a revolution was in progress on Long Island. Certain self-constituted officials visited the English towns, changed the names thereof, proclaimed the king, and threatened the Dutch settlements.

Let us turn aside, however, from the current of public events, in order to notice a few local items, marking more particularly the progress of the town of Breuckelen.

On the first of March in this year (1663), the following petition was presented

"To the Right Honble Director-General and Council of New Netherland:

"Shew with due reverence and respect, the undersigned, neighbors and inhabitants of the village of Breuckelen, your Honors' obedient servants, that there lies convenient to us a certain place near Breuckelen fit to be erected into a new village, for our advantage, being a woodland (as we) believe (is) known to your Honors, in which place there is sufficient accommodation where twenty or thirty persons can have a suitable place and lot; and as the valleys thereby furnish no nearer place (than) those adjoining between the 3d and 4th kills,[1] to supply the cattle with fodder, and is also the nearest spot, therefore we, the Petitioners, are under the necessity of turning to your Honors, humbly praying and soliciting that the aforesaid requested place may be granted to them, each his lot, as the valleys in the hay season be far from here, and they seek the nearest, in order to bring in the grass dry and in good condition (with God's blessing), for the preservation of the cattle, and all that is annexed thereto, that appertains to the farmers. Awaiting, therefore, a favorable answer, if your Honors the Director-General and Council, in your wise discretion, shall vouchsafe to grant the same, we remain your Honors' obedient servants.

	Albert Cornelissen,
Tietje Schiercks,	Barent B I Jansen,
Jan Jacobsen,	Jan Damen,
Joost Verstraalen,	Jan Peters, from Deventer,
Casper Pieters,	Jan Martyn,
Henrycus Teunis,	Theunis Cornelis,
Symon Clasen,	Tjerck Jansen,
Heyndryck Jansen Been,	Tonis Snysken, (?)
Tiercs Diercks,	Peter Peters,
Harmen Heyndricks,	Pieter Lambert,
Jan Hibon,	Symen Joosten,
Jores Jorise,	Heydrick Fallkers,
Cornelys van Borsem,	Piere Wouterse,
Lodewy(ck) Jongs,	Cornelys Janse Spuyler,
Yokam . . . uedden,	Barent Pjterse."[2]

The magistrates of Midwout, also, petitioned for a similar favor of erecting a village on the same parcel of land. It was, therefore, determined by the authorities that the land should be surveyed by the Surveyor, in order that an opinion might be formed as to the number of plantations which might advantageously be laid out on it.

On the 26th of May, Thomas Lambertsen, Evert Dircksen van As, Teunis Dircksen, Teunis Jansen, John Damen, Hendrick Jansen Been, George Probatskin, Peter Petersen, Teunis Cornelissen, Joost Fransen, Dirck Jans Hooglandt, Paulus Dircksen, Wynant

[1] Ante, pp. 116, 118.

[2] N. Y. Col. MSS., Part ii. x. 37.

Petersen, Dirck Paulusen and Hendrick Claesen, citizens of Breuckelen, petitioned the Council for leave to establish a "concentration," in the following terms:

"*Whereas*, we lately obtained from your Honors a certain piece of land, situated back of the Waale-boght, or at Marcus' plantation; and whereas, we, the petitioners, have our fencing stuff ready, and some of us have already sowed and planted, and others contemplate beginning their plantations, and inasmuch as (otherwise) we should be at a considerable distance from our property, we have agreed unanimously to solicit as a favor, that we may be permitted to make a concentration there, in order to protect our property."[1]

The petition was granted.

In the month of July, during the Indian troubles which prevailed, the Director proposed that Breuckelen should furnish 8, 10, or 12 men, to be "kept ready for the protection of one or the other place in danger, which may God avert!" A meeting of the inhabitants was forthwith held, at which every person present expressed a willingness to aid in protecting their neighbors on Long Island, but it was deemed that *the town was not strong enough to furnish so many men;* and a letter was despatched to the Director and Council to that effect; also refusing, from prudential motives, to cross the river to the defence of New Amsterdam. Letters expressing a similar resolution were also sent by the neighboring towns of Amersfoort, Gravesend, Midwout, and New Utrecht.[2]

In February, 1664, on petition of the magistrates of Breuckelen and the three adjoining Dutch towns, an ordinance was passed by the Council, providing for the registry of deeds, mortgages, and all legal writings relating to real estate in those towns, to be made, according to the practice of the Fatherland, before the Secretary and two of the magistrates of the town in which said property is situated, —no deed to be signed unless the original patent was exhibited.[3]

During the same month the people of Breuckelen were forbidden, under penalty of 100 guilders,[4] to remove their crops from the fields

---

[1] N. Y. Col. MSS., x., Part ii., 117.
[2] Ibid., x., Part ii. 191, 193, 195.
[3] Ibid., x., Part iii., 53, 55, 56.
[4] A guilder is equal to 41 cents, 6 mills, and a fraction $\frac{666}{1000}$.

until the tithes had been collected by Sheriff Hegeman. The same thing had occurred before; and in the following year, "some of the country people" of Breuckelen, having neglected to pay their tithes, were ordered to pay them within twenty-four hours, on penalty of execution. These tithes, probably, were not raised for church purposes exclusively, but for government. According to the laws of that day, lands were usually exempt from taxation for ten years, after which time they were taxed one-tenth of their produce.

But, to return to our narrative of the public events which were agitating the colony of New Netherland. Early in January, 1664, Captain John Scott, an adventurer of unsettled life and principles, acting under the *quasi* authority of the Duke of York, visited the discontented English villages on Long Island, stimulated them to the formation of a distinct and independent government, of which he was declared the temporary President, and proclaimed Charles the Second as their king. Having made this fair beginning, he set out with about 150 followers, horse and foot, to subjugate the neighboring Dutch towns. Coming first to Breuckelen, he raised the English flag and addressed the citizens, affirming that the soil they occupied belonged to the King of England, and absolving them from their allegiance to the Dutch Government. But his appeal fell dead upon the ears of the listening crowd, and the only answer made was a courteous invitation from Secretary Van Ruyven, to visit and confer with the Director-General. This Scott declined, saying: "Let Stuyvesant come here with a hundred men; I shall wait for him and run a sword through his body." Turning next to a lad near by, the son of Burgomaster Krygier, he commanded him to doff his hat to the royal standard. Upon the boy's refusal to do so, he struck him, whereupon one of the Dutch bystanders remarked that he ought to strike men, not boys. This speech provoked the ire of Scott's followers, four of whom fell upon the man, who was finally obliged to flee, after making a brief resistance with an axe. The English thereupon left, threatening to burn the town if he was not delivered up.[1] Passing next to Midwout, Scott repeated the scenes of Brooklyn; but the stolid Dutchmen, alike unmoved by his seduc-

---

[1] N. Y. Col. Doc., ii. 394, 399, 482, 483, 404.

tions and his threats, merely asked to see his commission, which he promised to produce on his return, in April. The next day the farce was repeated at Amersfoort and New Utrecht, where those who refused to salute the English flag were set upon and maltreated, to the engendering of much confusion and mutual enmity.

Learning of these transactions, Stuyvesant sent a commission to Long Island, to seek some settlement of these troubles. A meeting occurred (January 14) between the two parties at Jamaica, where a basis of agreement was agreed upon—although Scott had informed the Dutchmen that the King of England had granted Long Island to his brother, the Duke of York, who was determined, if it was not peaceably surrendered, to possess himself of it, and also of the whole province of Nieuw Netherland. Collisions and disturbances, however, continuing between the English and Dutch, induced the Director, in February, to call a meeting of delegates from the Dutch settlements on the island, for the purpose of making a proper representation to the States-General and W. I. Company, of their trials and dangers. This Convention, wherein Breuckelen was represented by Messrs. Willem Bredenbent, Albert Cornelis Wantenaer, and Joris Gysberts Bogert, voted a remonstrance and detailed statement of affairs, which was forwarded to the Fatherland.

In the succeeding month, the provisional arrangement agreed upon by the Dutch authorities and Captain Scott at Jamaica, in the preceding January, were formally ratified by commissioners from either side. It was the best the Dutch could do, in the unfortunate circumstances under which they were placed; but it was a virtual concession of their own weakness and inability to cope with their English neighbors. The valley of the Connecticut River, the fertile lands of Westchester, and now, last of all, the five English towns of Long Island, had slipped from their nerveless grasp. In this critical state of affairs, the principle of popular representation was, for the first time, fully recognized in the province. At the special request of the Burgomasters and Schepens, the Director convened a General Assembly of delegates from the several towns, to discuss and consider the affairs of Nieuw Netherland. This Convention, in which Breuckelen was represented by Willem Bredenbent and Albert Cornelis Wantenaer, assembled at the "Stadt Huys" (or City

Hall), in New Amsterdam, on the 10th of April, 1664. Within the first days of its session, however, advices were received from the Fatherland, announcing that the provincial despatches of November preceding had been duly received, and that certain prompt and important measures had been inaugurated towards a settlement of the difficulties pending between the English and Dutch. An additional military force was also sent out, and the Governor was directed to prosecute the war with the Esopus Indians to a complete and successful issue, and also to reduce to obedience the revolted English towns. Thinking this latter to be an undertaking easier commanded than accomplished, the Dutch authorities turned their chief attention to their relations with the savages, with whom, on the 16th of May, a satisfactory peace was concluded.

Unfortunately, however, their English enemies could not be so easily placated. In spite of all that Stuyvesant could do to effect a just and amicable arrangement of existing difficulties, it soon became evident that the English were predetermined, at all hazards, and by any means or pretext, to wrest the province of Nieuw Netherland from its lawful owners. Lulled to security—in spite of forewarnings—by advices from the Chamber at Amsterdam, stating that no apprehension need be entertained of any public danger or enemy from England, the honest burghers of the city of Nieuw Amsterdam suddenly found their city blockaded, and their communication with Long Island and the Jersey shore cut off, by a strong British fleet, anchored at the Narrows, in Nyack Bay, between New Utrecht and Coney Island. Simultaneously with his arrival, Col. Richard Nicolls, commander of the fleet, took possession of Staten Island, captured a couple of yachts, forbade the surrounding farmers to furnish any supplies to the garrison of Fort Amsterdam, and scattered broadcast his proclamations promising amnesty to those who should acknowledge, and the rigors of war to those who should deny the authority of the English king. The next morning, August 30th, Stuyvesant's indignant inquiry as to what all this meant, was peremptorily answered by a formal summons to surrender the city and the province to the English crown. The position of the Director-General was now trying in the extreme: for himself he had no care, and would willingly have risked his life in resisting the foe;

but such a course would have been pure madness. Help from abroad, or even from the neighboring Long Island towns, was utterly out of the question; the city was unprotected by proper defences, the fort quite untenable, and though the Burgomasters showed spirit, the people were hopeless and disposed to yield. For two days, the brave old man assented neither to the reiterated summons of Nicolls, nor to the murmurings or entreaties of the citizens. Finally, wishing to bring matters to an end, the English fleet moved up towards the city, two of the vessels lying broadside towards the fort, while others disembarked troops on the Long Island shore, just below Breuckelen, where, at "the Ferry," the New England and Long Island volunteers had already encamped. Even then, the lion-hearted Director could only answer the crowd of men, women, and children who surrounded him and implored him to submit, "I would much rather be carried out dead." The next day, September 5th, he reluctantly yielded to a remonstrance, signed by all the prominent men of the city, and on the 6th articles of capitulation were signed. On the 8th, occurred the final act in this political tragedy—briefly described as follows, in a letter from Secretary Van Ruyven to the town of Boswyck:[1]

"ANNO, SEPTEMBER 8, 1664, N. S.

"It has happened that the Nieuw Netherlands is given up to the English, and that Peter Stuyvesant, Governor of the West India Company, has marched out of the Fort, with his men, to Beur's Paeet (Beaver Lane) to the Holland shipping, which lay there at the time; and that Governor Richard Nicolls, in the name of the King of England, ordered a corporal's guard to take possession of the Fort. Afterwards the Governor, with two companies of men,[2] marched into the Fort, accompanied by the Burgomasters of the city, who inducted the Governor and gave him a welcome reception. Gov. Nicolls has altered the name of the city of Nieuw Amsterdam, and *named the same New York*, and the Fort, "Fort James."

"From your friend,

CORNELIS VAN RUYVEN."

---

[1] Similar letters were undoubtedly addressed by the Secretary to the magistrates of Brooklyn and the other Dutch towns.

[2] The New England and Long Island volunteers were kept at the ferry, on the Brooklyn side, "as the citizens dreaded most being plundered by them."

Thus, in the words of our latest State historian,[1] "The flag of England was at length triumphantly displayed, where for half a century that of Holland had rightfully waved, and from Virginia to Canada, the King of Great Britain was acknowledged as sovereign. Viewed in all its aspects, the event which gave to the whole of that country a unity in allegiance, and to which a misgoverned people complacently submitted, was as inevitable as it was momentous. But, whatever may have been its ultimate consequences, this treacherous and violent seizure of the territory and possessions of an unsuspecting ally, was no less a breach of private justice than of public faith. It may, indeed, be affirmed that, among all the acts of selfish perfidy which royal ingratitude conceived and executed, there have been few more characteristic, and none more base."

---

[1] Brodhead, i. 745.

CHAPTER IV.

ECCLESIASTICAL HISTORY OF BREUCKELEN.

1628-1664.

It has often been claimed as a peculiar distinction of the Puritan settlers of New England, that their prominent aim, and chief care, in settling those desert regions, was the establishment of religious and educational privileges. Yet, although the settlement of New Netherlands was undoubtedly undertaken rather as a commercial speculation, than as an experimental solution of ecclesiastical and civil principles and government, we find that the Dutch were equally anxious and careful to extend and to preserve to their infant settlements the blessings of education and religion. It is true that, in the earlier years of roving and unsystematized traffic which followed the discovery of Manhattan Island, there seems to have been no higher principle involved than that of gain. But as soon as a permanent agricultural and commercial occupation of the country was undertaken by the West India Company, the higher moral and spiritual wants and necessities of its settlers were fully recognized. Emigrants who went forth under their auspices, or those of the States General of Holland, were accompanied by a schoolmaster, being a pious church-member, who was to instruct the children and officiate at religious meetings by leading in the devotions and reading a sermon, until a regular pastor was established over them. *Ziekentroosters*, or "comforters of the sick," being persons adapted by their spiritual gifts and graces to edify and comfort the people, were also frequently commissioned as aids to the ministers. Two of these "comforters" accompanied Gov. Minuit in the year 1626, and by them the religious services of the colonists were conducted until early in 1628, when the learned and zealous Jonas Michaelius[1] came out from Amsterdam, under the auspices of the North Synod of Hol-

[1] N. Y. Col. MSS., ii. 759-70; Brodhead's N. Y., i. 183.

land, and "first established the form of a church," at Manhattan. He was succeeded, in 1633, by the Rev. Everardus Bogardus, and the congregation, who had hitherto worshipped in the upper loft of a horse-mill, now erected a small, plain church, together with a dwelling and stable for the Dominie's use.[1] This first church in Manhattan gave place, in 1642, to a new stone edifice within the fort (now the Battery), and which was much better suited to the size and dignity of the colony than the "mean barn" in which they had hitherto worshipped.

Dominie Bogardus was followed, in 1647, by the Rev. Johannes Megapolensis, a man eminent for his piety and talents, who served this church and congregation with fidelity until his death, in 1669.

For many years succeeding the first settlement of the country, the settlers on the western end of Long Island were dependent upon the city for all their civil and religious privileges. This state of things, with all its inconveniences, lasted until 1654, when the first church on Long Island was established at Midwout, now Flatbush; and the Governor designated Dominie Megapolensis, of New Amsterdam, with John Snedicor and John Stryker, commissioners to superintend the erection of a church edifice. In February, 1655, in compliance with a request from the people of Midwout, an order was issued requiring the inhabitants of Breuckelen and Amersfoort (Flatlands) to assist "in cutting and hauling wood" for the said church.[2] The Breuckelen people, however, while they expressed their perfect willingness to aid in the erection of the church itself, objected to work on the "minister's house," which it was proposed to add thereto, averring that the Midwout folks were able to do it themselves.[3] They were finally obliged to conform to the Governor's order, and the church, which was built in the form of a cross, 28 by 60 or 65 feet, and 12 to 14 feet between the beams, the rear to be used as a minister's dwelling, was the first house of worship erected in King's County. Its construction, as we shall see, occupied several years, although it was probably sufficiently advanced within the year to allow of its being used for worship.

---

[1] Rev. Thomas De Witt's Hist. Dis. in North Ref. Dutch Ch. of city of New York, 1857.

[2] N. Y. Col. MSS., vi. 15, Feb. 9, 1655.

[3] Ibid., p. 23.

On the 6th of August, 1655, by order of Governor Stuyvesant, the inhabitants of the country were convened for the purpose of ascertaining whether they approved of the Rev. Johannes Theodorus Polhemus, their "provisional minister," and what salary they were willing to pay him.[1] The Sheriff reported that they approved of Mr. Polhemus, and would pay him a salary of 1,040 guilders per year,[2] to be raised by a yearly tax.

Mr. Polhemus, a descendant of an ancient and highly respectable family in the Netherlands, had come to New Amsterdam during the preceding year from Itamarca, in Brazil, where he had been laboring as a missionary. He was immediately settled in Flatbush, where he subsequently received a patent for a part of the premises recently owned by the late Jeremiah Lott, Esq. He was an eminently pious and faithful preacher of the Gospel, and although, as we shall see in the following pages, his hearers in the town of Breuckelen were not altogether satisfied with him, it is evident that their opposition proceeded from no lack of personal respect, nor from any doubts of his Christian character.

In February, 1656, the magistracy of Midwout and Amersfoort asked permission to request a voluntary contribution from the people of the three Dutch towns, towards the proper maintenance of the Gospel.[3] To this the Breuckelen people respectfully objected, saying, "as the Rev. John Polhemus only acts as a minister of the Gospel in the village of Midwout, therefore the inhabitants of the village of Breuckelen and adjacent districts are disinclined to subscribe or promise any thing for the maintenance of a Gospel minister who is of no use to them." They therefore solicited "with reverence" that the Rev. Mr. Polhemus might be allowed to preach alternately in Breuckelen and Midwout, in which case they were "very willing to contribute cheerfully to his support, agreeable to their abilities." Otherwise they begged to be excused from contributing to his maintenance.[4] To this the Director and Council replied that they had "no objection that the Rev. Polhemus, when *the weather*

---

[1] N. Y. Col. MSS., vi. 71.

[2] Equal to about $416.

[3] Col. MSS., vi. 278, Feb. 8, 1656.

[4] Col. MSS., vi. 299, Feb., 1656. This remonstrance of Breuckelen was signed by Joris Dircksen, Albert Cornelissen and Joris Rappelje.

permits, shall preach alternately at both places." On the 15th of March following, the Sheriff and Commissioners of Midwout appeared before the Council, to whom they represented that *they* had accepted, and were satisfied with, the decree of the Council, but that it had met with serious objections from the people of Gravesend and Amersfoort, who had subscribed with the understanding

"that on Sundays, in the forenoon, they might hear the sermon at Midwout, both places being nearly at the same distance from one another as Breuckelen, at which place, if alternately, as the apostillé said, preaching was to be held, it would be inconvenient for the inhabitants, by reason of the great distance of the places, to come there to church in the morning and return at noon home to their families, inasmuch as Breuckelen is quite *two hours' walking* from Amersfoort and Gravesend; whereas the village of Midwout is not half so far and the road much better. So they consider it a hardship to choose either to hear the Gospel but once a day, or to be compelled to travel four hours, in going and returning, all for one single sermon, which would be to some very troublesome and to some utterly impossible."

All of which "being maturely considered by the Director-General and the Council," it was fully arranged that the Sunday sermon should be delivered in the morning at Midwout, as being at a nearly equal distance from the other three towns; but that the usual afternoon discourse should be changed to an evening service, to be held alternately in Breuckelen and Amersfoort,[1] and thus the matter was amicably settled. During the same month, also, the three towns were permitted, on application, to levy a tax for the purpose of paying the minister's tax.

In accordance with a resolution of the Council, November 29th, 1656, in regard to the apportionment of the Rev. Mr. Polhemus' salary among the three towns, it had been agreed that Midwout should give annually 400, and Brooklyn and Amersfoort 300 guilders each for that purpose. The good people of Breuckelen, however, had become quite dissatisfied with the style of Mr. Polhemus' clerical services, and the assessment of the tax occasioned much grumbling, which finally culminated in a plain-spoken protest to the

---

[1] Col. MSS., vi. 331, March 15, 1656.

Director and Council. This document, dated January 1, 1657, represents that:

"The Magistrates of Breuckelen find themselves obliged to communicate to your Honors that to them it seems impossible that they should be able to collect annually 300 guilders from such a poor congregation, as there are many among them who suffered immense losses during the late wars, and principally at the invasion of the savages, by which they have been disabled, so that many, who would otherwise be very willing, have not the power to contribute their share. We must be further permitted to say that we never gave a call to the aforesaid Reverend Polhemus, and never accepted him as our minister; but he intruded himself upon us against our will, and voluntarily preached in the open street, under the blue sky; when, to avoid offence, the house of Joris Dircksen was temporarily offered him here in Breuckelen. It is the general opinion and saying of the citizens and inhabitants of Breuckelen generally, with those living in their neighborhood, that they could not resolve, even when it was in their power to collect the money, to contribute any thing for such a poor and meagre service as that with which they thus far have been regaled. Every fortnight, on Sundays, he comes here only in the afternoon for a quarter of an hour, when he only gives us a prayer in lieu of a sermon, by which we can receive very little instruction; while often, while one supposes the prayer or sermon (whichever name might be preferred for it) is beginning, then it is actually at an end, by which he contributes very little to the edification of his congregation. This we experienced on the Sunday preceding Christmas, on the 24th of December last, when we, expecting a sermon, heard nothing but a prayer, and that so short that it was finished before we expected it. Now, it is true it was nearly evening before Polhemus arrived, so that he had not much time to spare, and was compelled to march off and finish so much sooner, to reach his home. This is all the satisfaction—little enough, indeed—which we had during Christmas; wherefore it is our opinion that we shall enjoy as much and more edification by appointing one among ourselves, who may read to us on Sundays a sermon from the 'Apostille Book,' as we ever have until now, from any of the prayers or sermons of the Reverend Polhemus. We do not, however, intend to offend the Reverend Polhemus, or assert any thing to bring him into bad repute. We mean only to say, that his greatly advanced age occasions all this, and that his talents do not accompany him as steadily as in the days of yore; yea, we discover it clearly, that it is not the want of good-will in Polhemus; but as we never did give him a call, we cannot resolve to contribute to his maintenance. The possibility of so doing being wholly out of the question, as explained to your Honors; and although the Magistrates of Breuckelen resolved to contribute something towards the salary of the aforesaid Polhemus, it would be on their own account, as the congregation can never resolve to join them. Many there are among them who cannot, and who rather need that others should come to their aid. To this (the consideration of the fact) should be added that many farms are unoccupied and waste: as the farms of Mr. Poulis; a farm lying near the shore, of Fred'k Lubbertsen; on another farm lives a poor person, who also has nothing, and cannot afford to give any thing; while (there is) Lodewyck, who lives on one of the farms for the poor, and whose land also lies waste, as also that of Peter Cornelissen and Elbert Elbertsen. So also the land of Black Hans, Grabie's (Gaby's) land, Peter Mallemacque, Peter Minuit, Jan Manty (Manje?) and many others; from all which your Honors may easily calculate what may here be given or expected. And suppose that every one of us was taxed, even then no person can be induced to contribute any thing for such a poor service as thus far has been obtruded on us. However, permit us to say in conclusion, and be it said in reverence, that as those of Midwout have engaged said Polhemus alone, without our knowledge, and without any previous communication (with us), we have no objection whatever. Nay, we are rather satisfied that the people of Midwout shall enjoy exclusively the whole service of the aforesaid Rev. Polhemus. And in case the aforesaid Polhemus should again desire to say his prayers here, in lieu of giving a sermon, as he did before, although we are unwilling to put ourselves under any obligation, still we are disposed to make him, from time to time, as opportunity shall offer, some allowance, as proof of our good-will, inasmuch as there are several among us who think and act favorably of the Reverend Polhemus, although they make no use of his services. With this conclusion, we commend your Honors to God's merciful protection, with the cordial wish of a Happy New Year, besides a prosperous and blessed administration, to Salvation; recommending ourselves to your Honors' favor, while we shall ever remain[1] Your obedient servants,

Albert Cornelissen, Jacob Dircks,
Willem Bredenbent, Peter Tonneman, Sec'y.

Done in Breuckelen, January 1, 1657."

---

[1] N. Y. Col. MSS., viii. 406.

But Gov. Stuyvesant was obdurate, and Sheriff Tonneman was instructed "to remind those of Breuckelen, once more, to fulfil their engagement, and to execute their promise relative to the salary of Mr. Polhemus."[1] The good minister, meantime, seems to have been put to much inconvenience, if not absolute suffering, by these quarrels among his parishioners; for on the 14th of December, 1656, he wrote to the Director that his house (at Flatbush) was not yet enclosed, and that, in consequence, himself, wife, and children were obliged to sleep in the cold upon the floor.[2] Forced to an unwilling compliance with this order, the people of Breuckelen contented themselves with reasserting, through their magistrates, that the arrangement of 300 guilders for Mr. Polhemus's salary was made without their consent—that they really were unable to pay it—but, unwilling to resist the Governor and Council, they would endeavor to raise the amount in some way. They took the opportunity, however, of notifying their Honors, that after the expiration of Mr. Polhemus's first year (on April 7, 1657), they should hold themselves excused from any further payment to him, so long as he should remain there, unless affairs at home, "in the Fatherland," should improve ("which God grant")—in which event, *possibly*, they might be willing to make and keep another contract with him.[3]

The order of the magistrates of Breuckelen, imposing an assessment upon the town to pay this ministerial tax, is especially interesting, on account of its being accompanied by a list of those inhabitants of the town designated as being "in easy circumstances and well off:"

"*Whereas*, the village of Breuckelen is taxed by the Director-General and Council, but finally with our general consent and agreement, with the sum and charge of 300 fl. provisionally for this year, as a supplement of the promised salary and yearly allowance of the Rev. minister De. J. Theodorus Polhemus, therefore have we, of the Court of Brooklyn, to raise said sum of 300 fl. aforesaid in the easiest manner, assessed and taxed each person, inhabitant of Breuckelen and its dependencies, as hereunder is more fully set forth and to be seen; all, according to our conscience and our opinion, in easy circumstances and well off: wherefore, Simon Jooster, our

[1] N. Y. Col. MSS., viii. 410. [2] Ibid., viii. 396. [3] Alb. Rec., iv.

court messenger, is hereby ordered and commanded, on sight and receipt hereof, to repair to the under-mentioned and named persons, and to notify each of their assessment and tax; and that each for himself in particular shall be bound, within eight days from now, to bring in and to deliver into the hands of Mr. A. Cornelissen, in Breuckelen, the half of his assessment either in wampum or country produce, such as corn, wheat, peas, maize, etc., that then all shall be credited and correctly entered on each one's account and assessment at the current price: the remaining half must be promptly paid next May of the present year, Anno 1657, in order to be able at that time to satisfy and give contentment to the said Polhemus. Thus done and enacted at the court held in Breuckelen, with previous approbation of the Director and Supreme Council in New Netherland, on Wednesday, the 7 February, A°. 1657.

Persons and inhabitants of *Breuckelen, and unto the Ferry:*

Albert Cornelissen hath promised for this year	*fl.* 12
Joris Dircksen, in like manner	12
Jan Eversen's farmer, named Bartel Clasen, taxed at	10
Theunis Jansen, on Frederick Lubbertsen's land, taxed at	10
Baerent Jansen	6
Jan Daeme(n)	6
Johannes Nevius, at the Ferry, is taxed at	15
Cornelis Dircksen, late ferryman	10
Adryaen Huybertsen	6
Claes de Mentelaer	6
Gerrit the Wheelwright	8
Outie, house carpenter	6
Jan Martyn	6
Egbert van Borstelen (or Van Borsum)	10
Louis; lives at present at the Poor's Bowery (or Poor Farm, at Newtown), but intends to return	10
Michael Tater	10
Pieter Cornelissen	6
Elbert Elbertsen, in the Bay	10
The Smith	6
Black Hans's land	6
Total	*fl.* 171

The persons taxed at the *Walebocht* are the following:

Joris Raphallie hath of his own free will promised to give and contribute	*fl.* 10
Hendrick de Copsteerdt's (the cupper's) land is taxed at	4
Peter Moelett (say Abram the Turk)	6
Jan de Clerck	6
Peter Jansen, resides on Lagebergh's land	8
Peter Montfoor(t)	10
Jan Martyn	8
Gabriel's land (Mr. Paulus Leendersen must answer for this)	10
Peter Meinst	8
Aert Theunissen (Middag)	8
Jan the chimney-sweeper	4
Nicholas, the Frenchman	6
Total	*fl.* 88

The taxed inhabitants at the *Gouwanes* are these following and undernamed persons:

William Bredenbent hath voluntarily promised to contribute	*fl.* 12
Jan Petersen is taxed at	8
Barent Bal, in a like sum	8
Theunis Niesen	12
Adam Brouwer	6
Johannus Marcus	4
Mr. Paulus (Van der Beeck)	10
Total	*fl.* 60

By order of the Schepens of the Court of Breuckelen, with the previous approbation of the Director-General and Supreme Council in New Netherland aforesaid.

(Signed) PETER TONNEMAN, Secretary."[1]

The troubles occasioned by this odious minister's-tax were, however, by no means at an end. In April, Mr. Polhemus petitioned the

[1] N. Y. Col. MSS., viii. 463, 464, 466.

Governor and Council that they would pay for him a debt of 100 guilders, alleging as an excuse that he had been obliged to contract it, inasmuch as he had only received some fl. 200 out of his fl. 1,000 salary, and had a large family to support.[1] The Council kindly allowed him the sum of 60 guilders. In the course of the next month, the court messenger reported "that several of the Breuckelen people were still unwilling to pay their share of the tax."[2] This was followed by several complaints from the minister, in which he represents that his house had not been finished according to contract, that he had served as pastor in the three villages from October, 1654, to April 7, 1657, without salary, and as he came to this country "naked," he has been obliged from time to time to get his supplies from the Company's stores, until his bill amounted to 942 guilders, which he wanted made up. By order of the Council, the sum was granted and his account was balanced.[3] Meanwhile, in the midst of this disaffection among the inhabitants of Breuckelen in regard to their minister, a new element of discord had arisen within the jurisdiction of the Dutch Government. The Quakers, banished incontinently from all the *self-righteous* colonies of New England (except, be it always remembered, from Rhode Island), ventured to find in New Netherlands the home and the liberty of conscience which was elsewhere denied them. Unfortunately they only stepped from the "frying-pan into the fire." Heavy fines, scourgings, solitary imprisonments and banishments were the only welcome that met them; and when the people of Flushing nobly protested against such intolerance as totally at variance with the law of Christian love and the rights of their charter, they brought down upon themselves a whirlwind of indignation and summary punishment from Governor Stuyvesant and his clerical advisers. In spite, however, of these severe measures against Flushing, the infection rapidly spread through Long Island. Jamaica, Gravesend, and Hempstead soon developed the germs of Quakerism, which no civil persecution has ever crushed out even to this day. Symptoms of disaffection also appeared at Brooklyn—or, rather, perhaps, as is usual in a disaffected community, the new principle of non-conformity was used

[1] N. Y. Col. MSS., viii. 515, 516. [2] Ibid., viii. 563. [3] Ibid., viii. 705.

by many as an excuse for their non-compliance in the matter of paying the minister's tax. Sheriff Tonneman complained to the Council of abuse received, while collecting the tax, from Lodewyck Jong, Jan Martyn, Nicholas the Frenchman, Abraham Jansen, the mulatto, and Gerrit the wheelwright. They were summoned before the Council, where the excuses they pleaded—of one that he was a Catholic, and the other that he did not understand Dutch—were pronounced "frivolous," and they were each condemned to pay a fine of twelve guilders ($4.80).[1] The principal malcontent, Jan Martyn, "of Harfleur" (*ante*, p. 80), who attempted to hire the public bellman to go around and defame Councillor Tonneman, was obliged to beg pardon, on bended knees, of the Lord and of the court, and was fined twenty-five guilders ($10) and costs.[2]

The inflexible Governor finally brought matters to a focus with the refractory Breuckelen people, by issuing an order, on the 6th of July, 1658, forbidding the inhabitants of the three towns to remove their grain from their fields, until their tithes were taken or commuted—which commutations were ordered to be paid within three days. This order was complied with; for when the Governor "put his foot down" in this manner, as was his wont, the people found it was useless to "kick against the pricks."

Previous to this time (1660), the only ministers of the Reformed Church in New Netherland were Megapolensis and Drisius, in the city of New Amsterdam, Schaats at Beverwyck, Polhemus at Midwout, and Welius at New Amstel. In the fall of 1658, however, a letter was sent to the Classis of Amsterdam of the Fatherland, by Messrs. Megapolensis and Drisius, giving an interesting account of the state of religion in the colony, and earnestly entreating that "good Dutch clergymen" might speedily be sent over.[3] These letters awakened the attention of the Classis to the spiritual necessities of New Netherland, and earnest representations on the subject were addressed to the College of the XIX. And, although it was difficult to prevail upon any settled clergyman to leave his charge in Holland and brave the trials of a newly settled country, yet one Her-

[1] N. Y. Col. MSS., viii. 563, 789, 804, 818.
[2] N. Y. Col. MSS., viii. 825.
[3] Brodhead, i. 643.

manus Blom, a candidate for the ministry, was induced to come out to New Amsterdam. Arriving here about the last of April, he shortly after received a call from the prosperous village of Esopus (now Kingston); and having accepted it, returned to Holland to pass his examination before the Classis, and receive ordination. Meanwhile the people of Breuckelen, in view of the badness of the roads to Flatbush, and the inability of the Rev. Mr. Polhemus, on account of his age and infirmity, to bestow any considerable portion of his labor upon them, had petitioned the Governor and Council for permission to have a minister resident in their town. The application was favorably regarded,[1] and when (March 1) Blom left Holland on his return to New Netherland, he was accompanied by the Rev. Henricus Selyns, under appointment to preach at Breuckelen.[2]

Mr. Selyns was the son of Jan Selyns and Agneta Kock, of Amsterdam, where he was born in the year 1636. Having been regularly educated for the ministry, he became, in due time, a proponent or candidate for full orders. "Tracing his ancestry, both on the father's and mother's side, clearly back, through a regular line of elders, deacons, and deaconesses, to the first institution of the Dutch Reformed Church as an independent establishment, and connected by blood and marriage with distinguished ministers of that church, he could not fail to imbibe its tenets and principles, and enter with confidence and honorable ambition upon the studies which were to fit him for its services."[3] Such were the antecedents of the man who, having accepted the call from Breuckelen, made through the Dutch West India Company to the Classis at Amster-

---

[1] Nicasius de Sille, the Fiscal, and Martin Kreiger, one of the Burgomasters, were appointed as a committee of inquiry by the Governor, upon whose favorable report the required permission was granted.

[2] The call of the Breuckelen church to Dominie Selyns was by him accepted, and approved by the Classis of Amsterdam, February 16, 1660 (–61).—Brooklyn Church Records.

[3] His paternal grandfather, Hendrick Selyns, was a deacon of the Amsterdam church in 1598; his father, an elder from 1639 to 1663; his maternal great-grandfather, Hendrick Kock, a deacon from 1584 to 1595; his grandfather, Hans Verlocken, in 1587–90; while his grandmother, Agneta Selyns, was a deaconess for several years in the same church. Triglandius, Lantsman, and J. Nieuwenhuysen, celebrated ministers of the Netherland church, were also his cousins.

dam, was, on the 16th February, 1660, peremptorily examined by that body, and admitted to the ministry with full powers,—engaging, however, to serve the Breuckelen church for the term of four years.

Messrs. Blom and Selyns arrived at New Amsterdam, bearing letters to the colonial churches from the Classis at Amsterdam, in which the former were earnestly exhorted "not to depart from the usual formulary of baptism." Governor Stuyvesant, by whom alone all public functionaries, ecclesiastical as well as civil, could be accredited, was then absent at Esopus, negotiating a peace with the Indians; and when that had been concluded, he paid a visit to Fort Orange. To both of these places the two young clergymen followed him, to deliver their letters,[1] so that it was not until the 7th of September, 1660, that Mr. Selyns was formally installed into the church at Breuckelen. "This ceremony," says his biographer, "measured by the usual standard of great events, was, indeed, insignificant; but viewed as the first installation of a minister in what is now a large and flourishing city, the third in size in the United States, and as populous as the famous city of Amsterdam herself at the present day, it was one which deserved, as it received, the attention of the authorities in an appropriate and becoming manner. It was, nevertheless, to that colony, an interesting event, and it was accompanied by proceedings calculated to give dignity and authority to the minister. The Governor deputed two of his principal officers to present the minister to the congregation—Nicasius de Sillé, a member of the Council, a man of no mean attainments, and well versed in the law, and Martin Krigier, burgomaster of New Amsterdam, who, on several important occasions, was the envoy of the Governor to the adjoining English colonies. After the presentation, Dominie Selyns preached his inaugural sermon, and then read the call of the Classis and their certificate of examination, with a testimonial from the ministers of Amsterdam, declaring that during the time he had dwelt among them, he had not only diligently used the holy ordinances of God for the promotion of his own salvation, but had also often edified their church by his acceptable preaching; and, more-

---

[1] N. Y. Col. MSS., xiii. 81, 84, 131, 132; xiv. 58.

over, had, by his life and conversation, demeaned himself as a godly and pious man—a character which he never forfeited."[1]

On the 7th, a letter was forwarded, "by a respectable person," to the Rev. Mr. Polhemus, informing him of Mr. Selyns' installation in the church at Breuckelen, and thanking him in courteous terms for his labors and attention to the congregation. This attention was appropriately acknowledged by the venerable pastor, who, on the 12th, sent to the new incumbent a list of church-members residing within this vicinity, numbering in all twenty-seven persons,

---

[1] On this occasion the Rev. Henry Selyns addressed the church as follows:

"I have appeared before you and the Consistory, according to the usages and ordinances of our Church, and now surrender to you my letter of call of the Honorable Classis of Amsterdam, together with the approbation of the Honorable the Directors of the Chamber of Amsterdam, also my classical and church attestations, which, with my call, appertain to your church." (Brooklyn Church Records.)

The above-mentioned "Letter of Call" is as follows:

"*Whereas,* it is indispensably required that the honor of God and the salvation of men be promoted to the best of our abilities, and that for this end religious meetings should be instituted and encouraged by the pure preaching of God's word, the lawful administration of the sacraments, the public invocation of the name of God, and whatsoever else belongs to a dutiful worship; and *whereas,* the situation of Breuckelen, in New Netherland, requires that a duly qualified person, as a lawfully ordained minister, should be sent there, who can there execute the ministerial functions in every particular in conformity with the Church government and the word of God, and in unison with the laudable usages of the Reformed Churches in this country, and who is able to maintain and defend these: Therefore it is that we, ministers of the word of God, and elders of the Church of Christ, belonging to the Classis of Amsterdam, after the invocation of the name of God, and in His fear, and with the approbation of the Noble Directors of the West India Company, and after a careful examination in the principal doctrines of the Reformed Christian Church, and after we had received satisfactory evidence of a pious life, and talents requisite for the gospel ministry, and after he had signed the Netherlandish Confession, the Christian Catechism, and the Canons of the National Synod, have, with the laying on of hands, ordained the reverend, pious, prudent, and learned minister, Henricus Selyns, to preach, both on land and water, and in all the neighborhood, but principally in that place (Breuckelen), the holy and only saving doctrine of the word of God in its purity; to administer the sacraments, as instituted by Christ, with propriety; publicly to lead the prayers of the congregation, to keep them (with the aid of his Consistory) in good order and discipline, all in conformity with the word of God, and the Canons of the Netherlandish Church, and the Christian Catechism: requesting all our brethren to acknowledge him as a lawful brother and ordained minister of the gospel of Christ; to honor him for the sake of his ministry; and to assist him, whenever it is in their power; so that he may labor unmolested (*i. e.,* by worldly cares, etc.), and cheerfully, in glorifying God's name, and in the conversion and salvation of souls.

"May the Almighty God, who has called this minister to the service of His Church, enrich him more and more with all talents, and with the blessings of the Holy Ghost; so that his labors may be crowned with abundant success, to the glory of His name

inclusive of one elder and two deacons.[1] The population of the village at this time was 134 persons, in thirty-one families; and the bounds of the new Dominie's charge included "The Ferry," "The Waal-boght," and "The Gujanes." Measures were taken for the speedy erection of a church, and in the mean time the congregation worshipped in a barn. As the people were not able of themselves to pay his entire salary, they petitioned the Council for assistance;[2]

---

and the salvation of men, and reward and adorn him, at the appearance of the Great Shepherd of sheep, with the unfading crown of immortal glory.

"Done in a Classical meeting in Amsterdam, on the 16th of February, 1660.

"In the name, and by order of all,

"PETRUS PROËLIUS, Eccles. Amstelodamensis, et Classis p. t. Deputatus.

"LAURENS VAN NOORDT, Eccles. in Diemen. et pro t. ad caus. sat. Indicas Deput.

"SAMUELL COOP, a groen Eccles. Amstelodamensis et p. t. Deputatus."

[ENDORSEMENT.]

"The aforesaid Act of the Classis of Amsterdam was approved by the Directors of the West India Company, Department of Amst., on the 26th March, 1660.

(Signed) "DAVID VAN BAERLE.
"EDWARD MAN."

The above translation of this document is from N. Y. Col. MSS., xiii. 69. Another version, by the late General Jeremiah Johnson, taken, probably, from the original Dutch records of the First Reformed Dutch Church of Brooklyn, is printed in the Magazine of the Reformed Dutch Church, vol. iii., for 1828–29, pp. 52, 54. This, although a more elegant translation, does not, in our opinion, present so faithful a transcript of the original as the one above printed.

[1] The list of church members at this period, together with other extracts from the Brooklyn Church Records, will be found in Appendix No. 6.

[2] Alb. Rec., xxiv. 383. Aug. 30, 1660, there appeared before the Council, "Joris Dirck and Joris Rapelje, magistrates of the village of Breuckelen, on Long Island, and represented that they, in conformity with the order of the Director-General, had convened all the inhabitants of the aforesaid village, and conversed with them, and inquired how much they would be able to contribute to the salary of the Rev. Mr. Selyns; and that, after all their endeavors, they could not succeed in obtaining more than 300 guilders annually (payable in corn, at the value of beavers); and that in addition they were willing to provide the Rev. Mr. Selyns with a comfortable dwelling. On being reminded that Dominie Selyns had been promised the annual salary of 100 fl., and had come hither in that expectation, and that the said sum ought to be collected,—in lieu of which the village tithes would be taken and contributed by the Company,—and that they ought to strive to make up the deficiency, they declared that it was totally impossible for the people of the village to raise the required amount, as the burden fell chiefly on a few individuals, the rest being poor people who had nothing but what was earned by their daily labor. To this it was replied (by the Council) that they (of Breuckelen) should have duly considered all these things before they requested or called a minister. In answer, they (the inhabitants of Breuckelen) said they had

and Stuyvesant agreed personally to contribute two hundred and fifty guilders, provided Mr. Selyns would preach a sermon, on Sunday afternoons, at his "bouwery" on Manhattan Island.[1] In this arrangement the Dominie acquiesced, and thereafter preached at the "Director's bouwery," which was a "sort of stopping-place and pleasure-ground of the Manhattans." Here his audiences consisted mostly of people from the city, and besides Stuyvesant's own household, about forty negroes who lived in that neighborhood, in what was known as the "negro quarter." After Selyns' installation at

---

hopes that their village would now daily increase, and that consequently they would be enabled in future to contribute more; and they earnestly requested that Dominie Selyns might come among them at the earliest opportunity."

[1] Extract from a letter of Dominie Selyns to the Classis at Amsterdam, dated "Amsterdam on the Manhattans, 4 October, 1660" (Doc. Hist. N. Y., iii. 108): "When we arrived in N. Netherland, we repaired forthwith to the Manhattans; but the negotiations for peace at the Esopus, where we were, and the public interests, necessarily retarded our progress thus long. We preached, meanwhile, here, and at the Esopus and Fort Orange; during our stay were provided with board and lodging. (See Alb. Rec., xxiv. 387.) Esopus needs more people, but Breuckelen more wealth; wherefore I officiate, Sunday afternoons, at the General's bouwerye, at the Noble General's private expense. Through the worshipful Messrs. Nicasius de Sille, Fiscal, and Martin Cregiers, Burgomaster, the induction (or call) in Breuckelen occurred with the Hon'ble General's open commission. Whereupon I was suitably received by the Magistrate and Consistory, and D[e] Polhemus was forthwith discharged. We do not preach in any church, but in a barn (Korenschuur), and shall, God willing, erect a church in the winter, by the co-operation of the people. The congregation is passable. The attendance is augmented from Middlewout, New Amersfoort, and frequently Gravesende but most from the Manhattans. To Breuckelen appertains, also, the Ferry, the Wale bocht, and Gujanus. The Breuckelen Ferry is about 2,000 paces, but the River of the Manhattans is 4,000 feet from the Breuckelen Ferry. I found at Breuckelen one elder, two deacons, twenty-four members, thirty-one householders (Huysgesins), and 134 persons. The Consistory will remain provisionally as it is. More material will be obtained through time and a better knowledge of the community. There can be no catechizing before the winter; but this shall be introduced either on week-days, or when there is no preaching at the Bowery. Christmas, Easter, Whitsuntide, and September will be most suitable for the Lord's Supper, as Thanksgiving is observed on these festivals. . . . . . . There is preaching in the morning at Breuckelen, but towards the conclusion of the Catechismal exercises of New Amsterdam, at the Bouwery, which is a continuation and the place of recreation of the Manhattans, where people also come from the city to evening service. In addition to the household, there are over forty negroes, whose location is the negro quarter. There is no Consistory here (*i. e.*, at the Bouwery), but the deacons of New Amsterdam provisionally receive the alms-offerings; and there are to be neither elders nor deacons there. Besides me, there are in New Netherland: D. D. Johannes Megapolensis and Samuel Drisius, in New Amsterdam; D. Gideon Schaets, at Fort Orange; D. Joannes Polhemus, at Middlewout; and N. Amersfoort and Hermans Blom, at the Esopus."

Breuckelen, Dominie Polhemus confined his services to Midwout and Amersfoort.

Under the able ministrations of the new pastor, the church in Breuckelen increased, until, in 1661, it numbered fifty-two communicants, many of whom were admitted on certificates from New Amsterdam and from churches in the Fatherland. The same year the village of Breuckelen received from the West India Company, on the request of Rev. Mr. Selyns, a bell for their church, which "might also be used, in time of danger, to call the county people thereabouts together." Esopus also received a similar present.[1]

It would seem, from the following petition, that the Rev. Mr. Selyns had not, as late as 1662, become an actual resident of the town over which he exercised a pastoral charge.

"MAY 25th, 1662.

"To the Noble, Great, and Respected, the Director-General and Council in Nieuw Netherlands:

"The undersigned, Schepens of the village of Breuckelen, represent, with all due respect, that they, the said petitioners, have been engaged, for some time past, in collecting, among their community, that which they had promised to contribute as their share towards the Rev. Mr. Selyns' salary; and they find that the community would be more willing and ready to bring in their respective quotas, if the aforesaid Rev. Mr. Selyns would come to reside within their village, inasmuch as they have already been at the expense of building a house for him. They therefore request your Honors to consent to and permit it, towards which end, expecting your Honors' favorable decision, etc.

"The delegated Schepens of the village of Breuckelen,

"WILLIAM GERRITSE VAN COUWENHOVEN.
"WILLEM BREDENBENT.
"JAN JORIS RAPALJE."

The petitioners were referred to Mr. Selyns, whose decision is not recorded, and unknown to us.[2]

September 21st, 1662, the Council "ordered that the inhabitants of Breuckelen pay 300 guilders to the Rev. Henry Selyns, who has

[1] Letter of Directors to Stuyvesant, dated December 24, 1660. (N. Y. Col. MSS., xiii. 143.)

[2] N. Y. Col. MSS., x. 137.

preached in said town since August 30, 1660, instead of the Rev. J. Polhemus," and that the book-keeper credit that amount to Selyns.[1] On the 12th of the same month the people of Flatlands had been permitted to build a church; making, with that of Bushwick, the fourth Dutch church within the county. During this year, also, complaint was made to the Consistory of the exposure of the graveyard to hogs and other animals; in consequence of which, the Consistory contracted for a clapboard fence, five feet high, to enclose the entire ground, for the sum of seventy guilders.[2]

The unfortunate burning of the town of Esopus, and the massacre of its inhabitants, by the Indians, June 7, 1663, was the occasion of the following proclamation from Governor Stuyvesant to the church at Breuckelen:

"As a sorrowful accident and wilful massacre has been committed by the Esopus Indians, who have with deliberate design, under the insidious cover of friendship, determined to destroy Esopus, which they effected on the 7th instant, killing and wounding a number of the inhabitants, and taking many prisoners, burning the town and desolating the place: Whereupon the congregation is directed and desired, by his Excellency the Governor-General, to observe and keep the ensuing Wednesday as a day of fasting, humiliation, and prayer to the Almighty, hoping that He may avert further calamities from the New Netherlands, and extend His fatherly protection and care to the country. And it is further ordered, that the first Wednesday in every month be observed in like manner. By order of the Director-General and Council, etc. Dated at Fort Orange, June 26, 1663."[3]

Early in the year 1664, Dominie Selyns addressed a petition to the Director and Council, complaining that, in consequence of the great depreciation which had taken place in seawant and beaverskins, he found his salary much reduced and insufficient to meet

[1] N. Y. Col. MSS., x. 216.

[2] Brooklyn Church Records.

[3] The cloud of war speedily passed over, however; for Wednesday, the 4th of July, 1663, was observed as a day of thanksgiving on account of a treaty of peace which had been made with these same Esopus Indians, and the release of the prisoners who had been taken by them; and likewise for the defeat of the English, who had been thwarted in an attempt to take possession of Long Island, by the opportune arrival of the Dutch fleet.

his wants. His application for redress was discussed at considerable length by the Council, who finally decided that any money paid to the Dominie on account of the 600 gl. allowed to him in the Fatherland, should be paid in beavers, at a rate not higher than 6 gl., and any commodities in seawant in proportion. The 600 gl. promised him here in New Netherland, was to be paid with beavers, in cash, at the value of 8 gl. per beaver, agreeably to the contract of August 30th, 1660.[1]

This year, also, the church of Breuckelen was called upon to part with its beloved pastor, Selyns. His time having expired, he yielded to the urgent solicitations of his aged father in Holland; and having duly obtained permission from the Lords Directors of the West India Company,[2] was most tenderly and respectfully dismissed from his church on the 17th of July, 1664, and sailed for home on the 23d, in the ship Beaver, the same vessel which had conveyed him to America.

After his departure, Charles Debevoise, the schoolmaster of the town and church sexton, was authorized to read prayers and a sermon from some approved author, each Sabbath, in the church, for the improvement of the congregation, until another minister could be found.

Selyn's pastoral duties at Breuckelen were always discharged "with zeal and fidelity. The records of the church at Breuckelen for this period, are still preserved in his own handwriting, and bear ample evidence of his devotion to his calling—chronicling, with rare simplicity, the occurrences in the government of the church and the occasions of discipline of his flock. Once we find him in collision with the magistrates of the town, in regard to an attempted jurisdiction on their part over an act of ecclesiastical censure exercised by him towards one of the church-members. In a respectful letter, he refused to appear before them or acknowledge their right to take cognizance of the sentence pronounced by him and his consistory. He maintained that the civil courts could not try offences arising purely out of the ecclesiastical relation; and that the complainant

[1] N. Y. Col. MSS., x. 33, 35, 100, 131.

[2] The petition of Dominie Selyns for permission to return home may be found (dated July 17, 1664) in N. Y. Col. MSS., x. 270.

having submitted himself to the canons of the church, by becoming one of its members, was thereby precluded from taking the matter before the courts. In this, as in some other trying occasions of his life, when he was brought in conflict with others upon questions of authority and power, he sustained the rights and privileges of his official position with equal firmness, dignity, and force of reasoning. His pen and logic were never to be despised by his opponents. In his controversy with the magistrates of Breuckelen, his arguments prevailed." During his ministry in Breuckelen, he married at New Amsterdam, on the 9th of July, 1662, his first wife, Machtelt, daughter of Hermann Specht, of the city of Utrecht, "a young lady, if we may trust his own description of her, of rare personal beauty and worth," whose portrait he has transmitted to us in a birth-day ode, which is said to be "one of the prettiest pictures that conjugal affection has ever drawn."

After his return to Holland, Selyns remained unsettled for two years; and in 1666, took charge of the congregation of Waverveen, near Utrecht, a rural village of no fame. In 1675, he became a chaplain in the army of the States; but with the exception of this temporary office, he seems to have passed sixteen years of his life in the obscurity of Waverveen, usefully and even contentedly employed; for, in 1670, upon the death of Megapolensis, of New York, he declined a call from that church to become associated with Rev. Mr. Drisius in its charge. The Rev. William Nieuwenhuysen took the place thus declined, and subsequently, upon the death of both Nieuwenhuysen and Drisius, the call was so urgently renewed to Selyns that he accepted, and again left his native land to spend, as it proved, the remainder of his life in America. He arrived at New York in the summer of 1682, and was received "by the whole congregation with great affection and joy." Selyns now occupied a position among the churches of the colony which was commensurate with his talents. His congregation possessed not only the advantage of being a metropolitan one, but it was the largest in numbers, and the most powerful in the social and political standing of its members. The times, also, were critical in respect to the ecclesiastical affairs of the Dutch; for, during his absence in Holland, the political and ecclesiastical relations of the province had entirely changed. British rule, while it allowed the Dutch to enjoy liberty of conscience in divine worship and church discipline, gave no legal sanction to the special authority of the Classis of Amsterdam over the churches of the Reformed Dutch faith. Still, the ecclesiastical authority of the Classis continued to be exercised and acknowledged among the Dutch themselves, as before the conquest. Ministers still received their appointment and ordination from that body, and rendered an account of their stewardship thereto. In the correspondence which was thus maintained between the colonial ministers and their Classis, the letters of Selyns hold no inferior position, not only for the historic light which they throw upon the public and religious affairs of the day, but for the catholic spirit which they exhibit towards other denominations and ministers. "In his confidential intercourse with his superiors, he might be expected to have exhibited some sectarian spirit in regard to their progress or merits; yet we find nothing of the kind in them, but, on the contrary, expressions of satisfaction at their success; and where he does condemn, it is easy to be seen that he does so on no narrow or selfish grounds. A character so liberal and amiable could not help endearing him to those around him, and inviting their confidence. We find him, accordingly, not only beloved by his own congregation, but on terms of friendship with the heads of the government and his colleagues in the other churches in New York, and in correspondence with distinguished men in the neighboring colonies. He was probably known to the ministers at Boston, at the time of his first residence in New Netherland, as we find among his poems one in Latin, upon some verses addressed by the Rev. John Wilson, the first minister of Boston, to Governor Stuyvesant. But his correspondence with them after his return to New York was frequent."

Troublous days, however, came to Dominie Selyns with the revolutionary outbreak which placed Jacob Leisler at the head of the government. It was natural that Selyns, as well as the other ministers, should look upon Leisler as a usurper, and that they should throw all the weight of their influence against him and his party. But they committed the error of continuing their opposition to him after his power had been fully established; thus themselves becoming traitors to his government, whom he felt justified in putting down at any cost. Dellius was obliged to escape to Boston; Varick, the minister of the four Dutch towns of Kings county, was imprisoned, tried, and convicted of treason, and sentenced to be deposed from his ministerial functions; Tesschenmaker was massacred at Schenectady, in February, 1690; and Van der Bosch, of Kingston, had been deposed previously; so that Selyns was, for a considerable time, the only Dutch clergyman on duty in the province. He "had committed no overt act rendering himself amenable to the law; but he was in such close communication and sympathy with the leaders of the opposition, that he was constantly watched. He was suspected of concealing Bayard, and his house was searched by public officers, for the purpose of discovering him. His service in church, of which Leisler was a member, was interrupted by Leisler himself, who there threatened openly to silence him. His letters to Holland and elsewhere were stopped in transit, and opened by order of the government. His feelings of hostility to Leisler were aggravated, no doubt, in a large degree by these circumstances, and were carried by him to the grave itself. He was one of those who approved and recommended the carrying into execution the sentence of that popular leader, when Sloughter wisely hesitated, and desired to wait until he could obtain the views of the home government on the propriety of the act. While Leisler was lying in prison, the helpless subject of a political prosecution, and the proper object of consolation from the ministers of religion, Selyns preached a sermon against him, from the verse of the Psalmist: 'I had fainted, unless I had believed to see the goodness of the Lord in the land of the living.' This proceeding on his part was, in the mildest view of the case, most injudicious and unwise. His opposition had already estranged from him the Leislerian portion of his congregation. He affected to call them men of inconsiderable influence. They, nevertheless, refused to contribute to his salary; and the refusal continued, under this fresh provocation, for several years. He appealed to the Classis to interfere, and even sought, through that body, the mandate of King William, supposing that, as a Dutchman, he could be induced by the ecclesiastical authorities at Amsterdam to compel the payment of his arrears. He intimated that he would, in consequence of withholding the salary, be forced to give up his ministry here and return to Holland. The Classis, in a proper spirit, advised him to pacify and win back the alienated hearts of his flock, and to suffer and forget all in love; and also addressed a letter in the same spirit to the consistory and congregation. The difficulty was thus finally arranged," although the divisions which arose at the Leislerian era laid the foundation of the political controversies which troubled the colony for more than a generation afterwards.

The great object of Selyns' labors, during the later years of his life, was the establishment of the liberties of his church by the procuring of a royal charter confirming its rights and privileges. This was at length accomplished, May 11th, 1696, by a charter under the royal seal, for the Reformed Protestant Dutch church in the city of New York, which is still in full force, and was virtually the charter of the Low Dutch Church in America.[1] Selyns had now attained his sixtieth year. "He had labored faithfully, zealously, and successfully. Amidst all his trials, no one had ventured to breathe a syllable against the purity of his life and conversation, or his fidelity to the spiritual interests of his congregation, which had increased from 450 to 650 members during his ministry among them." In 1699, he received an assistant, in the person of Rev. Gualterus du Bois, of Amsterdam; and shortly after, in July, 1701, he died at New York, in his sixty-fifth year. "In his domestic relations he appears to have been fortunate. Of his first wife we have already spoken. Upon her death, in 1686, he married the widow of Cornelius Steenwyck, Margaretta de Riemer, whom he himself describes as 'rich in temporal goods, but richer in spiritual.' This lady survived him several years. He had one child, a daughter, by his first wife, born while he was at Breuckelen; but from all omission of her name in his will, we infer she died while he was in Holland."

"His character, as we are able to view it through the long vista of time, and with an imperfect exhibition of its traits, presents him in a favorable light. He was a faithful and devoted minister, honest, sincere, and capable. He was learned in his profession, pious, and

---

[1] Liber vii. 25, Sec'y State's office. This charter antedates that of Trinity church, which was granted May 6, 1697.

pure in his life. He was free from that narrow feeling which begets prejudice from mere difference of opinion. But he was fond of the exercise of power. He was persevering, and pursued his object with determination, and sought it sometimes for the sake of

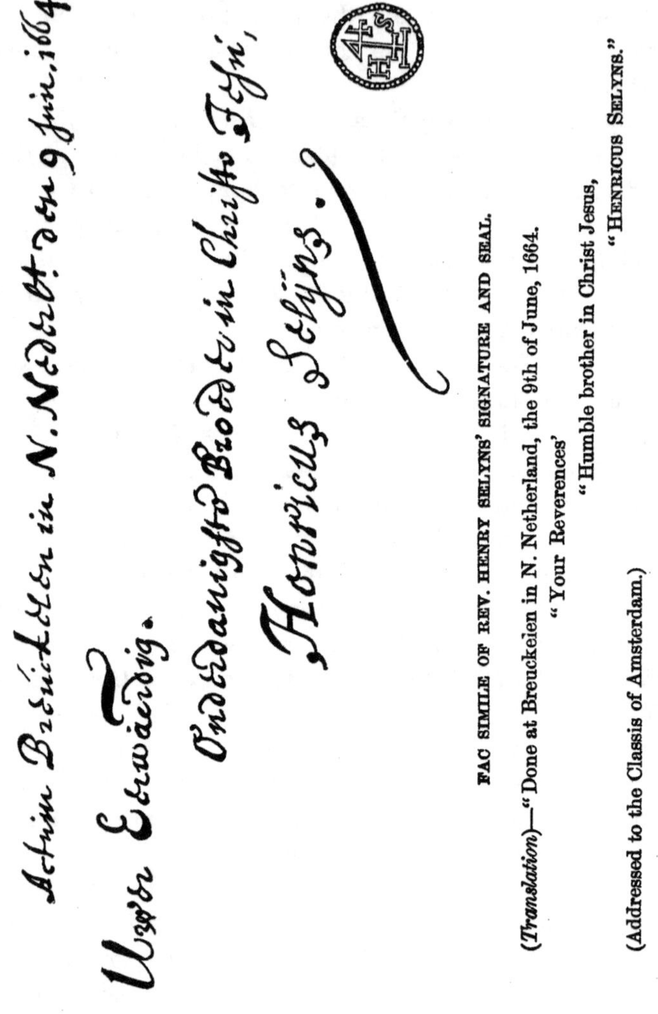

FAC SIMILE OF REV. HENRY SELYNS' SIGNATURE AND SEAL.

(*Translation*)—"Done at Breuckeien in N. Netherland, the 9th of June, 1664.
"Your Reverences'
"Humble brother in Christ Jesus,
"HENRICUS SELYNS."

(Addressed to the Classis of Amsterdam.)

success, when, perhaps, a wise regard for the feelings of others would have led him to abandon it. He may be justly regarded as one of the founders of the Dutch Church in America, who did more to determine its position in the country than any other man ; and in this circumscribed field, in which the great business of his life was concerned, his fame must mainly rest."

Although he corresponded extensively with men of genius and of learning, he never appeared as an author in print;[1] and his only literary remains are contained in a little volume of poems, of which a pleasant selection, translated by our fellow-citizen, Hon. Henry C. Murphy, has been published in one of the elegant volumes of the "Bradford Club."[2] We have drawn freely, in our sketch of the first pastor of Breuckelen, upon the elegant and careful memoir which Mr. Murphy has there given.

---

[1] Except as the author of a Latin poem eulogistic of the Rev. Cotton Mather's "Magnalia Americana," and which may be found, together with a translation, in the Hartford edition of that work (i. 23).

[2] Anthology of New Netherland; or, Translations from the Early Dutch Poets ot New York, with Memoirs of the Authors. By Henry C. Murphy. New York, 1865 79–183.

CHAPTER V.

CIVIL HISTORY OF BREUCKELEN.

1664—1674.

AMONG the first subjects that demanded the attention of the new authorities of the Province of New York was the formation of a uniform code of laws for the several plantations upon Long Island, now for the first time united under one and the same administration. In those communities formerly known as the "English towns" the English common law very generally prevailed, while the civil code of the Dutch towns had been modelled on that of the Fatherland. Fully alive to the difficulties which were incident to such a diversity of jurisprudence, the Governor convened an assemblage of delegates from the several towns, to deliberate upon and provide for the emergency. The Convention accordingly met at Hempstead on the 28th of February, 1665 (Breuckelen being represented by Frederick Lubbertsen and Jan Evertsen Bout), and then and there promulgated a body of laws and ordinances for the future government of the province. Of this code, called by way of distinction the "DUKE'S LAWS," copies were furnished to the deputies of each town, and duly filed in the clerks' offices of the several counties, where, or in some of them, they remain to the present day. These laws, with occasional additions and alterations, continued in force until the first Provincial Assembly, convened by Governor Dongan in 1683. Designed to operate in a newly settled country, and among a population composed of different nationalities, holding various and conflicting opinions concerning law and government, it was hardly to be expected that they would be satisfactory to all; yet they were, on the whole, as just and reasonable as those enjoyed by any of the neighboring colonies.

The delegates composing this Provincial Assembly were so favorably impressed with the Governor, and with his representation of the liberal intentions of the Duke of York towards his new subjects, that they prepared and presented an address to his royal highness, abounding with expressions of loyalty and esteem. The people whom they represented, however, were far from being perfectly satisfied with some of the laws which had been adopted, and deemed the address of their deputies as too servile in its tone. So open and severe was the censure cast upon their action, that Government felt called upon to interfere; and, at a court of assize held in Fort James, October, 1666, it was decreed, "that whoever thereafter should in any way detract or speak against the deputies signing the address to his royal highness, at the next general meeting at Hempstead, should be presented to the next court of sessions, and, if the justices see cause, they should then be bound over to the assizes, to answer for the slander, upon plaint or information."

At this Convention of 1665, Long Island and Staten Island were duly erected into a shire, called, in honor of the Duke of York, YORKSHIRE, which was further subdivided into separate districts, denominated *Ridings*;—the towns now included in Suffolk County constituting the *East Riding*; Kings County, Newtown, and Staten Island, the *West Riding*; and the remainder of Queens County, the *North Riding*.

Nicolls retained the government of the province until 1668, and was then succeeded by Governor Francis Lovelace.

During their terms of office, Long Island, as well as the rest of the province, enjoyed a high degree of tranquillity and prosperity, and the records of that day contain little or nothing of interest concerning the town of Breuckelen.

In September, 1665, Governor Nicolls commanded the Constable and Overseers of Breuckelen to make proper provision for the horses of such persons as might come to Breuckelen and the Ferry to attend the assizes.[1]

In 1666, the town was directed to pay over the grain, collected for its rate, to Captain Delavall, in the city.[2]

February 7, 1666, the town of Jamaica having purchased[3] from Indians a tract of land called Seller's Neck, lying southwest of Jamaica, had allowed the town of Breuckelen to have one-third of

[1] Council Minutes, ii. 14. [2] Ibid., 110. [3] See Annals of Newtown, p. 63.

it, which the latter town had been somewhat dilatory in paying for. On the above-named day they were reminded of their delinquency by a special order from the Governor, which had its desired effect, as, on the 1st of March ensuing, they paid the sum of £12, being their third of the purchase.[1]

February 19, 1667, in a rate levied by the Governor on the towns of the West Riding, "for a Sessions House, which long since ought to have been provided," they were rated in the following proportion—

	£	s.	d.		£	s.	d.
Gravesend.......	16	04	05	*Breuckelen*.......	15	03	11
Newtown........	26	02	03½	Flatbush.........	19	03	08
Bushwick........	5	11	02⅓	New Utrecht.....	7	00	00
Amersfoort......	13	19	07½	Staten Island.....	6	14	10½
				Total.......	£110	00	00

which was to be paid to Alderman Oloff Stevens, "in good corn."[2]

October 18, 1667, Richard Nicolls, Governor of New York, granted to the inhabitants of Breuckelen the following full and ample patent, confirming them in their rights and privileges:

L. S. "RICHARD NICOLLS, ESQ., *Governor-General under his Royal Highness James Duke of Yorke and Albany, etc., of all his Territorys in America*, To all to whom these presents shall come, sendeth Greeting—Whereas there is a certain town within this government, situate, lying, and being in the West Riding of Yorkshire, upon Long Island, commonly called and known by the name of Breuckelen, which said town is in the tenure or occupation of several freeholders and inhabitants, who, having heretofore been seated there by authority, have been at very considerable charge in manuring and planting a considerable part of the lands belonging thereunto, and settled a competent number of families thereupon. Now, for a confirmation unto the said freeholders and inhabitants in their

[1] Council Minutes, ii. 129. See also Furman's Notes, 13 (*note*). At the annual town meeting, April, 1823, a committee was appointed to "discover and obtain possession of all common lands and meadows belonging to the town, which are lying at a place called Seller's Neck, in the town of Jamaica, in Queen's County." (Brooklyn Town Records, 1st Book, loose page.) We are uninformed as to what was the result of their investigation. Furman states his opinion that this Seller's Neck was apportioned among the freeholders, from the fact that, on May 10, 1695, John Damen, one of the patentees of the town, sold to William Huddlestone all his interest in the said meadow.

[2] Council Minutes, ii. 198.

possessions and enjoyment of the premises, Know ye, That by virtue of the commission and authority unto me given by his Royal Highness, I have given, ratified, confirmed, and granted, and by these presents do give, ratify, confirm, and grant, unto Jan Everts, Jan Damen, Albert Cornelissen, Paulus Veerbeeck, Michael Eneyl (Hainelle), Thomas Lamberts, Teunis Guysbert, Bogart and Joris Jacobson, as patentees, for and on the behalf of themselves and their associates, the freeholders and inhabitants of the said town, their heirs, successors, and assigns, all that tract, together with the several parcels of land which already have or hereafter shall be purchased or procured for and on behalf of the said town, whether from the native Indian proprietors or others, within the bounds and limits hereafter set forth and exprest, viz., that is to say, the town is bounded westward on the farther side of the land of Mr. Paulus Veerbeck, from whence stretching southeast, they go over the hills, and so eastward along the said hills to a southeast point which takes in all the lotts behind the swamp, from which said lotts they run northwest to the River[1] and extend to the farm, on the t'other side of the hill, heretofore belonging to Hans Hansen, over against the Kicke or Looke-out,[2] including within the said bounds and limitts all the lotts and plantations lying and being at the Gowanis, Bedford, Wallaboucht, and the Ferry.—All which said parcels and tracks of land and premises within the bounds and limits afore-mentioned, described, and all or any plantation or plantations thereupon, from henceforth are to bee, appertaine, and belong to the said town of Breucklen, Together with all havens, harbours, creeks, quarryes, woodland, meadow-ground, reed-land or valley of all sorts, pastures, marshes, runs, rivers, lakes, hunting, fishing, hawking, and fowling, and all other profitts, commodities, emoluments, and hereditaments, to the said lands and premises within the bounds and limits all forth belonging, or in any wise appertaining,—and withall to have freedome of commonage for range and feed of cattle and horse into the woods, as well without as within these bounds and limitts, with the rest of their neighbours,[3]—as also one-third part of a certain neck of meadow-ground or valley called Sellers neck, lying and being within the limits of

[1] According to the New York doctrine, this boundary of the town can only be correct when the tide is flood; for, when the water is low, the town is bounded by property belonging to the Corporation of the city of New York, and not by the river.—Furman's Notes, p. 12.

[2] See *ante*, page 113.

[3] This town enjoyed this privilege in common with the other towns on Long Island, and their cattle which ran at large were marked with the letter "N."—Furman's Notes, p. 13.

the town of Jamaica, purchased by the said town of Jamaica from the Indians, and sold by them unto the inhabitants of Breucklen aforesaid, as it has been lately laid out and divided by their mutual consent and my order, whereunto and from which they are likewise to have free egress and regress, as their occasions may require. To have and to hold all and singular the said tract and parcell of land, meadow-ground or valley, commonage, hereditaments and premises, with their and every of their appurtenances, and of every part and parcell thereof, to the said patentees and their associates, their heirs, successors, and assigns, to the proper use and behoof of the said patentees and their associates, their heirs, successors, and assigns forever. Moreover, I do hereby give, ratify, confirm and grant unto the said patentees and their associates, their heirs, successors, and assigns, all the rights and privileges belonging to a town within this government, and that the place of their present habitation shall continue and retain the name of Breuckelen, by which name and stile it shall be distinguished and known in all bargains and sales made by them, the said patentees and their associates, their heirs, successors, and assigns, rendering and paying such duties and acknowledgments as now are or hereafter shall be constituted and established by the laws of this government, under the obedience of his Royal highness, his heirs and successors. Given under my hand and seal at Fort James, in New York, on the Island of Manhattat, this 18th day of October, in the nineteenth year of the reign of our Sovereign Lord, Charles the second, by the grace of God, of England, Scotland, France, and Ireland, King, Defender of the Faith, etc., Annoque Domini, 1667.

"RICHARD NICOLLS.

"Recorded, by order of the Governor, the day and year above written.

"MATTHIAS NICOLLS, Sec'ry."

There was, unquestionably, a General Patent or Charter of this town under the Dutch government, which is now lost. The Nicolls Charter, above given, is evidently confirmatory of some such former part; and the same is also referred to by conveyances between individuals.

Adam Brouwer, of Breuckelen, miller, being complained of by the inhabitants, constables, and overseers of the town, that he would not at all times grind corn for some of them, "on frivolous pretences," and being apparently forgetful of former court action on a similar charge, was warned by Governor Lovelace (November 12,

1668), that as long as he should keep the mill, he must "grind for all persons, without distinction or exception, according to custom, the first come to be first served," under penalty.[1]

January 4, 1668, one Robert Hollis was granted the exclusive privilege of selling strong drink in Breuckelen.[2]

During this year, also, the little village-hamlet of Bedford[3] was

---

[1] Brouwer, although a respectable citizen, in good circumstances, seems to have been rather fractious and troublesome at times, if we may judge from this and other items recorded concerning him. In February, 1667 (-8), he had been ordered under arrest for seditious speeches; and in September, 1669, he was fined 500 guilders for an assault on Gerrit Coosen. (Council Minutes, ii. 282, 195, 537.)

[2] July 18, 1669, Robert Hollis received a patent for a piece of land in Breuckelen, "lying and being to the south of Jan Martyn's, and the north of Jan Damen's, containing in breadth (an east line being run on each side) 40 rod, and in length 200 rod, in bigness about 26 acres or 13 morgen," sold in 1647, by Jan Misroel, to the said Hollis. (Council Minutes, ii. 320.)

[3] The settlement of the locality, which retains, even at the present day, its ancient name of *Bedford*, seems to have commenced in 1662; for on the 18th of March, in that year, Jan Joris Rapalje, Teunis Gysbert (Bogaert), Cornelis Jacobsen, Hendrick Sweers, Michael Hans (Bergen), and Jan Hans (Bergen), made a humble request to the Director and General for "the grant of a parcel of free (unoccupied) woodland, situated in the rear of Joris Rapalje, next to the old Bay road." The request was granted to the suppliants, provided that they placed their dwellings "within one or the other concentration, which shall suit them best, but not to make a new hamlet." (N. Y. Col. MSS., x. Part i. 88. By this grant the parties are supposed to have obtained 20 morgen (or 40 acres) of land apiece at Bedford. (See also ibid., xxii. 145, 146; xxiv. 60.)

Feb. 18, 1666, a patent was granted to Thomas Lamberts, to confirm to him a certain parcel of land lying in the Walleboght, within the limits of a certain village known by the name of New Bedford, on Long Island, "being on the south side of the land belonging to Jan Lourensen, and on the north side of that which belongs to Michael Hansen (Bergen); containing in breadth, 24 rods; and in length, upon an east line, 500 rods: which in all, by estimation, amounts to about 40 acres of ground," as granted by Governor Stuyvesant, May 15, 1664, to said Lamberts.

Feb. 18, 1666, a patent was granted to Thomas Lamberts, confirming to him a parcel of land, "being on the south side of the land belonging to Jan Laurensen, and on the west side of the cart-way, containing, by estimation, 3 acres or thereabouts." Also "a certain plot of ground, lying on the south part of New Bedford aforesaid, being on the north side of the above-mentioned land, and on the west side of the cart-way, having a house and barn standing thereon; containing, in length, 24 rod; and in breadth, on the east and west sides, 16 rod," as occupied by said Lamberts.

May 14, 1700, Thomas Lambertse, of Bedford, conveyed to Leffert Peterse (the ancestor of the *Lefferts* family), of Flatbush, the premises covered by the last-mentioned patent of Feb. 18, 1666. (Lib. ii. 213, Kings County Conveyances.)

Dec. 3, 1667, a patent was granted to Charles Heynant, described as an inhabitant of Bedford, within the jurisdiction of the town of Breucklyn, in the West Riding of Yorkshire, upon Long Island, having a lot of ground in the place aforesaid, but having not a sufficient quantity of woodland belonging thereto, granting to him "an addition of about 3 morgen, or 6 acres, of land adjoining his said lot."

honored by the establishment of an inn or ordinary "for man and beast:"

"License granted to Thomas Lamberts, of Bedford, to sell beer, wine, and other liquors.

"Whereas, Thomas Lamberts, of Bedford, within the jurisdiction of Breuckelen, in the West Riding of Yorkshire, upon Long Island, is willing to undertake the keeping of an Ordinary, for the accommodation of strangers, travellers, and other persons passing that way, with diet and lodging and horse meals, I do hereby give him license to sell beer, wine, or any other strong liquors for their relief. And for his further encouragement therein, do think fit to order that no person living in the said village of Bedford have privilege so to do but himself. This License is to continue for one year after the date hereof, and no longer. Given under my hand, at Fort James, in New York, this 17th day of December, 1668.

"FRANCIS LOVELACE."

In the year 1670, the inhabitants of Breuckelen, being desirous of enlarging the bounds of their common lands, and of extinguishing the Indian title to the same, applied to Governor Lovelace, and obtained from him the following permission to purchase from the native proprietors a large tract of land in and about the hamlet then and since known as Bedford:

"*L. S.* *Whereas*, the inhabitants of Breucklyn, in the west Riding of Yorkshire, upon Long Island, who were seated there in a township by the authority then in being, and having bin at considerable charges in clearing, ffencing, and manuring their land, as well as building ffor their conveniency, have requested my lycense, for their further security, to make purchase of the said land of some Indians who lay claim and interest therein; these are to certify all whom it may concerne, that I have and doe hereby give the said inhabitants lycense to purchase their land according to their request, the said Indians concerned appearing before me as in the law is required, and making their acknowledgments to be fully satisfyed and paid

The *Bedford* settlement, of which these notes serve to show the beginnings, was located at the intersection of the old highway to Jamaica with the "Clove Road" to Flatbush, on the south; and with the "Cripplebush Road" to Newtown, on the north; and extending about a quarter of a mile each way from that point.

for the same. Given under my hand and seal at ffort James, in New Yorke, this ffirst day of May, in the 22nd yeare of his Majestyies reigne, Annoque Dom. 1670.

"FFRANCIS LOVELACE."

The purchase was accordingly made, and the following is a copy of a deed from the Indians for the same:

"To all people to whom this present writing shall come, PETER, ELMOHAR, JOB, MAKAQUIQUOS, and SHAMESE, late of Staten Island, send Greeting; *Whereas* they, the said PETER, ELMOHAR, JOB, MAKAQUIQUOS, and SHAMESE, afore-mentioned, doe lay claime to the land now in the tenure and occupation of some of the inhabitants of Breucklyn, as well as other lands there adjascent, as the true Indian owners and proprietors thereof, Know Yee, that for and in consideration of a certaine sum of wampum and diverse other goods, the which in the Schedule annext are exprest, unto the said Sachems in hand payed by Monsieur Machiell Hainelle, Thomas Lambertse, John Lewis, and Peter Darmantier, on the behalf of themselves and the inhabitants of Breucklyn, the receipt whereof they doe hereby acknowledge, and themselves to be fully satisfyed and payed therefor; have given, granted, bargained, and sold, and by these presents doe fully, freely, and absolutely give, grant, bargain and sell unto the said Monsieur Machiell Hainelle, Thomas Lambertse, John Lewis, and Peter Darmantier, ffor and on behalf of themselves and the inhabitants aforesaid, their heyrs and successors; all that parcell of land and tract of land in and about Bedford, within the jurisdiction of Breucklyn, beginning ffrom Hendrick Van Aarnhem's land by a swamp of water, and stretching to the hills, then going along the hills to the port or entrance thereof,[1] and soe to the Rockaway ffoot-path, as their purchase is more particularly set fforth; To have and to hold all the said parcell and tract of land and premises within the limits before described unto the said Monsieur Machiell Hainelle, Thomas Lambertse, John Lewis, and Peter Darmantier, ffor and on behalf of the inhabitants aforesaid, their heyres and successors, to the proper use and behoof of the said inhabitants, their heyres and successors forever; in witness whereof the partyes to these presents have hereunto sett their hands and

[1] This port "or entrance," as it is called, is situate in the valley on the Flatbush Turnpike, near the "Brush," or "Valley Tavern," and a short distance beyond the three-mile post from Breuckelen ferry. A freestone monument was placed here, to designate the patent line between Breuckelen and Flatbush.

seales, this 14th day of May, in the 22nd yeare of his Majestyes reigne, Annoque Dom. 1670.

"Sealed and Delivered in the presence of Mathias Nicolls, R. Lough, Samuel § Davies, John Garland.

his marke.

"The mark of P PETER, [L. S.]

"The mark of o ELMOHAR, [L. S.]

"The mark of N JOB, [L. S.]

"The mark of ? MAQUIQUOS, [L. S.]

"The mark of 7 SHAMESE, [L. S.]

"This deed was acknowledged by the within written Sachems before the Governor in the presence of us, the day and year within written.

"MATHIAS NICOLLS, Secretary.

"The mark of § SAMUEL DAVIES.

"Recorded by order of the Governor.

"MATHIAS NICOLLS, Secretary.

" *The Inventory or Schedule Referred to in the Deed.*

"The payment agreed upon ffor the purchase of the land in and about Bedford, within the jurisdiction of Breucklyn, conveyed this day by the Indian Sachems, proprietors, is, viz:

"100 Guilders Seawant,

"Half a tun of strong beer,

"2 half tuns of good beer,

"3 guns, long barrells, with each a pound of powder, and lead proportionable—2 bars to a gun—4 match coates."

August 10th, 1671. Adriaen Hegeman, Schout, and Albert Cornelissen Wantenaer, and others, Schepens of Breuckelen during the Dutch government, had levied a rate on the town, by consent of the Governor, for the purpose of building a "minister's house," but had not collected the whole amount. The government being now changed, they were held somewhat liable for the amount, and ordered by the court to pay for the work done on the house. Governor Lovelace ordered that they should be acquitted from the said obligation, and the business should be undertaken by the present Overseers of Breuckelen, who were to levy sums in arrears upon persons and estates, if found; if not sufficient, however, they were directed to make a new rate upon the town.[1]

This year, also, Breuckelen, with five other towns in the West Riding, petitioned the Court of Sessions "for liberty to transport wheat." Their petition was referred to the Governor.

In the year 1673, however, by an event as sudden as it was unexpected, the whole of New Netherland passed again under the control of the States-General. Early in that year, news was received that England and Holland were again involved in war. Orders were also forwarded to Gov. Lovelace to put the province in a proper state of defence; but so lacking was he in the means necessary to fortify the city of New York, that a Dutch fleet, under Captains Binckes and Evertsen, returning from a predatory excursion against the French and English West India trade, entered the harbor on the 30th of July, and captured the place without firing a gun. Captain Anthony Colve was appointed Governor of the province by the naval commanders, and immediately began to reinstate the Dutch government. The city was denominated *New Orange* and the fort *William Hendrick*, in honor of the *Staadt Holder*. On the 14th of August, 1673, the new Governor issued a proclamation requiring each of the Long Island towns to send two deputies to the city, with full powers to tender their submission to the States-General and the Prince of Orange. The five Dutch towns, rejoiced to find themselves once more under their old masters, submitted with alacrity; but the other towns showed an inclination to evade the order and to seek the protection of their former ally, the English Colony of Connecticut; and eventually, in spite of Gov. Colve's efforts to the contrary, Southampton, Easthampton, and Southold succeeded in joining themselves to the jurisdiction of that colony. In Breuckelen and the adjoining hamlets, fifty-two out of eighty-one men took the oath of allegiance, and the remainder were ordered to comply.[2]

In October following, a code of "Provisional Instructions" was received from the new governor, for the guidance of the magistrates in the future government of their towns, although in some minor

---

[1] General Entries, iv. 12.

[2] N. Y. Col. MSS., xxiii. 14, 40, 51; N. Y. Col. Doc., ii. 573, 580, 586, 589, 596.

affairs the people were allowed to adhere to the laws formerly in force. In fact, the transient rule of the Dutch afforded opportunity for but few legislative changes.[1]

---

[1] Provisional Instructions for the Sheriff and Magistrates of the Villages of Midwout, Amersfoort, Breuckelen, New Utrecht, and Gravesend, and for the Magistrates of Boswyck (N. Y. Col. MSS., xxiii. 93):

Art. 1. The Sheriff and Magistrates, each in his quality, shall see to the maintenance of the Reformed Christian Religion, in conformity with the (canons of) the Synod of Dordrecht; and shall not permit that any thing contrary to it shall be attempted by any other sects.

Art. 2. The Sheriff shall, as often as possible, be present at and preside in all the meetings. However, if he acts for himself as a party, or defends the rights of the Lord's patrons, or steps forward in the cause of justice, he shall, in such cases, rise from his seat and leave the bench, and shall then have no advisory, much less a conclusive, vote, while in his stead the oldest Schepen shall preside.

Art. 3. All cases relating to the police, to the security and peace of the inhabitants, and to justice between man and man, shall be definitely determined by the magistrates of each of the aforesaid villages, to the amount of 60 guilders, or less, in beavers. If the sum is larger than that, the aggrieved party may appeal to a council (consisting of) the Sheriff and a Commissioner of the Counsellors (magistrates) of the village, subject to his (the Sheriff's) jurisdiction (for which purpose one person shall be annually chosen in each village), who shall meet at some convenient place selected by them, and who shall have the power to pronounce a definitive sentence to the amount of 240 guilders, in beavers, and under. But in all cases exceeding that sum, each party shall be entitled to the right of appeal to the Governor and Council.

Art. 4. In case of a disparity of votes, the minority shall submit to the majority; but they who have a dissentient opinion, are permitted to have it recorded on the protocol, but they shall not divulge it outside of the meeting, under penalty of an arbitrary correction.

Art. 5. If at any such meeting, cases occur in which any of the magistrates are concerned as parties, the magistrate in such case shall be obliged to leave his seat and absent himself, as was before said of the Sheriff in the 2d article.

Art. 6. All the inhabitants of the aforesaid villages may be summoned before the Sheriff and Schepens, or before the Committee of Counsellors, who shall hold their meetings as often as may be required.

Art. 7. All criminal derelictions shall be referred to the Governor-General and the Council; provided that the Sheriff is under obligation to apprehend the criminals, to arrest and secure them, and conduct them in safety to the Chief Magistrate, with correct information of the committed crime, at the expense of the delinquent or of the Attorney-General.

Art. 8. Smaller derelictions, such as quarrels, injuries, scoldings, threatenings, blows, and similar trespasses, are left to the jurisdiction of the magistrates of each village.

Art. 9. The Sheriff and Schepens are authorized to issue orders relative to the welfare and peace of the inhabitants, such as the laying out and making of roads, the surveying of lots and garden-spots, and whatever has any relation to agriculture; also with respect to keeping the Sabbath, building of churches, school-houses, and similar public works; also about fighting, throwing stones, and similar petty crimes—provided that such orders are opposed, but, as far as possible, consonant with the laws of our Fatherland and the statutes of this province; and therefore all such orders of any

On the 15th of December, his Excellency, Gov. Colve, accompanied by some of his officers and prominent citizens, repaired to the village of Midwout, where, by his order, all the magistrates and field-officers of the Dutch towns on Long Island had assembled. He then and there informed them that he had learned that the New England troops were even then on their way to assail the province; and, although he did not fully credit the report, yet he deemed it necessary to remind them of their allegiance and duty, as well as to recommend them, with all possible speed, to thrash out and transport all their grain to New York. He also commanded them not to be remiss in proceeding immediately, with the people of their villages, to the city whenever he should summon them; advising meanwhile they should maintain a strict guard, and that, from time to time, they should send out one or two mounted patrols towards the neighboring English villages, to keep a lookout. All of which was unanimously promised by the authorities, who also thanked the Governor

---

importance, before being published, shall be submitted to the Chief Magistrate for his approval.

Art. 10. The aforesaid Sheriff and Schepens shall see that all placards and ordinances which are ordained and published by the Chief Magistrate are well observed and executed, and shall not allow that they shall be disobeyed by any one; that transgressors shall be prosecuted, and that all and every law, as may from time to time be issued by the Governor-General, shall be promptly enforced.

Art. 11. The Sheriff and Schepens shall acknowledge for their sovereign their High and Mighty Lords the States-General of the United Netherlands, and His Serene Highness the Lord Prince of Orange, and shall defend and maintain their high jurisdiction, rights, and domains in this country.

Art. 12. The election of all inferior officers and assistants, for the service of the aforesaid Schout and Schepens (the office of secretary only excepted), shall be made and confirmed by the Schepens themselves.

Art. 13. The Sheriff, either personally or through his assistants, shall execute all the judgments of the Schepens, discharging no individual except with full consent of the Court. He shall furthermore take due care to keep his jurisdiction free from every sort of villany in trading, brothels, and similar impurities.

Art. 14. The Sheriff shall receive half of all the civil fines during his term of service, besides one-third of what falls to the share of the respective villages in criminal cases, but he shall not accept, either directly or indirectly, any presents, which are by law forbidden.

Art. 15. Previous to the annual election, the Sheriff and Schepens shall make, in nomination for Schepens, of a double number of the best qualified, honest, intelligent, and wealthiest inhabitants (but only those belonging to, or well affected toward, the Reformed Christian Religion), and shall present it the Governor, who shall then make a selection, and, if he deem it best, confirm some of the old Schepens.

Done at Fort William Hendricks, October 1, 1673.

for his prudent precautions, and promised to abide by his orders. And, agreeably to the petition of some of the "country people," that they might be permitted, for their better safety, to remove their families and property into the city, and that some accommodation might be apportioned to them for a season, the Hon. Cornelius Steenwyck, of the Council, Cornelis Van Ruyven, and Johannes Van Brugh, Burgomaster, were appointed to look up the proper houses and accommodation, and to make the necessary provision at the ferry for the safe and speedy passage of goods, etc., over the river.

The inhabitants of Breuckelen, Boswyck, and the other Dutch towns were not slow in complying with these propositions of the Governor, and so active and general was the emigration to the city, as to threaten the total depopulation of the west end of Long Island. In this emergency, Gov. Colve, on the 26th of December, issued an order, wherein he states that he "deemed it necessary that, for the present, in each of those villages, a few males should remain, to prevent further losses, until we have received further information of the arrival or the designs of the enemy. And in order that this may be most safely effected for the public welfare and in good order, therefore the respective captains, lieutenants, and ensigns of the aforesaid villages are hereby commanded to appear with their companies, all armed, on Friday, the 29th of this month, in the forenoon, within this city of New Orange and before the fortress William Hendricks, leaving six men in each village. This being done, then immediately one-third portion of each company shall be discharged to depart to their several villages, there to remain until relieved by another corporalship, which shall be done (until further orders) every third day. Also, the officers are hereby authorized to give such orders about thrashing grain and foddering the cattle, as each one shall deem advisable within his own jurisdiction; above all, taking especial care that a vigilant watch is maintained and patrol kept up both day and night, so that they may not be surprised by the enemy or separated from us."[1]

But another change in the political condition of the country was at hand, and the second epoch of Dutch power was terminated, in

---

[1] N. Y. Col. MSS., xxiii. 185.

February, 1674, by a treaty of peace between England and Holland, by which New Netherlands was given to the English in exchange for Surinam. The new governor, Sir Edmund Andros, arrived at New York on the 31st of October, received a formal surrender of the place, and re-established the English government. The Duke's laws were reinstated and confirmed, together with such grants and privileges as had been previously enjoyed under his royal highness; all legal judicial proceedings during the Dutch government were pronounced valid, and the inhabitants secured in their lawful estates and property. A special order, also, of November 4th, reinstated in office, for a period of six months, the officials of the several towns who were serving when the Dutch came in power. The fort again became *Fort James*, and *New Orange* resumed its former name of NEW YORK.

CHAPTER VI.

ECCLESIASTICAL HISTORY OF BREUCKELEN.

1664–1803.

After Domine Selyns' return to Holland, in 1664, the church at Breuckelen came again under the pastoral charge of Domine Polhemus, the minister of the associated churches of the four Dutch towns of the county. The labors of this venerable and faithful servant of God ceased only with his life; and his death, on the 9th of June, 1676, is commemorated on the records of the church at Breuckelen in the following respectful and affectionate terms:

"It has pleased the Almighty God to remove from this world of care and trouble our worthy and beloved pastor, Johannes Polhemus, to the abode of peace and happiness in His heavenly kingdom; by which our church is deprived of his pious instructions, godly example, and evangelical ministrations, particularly in the administration of the holy sacrament of the Lord's Supper."

During his ministry, in the year 1666, the first church edifice in Breuckelen was erected in the middle of the highway, now Fulton avenue, near Lawrence street. Tradition says that it was built on the walls of a stone fort, constructed in the early days of the settlement for protection against the savages. This first church remained in existence just a century, being pulled down in the year 1766.

By the death of Domine Polhemus, the churches of Kings County were deprived of the regular preaching of the Gospel, and the Breuckelen church invited the Rev. Mr. Nieuwenhausen, of New Amsterdam, to supply their pulpit, which he did until the year 1677. In that year the collegiate churches of the county extended a call to the Rev. Casparus Van Zuren, from Holland, who was installed on the 6th of September at Flatbush, and of whom little is known, except that he was an industrious and systematic man.[1]

[1] As evidenced by the very copious minutes which he has left upon the Flatbush Church Records, of the services which he performed, lists of baptisms, marriages, elections of officers, etc. See Strong's Hist. of Flatbush, p. 80.

When the pulpit of the church in New York was vacant, he preached there every Wednesday by invitation, without failure on account of weather; for which he received compensation and a vote of thanks from the New York Consistory. He also preached (1680–2) for the Dutch church at Bergen. In 1685 he returned to Holland, where he resumed his former charge over the church at Gonderac.[1]

The records of the church at Flatbush during Van Zuren's pastorate present the following minutes, which may not be uninteresting to our readers:

"Respecting another difficulty, touching the preaching at Flatbush beyond the usual turn. It was asked, inasmuch as this (*i. e.*, a similar case) had occurred at a previous meeting, on the 15th November, 1679, whether, when the town which has the turn shall neglect to fetch the minister, or be hindered by foul weather, such ought to pass for a turn for Flatbush—which appeared improper, because in such case the minister would then (only) sit still. After some debate between Flatbush and the other towns, the minister observed that the service on the Lord's day might not be neglected; for it could not injure the other towns that Flatbush had an extra turn, for the other towns thereafter again took their course (*i. e.*, their respective turns). That the minister not being fetched by anybody, evidently belonged no more to the one than to the other, and in such a case he stood free on his own feet to give the extra turn to whom he pleased; that Flatbush received profit, but the other towns no injury, (and) that this was unjust no one could pretend; and that Flatbush was not obligated to the other towns, but to the minister whom they remunerated, which was evident, inasmuch as they had purchased a piece of land 16 rods long and 12 broad, adjoining the parsonage; and this ought to be duly considered, although no person ought to be a judge in his own

[1] The two self-righteous Labadist travellers, whose journal forms the first volume of the Collections of the L. I. Hist. Society, have left us a brief glimpse of Van Zuren: "While we were sitting there, Do. Van Suren came up, to whom the farmers called out as uncivilly and rudely as if he had been a boy. He had a chatting time with all of them. As Jan Theunissen had said to us in the house, that if the Domine only had a chance ever to talk to us, Oh, how he would talk to us! that we avoided him, and therefore could not be very good people; now, as we were there, we sat near him and the boors and those with whom he was conversing. He spoke to us, but not a word of that fell from him. Indeed, he sat prating and gossiping with the boors, who talked foully and otherwise, not only without giving them a single word of reproof, but even without speaking a word about God, or spiritual matters. It was all about horses, and cattle, and swine, and grain, and then he went away."

case; therefore the minister advised that this difference be referred and submitted to the Honorable the Consistory of New York."[1]

On the 14th of October, 1680, the following was agreed to, being article 7 of a new agreement with the minister, viz.:

"Those of Flatbush shall provide that the minister's field be enlarged two morgen, in order that the minister may keep a horse and suitably attend to the service of the Church, and also make all necessary repairs to the fences, dwelling, kitchens, well, and appurtenances, with earnest desire and integrity of heart."

The interference of the British authorities, who then held the Dutch colonies in subjection, with the concerns of the Reformed Dutch churches, produced much uneasiness and a considerable show of opposition among the inhabitants of the four towns. And in 1680 the Church Council, assembled in synod at Flatbush, formally resolved that the charge and management of church lands and property belonged to the Church Council, and was secured to them by the Charter of Freedoms; and furthermore, that the English officials were, by their oaths of office, bound to *protect* and not to abridge the rights of the church.[2] They also chose church masters, to take charge of the church property; and these officers were reappointed for several successive years.

In a MS. of the Rev. Peter Lowe, quoted by some writers, "a

---

[1] Translation of the second resolution of the session of the four towns, held at Flatbush the 1st of February, 1680.

[2] Translation. "In Synedrio Midwoudano. The following was done on the 1st of February, 1679 (–80):

"*Whereas* the Church Consistory judged that the charge of the goods and lands of the Low Dutch Church ought to be intrusted to the Hon. the Church Council, because it accords with the freedoms granted to us in this land,

"*Therefore*, the said Consistory provide (as it may not accord with their service in the church) that the right of choosing *Church-Masters* should be given to them, in connection with the Hon. Constables and Overseers, not because they judged that the English officers had any power over the church, or church property, as that would be contrary to the Dutch freedom, but simply to cause the aforesaid officers faithfully to maintain and protect the church and church property, which is not contrary to their oath or trust, etc.

"Whereupon, collectively with the Hon. Magistrate and Church Council, Joseph Hegeman, Adriaen Reijersz, Dirck Jansz Vander Vliet, were appointed as *Church-Masters* in the place of the retiring officers."

This action was continued in 1680, 1681, 1683.

Mr. Clark" is mentioned as the immediate successor of Domine Van Zuren. But of him nothing is known, and if such a person existed, it is quite probable that he was merely a temporary supply. At all events, in the carefully prepared "History of the Reformed Dutch Church in North America," by the Rev. Dr. DeWitt, which we may safely assume to be the highest authority on these points, we find the name of the Rev. RUDOLPHUS VAN VARICK as minister of Kings County from 1685 to 1694. During the Leislerian troubles, in 1689, Mr. Varick, as well as the other Dutch ministers, stood out against the authority of Leisler, and was treated with much harshness, being dragged from his home, cast into the jail, deposed from his ministerial functions, and fined heavily. These severities, which were heaped upon him for alleged treasonable utterances against Leisler, undoubtedly hastened his death.[1] His congregation, also, were divided, and many of them refused to pay his salary according to the terms upon which they called him from Holland,—especially, as he says, in a petition to the Governor, Sept. 11th, 1691, for the six months of his imprisonment. The Court ordered the arrears of salary due him by his congregation to be collected, *by distress, if necessary.*[2] Mr. Varick was naturalized on the 29th of July, 1686, and his posterity are to be found on the island.[3]

He was succeeded by the Rev. WILHELMUS LUPARDUS, whose ministry was terminated by death in 1701 or 2.

Being thus again deprived of a regular ministry, the people of the four towns empowered the elders of the churches within said towns to procure a minister, "either out of the province or out of Holland," and the elders, after much deliberation, determined upon the Rev. BERNARDUS FREEMAN, of Schenectady, and applied to the Gov-

---

[1] This is Secretary Clarkson's statement (Doc. Hist. N. Y., ii. 431, 432), but another party, not so favorably inclined, says that Varick was, at first, in favor of the revolution of Leisler, and influenced Kings County to act unanimously in its favor; but that, afterwards, he was won over to a contrary opinion, and created a diversion in the popular mind. The same authority says that he was suspected by the people of conspiring to seize the fort in New York, was arrested, and released, after a time, upon his submission to Leisler; that he favored the execution of the latter, "made intolerable sermons" against him, and cherished animosity even to his dying day.

[2] Council Minutes, vi. 55.

[3] May 19, 1690, in an address to William and Mary, he styles himself 'Pastor Ecclesiæ Belgicæ in Insulâ Longâ."

ernor, Lord Cornbury, for permission to call him. Their action, however, well-meant as it undoubtedly was, gave rise to a contention which was destined to distract and agitate the inhabitants of Kings County for many succeeding years. The people, always jealous of the English power, to which they were unwilling subjects, and particularly sensitive to any interference of that power with their ecclesiastical affairs, were highly indignant because the elders had seen fit to ask the Governor's permission to call Mr. Freeman. In Flatbush, the disaffected even went so far as to convene a town meeting, whereat the regular elders of that church were deposed from office and new ones elected in their stead, who were instructed forthwith to send for Mr. Freeman; while at Breuckelen certain busybodies went around endeavoring to gain signatures to a petition or call to the said Freeman, and also for the choosing of three new elders from that town, as had been done at Flatbush.[1] Their discontent was undoubtedly encouraged by some inconsiderate acts of Domine Freeman, and his evident desire to come among them—although in direct opposition to the expressed desire of his own church at Schenectady.[2]

The legal examination of the contending parties before the Council, resulted in the following order from Governor Cornbury:

> "I having duly Considered the Within petition, and having been well Informed that Mr. Bar. ffreeman has misbehaved himself by promoting and Encouraging the unhappy divisions among the people of this province, do not think it Consistent with her Majestie's Service that the s[d] ffreeman should be admitted to be called, as is prayed by the s[d] petition, And the petitioners are hereby required not to call or receive the s[d] ffreeman. But they are hereby left at Liberty to send for such Minister as they shall think fitt, from holland or any other place, as hath been customary."[3]

The opposition which Mr. Freeman met with from the Governor, the people of his charge at Schenectady, and the disaffected minority in Flatbush and Breuckelen, although it retarded, did not defeat his settlement in Kings County. Late in the year 1705, he received the following commission as minister there:

---

[1] Doc. Hist. N. Y., iii. 139, 140, 141, 142.

[2] Ibid., iii. 143, 144.

[3] The above order is on a scrap of paper without date. Dr. Strong (Hist. Flatbush) states that it was made on 23d Oct., 1702.

"By his Excellency Edward Viscount Cornbury Capt Gen^{ll} & Govr in Cheife of ye Provinces of New York, New Jersey, & of all The Territories and Tracts of Land Depending Thereon in America & Vice Admirale of ye same, &c.

"To Mr BERNARDUS FREEMAN Greeting—

"You are hereby Licenced, Tollerated, and allowed to be Minist^r of the Dutch Congregation at New Uytrecht, Flackbush, Bruyckland, and Buswick, in Kings County, upon The Island of Nassaw, in the s^d Province of New York, and to have & Exercise the free Liberty and use of yor Religion, according to ye Laws in such case made and Provided for, & During So Long Time as to me shall Seem meet, & all P'sons are hereby Required to Take Notice hereof accordingly. GIVEN under my hand & seal at Fort Anne, in New York, This 26th day of Decem^r, in the fourth year of her Maties Reigne Annoq: D^m 1705. "CORNBURY.[1]

"By his Excell^{ns} command.

"WILLIAM ANDERSON, D^y Sec^y."

In compliance with this order, Mr. Freeman s installation ceremonies took place at New Utrecht;[2] but his troubles were not yet ended. While his adherents had been foisting him into the pastorate, his opponents had made formal application to the Classis at Amsterdam for a minister, and in response to their request the Rev. VINCENTIUS ANTONIDES arrived from the Fatherland on the first of January, 1705–6,[3] and was duly installed at Flatbush, assuming the charge of the four churches, to which, in 1702, had been added the newly formed church of Jamaica.

The controversy between the two parties rapidly increased in bitterness and extent. Freeman's adherents, conscious of the protection of the Governor and Council, formally demanded that the church books, lands, and stock should be delivered into their keeping; to which the "original" church party very naturally demurred. On petition of Domine Freeman's party, the Governor then issued a warrant to the authorities of the Flatbush and Breuckelen churches, to deliver up said property and books to Mr. Freeman.[4]

---

[1] N. Y. Doc. Hist., iii. 145. [2] Ibid., iii. 147.

[3] Prime says, "in Nov., 1705," which does not agree well with the date of the above commission.

[4] N. Y. Doc. Hist., iii. 146, 147.

To this the elders of the churches of Breuckelen, Flatbush, and Flatlands replied by a counter petition, in which they recite the circumstances attending Domine Antonides' settlement; assert that Mr. Freeman was "only called minister for the town of New Utrecht," and "has entered upon two of the said churches without any lawful call, and has continually obstructed their minister," etc., and conclude by requesting that a council may be called, composed of some of her Majesty's Council and the Deputies of the Dutch churches of the province, by whom the matter may be fully examined and decided.[1] The council was granted, to which were forthwith presented various and divers petitions from both of the contending parties, as well as the following documents, which we copy verbatim:

PROPOSALS

"Offered by Cornelius Seabring, Ingelbert Lot, and Cornelius Van Brunt, in behalf of themselves and others, Members of ye Dutch Churches of Flatbush, Brookland, and New Utrecht, in Kings County, on the Island of Nassau (who have hitherto adhered to the Interest of Domine Bernardus Freeman, their Minister) pursuant to a due authority to them the s^d Seabring, Lot, & Van Brunt, for that purpose given; for the more perfect and effectuall accommodation of the Difference between ye said Members, and others, Members of ye s^d Churches, who have hitherto adhered to the Interest of Domine Vincentius Antonides, in the articles following:

"1. First, that all differences and Animosities between the s^d Members which have hitherto hapend, be on either side no further talked of, but entirely buryed in Oblivion.

"2dly. That Domine Bernardus Freeman, from the time the agreem^t intended shall take effect, may in all things relating to the three Dutch Churches of Flatbush, Brookland, and New Utrecht, or any other Neighboring Churches, be admitted and put into equal State and Condition wth Domine Vincentius Antonides (to wit) in Service, in Sallary, in House & Land, and all other Proffits.

"3. That in order to put an End to ye Dispute concerning the present Consistory of Flatbush & Brookland, those persons wch M^r. Freeman now

[1] N. Y. Doc. Hist., iii. 148, date January 27, 1708–9.

Deems to be a Consistory, & those persons wch M^r^. Antonides now Deems to be a Consistory, Do severally Elect two Elders and Deacons of each part, in the presence & wth the concurance of one or both Ministers, if they both please to attend, and that those Eight Elders & Deacons so to be elected, shall from thence forth be and remain Elders and Deacons for the s^d^ two Churches of fflat Bush & Brookland for the first ensuing year & that at the end of ye s^d^ year to comence from the s^d^ election, half of them shall be removed & four others chosen in their stead, and at the end of two years after s^d^ first election, the other half shall be removed, & other four shall be chosen in their stead, & so successively every year according to ye usuall custom, the said Elections to be made by the votes of both the s^d^ Ministers and the Consistory for the time being: and that whenever the s^d^ Ministers shall meet upon any such or other Publick Service, the one shall preside one time and ye other the next time, & so alternately.

"4. That to the time of ye Election of ye s^d^ New Consistory, so to be made by both parties as aforesaid, each party shall, of their own parts respectively bear pay and discharge the Sallary, Perquisites, and other things due to ye respective Ministers, vizt, Those who have hitherto sided with Mr Freeman shall clear all arrears to him: & those who have hitherto sided with Mr Antonides, all arrears to him.

"New York March 5th 1708. "CORNELIS SEBERINGH,

"Endorsed, 'Proposals on the part of Mr Freeman's friends. 1708.' "ENGELBARDT LOTTE,

"CORNELIS VAN BRUNT."

ARTICLES

"Exhibited by the Elders & Deacons of the Dutch Reformed Protestant Church of the Towns of Brookland, fflatbush, and fflatlands, on the Island of Nassau, for the Reconciling the differences wch have of late been amongst the Dutch Churches on the said Island.

"1st That all parties do consent that Mr Antonides, according to the rules of the said Church, is the duely called Minister of Brookland, flatbush and flatlands, and that the Elders & Deacons wch were lately chosen by Mr Antonides with the assistance and consent of those Elders & Deacons wch he formed there at his arrivall are yet still the true Elders & Deacons, and that what ever has been acted to the contrary by Mr Freeman & others was always null & void & is so still; That therefore the collections gathered in the Churches of Brookland & flatbush by the friends of Mr Freerman be delivered to the Consistory of Mr Antonides to be disposed of according to the rules of the Church.

"2dly That all parties do consent that the Call made for Mr Freerman by those of New Utrecht does limit him to the Congregation of that Town only.

"3dly That all parties do consent, that no such lycence, or the other orders wch the Lord Cornbury has granted to Mr Freeman whereby the Effects of the sd Churches at his pleasure were to be delivered up to Mr Freeman, never were nor yet are of any force or validity in the Dutch Churches of this Province, but Tended to the ruin of the liberty of the said Churches in this Country; That they do allso reject this Position, That all the Ecclesiasticall Jurisdiccon of the Dutch Churches in this Province is wholly in the Power of the Govr according to his will & pleasure, That yet nevertheless all parties do firmly own that the Dutch Churches in this Province are accountable to the Govt for their peaceable & good behaviour in their Doctrin, Disciplin, and Church Government; that is to say, as farr as it does consist with the Rules & Constituçons of their own nationall Church always enjoyed at New York, As well as they have the right and Priviledge to be protected by the Civill Govt in the free exercise of their Religion according to their own Constitution.

"4^{thly} That all parties consent to subscribe the Church Orders of the Classis of Amsterdam, & those practiced on the Island of Nassauw not being contradictory thereto, & that in case any matter in difference cannot be decided amongst themselves the same be referred to the other Dutch Churches of this Province & if not by them decided the same to be submitted to the Classis of Amsterdam, whose decision is to be binding.

"5^{thly} That all parties reject the expression made by Mr. Freerman at a certain time, vizt that when the Church Orders were for his advantadge he observed them, but if they were against him he went round about the same, & could tread them under his feet.

"6^{thly} That then Mr Freeman shall be in a condicon to be called to those congregacons on the sd Island where he is not yet called according to the rules of the Church, and shall be called accordingly, Provided Mr Freerman's friends do first find out sufficient means thereto and a dwelling house and do perswade the Congregacons aforesaid to desire the Consistory to call him in an Ecclesiasticall manner.

"7^{thly} To the end that there may be a perfect peace in all the Dutch Churches on the said Island all parties, together with the freinds of Mr Freerman at Jamaica are to consent that the Elders & Deacons that were there when Mr Du Bois preached there the last time are yet the true Elders and Deacons & that then both Ministers may be called there.

"8thly That all parties consent that these articles being interchangeably signed be read to the respective Congregations from the Pulpit & authentiq copies thereof sent to the other Dutch Churches in this Province to be by them kept & that notice hereof be given to the Classis of Amsterdam with the request of both parties for their approbacon.

"Lastly. If Mr Freerman & his friends should not be pleased to consent to the above articles that then Capn Joannes De Peyster be desired to produce the resolucon of the Classis of Amsterdam, whereby Peace is said to be recommended according to the order of the said Classis, as Mr Freerman intimates in his letter without date to Mr Antonides that Capt. De Peyster aforesaid had shewn the same to him, together with the means to attain such a Peace.

"New-York 4th March 170 8/9.

"By order of the said Elders and Deacons,

"Abrah: Gouverneur,
"Joseph Hegeman,
"Geronemus Remsen,
"Pieter Melijus.

"Endorsed,

"'Proposals on the part of Mr Antonides's friends. 1708.'"[1]

After a full and patient hearing of all the testimony in the case, the Council sent in majority and minority reports to the Governor. The former, signed by Messrs. Rip Van Dam, A. D. Philipse, J. V. Courtlandt, and Leendert Hugyen De Kley, finds "that Mr. Antonides is duly and regularly called minister of the said towns of Brookland, Flatbush, and Flatlands, according to the discipline, practice, aud constitution of the Dutch churches of the towns aforesaid, and that Mr. Freeman is duly called minister of New Utrecht, on the said island, and we believe is likewise minister of Bushwick, though it has not been proved before us."[2] The minority report, by Messrs. D. Provoost, A. D. Peyster, and Jo. D. Peyster, finds that "Mr. Freeman is justly and legally called and entitled to the ministry of the churches of Breukland, Flatbush, New Utrecht, and Boswyck."[3] The majority report, however, in favor of Mr. Anton-

[1] N. Y. Doc. Hist., iii. 151–154.

[2] Ibid., iii. 159.

[3] N. Y. Doc. Hist., iii. 160, 161, date Oct. 6, 1709: "and that the said Mr. Antonides is not Legally called thereto, for the Reasons Following—

"First, that the Persons whoe pretend to haue Called Mr Antonides were not at that time the Elders & Deacons of the said Churches according to ye Rules & Methides, was accepted by the Governor and Council,[1] and Governor Lovelace thereupon promulgated an order to the effect that "His Honor having considered the said report and the matters therein contained, does think fit to order and direct, and does hereby order and direct, that from this time forward Mr. Freeman and Mr. Antonides shall preach at all the said churches in Kings County alternately, and divide all the profits equally, share and share alike; and to avoid all further disputes between the said ministers, Mr. Freeman shall preach next Sunday at Flatbush, and the Sunday following Mr. Antonides shall preach at Flatbush, and so on in the other churches, turn by turn; if either of them refuses to comply with this order, to be dismissed."[2]

The doughty Domine Antonides, however, was not so easily satisfied, and firmly but courteously refused to obey the order, saying that "to the end that he may not be wanting in his duty to God, his said Churches, nor give any Just cause to incur his honour's displeasure, he humbly beggs leave to Represent that he cannot comply with the said Order unless he breaks thro' the Rules &

---

ods prescribed by the Sinod of Dort for the Governmt: of the Dutch Reformed Churches, they having Continued as Such Some three years, Some four years, whereas by the Constitution of the said Sinod they could haue continued but two years——

"SECONDLY, that the call on which Mr Antonides came over is Expressed to bee made by a Generall towne meeting (which appears to haue been the usuall way in Such Cases) and that apears utterly false by the Examinations, for that the pretended authority for making that call apears not to be given in a publiq meeting, but to be obtained Privatly & Clandestinely by Procuring Subscriptions in Going from house to house & there using false Insinuations concerning Mr Freeman.

"THIRDLY, that the said pretended call mentions the having obtained the Govrs License, & aprobation for making the said call, whereas it appears by the oath of the Lord Cornbury Govr & thire own confession that the Lord Cornbury, did not give any License to make that call,

"FOURTHLY, that on the contrary it apears that Mr Freeman was called by a generall Towne Meeting Publiqly assembled (as has alwaies been Customary) for which the Express License & aprobation of the Lord Cornbury then Governour had bein first obtained.

"FIFTHLY, that the having a License from the Govr was Esteemed necessary even by Mr Antonides himselfe & those that sided with him, Since both he & they frequently aplyed to obtain Such a License; as appears by Seaverall letters to the Late Lady Cornbury, & Mrs Peartree, under the hand of the said Antonides & of the Said pretended Elders for the truth of which wee the Subscribers refer our Selves to the Examinations & the Respective papers produced at the taking thereof."

[1] Council Minutes, N. Y. Doc. Hist., iii. 162, date Oct. 20, 1709.

[2] N. Y. Doc. Hist., iii. 165.

Discipline of the Dutch Reformed Protestant Churches, the Constitucon whereof not admitting any minister to assume a right to any Church but where he is Regularly called to, which the said order seems to Direct."[1]

The only reply which the intractable domine received, was notice that the Governor "had already determined the matter, and would hear nothing further."[2] Still, he and his friends continued to worry the Governor with petition after petition, and finally (April 18, 1710), in the interval between Gov. Lovelace's term and the arrival of the new Governor, Robert Hunter, the question was again brought up in the Council, of which the Hon. Gerardus Beekman was president *pro tem.* It was then and there determined that the majority report rendered to the Council in 1709, in favor of Mr. Antonides, should be confirmed. Mr. Antonides had at length triumphed; but a few days thereafter Mr. Freeman surreptitiously obtained an order from Mr. Beekman, the President of the Board, authorizing him to preach "alternately with Mr. Antonides, in Flatbush and Brookland churches." This *outside* movement on the part of Mr. Beekman gave great umbrage to the adherents of Mr. Antonides, who earnestly protested against it, and requested that the order thus illegally granted might be recalled.[3] The Council also felt insulted by the unwarrantable act of their President, and on his refusing, at their next sitting, to recall his order to Domine Freeman, "they declared they would not meet in council till it was done; telling the President, if he could do what he had done as aforesaid without them, he might do all other acts of government without them, and that then they saw no business they had to convene in council. And thereupon the Council broke up."[4]

---

[1] N. Y. Doc. Hist., iii. 166. [2] Ibid., iii. 167. [3] Ibid., iii. 172—date June 12, 1710.

[4] Council Minutes, x.; N. Y. Doc. Hist., iii. 173. The following document relative to the above is taken from Doc. Hist. N. Y., iii. 174, 175:

"H. FFILKIN TO SECRETARY (CLARKE) EXPLANATORY OF THE QUARREL BETWEEN HIM AND LT. GOV. BEEKMAN.

"SIR—I am in expectation of a complaint coming to his Excellency by Coll. Beeckman against me, and that his Excellency may be rightly informed of the matter, my humble request to you is, that if such a thing happen, be pleased to give his Excellency an account thereof, which is as follows: A ffriday night last, the Justices of the County and I came from his Excellency's; Coll. Beeckman happened to come over in the fferry boat along with us, and as we came over the fferry, Coll. Beeckman and we went into the fferry house to drink a glass of wine, and being soe in company, there happened a

The difficulty being laid before Governor Hunter, as soon as possible after his arrival, occasioned the following kindly and prudent communication from him to the Justices of Kings County:

"New York 15th Septr 1710.

"GENTLEMEN

"The Controversy between Mr ffreeman and Mr. Antonides concerning the Churches in your County looking now with a fairer aspect towards a Reconciliation than hitherto they have; to the end that nothing may be done to impede so good a work, I desire you to permit M^r ffreeman and Mr Antonides to preach to-morrow in the Respective Churches wherein in Course it is their Turn to preach and that no molestation be given to either of them therein, having good hopes that before the next Sunday everything will be so disposed that this unhappy dispute will be accommodated to the Satisfaction of both those Gentlemen, and to the generall approbation of all their Congregations, whereby their present devisions may be healed, and the disagreing partys united into one mind. And that no misinterpretations may be made hereof on either hand, I desire you to let each party and their respective Congregations know that I am so farr from determining any one point in dispute, that the Right of either of them is as entirely reserved to them as it was before and that after to-morrow no further use be made hereof.

---

dispute between Coll. Beeckman and myself, about his particular order that he lately made to Mr ffreeman, when he was President of the Councill, without the consent of the Councill: Coll. Beeckman stood to affirm there, before most of the Justices of Kings County, that said order that he made then to Mr. ffreeman as President only, was still in force, and that Mr ffreeman should preach at Broockland next Sunday according to that order: whereupon I said it was not in fforce, but void and of noe effect, and he had not in this County any more power now than I had, being equall in commission with him in the general commission of the peace and one of the quorum as well as he; upon which he gave me affronting words, giving me the lie and calling me pittifull fellow, dog, rogue, rascall, &c., which caused me, being overcome with passion, to tell him that I had a good mind to knock him off his horse, we being both at that time getting upon our horses to goe home, but that I would not goe, I would fight him at any time with a sword. I could wish that these last words had been kept in, and I am troubled that I was soe overcome with passion and inflamed with wine. The works of these Dutch ministers is the occasion of all our quarrels. And this is the truth of the matter, there were no blows offered, nor noe more done. Mr ffreeman has preached at Broockland yesterday accordingly, and the Church doore was broke open, by whom is not yet knowne. Soe I beg your pardon ffor this trouble, crave your favour in this matter, and shall always remaine,

"Sir, your ffaithful and humble servant,

"(June, 1710.) "H. FILKIN."

"I desire you to tell Mr Antonides and Mr ffreeman that I would speak with them here on Monday next.

"I am sincerely, Gentlemen,

"Your very humble Serv^{r}

"Ro. Hunter."[1]

The "good hopes" of the worthy Governor were not destined to be realized—dissension still prevailed, and on the 27th of November his Excellency desired the members of the Council to favor him with their opinions as to what should be done in the case. The members of the Council, with but one dissenting voice, advised that "the order made in Council in this matter on the 18th of April last, be confirmed, whereby Mr. Antonides was to be protected in the free exercise of his ministerial functions in the towns of Flatbush, Flatlands, and Brookland," etc. On the 30th of April, 1711, in consequence of a complaint that Domine Freeman had "lately preached in the churches of Kings County to which Mr. Antonides is called, and that many violent proceedings are taken, to the great disturbance of the public peace of the said churches and county;" and, furthermore, that the town of Flatbush had lately elected Church-Masters, "after a new and unprecedented manner," etc., a Council order was issued, ordering "that Mr. Freeman does not *presume* to preach in any of the churches to which Mr. Antonides is called, and that none of the said Church-Masters so newly elected presume to intermeddle in the affairs of the said church, or in any lands, houses, or other effects, thereto belonging."[2]

The next item recorded, is an application of Antonides and his Consistory for a charter, as follows:

"To his Excellency Robert Hunter Esqr Captn Gen^{ll} & Govr in Chief in in and over her Maties Province of New York &c &c &c.

"The humble Peticon of Vincentius Antonides Minister of the Reformed Protestant Dutch Churches of Flatbush Brookland & flatlands in Kings County on the Island of Nassau in the Province of New York Joannes Cornel Rynier Aarsen, & Henry Filkin Elders of the said Church at Flatbush Benjamin Hegeman Cornelis Cornel & Jan Bennet Deacons thereof—Michiel Hansen Jan Dorlant & Cornelis Van Duyn Elders of

[1] Doc. Hist. N. Y., iii. 175.

[2] Ibid., iii. 177.

the said Church at Brookland Nicolas Van Dyk Isaak Remse & Jan Rapalie Deacons thereof, Jan alberts ter heunen Lucas Stevense H Gerrit Stoothof Elders of the said Church in Flatlands, Harman Hooglant Alexander Simson & Jan Amerman Deacons of the same.

"Most Humbly Sheweth,

"That for many years last past at the charge of sundry of the Inhabitants of the said Towns & of other Pious persons there hath been erected in each of the said Towns a Church for the Publicq worship of Almighty God and other Divine Service to be celebrated therein after the manner of the Dutch nationall Churches of the Provinces of the United Netherlands acording to their Profession and Discipline Established by the nationall Synod of Dort held in the year 1618 & 1619 which said three Churches since the settlement have always Joyned together in the calling & paying of one Minister for them all.

"And whereas the said Minister Elders & Deacons respectively for the use of their said churches by virtue of sundry mean conveyances in the Law are possessed of sundry parcells of Lands & Tenements respectively for every particular Church aforesaid That is to say for the Church of Flatbush two Lotts of land situate lying and being in the said Town on the north side of Col. Gerardus Beekman Jacob Hendrickse & Roelof van Kerck on the south of the lane that leads to Gouwanes conteining one hundred & eighteen acres as allso two Lotts of meadow the (whole) being in the bounds of the said Town over the fresh creek broad 7 Rodd laid out by N° 19 and the other over the Second Creek broad 12 Rod N° 15 both stretching from the woods to the Sea Allso oneother Lot of Land in the said Town to the north of Peter Stryker and to the South of the highway that Leads to the New Lotts Containing fourty eight acres Allso one other Lot to the South of Peter Stryker & matty Luyster and to the North of the Lane that leads to the New Lotts conteining fourty eight acres Allso two Lotts of meadow the one over the fresh creek broad 7 Rodd N° 20 and the other over the Second creek broad 13 Rodd N° 11 Allso one Lot of Land lying amongst the new Lotts of the said Towns to the west side of Rem Remsen to the East of Elsie Snediker conteining thirty four acres as *Allso* the Church and ministers Dwelling howse in the said Town together with the orchard gardens and yard adjoyning conteining ten acres, Allso one howse & Lot of ground in the said Town called the School howse conteining Eight acres, together with the Lands and meadows in right thereof laid out for the use of the said Church out of the comons of the said Town.

"And for the Church of Brookland one Lot of Land in the said Town in breadth Eight Rodd Long thirteen Rodd & a half bounden on the South West by the highway on the north west by Jacobus Beavois and on the south east by Charles Beavois ALLSO one church yard elleaven Rodd square bounded on the north east by the highway on the south east by a Small Lane to the South West by Joris Hanssen & to the north west by Albertie Barents and the Church in the said Town Standing in the middle of the highway.

"And for the Church of Flatland, One Lot of Land at a place called Amesfoorts Neck containing Twenty Acres laid out by N° 10 And ALLSO the Church in s[d] Town & one howse called the School howse with the Land adjoyning Containing two acres or thereabouts therefore for the advanceing of Piety & Religion and that the said Lands may be the better administered and the Revenue thereof duly applyed for the Maintenance of the minister or ministers for the time being & other Pious Charitable uses—

"They do most humbly Pray that the said Minister Elders & Deacons & their Successors may be by her Majesties Grant or Charter under the Seal of this Province Made One body Politick and Corporate in the same, and in like manner and as near as may be to the Charter heretofore granted to the Minister Elders & Deacons of the Reformed Protestant Dutch Church of the City of New York, save only that the severall Lands & Tenemens aforesaid now in their Possession be therein reserved to the use of Each respective Church aforesaid paying to her Matie her heirs and successors the Proporcon of the Quitrents they now pay in each respective Town aforesaid

"And yor Petion[rs] as in Duty bound shall ever Pray &c

"LUYCAS STEUENS,	"V. ANTONIDES,
"GERRIT STOOTHOF,	"REYNIER AERTSÈN,
"CLAES VAN DYCK,	"JOHANNES CORNELL,
"HERMANUS HOOGLANDT,	"HEN: FFILKIN,
"JAN AMEARMAN,	"ALEXANDER SIMPSON (mark),
"MIGGUEL HANSEN,	"BENJAMIN HEGEMAN,
"JOHN DORLAND (mark),	"CORNELIS CORNEL,
"CORNELIS VAN DUYN,	"Dit is het IB eigen gestelt handt merk van
"ISAACK REMSEN,	
"JAN RAPALE,	"JAN BENNIT.

"Kings County the 1 Aug[st] 1711.

"Read in Council 8 Aug 1711. & referred."

Contrary to the order of April 18th, 1710, and the subsequent confirmatory orders, Mr. Freeman once more intruded his ministrations upon the congregation at Flatbush, in September, 1713;[1] but this is the last recorded belligerent act of the controversy which had now agitated the churches of Kings County for upwards of thirteen years, and vexed the souls of four royal governors and their councils. Near the close of the year 1714 the long contest was happily terminated by a convention of delegates from the several congregations, who mutually agreed to lay aside their ancient differences, and acknowledge Messrs. Freeman and Antonides as their ministers.[2] Breuckelen, Bushwick, Flatbush, Flatlands, New Utrecht, and even Jamaica, were all included within the charge, and both the domines resided at Flatbush, in the pleasant and harmonious discharge of their duties. They were esteemed as men of respectable talents and acquirements.

During their ministry the Reformed Dutch Churches of New Netherlands were sadly agitated by the question concerning the organization of a *Cœtus*, or assembly of ministers and elders, in this country, subordinate to the Classis of Amsterdam.[3]

---

[1] Strong's Hist. Flatbush, p. 46.

[2] This Convention agreed upon the proportion of salary to be raised by the different churches for the support of the ministers, and the times and places of preaching and of communion. It was arranged that one minister should preach on one Sabbath in Bushwick, and the other in New Utrecht; the next Sabbath, one in Brooklyn, and the other in Flatlands; on the third Sabbath, one in Flatbush, the other in Jamaica; and so on, in regular rotation. As to communions, Bushwick, Brooklyn, and Flatbush were to commune together; Flatlands, Gravesend, and New Utrecht, together; and the congregations of Queens County should form another communion.

[3] The movement towards the formation of a *Cœtus* was initiated in 1737, by a convention of ministers at New York, at which Domine Freeman attended on behalf of the Dutch churches of Long Island. A plan was formed, and having been generally adopted by the churches, was ratified by a second convention, held in April, 1738, at which Freeman again appeared as delegate. The approval of the Classis of Amsterdam did not, however, reach this country until 1746, being brought over by Rev. Mr. Van Sinderen · and the first meeting of the new *Cœtus* was held in September, 1747, at the city of New York, being the first judicial organization, higher than a Consistory, established in the American Dutch Church. The *Cœtus* plan, however, met with opposition from several churches and ministers, and gave rise to differences which seriously agitated the Reformed Dutch denomination for many years thereafter. The contest related principally to the question of the right of ordination, and the exercise of church authority: the "*Cœtus party*" claiming that, in view of the increase of churches in this country, and the inconvenience of importing all their ministers from Holland, it would be better to have a regular organization into classes and synods, similar in all respects

FREEMAN was born at Gilhius, Holland; received a call to Schenectady, to which charge he was ordained by the Classis of Linge, March 16, 1700. He first officiated at Schenectady, July 28th of that year, learned the Mohawk language, and made many Indian converts. On the 25th of August, 1705, he married Magretia Van Schaick of New York, who died January 18th, 1738, leaving him a handsome fortune. In 1721 he published a volume of sermons in Dutch, entitled "The Balances of God's Grace," which was printed in Amsterdam, and another entitled "De Spiegel der Selfkennis" (or Mirror of Self-knowledge), being a collection, in the Dutch language, of ancient moral and philosophical maxims, which was subsequently translated by General Jeremiah Johnson, and which is described as displaying a great amount of learning and research. In 1735 he purchased seven acres of land at Flatbush, and built a house, which is still standing, although altered; and died in the year 1741. His only child, Anna Margaretta, mar-

---

to those of the mother country; and the "*Conferentie party*," as they were called, that all ministers should be ordained by, or under the authority of, the Classis at Amsterdam. This unhappy controversy continued until 1772; and so alienated and embittered were the opposing parties, that many would not worship together with, or even speak to, those of the other party. "Sometimes" (says Strong, Hist. Flatbush) "they would not turn out when they met on the road. On one occasion, it is said that two of these redoubtable opponents, belonging to Flatbush, meeting in their wagons, and both refusing to give the road, they each deliberately took out their pipes and began to smoke! How long they continued at this very pacific employment is not stated, nor is it said whether the difficulty between them was lost sight of by the cloud of smoke obscuring their vision, or whether their pipes were ever turned into the calumet of peace."

ried her cousin, David Clarkson, a son of the Secretary of the Province, and left numerous descendants.

Freeman's successor, in 1742, was the Rev. JOHANNES ARONDEUS, from Rotterdam, who seems to have possessed a contumacious spirit, and to have led an irregular life. He quarrelled with his new colleague, Van Sinderen, very soon after the latter's arrival; and, in May, 1747, he went off secretly, as was alleged, to the Raritan, where he was installed as minister; returning, however, July 31, 1748, to Kings County, where he resumed his functions, especially at Brookland and New Utrecht. His outraged parishioners brought charges against him (September 27, 1748) before the *Cœtus*. These he refused to notice; whereupon he was declared to be an unlawful minister of Kings County, but replied that he should continue to perform service there. On appeal to the Classis of Amsterdam (January 12, 1751), the action of the *Cœtus* was confirmed, and the latter, on 16th April, 1752, passed sentence upon Arondeus—(1), that his Consistory was unlawful; (2), that he should not administer the word of sacraments; and (3), that the church property should be restored to Van Sinderen. Their action was, however, totally disregarded by Arondeus. Proposals of peace for Long Island were offered (December 5, 1752) by the Classis of Amsterdam. On the 20th of September, 1753, the *Cœtus* confirmed anew their former sentence, averring, in reply to his appeals, that (1), he misbehaved to his servant-maid; (2), that he was a drunkard; and (3), that he kept alive the flames of discord. The last time he baptized a child, in Queen's County, was at Jamaica, in April, 1754. He probably remained on the island, leading the same dissolute life, for some time; for, in October, 1772, the Synod cautioned the people against "one Johannes Arondeus, who claims to be a minister of the Church, but has no ecclesiastical attestation."

FAC-SIMILE OF AUTOGRAPH OF REV. JOHANNES ARONDEUS.

Mr. ANTONIDES died in 1744. In a New York paper of that date we find his death thus noticed: "On the 18th of July, 1744, died at his house at Flatbush, the Rev. Mr. VINCENTIUS ANTONIDES, in the 74th year of his age. He was a gentleman of extensive learning; of an easy, condescending behavior and conversation, and of a regular, exemplary piety, endeavoring to practise, himself, what he preached to others; was kind, benevolent, and charitable to all, according to his abilities; meek, humble, patriotic, and resigned under all afflictions, losses, calamities, and misfortunes which befell him in his own person and family, which were not a few; and after a lingering disease, full of hopes of a blessed immortality, departed this life, to the great and irreparable loss of his relations and friends, and to the great grief of his congregation and friends." He was succeeded by the Rev. ULPIANUS VAN SINDEREN,[1] a native of Holland, in the year 1746. He began to preach at Flatbush, April 19, 1747. In October of the following year he married (his first wife) Cornelia Schenck, who was subsequently killed by being thrown out of a wagon.

FAC-SIMILE OF AUTOGRAPH OF REV. VINCENTIUS ANTONIDES.

Upon the deposition from the ministerial office of the Rev. Mr. Arondeus, his place was filled by the Rev. ANTONIUS CURTENIUS,[2] from Hackensack, N. J., where he had preached since 1730, and was installed as Van Sinderin's colleague, May 2, 1755. He died in October, 1756, at the age of fifty-eight years. In a newspaper of the day we find the following notice of this gentleman: "On Tuesday, the 19th ultimo, the Reverend Mr. ANTHONY CURTENIUS departed this transitory life, at Flat-Bush, Long Island, in the 59th Year of his Age, after an Illness of about four Weeks, being Pastor of the five Dutch Reformed Churches in Kings County, on Long Island. He was a Gentleman regularly educated, and remarkable for his indefatigable Diligence in the Ministration of his Function. His Actions in all the Affairs of Life have ever been accompanied with the strictest Rules of Justice; so that none could with more

---

[1] His great-grandson, Adriaen Van Sinderen, a prominent and highly respected citizen of Brooklyn, was the founder and first president of the Long Island Bible Society.

[2] So named from Curten, a town of Holland.

Propriety claim the Title of a Preacher and a sincere Christian, which not only his Morals manifested, but his Glorious Resolutions to launch into endless Eternity, saying with *St. Paul, O Death! where is thy Sting? O Grave! where is thy Victory?* His Remains were decently interred on Thursday following, in the Church of the above-named place. His Death is universally lamented by his Relations, and all those that knew him, particularly his Congregation, who are highly sensible of the Loss of so inestimable a Shepard, whose every Action displayed the Christian."[1]

His place was supplied by the Rev. JOHANNES CASPARUS RUBEL, a native of Hesse Cassel, in Germany, who had been settled at Red Hook, Dutchess County, from 1755 to August, 1757, when he was called to be colleague pastor with Domine Van Sinderen, over the churches of Kings County. He was educated in Germany, and came to this country (1751), with others of the German Reformed Church, under the auspices of the Classis of Amsterdam, from which body he received an annual salary of £15, while settled over the German Church at Philadelphia. Even then he was so insubordinate to his superiors, that the German *Cœtus* styled him "the rebellious Rubel," and voted, April 9, 1755, that he ought to withdraw from his charge. He, at first, desired to avail himself of the six months' notice; but finally gave his farewell discourse, April, 1755, left Pennsylvania, and settled at Rhinebeck. He was naturalized on the 23d of December, 1765; and in June, 1769, styled himself "Ecclesiastes in Kings County and in the Manor of Cortland;" and in August, 1770, "Minister of Clarkstown"—probably on the strength of his having occasionally filled a pulpit there.

Both of these gentlemen continued in the work of the ministry until after the close of the Revolutionary war. In politics they differed extremely, Mr. Van Sinderen being a firm Whig, while Mr. Rubel was as decided a loyalist.[2] In Colonel Graydon's Memoirs we find the following brief but spirited picture of the two pastors:

"The principal person in a Low Dutch village appears to be the

[1] His funeral eulogy was printed, in Dutch, at New York, by H. Goelet; price, three coppers.

[2] On a fast-day appointed by the Provincial Congress, it is said that he took occasion to preach, at Flatbush, from the text, "Honor the king;" and, among other things, remarked that "people could do as well without a head as without a king." (Strong's

Domine or minister, and Flatbush, at this time, revered her domine, Rubel, a rotund, jolly-looking man, a follower of Luther, and a Tory.[1] . . . . At Flatlands there was also a domine, Van Zinder(en), a disciple of Calvin, and a Whig. He was, in person and principle, a perfect contrast to Mr. Rubel, being a lean and shrivelled little man, with a triangular sharp-pointed hat, and silver locks which 'streamed like a meteor flowing to the troubled air,' as he whisked along with great velocity in his chaise through Flatbush. He was distinguished by a species of pulpit eloquence which might be truly said to 'bring matters home to men's business and bosoms.' Mr. Bache assured me that, in once descanting on the wily arts of the devil, he likened him to my landlord, 'sneaking and skulking about to get a shot at a flock of snipes,' in shooting of which, it seems, Jacob was eminently skilful."[2]

PORTRAIT OF REV. ULPIANUS VAN SINDEREN.

In the minutes of the Particular Synod at New York, May 14, 1784, we find a complaint from the Consistory of Flatbush and the other churches of Kings County, concerning the unchristian conduct of both of their ministers, Van Sinderen and Rubel, and requesting to be released from them; one (Van Sinderen) being useless from advanced age, and the other (Rubel) being of notoriously bad hab-

Hist. Flatbush, 93.) When the famous privateer boatsman, Captain Marriner, made a descent on Flatbush and captured several noted British officers, Domine Rubel gave the alarm by ringing the church bell. (See Onderdonk, Kings County, section 845, p. 179.)

1 See Strong's Flatbush for particulars.

2 See Strong's Flatbush, which relates that he was "too much in the habit of introducing the occurrences of the week previous in his sermons on the Sabbath, and often would allude to very trifling circumstances. On one occasion, a good elder, who had borne with the Domine in this particular till his patience was exhausted, very injudiciously, under the excitement of his feelings, rose in his seat during divine service, and interrupted Mr. Van Sinderen by saying that they had called him to preach the gospel, and not to detail to them such matters. The Domine, indignant at being stopped in his discourse, leaned over the pulpit and replied: 'You, Philip Nagle, if you can preach the gospel better than I can, come up here and try!'"

its. Several witnesses testified to the unchristian and intemperate language used by Rubel, both in and out of the pulpit, in regard to Americans who opposed the King of Great Britain, calling them "Satan's soldiers," and saying "that they were accursed, and many were already in hell, and those who were not dead would go there, and that he could prove it by the Bible," etc. Also, that he quarrelled frequently with his wife, towards whom he not unfrequently used personal violence; that he drank freely, and led a bad life, keeping much company with the Hessian officers quartered in the town of Flatbush, who were great swearers and drunkards. All the witnesses, however, agreed that they had nothing against Van Sinderen except his age, and that the breach between him and Rubel had gone so far that the old domine could not control his temper whenever he met the latter. The matter was referred to the General Synod, before whom Rubel was cited to appear, but replied only by an angry letter. He was, therefore, deposed in May, 1784. In May, 1788, he appeared before the Synod, desiring to be reinstated, but evincing no spirit of contrition. He continued to reside at Flatbush, devoting his time to the preparation of quack medicines, and in his advertisements styles himself "Minister of the Gospel and Chymicus."[1] In 1788 he published a pamphlet, in Dutch and English, showing, as he pretended, how he had been defrauded of his living by a wicked man in New York. He had a daughter, who was seduced by a Hessian officer during the war; and the old man's unhappy life ended in 1797, his solitary tombstone still existing in the Flatbush churchyard.[2]

Mr. Van Sinderen, at the request of the Consistory, resigned his pastoral charge in June, 1784, although he received a stated salary until his death, at Flatlands, on 23d of July, 1796, in his

---

[1] "March 28, 1778. It has pleased Almighty God to give me the wisdom to find out the *Golden Mother Tincture*, and such a *Universal Pill* as will cure most diseases. I have studied European physicians in four different languages. I don't take much money, as I want no more than a small living, whereto God will give his blessing.—JOHANNES CASPARUS RUBEL, Minister of the Gospel and Chymicus."

[2] "*Tot gedachtenis van Joh's. Casp's Rubel. V. D. M.—Geboren den 6de March, O. S.,* 1719.—*Overleden den 19de Maii,* 1797." (TRANSLATION): To the memory of John Caspar Rubel, minister of God's word. Born, March 6th, 1719, O. S. Died, May 19th, 1797.

89th year. He was a learned but eccentric man, and for this reason, perhaps, was sometimes considered "deficient in sound judgment."[1]

With Messrs. Van Sinderen and Rubel, the European Dutch ministry in Kings County ceased.[2]

In 1785, the Rev. MARTINUS SCHOONMAKER, who was then officiating at Harlem and Gravesend, accepted a call to take charge of the collegiate churches of the county, to which the church at Gravesend was then added; and, on the 28th of October, 1787, the Rev. PETER LOWE was ordained at New Utrecht as his colleague. The former officiated in the Dutch language until his death, in 1824; and the latter, in the English tongue. In their regular rotation through the county, four churches would be closed, and two open, for divine worship on the Sabbath. Such, however, is the peculiar position of the county, and the easy communication between the several towns, that, with the exception of Bushwick and Gravesend, each of the others could quite conveniently follow the ministers, who consequently preached to full and crowded houses.

The Rev. Martinus Schoonmaker, second son of Joachim and Lydia Schoonmaker, was born at Rochester, Ulster County, N. Y., March 1, 1737; commenced his classical studies with Domine Goetchius, of Schraalenburgh, N. J., 1753; and his theological, with the Rev. Mr. Marenus, of Aquackanock, in 1759. On the 27th of June, 1761, he married Mary (daughter of Stephen and Ann) Basset, of that place; and was licensed to preach in 1763, first accepting a call from the congregations of Harlem and Gravesend. In 1781, he accepted a call from the particular churches of Gravesend, Success, and Wolver Hollow, which charge he retained until

---

[1] The following is the inscription on his gravestone at Flatbush: "*Hier leyt het Liechaem van den Wel-Erwaede Heer Ulpianus Van Sinderen, in zyn leeven Predicant in Kings County. Overleeden den* 23 *July*, 1796, *oud Zynde* 88 *Jaeren* 7 *Maanden en* 12 *daegen*." (TRANSLATION): Here lies the body of the very worthy Mr. Ulpianus Van Sinderen, in his lifetime preacher in Kings County. Died, July 23, 1796, aged 88 years 7 months and 12 days.

[2] During the pastorship of Rubel and Van Sinderen, "the seats in churches were all numbered in the pews or ranges. Men and women sat separately, and it rarely happened that two persons of the same family sat together. In several churches women sat in their own chairs, in the ranges of chairs. Every church had a free pew for justices and judges."

1784, when he was elected to the pastorate of the six collegiate churches of Kings County, at a salary of £150 per annum. He fixed his residence at Flatbush, where he spent the remainder of his life in the faithful discharge of his labors as a minister of God. "His labors in the ministry," says his successor, "for sixty-one years, were arduous, yet was he never known to faint in his Master's cause; and few men have gone to the grave with a character more unblemished, or one more universally respected and beloved."

Mr. Schoonmaker left six sons and five daughters, nine of whom arrived to mature age, and seven of them survived their father. He had, at the time of his death, fifty-nine grandchildren and twenty-one great-grandchildren. His wife died in 1819, aged eighty years.

For the following very interesting sketch of Domine Schoonmaker, and some of the customs and manners of the people during his pastorate, we are indebted to an article in the Christian Intelligencer of October 23, 1858, by the Rev. Peter Van Pelt:

"Domine Schoonmaker resided at Flatbush, central and convenient for his other churches. He was a man of reserved and retiring habits; more so, perhaps, from the circumstance that it was exceedingly difficult for him to hold even a common conversation without mangling most horribly the English language. Fluent and ready in the language in which he was educated, he displayed, by his manner and gestures, all the dignity and sincerity applicable to his position and functions. Courteous and polite, he was a relic of the old school, and universally respected. Indeed, it may be questioned whether the venerable old minister had a solitary enemy. An anecdote has been related, and many years ago was in common circulation, which some may consider a slander upon his abilities and acquirements. I would rather regard it as an innocent and harmless witticism of some wag, and probably one of his best friends. Having celebrated a marriage, at the close of the ceremony, for the benefit of the spectators, he attempted to terminate it in English with the sentence, 'I pronounce you man and wife, and one flesh; whom God hath joined together, let no man put asunder.

His English failed him; yet conscious of perfect rectitude, and the propriety of a shorter translation, with much solemnity and emphasis, and an appropriate *congee*, he exclaimed, '*I pronounce you two to be one beef!*'

"It was in 1819 that I last heard, or recollect to have seen, the venerable old domine. It was at the funeral of one of his old friends and associates. A custom had very generally prevailed, which, though then very rarely observed, yet in this instance was literally adhered to. The deceased had, many years before, provided and laid away the materials for his own coffin. This one was of the best seasoned and smoothest boards, and beautifully grained. Other customs and ceremonies then existed, now almost forgotten. As I entered the room, I observed the coffin elevated on a table in one corner. The Domine, abstracted and grave, was seated at the upper end; and around, in solemn silence, the venerable and hoary-headed friends of the deceased. All was still and serious. A simple recognition, or a half-audible inquiry, as one after another arrived, was all that passed. Directly, the sexton, followed by a servant, made his appearance, with glasses and decanters. *Wine* was handed to each. Some declined; others drank a solitary glass. This ended, and again the sexton presented himself, with *pipes and tobacco.* The Domine smoked his pipe, and a few followed his example. The custom has become obsolete, and it is well that it has. When the whiffs of smoke had ceased to curl around the head of the Domine, he arose with evident feeling, and in a quiet, subdued tone, made a short but apparently impressive address. I judged solely by his appearance and manner; for although boasting a Holland descent, it was to me 'speaking in an unknown tongue.' A short prayer concluded the service; and then the sexton taking the lead, was followed by the Domine, the doctor, and the pall-bearers, with white scarfs and black gloves. The corpse and a long procession of friends and neighbors proceeded to the churchyard, where all that was mortal was committed to the earth, till the last trump shall sound and the grave shall give up the dead. No bustle, no confusion, no noise nor indecent haste, attended that funeral."

Domine Schoonmaker died on the 20th of May, 1824, aged eighty-seven years, and with him ceased the regular public and official use of the Dutch language in all the pulpits of the Dutch Reformed churches.[1]

The Rev. PETER LOWE was born April 30th, 1764, at Esopus (now Kingston), N. Y., where he received his academic education. He pursued his theological studies with Rev. Dr. Livingston, of New York; and, soon after his licensure, received several calls, finally giving the preference to that from the six churches of Kings County. In this relation he faithfully discharged the functions of the holy ministry for twenty-one years; until, the collegiate connection between the six churches being dissolved, by mutual consent, for the sake of a more frequent supply of the word and ordinances, he accepted the call from Flatbush and Flatlands, where he continued to labor more than nine years, with increasing usefulness, until his death, from cancer, in June, 1818, and in the fifty-fifth year of his age. He was frank, generous and affectionate in disposition; cheerful in his religion, modest and peaceful in temper, agreeable in conversation; sound and solid in his ministerial advice and public preaching. He was industrious, systematic, and active in habit, and had learned the art of book-binding, which he turned to good account in collecting and binding up all the church records which he could find. He built two dwellings, in succession, at Flatbush, and ornamented the grounds with shrubbery, trees, and flowers, of which he was extremely fond. His garden was his favorite place of meditation, from which he was wont to go to his lecture.

REV. PETER LOWE.

The old Brooklyn church was a large, square edifice, with solid and very thick walls, plastered and whitewashed on every side up

[1] "In 1792, it was resolved that divine service, which had heretofore been maintained in the Dutch language, should be thereafter performed in *English*, in the afternoon, whenever Mr. Lowe should preach at Brooklyn, Flatbush, and New Utrecht. But Mr. Schoonmaker continued to preach in Dutch to the time of his death, having never attempted to preach in English but once (in 1788)."—Prime, 328.

THE BROOKLYN CHURCH, AND DUFFIELD HOUSE, 1776.

(Fulton Avenue, between Bridge and Lawrence Streets.)

Page 193.

to the eaves; the roof, as usual, ascending to a peak in the centre, capped with an open belfry, in which hung a small, sharp-toned bell, brought from Holland shortly after its erection.[1] Its interior was plain, dark, and very gloomy; so that, in summer, one could not see to read in it after four o'clock in the afternoon, by reason of its small windows. These were six or eight feet above the floor, and filled with stained-glass lights from Holland, representing vines loaded with flowers.[2] This church, the second which had occupied the same site, was built in 1766, in the middle of the road leading from the Ferry into the country, which road is now known as Fulton avenue, and immediately opposite to a burying-ground yet remaining on the west side of that avenue and between Bridge and Lawrence streets.[3] It was unprotected by fence or enclosure. The road was spacious, and a carriage and wagon-track passed around each end, forming an oblong circle, remitting at either end.[4]

The old town, it will be remembered, comprised, at this time, several divisions or settlements, each possessing local names which yet cling to them, in spite of the streets, squares, and avenues of the new city of Brooklyn—*Gowanus, Red Hook, Bedford, Cripplebush, Wallabout*—and for all these the old church occupied a very central position.

"The Collegiate Domines," says Mr. Van Pelt, "had many pious people and firm friends in Brooklyn. Almost every house was as open to them as their own homes, and one in particular, opposite the church, was especially designated 'The Domine's House.' This was convenient for rest between services on the Sabbath; for receiving applications for baptism, membership, etc; for meeting the Consistory, Church-Masters, and others; and for attending generally to official duties."

The collegiate connection between the Dutch churches of the county, so far as related to the service in English, was gradually given up after the commencement of the present century. The Rev. JOHN B. JOHNSON was called to Brooklyn in 1802; Dr. BASSETT to

[1] This bell was afterwards (1840) in the belfry of the district school-house in Middagh street, Third Ward of Brooklyn. See, also, page 143.

[2] Furman's MSS.

[3] *Ante*, p. 166.

[4] "And a miserable road it was, filled with mud-holes and large rocks."—Furman's MSS.

Bushwick, in 1811; and Mr. BEATTIE, in 1809, to New Utrecht: while Domine Schoonmaker remained at Flatbush, continuing the Dutch service alternately among the six towns; but on the day that he preached at Bushwick, Dr. Bassett supplied Gravesend, which place, as to amount of service, remained precisely the same.

The new pastor of the Brooklyn church, JOHN BARENT JOHNSON, was a native of this town, where he was born, March 3, 1769, his father, Barent Johnson, being a prosperous farmer, of Dutch descent, and his mother, Maria, the daughter of Captain John Guest, of New Brunswick, who commanded a vessel which sailed between New York and Antigua. Having lost both parents before his ninth year, he was brought up by a cousin, who was also his father's executor. In his seventeenth year, while at school in Flatbush, he became acquainted with the Rev. Dr. John H. Livingston, who was spending the summer there. Discovering in him more than ordinary talents, the Doctor encouraged him to undertake a course of liberal studies, offering him, at the same time, a residence in his own family and the superintendence of his education. The offer, thus kindly made, was gratefully accepted by young Johnson, who was shortly prepared to enter college. In 1788 he matriculated at Columbia College, and in the same year became a communicant in the Reformed Dutch Church. After his graduation he pursued a course of theological studies with his old friend, Dr. Livingston; was licensed by the Classis of New York, April 21, 1795; and preached his first sermon on the succeeding Sabbath, in that city, for the Rev. Dr. Kuypers. On the 5th of June, 1796, Mr. Johnson was ordained to the work of the ministry, and settled as colleague pastor with Mr. Bassett (who preached the ordination sermon) over the Reformed Protestant Dutch Church of Albany. In 1802 he was called to the Reformed Dutch Church of Schenectady, and also to that in Brooklyn. Deciding in favor of the latter, he preached his farewell sermon to the Albany church on the 26th of September, 1802, and on the 24th of the ensuing October was duly installed over his new charge at Brooklyn.[1] "Among other marked features of this sermon

[1] On this occasion the Rev. Dr. Linn presided, assisted by the Rev. Mr. Schoonmaker. In the afternoon Mr. Johnson preached from 2d Timothy, iv. 2.

—which was a very able, earnest, and eloquent discourse—is a fine tribute to the Heidelberg Catechism, and a plea for its faithful and regular exposition in our churches." His health, somewhat impaired before his removal from Albany, now began to fail rapidly; and the loss of his wife, in March, 1803, undoubtedly contributed to hasten his own death. He died at the house of his brother-in-law, Peter Rosevelt, Esq., in Newtown, August 29th, 1803, leaving three children, two of whom still survive in the ministry of the Episcopal Church—one at Jamaica, L. I., and another as a professor in the Episcopal Theological Seminary in New York.

From a sketch of Mr. Johnson, from the pen of Hon. Teunis Van Vechten, for Rev. Dr. Sprague's Annals of the American Pulpit, we learn that he was a man of unusually prepossessing personal appearance, and easy and graceful manners. "His countenance had an expression of great benignity, united with high intelligence. His manners were bland and courteous, and predisposed every one who saw him to be his friend; and his countenance and manners were a faithful index to his disposition. He was acknowledged, on all hands, to possess an uncommonly amiable and generous spirit. He had the reputation of an excellent pastor. He mingled freely, and to great acceptance, with all classes of people. He was particularly attentive to the young, and had the faculty of making himself exceedingly pleasant to them. This I know from personal experience.

"As a preacher he was undoubtedly one of the most popular in the Dutch Church at that day. Of his manner in the pulpit I retain a very distinct recollection. His voice was a melodious one, and though not of remarkable compass, yet loud enough to be heard with ease in a large church. His gesture was natural and effective, and sometimes he reached what I should think a high pitch of pulpit oratory."

At the death of General Washington, the Legislature of the State, then in session, requested of the Consistory the use of this church (the Albany church) for the celebration of appropriate funeral services, and invited Mr. Johnson to deliver the eulogy on that occasion. The service was accordingly held, February 22d, 1800, and, as might be supposed, was one of universal interest and solemnity. The church was hung with black, and crowded by a mourning people. The oration by Mr. Johnson was a masterly effort, and produced a great sensation. It was published by vote of both Houses; Hon. Stephen Van Rensselaer being then president of the Senate, and Hon. Dirck Ten Broeck, speaker of the House. Mr. Van Vechten says of it: "The exordium was spoken of at the time as a rare specimen of eloquence, and the whole performance was of a very high order. I speak with confidence concerning this, as it was published, and I have had an opportunity of reading it since I have been more competent to judge of its merits than I was when it was delivered." Mr. Van Vechten closes his sketch of Mr. Johnson in these words: "He left an excellent name behind him, and the few who still remember him cherish gratefully the recollections of both his gifts and his graces."[1]

---

[1] See Rev. Dr. E. P. Rogers' Hist. Discourse on the Reformed Protestant Dutch Church of Albany, 1858.

CHAPTER VII.

CIVIL HISTORY OF BROOKLAND.

1675—1775.

THE only excitement which occurred in Breuckelen, during the year 1675, was a painful apprehension, shared by its inhabitants in common with those of neighboring towns, that they might become involved in the Indian outbreak known as "King Philip's War," which it was feared would extend to the Long Island tribes. Proper measures being taken, however, by the provincial government, and in the several towns, fear was somewhat allayed, and the speedy defeat which overtook that notorious chieftain, restored tranquillity to the public mind.

Breuckelen had, at this time, attained the leading position among the Kings County towns, in respect of population and wealth, as evidenced by the "Assessment Rolls of the 5 Dutch towns up to August 19, 1675," which afford the following total valuation at a rate of one stiver on the pound :[1]

Towns.	No. of Persons Assessed.	£	*s.*	*Guil.*	*Stiv.*	Equal to £	*s.*	*d.*
Boswyck	36	3,174	10	158	148	13	4	6
Breuckelen	60	5,204	00	260	4	21	13	8
Middlewout	54	5,079	10	253	19–8	21	3	4
Amersfoort	35	4,008	10	200	8–8	16	14	0
New Utrecht	29	2,852	10	142	12–8	11	17	8
Total		20,319	10	1,015	19	84	13	2

Also, when, in the course of the same year, it became necessary to build a new dock at New York, the Governor and Council required the Kings and Queens County towns to furnish timber for the undertaking, and Breuckelen's tribute was the largest,[1] that of Flatbush being the next in amount.[2]

---

[1] N. Y. Col. MSS., xxiv. 136; and N. Y. Doc. Hist., iv. 141–161.
[2] Council Minutes, iii. 171.

Breuckelyn's importance was further increased by its appointment as a *market town.* The record concerning this is as follows:

"Upon a proposall of having a ffayre or markett in or neare this Citty (New York); It is ordered, that after this season, there shall yearely be kept a ffayre and markett at Breucklyn, near the fferry, for all graine, cattle, or other produce of the country; to bee held the first Monday, Tuesday and Wednesday in November, and in the City of New Yorke the thursday, ffriday, and Saturday following."[1]

A pleasant glimpse of the neighborly feeling existing between the people of the neighboring towns, and of the comparative simplicity of the times, is afforded by the following:

"A recommendation on the behalfe of Capt. Jacques Corteleau, and the inhabitants of New Utrecht, to the Constables and Overseers of Bruyckline—

"Whereas, Capt. Jacques Corteleau, having (through misfortune by ffire) sustained great losses; and being intended speedily to build him another House, towards the effecting of which divers good and Charitable People (his Neighbors round about) have already contributed their Assistance, That the same may be the Sooner accomplished, for his more comfortable accomodation, I do hereby recommend to you, that you encourage the People of yor Towne, to assist him with one Daye's worke, towards perfecting the said Building, this or the next weeke, as he shall direct; and that you likewise assist his Neighbo^rs^, in the Neighboring Towne of New Utrecht, in their present distresse if requested thereunto by them, in the which you will do a good and Charitable worke: Given under my hand in New Yorke, the 1st day of May, 1675. "E. ANDROS.[2]

"To the Constables & Overseers of Breucklyn."

An assessment on the town of Breuckelen, made up to September, 1676, was levied on 57 persons, who represented 70 polls, 1,232 acres of land, 85 horses, 292 cows, 35 hogs, 38 oxen, and 25 sheep.[3]

---

[1] Ext. from orders made at Court of Gen'l Assizes, beginning 6th and ending 13th Oct., 1675 (Valentine's Manual, 1845, p. 311). By another clause in this order, all persons and goods going to or coming from this fair, were exempted from arrest for debt. This order was to remain in force for three years from the 24th of March ensuing.

[2] Warrants, Orders, and Passes, iii. 90.

[3] See Appendix No. 7.

In May, 1682, Governor Andros, whose arbitrary character and government had rendered him unpopular in the province, left the country, and was succeeded, on the 25th of August, 1683, by Col. Thomas Dongan. The province of New York had for many years suffered from many grievances, due to the unlimited authority which was vested in its chief magistrate; and as early as 1681, the popular feeling on the subject found expression in a petition for redress to the Duke of York. His Royal Highness prudently assented, and Gov. Dongan brought with him special instructions to institute a General Assembly, similar to that of the New England colonies. This first Colonial Legislature, composed of the Governor, Council, and seventeen members, chosen by the people, held its first session from October 17th to Nov. 3d, 1683. It straightway adopted a "charter of liberties," providing that the supreme authority, under the duke, should be vested in the Governor, Council, and a legislature elected by the people, according to the laws of England, which should convene, at least, triennially. It furthermore established the right of trial by jury of twelve, and interdicted the molestation or prosecution of any person for any difference of opinion or action concerning religious affairs, so long as they professed a faith in God by Jesus Christ, and did not actually disturb the peace. Other important changes in the organization of the province were also made. The ridings were abolished and rearranged into counties; Breuckelen, Boswyck, Amersfoort, Flatbush, New Utrecht, and Gravesend being comprised in the new County of Kings, while Newtown was transferred to Queens County. In each of the twelve counties into which the province was divided, the Court of Sessions was to meet twice a year, and the Court of Oyer and Terminer annually. In each town, a *Commissioners'* Court was established, which was to be held on the first Wednesday in every month, for the hearing of small causes, and actions for debt and trespass, not exceeding 40*s*. Another change in the form of town government was the establishment of assessors and supervisors, the latter having supervision of public affairs and town expenses.

In pursuance of royal instructions, and with the view of definitely fixing the amount of quit-rent, to be paid to the government by each of the towns, in acknowledgment for their lands, Gov. Dongan, on the 31st of March, 1684, issued an order to all the towns to bring in their patents and Indian deeds, for examination preparatory to the granting of new charters.[1] Breuckelen, together with Boswyck, complied with this order on the 16th of April following,[2] and desired some arrangement to be made concerning quit-rent. Owing, however, to the difficulties attendant upon the settlement of a dispute which had previously arisen between the towns of Newtown, Boswyck, and Breuckelen, concerning their bounds,[3] no immediate action could be taken in reference to the new patents and quit-rents of the three places. And it was not until May 3, 1686, that Breuckelen received from Gov. Dongan the following Patent:

"L. S. THOMAS DONGAN, *Lieutenant Governor and Vice Admiral of New York, and its dependencies under his Majesty James the Second, by the grace of God, of England, Scotland, France and Ireland, King, Defender of the Faith, &c.—Supreme lord and proprietor of the Colony and province of New York and its dependencies in America,* &c. To all to whom this shall come sendeth greeting, whereas the Honorable Richard Nicolls, Esq., formerly Governor of this province, did by his certain writing or patent under his hand and seal, bearing date the 18th day of October, Annoque Domini, one thousand six hundred and sixty seven, ratifie, confirm and grant unto Jan Everts, Jan Damen, Albert Cornelissen, Paulus Verbeeck, Michael Enyle (Hainelle), Thomas Lamberts, Teunis Gysberts Bogart, and Joris Jacobsen, as patentees for and on behalf of themselves and their associates, the freeholders and inhabitants of the town of Breucklen, their heirs, successors and assigns forever, a certain tract of land, together with the several parcels of land which then were or thereafter should be purchased or procured for and on behalf of the said town, whether from the native Indian proprietors, or others within the bounds and limitts therein sett forth and expressed, that is to say, the said town is bounded westward on the further side of the land of Mr. Paulus Verbeeck, from whence stretching southeast they go over the hills and so eastward along by the said hills to a southeast point, which takes in all the lotts behind the swamp, from which said lotts they run northwest to the River, and extend to the farm on the other side of the hills heretofore belonging to Hans Hansen,

[1] Council Minutes, v. 63. [2] Ibid., v. 71.

[3] N. Y. Col. MSS., xxxiii. 68, 233, xxxiv. 15, xxxv. 146, 152. For account of this dispute, see Riker's excellent history of Newtown.

over against Keak or Look-out, including within the said bounds and limitts all the lots and plantations, lying and being at the Gouwanes, Bedford, Wallabocht and the ferry, all which said parcels and tract of land and premises within the bounds and limitts aforementioned described, and all or any plantation or plantations thereupon, from henceforth are to be, appertain and belong to the said town of Breucklyn, Together with all harbor, havens, creeks, quarries, woodland, meadow ground, reed land or valley of all sorts, pastures, marshes, waters, rivers, lakes, fishing, hawking, hunting, fowling and all other profits, commodities, emoluments, and hereditaments to the said lands and premises within the bounds and limitts set forth, belonging, or in any wise appertaining, and with all to have freedom of commonage for range and feed of cattle and horses, into the woods with the rest of their neighbors, as also one third part of a certain neck of meadow ground or valley, called Seller's neck, lying and being within the town of Jamaica, purchased by the said town of Jamaica from the Indians, and sold by them unto the inhabitants of Breucklen aforesaid, as it was laid out aforesaid, and divided by their mutual consent and order of the Governor. To have and to hold unto them the said patentees and their associates, their heirs, successors and assigns forever, as by the said patent reference being thereunto had, doth fully and at large appear. And further, in and by the said patent, the said Governor Richard Nicolls, Esq., did erect the said tract of land into a township by the name of Breucklen aforesaid, by that name and style to be distinguished and known in all bargains, sales, deeds, records and writings whatsoever; and whereas the present inhabitants and freeholders of the town of Breucklen aforesaid, have made their application to me for a confirmation of the aforesaid tract of land and premises in their quiet and peaceable possession and enjoyment of the aforesaid land and premises. Now Know Ye, That I, the said Thomas Dongan, by virtue of the commission and authority derived unto me, and power in me residing, have granted, ratified and confirmed, and by these presents do grant, ratifie and confirm, unto Teunis Gysberts (Bogart), Thomas Lamberts, Peter Jansen, Jacobus Vander Water, Jan Dame(n), Joris Jacobs, Jeronimus Rapalle, Daniel Rapalle, Jan Jansen, Adrian Bennet, and Michael Hanse (Bergen), for and on the behalf of themselves and the rest of the present freeholders and inhabitants of the said town of Breucklen, their heirs and assigns forever, all and singular the afore-recited tract and parcels of land set forth, limited and bounded as aforesaid; together with all and singular, the houses, messuages, tenements, fencings, buildings, gardens, orchards, trees, woods, underwoods, pastures, feedings, common of pasture, meadows, marshes, lakes, ponds, creeks, harbors, rivers, rivulets, brooks, streams, highways and easements whatsoever, belonging or in any wise appertaining to any of the afore-recited tract or parcells of land and divisions, allotments, settlements made and appropriated before the day and date hereof. To Have and To Hold, all and singular, the said tract or parcels of land and premises, with their, and every of their appurtenances unto the said Tunis Gysberts (Bogart), Thomas Lamberts, Peter Jansen, Jacobus Vander Water, Joris Jacobs, Jeronimus Rappalle, Daniel Rappalle, Jan Jansen, Adrian Bennet and Michael Hanse (Bergen), for and on behalf of themselves and the present freeholders and inhabitants of the town of Breucklen, their and every of their heirs and assigns forever, as tenants in common without any let, hindrance, molestation, right o: survivorship or otherwise, to be holden in free and common socage according to the tenure of East Greenwich, in the County of Kent, in his Majesty's kingdom of England. Yielding, rendering and paying therefor yearly and every year, on the five and twentyeth day of March, forever, in lieu of all services and demands, whatsoever, as a quit rent to his most sacred Majesty aforesaid, the heirs and successors, at the city of New York, twenty bushels of good merchantable wheat. In testimony whereof, I have caused these presents to be entered and recorded in the Secretary's office, and the seal of the Province to be hereunto affixed this thirteenth day of May, Anno. Domini, one thousand six hundred and eighty six, and in the second year of his Majesty's reign.

"THOMAS DONGAN."

On the 13th of the ensuing October, Messrs. Jacobus Vande Water, Jeronimus Rapallie, and Teunis Gysbertse Bogart, deputies from the town of Breucklen, appeared before the Governor, and formally agreed, on behalf of the town, to the annual payment of the quit-rent above mentioned.[1]

---

[1] This quit-rent has been regularly paid to the 25th day of March, 1775, as will appear from the following copies of the collector's receipts, viz.:

"June 8, 1713. Paid to Benjamin Van de Water, Treasurer, the sum of £96 *7s.* *1d.*, for upwards of 16 years' quit-rent.

"Received of Charles De Bevoice, collector for Brooklyn, twenty bushels of wheat, in full for one year's quit of the said township, due the 25th of March last, New York, 6th of April, 1775. JOHN MOORE, D. R. Gen."

After the independence of the State of New York, the payment of quit-rent was revived, and on the 9th day of Nov., 1786, the arrears of quit-rent were paid up, and all future quit-rents were commuted for, as will appear from the following copy of the Treasurer's receipt, viz.:

The oath of allegiance was this year taken by the following inhabitants of Breucklyn:

Thomas Lambertse, 36 years[1]	Theunis Tobiassen, native
Jooris Hanssen, native	Pieter Corsen, native
Hendrick Vechten, 27 years	Theunis Janse Couverts, 36 years
Claes Arense Vechten, 27 years	Aert Simonssen, native
Jan Aertsen (Middag), 26 years	Adam Brouwer, Junior, native
Hendrick Claasen, 33 years	Alexander Shaers, native
Jacob Hanssen Bergen, native	Willem Pos, native
Jooris Martens, native	Jan gerrise Dorland, 35 years
Hendrick Thyssen, 21 years	Johannis Casperse, 35 years
Mauritius Couverts, native	Claes Barentse Blom, native
Willem Huijcken, 24 years	Pieter Brouwer, native
Theunis Gysbertse Bogaert, 35 years	Abram Brouwer, native
Willem Bennitt, native	Jan Bennit, native
Hendrick Lambertse, native	Barent Sleght, native
Jan Fredricks, 35 years	Jacobus Vande Water, 29 years
Jan Couverts, native	Benjamin Vande Water, native
Luijcas Couverts, 24 years	Pieter Weijnants, native
Frans Abramse, native	Joost Franssen, 33 years
Gerrit Aerts Middag, native	Hendrick Aaten, native
Simon Aertsen, 23 years	Jan Janse Staats, native
Matthys Cornelisen, 24 years	Claes Simons, native
Ephraim Hendricks, 33 years	Anthonij Souso, 5 years
Claes Thomas Van Dyck, native	Joost Casperse, 35 years
Jeronimus d'Rapale, native	Thijs Lubberse, 50 years
Jeronimus Remsen, native	Paulus Dirckse, 36 years
Casper Janssen, native	Adam Brouwer, 45 years
Achias Janse Vandijck, 36 years	Josias Dreths, 26 years
Jacob Joorissen, native	Pieter Van Nesten, 40 years
Jacobus d'Beauvois, 28 years	Jan Theunisen, native

"Received Nov. 9th, 1786, from Messrs. Fernandus Suydam and Charles C. Doughty, two of the Trustees of the township of Brookland, public securities, which, with the interest allowed thereon, amount to one hundred and five pounds ten shillings, in full for the arrears of quit-rent, and commutation for the future quit-rent, that would have arisen on the patent granted to the town of Brookland, the 13th day of May, 1686.

"GERARD BANCKER, Treas'r."

[1] In this, as in the case of all those who emigrated to this country from Europe, the *number of years of their residence here* is appended to their name.

Harmen Joorissen, native	Dirck Janse Woertman, 40 years
Jacob Willemse Bennit, native	Daniel D'Rapale, native
Jacob Brouwer, native	Gijsbert Boomgaert, native
Bourgon Broulaet, 12 years	Volkert Vanderbraats, native
Jan Damen, 37 years	Jan Buijs, 39 years
Cornelis Subrink (Sebring), native	Gerrit Dorlant, native
Hendrick Sleght, 35 years	Adriaen Bennet, native
Abram Remsen, native	Thomas Verdon, native
Machiel Hanssen, native	Pieter Janse Staats, native[1]

1687. The Clerk's office of Kings County was kept in this town, by the Deputy Register, Jacob Vandewater, who saw also a Notary Public here at the same period. The Register, Samuel Bayard, Esq., resided in the city of New York.

The popular hopes which had been excited by the appointment of the Colonial Assembly, proved delusive, for after its third annual session, it was prohibited by the Duke of York, who, under the title of James II., had succeeded to the throne of England, and had begun to disclose his true character, and his intention to establish an arbitrary and Catholic government over the Protestant province of New York. The gloomy apprehensions of the people, however, were suddenly relieved, in 1689, by the news of his abdication, and the succession of their Protestant majesties, William and Mary, to the throne; and the citizens of New York, suspicious of the hireling officials of the late king, suddenly deposed them, and intrusted the government of the colony to Capt. Jacob Leisler, who held it in the name of the new sovereigns. Beginning, however, with the best intentions, Leisler was finally swept into the assumption of extreme power, whereby he incurred enmity which finally brought him to the scaffold on an unmerited charge of high treason. The administration of his successor, Gov. Henry Sloughter, which commenced in March, 1691, was distinguished by the reconstruction of the provincial government, upon a basis which remained intact and uninterrupted to the close of the American Revolution. Among other

[1] "The Roll off those who have Taken the oath off Allegiance in the Kings County in the Province off New Yorke the 26th 27; 28; 29 and 30th day off September In the Third Yeare off his Mayt[sh] Raigne Annoque Domine 1687."—MSS. in Sec'y of State's office. See Doc. Hist. N. Y., i. p. 659.

changes, courts of common pleas and general pleas were organized in every county; the form of municipal or town government was revised, and assumed more nearly its present form; the commissioners' court was replaced by the assumption of its duties by the justices; the number of supervisors in each town was reduced to one; and three surveyors of highways were added to the town officers.

May 6th, 1691, an act was passed by the General Assembly, confirming to all the towns of the colony their respective grants and patents, by which law both of the patents of Brooklyn were confirmed.

Governor Sloughter died suddenly in July, 1691, and was succeeded by Col. Benjamin Fletcher, who arrived August 30, 1692, and whose avaricious and arbitrary character very soon rendered him quite unpopular with the people.

At a Court of Sessions, held at Flatbush, November 8, 1692, the following regulation was promulgated:

> "The Courte doe order that there be a good pare of stocks and a good pound made in every town within Kings County, and to be always kept in sufficient repairs, and that there be warrants issued to the Constables of every towne to see the order of the Court performed, as they will answer the contrary at their perill."

The retailing of liquors within the county was also forbidden, excepting under a license from the Justices of the County.[1]

April 10th, 1693, the name of Long Island was changed to the "Island of Nassau," which alteration was neither popular nor generally adopted, and gradually became obsolete by disuse, although the act, it is believed, was never explicitly repealed.

The town of Breuckelen having acquired a large amount of common land, by the purchase from the Indians in 1670, the inhabitants thought best to adopt some measures for its proper division, together with their other common lands. Accordingly,

> "at a Town meeting held the 25th day of February, 1692–3, att Breuck-

---

[1] Ct. Sess. Rec., Old Road Book.

lyn, in Kings County. Then Resolved to divide their common land and woods into three parts, in manner following to wit:

"1. All the lands and woods after Bedford and Cripplebush, over the hills to the path of New lotts shall belong to the inhabitants and freeholders of the Gowanis, beginning from Jacob Brewer and soe to the uttermost bounds of the limits of New-Utrecht.

"2. And all the lands and woods that lyes betwixt the abovesaid path and the highway from the ferry toward Flattbush, shall belong to the freeholders and inhabitants of Bedford and Cripplebush.

"3. And all the lands that lyes in common after the Gowanis, betwixt the limits and bounds of Flatbush and New Utrecht shall belong to the freeholders and inhabitants of Brooklyn, fred. neck (Frederick Lubbertsen's Neck, *ante*, pp. 63, 66) the ferry and the Wallabout."

This proceeding of the town was duly approved of by the Court of Sessions, held at Flatbush, on the 10th of May, 1693.[1]

There was, during this year, considerable commotion and disturbance among the Dutch towns of the county (more especially, however, in Bushwick), arising from some political causes not now fully understood.[2] At a meeting of the Kings Co. Justices, Oct. 11, 1693, "John Bibout, off Broockland, in the county afforesayde, weeaver, being committed bye the said justices to the common jail off Kings County ffor divers scandalous and abusive wordes spoken bye the sayde John against theire majesties justices of the peace for the county aforesaid, to the contempt of their majesties authority and breache off the peace; the sayd John havinge now humbly submitted himselfe and craves pardon and mercy off the sayd justices ffor his missdemeanor, is discharged, payinge the officers ffees, and being on his good behavour till next cort of sessions, in November next ensuing the dayte thereoff."[3] During the same month, one Hendrick Claes Vechte, of this town, was also imprisoned by order of the justices, on a charge "of raising of dissension, strife and mutiny, among their

---

[1] See Appendix 8.

[2] These difficulties, so far as we can learn, seem to have been caused by the very arbitrary measures resorted to by the county justices, in order to support their authority. The arrest and confinement of individuals on the charge (often frivolous) of having uttered words against them and subversive of the government, were matters of frequent occurrence, tending to betray the people into the commission of excesses and outbreaks of exasperation and defiance.

[3] Old Road Book, p. 19.

majesties subjects." Subsequently, upon his confession of error, he was released, on payment of a smart fine.[1]

The following year, 1694, was also characterized by a continuance of the same troubles between the people and their rulers, as we have mentioned in the previous year; and Volkert Brier, Constable of Brookland, was fined £5 and costs of court, amounting to £1, "for tearing and burning an execution directed to him as constable," by Justice Hegeman. He afterwards petitioned the Governor for a remission of his fine, in words as follows:

"To His Excellency,—The humble peticon of Volkert Brier, inhabitant of the towne of Broockland, on the Island of Nassau.

"May it please your Excellency your peticoner being fined five pounds last Court of Sessions, in Kings County for tearing an execucon directed to him as Constable, Your peticoner being ignorant of the crime, and not thinking it was of force when he was out of his office, or that he should have made returne of it as the lawe directs, he being an illiterate man could not read said execucon nor understand any thing of lawe: humbly prays y^r Excellency yt you would be pleased to remit said fine of five pounds, y^r peticoner being a poor man and not capacitated to pay said fine without great damage to himself and family. And for y^r Excellency y^r peticoner will ever pray, &c."[2]

"At a Court of Sessions ffor Kings County, November 12, 1695. Ordered that the Constable of every towne within Kings County shall every Sunday or Sabbath daye tayke lawe ffor the apprehendinge off all Sabbath breakers, and that they or their deputyes goe with their staves each Sabbath daye in and about theire respective towns during their time of servitude as Constable, and searche all ale-houses, taverns and other suspected places ffor all prophaners and breakers off the Sabbath day, & then to apprehend and bring them before any one of his Majesties Justices of the County aforesaid, too bee punished accordinge to lawe.

"Ordered that ffor every neglect or default, the constable shall pay a ffine of six shillings.

"Ordered that Mad James bee kept by Kings County in general, and that the deacons off each towne within the sayde county doe fforthwith meete together and consider about their proporcons ffor maintenance of sayd James."

---

[1] Ct. Sessions Rec., Old Road Book, p. 14.

[2] Ibid., pp. 25, 26.

All the king's highways in the county were likewise to be continued and confirmed, as they had been for twenty years past, and were to be laid out four rods wide, at least.[1]

Another emeute of the disaffected people of Kings County occurred about 8 o'clock in the evening of the 14th of September, 1697 (or 6?), when John Rapalje, Isaac Remsen, Jooris Vannesten, Joras Danielse Rapalje, Jacob Reyerse, Aert Aertsen, Theunis Bujs, Garret Cowenhoven, Gabriel Sprong, Urian Andriese, John Willemse Bennett, Jacob Bennett and John Meserole, jr.—most of whom will be recognized as inhabitants of Breuckelen and Boswyck —"met, armed, at the courthouse of Kings, where they destroyed and defaced the king's arms which were hanging up there."[2]

November 11, 1697, negroes were forbidden to be brought over from New York on the Sabbath, without tickets or passes. Similar legislation was made in the succeeding years, negroes being forbidden to "run about on the Sabbath," or to purchase liquors. It was further "ordered that no people shall pass on the Sabbath day, unless it be to or from church, or other urgent and lawful occasions, according to act of assembly, upon penalty aforesaid of fine and imprisonment."[3]

"At a towne meeting held this twentieth day of Aprill, 1697, at Bedford, within the jurisdiction of Broockland, in Kings County, upon the Island of Nassau, Resolved by all the ffreeholders of the towne of Broockland aforesaid, that all their common land not yet laid out and divided, belonging to their whole patent, shall be equally divided and laid out to each ffreeholder of said towne, his just proporcon in all the common lands abovesaid, except those that have but an house and home lott, which are only to have but half share of the lands aforesaid. And for the laying out of the said lands there are chosen and appointed by the ffreeholders abovesaid, Capt. Henry Ffilkin, Jacobus Vanderwater, Daniel Rapalle, Joris Hansen, John Dorlant and Cornelius Vanduyne. It is further ordered that noe men within this township abovesaid, shall have priviledge to sell his part of the undivided lands of Broockland not yet laid out, to any person living without the township

---

[1] Rec. Ct. Sess., Old Road Book.

[2] Ct. Sess. Rec., Old Road Book, 38—contains the original depositions of Justices Hegeman, Filkin, and Stillwell.

[3] Ct. Sess. Rec., Old Road Book.

abovesaid. It is likewise ordered, consented to, and agreed by the towne meeting aforesaid, That Capt. Henry Ffilkin shall have a full share with any or all the ffreeholders aforesaid, in all the common land or woods in the whole patent of the towne of Breuckland aforesaid, besides a half share for his home lott; To have and to hold to him, his heirs and assigns forever. It is likewise ordered, that noe person whatsoever within the common woods of the jurisdiction of Broockland aforesaid, shall cutt or fall any oake or chesnut saplings for firewood during the space of four years from the date hereof upon any of the said common lands or woods within the jurisdicon of Broockland patent, upon the penalty of six shillings in money for every waggon load of saplings abovesaid soe cutt, besides the forfeiture of the wood or timber soe cutt as abovesaid, the one-half thereof to the informer, and the other half for the use of the poor of the towne of Broockland aforesaid.

"By order of the towne meeting aforesaid.

"and JUSTICE HENRY FFILKIN.

"JACOBUS VANDEWATER, Towne Clerk."[1]

The following record is curious, as illustrative of the ancient practice of tradesmen cutting down timber in the public woods, and of the regulations adopted respecting the same:

"Att a meeting held this 29th day off Aprill (1699), in Breucklyn, Present, Benjamin Vande Water, Joris Hanssen (Bergen), Jan Gerritse Dorlant, being choisen townsmen in the presence and with the advice off the Justices of this towne. Considering the greate inconvenience, lose and interest that the inhabitants off this towne have by reason that the tradesmen here living in this towne doe ffall and cutt the best trees and sully the best of our woods, and sell the worke thereoff made, the most part to others living withoute the towne, and that the shoemakers and others doe cutt and fall all the best treese ffor the barke, and the wood lyes and rott, and that some persons doe cutt and ffall trees for timber and ffensing stuff, and leave the trees in the woods soe cutt until they are spoilt, and that people off other towns come and cutt and ffall trees for timber, ffensing stuff, and ffire woods, and transport the same away out off our townes, bounds and limitts, and that without leave or consent off the towne, soe that in the time off ffew yeares there shall bee no woods leaved ffor the inhabitants ffor timber or ffensing stuff, to the ruine off the said towne. It

[1] Furman's Notes, p. 116.

is thereffore ordered, That ffrom the date hereoff no tradesman shall make any worke ffor to sell to others without thee tówne, ffrom wood soe cutt as afforesaid as only ffrom old wood.

"That no shoemaker or others shall cutt or ffall any trees ffor to barke in the common woods uppon the penaltie off ffive pounds ffor every tree soe cutt.

"That no men shall leave any timber, ffensing stuffe, or other wood in the woods longer as six weeks affter itt is cutt, uppon the penaltie, that itt shall be ffree ffor others to take and carry the same away as theire owne wood. And that iff any one off other townes shall be ffounden within our townes limitts to cutt or carry away any sorts off woods ffor timber, ffensing stuff or ffire wood, that itt shall bee ffree ffor any one off this towne to take it away and to take out writ to arrest, or to apprehend such offender or offenders presently, and that the Justices off this towne shall answer the action as iff itt were done by theire owneselves."[1]

These proceedings were also recorded, by order of the Court of Sessions.

Further action was had in the matter of the common lands, during the year 1701, as appears by the following record;

"Towne Meeting held this 5th day off May, 1701, by order off Justices Cornelis Sebringh and Machiell Hanssen (Bergen). We the major part off the ffreeholders off Breucklyn doe hereby nominate, constitute, and appoint Capt. Jooris Hanssen (Bergen), Jacob Hanssen (Bergen), and Cornelis Van Duyn, to bee trustees of our Common and undivided lands, and to deffend and maintaine the rights and privileges off our General pattent, as well within as without."

Again, at a

"Towne meeting held this second day off February, 1701–2, by order off Justice Cornelis Sebringh. Purposed iff the order off Bedford, made the 12th day off April, 1697,[2] shall bee conffirmed concerning the lying out of the common or undivided lands, or that the said land shall bee lyed out according to the last tax, concerning the deffending off our limitts.

---

[1] As we understand this clause, the Justices of Brooklyn were to have cognizance of the offence, as much as if the offenders resided within the town.

[2] See *ante*, p. 208.

"Resolved by the ffreeholders aforesaid, that the chosen townsmen shall ley out the commens according as by the said order off Bedford was concluded, with the ffirst opportunitie, and that all the lotts joyning to the common woods shall be surveyed according to their grants."

These lands were accordingly surveyed, during the same month, by Messrs. Pieter Corteljeau and S. Clowes, surveyors, and were by them divided into three divisions. The first, or west division, consisting of 62 lots, containing about 5 acres each, comprised near 310 acres. The second, or middle division, consisted of 62 lots, of about 10 acres each, amounting to 620 acres; and the third, or east division, also of 62 lots, of about 10 acres each, also comprised about 620 acres. The total number of acres was about 1550.[1]

The common lands having been thus equitably divided among the freeholders, and a portion annexed to each house in town,[2] the following resolution was adopted for the better protection of those inhabitants to whom portions had been allotted in their enjoyment of the same:

"Att a Towne meeting held att Brookland, in Kings County, this 14th day of March, 1701–2. Present Machiel Hanssen (Bergen), Cornelis Sebringh, and Hendrick Vechten, Esquires, Justices.—Resolved, by the major part of the freeholders of the saide towne of Brookland, that every man that has now a right, lott, or lotts laid out in the quondam Common and undivided lands of Brookland aforesaid, shall forever free liberty have for egress or regress to his said lotts for fetching off wood or otherwise, over all or any of the said lott or lotts of the said freeholders in the lands aforesaid. And further, that if any of the said freeholders shall at any time or times hereafter, come by any loss or trouble, cost or charges by lawe or otherwise, of, for or concerning the title of any of their said lott or lotts, by any person or persons, either within the township of Brookland afforesaid or without, that it shall be defended and made goode (if lost), att all the proper costs and charges of all the freeholders of said towne equally."

---

[1] Furman's Notes, 45.

[2] This appears evident from the fact that a deed, dated April 17, 1705, after conveying a house and lot of land in this town, conveys "alsoe all the rights and priviledges in the common woodlands of the towne of Broockland aforesaid, to said house belonging as per record of said towne may appear."

Owing to the complete absence of the town and county records, from the year 1700 to the close of the American Revolution, we are unable to glean much material for a history of Breucklyn during that period. The slender data on which we are obliged to base our chronicle of the progress of the place, are mostly derived from provincial records, stray deeds and documents, newspapers, letters, etc. Two bitter controversies agitated the public mind during that period: the first between this town (together with Flatbush and Bushwick) and Newtown, concerning their respective bounds, which ended only in 1769;[1] and the second between this town and the city of New York, relative to town and ferry rights, which has not yet (1867) ended. This latter topic, however, will be more fully discussed in another portion of this work.

April 21, 1701, a piece of land, about 200 feet square, lying within the limits of the subsequent village of Brooklyn, was sold for £75, "current money of the Province of New York."[2]

August 30, 1701, John Bybon sold to Cornelius Vanderhove, for £37 10s., the one equal half part of a brew-house, situate at Bedford, in the town of Brookland, fronting the highway leading from Bedford to Cripplebush; together with one equal half part of all the brewing-vessels, etc.[3]

In the year 1703, "Brookland's improveable lands and meadows, within fence," were surveyed, and found to amount to 5,177 acres.[4] The greatest landowner, at that time, was Simon Aerson, who owned 200 acres.

On the 28th of March, 1704, the main road or "king's highway," now called *Fulton street* and *Fulton avenue*, was laid out by Joseph Hegeman, Peter Cortelyou, and Benjamin Vandewater, commissioners, appointed by act of the General Assembly of the Colony of New York, for the laying out, regulating, clearing, and preserving of public highways in the colony. The record of this road, which now forms the chief thoroughfare of the city of Brooklyn, is as follows:

"One publique, common and general highway, to begin ffrom *low water marke* at the ferry in the township of Broockland, in Kings County, and

[1] See Appendix No. 7.

[2] Furman's Notes, 91.

[3] Furman's Notes, 91.

[4] N. Y. Col. MSS., lxxii. 31.

ffrom thence to run ffour rod wide up between the houses and lands of John Aerson, John Coe, and George Jacobs, and soe all along to Broockland towne aforesaid, through the lane that now is, and ffrom thence straight along a certaine lane to the southward corner of John Van Couwenhoven's land, and ffrom thence straight to Bedfford as it is now staked out, to the lane where the house of Benjamin Vandewater stands, and ffrom thence straight along through Bedfford towne to Bedfford lane, running between the lands of John Garretse, Dorlant and Claes Barnse, to the rear of the lands of the said Cloyse, and ffrom thence southerly to the old path now in use, and soe all along said path to Philip Volkertses land, taking in a little slip of said Philip's land on the south corner, soe all along said road by Isaack Greg's house to the Fflackbush new lotts ffence, and soe all along said ffense to the eastward, to the northeast corner of Eldert Lucas's land, lying within the New lotts of Fflattbush aforesaid, being ffour rod wide all along, to be and continue forever."

In 1706, all the real and personal estates of the town of Brooklyn were assessed £3,122 12s., the tax on the same being £41 3s. 7½d., and the whole county tax, £201 16s. 1½d. There were at this time 64 freeholders in the town. In 1707, the real and personal estates were assessed at £3,091, 11s., on which the government tax was £116 7s. 3d., payable in two instalments, and the county tax was £448 3s. 7d.

1717. November 21, a bill was brought into the Assembly to erect Kings and Queens Counties into one by the name of *St. George's County*; also, to elect six members from said county to the Assembly.

1721. Private encroachments on the old road or "king's highway" (now Fulton street and avenue), leading from the ferry to the old Dutch church, or Brooklyn parish, and which had been laid out seventeen years before, in 1704, gave rise to much contention in the town. At the April term of the General Sessions of the Peace for Kings County, indictments were found for encroaching thereon, against John Rapalje, Hans Bergen, James Harding, and others. These indictments seem to have been predicated as well on the application of Rapalie and Bergen, as upon complaints from other citizens.[1] Some of the parties thus indicted, and who considered them-

[1] "Fflatbush, April 19, 1721. John Rapalje and Hans Bergen, of the fferry, desires of the grand jury that the Commissioners now being should be presented for not doing

selves aggrieved, together with others who feared being placed in the same position, applied to the Colonial Legislature, and obtained, July 27, 1721, the passage of a law[1] to "continue the common road or king's highway, from the ferry, towards the town of Breuckland, on the Island of Nassau, in the Province of New York," with the following preamble:

"*Whereas*, several of the inhabitants on the ferry, on the Island of Nassau, by their petition preferred to the General Assembly, by setting forth, that they have been molested by prosecutions, occasioned by the contrivance and instigations of ill and dissaffected persons to the neighbourhood, who would encroach upon the buildings and fences that have been made many years, alledging the road was not wide enough, to the great damage of several of the old inhabitants, on the said ferry; the said road as it now is, has been so for at least these sixty years past, without any complaint, either of the inhabitants or travellers."

The law then proceeds to establish the road "forever" as it then was, from the ferry upwards to the town of Breuckland, as far as the swinging gate of John Rapalje, just above the house and land belonging to James Harding. Providing, however, against a possible "jam" near the ferry—although, perhaps, scarcely anticipating the great thoroughfare which now exists at that locality—the law enacts that, if a majority of the inhabitants of the town should "*adjudge that part of the road near to the ferry* to be too narrow and inconvenient," they might cause the Sheriff to summon a jury of twelve, to appraise the land necessary to be taken in the widening, and that said appraisement should be levied and collected upon the town, and paid to the owners. This, however, was never done, and the old lane continued to serve the economical townsfolk of Brooklyn. Its appearance may be understood by a glance at Guy's picture of Brooklyn, which represents it at its passage at Front street,

their duty in laying out the King's highway according to ye law, being the King's highway is too narrow from the ferry to one Nicalus Cowenhoven, living at Brooklyn; and if all our neighbours will make ye road according to law, then ye said John Rapalje and Hans Bergen is willing to do the same as aforesaid, being they are not willing to suffer more than their neighbours. As witness our hands the day and year first above written.

JAN RAPELJE.
HANS BERGEN."

[1] N. Y. Col. Doc., v. 621.

but so narrow as hardly to lead one to suppose that it was a street. The "swinging gate" here referred to was on the east side of the present Fulton street, about where Sands street now enters, and there commenced the four-foot road. On Ratzer's map, prepared in 1766–7, this road is laid down, with the buildings thereon, showing conclusively that it was then the same as Fulton street before the widening in 1839.

For the few remaining incidents of interest in the history of the town, previous to the Revolutionary period, we are indebted mainly to the New York newspapers of the day.

1732, March 27. The *New York Gazette* contains an advertisement by Edward Willett, offering to sell, on reasonable terms, a very good negro woman, aged twenty-seven, with two fine children. She is described as understanding all sorts of business in city or country, and speaks very good English and Dutch.

1732, July 17. Edward Willett advertises for sale the large, well-furnished house where Mr. James Harding lately lived, near the ferry, at Brooklyn, finely situated for a gentleman and a country-seat, or a public house. With it was also a "large barn, well covered with cedar;[1] a large, handsome garden; and ten acres of good land, in a fine young orchard."

Brooklyn's relative population in 1738, as compared with the other Kings County towns, is exhibited in the following table:

Towns.	White males above ten yrs.	White females above ten.	White males under ten.	White females under ten.	Black males above ten.	Black females above ten.	Black males under ten.	Black females under ten.	Number of whole.
Flatlands......	83	76	32	27	19	19	7	5	268
Gravesend.....	75	70	22	25	15	16	6	6	235
Brookland.....	191	196	66	84	74	49	31	30	721
Flatbush......	148	138	56	64	44	41	18	31	540
N. Utrecht.....	72	65	26	32	36	23	17	11	282
Bushwick......	85	86	33	32	22	21	5	18	302
	654	631	235	264	210	169	84	101	2,348

Total of Whites, 1,784. Total of Blacks, 564.

PETER STRYCKER, Junr Sheriff.[2]

[1] Dwellings and barns were, at this period, very generally covered with straw thatch.
[2] N. Y. Col. MSS., lxxii. 31.

March 20, 1745–6. The General Assembly of the Province met at the house of the Widow Sickle, in this town, in consequence of the prevalence of the small-pox in the city of New York, and continued sitting at Brooklyn, by several adjournments, until the 8th day of October.

1752. The Colonial Legislature, during the prevalence of the small-pox in New York, held their session at Brooklyn in a large building on the west side of Fulton street, just below Nassau. This very ancient edifice was constructed of small brick, said to have been brought from Holland, and was demolished in 1832. At this house, also, on the 4th of June, 1752, 2,541 bills of credit issued by the colony of New York, and amounting to £3,602 18s. 3d., were cancelled by the Colonial Commissioners. The building was further honored by being made Gen. Putnam's headquarters during the stay of the American army on Long Island, in 1776.

1757, January 24. Jacob Brewster, at Brooklyn ferry, offers for sale a pole-chair, or curricle, with excellent good harness and extraordinary horses.

1757, March 14. Garrett Rapelje, of New York, offers for sale a new house on the Jamaica Road, about a mile from Brooklyn ferry, with forty acres of land, west side of John Conover's, and adjoining the place now in possession of Capt. Pikeman. Some of the land has a prospect of the Narrows, New York, and Turtle Bay.

1758. This year the sum of £122 18s. 7d. was assessed in two assessments, by the Justices of the Peace on this town, towards building "a new court-house and gaol" for Kings County. The whole amount assessed on the county was £448 4s. 1d.

1759, Nov. 26. "On Sunday week last past, a large bear passed the house of Mr. Sebring, Brooklyn, and took the water at Red Hook, attempting to swim across the bay, when Cornelius Sebring and his miller immediately pushed off in a boat after him. The latter fired and missed, on which Mr. S. let fly, and sent the ball in at the back of his head, which came out of his eye, and killed him outright."—*N. Y. Gazette.*

1761, Nov. 5. "On Tuesday morning, a grist-mill of one Mr. Remsen, on Long Island, a few miles from this city, accidentally took fire and was entirely consumed, with a large quantity of grain."

—*N. Y. Post Boy.* This mill was probably the one at the Wallabout Bay.[1]

1764, April 16. James Degraw, Brooklyn, offers for sale his farm opposite the church, and joining Mr. Harvey's, a mile from the ferry. It is convenient for the New York market, having ten acres of land and forty fruit-trees.

1764, Oct. 11. Aris Remsen offers twenty shillings reward for the apprehension of a runaway negro named Harry. "He had on a Scotch bonnet, short, wide trowsers, and half-worn shoes, with steel buckles. He is apt to get drunk, and stutters. He speaks good English, French, Spanish, and a little of other languages."

1765, Feb. 28. "James Leadbetter and Thomas Horsfield have opened their brewery in Brooklyn, where may be had English ale, table, ship, and spruce beer."—*N. Y. Gazette.*

VIEW OF BROOCKLAND, IN 1766-7.[2]

1767, Jan. 8. "Last week, on Wednesday, a very valuable negro fellow of Mr. Samuel Waldron, who keeps the Brooklyn ferry, in pushing off the boat from the ferry stairs with an oar, lost his purchase and fell out of the bow of the boat, and by a sudden rise of the sea, his head was crushed between the boat and dock, so that he died in a few minutes after he was taken up."

1767, February. "JOYCE's great wound BALSAM is a corrector of coughs and colds, and cures ulcers and fistulas; and has many other virtues too tedious to mention. Sold at Edward Joyce's shop, near

---

[1] *Ante*, p. 81.

[2] From Rutger's map, of that date.

Brooklyn ferry." The same remedy, under the name of the "great American balsam," is again advertised in January, 1769, by Edward Joyce, *Surgeon*, as for sale by him, and also at Capt. Koffler's at Brooklyn ferry.

1767. Israel Horsfield, sen., Brooklyn ferry, advertises to sell at outcry to the highest bidder, Sept. 8th, at the brew-house, "two negro men, one of which has lived with a ship-carpenter, and is a good caulker, and has lately lived with a brewer and malster, and is very handy." On the 2d of November following, Mr. Horsfield offers for sale his brew-house, malt-house, drying kiln, dwelling, and store-house, built of brick, one and a half feet thick, after an English plan; a horse-mill, for grinding malt and pumping water, a copper kettle holding thirty-six barrels, two lead cisterns, which will steep seventy bushels of barley each.

1767, Nov. 16. Francis Koffler[1] offers a reward for a runaway indentured Irish servant, John Miller, "which kept the bar and made punch at his house," at Brooklyn ferry, and who is particularly described as wearing "deer-skin breeches, speckled yarn stockings, double-soled shoes with brass buckles, and a beaver hat."

1768. A New York paper chronicles the fact that, "in the hard gale of wind and snow-shower we had here on Saturday night (March 19th), a servant man and valuable slave of Mr. Pikeman, of Long Island, were drowned in a periauger, going across the river with manure for their master's farm."

1768. "To be run for, April 5th, at Mr. James Noblett's, Brooklyn, a neat saddle, with hog-skin seat, valued at £5, the best two out of three single mile heats; free for any horse not more than quarter blood, carrying ten stone. Entrance fee 5s., cash."

1768. "*Liberal Reward.* On July 8th. the house of Widow Rapelye, Brooklyn ferry, was broken open and robbed of one gold ring, marked M. D., heart in hand; seven silver spoons, marked J. R. D.; one pair gold sleeve-buttons; two Johannesses; one doubloon; two

---

[1] This gentleman's obituary is found in the N. Y. Journal of Aug. 29, 1771: "Last Friday, departed this life, after a lingering sickness, at Brooklyn, in an advanced age, Captain Francis Koffler, an honest, upright man, greatly lamented. In the last war he had command of several privateers out of this port, and acquired great honor by the bravery and resolution with which he acted in the several engagements he was in."

New York £5 bills; one of 40s.; and about £40 in Jersey bills and dollars." Speedy justice overtook the thief, "Garret Middagh's negro fellow, Cæsar," who was tried on the 1st of September following, convicted, and *executed* on the 15th of the same month, at Flatbush, the county town.

1770, Feb. 25. The *New York Mercury* states that Thomas Horsfield's malt-kilns, at Brooklyn ferry, were burned. Loss, £500.

1770, March 22. "On Monday last was celebrated the Anniversary of the repeal of the Stamp Act, by a number of gentlemen, who dined at Mr. Waldron's, Brooklyn ferry, and spent the day in great cheerfulness and good order, and drank the usual toasts."—*N. Y. Journal.*

1771, Aug. 7. Ares Remsen, at the Wallebocht, offers 20s. reward for a runaway "negro man, Newport, Guinea-born, and *branded* on the breast with three letters. He speaks good English, and is a great talker."

1773, March 4. Sunday, Feb. 24th, was "the coldest day for more than half a century. The harbor was so full of ice last Thursday, that many people walked over to Brooklyn and back again. By the fall of a little rain at night, scarcely any ice was to be seen next morning."—*N. Y. Journal.*

1774, Feb. 21. "A Ferry is now established from the Coenties Market, New York, to the landing place of P. Livingston, Esq., and Henry Remsen, on Long Island, and another from Fly Market, and a third from Peck Slip to the present ferry-house at Brooklyn."—*N. Y. Mercury.*

The "landing place of P. Livingston, Esq., and Henry Remsen" was near the foot of the present Joralemon street.[1] This ferry was called "St. George's Ferry," but did not exist long, being discontinued in 1776, and the ferry-house, together with Livingston's distillery, was burned after the war.

1774, March 31. "Many persons have been misled by an opinion that the church proposed to be erected by lottery, at Brooklyn, is to be under the ministry of the Rev. Mr. Bernard Page. It will be a truly orthodox church, strictly conformable to the doctrine and dis-

---

[1] *Ante*, pp. 72, 73.

cipline of the constitutional Church of England as by law established, and under the patronage of the Rev. Rector and Vestry of Trinity church."—*Rivington's Gazette.*

1774, May 9. John Cornell announces, in the *N. Y. Mercury*, that he "has opened a tavern on Tower Hill, Brooklyn, near the new ferry, called 'St. George's.' Companies will be entertained if they bring their own liquor, and may dress turtle, etc., at the said house on the very lowest terms." And, in August following, he advertised that "there will be a *bull baited* on Tower Hill, at three o'clock in the afternoon, every Thursday during the season."

"Tower Hill" was a slight eminence on the Heights, on the site of the old "Colonnade Row," on Columbia, between Middagh and Cranberry streets.

CHAPTER VIII.

THE DOMESTIC HISTORY OF THE PEOPLE, FROM THE SETTLEMENT OF THE COUNTRY TO THE REVOLUTIONARY PERIOD.

THE unsettled and wandering life led by the earliest Dutch traders in the New Netherlands, had a natural tendency to assimilate their habits and customs to those of the untutored savages with whom they associated. Freed from the restraints of civilization, they cohabited with the native girls, and every change of temporary location which occurred in the course of their traffic, afforded them the opportunity of selecting new companions, while former ties were carelessly sundered. The children, in these cases, remaining with their mothers, were left to be brought up amid the influences of savage life. Under such circumstances, fostered alike by the recklessness of the white, and the loose morality of the Indian, it can scarcely be a matter of surprise that the life of the former presented little or no trace of the *domestic* civilization which should have been a distinguishing mark between him and his red neighbor.

The domestic history of the country, however, commenced with the arrival of the thirty families brought over in the good ship "New Netherland," in the year 1623. Rapidly, under the repeated blows of the stalwart woodsman's axe, the forests bowed their lofty heads, and the sun, for the first time in many centuries, peeped in here and there upon the little "clearings" where the settler had commenced to raise his first scanty crop of maize or vegetables. Fences, too, divided men's possessions from their neighbors', or restrained the cattle (imported from Europe) from extensive wanderings into the neighboring woods after food, as had been their wont during the first busy days which had succeeded the disembarkation. Houses, or at least temporary shelter, were also furnished—and the foot of civilization was, at length, firmly planted on these hitherto silent shores.

The first dwellings of these pioneer families were mostly constructed, as we learn, in the Indian fashion, of saplings and bark; with here and there a wooden chimney, or glazed window,—improvements suggested by the experience of civilization. Others again, consulting comfort rather than show, constructed cellars, sided with bark and covered with thatched reeds, which, although deficient in light, were snug and warm. In a few years, however, the establishment of a saw-mill on Manhattan Island, supplied timber for more substantial abodes; and the improving circumstances of the settlers were gradually evidenced by the appearance of a better class of dwellings, one story in height, with two rooms on a floor, and a garret overhead. These humble cottages were roofed with straw thatch, and had fireplaces constructed of stone, to the height of about six feet, having an oven of the same material at the side of the fireplace, and extending beyond the rear of the house. But, in the absence of bricks, the chimneys above the stone-work were made of boards, plastered inside with mortar. Each dwelling was surrounded by strong palisades, as a protection against the savages.

The furniture within these humble edifices was of the simplest sort, and such merely as was necessary to the every-day purposes of life. The great chest, with its precious stores of household goods, was the most imposing article of furniture. Tables were of domestic manufacture; stools, rough-hewn from forest wood, answered the uses of chairs; while rude shelves assumed the office of a cupboard. The "slaap-banck," or sleeping-bench, usurped the offices of a bedstead, but upon it the ample feather-bed lay in state, and made up in comfort what was wanting in display.

Such was the general character of the dwellings of New Netherland, for some thirty years succeeding its settlement, during which time many of its industrious citizens had accumulated considerable wealth, their children had grown up, and the community had gradually developed the shades of social distinction, consequent upon the advancing prosperity of its members. As early as the year 1656, several of the merchants of New Amsterdam had erected stone dwelling-houses, and there had been a corresponding advance in the style of living, among all classes. In the interior decorations of their abodes this was plainly seen; great high-post bedsteads, with their dimity curtains, adorned the parlors of the wealthy; and cupboards of nut-wood, imported from the "Fatherland," were not unfrequently seen, while silver-plate was, in a few rare instances, displayed. Schools, also, had been established, and the youth of both sexes, now growing up to maturity, swayed no inconsiderable social influence, as was evidenced by the improved standard of taste which gradually became apparent in the domestic arrangements of private dwellings, both externally and internally. In the city, or rather the village of New Amsterdam, as it then was, public attention was directed towards certain needed municipal reforms—and the magistrates decreed the abolition of wooden chimneys, as well as "little houses," hay-barracks, and hog-pens, all of which had hitherto been paraded along the line of streets, and gradually the town became characterized by a much greater cleanliness and propriety of appearance. Other and larger houses were now erected, and after the establishment of a brick-yard at New Amsterdam, by DeGraff and Hogeboom, in the year 1660, brick houses became the fashion with all who could afford the additional expense.[1]

Still, the best edifices of that day would be deemed extremely cheap, as compared with those of a more recent period,—rarely exceeding $800, while those of an ordinary character were rated at from $200 to $500 of our present currency. Rents ranged from $25 to $100; and as barter was then, by reason of the want of a well-established system of currency, commonly provided for in all agreements, payments were frequently made partly in trade and partly in beaver-skins, which, in wholes or halves, then passed as a current medium of exchange, as regularly as bank-bills of the present day.

Thus far, we have described the buildings erected on Manhattan Island, and it is probable that those edifices which succeeded the

---

[1] It was in those days thought that the baking of brick of greater thickness than two inches, could not be effectual, and thus we find the brick of olden times to be relatively a third smaller than those of later days. They wasted none, and those which, from greater exposure to the heat, were burnt black, were built into the fronts of houses in ornamental figures of diamonds, crosses, or squares, or perhaps the whole front chequered, as suited the taste of the owners. This custom is believed to have been peculiar (in the American settlements) to the Dutch of New Netherland, and their descendants, as travellers, at a period much later than the one now spoken of, remark upon the appearance of this city, in that particular, as being unlike that of any other place they had visited in the colonies. Valentine's Corp. Manual, N. Y., 1861.

first rude cabins of the settlers on the shores of the Waale-boght and at "the Ferry," partook of the same general characteristics. The farm-houses on Long Island, however, were more generally constructed, in a rough but substantial manner, of stone—lighted by narrow windows, containing two small panes of glass—and protected against the "overloopen" or escalading of any savage foe, by strong, well-pointed palisades. Snugness, economy, safety, were the characteristics of these country dwellings.

An interesting glimpse at the construction of the ordinary country houses of the day, is afforded by the following translation of a contract for the erection of a ferry-house, or tavern, on the Long Island side, for Egbert Van Borsum, the ferry-master, in 1655:

"We, Carpenters Jan Cornelisen, Abram Jacobsen, and Jan Hendricksen, have contracted to construct a house over at the ferry of Egbert Van Borsum, ferry-man, thirty feet long and eighteen feet wide, with an outlet of four feet, to place in it seven girders, with three transome windows and one door in the front, the front to be planed and grooved, and the rear front to have boards overlapped in order to be tight, with door and windows therein; and a floor and garret grooved and planed beneath (on the under side); to saw the roof thereon, and moreover to set a window-frame with a glass light in the front side; to make a chimney mantel and to wainscot the fore-room below, and divide it in the centre across with a door in the partition; to set a window-frame with two glass lights therein; further to wainscot the east side the whole length of the house, and in the recess two bedsteads, one in the front room and one in the inside room, with a pantry at the end of the bedstead (betste); a winding staircase in the fore-room. Furthermore we, the carpenters, are bound to deliver all the square timber—to wit, beams, posts, and frame timber, with the pillar for the winding staircase, spars, and worm, and girders, and foundation timbers required for the work; also the spikes and nails for the interior work; also rails for the wainscot are to be delivered by us.

"For which work Egbert Van Borsum is to pay five hundred and fifty guilders (two hundred and twenty dollars), one-third in beavers, one-third in good merchantable wampum, one-third in good silver coin, and free passage over the ferry so long as the work continues, and small beer to be drunk during work.

"We have subsequently contracted with said Egbert Van Borsum to build a cellar-kitchen under said house, and to furnish the wood for it—to wit, beams and frame timber. There must be made two door-frames and two circular frames with windows therein, with a stairway to enter it, and to line the stairs in the cellar round about with boards, with a chimney mantel in the kitchen, and to groove and plane the ceiling. Egbert must excavate the cellar at his own expense. The carpenters must furnish the nails. For this work one hundred guilders (forty dollars) are promised, together with one whole good otter skin. Moreover, Egbert must deliver all the flat wood-work required for the house—to wit, boards and wainscotting.

"Dated 26th April, 1655, at New Amsterdam.

(Signed) "JAN CORNELISEN CLEYN.

"'X,' The Mark of Egbert Van Borsum."

"The word 'betste,' equivalent to the present 'bedstead,' which occurs in this contract," says the source from which we extract the foregoing document, "requires some explanation, as its modern signification is very different from that which it had in those days. The 'betste' was then a part of the house, being constructed like a cupboard in a partition, with doors closing upon it when unoccupied, so that the sleeping apartment of an inn could accommodate several travellers with sleeping accommodations, and yet, in the daytime, the room would answer for a public room, and afford a neat and unencumbered appearance. In houses of more humble pretensions, the 'slaap-banck,' or 'bunk' of modern parlance, was the place of sleeping for travellers.

"To illustrate in a manner which, we doubt not, will give a fair idea of the customs of the Dutch taverns of New Netherlands, such as Van Borsum's, we give the following extract from the journal of one of our citizens,[1] who, as a matter of curiosity, visited a part of the Netherlands, where customs have not changed for centuries.

"It was the business of the good vrow, or her maid, to show up the traveller, and open the doors in the smooth partition of the box which was to receive his weary limbs for the night, and which otherwise he might not be able to discover, and after he crept into it, to come back again and blow out the candle, and in the morning

---

[1] Hon. Henry C. Murphy, of Brooklyn.

to draw the curtains of the window at the hour he fixed to rise. There was generally one room in which all the guests were received, and where there was a pleasant reunion in the evening, and all the visitors ate, drank, and smoked. It had in one corner a closet, which, when opened (and, honestly, it was not unfrequently opened), disclosed sundry decanters, glasses, and black bottles; and, on one side of the room, a rack in which were suspended, by their bowls, a score or two of very long pipes, each one inscribed with the name of a neighbor, its owner. This was the room of Mynheer, the landlord, who found all his occupation here in attending to the pleasure of his guests. He had no care beyond this: his vrow was the head of the house; she attended to all the wants of the guests, and gave them the information which they might desire. She was always on the spot, as when, with a '*wel te rusten*,' like a good mother, she bade you good-night, and when, with a '*hoo-y-reis*,' like an old friend, she bade you good-by."

A very interesting description of the manner in which the old farmers of Breuckelen lived, is given by the Labadist travellers, who visited this country in the year 1679. Among others, they visited Simon de Hart, whose old house is yet standing near the Gowanus Cove, at the foot of the present Thirty-eighth street.

"He was very glad to see us, and so was his wife. He took us into the house and entertained us exceedingly well. We found a good fire, half-way up the chimney, of clear oak and hickory, of which they made not the least scruple of burning profusely. We let it penetrate us thoroughly. There had been already thrown upon it, to be roasted, a pail full of *Gowanes* oysters, which are the best in the country. They are fully as good as those of England, and better than those we eat at Falmouth. I had to try some of them raw. They are large and full, some of them not less than a foot long, and they grow sometimes ten, twelve, and sixteen together, and are then like a piece of rock. Others are young and small. In consequence of the great quantities of them, everybody keeps the shells for the purpose of burning them into lime. They pickle the oysters in small casks, and send them to Barbadoes and the other islands. We had for supper a roasted haunch of venison, which he had bought of the Indians for three guilders and a half of *seewant*, that is, fifteen stivers of Dutch money (15 cents), and which weighed thirty pounds. The meat was exceedingly tender and good, and also quite fat. It had a slight aromatic flavor. We were also served with wild turkey, which was also fat and of a good flavor, and a wild goose, but that was rather dry. Every thing we had was the natural production of the country. We saw here, lying in a heap, a whole hill of watermelons, which were as large as pumpkins, and which Simon was going to take to the city to sell. They were very good, though there is a difference between them and those of the Carribby islands; but this may be owing to its being very late in the season, and these were the last pulling. It was very late at night when we went to rest in a Kermis bed, as it is called, in the corner of the hearth, alongside of a good fire." Early the next morning, they relate that their host and his wife went off to the city, probably in their own boat, with their marketing.[1]

On another occasion they visited Jacques Cortelyou, in New Utrecht, who had just built an excellent stone house, the best dwelling in the place. "After supper," they say, "we went to sleep in the barn upon some straw spread with sheepskins, in the midst of the continuous grunting of hogs, squealing of pigs, bleating and coughing of sheep, barking of dogs, crowing of cocks, cackling of hens, and especially a goodly quantity of fleas and vermin, of no small portion of which we were participants, and all with an open barn-door, through which a fresh north wind was blowing. Though we could not sleep, we could not complain, inasmuch as we had the same quarters and kind of bed that their own son usually had, who now, on our arrival, crept in the straw behind us."[2]

To return to the domestic architecture of the Dutch on Long Island, we may observe that most of their dwellings were of wood, some few being of brick, and here and there was to be found a substantial stone house. These were all one-story edifices, with either an "overshot," or projecting roof, forming a piazza both on the front and rear; or the "overshot" in front, with the roof extending on the rear until within a few feet of the ground. The low-browed rooms

[1] Coll L. I. Hist. Soc., i. 122, 123.

[2] Ibid., i. 178.

were unceiled, showing overhead the broad, heavy oak beams, upon which the upper, or garret floor was laid. The fireplaces were usually very large, generally extending, without jambs, to a width sufficient to accommodate the whole family with seats near the fire. The chimneys were capacious, and in them the meat was hung for roasting, or to be "cured" by smoking. The jambs, when the fireplace had any, were usually set around with glazed earthenware tiles, imported from Holland, representing scenes and Scriptural subjects, which formed a never-failing source of amusement and instruction to the children, who frequently gained their first Bible instruction from these tile-pictures, aided by the explanations of the elder members of the family. Some of these tiles were of a sort of porcelain or china, with bright-colored pictures of birds and flowers; but these were only found in the houses of the better classes, and were comparatively rare,—those in ordinary use being of a blue delft ware.

Frequently the barns were quite closely connected to the dwelling-houses.

Previous to the English conquest of the Netherlands, the domestic habits and customs of the Dutch were simple and somewhat democratic in their character. The Fatherland was a republic, and the accident of family descent, that element which prevailed so greatly in the formation of English society, could not be recognized, or its distinctions claimed by her colonists in the New World; for it was within the recollection of the older citizens that all had come hither in search of fortune, and had brought little with them in the beginning. Some, indeed, through industry or peculiar sagacity, had attained positions of wealth, and consequently of increased influence, yet it might justly be said of the Dutch community, that its social circles were open to all of good character, without regard to business pursuits, or any factitious considerations. Rich and poor mingled together with a freedom and a heartiness of enjoyment which can hardly be expected to exist, except in the formative stage of society—and which, in the natural course of events, could not last long. The advent, however, of the English, many of whom possessed high social connections at home, with all their corresponding habits, etc., infused a change into the social life of the colony, and necessarily developed an aristocratic state of society previously unknown.

In the "best room" of every house, whether of the wealthy or humbler class, the *bedstead* was a principal object, and, with its furniture and hangings, formed the index of the social standing of its owner. Upon it, according to the old Dutch fashion, were two feather beds—one for the sleeper to lie upon, and another, of a lighter weight, to be used as a covering. The pillow-cases were generally of check patterns; and the curtains and valance were of as expensive materials as its owner could afford; while in front of the bed a rug was laid, for *carpets* were not then in common use. Among the Dutch, the only article of that sort, even up to the time of the Revolution, was a drugget cloth, which was spread under the table during meal-time, when, upon "extra occasions," the table was set in the parlor. But even these were unknown among the inhabitants of Breuckelen and the neighboring towns. The uniform practice, after scrubbing the floor well on certain days, was to place upon the damp boards the fine white beach-sand (of which every family kept a supply on hand, renewing it by trips to the seashore twice a year), arranged in small heaps, which the members of the family were careful not to disturb by treading upon; and, on the following day, when it had become dry, it was swept, by the light and skilful touch of the housewife's broom, into waves or other more fanciful figures. Rag carpets did not make their appearance in Kings County until about the beginning of the present century.

Chairs, straight and high-backed, and ungainly to modern eyes, were mostly of wood, sometimes covered with leather and studded with brass nails, but more frequently seated simply with matted rushes. *Tables*, for other than kitchen use, were unknown to the earlier Dutch, and for many years to their successors. In the principal room, which held the fine bed, and was, also, tea and dining room on special occasions, was generally a round tea-table, with a leaf which could be turned up perpendicularly when not in use, and a large square table, with leaves, for use at tea-parties. *Looking-glasses*, in the early days, were generally small, with narrow black frames; and *window-curtains* were of the simplest and cheapest description, being no better in the best apartments than a strip of ordinary cloth run upon a string. *Clocks* were rare, and most families marked their time by the hour-glass,—the great eight-day clock, which we sometimes see as heir-looms in our oldest families, being first introduced in this country about 1720. *Earthenware*, during the Dutch dynasty, and for some twenty years thereafter, was not used in the ordinary table service, wooden and pewter being then universally in use by all classes. The few articles of china, kept by some for display upon the cupboard, were rarely used on the table; and, though earthenware came into partial use about 1680, *pewter* was still the most common up to the period of the Revolution. Among the wealthy, blue and white china and porcelain, curiously ornamented with Chinese pictures, were used "for company." The teacups were very diminutive in size, for tea was then an article of the highest luxury, and was sipped in small quantities alternately with a bite from the lump of loaf-sugar which was laid beside each guest's plate. *Silverware*, in the form of tankards, beakers, porringers, spoons, snuffers, candlesticks, etc., was a favorite form of display among the Dutch, inasmuch as it served as an index of the owner's wealth, and was the safest and most convenient form of investment for any surplus funds. Of *books* our ancestors had but few, and these were mostly Bibles, Testaments, and Psalm-Books. The former, many of which still exist among the old families, were quaint specimens of early Dutch printing, with thick covers, and massive brass, and sometimes silver, corner-pieces and clasps. The Psalm-Books were also adorned with silver edgings and clasps, and when hung by chains of the same material to the girdle of matrons and maidens fair, were undoubtedly valued by their owners quite as much for the display which they made as for their intrinsic value. It is an interesting fact, that the merchants who kept school-books, psalm-books, etc., as a part of their stock, about the middle of the last century, were provided with about an equal number of books in the Dutch and English language; showing that, even at that late period after the termination of the Dutch power, the greater part of the children of Dutch descent continued to be educated in the language of the Fatherland. *Spinning-wheels* were to be found in every family, many having four or five—some for spinning flax and others for wool. A Dutch matron, indeed, took great pride in her large stock of household linen, which was then cheaper than cotton; and it was the ambition of every Dutch maiden to take to her husband's house a full and complete stock of such domestic articles.[1]

As to the means of *travelling*, the lumber-wagon, and in winter the sleigh, running upon split saplings, and drawn, at a uniform dog-trot pace, by pot-bellied nags, seem to have been the only conveyance possessed by the Dutchmen who did not wish to ride horseback or to walk. During the early part of the seventeenth century, the two-wheeled one-horse chaise came gradually into use, and was the fashionable vehicle up to the time of the Revolution. In riding horseback, the lady did not, as now, ride alone; but was mounted upon a pillow or padded cushion, fixed behind the saddle of the gentleman or servant, upon whose support she was therefore dependent; and this was the common mode of country travel for ladies at that day, when roads were generally little else than bridle-paths. Side-saddles only came into partial use in the eighteenth century.

The *manners* of the people were simple, unaffected, and economical. Industry was cultivated by all; every son was brought up to the exercise of some mechanical employment, and every daughter to the knowledge of household duties. In those days, farmers made their own lime, tanned their own leather, often made their own shoes, did their own carpentering, wheelwrighting, and blacksmithing; while the females spun wool and flax, frequently taking their spinning-wheels with them when they went abroad to spend an afternoon with a neighbor's wife.

In regard to the *agriculture* of the country during its earlier years, we can learn but little. It was probably as good as that of the "Fatherland" at that day, all due allowance being made for the novel and peculiar circumstances which surround the settler in a

---

[1] Furman's Notes (p. 100) preserves the inventory of the estate which a bride in Brooklyn brought to her husband, in the year 1691. The husband, by various records, appears to have been a man of considerable wealth, notwithstanding which, the following inventory was thought by both of them of sufficient importance to merit being recorded, viz.:

"A half-worn bed, pillow, 2 cushions of ticking with feathers, one rug, 4 sheets, 4 cushion-covers, 2 iron pots, 3 pewter dishes, 1 pewter basin, 1 iron roaster, 1 schuyrn spoon, 2 cowes about 5 yeares old, 1 case or cupboard, 1 table."

new and unimproved country, amid the vicissitudes of an untried climate, and the constant danger of molestation and violence from savage foes.

We may mention, however, in this connection, that at the period of the Revolutionary War, the farmers of Kings County were in the habit of raising their own *tobacco*, and that during the century previous the cultivation of that weed was extensively carried on as an article of exportation,—some of the best tobacco exported to Europe from the American colonies, being raised on the Dutch tobacco plantations around the Wallabout, in the town of Brooklyn.

The farmers of this vicinity, also, for some time previous to the Revolution, had been in the habit of raising *cotton*,—although probably to a very limited extent, and solely for the domestic uses of their own households. Furman says, in 1836,[1] "we have now a bedspread in our family, made of cotton and wool, colored blue and white, and woven in neat and handsome figures, the *cotton* of which, as well as the wool, was raised on my grandfather's farm in Kings County, L. I., in the year 1775, and which was cleaned, colored, and woven by the women of his family. It is now in use, and in good condition, and is one of the best fabrics I ever saw."

Slavery was also a feature of the domestic history of ante-revolutionary times. It had existed from an early period, and formed a considerable branch of the shipping interests of the Dutch. The mercantile value of a prime slave was from $120 to $150, both under the Dutch and English dynasties. And when, from time to time, by natural increase and by importation, the number of slaves accumulated beyond the demand, the slave-trade decreased.[2] Almost every domestic establishment of any pretensions in city or country was provided with one or more negro servants. These did the most of the farm labor, and their number was considered as a significant indication of the relative wealth of different families.[3]

These slaves were, as a general thing, kindly treated and well

---

[1] MSS. Notes, iv. 381.

[2] N. Y. Doc. Hist., i. 707.

[3] In N. Y. Doc. Hist. is a census of negroes in the province of New York, taken in 1755, from which we learn that there were then in Brooklyn 133 slaves (53 of whom were females), owned by *sixty-two* persons, among whom John Bargay and Jacob Bruington were the largest holders, the former having *seven* and the latter *five* slave servants.

cared for; but, after all, the institution of slavery was one that commended itself to the Dutch mind rather as a necessity than as a desirable system. In the city, the association of so many blacks gave rise to much trouble, and even to several outbreaks during the half century preceding the Revolution, which seriously affected the public peace; and in the rural districts, especially on Long Island, the intercourse of the city negroes with their own house and farm servants, was strongly deprecated and discouraged. After the Revolution, and under the beneficent influences of a more enlightened State legislation, slavery gradually disappeared. The last public sale of human beings in the town of Brooklyn, is believed to have been that of four slaves belonging to the widow Heltje Rappelje, of the Wallabout, in the year 1773. It occurred at the division of her estate, and was even at that time considered an odious departure from the time-honored and more humane practice, which then prevailed, of permitting slaves who wished to be sold, or who were offered for sale, to select their own masters.[1]

Some of the peculiar *funeral* customs of the Dutch will be found incidentally mentioned in another portion of this work.[2] In this connection we may be permitted to quote the following from Furman:[3] "Among our Dutch farmers in Kings County, it has been from time immemorial, and still is a custom, for all the young men, after becoming of age, to lay up a sufficient sum of money in gold to pay the expense of their funerals. In many families the money thus hallowed is not expended for that purpose, but descends as a species of heir-loom through several generations. I have seen gold thus saved from before the Revolution, and now in the hands of the grandson, himself a man of family, having sons grown up to manhood, and which consisted of gold Johannes or Joes ($16 pieces), guineas, etc."

It seems to have been customary, also, among the Dutch, about the close of the last century, to designate a widow as "the last wife"

---

[1] Reminiscences of Jeremiah Johnson. This Heltje was the widow of Jeronimus Rapalje, who sold to Martin Schenck (son-in-law) his farm of 300 acres or more, in the Wallabout. She died in the Wallabout in 1773, aged 93 years, and her estate was sold and divided between her other heirs at law—Johannis Alstine, Thomas Thorne, Aris Remsen.

[2] See sketch of Domine Schoonmaker, *ante*, p. 191.

[3] MSS. Notes, vii. 240.

of her deceased husband, and a widower as "the last man" of his deceased wife.

A well-known investigator of ancient deeds, wills, etc., in Williamsburgh,[1] makes the remark "that the old Dutch wills seem not to trust the widow in a second marriage. The restraints placed upon remarriages, by wills, were generally in favor of the children of the first marriage; and the widows thus restricted generally signed consents to accept the bequests in lieu of dower, for the good reason that propriety did not allow them to refuse so soon after the death of their first husband, and because the devises and bequests in lieu of dower vested an estate for life, or three-thirds of the estate subject to a contingency in their own control, instead of one-third absolutely. The will of Cornelius Van Catts, of Bushwick, dated in 1726, and expressed in a sort of half Dutch dialect, devises to his wife, Annetjie, his whole estate to her while she remains his widow—both real and personal. "But if she happen to marry, then I geff her nothing of my estate, neither real or personal. I geff to my well-beloved son, Cornelius, the best horse that I have, or else £7 10s., for his good as my eldest son. And then my two children, Cornelius Catts and David Catts, all heef (half) of my whole effects, land and moveables, that is to say, Cornelius Catts heef of all, and David Catts heeff of all. But my wife can be master of all, for bringing up to good learning my two children (*offetten*) school to learn. But if she comes to marry again, then her husband can take her away from the farm, and all will be left for the children, Cornelius Catts and David Catts, heeff and heeff."

So also in the will of John Burroughs, of Newtown, July 7, 1678, he devises to his son John his then dwelling-house, barn, orchard, out-houses, and lands, etc. "But not to dispossess my beloved wife during the time of her widowhood. But if she marry, then her husband must provide for her, as I have done." So also the will of Thomas Skillman, of Newtown, in 1739.

We cannot more appropriately conclude this brief sketch of Dutch domestic life, than by reproducing an article written by Hon. HENRY C. MURPHY, of Brooklyn, descriptive of Dutch *nomenclature*, etc. It

---

[1] J. M. Stearns, Esq., of Williamsburgh.

originally formed one of a series of letters written for the columns of the *Brooklyn Eagle*, during Mr. Murphy's residence as U. S. Minister at the Hague; and is so especially full of information concerning names and families familiar to Brooklyn and Kings County, that it cannot fail, we think, to interest our readers.

"The great body of Netherlanders who settled permanently in America, belonged, without exception, to the industrial classes. The most distinguished families amongst us, those whose ancestors filled the most important positions in the new settlement, as well as others, were from the great body of burghers. The only Governor who remained in the country, Peter Stuyvesant, was the son of a minister of Scherpenzed, in Friesland; and the only patroon who settled upon his estates, Kiliaen Van Rensselaer, was a merchant of Amsterdam. Although the Republic confirmed no titles, it protected the old nobility in their estates, and they and their families were content to leave the distant enterprises in the hands of the other classes, and remain in the province.

"Returning now to the consideration of names, in order to show what difficulties the peculiar systems adopted in this country (Holland), and continued by the settlers in our own home, throw in the way of tracing genealogies, it is to be observed that the first of these, in point of time, was the patronymic, as it is called, by which a child took, besides his own baptismal name, that of his father, with the addition of *zoon* or *sen*, meaning son. To illustrate this: if a child were baptized Hendrick and the baptismal name of his father were Jan, the child would be called Hendrick Jansen. His son, if baptized Tunis, would be called Tunis Hendricksen; the son of the latter might be Willem, and would have the name of Willem Tunissen. And so we might have the succeeding generations called successively Garret Willemsen, Marten Garretsen, Adrian Martensen, and so on, through the whole of the calendar of Christian names; or, as more frequently happened, there would be repetition in the second, third, or fourth generation, of the name of the first; and thus, as these names were common to the whole people, there were in every community different lineages of identically the same name. This custom, which had prevailed in Holland for centuries, was in full vogue at the time of the settlement of New Netherland. In writing the termination *sen*, it was frequently contracted into *se*, or *z*, or *s*. Thus the name of William Barrentsen, who commanded in the first three Arctic voyages of exploration, in 1594, '5, and '6, is given in the old accounts of those voyages, Barentsen, Barentse, Barentz, Barents, sometimes in one way, sometimes another, indifferently. Or, to give an example nearer home, both of the patronymic custom and of the contraction of the name, the father of Garret Martense, the founder of a family of that name in Flatbush, was Martin Adriaense, and his father was Adriæ Ryerse, who came from Amsterdam. The inconveniences of this practice, the confusion to which it gave rise, and the difficulty of tracing families, led ultimately to its abandonment both in Holland and in our own country. In doing so, the patronymic which the person originating the name bore, was adopted as the surname. Most of the family names thus formed and existing amongst us, may be said to be of American origin, as they were first fixed in America, though the same names were adopted by others in Holland. Hence we have the names of such families of Dutch descent amongst us as Jansen (*anglice*, Johnson), Garretsen, Cornelisen, Williamsen or Williamson, Hendricksen or Hendrickson, Clasen, Simonsen or Simonson, Tysen (son of Mathias), Aresend (son of Arend), Hansen, Lambertsen or Lambertson, Paulisen, Remsen,[1] Ryersen, Martense, Adriance, Rutgers, Everts, Phillips, Lefferts, and others. To trace connection between these families and persons in this country, it is evident, would be impossible for the reason stated, without a regular record.

"Another mode of nomenclature, intended to obviate the difficulty of an identity of names for the time being, but which rendered the confusion worse confounded for the future genealogist, was to add to the patronymic name the occupation or some other personal characteristic of the individual. Thus Laurens Jansen, the inventor of the art of printing, as the Dutch claim, had affixed to his name that of Coster—that is to say, *sexton*—an office of which he was in possession of the emoluments. But the same addition was not transmitted to the son; and thus the son of Hendrick Jansen Coster might be called Tunis Hendricksen Brouwer (brewer), and his grand-

[1] It is generally supposed that the name Rembrandt was shortened into *Rem*, and the son then became Remson or Remsen.

son might be William Tunissen Bleecker (bleacher). Upon the abandonment of the old system of names, this practice went with it; but it often happened that, while one brother took the father's patronymic as a family name, another took that of his occupation or personal designation. Thus originated such families as Coster, Brouwer, Bleecker, Schoonmaker, Stryker, Schuyler, Cryger, Snediker, Hegeman, Hofman, Dykman, Bleekman, Wortman, and Tieman. Like the others, they are not ancient family names, and are not all to be traced to Holland as the place where they first became fixed. Some of them were adopted in our own country.

"A third practice, evidently designed, like that referred to, to obviate the confusions of the first, was to append the name of the place where the person resided—not often of a large city, but of a particular, limited locality, and frequently of a particular farm or natural object. This custom is denoted in all the family names which have the prefix of *Van*, *Vander*, *Ver* (which is a contraction of *Vander*), and *Ten*—meaning, respectively, *of*, *of the*, and *at the*. From towns in Holland we have the families of Van Cleef, Van Wyck, Van Schaack, Van Bergen, and others; from Guelderland, those of Van Sinderen, Van Dyk, and Van Buren; from Utrecht, Van Winkel; from Friesland, Van Ness; from Zeeland, Van Duyne. Sometimes the *Van* has been dropped, as in the name of Boerum, of the province of Friesland; of Covert, of North Brabant; of Westervelt, of Drenthe; of Brevoort and Wessels, in Guelderland. The prefixes, *Vander* or *Ver*, and *Ten*,[1] were adopted where the name was derived from a particular spot, thus: Vanderveer (of the ferry); Vanderburg, of the hill; Vanderbilt (of the bildt—*i. e.*, certain elevations of ground in Guelderland and New Utrecht); Vanderbeck (of the brook); Vanderhoff (of the court); Verplanck (of the plank); Verhultz (of the holly); Verkerk (of the church); Ten Eyck (at the oak); Tenbroeck (at the marsh). Some were derived, as we have observed, from particular farms, thus: Van Couwenhoven (also written Van Cowdenhoven—cold farms). The founder of that family in America, Wolphert Gerrissen Van Cowenhoven, came from Amersfoort, in the

[1] The prefixes *vander* and *van de* ought to be written separately, and *not* with capital letters, as, van Anden, and not Vananden; van der Chys, and not Vanderchys; de Witt, and not Dewitt. The prefix *von* is German.

province of Utrecht, and settled at what is now called Flatlands, in our county, but what was called by him New Amersfoort. Some names, in the classification which I have attempted, have undergone a slight change in their transfer to America. Barculo is from Borculo, a town in Guelderland; Van Anden is from Andel, in the province of Groningen; Snediker should be Snediger; Bonton, if of Dutch origin, should be Bonten (son of Bondwijn or Baldwin), otherwise it is French. Van Cott was probably Van Catt, of South Holland. The Catti were the original inhabitants of the country, and hence the name. There is one family which has defied all my etymological research. It is evidently Dutch, but has most likely undergone some change, and that is the name of Van Brunt. There is no such name now existing in Holland. There are a few names derived from relative situation to a place: thus Voorhees is simply *before* or in front of *Hess*, a town in Guelderland; and Onderdonk is *below Donk*, which is in Brabant. There are a few names more arbitrary—such as Middagh (midday); Conrad (bold counsel); Hagedorn (hawthorn); Bogaert (orchard); Blauvelt (blue-field); Rosevelt (rose-field); Stuyvesant (quicksand); Wyckoff (parish-court); Hooghland (highland); Dorland (arid land); Opdyke (on the dyke); Hasbrook (hare's marsh)—and afford a more ready means of identification of relationship. The names of Brinkerhoff and Schenck, the latter of which is very common here, may be either of Dutch or German origin. Martin Schenck was a somewhat celebrated general in the war of independence. Ditmars is derived from the Danish, and Bethune is from a place in the Spanish Netherlands, near Lille. Lott is a Dutch name, though it has an English sound. There is a person of that name, from Guelderland, residing in the Hague. Pieter Lots was one of the schepens of Amersfoort in 1676, and I infer from the patronymic form of his name that Lott is a baptismal name and is derived from Lodewyck or Lewis, and that Pieter Lots means Peter the son of Lodewyck or Lot, as the former is often contracted. Some names are disguised in a Latin dress. The practice prevailed, at the time of the emigration to our country, of changing the names of those who had gone through the university and received a degree, from plain Dutch into sonorous Roman. The names of all our early ministers were thus altered. Johannes or Jan Mecklenburg became Johannes Megapolensis; Evert Willemse Bogaert became Everardus Bogardus; Jan Doris Polheem became Johannes Theodorus Polhemius. The last was the founder of the Polhemus family of Brooklyn. The records here show that he was a minister at Meppel, in the province of Drenthe, and in 1637 went as such to Brazil, under the auspices of the West India Company, whence he went to Long Island. Samuel Dries (who, by the way, was an Englishman, but who graduated at Leyden) was named Samuel Drisius. It may, therefore, be set down as a general rule, that the names of Dutch families ending in *us* have been thus latinized.

"There were many persons who emigrated from Holland who were of Gallic extraction. When the bloody Duke of Alva came into the Spanish Netherlands in 1567, clothed with despotic power over the provinces by the bigoted Philip II., more than 100,000 of the Protestants of the Gallic provinces fled to England, under the protection of Queen Elizabeth, and to their brethren in Zeeland and Holland. They retained their language, that of the ancient Gauls, and were known in England as Walloons, and in Holland as Waalen, from the name of their provinces, called Gaulsche, or, as the word is pronounced, Waalsche provinces. The number of fugitives from religious persecution was increased by the flight of the Protestants of France at the same time, and was further augmented, five years later, by the memorable massacre of St. Bartholomew. When the West India Company was incorporated, many of these persons and their descendants sought further homes in New Netherland. Such were the founders of the families of Rapelye, Cortelyou, Dubois, De Bevoise, Duryea, Crommelin, Conselyes, Montague, Fountain, and others. The Waalebocht, or Walloon's Bay, was so named because some of them settled there.

"In regard to Dutch names proper, it cannot fail to have been observed that they are of the simplest origin. They partake of the character of the people, which is eminently practical. The English, and, in fact, all the northern nations of Europe, have exhibited this tendency, more or less, in the origin of family designations, but none of them have carried it to so great a degree as the Dutch. We have in our country, both in Dutch and English, the names of

White (De Witt), Black (Swart), and Brown (Broom), but not, according to my recollection, the names of Blue, Yellow, and Red, which exist here.

"Allied to the subject of family names is that of family arms. It was not until the present monarchical *régime* that they were regulated by government. Before the independence of the country, titles, it is true, were conferred by the dukes of Burgundy and of Hainault, by the Elector of Bavaria, by the House of Austria, and by the counts of Holland, all of whom had dominion in some or other of the provinces; but family devices were not regulated. Of older date than these were the nobility of Friesland, which continues to this day, and whose members, discarding the modern names of count and baron, adhere to the ancient title of '*Jonkher*,' and their arms constitute a considerable number. In the time of the Republic no titles were conferred, and the citizens were prohibited from receiving any such from foreign powers, unless by consent of the States-General. The old nobility were, during its existence, protected in their estates and titles, but lost political caste as a privileged class. The States-General, on several occasions, granted to various ambassadors of the Republic of Venice, with which they were assiduous to cultivate a friendly intercourse, the right to quarter the arms of the United Provinces upon their own. On one occasion they decreed to one of these distinguished persons the right to quarter the lion, from the arms of the Republic, on his own; and in another instance, half the lion: but they gave no title or right of arms to Dutch citizens. The number of those, therefore, who were entitled to these family symbols in Holland, at the time of the settlement of the New Netherlands, was very few; and there are not half a dozen bearing the name of any of those who settled in our country. Some of their names have since been ennobled under the monarchy. When Louis Bonaparte ascended the throne of Holland, he promulgated a decree establishing a nobility as a part of the State, and an heraldic college; but the measure did not meet the approbation of Napoleon, and it was soon after abandoned. On the establishment of the present dynasty, after the downfall of Napoleon, this measure was renewed, and titles and houses and decorations have been scattered broadcast over the land; although the constitution of 1848, one of the consequences of the French revolution in that year, abolished the political importance of the nobility, inaugurated by the new system. It would be absurd to connect these late creations with their relatives, if there be any such, in America. I might give the escutcheons of the few of the old noblesse whose names exist in our country; but it would be of no account—two or three at the outside, and these of dubious relationship—and certainly with no satisfactory result. In fact, in whatever light you regard the subject, the grand truth, to which I have already referred, stands boldly prominent, that our settlers belonged to no privileged class. They came from the towns, where an uncommon commercial activity had arisen, consequent upon the independence of the country. They came from the fields, where the lands were held by the proprietors in a kind of feudal tenure which exists even to this day in a large portion of the country. They went to America to make their fortunes in trade, or to secure a landed estate which would belong to them and their children. They went there carrying with them free and tolerant principles. In conversing on the subject of their emigration, not long since, with a distinguished scholar of this city (the Hague), he asked me if the descendants of the Dutch in America were not very conservative in their feelings. He judged from the national character. I answered that they were eminently so, but that they were *republicans*. He smiled, and asked me further if they were not Calvinists. I told him I believed that they adhered, more closely than the Church here, to the faith and practice of their fathers. And so it is, I believe, in political and religious matters: the Dutch of America retain the ancient principles of the Fatherland more strongly than the Dutch of Holland; and in this they show that they have sprung, not from privileged, but from republican loins."

16

CHAPTER IX.

BROOKLYN DURING THE REVOLUTION.

PART I.

THE BATTLE OF BROOKLYN.*

AUGUST 27, 1776.

BROOKLYN, at the commencement of the Revolutionary War, was a pleasant but quiet agricultural town, numbering between three and four thousand inhabitants, who were mostly grouped within three or four hamlets or neighborhoods. Near "the Ferry" a few houses were clustered around the old ferry tavern, whose reputation for excellent dinners made it a favorite resort of British officers and the "young bucks" of New York; but the whole number of dwellings in this portion of the town (now embraced within the 1st, 2d, 3d, and 4th wards of the city), at that time, scarcely exceeded fifty. Along "the Heights," whose precipitous banks were crowned with goodly groves of cedar, were a few private residences, among which that of Philip Livingston, Esq., was most conspicuous for size and elegance; while the whole of that now thickly-builded portion of the city, embraced between the East River, Joralemon and Fulton streets, was occupied only by thrifty fruit-orchards, extensive market-gardens, and choice pasture-land. From either side of the ferry, along the shores of the Wallabout to Bushwick, and along the East River to Gowanus, were scattered the substantial farm-houses of old Dutch families. Nearly a mile and a half back from the ferry, and in the middle of the road to Jamaica, stood the ancient stone church, around which was gathered the village proper of Brooklyn.

* We have preferred to call this the "Battle *of Brooklyn*," because that term more completely describes the *locale* of the battle, which was fought entirely within the limits of the old town, now included in the present city of Brooklyn.

Another mile and a quarter beyond, on the same road, a few farm-houses formed the neighborhood known then and now as Bedford.

The people of Brooklyn, like those of the other towns in Kings County, were mostly Dutch, whose sympathies were but slightly enlisted in behalf of the Revolutionary cause, and in whom the fear of pecuniary loss and personal inconvenience quite outweighed the more generous impulses of patriotism. Therefore it was, that while we find the inhabitants of Suffolk County, and other portions of the State, cordially responding to the first outbreak of rebellion in Massachusetts,—sympathizing, in 1774, with their fellow-citizens of New England in regard to the odious Boston Port Bill, etc.,—the people of Kings County seem to have viewed the approaching storm with perfect indifference, and to have acted tardily in defence of their rights.

Yet, in spite of this general apathy, Brooklyn could not avoid becoming somewhat inoculated with the Revolutionary spirit which pervaded the land. In 1775 the names of "Whig" and "Tory" began to be used, and political sentiment divided families and friends. The Whigs united in articles of association for common defence, and met weekly in small parties for purposes of military drill, under the supervision of officers, some of whom were veterans of the early French wars. Many long fowling-pieces were cut down and fitted with bayonets, and those who had two guns loaned to those who had none. Elijah Freeman Payne, the teacher of the Wallabout school, left his charge, and hastened to join the American army at Boston, and the school remained closed until 1777.[1] In every quarter of the political horizon gathering clouds betokened the approach of the storm of war.[2]

The first action of the county was in response to a call from a

---

[1] MSS. of General Jeremiah Johnson.

[2] The following officers of Brooklyn militia companies had, at this time (March, '76), signed the Declaration and taken their commissions, viz.: *Half of Brooklyn.* Barent Johnson, *Captain;* Barent Lefferts, 1*st Lieut.;* Jost Debevoice, 2*d Lieut.;* Martin Schenck, *Ensign.*—*Half of Brooklyn.* Fer'd Suydam, *Captain;* Simon Bergen, 1*st Lieut.;* Wm. Brower, 2*d Lieut.;* Jacob Stellenwert, *Ensign.*

The following were the superior or regimental officers of Kings County militia:

Rutgert Van Brunt, *Col.;* Nich. Cowenhoven, *Lieut.-Col.;* Johannes Titus, 1*st Major;* John Vanderbilt, 2*d Major;* Geo. Carpenter, *Adj.;* Nich. Cowenhoven, *Q. M.* —Onderdonk, Kings County, p. 120.

Committee of Correspondence to the several counties of the colony, requesting them to appoint delegates to a general Provincial Convention to be held in the city of New York, on the 20th of April, 1775. At a meeting of the Committee chosen by the several towns of Kings County, at the County Hall in Flatbush, on the 15th of April, all the towns were represented, except Flatlands, which "would not put a negative on the proceedings, but chose to remain neutral." The Brooklyn delegates, on this occasion, were Simon Boerum,[1] Henry Williams, Jeremiah Remsen, John Suydam, Johannes Bergen, Jacob Sharpe, and Rem Cowenhoven. Mr. Boerum was appointed chairman, when it was "resolved, unanimously, that Simon Boerum, Richard Stillwell, Theodorus Polhemus, Denys Denice, and Jeremiah Vanderbilt, or a major part of them, be appointed Deputies to the Convention for choosing Delegates to the Continental Congress, to be held at Philadelphia in May."[2]

This Convention closed its session at New York, on the 22d of April; but, on the next day, the news of the battle of Lexington reached the city, where it created such a profound sensation that, on the 28th, the New York Committee again sent circulars, together with forms of association, to each county, requesting them to choose Deputies to a Provincial Congress to be held on the 24th of May, in order "to deliberate on and direct such measures as may be expedient for our common safety:"

"At a general Town Meeting, regularly warned, at Brooklyn, May 20, '75, the Magistrates and Freeholders met, and voted Jer. Remsen, Esq., into the chair, and Leffert Lefferts, Esq., Clerk.

"Taking into our serious consideration the expediency and propriety of concurring with the freeholders and freemen of the City and County of N. Y., and the other Colonies, Townships, and Precincts, within this Province, for holding a Provincial Congress to advise, consult, watch over and defend, at this very alarming crisis, all our civil and religious rights, liberties and privileges, according to their collective prudence.

---

[1] Simon Boerum's name appears as a Delegate from Kings County, in the first Continental Congress. He died at New York, in 1775; and as the British held possession of Long Island until Nov. 25, 1783, no one appears in his place.—Furman's Notes, viii., p. 223.

[2] Onderdonk's Rev. Incidents Kings County, sec. 770.

"After duly considering the unjust plunder and inhuman carnage committed on the property and persons of our brethren in the Massachusetts, who, with the other N. England Colonies, are now deemed by the Mother Country to be in a state of actual rebellion, by which declaration England hath put it beyond her own power to treat with New England, or to propose or receive any terms of reconciliation, until those Colonies shall submit as a conquered country. The first effort to effect which was by military and naval force; the next attempt is, to bring a famine among them, by depriving them of both their natural and acquired right of fishing. Further, contemplating the very unhappy situation to which the powers at home, by oppressive measures, have driven all the other Protestant Provinces, we have all evils in their power to fear, as they have already declared all the Provinces aiders and abettors of rebellion: Therefore,

"1st, *Resolved*, That Henry Williams and Jer. Remsen, Esqrs., be now elected Deputies for this Township, to meet, May 22, with other Deputies in Provincial Convention in N. Y., and there to consider, determine and do, all prudential and necessary business.

"2d, *Resolved*, That we, confiding in the wisdom and equity of said Convention, do agree to observe all warrantable acts, associations and orders, as said Congress shall direct.

"Signed by order of the Town Meeting,

"LEFFERT LEFFERTS, Clerk."[1]

Delegates were similarly appointed by the other Kings County towns; but their zeal was lukewarm, and their subsequent attendance so irregular, that in February, 1776, the Convention were obliged to request their more regular appearance.[2] It is probable that they but reflected the spirit of their constituency; for, during the previous winter of 1775–6, many portions of the province, especially on Long Island, had given such evident signs of dissatisfaction to the American cause as raised the brightest hopes of the loyalist leaders, and excited the apprehensions of the

---

[1] Onderdonk, sec. 771.

[2] It is to the credit of Brooklyn that the names of her delegates do not appear among those who are recorded as having complied with this pointed rebuke from the Convention. It may be fairly presumed, therefore, that they had regularly attended to their duties. (See Onderdonk, Rev. Inc. Kings County, sections 772, 784.)

Continental Congress, which took prompt measures to arrest its spread and break its power by disarming the Tories.[1] About the same time, the realities of war seemed to be brought nearer home to the vacillating patriots of Kings County. Washington, then in command of the patriot army at Boston, which had recently been evacuated by the British, received intelligence of an intended secret expedition by the fleet and troops under Sir Henry Clinton. Rightly divining that the British Ministry had resolved to retrieve the loss of Boston, by removing the seat of war to New York, and thus cut off all intercourse between the New England and the Southern colonies, he at once comprehended the necessity of immediately thwarting the intended manœuvre. Just at this juncture came an urgent request from the sagacious General Charles Lee, at that time in Connecticut, proposing to raise a volunteer force in that colony, and march them to the defence of New York city. The well-timed offer was accepted; and within a fortnight, General Lee, who had been ably seconded by the exertions of the indefatigable Governor Trumbull of Connecticut, was *en route* for New York, at the head of twelve thousand men. His arrival there (February 3, 1776) was unexpected and sudden, and his first measures so energetic as to reassure the friends of liberty, and effectually to crush out the spirit of Toryism, which had needed but a breath to kindle it into a flame. On the same day on which Lee entered the city, the British general, Clinton, arrived at Sandy Hook, whence he sailed for North Carolina.

Lee lost no time in initiating a system of garrison and fortification of the city and its approaches. On the 18th of February, he posted 400 of the Pennsylvania troops in Brooklyn, from the Wallabout to the Gowanus—those who could not find lodgment being billeted on the inhabitants, who were allowed 7s. per week for boarding the officers, and 1s. 4d. for privates.[2] In the midst of his labors, he was superseded (March 6) by Gen. Lord Stirling, and moving southward, was soon engaged in battle, in Charleston harbor, with Gen. Clinton.

Stirling vigorously prosecuted the defences planned and begun by

[1] Sparks' Writings of Washington, iii. 398–400, 440, 469, 470; iv. 86.

[2] Onderdonk, Kings Co. sec. 775.

Lee. The fortifications in progress of erection on Long Island were under the supervision of Col. Ward, in command of 519 men, and the inhabitants of Kings County were ordered by Congress to assist him, by "turning out for service at least one-half their male population (negroes included) every day, with spades, hoes, and pickaxes;" and by furnishing brush for fascines, wood for pickets, and other necessary timber. Col. Ward was also ordered to detail two parties of thirty men each, with three days' provisions, for the especial purpose of interrupting the communication of persons on shore with the British ship of war Phœnix, by scuttling all boats on the beach below the Narrows, and by seizing pilots—especially one Frank Jones—who decoyed vessels into the hands of the enemy. Six of the Kings County horsemen were detailed as a corps of observation, on some high point at the west end of Long Island, to give information of the entrance of the enemy into Sandy Hook, or their appearance on the coast.[1] Capt. Waldron's troop of light-horse, belonging to Brooklyn,[2] were employed as videttes along the southern coast of the county until April 10th, when they were relieved by Col. Hand's regiment of riflemen, who were stationed at New Utrecht. Upon Brooklyn Heights a battery of eight guns had been erected (as early as March 24), on land then belonging to Jacob Hicks and others. This work, open in the rear, was nearly opposite Fly Market, at Coenties slip, and was named *Fort Stirling.*[3] It was proposed to erect a citadel in its rear covering about five acres, and to be called *The Congress*, which, however, was not done.

On the night of the 10th, a body of one thousand Continental

---

[1] Onderdonk, Kings Co., sec. 777, 778, 779.

[2] Capt. Waldron's company consisted of the following individuals:

Adolph Waldron, *Captain;* William Boerum, 1*st Lieut.;* Thomas Everitt, 2*d Lieut.;* Jacob Sebring, jr., *Cornet;* Isaac Sebring, *Q. M.* Samuel Etherington, John Reade, Rob. Galbraithe, Rem A. Remsen, David Titus, Jos. Smith, Jacob Kemper, John Guest, Nich. Van Dam, Geo. Powers, William Everitt, John Hicks, Wm. Chardavoyne, Thos. Hazard. This Capt. Waldron was an innkeeper at Brooklyn ferry (*ante*, pp. 217, 219), and resided, during the war, at Preakness, N. J.—Onderdonk, Kings Co., sec. 773, 779.

[3] We are inclined to believe, from the best evidence we can obtain, that this was the same "half-moon fort" upon the edge of the Heights (on the line of present Columbia, between Orange and Clark streets,) which was subsequently garrisoned by Hessian troops, during the British occupation of the town.

May 22d, this fort was garrisoned by Lt. Randell and twelve men, with four 32-pounders and two 18's.—Force, Am. Archives, v. 480.

troops took possession of Governor's Island and constructed a redoubt upon its west side, a little southeast of Castle William.[1] On the same night a regiment occupied Red Hook, the extreme point of land north of Gowanus Bay, where they constructed a redoubt for one 3-pounder and four 18's. This redoubt, named *Fort Defiance,* was near the intersection of present Conover and Van Dyke streets, south of the Atlantic Docks.[2]

On the 14th of April, Washington arrived at New York, and his presence gave a new impulse to the work of defence, which had been so admirably planned and prosecuted by Generals Lee and Stirling; and, towards the latter part of May, he went to Philadelphia, leaving Gen. Putnam in command at New York, and Gen. Greene stationed at Brooklyn, in charge of the work of fortification there. On the 29th of June, Gen. Howe arrived from Halifax, and on the 8th of July, landed 9,000 troops upon Staten Island, where, within a few days, he was joined by his brother, Admiral Howe, with a large force of English regulars and Hessians, and on the 11th by the fragments of the defeated armies of Clinton and Parker, making the whole British force at that place, on shore and water, about 30,000 men. On the 12th of July, the Rose and Phœnix, ships of war, passed the American batteries, and went up the Hudson to Haverstraw, with the twofold object of arming the Tories of Westchester and keeping open a communica-

---

[1] *Gaine.*

[2] Maj. Shaw, June 11, '76, writes to his family: "I am now stationed at Red Hook, about four miles from New York. It is on an island [the connection between Red Hook and the main land was so slight, and it was so nearly surrounded by water, as to make it seem an island—see Appendix, No. 5], situated in such a manner as to command the entrance of the harbor entirely, where we have a fort with four 18-pounders, to fire *en barbette,* that is, over the top of the works, which is vastly better than firing through embrasures, as we can now bring all our guns to bear on the same object at once. The fort is named Defiance. It is thought to be one of the most important posts we have. There are two families here—Mr. Van Dyke and his son—good, staunch Whigs, and very clever folks, between whom and our people a very pleasant intercourse subsists. I rode out with the young man, about a week ago, to a place called Flushing, sixteen miles off, where, and in most of the country towns about, the Tories from the city have taken shelter. It is almost incredible how many of these vermin there are. Scarce a house we rode by, but Mr. Van Dyke would say, 'There lives a rascally Tory.'"—Quincy's Mem. of Samuel Shaw, p. 13. Capt. Foster was in command here on May 22, '76.—Force, v. 480.

When the Rose and Phœnix ran past the American batteries, on the 12th of July, they did not compliment this Red Hook redoubt so much as to return her fire—being, as Shaw relates, two miles distant.—Onderdonk, sec. 187.

tion with Carleton, who was coming southward by way of Lake Champlain. Meanwhile, the patriots were busily hurrying forward the completion of their defences, before the battle which was so unmistakably approaching. Hulks of vessels were sunk in the channel between Governor's Island and the Battery, and *chevaux-de-frise* formed to oppose the passage of the British vessels up the East River.[1] A large force of troops was concentrated at Brooklyn, under Gen. Greene; Sullivan, with his army, was called from the north, while from Pennsylvania, Maryland, New York, and New England troops and militia gradually augmented the American army, by the first of August, to some 27,000 men; of whom, however, nearly one-fourth were unfitted for active service by sickness. Bilious fever prostrated Gen. Greene about the middle of August, and Sullivan succeeded him at Brooklyn. Governor's Island and Paulus Hook (now Jersey City) were garrisoned, while Gen. George Clinton, at the head of some New York militia, guarded Westchester and King's Bridge from the approach of the British, and Gen. Parson's brigade performed the same service on the East River, at Kip's Bay.

We have evidence, however, that disaffection was still rife in this county; and that, while the patriot hosts were making this the scene of their most strenuous labors in the defence of a nation's existence, the actual inhabitants and inheritors of its soil were sadly lacking in spirit and unanimity of feeling.[2] We have previously seen that its representatives had been so irregular in their attendance upon the

---

[1] The channel between Long Island and Red Hook was left open, and the British vessels passed up there in the attack, Aug. 27, 1776.

[2] July 30, 1776. The Convention received a letter from the captains of the Kings County Militia, requesting to be excused from making a draft of every fourth man (according to Resolutions of Convention, July 19), and saying that they will turn out their whole militia or command to drive stock into the interior, and to guard the coast, etc. It was signed by Jno. Vanderbilt, Lambert Suydam, Barent Johnson, John Titus, Corn. Vanderveer, Rem Williamson, Bernardus Suydam, Adrian Van Brunt, *Captains;* but their request was not granted by the Convention.—Force's Am. Archives, vol. i., Fifth Series, p. 1460.

"A Roll of the commissioned officers, non-commissioned officers, and privates of the Troop of Horse in King's County, which were upon duty to drive off the stock, commenced August 14, 1776. *Upon duty and came over from L. I.:* Daniel Rappelye, 1*st Lieut.;* Jacob Bloom, 2*d Lieut.;* Peter Vandervoort, *Ens.;* Hendrick Johnson, *Sgt.;* John Blanco, *Trumpeter;* Reyer Suydam, John Vanderveer, *Privates. Upon duty, but remained upon L. I.;* Lambert Suydam, *Capt.;* Peter Wyckoff, *Quartermaster;* Hen-

sessions of the Convention, as to call forth the special animadversion of that body; and now, when every American heart should have been nerved to still greater fortitude, the county towns appeared still more "shaky" in their allegiance. On August 14th, Mr. Polhemus appeared in Convention and informed them that Kings County had held no election for deputies since May previous, but that the County Committees had met and requested him to attend as a member until another election. The Convention allowed him to represent the county, except in matters relating to the formation of Government.[1] Subsequently, an election held by Kings County, on 19th of August, was declared defective, inasmuch as the Deputies were not authorized to frame a new form of government. A new election was therefore ordered for the 24th of August, but was never held,[2] as Kings County was then the theatre of actual hostilities. The rumors of disaffection in the country were at this time so strong, that the Provincial Congress ordered a committee to repair thither, and if the reports proved to be well-founded, to disarm and secure the disaffected citizens, remove or destroy the crops, and even, if necessary, "*lay the whole county waste.*"[3] The arrest and disarming of the Tories, in accordance with these instructions, was energetically prosecuted, and produced a salutary effect, which would probably have proved permanent, but for the disastrous result of the subsequent battle of the 27th.

Among the other approaches to the city, that by Long Island had been amply provided for by the skill and forethought of Gens. Greene and Sullivan. In addition to the battery at Red Hook and Fort Sterling, previously mentioned, and which were the first works erected at Brooklyn, the following strong line of fortifications was constructed across the island from the Wallabout to the head of Gowanus Creek.

---

drick Suydam, *Clerk;* John Nostrand, Jacob Suydam, Isaac Snediker, Isaac Boerum John Ryerson, Rutgert Vanbrunt, Chas. De Bevois, Benjamin Seaman, Roelof Terhune, Andrew Casper, Thos. Betty, Martin Kershaw, Peter Miller, Hendrick Wyckoff, *Privates.* (Signed) "DANIEL RAPPELYE, Lt."
—Force's Am. Archives, vol. i., Fifth Series, 953.

[1] Ibid., i. 1506, date Aug. 17, 1776.

[2] Ibid., i. 1525, date Aug. 21, 1776.

[3] Ibid., i. 1497, date Aug. 19, 1776. Messrs. Duer and Hobart and Colonels Remsen and DeWitt were appointed said committee.

These fortifications were:

1. A redoubt, mounting five guns, and called *Fort Putnam*, which was erected upon a heavily-wooded hill overlooking the Wallabout, now known as *Fort Greene*, or *Washington Park*.[1] When cleared of its trees, this was a fine position, commanding the East River and the roads leading into Brooklyn from the country.

2. A line of intrenchment extending northwesterly from Fort Putnam down the hill to a spring, then on the verge of the Wallabout.[2]

3. A line of intrenchment, extending in a zigzag course southwesterly from Fort Putnam across the old Jamaica turnpike (now Fulton avenue),[3] and along the crest of the high land between and nearly parallel with Nevins and Bond streets to the head of Gowanus Creek (Freeck's mill-pond), at about the junction of present Bond and Warren streets.[4]

4. Upon the land then belonging to John Johnson, and about midway between Fort Putnam and the Jamaica Turnpike[5] (at junction of present DeKalb avenue and Hudson street), and adjoining the line of intrenchment, was another small redoubt.

5. On "Bergen's Hill," between Smith and Court street, in the vicinity of First Place, was another redoubt, mounting four guns, which was probably the one named *Fort Box*.[6] It was subsequently strengthened and occupied by the British; and as late as 1852, but-

---

[1] This hill, at the time of the Revolution, belonged to John Cowenhoven, sen., his son, Rem Cowenhoven, and Casper Wooster, and was known, from its heavy timber, as "Cowenhoven's *boschje*," or woods.

[2] Lossing (Field Book of the Revolution, ii. 806) says that the site of this spring was marked (in 1852) by a pump in a tannery near the intersection of Flushing avenue and Portland street.

[3] The large sycamore-tree, just above "The Abbey" on the north side of Fulton, a little above its junction with De Kalb avenue (and which was cut down in the fall of 1859—Ed.), is believed to have marked the point where the line of intrenchment (which was also renewed in the war of 1812–14) crossed the Jamaica road.—Furman MSS., vii. 251. No. 159 Fulton avenue now (1867) marks the site of the tree above mentioned.

[4] Lossing says, "across the Flatbush road, near the junction of Flatbush avenue and Powers street, to Freek's Mill Pond, at the head of Gowanus Creek, near the junction of Second avenue and Carroll street;" but this would have carried the line of intrenchment along the low lands, which was not probable.

[5] Lossing says, "a little eastward of Fort Putnam, near the Jamaica road."

[6] Lossing says, "between Smith street and First avenue, not far from the termination of Hoyt street at Carroll."

tons marked "42" (42d Highlanders) were found on its site. In 1812, this fortification was restored and called "Fort Lawrence."

6. On the land of Johannes Debevoise and Rutgert Van Brunt, half way between the Jamaica road and Brower's mill-pond, probably between Atlantic and Pacific, Nevins and Bond streets, a redoubt was erected, mounting five guns, and called *Fort Greene*.

7. About at the junction of Clinton and Atlantic streets, on a very steep conical hill, called *Ponkiesbergh*, and otherwise known as "Cobble Hill," was a fort of three guns. Its trenches ascended spirally to the top, where a platform was laid for the cannon; from which circumstance it derived the nickname of "Corkscrew Fort." It commanded Fort Stirling, on the Heights, and on that account was made lower by the British during their subsequent occupation, for fear that it might fall into the hands of the Continentals, in which case Fort Stirling would have been untenable.[1]

---

[1] The precise location of this fort cannot now be ascertained. Lossing (*Field Book of Rev.*, ii. 806) and Dawson (*Battles of America*, i. 144) describe it as being "at the head of the tunnel of the Long Island R. Road, in the vicinity of Boerum and Atlantic streets," which is manifestly incorrect. Gen. J. G. Swift, under whose superintendence the lines were reconstructed, and Cobble Hill Fort rebuilt during the war of 1812, in a letter to the author, designates the spot as marked (1860) by a little willow-tree on the south side of Atlantic street, near Clinton. The Savings Bank, on the corner of these streets, is also pointed out as the site; and Furman, MS. Notes (Oct., 1835), says that "about 40 years ago, it was currently reported about Kings County, that the spot of ground *about* 100 *feet northeasterly from the corner of Atlantic and Court streets, then in the old Red Hook lane, and near the foot of a fortification then known as Cobble Hill Fort*, and afterwards, in the war of 1812, as Fort Swift, was haunted by the spirit of a murdered man." As nearly as we can describe it, Cobble Hill rose from old Red Hook Lane, now swallowed up by Court street, on the block now bounded by that street, Atlantic, Pacific, and Clinton streets, and was nearer to the Court street end of the block. As before stated, this fort was strengthened in 1814, and called Fort Swift. Fort Putnam was also strengthened and called Fort Greene.

In describing the sites of these fortifications we differ, as will be seen, from Mr. Lossing; but we do so with the respect which is due him as having been the *first* to attempt their precise location. In addition to a better opportunity for extended examination, and with that more intimate acquaintance with the topographical peculiarities of the region, which a local historian may be presumed to have, we have also enjoyed the advice and assistance of Mr. SILAS LUDLAM, the well-known City Surveyor, whose father, Stephen Ludlam, surveyed the old lines when they were comparatively plain, the field-notes of which survey are still in his son's possession. From Mr. Ludlam's extensive collection of farm maps, etc., as well as from his long acquaintance with, and recollection of, Brooklyn *as it was* before brick and mortar had completely changed its features, we have gleaned many facts of great use to us, both in this and other portions of our work.

All Long Island and Brooklyn historians, previous to Mr. Lossing, have been contented with rehearsing the statements of Gen. Jeremiah Johnson, who has preserved

As we have already seen, the whole British naval and military force which had been concentrated in the Bay of New York and on Staten Island before the 13th of July, gave, as yet, no indication of the course or manner of their intended attack. Their movements seemed alternately to indicate an immediate readiness, and then a certain indecision. At this time, also, dispatches were received from England, announcing an important change in the French ministry, and the prospect of a general continental war, in which England would be involved. The conjecture that the tenor of these dispatches rendered the British commanders exceedingly cautious, and even anxious for a reconciliation, was further strengthened by the arrival, on the of 17th of August, of a flag of truce from the British fleet. It was borne by Lord Drummond, who had already twice violated his parole given to the American general while engaged in similar diplomatic errands, and the conciliatory overtures which he presented were indignantly spurned by Washington, who availed himself of the opportunity to administer his lordship a severe rebuke for his former duplicity.

Washington, meanwhile, lost no time in providing against every

---

much relative to our Revolutionary period that history will not willingly let die, but whose description and maps of localities are too vague to be entirely satisfactory. The industrious Furman, who possessed the inborn antiquarian spirit of *accuracy in details*, has preserved, in manuscript, much interesting material relative to these points, which we have very freely drawn upon in the compilation of this history.

That these defences were by no means despicable, is sufficiently evidenced by the fact that some of them were retained and strengthened by the British during their subsequent occupation of the island. Major Holland, of the British engineers, testified that they were well and solidly made, and according to the rules of fortification, and that they could have been held by a sufficient force for a long time, but that they had not been entirely completed. We also have the following direct testimony of Lieut. Anbury, an experienced British officer, published in his Travels in North America (vol. ii. 540): "At a small distance from the town (Brooklyn) are some considerable heights, commanding the city of New York. On these is erected a strong regular fort (now Fort Greene) with four bastions. To describe the works thrown up by the Americans on this Island, would be bestowing more attention on the subject than it deserves, as they actually cover the whole. They are not only on grounds and situations that are extremely advantageous and commanding, but works of great strength, that I am at a loss to account for their so hastily abandoning them, as they were certain by such a step to give up New York. I am induced to believe that Gen. Washington thought the Americans were so panic-struck after the engagement, as our troops pursued them close to their lines, that they would not stand an assault; and if his lines were carried he was sensible there was no place of retreat, and that his army must inevitably have been destroyed."

possible contingency of attack. Tories were transferred from New York to the care of Gov. Trumbull, of Connecticut, accompanied with paternal requests for their kind treatment. Measures were taken to quench the rising flame of loyalty in New Jersey; suspected persons in Kings County, on Long Island, were disarmed, and a committee, as we have already seen, was sent by Congress to enforce the suppression of toryism at every hazard. The public archives were carefully conveyed from New York to the care of Congress, at Philadelphia, the officers' wives in camp were removed from danger, and the most liberal and tender measures for the protection and relief of women and children in the menaced city were suggested by Washington and promptly carried out by Congress. At New Utrecht, Col. Hand, with his corps of Pennsylvania riflemen, was posted on the hill above the present site of Fort Hamilton, in order to serve as a check to, and to give information of, any landing in that quarter.

The rejection of their overtures seems to have decided the British generals in their action. At dawn on the 22d of August, information was received at the American headquarters from Brig.-Gen. William Livingston, then in camp at Elizabeth, N. J., that Lord Howe had landed a large force at Gravesend Bay, on Long Island, and that 20,000 men had gone to take possession of that island, while 15,000 were to attack Bergen, Elizabethtown Point, and Amboy. These reports, although exaggerated, had a substratum of truth, as was evidenced, at sunrise, by the roar of cannon and dense columns of smoke arising from near the Narrows.[1]

---

[1] The British fleet, after taking position to cover the landing of the troops, shelled the heights and woods on the Long Island shore, in order to drive out any force which might be there concealed. It was this preliminary bombardment which startled the expectant American army, and which may possibly afford an explanation of the following curious circumstance as related by Judge Furman (MS. Memoranda, viii., p. 396):

"In the month of August, '76, on the second or third day before the landing of the British troops upon Long Island, an apparent cannonading was heard. So very distinct was this cannonading, and so very regular was it and continuous, that all the inhabitants of the island residing between the distance of two miles from the city of New York and about thirty-five miles down the island, were satisfied that the British had landed and attacked the American army. Those residing at the west end of the island immediately commenced moving their families and driving their cattle towards the interior; and in such numbers, that my aunt Tyler, then a young girl, and living at her home in New Lots, nine miles from Brooklyn ferry, tells me she was awakened the next morning by the lowing of cattle, and upon arising, she found the roads blocked up with cows, horses, sheep, &c., which had been driven up during the night to escape the plunder

About nine o'clock A. M. four thousand light infantry, with forty pieces of cannon, crossed over from Staten Island in flat-boats, under the guns of the Rainbow and other men-of-war which lay anchored where Fort Lafayette now rises in the centre of the Narrows, and landed at Denise's ferry (now Fort Hamilton) in the town of New Utrecht.[1] An hour after the landing of this first division, a second, comprising English and Hessian troops, left the British ships and transports, and in regular rows of boats, under command of Commodore Hotham, passed over and landed in the bend of Gravesend Bay, at a place now known as Bath, in front of New Utrecht. The embarkation of the entire force, comprising 15,000 men, under cover of the *Phœnix*, *Rose*, and *Greyhound*, was safely completed by noon. The main part of the invading army quickly extended itself over the plain bordering on Gravesend Bay; and the country people, following the dictates of their fears or their consciences, either made haste to place themselves under British protection, or abandoned their farms and sought refuge within the American lines.

Col. Hand's riflemen, on the hill overlooking the scene, could, of course, offer no effectual resistance, and setting fire to the wheat and hay stacks, to prevent their falling into the enemy's hands, fell back towards Flatbush, where they took position behind a redoubt between that village and the Brooklyn lines.

Howe established his quarters at New Utrecht, and dispatched Lord Cornwallis, with the reserves, Col. Donop's corps of Hessian yagers and grenadiers, with six field-pieces, to Flatbush, and with instructions not to attack the place if he should find it occupied by the enemy. Taking his position at Gravesend, Cornwallis pushed forward Donop's corps to Flatbush, which the latter reached towards evening,—the three hundred American riflemen, who had occupied it,

---

of the British, as they supposed. In the morning, however, it was discovered that the British army had not stirred a foot from their encampment on Staten Island, and that not a single cannon had been fired! (?) The next day after—as if, indeed, it had been intended by a good Providence as a warning to the people of what was fast approaching—the roads between the city of New York and Jamaica, nine miles distant, were covered with the British light horsemen, in their scarlet cloaks."

[1] On the farms of Isaac Cortelyou and Adrian Van Brunt, which lay west of the Bath House, *i. e.* between the Cortelyou road and the Bath road, anciently called DeBruyn road.—Onderdonk, K. Co., sec. 801.

retiring before him, "a few cannon-balls being sent after them," to accelerate their steps. Early on the following morning (23d), however, these same riflemen attacked the right wing of the Hessian outposts, but retired on being confronted with a field-piece. On the afternoon of the same day, another attack was made upon the left of the Hessian line, which was driven back upon the main body, south of the village church, where the skirmish raged furiously for over an hour. Under the galling fire of the American sharp-shooters, the Hessians were compelled to seek shelter in some of the houses, cutting loop-holes in the walls, from whence they could fire upon their assailants. Finally, the Hessian guns were brought into position, before which the Americans fell back, but not until they had set fire to several dwelling-houses.[1] On the 25th, a stronger force of riflemen, with some cannon, opened with ball and grapeshot upon the village, from the edge of the neighboring woods, but their fire was soon silenced by the superior metal and service of the Hessian guns. These foreign troops, who had now been since the 22d continually in the advance, and who were severely harassed by the unremitting activity of their lively foes—a species of fighting for

---

[1] (Gen. Sullivan's account): "On Friday, 23d, a party of British took possession of Flatbush, which brought on a hot fire from our troops, who are advantageously posted in woods and on every eminence. An advanced party are encamped a little to the N. W. of Flatbush church, and have a battery somewhat west of Jer'h Vanderbilt's, whence they fire briskly on our people, who often approach and discharge rifles within 200 yards of their works. One of our gunners threw a shell into Mr. Axtell's house, where a number of officers were at dinner, but we have not heard what damage it did.

"*Aug.* 23. This afternoon the enemy formed and attempted to pass the wood by Bedford (Flatbush), and a smart fire between them and the riflemen ensued. A number of musketry came up to the assistance of the riflemen, whose fire, with that of the field-pieces, caused a retreat of the enemy. Our men followed to the house of Judge Lefferts (where a number of them had taken lodgings), drove them out, and burned the contiguous buildings. We have driven them half a mile from their former station."

Washington disapproved of this wasteful and scattering fire upon the enemy.

Strong, in his *Hist. of Flatbush*, says the British encamped in a diagonal direction across that village, their tents extending from the little lane over the farms of Hendrick Vanderveer, of J. C. Bergen, of Jacobus Vandeventer, and so on, in a northeasterly line towards the road to New Lots. The main body were posted on the south of the church and west of the main street. They soon gained possession of the intrenchment erected by the Americans in the north of the village. They also knocked out large port-holes in the stone house of Adrian Hegeman, now occupied by Mrs. Cynthia Lefferts. The house of Lefferts Martense, on the opposite side of the road, built of wood, was also fortified. It fronted south, and in the roof, on the north side, which extended nearly to the ground, they cut holes through which to discharge muskets.

which their experience in the regular methods of European warfare had totally unfitted them—were allowed to rest from the 24th to the 25th; but were again alarmed at 2 o'clock on the morning of the 26th, and returned to their position in the front; against which, on the afternoon of the same day, the Americans made such an imposing demonstration, that Cornwallis, in pursuance of previous imperative orders from Howe, directed Donop, much to the latter's disgust, to fall back upon the main body at Flatlands.

On the 25th of August, the same day on which General Putnam took command within the American lines, General Von Heister,[1] the veteran commander-in-chief of the British auxiliaries, with General Knyphausen, and two full brigades of Hessians, landed at New Utrecht, and advanced on the middle road towards Flatbush,—Lieutenant-Colonel Dalrymple being left in charge of the reserves on Staten Island. The invading army on Long Island, which now numbered "upwards of twenty thousand" rank and file,[2] was unequalled for experience, discipline, and *materiel* of war, and was supported by a fleet in the Bay of New York, numbering over four hundred ships and transports, and by ten ships of the line, twenty frigates, together with bomb-ketches and other small vessels. Opposed to this splendid army, the Americans had only some eight thousand men,[3] mostly volunteers or militia, without cavalry, with but slender stores of light-artillery, and unsupported by a single vessel.

Meanwhile, on the 23d of August, Gen. Howe issued the following proclamation to the people of the island:

A PROCLAMATION

By his EXCELLENCY, *the* HON. WM. HOWE, *General and Commander-in-Chief of all His Majesty's forces within the Colonies lying on the Atlantic Ocean, from Nova Scotia to West Florida, inclusive, &c., &c.*

---

[1] Lossing (*Field-Book of Rev.*, ii. 804) says: "Lieutenant-General De Heister was an old man, and warmly attached to his master, the Landgrave of Hesse Cassel. The long voyage of fourteen weeks dispirited him, 'and,' says Sir George Collier, 'his patience and tobacco became exhausted.' A sniff of land-breeze revived him. 'He called for Hock, and swallowed large potations to the health of his friends.'"

[2] Lord Howe's Observations, in Narrative, p. 45.

[3] Bancroft, ix. 90, *note;* Almond's Debates, xiii. 9, 54, 314.

Whereas, it is represented that many of the loyal inhabitants of this Island have been compelled by the leaders in rebellion, to take up arms against His Majesty's Government, Notice is hereby given to all persons so forced into rebellion, that on delivering themselves up at said quarters of the Army, they will be received as faithful subjects, have permits peaceably to return to their respective dwellings, and meet with full protection for their persons and property. All those who choose to take up arms for the restoration of order and good government within this Island, shall be disposed of in the best manner, and have every encouragement that can be expected.

Given under my hand at Head Quarters on Long Island, Aug. 23, 1776.

WM. HOWE.

By His Excellency's command, ROB'T MACKENSIE, *Sec.*

A few persons availed themselves of this offer; but the majority, although by no means averse to British rule, were probably unwilling to declare themselves until they were certain which would prove the winning side.

In the city of New York, during the night succeeding the landing, all was confusion and alarm. The camp and its various outposts were the scene of vigilant activity and preparation, for a rumor had spread that vessels had been detached from the British fleet, with the intention of circumnavigating Long Island, and by thus stealing a passage through the Sound and East River, to cut off all communication with the Westchester main. Under the supposition, also, that the enemy would immediately march upon the American lines at Brooklyn, Washington had that same evening sent over six regiments to re-enforce those defences; and early next morning, in the momentary expectation of an attack, he addressed an earnest appeal to the troops at Brooklyn, reanimating their hopes and encouraging them to make a bold stand.[1] Cornwallis, meanwhile, was resting

[1] The following extract is from the General's Orderly-book, August 23d: "The enemy have now landed on Long Island, and the hour is fast approaching in which the honor and success of this army, and the safety of our bleeding country, will depend. Remember, officers and soldiers, that you are freemen, fighting for the blessings of liberty; that slavery will be your portion, and that of your posterity, if you do not acquit yourselves like men. Remember how your courage and spirit have been despised and traduced by your cruel invaders; though they have found, by dear experience at Boston, Charlestown, and other places, what a few brave men, contending in

almost idly at Flatbush, apparently kept in check by Hand's riflemen, but really in obedience to Howe's imperative orders. His caution may be counted among the several providences which seemed to watch over the American army, and saved it from what might otherwise have been total annihilation. For had he, at this juncture, made one vigorous push, he would, with the force at his command, almost certainly have made himself master of works scarcely in a state of completion, and an enemy poorly organized or prepared to receive him. Gen. Greene, under whose supervision the American defences had been constructed, and who had made himself thoroughly acquainted with the whole detail of the army, and with every important point and pass on the west end of Long Island, had been prostrated by illness a few days previous. Sullivan, who succeeded him (on the 20th), was faithful and brave, but was personally unknown to the troops under his command, and had but little opportunity to acquaint himself fully with the field of operations. As a consequence, when Gen. Washington visited the lines on Long Island on the 24th, he found things at "loose ends." Disorder was perceptible in every department—detachments skirmished with the enemy's vanguard, or picked off his sentries, without any orders and with little method—others were little better than marauding parties, who burned the houses of friend and foe alike, and robbed dwellings, barns, and hen-roosts with impunity. Annoyed and alarmed that such a state of things should exist in the face of an approaching army, Washington immediately resolved to place some one in command better fitted, by local knowledge and personal influence, to regulate and harmonize the diverse elements of which the army was composed. Gen. Putnam, whose brave heart had been aching

---

their own land, and in the best of causes, can do against hirelings and mercenaries. Be cool, but determined; do not fire at a distance, but wait for orders from your officers. It is the general's express orders, that if any man attempt to skulk, lie down, or retreat without orders, he be instantly shot down as an example. He hopes no such will be found in this army; but, on the contrary, that every one for himself resolving to conquer or die, and trusting in the smiles of Heaven upon so just a cause, will behave with bravery and resolution. Those who are distinguished for their gallantry and good conduct may depend on being honorably noticed and suitably rewarded; and if this army will but emulate and imitate their brave countrymen in other parts of America, he has no doubt they will, by a glorious victory, save their country and acquire to themselves immortal honor."

for several days to have a hand in the approaching fight, was made quite happy by being appointed to the command on Long Island,[1] and on the 25th he entered upon its duties, under minute and wholesome instructions from the commander-in-chief. Prominent among these were strict orders for the suppression of the prevailing looseness and laxity of *morale* so evident among the troops. "Shameful it is," said Washington, "to find that those men who have come hither in defence of the rights of mankind, should turn invaders of them, by destroying the substance of their friends. . . . The distinction between a well-regulated army and a mob, is the good discipline and order of the former, and the licentious and disorderly behavior of the latter." Gen. Sullivan, with Brig.-Gen. Lord Stirling as his second, was assigned to the command of the troops outside of the lines at Brooklyn.

This series of works (described, *ante*, pp. 251, 252), which extended over a mile and a half in length, and mounted twenty large and small cannon, and which was defended by ditches and felled trees, with *abatis* of sharpened stakes, formed simply the *interior* or intrenched line of defence of the American army. Its *exterior* line of defence, at a distance of about two miles from the intrenchments, was that furnished by the natural topographical peculiarities of the country.

In the rear of Brooklyn a series of hills, now known as the Mount Prospect range, extends northeasterly from the Narrows towards the Jamaica road at East New York, and, in broken elevations, continues further on beyond that point. This range was, at that time, thickly covered with woods, pierced, at different points, with roads, all of which offered obvious routes for the British approach to Brooklyn. These were:

1. *Martense's Lane*, extending along the southern border of the present Greenwood Cemetery, from the old Flatbush and New Utrecht road to the coast road, which ran along Gowanus Bay, on about the line of the present Third avenue.

2. The *Flatbush Pass* and road, at the junction of the Brooklyn

---

[1] *Letter of Adjt.-Gen. Reed to his wife*, Aug. 24: "Gen. Putnam was made happy by obtaining leave to go over. The old man was quite miserable at being kept here."

THE BATTLE PASS (IN PROSPECT PARK), BROOKLYN.

(From a Sketch by G. L. BURDETTE, taken in **1792**.)

Page 261.

and Flatbush turnpike with the Coney Island Plankroad, and now within the limits of Prospect Park. The defences of this pass were, *first*, a sort of crescent-shaped intrenchment, just within the village of Flatbush, and lying diagonally across the main street, a little south of Judge Martense's house, with a ditch of considerable depth on its northerly side;[1] and, *secondly*, a small redoubt, mounting a few small pieces of artillery, at the "Valley Grove," to guard the passage through the "Port Road,"[2] and by the direct route to Brooklyn. Near this redoubt stood an immense white-oak tree, mentioned in Governor Dongan's Patent as one of the boundary marks between Brooklyn and Flatbush.[3] This, in obedience to the stern exigencies of war, was felled across the road, where, in consequence of the then dense woods on the south and the swamp on the north, it formed a very considerable obstacle to an enemy's advance.

3. The *Bedford Pass*, at the intersection of the old "Clove Road" with the Flatbush and Brooklyn boundary-line, half a mile south of the hamlet of Bedford.

4. And three miles east of Bedford, on the old Jamaica turnpike, and just at the present entrance to the "Cemetery of the Evergreens," was a road through the hills, known as the *Jamaica Pass*.

The natural line of defence afforded by this range of heavily wooded hills could not, of course, with the small force at the disposal of the American generals, be properly occupied by any continuous line of troops. All that could be done, under the circumstances, was to post strong picket-guards (for they could scarcely be called more than that) at its most defensible points; nor was it expected by Washington that the attenuated line of troops (scarcely twenty-five hundred in all) which held the ridge for a distance of over five miles, would do more than a picket-guard's duty, in discovering the approach of the British and harassing them on their march. The extreme right of the American line, which was com-

---

[1] Strong's Hist. Flatbush.

[2] The "Port Road" was a lane diverging from the Flatbush turnpike, near the present city line, and extending to the East River, across Freecke's mill-dam. It followed the general line of the present First street, and remains of it are still to be seen near Fifth avenue. (*Ante*, 159, *note*.)

[3] This tree was in the present Prospect Park, nearly in the centre of the Flatbush road, and about opposite the west end of the old toll-gate house. It is hoped that its position will be carefully indicated, in some permanent manner, by the Park Commissioners.

manded by Gen. Lord Stirling, was at the Red Lion Tavern, where Martense's Lane enters the shore road. Along this lane, which cuts eastwardly through the Greenwood Hills, were stationed one hundred and twenty of Colonels Atlee's and Kichline's Pennsylvania musketeers and riflemen, who sheltered themselves behind stone walls and among the trees, rocks, and hollows of that locality, as their fancy or experience dictated. The left of this line rested, or was supposed to rest, upon the right of General Sullivan's command, consisting of Henshaw's Massachusetts and Johnston's New Jersey regiments, which formed the centre of the American line, at the junction of the Port Road with the Flatbush road, near the intersection of the present Flatbush avenue with the city line. Here were the defences mentioned on page 261, and here it was supposed, from the previous demonstrations made by the Hessians, would be the main point of attack. At this point the range of hills formed an obtuse angle, forming two sides of an immense amphitheatre, looking down upon a broad and beautiful plain, upon which rested, in slumberous quiet, the villages of Flatbush, Flatlands, New Utrecht, and Gravesend; while in the further distance were to be seen the town of Jamaica and the blue waters of ocean. Sullivan's arrangement of his troops corresponded with the configuration of the summit of the hills upon which he had taken position; the regiment on his right stretching along the brow of the hill on either side of the Flatbush road, three or four hundred feet south of its junction with the Port Road (*note*, p. 261), and facing obliquely to them were the two regiments on the left, extending nearly a mile to the east of the Flatbush road, while Colonel Miles' First Pennsylvania regiment, with some Connecticut levies, continued the line still another mile further eastward, occupying the Bedford Pass (page 261) and the woods beyond towards the Jamaica Pass.[1] It will be seen, there-

[1] An American officer of distinction in the battle writes the following to the Connecticut Courant (No. 673), as a corrective to some high encomiums which he had seen on Colonel Miles:

"The enemy were some days encamped at Flatbush, about 3½ miles S. and E. of our lines. Within half a mile of the enemy is a ridge of hills, covered with woods, running from the narrows about N. E. toward Jamaica about 6 miles. Through this woods are three passes, which we kept strongly guarded, 800 men at each, to prevent the enemy penetrating the woods. The night before August 27, on the west road were posted Col. Hand's regiment, a detachment from Penn. and N. Y.; next east were posted Col.

fore, that while Sullivan's right rested, but imperfectly, upon Stirling's left, his own left wing was entirely unsupported, or, as the military phrase is, "hung in air." Yet, both the officers who planned and the men who held these positions, seemed entirely unconscious of the appalling danger which menaced them if the enemy should turn their flank. As we have before remarked, it is hardly probable, from the extremely limited force which could be employed to occupy so widely extended a line, as well as from the comparatively slight nature of the fortifications thrown up at different points, that Washington intended that the Mount Prospect ridge should be held otherwise than as a picket-line, from whence the men were to fall back upon the fortified works at Brooklyn, without risking any very serious engagement with the enemy.

Beyond and to the eastward of this range of hills was a flat country, traversed by several roads, reconnoitred by mounted patrols under Colonel Wyllys of Connecticut. In addition to these, General Woodhull, former president of the New York Convention, had charge of the local militia, who were occupied in removing the live-stock to Hempstead and destroying forage, in order to prevent its falling into the hands of the enemy.

Thus, on the evening of the 26th of August, in the impenetrable shadow of the woods which crowned the summit and slopes of the Flatbush hills, these few regiments of raw, undisciplined troops awaited the coming of their foe, whose tents and camp-fires stretched along the plain beneath them, in an unbroken line, from Gravesend to Flatlands.

The position of the British army was now as follows: the left wing, under Gen. Grant, rested on New York Bay; the Hessians, under De Heister, formed the centre, opposite to Sullivan's position, at Flatbush Pass; while the right wing, which was designed to bear the brunt of the coming battle, and was composed of the choice battalions under Gen. Clinton and Earls Cornwallis and Percy, stretched

---

Johnson of Jersey and Lieut.-Col. Henshaw of Mass.; next east were posted Col. Wyllys and Lieut.-Col. Wills of Conn. East of all these Col. Miles of Penn. was posted toward Jamaica, to watch the motion of the enemy and give intelligence. Col. Miles' guard on the east of the woods, by some fatality, what I don't know, suffered the enemy to march their main body to the east of the woods and advance near two miles in rear of our guards in the woods without discovery."

along the eastern foot of the range of hills from New Utrecht to Flatlands, idly skirmishing and occupying the attention of the Americans.

Gen. Howe, meanwhile, had been informed of the unguarded state of the road at Bedford,[1] "and that it would not be a difficult matter to turn the Americans' left flank, which would either oblige them to risk an engagement, or to retire under manifest disadvantage." In view of this fact, he adopted the following plan of attack, viz.:

(1.) Gen. Grant, with two brigades, one Highland regiment, and two companies of New York Provincials, was to move forward upon the coast-road, towards Gowanus, while some of the ships-of-war were to menace New York, and to operate against the right of the American fortified lines.[2] While the attention of the Americans was thus diverted by the threatened danger to the city and to their rear,

(2.) The German troops, under Gen. De Heister, were to force the Flatbush Pass and the direct road to Brooklyn, by assault; and,

(3.) At evening gun-fire, the right wing, under Clinton, Cornwallis, and Percy, accompanied by Howe himself, was to move, in light marching order, from Flatlands, across the country to New Lotts,

---

[1] Stedman (i., p. 194) attributes the information to Generals Sir Henry Clinton and Sir William Erskine, whereas Onderdonk (Kings Co., sec. 802) says it was furnished by disaffected inhabitants.

[2] (Extract from Lord Howe's letter): "Being informed next day (26th) by Gen. Howe of his intention to advance with the army that night to the enemy's lines, and of his wishes that some diversion might be attempted by the ships on this side, I gave direction to Sir Peter Parker for proceeding higher up in the channel towards the town of New York next morning, with the Asia, Renown, Preston (Com. Hotham embarked in the Phœnix, having been left to carry on the service in Gravesend Bay), Roebuck, and Repulse, and to keep those ships in readiness for being employed as occasion might require; but the wind veering to the northward soon after the break of day, the ships could not be moved up to the distance proposed: therefore, when the troops under Gen. Grant, forming the left column of the army, were seen to be engaged with the enemy in the morning, the Roebuck, Capt. Hammond, leading the detached squadron, was the only ship that could fetch high enough to the northward to exchange a few random shots with the battery on Red Hook; and the ebb making strongly down the river soon after, I ordered the signal to be shown for the squadron to anchor."

From the Journal of a British Officer, we learn that "the Admiral directed Sir Geo. Collier to place the Rainbow, at dawn of day, in the Narrows, abreast of a large stone building called Denyse's (now Fort Hamilton), where he understood the rebels had cannon and a strong post, in which situation she would also be able to enfilade the road leading from New York, and prevent re-enforcements being sent to the rebel outposts, as well as to their troops who were stationed to oppose the landing."

in order to secure the passes between that place and Jamaica, and to turn, if possible, the American left.

Accordingly, late on the afternoon of the 26th, De Heister and his Hessians took post at Flatbush, and relieved Lord Cornwallis, who withdrew his division (leaving only the 42d Regiment) to Flatlands, about two miles southeast of Flatbush. At about 9 o'clock of the same evening the vanguard of the right of the army, consisting of a brigade of light infantry and the light dragoons, under command of Gen. Sir Henry Clinton, moved eastward on the road to New Lotts. He was followed by Lord Percy, with the artillery and grenadiers, and Lord Cornwallis, with a reserve, the 71st Regiment, and fourteen field-pieces, accompanied by the commander-in-chief, Lord Howe. The troops were withdrawn under cover of the darkness, and with great caution, from their respective encampments, in which the tents were left standing, the fires burning, and every appearance of actual occupation maintained. The intended route of march was known only to a few of the principal officers, and, guided by a resident Tory, the army moved over the country, through fields and by-ways, so silently that their footfalls could scarcely be heard at ten rods' distance,[1] moving slowly, in order to give time for the light troops in the advance to secure and occupy all the points of the anticipated attack. Passing thus noiselessly along, irresistibly sweeping into its grasp every human being that it met who might give information to the enemy, the head of the column reached the vicinity of Schoonmaker's Bridge, which spans the head of a little creek near the village of New Lotts, and a short distance southwest of the present East New York.[2] Here was a point of defence of which the British commander expected the Americans would avail themselves, and he made his dispositions accordingly—throwing out skirmishers, and taking such other precautions as seemed necessary.

---

[1] They were seen by Captain Cornelius Vanderveer, who stated that although he was near the fence fronting his house, on the road, he could scarcely hear them.—Strong's Flatbush, p. 145.

[2] The exact route taken by the British army on this eventful morning, is a matter of much dispute among those who have most carefully examined the subject. J. C. Brevoort doubts whether the enemy crossed Schoonmaker's Bridge, the approach to which is through deep sand. In which opinion he is sustained by Ward and others.

To his surprise, the place was found to be entirely unoccupied, and the country open to the base of the Bushwick hills, where the Jamaica road enters upon the plains. Crossing the fields from the New Lotts road, in a direct course, to this point, the army halted, at two o'clock of the morning of the 27th, at William Howard's Half-way House, which yet stands at the corner of the present Broadway and the Jamaica and Brooklyn road. In front of them, on this road, was the Jamaica Pass (*ante*, 261), a winding defile, admirably calculated for defence, and where the British expected, as a matter of course, that their passage would be hotly contested. The perfect success of the flank movement which Howe was now performing, demanded that this pass should be turned without risking an engagement, or even attracting the attention of those who, as it was supposed, defended it. Here his Tory guides seem to have been at fault, and, at their recommendation, perhaps, he pressed into his service William Howard, the innkeeper, and his son, then a lad of fourteen years.[1] Father and son were compelled, at the point of the

---

[1] William Howard, æ. 87, says the British army was guided by N. W. along a narrow road across Schoonmaker's Bridge (where a small force might easily have brought the whole British army to a stand). Thence they turned off east of Daniel Rapalje's (threw open the fence) and crossed the fields to the south of Howard's Half-way House, where they halted in front of his house. About 2 o'clock in the morning, after the market wagons had passed, Howe (?), with a citizen's hat on and a camlet cloak over his uniform, entered Wm. Howard's tavern, attended by Clinton and two aids, and asked for something to drink, conversed with him, and asked if he had joined the association. Howard said that he had. "That's all very well – stick to your integrity. But now you are my prisoner, and must lead me across these hills out of the way of the enemy, the nearest way to Gowanus." Howard accordingly conducted the army by a passage-way between his house and horseshed *over the hills* and woods *east of his house, till they came to the cleared land north of the woods.* The horses drew the artillery up the hill in a slanting direction, and halted on the brow to breathe a little. The army *then proceeded west* and came out at Baker's tavern, by the Gowanus road. The British took Adj. Jeronimus Hoogland, (Lieut. Troup), and Lieut. Dunscomb, American patrols, at the big white-oak (since struck by lightning), in the middle of the road, by the mile-post, a little east of Howard's. Isaac Boerum, a trooper of New Lotts, was also taken in Bushwick, and died of small-pox in prison."—Onderdonk, Kings Co., sec. 805.

Lossing says (Field Book of Rev., ii. 807) that in 1852 William Howard, a son of this old Whig tavern-keeper, was still living, æ. 90, in the old tavern (Howard's Half-way House) still (1867) standing, although considerably altered, at the corner of Broadway and Fulton avenue. The part nearest the corner is *the* building, the other part being a house of Joseph Howard. He well remembered the above scene described in his father's statement.

REFERENCES

TO THE

MAP OF BEDFORD CORNERS IN 1766–67 AND 1867.

THAT portion of the Map printed in black is from Ratzer's Survey of 1766-67, and shows the farm lines, roads, houses, etc., etc., as then existing. Over this have been printed, in red, the street lines of the present city. The *large* figures are designed to indicate the several farms; and the *small* figures, the houses, etc. etc., at the period of the Revolution; those shown *in outline* having been erected since 1776.

REFERENCES TO THE LARGE FIGURES.

1. P. Reid (?).
2. Teunis Tiebout, 1776.
3. Peter Stothoff.
4. Jeremiah Meserole.
5. —— Johnson.
6. Jacob Ryerson.
7. Rem Remsen, afterwards Barent Lefferts. House pulled down about 1840.
8. Barent Lefferts.
9. Michael Vandervoort, 1776: afterwards Jacobus De Bevoise. House pulled down recently.
10. Cornelius Vanderhoef, afterwards Leffert Lefferts.
11. Jeronimus Remsen, afterwards Barent Lefferts and Rem Lefferts. House pulled down 1838.
12. Lambert Suydam, afterwards Daniel Lott, now Chas. Betts. House pulled down 1856.
13. Abraham Van Enden, afterwards Benjamin Hinchman. House pulled down 1819.
14. Nicholas Blom, afterwards Charles Turnbull, Leffert Lefferts, Sr., 1791, and John Lefferts. House rebuilt about 1787.
15. Peter Vandewater. Hendrick Suydam, 1791; Leffert Lefferts, Jr., 1835.
16. Andris Andriese, Leffert Lefferts, Sr., 1774; Leffert Lefferts, Jr.
17. Benjamin and Jacobus Vandewater to Hendrick Fine, 1743; Fine to Jacobus Lefferts, 1753; L. Lefferts, Sr. and Jr.
18. H. Fine to Jacobus Lefferts, 1753. Partly from Executors of Andris Andriese. House built about 1750.
19. Peter Vandewater, Robert De Bevoise.
20. Isaac (?) Selover.
21. Rem Cowenhoven, Teunis Tiebout, Nicholas Cowenhoven.
22. Rem Vanderbeck and Lambert Andriese, afterwards Barent Lefferts.
23. John Cowenhoven, Isaac Cortelyou, and others, being part of first division Brooklyn Wood-lands.

REFERENCES TO THE SMALL FIGURES.

1. The Tiebout house, afterwards occupied by Nicholas Cowenhoven, subsequently by Robert Wilson.
2. The Selover house.
3. Rem Vanderbeck, afterwards Robert De Bevoise.
4. Judge Leffert Lefferts' house, built in 1838, now the residence of J. Carson Brevoort, Esq.
5. Judge Leffert Lefferts' old house, built about 1753.
6. N. Blom's house, rebuilt, 1787, by Charles Turnbull, an officer of the British army afterwards occupied by John Lefferts.
7. Abm. Van Enden's, then B. Hinchman's, and more recently J. P. Brinckerhoff's.
8. Lambert Suydam, afterwards Daniel Lott.
9. Jeronimus Remsen, then Barent Lefferts, then Rem Lefferts.
10. The old Bedford village school—afterwards Public School No. 3.
11. Old house pulled down in 1841.
12. Michael Vandervoort, afterwards Jacobus De Bevoise.
13. Bedford village burial-ground—the Lefferts' family burying-ground in the rear.
14. Old Remsen (?) family burying-ground.
15. Two acres bought by Brooklyn and Jamaica Turnpike Co., for a gravel bank.
16. Negro burying-ground.

BEDFORD CORNERS, IN 1776.

(Looking east, along the road to Jamaica.)

Page 267

sword, to lead a detachment of the troops around the Pass, through a bridle-path, known as the "Rockaway Path,"[1] which traversed the present Evergreen Cemetery. Much to the surprise of the British generals, the pass which they had so carefully flanked was found to be entirely unguarded,[2] and the fact was immediately communicated to the main body, then halted on the (East New York) plains. Clinton promptly pushed forward a battalion of light infantry to secure the pass, and at daybreak he followed with his own command along the Jamaica road, and so completely possessed himself of the heights, as virtually to decide the fortunes of the day. He was followed by Lord Percy with the main body, consisting of the Guards, the 2d, 3d, and 5th Brigades, with ten field-pieces, who halted in his rear at an hour before daylight. They in turn were followed by the 49th Regiment, with four medium 12-pounders and the baggage, under its own escort. Being now in position on the Bushwick hills, where they breakfasted, the troops resumed their march along the Jamaica turnpike to Bedford, which they reached about half-past eight o'clock, while the Americans were as yet unaware that they had left Flatlands.[3] Pressing forward now with renewed energy, the head of the column, by nine o'clock, had reached and occupied the junction of the Flatbush road and the Jamaica turnpike. The British line now extended from that point to Bedford, and at the distance of half a mile from the rear of the Americans, who were contesting the possession of the Flatbush hills with De Heister—all unconscious that the trap had sprung upon them, and that they were hemmed in on all sides. But so it was. Sullivan, indeed, seems to have been so completely duped by the feint which Grant was making

---

[1] The course of this "Rockaway footpath," which formed one of the boundaries of the original Indian purchase of Bedford (*ante*, 159), is accurately traced upon the Battle Map which illustrates this chapter.

[2] The Hessian account says that "he learned in a distance of one mile and a half from it, by a reconnoitring party, as others say by a captured American picket,"—most probably the latter.

[3] We have it, on excellent authority, that when the British column reached "Bedford Corners," the profound silence and secrecy which had previously characterized their movements, gave way to a feeling of exultant joy. They felt assured that the great object of their long and wary night-march was fully accomplished; their bands struck up lively strains of martial music, and, with elastic step, the troops pressed eagerly forward towards Brooklyn.

on his right in the direction of Gowanus, that he quite neglected to send out any fresh patrols towards Jamaica, although he had foretold that the real danger would come from that quarter. [1]

Fatal mistake! The battle was lost before it had been begun.

All these movements had not been unobserved by Washington, who, although receiving hourly reports from Putnam's camp, could not rest satisfied without a personal inspection of the state of affairs. All the previous day (26th) he had spent on Long Island, visiting the redoubts and guard-posts, reconnoitring the enemy, and thoroughly acquainting himself with the relative position of the two armies. The movements which he had observed towards evening, on the centre and right of the British force, were ominous of an immediate conflict. He, too, shared the general apprehension that the city of New York would be attacked by the enemy's fleet; and the Southern brigades of the troops on Long Island, although the choicest, best equipped and officered in the army, had as yet never engaged in battle. What wonder, then, that his mind, as he returned to New York that evening, was filled with anxious thoughts and apprehensions of the morrow? At no period in his previous career had the responsibilities of his position and the welfare of his beloved country weighed so heavily upon him as on the eve of what was to be the first pitched battle of the Revolution, and upon the event of which the destiny of America seemed to be staked. Yet his heart was buoyed up by a firm reliance on Him who doeth all things well—faith was triumphant o'er his fears, and after supping cheerfully with his military staff, he calmly remarked, as he withdrew at an early hour to his chamber, "The same Providence that rules to-day will rule to-morrow, gentlemen. Good-night."

Let us now return to the operations of the left wing and centre of the British army. Almost simultaneously with the march of the right wing on the previous evening, the left, under Gen. Grant, had advanced towards Brooklyn, partly by the Coast Road,[2] and partly by

---

[1] See his letter to Washington.

[2] This was not the present road along the verge of the high bank from Yellow Hook to Gowanus; but a road which ran along the slopes further inland, nearly on the line of present Third avenue. (See the Battle Map illustrating this chapter.)

way of Martense's Lane.[1] At midnight they reached the lower pass in the Lane, where they met a guard (probably a portion of Atlee's Pennsylvania regiment) commanded by Major Bird,[2] who retreated before them, and sent an alarm to Gen. Putnam, within the lines. About 3 o'clock on the morning of the 27th, Stirling, who was occupying the junction of the Gowanus and Port roads, was informed by Putnam in person of the enemy's advance, and requested to check them with the two regiments nearest at hand. These happened to be Hazlet's Delaware battalion and Smallwood's Maryland regiment,[3] which promptly turned out, and, with Lord Stirling at their head, were soon *en route* for the Narrows, closely followed by General Parsons with Colonel Huntington's Connecticut regiment of two hundred and fifty men. Within half a mile of the Red Lion Tavern they came up with Col. Atlee's regiment, slowly retiring before the advancing British column, whose front was then just coming into sight through the gray dawn of morning, a little in advance of the present entrance to the Cemetery.[4] The American line of battle was promptly formed across the Coast Road, reaching from the bay on the east to the crest of the hills which form the

---

[1] In Gen. Stirling's letter to Washington, written from the enemy's fleet, where he was then a prisoner of war, he says "the enemy were advancing by the road from Flatbush to the Red Lion."

[2] Major Byrd, or Bird, was an officer in Atlee's regiment, and was taken prisoner.

Also see the following extract from a letter written by an officer in Col. Atlee's battalion, dated Aug. 27: "Yesterday about 120 of our men went as a guard to a place on Long Island called Red Lion; about eleven at night the sentries descried two men coming up a water-melon patch, upon which our men fired on them. The enemy then retreated, and about one o'clock advanced with 200 or 300 men, and endeavored to surround our guard, but they being watchful, gave them two or three fires, and retreated to alarm the remainder of the battalion, except one lieutenant and about fifteen men, who have not been heard of as yet. About four o'clock this morning, the alarm was given by beating to arms, when the remainder of our battalion, accompanied by the Delaware and Maryland battalions, went to the place our men retreated from. About a quarter of a mile this side we saw the enemy, when we got into the woods (our battalion being the advanced guard) amidst the incessant fire of their field-pieces, loaded with grape-shot, which continued till ten o'clock," etc.—Onderdonk, sec. 813.

[3] The commanders of these regiments were then absent in New York, in attendance upon a court-martial, and did not arrive on the ground until the battle had begun.

[4] Authentic neighborhood tradition locates the scene of this first skirmish in the vicinity of 38th and 39th streets, between 2d and 3d avenues. At this spot the old road ran along the edge of a swamp (now filled up, but then known as the swamp of Simon de Hart (*ante*, pp. 49–55 and map), and here several lives were lost. See, also, Cleveland, in "Greenwood Illustrated," p. 88.

western boundary of Greenwood Cemetery. Placing Atlee's force in ambush as skirmishers, in an orchard[1] on the south side of the Coast or Gowanus road, near its intersection with the present 18th street, Stirling, at the head of Hazlet's and Smallwood's regiments, took his position on the slopes of the hills, between 18th and 20th streets, a little to the northwest of "Battle Hill," in Greenwood.[2] A company of riflemen were posted, partly on the edge of the woods and partly along a hedge near the foot of the hill, and some of the Maryland regiment took position at a wooded hill on a curve of the road at the foot of the present 23d street, then called "Blokje's

[1] This was Wynant Bennett's orchard, a few trees of which yet remain in the southwest part of Greenwood Cemetery.

[2] Traditions current among the old inhabitants of the Gowanus neighborhood, and worthy of credit, especially mark "Battle Hill" as a place of historic interest. Here it is said a small body of riflemen had been stationed, among the trees which then crowned that eminence; and when the right wing of the British army (under Cornwallis), unconscious of their presence, had approached within range, these unerring marksmen commenced their fire, each ball bringing down an officer. Unfortunately for them, the hill was surrounded before they could escape, and they were all shot down. "Here, too, in all probability, they were afterward interred; and thus enriched by the blood of patriots—thus mingling with their dust—we may safely suppose that this mount of burial received its first consecration."

Furman, in his Notes on Brooklyn, written in 1824, when opportunities for learning authentic facts were good, relates the following: "In this battle, part of the British army marched down a lane or road (Port Road) leading from the Brush tavern (at Valley Grove) to Gowanus, pursuing the Americans. Several of the American riflemen, in order to be more secure, and, at the same time, more effectually to succeed in their designs, had posted themselves in the high trees near the road. One of them, whose name is now partially forgotten, shot the English Major Grant: in this he passed unobserved. Again he loaded his deadly rifle and fired: another English officer fell. He was then marked, and a platoon ordered to advance and fire into the tree; which order was immediately carried into execution, and the rifleman fell to the ground, dead. After the battle was over, the two British officers were buried in a field near where they fell, and their graves fenced in with some posts and rails, where their remains still rest. But, 'for an example to the rebels,' they refused to the American rifleman the rites of sepulchre; and his remains were exposed on the ground till the flesh was rotted and torn off his bones by the fowls of the air. After a considerable length of time, in a heavy gale of wind, a large tree was uprooted; in the cavity formed by which some friends to the Americans, notwithstanding the prohibition of the English, placed the brave soldier's bones to mingle in peace with their kindred earth."

Mr. H. E. Pierrepont, of this city, informs us that along the line of trees and hedge at the funeral entrance of Greenwood Cemetery, the American riflemen, as tradition relates, made a desperate stand. And old Mr. Garret Bergen used to relate, as a boyish recollection, that so deadly and determined was their fire, which seemed mainly directed at the officers, that a British officer came rushing into his father's house, and dropping into a chair, exclaimed that "he'd be d—d if he was going to expose himself to that fire; that the d—d rascals picked out all the officers."

Barracks."[1] Then, as the patriots awaited the enemy's attack, Stirling addressed them in a brief and pithy speech, and reminding them that he had heard Gen. Grant, the commander of that advancing column, boast in the British Parliament, only a few months before, that the Americans could not fight, and that, with 5,000 men, he would undertake to march from one end of the continent to the other, he exclaimed, as he pointed to the head of Gowanus Bay, "Grant may have his 5,000 men with him now—we are not so many—but I think we are enough to prevent his advancing further on his march than that mill-pond."

Just then the British vanguard came within range of Atlee's men, who gave them two or three rounds with spirit, and fell back on Blokje's Barracks, which brought him on the left of Stirling, who was on the hills. At this moment Col. Kichline's rifle corps, Col. De Haas' battalion, and Capt. Carpenter, with two field-pieces, came up. Gen. Stirling immediately posted a portion of Kichline's riflemen behind a hedge at the foot of the hills, and a portion in front of the wood, while a detachment of light troops were ordered to occupy the orchard just left by Atlee, and behind some hedges. It was now broad daylight, and a brisk skirmishing was maintained for two hours between the British and American light troops, until Carpenter managed, with some difficulty, to get his two cannon into position on the hill, and then his fire, combined with Kichline's rifles,

---

[1] Near the intersection of 3d avenue and 23d street, the old road passed over a small hill known as "*Blokje's Berg*," north of which was a ditch which drained a morass and swamp lying east of said hill, into Gowanus Cove. The road crossed the ditch on a small bridge. The British column is said to have advanced as far as this hill, when it was checked by the Americans who had taken a position on the north side of this ditch and morass, the easterly end of which abutted on the woods. Owing to the strong natural impediment which the morass and ditch afforded to the advance of the British, the American riflemen were enabled to make fearful havoc among the ranks of the foe, before they could be dislodged. Many of the British were killed and buried in pits along the borders of the morass. (See *ante*, pp. 58, 59.)

In advancing from the Narrows, the British compelled many of the residents to accompany them in the capacity of guides. Peter Bennet, of Gowanus, stated that himself and one of his neighbors, acting in this capacity, under compulsion, in guiding a small detachment across the fields in the vicinity of the swamp at Blokje's Berg, stumbled upon a body of American riflemen, sheltered behind one of the hedges which formed a farm boundary, who shot down nearly the whole body of the enemy in their front, leaving himself and fellow guide standing almost alone. It is needless to say that the few survivors beat a hasty retreat.—Communicated by Hon. T. G Bergen, of New Utrecht.

proved too hot for the British, who finally relinquished the orchard, which was immediately reoccupied by Atlee's men. One of Grant's brigades was now formed upon the hills in two lines, some six hundred yards opposite to Stirling's right, the balance of his force facing Stirling's left, in a single line, across the Greenwood hills.[1] He also pushed forward a howitzer to within three hundred yards of the American right, and a battery of two guns opposite to their left. The battle, however, was rather spiritless, as Stirling's object was mainly to keep Grant in check for a time, while Grant's instructions were not to force an attack until warned by guns from the British right wing that Clinton had succeeded in gaining the rear of the American lines. Meantime, the sky was lowery, and a fresh breeze from the northeast hindered the advance of the British ships, with the exception of the inferior Roebuck, which, beating up against wind and tide, opened a fire upon the Red Hook battery, and received a brisk and effective return.

Leaving Grant and Stirling thus engaged, let us return to the centre of the American lines, on the Flatbush hills, where sunrise found Sullivan's men yet awaiting, as they had awaited ever since the 23d, the attack of the British force in their front. De Heister, at daybreak, opened a cannonade from his position at Flatbush upon the redoubt on the neighboring hill, where Hand's rifle-corps were posted, supported by the troops of Cols. Wyllys and Miles, on the Bedford road. Hearing this, Gen. Sullivan hastened forward with

---

[1] Mr. T. W. Field, the closest student of our Revolutionary battle-ground, and whose monograph on the subject will shortly be put to press, gives the following lucid statement, which will do much to clear up the confusion which has hitherto prevailed among historians in regard to the position of the American line on the right:

"Lord Stirling's line at this time formed two sides of a triangle, of which the hypothenuse was a line drawn from the Flatbush Road, near its junction with the Port Road, to the shore of the bay near the foot of Twenty-third street. The obtuse angle at the centre was yet unprotected by the two-gun battery which had been ordered up. From this point to the shore of Gowanus Bay was a distance of half a mile, along which the front was now warmly engaged. The right wing, resting on the bay, occupied the deep cut in the road at Blokje's Barracks. The security of this position from an assault in front, increased by a salt creek setting up into the land four or five hundred feet, made it one of no insignificant strength, so that, later in the day, the torrent of war sweeping around it left it unassailed. From the top of the hills the line bent northerly along the high ground to near the junction of Fifth avenue and Third street. This portion of the line was comprised of reserves—a portion of the Delaware Battalion and such supporting troops as Putnam could spare from the intrenchments. The left

four hundred riflemen, on a reconnoissance along the slope of the hills in part of his lines, and to the eastward of his centre, being all this time utterly ignorant of the fact that Clinton had gained his rear. De Heister, however, did not advance, but continued to blaze away at the redoubt, in order to keep the attention of the Americans in that direction, until late in the forenoon, when signal-guns from the northward assured him that Clinton had gained the American rear. Then, ordering Count Donop to charge the redoubt, he followed with the remainder of his division. The redoubt was quickly carried, and the impetuous Hessian yagers eagerly pressed forward into the woods south of the Port Road, driving the American riflemen before them, and taking possession of the coverts and lurking-places from which they dislodged them; so that, in a brief space of time, the latter found themselves more than matched by their German foes. The grenadiers followed the yagers into the woods, admirably preserving their lines, and slowly but surely pressing back the Americans at the point of the bayonet upon the main body, now fatally weakened by the withdrawal of four hundred men, which formed Sullivan's reconnoissance. That general, alarmed by Clinton's cannon, which revealed to him the fact that his flank had been turned, and fully alive to the danger of his position, was now in full retreat for the American lines. But, as his imperilled troops hurried down the rough and densely wooded slope of Mount Prospect, they were met on the open plain of Bedford by the British light infantry and dragoons, and hurled back again upon the Hessian bayonets, which bristled along the woods. Meanwhile, a heavy force from Clinton and Cornwallis' left, near Bedford, had cut the American lines at the "Clove Road," and Col. Miles' panic-stricken troops were flying for their lives. Parties of Americans, also, retreating from the onset of the Hessians towards the Bedford road,

wing, it will thus be seen, occupied a long, irregular line, in which were breaks of fearful length, which the Hessians, later in the day, took fatal advantage of. In consequence of the peculiar formation of the line, the extreme left wing was much nearer the extreme right than the centre, and when called into action to re-enforce the front, actually exchanged positions. From this circumstance, the accounts of the Gowanus battle have been found so conflicting as to be almost incomprehensible, and its varying phases can only be thus explained. It was thus that a portion of the Delaware regiment met and repulsed the advanced squads of the Second British Grenadiers on the extreme left, near Tenth street and Fifth avenue."

found themselves face to face with the dense columns of British troops, and turning back in dismay, became mingled hopelessly with the troops from the extreme left of Sullivan's line, who were hurrying forward to escape by the same road. The confused strife—for a battle it was not—which ensued is too terrible for the imagination to dwell upon. Broken up into small handfuls, the unfortunate Americans, fighting hopelessly but desperately, were tossed to and fro between British and Hessian bayonets. No mercy was shown;[1] the hireling mercenaries of Britain glutted themselves

---

[1] An officer in Gen. Frazer's Bat., 71st Reg't, writes: "The Hessians and our brave Highlanders gave no quarters; and it was a fine sight to see with what alacrity they dispatched the rebels with their bayonets, after we had surrounded them so they could not resist. We took care to tell the Hessians that the rebels had resolved to give no quarter—to them in particular—which made them fight desperately, and put to death all that came into their hands."

Another British officer of rank, and more humane and generous of heart, writes: "The Americans fought bravely, and (to do them justice) could not be broken till they were greatly outnumbered and taken in flank, front and rear. We were greatly shocked at the massacre made by the Hessians and Highlanders, *after* victory was decided."

Max von Elking (Hist. of the German Auxiliary troops in the North American War of Independence, i. 33 *et alios*), in reference to this point, says: "Great excitement and rage on the part of the Hessians cannot be denied, but it was chiefly caused by some squads of the enemy (Americans), who, after being surrounded and having asked for quarter, fired again upon the unsuspecting Hessians, who had advanced towards them (to accept their surrender). The British surpassed the Hessians in that respect. Col. von Heeringen, in his letter to Col. von Lossberg, remarks, 'The English did not give much quarter, and continually incited our troops to do the same.' We have seen in his letter, as previously quoted, how treacherously Col. John acted towards the Hessian grenadier, and how the Pennsylvania regiment, after having been surrounded, gave another volley. The natural consequence of this was an increase of the fury of well-disciplined troops, unused to such a manner of fighting. That the Hessians did not massacre all their enemies, we have seen from the fact that the regiment Rall, encountering a squad of Americans, made them prisoners without any cruelty." Many Americans did not accept quarter from the Hessians. 'They were so much frightened,' writes Lieut. Ruffer in his diary, 'that they preferred being shot down to taking quarter, because their generals and officers had told them that they would be hanged.'

"The conquerors showed their contempt for the conquered by putting them to the guns, which they had to draw, over very bad roads, to the ships; although this appears to have been more the result of necessity than of insolence, as there were no horses, and the English and German troops, already very exhausted, would otherwise have been obliged to do it themselves." "Howe treated the captive generals with great civility; Stirling and Sullivan dined with him almost every day."

Max von Elking gives what may be considered the Hessian version of this engagement: "As soon as Gen. von Heister heard the reports of artillery on his right, and

with blood. The unequal fight was maintained by the heroic band, with all the ferocity of despair, from nine o'clock until twelve, when

---

knew, from its direction, that the flanking movement had succeeded, he formed quickly for the attack. In front were the grenadiers, in three divisions, and in front of them, as flankers, a company of yagers under Capt. Wredon. The brigade von Mirbach covered the left flank. The troops advanced bravely, with martial music sounding and colors flying, and ascended the hills in the best order,—the men dragging the cannons with the greatest caution through the dense forest. When, with but little loss by the enemy's (American) artillery, the troops had reached the crest of the hill, the line was formed with as much care as on the parade-ground. The Americans (rifle skirmishers) were quickly driven back by the advancing flankers—many were killed or captured—while the Hessian regiments followed with closed ranks and shouldered muskets. 'The enemy,' wrote Col. von Heeringen to Col. von Lossberg, 'had almost impenetrable thickets, lines, *abatis*, and redoubts before him. The riflemen were mostly pierced by the bayonets to the trees. These terrible men deserve more pity than fear,—they want nearly fifteen minutes for loading their pieces, and during that time they feel our balls and bayonets.' The yagers of the left wing, eager for the combat, rushed forward so rapidly that their captain could not restrain them. They penetrated the works of the American encampment, and saw it on their left, a redoubt to their right. The Americans, surprised by the sudden appearance of the Hessians, rallied into groups of fifty to sixty men; but having no time to form, were shot down, dispersed, or captured. This happened in view of the garrison within the enemy's lines.

"The Americans supposed that the Hessians would not give quarter. Every one of them tried to sell his life as dearly as possible, or to save it by flight, while the Hessians grew more exasperated and angry in consequence of this apparently obstinate and useless resistance. Therefore ensued a violent contest, here in larger or smaller crowds, there in wild and irregular rout. A part tried to escape into the woods, but a great many fell into swamps and perished miserably, or were captured. Only a small number succeeded in cutting their way through and reaching their lines. The Hessians fired only once, and then attacked with their bayonets."

Lord Percy writes from the camp at Newtown, Sept. 4: "It was the General's orders that the troops should receive the rebels' first fire, and then rush on them before they had recovered their arms, with our bayonets, which threw them into the utmost confusion."

The Hessian account also mentions that "in this first battle in which the auxiliaries were engaged in the New World, all the German field-officers and aids were on foot, as their own horses had not been brought over from the old country, and new ones had not yet been provided. Col. Donop's aid thus writes in his diary: 'Almost all the officers of the staff and the subaltern officers were on foot, their cloaks rolled up on their shoulders, and a large canteen, filled with rum and water, suspended from their sides. I had to do the same, although I acted as an aid; and whenever my brigade general, Col. von Donop, wished to send a dispatch, he alighted and gave me his old but good steed, which he had brought over from Hessia.' Another novelty was that many officers, while marching or fighting, had their rifles over their shoulders. Col. Donop himself carried one, and would have probably been lost without it. During the skirmishing a rifleman near by aimed at him, but he, anticipating him, shot him through the head. The officers of skirmishers also carried muskets and bayonets, and the privates were allowed to do what their discipline had previously forbidden, viz., to carry their sabres across their breasts, in order to unbutton, in the unaccustomed heat, their coats, made of a coarse, heavy cloth."

the survivors surrendered, and the enemy was victorious.[1] The few who, nerved by their horrible situation, succeeded in cutting their way through the gleaming wall of bayonets and sabres which encircled them, were pursued within musket-shot of the American lines by the grenadiers, who were with the utmost difficulty restrained by their officers from storming Fort Putnam.[2] Other fugitives, less fortunate, were skulking along the hills and seeking, amid the swamps and thickets, a temporary respite from capture. Some in larger bodies, had succeeded in getting through the Hessian skirmish line, which now occupied the strip of woods between the Port Road and salt meadows, and were pouring across the dam of Freeke's Mill.[3] But, upon this confused and panic-stricken crowd, the Hessians opened a destructive fire from some guns posted on the hills, near the Ninth avenue; and to escape this new horror, many diverged to the south; some being shot and others drowned while struggling through the mud and water of the creeks which abound in that vicinity. Gen. Sullivan was captured by three fusileers of the Regiment von Knyphausen, concealed in a cornfield,

---

[1] The most sanguinary conflict occurred after the Americans had left the Flatbush Pass, and attempted to retreat to the lines at Brooklyn. The place of severest contest, and where Sullivan and his men were made prisoners, was upon the slope between the Flatbush avenue and the Long Island railway (Atlantic street), between Bedford and Brooklyn, near "Baker's Tavern," at a little east of the junction of these avenues.—Lossing, Field-Book of Rev., ii. p. 810. "Between Washington avenue and Third street, the low ground in the neighborhood of Greene and Fourth avenues, and the heights overlooking Flatbush."—T. W. Field.

[2] Gen. Robertson says: "The battalion of grenadiers, led by Col. Stuart, and 33d regiment, ran across a field beyond the Flatbush road towards the principal redoubt (Fort Putnam, now Fort Greene). Gen. Vaughan asked if he should attack the lines (which were semicircular and the parapets lined with spears and lances), but he was ordered back." The London Chronicle says: "Col. Monckton and Gen. Vaughan led the grenadiers and light infantry. They saw the advantage, and told Howe the rebels were shut up between the British and the sea. Vaughan stormed with rage at being stopped, and sent word to Howe that he could force the lines with inconsiderable loss."

It is further stated that the American cannon not being well pointed, a large number of the shot overreached the British; but some were killed and wounded by the fire of small-arms from the lines. It was stated by several of the militia that the bullets whistled over their heads as they stood in the ditch. Gen. Putnam rode along the lines, ordering them *not to fire till they could see the whites of the enemy's eyes.* A wounded British officer was brought into Boerum's bolt-house, which was used as a hospital, and where were several rows of beds occupied by the wounded.—See Onderdonk, Kings Co., sec. 805.

[3] *Ante*, pp. 99, 100.

about three hundred feet from the position of Colonel von Heeringen.[1]

Before midday the terrible struggle was over. The Hessian riflemen were rapidly extending their skirmish lines over and through the hills towards Gowanus, the British right wing was now massed in force upon the scene of its victory, and Earl Cornwallis was pushing, with a heavy column, down the Port Road, upon the left and rear of Stirling, whose long thin line had been anxiously awaiting, since early dawn, the impending onset of actual battle.

While this was going on, a similar scene was enacting in the direction of Gowanus. It was at early dawn, as we have seen, that Washington and the inhabitants of the city were aroused by the rattle of musketry which announced the advance of Grant's division near Greenwood. In the city all was anxiety and trepidation, for the appearance and movements of the British fleet betokened the attack which had been so long anticipated. Washington was in the saddle by daybreak, and the drum-beat resounded from all the alarm-posts. But as the hours passed, and the vessels, with the exception of the Roebuck, remained quietly at anchor, Washington, relieved of his anxiety as to the immediate danger of the city, hastened over to the lines at Brooklyn, where, from the eminence upon which Fort Putnam stood, he became the agonized witness of the rout and slaughter of Sullivan's command, to whom he could send no succor without unduly weakening the lines. As, with troubled spirit, he gazed upon the scene, he observed, emerging from the woods on his left, a heavy British column, which descended the hills in the direction of Stirling's division. It was Earl Cornwallis, who had been detached, with the larger part of the right wing of the British army, to co-operate with General Grant in his movements on Gowanus Bay, by occupying the junction of the Port and Gowanus roads. Stirling, meanwhile, doubtless wondering at Grant's forbearance, was totally unconscious of Cornwallis'

[1] Heeringen, in his report, thus speaks of his prize: "John Sullivan is a lawyer, and had previously been a servant; but he is a man of genius, whom the rebels will badly miss. He was brought before me. I ordered him to be searched, and found upon his person the original orders of General Washington, from which it was evident that he had the best troops under his command, that every thing depended upon the maintaining possession of the woods, and that he had 8,000 men."

movement upon his rear, until startled by the signal-guns with which the earl announced his approach to Grant. Then, as the truth burst upon him, he found that his retreat towards the lines at Brooklyn was intercepted, and that he was fairly trapped between two superior forces of the enemy. At the same time came tidings of the defeat of Sullivan upon his left. Grant, largely re-enforced,[1] was now in full motion, and pressing fiercely on his front. Colonel Atlee and his corps were made prisoners, after a series of spirited and desperate skirmishes; General Parsons' command, on the extreme left, had mostly been taken prisoners;[2] and Stirling, finding that he was fast being surrounded, saw that his only chance of escape was to drive Cornwallis, who then was occupying the "Cortelyou house" as a redoubt, up the Port Road towards Flatbush, and by getting between him and Fort Box, on the opposite side of the creek, to escape, under cover of its guns, across Brower's mill-dam.[3] He knew that his attack upon the earl would, at all events, give time for escape to his countrymen, whom he saw struggling through the salt morasses and across the narrow causeway of Freeke's mill-pond.

---

[1] This re-enforcement consisted of 2,000 men, who landed in boats, in Bennet's Cove, between ten and eleven o'clock A. M. See Colonel Smallwood's letter, Onderdonk, sec. 811, also sec. 810 and 813, and Bancroft, ix. 92, who says that Admiral Howe, "having learned that Grant's division, which halted at the edge of the woods, was in want of ammunition, went himself with a supply from his ship, sending his boat's crew with it on their backs up the hill, while further supplies followed from the storeships."

During this re-enforcement Lieut. Wragg and twenty of the British marines, mistaking Colonel Hazlet's Delaware regiment, who had just been ordered up from the left to the front (*ante*, p. 272, *note*), received several fires from them without returning them, and, on advancing towards them to correct their supposed error, were captured and marched to the rear under the charge of Lieut. Popham, whose amusing account of the affair will be found in Onderdonk, sec. 818. Original MSS. in library of L. I. Historical Society. See also Onderdonk, sec. 806, 819; also, *post*, p. 281 of this work.

[2] Parsons, it seems, had "left his men in quest of orders, was intercepted, concealed himself in a swamp, and came into camp the next morning by way of the East River." Bancroft, ix. 92; Penn. Journal, Sept. 11, '76.

[3] "The lines between Box Fort and the creek were not completed the day before. There was an opening adjoining the creek which it was thought the enemy were acquainted with; for when they came to it, and found the entrance closed with a breastwork and other defences, they appeared confounded."—Account in Independent (Boston) Chronicle, September 19, '76. Also, see Life of Stephen Olney of Rhode Island, p. 175: "All that seemed to prevent the enemy from taking our main fort was a scarecrow row of palisades, from the fort to low-water in the cove, which Major Box had set up that morning."

The generous thought was followed by heroic action. Quickly changing his front, and leaving the main body in conflict with General Grant, Stirling placed himself at the head of Smallwood's regiment, and forming hurriedly (in the vicinity of the present Fifth avenue and Tenth street), the column moved along the Gowanus road, in face of a storm of fire from cannon, musketry, and rifles. Driving the enemy's advance back upon the stone house, from the windows of which the bullets rattled mercilessly into their ranks, they pushed unfalteringly forward, until checked by a fire of canister and grape from a couple of guns which the British hurriedly wheeled into position near the building. Even then they closed up their wasted ranks and endeavored to face the storm, and again were repulsed. Thrice again these brave young Marylanders charged upon the house, once driving the gunners from their pieces within its shadow; but numbers overwhelmed them, and for twenty minutes the fight was terrible. Washington, Putnam, and the other general officers who witnessed it from the ramparts of Ponkiesbergh Fort, saw the overwhelming force with which their brave compatriots were contending, and held their breath in suspense and fear. As they saw the gallant Marylanders attempt to cut their way through the surrounding host, Washington wrung his hands, in the intensity of his emotion, and exclaimed, "Good God, what brave fellows I must this day lose!" Driven back into a neighboring cornfield, some were captured, some were bayoneted, while a few escaped across the Gowanus marsh. While Stirling was thus keeping Cornwallis in check, a large portion of those whom he had left fighting with Grant had found safety by wading or swimming across Gowanus Creek, which they did with difficulty, it is true; but they finally reached the lines, carrying with them the tattered colors of Smallwood's regiment and over twenty prisoners. A few were lost, either in the creek or on its marshy margin.[1] Less fortunate than those whom his intrepidity had saved, Stirling found escape impossible. Deprived of nearly

---

[1] The statement—founded partially on General Howe's official dispatches, and partly on the local traditions of the neighborhood—that *large numbers* were drowned in attempting to cross the marsh, is probably somewhat exaggerated. Colonel Hazlet, of the Delaware regiment, states that the retreat "was effected in good order, with the loss of one man drowned in passing." Colonel Smallwood, who covered the retreat, instances only seven, two of whom were Hessian prisoners.

all his men—more than 250 of whom belonged to Smallwood's gallant Maryland regiment, the flower of the American army[1]—he fled over the hills, until unable to elude pursuit; but disdaining to yield to a British subject, he sought out and surrendered himself to De Heister, and was immediately sent on board the British flagship Eagle, where he found Sullivan and others fellow-prisoners of war.

Thus ended the battle at high noon. Ere evening drew its pall around the battle-field, fully one-half of the five thousand patriot army, which had that morning gone forth to battle for their country, were dead, wounded, or imprisoned.

The victorious Britons, as we have already seen, were with difficulty restrained from carrying the rebel lines by storm; and it is quite probable that, in the heat and flush of the moment, they would have succeeded. Yet the struggle would have been fearfully desperate, and the victory dearly bought. For behind those redoubts were 3,000 determined troops, animated by the presence of Washington and Putnam, and rendered desperate by the rout and misfortunes of their brave compatriots under Sullivan and Stirling, to which they had just been witnesses. Ignorant of their real force, but knowing that desperation would nerve them with new strength, Howe, profiting by the wholesome experience which he had gained at Bunker Hill a short time before, wisely declined the attempt. His artillery was not up; he yet lacked fascines for filling the ditches, axes for cutting the *abatis*, and scaling-ladders to mount the parapets.[2] Preferring, therefore, to save the further loss of blood, and to secure his already certain victory by regular approaches, he withdrew his troops to a hollow way in front of the

---

[1] Composed chiefly of young men of the most prominent and influential families of Maryland. Two hundred and fifty-six of them were slain in the desperate struggle with Cornwallis' grenadiers, near the Cortelyou house. These noble martyrs of the Maryland and Delaware regiments were buried on a small island of dry ground, scarcely an acre in extent, which formerly rose out of the marshy salt-meadow on the farm of Adrian Van Brunt. This spot, then, and for some time afterwards, covered with trees and undergrowth, was carefully preserved intact from axe or plough during Mr. Van Brunt's lifetime; but the remorseless surveyor's lines have passed over it, and its site is now far below the grade of surrounding streets. Third avenue intersects its westerly end, and Seventh and Eighth streets indicate two of its sides. (T. W. Field, the late T. G. Talmadge, and others.)

[2] Testimony of Captain Montressor before a Parliamentary Committee in 1779.

American lines, out of range of their musketry, and encamped for the night.[1]

The strength of the American force engaged in this memorable conflict was about 5,000, while that of the British was fully treble that number. The precise loss of the former, on this occasion, was never known, owing to the capture of Generals Sullivan and Stirling, and the consequent absence of reliable returns from their divisions.[2] It was estimated, in General Howe's official dispatches,

---

[1] "Reliable reports say that General Von Heister learned, from the troops who pursued the retreating Americans to their lines, that the left part of the camp of the enemy near the river was open for a distance of several hundred paces. Accordingly, when the wings had again united with the centre, he reported the fact to General Howe, and made a proposition to profit by the confusion of the enemy and the valor of the troops, to attack the camp forthwith, at this weak point; but Howe manifested a number of scruples, and so missed the golden opportunity of completing his victory." —Von Elkin's Account.

[2] The prisoners comprised three generals, Stirling, Sullivan, and Woodhull, three colonels, four lieutenant-colonels, three majors, eighteen captains, forty-three lieutenants, one aid, eleven ensigns, and 1,011 men. In addition to these were taken fifteen cannon, one howitzer, some stands of colors, ammunition-wagons, pioneers' tools, etc. The Hessians alone took one stand of colors, five guns, and five hundred prisoners, among them General Sullivan and thirty-five officers.—Howe's Return of Prisoners; Onderdonk, sec. 821; and Hessian account in Von Elkin's work, which furthermore says: "Amongst the prisoners are many, so-called, colonels, lieut.-colonels, and majors, and other officers, who have all previously been tailors, shoemakers, barbers, etc. Some of them have been badly beaten by our men, because the latter did not consider them real officers. I did not find among the captured officers a single one who had been in foreign service before. They are all rebels and settled citizens. My Lord Stirling is nothing but an '*echappê de famille.*' He resembles my Lord Granby as one egg the other. General Putnam is a butcher by profession. The rebels desert frequently. It is not uncommon to see colonels, lieutenant-colonels, and majors coming into our lines with a number of men. The captured colors, made of red damask, with the motto '*Liberty,*' came with sixty men to the regiment Rall; they carried their muskets upside down, their hats under their arms, fell upon their knees, and begged for quarter. Not a single regiment is regularly uniformed or armed; every one has his private musket, just as the Hessian citizens march out on Whitsuntide, except Stirling's regiment, which had a blue and red uniform, was three battalions strong, and consisted mostly of Germans enlisted in Pennsylvania. They were tall, fine men, and had very fine English muskets, with bayonets." It was this regiment which was mistaken by the second battalion of grenadiers as Hessians. (See *ante*, pp. 273, 278.) "The rebels' artillery is poor, their cannons being mostly of iron, and mounted on naval gun-carriages." Bancroft, Hist. U. S., ix. 95, says: "The total loss of the Americans, including officers, was, after careful inquiry, found to be less than a thousand, of whom three-fourths were prisoners. This is the account always given by Washington, alike in his official report and in his most private letters. Its accuracy is confirmed by the special returns from those regiments which were the chief sufferers. More than half of this loss fell upon Stirling's command; more than a fourth on the Maryland regiment alone." In

at 3,300; and the British loss, in killed, wounded, and prisoners, at 367.[1]

The night (27th) which followed the battle was one of great anxiety to Washington. His fatigued, wounded, and dispirited soldiers were but poorly sheltered against the heavy storm which seemed to be gathering; the enemy was encamped before the lines; the morrow would probably bring a renewal of the conflict. But his energy again triumphed over his fears. The long hours of night—yet all too short for the work in hand—were occupied with efforts to strengthen his position; troops were ordered over from New York, from Fort Washington, and Kingsbridge; nothing was left undone that human effort and foresight could accomplish.

The morning sky of the 28th was lowering and heavy, with masses of vapor which hung like a funeral-pall over sea and land. At four o'clock, and in the midst of a thick-falling mist, Washington visited every part of the works, encouraging his suffering soldiers with

---

the absence of authorities on which Mr. Bancroft bases his estimate, we must consider it as considerably underrated. The stress which he lays upon this being the "account always given by Washington," etc., is, in our opinion, of little importance. It was *policy* on the part of that general, in the peculiarly demoralized and critical condition of his army after its first pitched battle, to give the lowest reasonable estimate of losses sustained.

Dawson (Battles of the U. S., 148), usually accurate, gives the American loss, in killed, wounded, and prisoners, as between 1,100 and 1,200 men, more than a thousand of whom were prisoners. A thousand prisoners would leave only 200 men to be killed and wounded out of the whole 1,200, whereas *the Maryland battalion alone* lost *two hundred and fifty-six men*, without taking into account the number killed in other parts of the field.

In consequence of the large and rapid desertion which occurred after the battle; the demoralization of the troops; the absence, as far as we can learn, of any full and accurate reports from regimental and other officers; the capture of the three general officers (Sullivan, Stirling, and Woodhull) who were best fitted, by education and personal knowledge, to furnish reliable reports, etc., we find it impossible to arrive at any very decisive conclusion as to the actual losses of the Americans. Our own examination of the matter inclines us to accept the British and Hessian estimate as being most nearly correct. As *masters of the field* they had the best opportunity of knowing the facts, nor can we see that they have been guilty of much exaggeration.

[1] Of the British, five officers and fifty-six subaltern officers and privates were killed, twelve officers and two hundred and forty-five subalterns and privates wounded, and one officer and twenty marines taken prisoners. The Hessian loss consisted of two privates killed, three officers (one of whom was Captain Donop) and twenty-three men wounded.

words of hope, and carefully inspecting the state of the defences. By the gradually increasing light of morning was revealed the encampment of over 15,000 troops of Britain. It is no wonder that "there was gloom everywhere—in the sky, on the land, on the water, and over the spirits of the Republicans. They almost despaired, for the heavy rains had injured their arms and almost destroyed their ammunition; but when, at five o'clock, Mifflin crossed the East River with the choice regiments of Magaw and Shee, and Glover's battalion of Marblehead fishermen and sailors, in all more than a thousand strong, all fresh and cheerful, there was an outburst of joy, for they seemed like sunshine as they passed the lines of sufferers and took post on the extreme left, near the Wallabout." Their arrival increased the American force to nine thousand. The British cannonade opened at ten o'clock upon the American lines, and was followed through the day by frequent skirmishes. The rain fell copiously, much to the discomfort of the Americans, who, in some parts of the trenches, stood up to their waists in water and mud. It served, however, to keep the British within their tents until near evening, when they broke ground within five hundred yards of the American lines, and commenced regular approaches by trenches. This night, also, they threw up a redoubt east of Fort Putnam (now Fort Greene), on the land of George Powers, from which they opened a fire upon the fort.[1] During this day, also, occurred the capture of General Woodhull, by a party of provincial loyalists under Captain De Lancey, about two miles beyond Jamaica. From wounds, barbarously inflicted upon him after his surrender, he died a few days later.

At midnight a dense fog arose, which remained motionless and impenetrable over the island during nearly the whole of the next

---

[1] "A strong column menaced this on the 29th. The Americans were here prepared to receive them, and orders were issued to reserve their fire till they could see the whites of their eyes. A few British officers reconnoitred the American lines, when one, coming too near, was shot by Wm. Van Cott of Bushwick, who then put up his gun, and said he had done his part. Several of the men were killed, after which the British fell back to their first position. An American rifleman leaped over the lines and took the officer's sword, watch, hat, and cash. This afternoon Captain Rutgers was killed: few Americans fell within the lines."—Reported by Lt. Thos. Skillman, of Capt. John Titus' company in '76. (General Johnson, in Williamsburgh Gazette, April 3, 1839.)

day. In the afternoon of the 29th, General Mifflin, Adjutant-General Reed, and Colonel Grayson reconnoitred at the outposts on the western extremity of the American lines, near the Red Hook. While there, a gentle shift of wind lifted the fog from Staten Island and revealed to them the British fleet in the Narrows, and boats passing to and from the admiral's ship and the other vessels. These signs of activity, together with a knowledge of the fact that a portion of the fleet had passed around the island and were anchored in Flushing Bay, betokened a movement upon the city, and the three officers lost no time in hastening back to camp.[1] The news which they brought was probably not unexpected to Washington; for, unknown to his aids, he had already made provision, earlier in the day, for the concentration in the East River, at New York, of every kind of sail or row boats, which were to be ready by dark;[2] but he immediately convened a council of war at five o'clock the same evening,[3] for the danger was indeed imminent. If the British should occupy the Hudson and the East River—as any moment, on a change of mind, they might do—they would, by securing the position of Kingsbridge, be able to cut off all communication between Manhattan Island and the Westchester main; thus

---

[1] Reed's Reed, i. 225; Col. Graydon's Memoirs, 166, Littel's ed.; Bancroft, Hist. U. S., ix. 105–107, *note*, in which much unnecessary space is given to a denial that Gen. Reed could have been enabled to see the British fleet, by a "lifting of the fog," and to an accumulation of evidence that "that fog did not rise till the morning of the thirtieth." Now, any one who has lived on the west end of Long Island, will readily understand that it is no unusual thing in summer for wet and rainy, "drizzly" days, such as the 28th and 29th had been, to be accompanied and followed by a misty vapor, or sea-fog, breaking away at times and again settling heavily down upon the horizon; nor is it difficult to believe that a momentary lifting of such a fog permitted the three American officers to catch a glimpse of the British fleet. This same heavy vapor, deepening with the approach of evening, easily settled down by midnight of the 29th into the fog which so favored the American retreat, and which, accumulating in density as the dawn of day approached, is naturally spoken of by witnesses as having risen on the "morning of the 30th."

[2] Force's American Archives, fifth series, i. 1211; Heath's Memoirs, 57; Memorial of Hugh Hughes (acting Quartermaster-General in New York), 32.

[3] The old Cornell house, afterwards known as the Pierrepont mansion, which formerly stood on the line of the present Montague street, near the little iron foot-bridge which spans the carriage-way, was the headquarters of Washington during this important contest. It was a spacious and costly house, having large chimneys, from which it was known as "the Four Chimnies," and upon its roof a telegraph was arranged, by which communication was held with New York city. It was here (and not at the old

imprisoning that portion of the American army in New York, and separating it from that on Long Island.

The deliberations of this council were brief, and their decision unanimous in favor of an evacuation of Long Island and a retreat to New York on that very night.[1] To effect the withdrawal of some nine thousand men, with their arms and munitions of war, and that, too, in face of an enemy at work in their trenches, so near that the sound of their pickaxes and spades could be distinctly heard,—to march them a considerable distance to the river, and to transport them across its strong, broad current,—necessitated the greatest skill and secrecy. Orders were immediately issued to Colonel Glover to collect and man with his regiment of hardy mariners all the boats of every kind which could be found, and to be in readiness by midnight for the embarkation, which was to be superintended by General McDougal. In order to have the army in proper marching condition, without divulging the plan of retreat, the officers were directed to hold their men in readiness for an attack upon the enemy's lines that night. The order excited general surprise, but by eight o'clock the army was ready for movement. That the enemy's suspicions might not be excited, General Mifflin was to remain within the lines, and within 250 yards of the British advanced works, with Colonel Hand's rifle-corps and the battered remnants of the Delaware and Maryland regiments, who, with barely a respite from the terrible battle of the 27th, had now cheerfully consented to cover the retreat of their fresher but less experienced companions in arms.[2] By nine o'clock the ebb-tide,

---

Dutch church in Fulton street, as has been erroneously stated by Lossing and Onderdonk, which was merely the *alarm-post* of the American army) that the council of war was held which determined upon the retreat, and from which the orders for that movement were promulgated. This is on the authority of Colonel Fish, the father of Governor Hamilton Fish, and one of Washington's military family, who, in 1824, during Lafayette's visit to Brooklyn, called the attention of the distinguished visitor to the fact, and designated the very positions in the room occupied by the members of that council.

[1] Proceedings of a Council of War held at Headquarters at Brooklyn, August 29th, 1776. (Onderdonk, sec. 161; Force's American Archives, fifth series, i. 1246.) This council was composed of His Excellency General Washington; Major-Generals Putnam and Spencer; Brigadier-Generals Mifflin, McDougal, Parsons, Scott, Wadsworth, and Fellows.

[2] Colonel Smallwood's letter, and Colonel Hazlet's letter to Thomas Rodney. Onderdonk, sec. 809.

with heavy rain and an adverse wind, rendered the sail-boats of little use; but, by eleven, the northeast wind, which had prevailed for three days, died away, the surface of the water became smooth, and with a southwest breeze favoring, both the sail and row boats were able to cross the river full laden.

By ten o'clock the troops began to move from the lines; and as each regiment left its position, the remaining troops moved to the right and left and filled up the vacancies.[1] Washington, taking his position at the ferry stairs, at the foot of Fulton street, Brooklyn, superintended the embarkation; and the whole movement was conducted with such order and quiet, that it failed to attract the notice of the British sentinels. The intense darkness of the night, and the thick fog which had settled down over every thing, favored the patriot hosts. At a little past midnight they were suddenly startled by the deep roar of a cannon—whether from the British or American lines no one could tell.[2] "The effect," says one who heard it, "was at once alarming and sublime;" but the deepest silence

---

[1] In Onderdonk's Rev. Reminiscences of Kings County, sec. 820, will be found an interesting account of the battle by James S. Martin of Connecticut. He thus speaks of the retreat: "We were strictly enjoined not to speak, or even cough, while on the march. All orders were given from officer to officer, and communicated to the men in whispers. What such secrecy could mean we could not divine. We marched off in the same way we had come on the island, forming various conjectures among ourselves as to our destination." A correspondent in the Independent (Boston) Chronicle, Sept. 19, '76, says of the retreat: "We went over with boats about 7 o'clock. The brigades were ordered to be in readiness with bag and baggage to march, but knew not where or for what; the 2d did not know where the 1st had gone, nor the 3d the 2d. The last marched off at the firing of the 3 o'clock (British) gun on Friday morning. The night was remarkably still, the water smooth as glass, so that all our boats went over safe, though many were but about 3 inches out of water. At sunrise a great fog came up. We left half a dozen large guns. 3 or 4 men were missing who came off in a batteau. On Friday or Saturday the British vessels came up to the desired place."—Onderdonk's Rev. Rem. Kings County, sec. 821.

Statement of Samuel Mills of Jamaica, L. I., a private in Colonel Lasher's First New York regiment: "When it was known that the Americans were retreating, the grenadiers (of which there were 120 in the regiment) were stationed at regular distances inside the American lines, each one having 6 hand-grenades besides their other arms. In the afternoon and evening, previous to crossing over to New York, the soldiers were continually marching and countermarching; one regiment would march up and two down; one up and two down: so that the troops were kept in ignorance of what the final move would be, but generally supposed that an attack of the British would take place the next day."

[2] Graydon's Memoirs, 147.

ensued, and the retreat went bravely on. As the night wore away the tide was turning and a northeast wind began to rise, yet a large proportion of the troops had not been transported over the river. Fearful of delay, Washington sent his aide-de-camp, Colonel Alexander Scammel, to hasten the troops who were on the march. Scammel, by mistake, communicated the order to General Mifflin, who, although somewhat surprised, obeyed, and evacuated the lines with his whole force. Their arrival at the ferry, where several regiments were already waiting to embark, created much alarm and confusion.[1] Sharp words passed between Washington and Mifflin in the annoyance of the moment. "It's a dreadful mistake," said Washington, when he found out that it was Scammel's blunder, "and unless the troops can regain their posts before their absence is discovered by the enemy, the most disastrous consequences are to be apprehended." With heroic cheerfulness Mifflin's troops immediately returned to the lines, and remained there for several hours, until a second order, when they "joyfully bid those trenches a long adieu."[2] Washington, who, since the morning of the 27th, had scarcely left the lines on Long Island, and for forty-eight hours preceding that had hardly been off his horse or closed his eyes, embarked with the last company.

---

[1] It is related, on the authority of Col. Fish, one of Washington's aids, Judge Daggett of New Haven, and others, that the crowd and confusion among the troops who were, at this juncture, huddled on the beach, was extreme, and bordered on a panic; and that Washington, annoyed and alarmed at its probable consequences, sprang to the side of a boat into which the men were crowding, and, holding aloft a large stone with both hands, ordered them, with an impassioned oath, to leave the boat instanter, or he would "sink it to hell." It is needless to say that the towering figure and wrathful eye of their revered general restored the scared troops to their senses, and the embarkation proceeded with more order than before.

[2] Colonel Hand's Account of the Retreat: "In the evening of the 29th of August, 1776, with several other commanding officers of corps, I received orders to attend Major-General Mifflin. When assembled, General Mifflin informed us that, in consequence of the determination of a board of general officers, the evacuation of Long Island, where we then were, was to be attempted that night; that the commander-in-chief had honored him with the command of the covering-party, and that our corps were to be employed in that service. He then assigned us our several stations which we were to occupy as soon as it was dark, and pointed out Brooklyn church as an alarm-post, to which the whole were to repair and unitedly oppose the enemy, in case they discovered our movement and made an attack in consequence. My regiment was posted in a redoubt on the left, and in the lines on the right of the great road below Brooklyn church. Captain Henry Miller commanded in the redoubt. Part of a regi-

Meanwhile, a Mrs. John Rapalje, living near the ferry at Brooklyn, and whose husband had been sent into the interior of New Jersey on suspicion of Toryism, shrewdly surmised, from the accumulation of boats on the beach and other movements which came within her

---

ment of the Flying Camp of the State of New York were, in the beginning of the night, posted by me. They showed so much uneasiness at their station, that I petitioned General Mifflin to suffer them to march off, lest they might communicate the panic with which they were seized to my people. The general granted my request, and they marched off accordingly. After that nothing remarkable happened at my post till about two o'clock in the morning, when Alexander Scammell, since Adjutant-General, who that day acted as A. D. C. to the commander-in-chief, came from the left, inquiring for General Mifflin, who happened to be with me at the time. Scammell told him that the boats were waiting, and the commander-in-chief anxious for the arrival of the troops at the ferry. General Mifflin said he thought he must be mistaken; that he did not imagine the general could mean the troops he immediately commanded. Scammell replied he was not mistaken; adding that he came from the extreme left, and had ordered all the troops he had met to march; that in consequence they were then in motion, and that he would go on to give the same orders. General Mifflin then ordered me to call in my advanced pickets and sentinels, to collect and form my regiment, and to march as soon as possible, and quitted me. Having marched into the great road leading to the church, I fell in with the troops returning from the left of the line. Having arrived at the left of the church, I halted to take up my camp equipage, which, in the course of the night, I had carried there by a small party. General Mifflin came up at the instant, and asked the reason of the halt. I told him, and he seemed very much displeased, and exclaimed: 'Damn your pots and kettles, I wish the devil had them; march on!' I obeyed, but had not gone far before I perceived the front had halted, and hastening to inquire the cause, I met the commander-in-chief, who perceived me, and said, 'Is not that Colonel Hand?' I replied in the affirmative. His Excellency said he was surprised at me in particular; that he did not suppose I would have abandoned my post. I answered that I had not abandoned it; that I had marched by order of my immediate commanding officer. He said it was impossible. I told him I hoped, if I could satisfy him I had the orders of General Mifflin, he would not think me particularly to blame. He said he undoubtedly would not. General Mifflin then coming up, and asking what the matter was, his Excellency said, 'Good God! General Mifflin, I am afraid you have ruined us by so unseasonably withdrawing the troops from the lines.' General Mifflin replied, with some warmth, 'I did it by your order.' His Excellency declared it could not be. Gen. Mifflin swore, 'By God, I did,' and asked: 'Did Scammel act as an A. D. C. for the day, or did he not?' His Excellency acknowledged he did. 'Then,' said Mifflin, 'I had orders through him.' The general replied it was a dreadful mistake, and informed him that matters were in much confusion at the ferry, and unless we could resume our posts before the enemy discovered we had left them, in all probability the most disagreeable consequences would follow. We immediately returned, and had the good fortune to recover our former stations and keep them for some hours longer, without the enemy perceiving what was going forward."

Colonel Tallmadge: "As the dawn approached, those of us who remained in the trenches became very anxious for our safety, at which time there were several regiments still on duty, and a dense fog began to rise and seemed to settle over both encampments. So dense was the atmosphere that a man could not be discerned six

observation, that a retreat had been decided upon by the Americans. With vengeful readiness, therefore, she secretly sent her slave, on the evening previous, to inform the British commander of the facts. The negro, however, first came upon a Hessian guard, who, not understanding his language, and believing him to be a spy, detained him until morning, when he was handed over to a British officer who was making his round of inspection at daylight. Howe was astonished at the negro's story. A company, under Captain Montressor, was detached to reconnoitre the American works, which they found deserted.[1] Detachments hurried off in hot pursuit; but they only reached the ferry in time to see the heavily-laden rear boats of the retreating army disappear in the impenetrable fog which yet hung over the river.[2] Nobly had the

---

yards off. When the sun rose we had orders to leave the lines, but before we reached the ferry the regiment was ordered back again. Colonel Chester faced about and returned to the lines, where the regiment tarried till the sun had risen; but the fog remained as dense as ever. Finally a second order came, and we joyfully bade those trenches a long adieu. When we reached Brooklyn ferry the boats had not yet returned from their last trip, but they soon appeared. I think I saw General Washington on the ferry-stairs when I stepped into one of the last boats. I left my horse at the ferry, tied to a post. The troops having all safely reached New York, and the fog continuing thick as ever, I got leave to return, with a crew of volunteers, for my favorite horse. I had got off with him some distance into the river before the enemy appeared in Brooklyn. As soon as they reached the ferry we were saluted merrily from their musketry, and finally by their field-pieces. When the enemy had taken possession of the heights opposite the city of New York they commenced firing from the artillery, and the fleet pretty soon were in motion to take possession of those waters."

[1] A British account of the battle, in the Parliamentary Register, vol. xiii., says: "They were reconnoitring before daybreak, and at four o'clock discovered the lines were evacuated. The pickets marched twenty-five minutes after. General Robertson heard of the retreat at seven o'clock, and his brigade was ordered to march at eight; but, while marching to the ferry, he was ordered towards Hell-Gate to meet Lee, reported to be landing there with an army. We were on the rear of the enemy; some were killed or taken prisoners in Brooklyn. We saw three or four boats afloat—some boats not off. The *debris* of their rearguard embarked about eight or nine o'clock."

The Hessian account (Max von Elking) says that the British "were astonished, on the following morning (30th), to see the lines deserted, which were immediately occupied by the Hessian regiments von Donop and von Lossberg. Col. von Heeringen, who had, in the night between the 29th and 30th, occupied a hill near the Hudson, had first discovered the desertion of the American lines, and sent Lieut. Zoll to report it to Howe. The English headquarters was so much vexed by the escape of the Amercans, that it deeply regretted having prevented the troops from storming the heights on the 27th."

[2] Washington's letter to Congress, Aug. 31, 1776. The guns of Fort Stirling were

"fishermen-soldiers of Marblehead and Salem" labored at their muffled oars during the long hours of that perilous night; naught, save a few heavy cannon, was left behind; none, save a few lagging marauders, were captured; and when the fog at last rolled away, the American army was joyously moving towards the upper portions of Manhattan Island. "That retreat, in all its circumstances, was truly wonderful. Surely that fog was the shield of God's providence over those men engaged in a holy cause. If 'the stars in their courses fought against Sisera,' in the time of Deborah, these mists were the wings of the cherubim of Mercy and Hope over the Americans on that occasion."[1]

The British, following close upon the heels of the retreating Americans, took possession of their deserted intrenchments, which were garrisoned with English and Hessian troops, while the remainder of the army was quartered at Bushwick, Newtown, Hell-Gate, and Flushing. Howe established his headquarters at Newtown, whence he dated his official dispatches announcing the results of the battle; and, for the period of seven years, two months, and ten days from this time, Long Island and New York city were held in possession by the British.

The defeat of the American army, and its subsequent retreat from Long Island, produced results most disastrous to the patriot cause. "Our situation is truly distressing," wrote Washington, two days after the battle. "The check our detachment sustained on the twenty-seventh ultimo has dispirited too great a proportion of our troops, and filled their minds with apprehension and despair. The militia, instead of calling forth their utmost efforts to a brave and manly opposition in order to repair our losses, are dismayed, intractable, and impatient to return. Great numbers of them have

---

unspiked and turned on the boats of the retreating Americans. Three persons, who left the island last, in a batteau, fell into the enemy's hands.—N. E. Chronicle.

[1] Lossing's Life of Washington, p. 282, who also says that in a letter written by the Rev. John Woodhull, of Leacock, Pa., to his wife, dated Sept. 2d, 1776, he mentions that, for almost a week previous to the battle on the 27th, the wind "had been contrary" for the British fleet, and prevented their coming up the bay. This prevalence of a northerly wind at New York, for so long a time, in August, is unprecedented. In the same letter he says, after speaking of the retreat: "A great fog favored us, the *only* fog that has been here for a long time."

gone off; in some instances almost by whole regiments, by half ones, and by companies, at a time. . . . I am obliged to confess my want of confidence in the generality of the troops. . . . Till of late, I had no doubt in my own mind of defending this place (New York city); nor should I have yet, if the men would do their duty; but this despair of." And two days later he wrote again in the same desponding strain: "Our affairs have not undergone a change for the better, nor assumed a more agreeable aspect than before. The militia, under various pretences, are daily diminishing; and in a little time, I am persuaded, their numbers will be very inconsiderable."

These gloomy forebodings, which so deeply shadowed the generally buoyant and hopeful heart of the commander-in-chief, were by no means groundless. His own army, demoralized by defeat, were gradually slipping away to their homes, carrying with them, wherever they went, the panic with which they had been infected. The enemy, flushed with their late victory, had occupied and garrisoned the American works at Brooklyn; and within a week after the battle their whole force, except four thousand troops left on Staten Island, were in full occupation of Long Island. Their heavy vessels had anchored near Governor's Island, within easy gunshot of the city;[1] while a forty-gun ship[2] had passed the American battery at Stuyvesant Point, and was anchored in Turtle Bay, on the East River, ready to act in conjunction with

---

[1] Upon their approach, the small garrisons at Governor's Island and at Red Hook removed to the city. One man, at Governor's Island, lost an arm, by a ball from a British ship, while embarking.

[2] The Rose, which had taken this position the night after the battle. General Johnson, who incorrectly states the date as the 15th of September, says that she "passed up Buttermilk Channel, and anchored opposite Bushwick Creek, near the shore. On the 16th (?) the Americans brought two 32-pounders to Burnt Mill Point (Stuyvesant's Point, where the Novelty Ironworks now stand), and towards night commenced firing upon the Rose." They fired eighteen shots, and hulled the frigate with seventeen balls, and would have sunk her if daylight had not shut in. The first shot struck her railing at the gangway, and killed a cow taken from Jacob Polhemus, who was on board and saw his cow shot. The frigate removed at night, and anchored between Blackwell's and Long Island, where her hull was protected by the land."

Lossing says that Major Crane of the artillery, acting under orders from Washington, posted two guns upon the high bank at Forty-sixth street, New York, with which he annoyed the frigate, as above described.

several other British ships already in the Sound. Their movements were such as to induce the belief that they intended shortly to make an attack upon the city, which Washington foresaw could not be successfully defended in the present dispirited condition of his troops, scantily supplied as they were with provisions, clothes, and ammunition. The counsels and opinions which agitated the American camp, at this critical juncture of affairs, were diverse. Suffice it to say that the untoward circumstances which surrounded them, as well as the increased activity of the enemy, combined to urge them to a prompt retreat from the city. Of this retreat, which forms so interesting a link in the history of our Revolution, we shall not speak at length. Suffice it to say that on the 13th of September the main body of the army moved towards Mount Washington and Kingsbridge, leaving a rearguard of four thousand men, under General Putnam, in the city. On the 16th Washington established his headquarters at the Morris mansion on Harlem Heights.

On the 15th occurred the occupation of New York island by the British, which is thus described by Gen. Jeremiah Johnson, an eye-witness: "In the evening of the 14th,[1] the Phœnix and Dutchess of Gordon frigates passed New York, with a large number of batteaux: the frigates anchored opposite Kip's Bay,[2] where the Rose joined them. The batteaux were placed near the (Long Island) shore, at the house of Peter Kolyer.[3] Early on the morning of the 15th, a division of the British army marched from Brooklyn, through Bushwick, to the shore at Mr. Kolyer's, where they embarked on board of the batteaux at high-water. About 7 o'clock the ships opened a heavy fire of round and grape shot upon the shore, to scour off the enemy. The firing continued an hour and a half: when the leading boats passed the ships, the firing ceased. The boats passed to the shore, and all the troops landed in safety. We may be incorrect as to dates, but the facts are as stated. I saw the scene. It was a fine morning, and the spectacle was sublime. Thomas Skillman, of Bushwick, and John Vandervoort, and Jacob Bloom, of Brooklyn, with their families, were at Kip's Bay, in the house of Mr.

---

[1] We correct Gen. Johnson's dates.
[2] Foot of 34th street, New York.
[3] On site now occupied by residence of Mr. Samuel Sneeden, Greenpoint.

Kip, when the cannonading of the three British frigates, which lay opposite the house, commenced. The cannon-balls were driven through the house. This induced them to take to the cellar for safety, where they were out of danger. After the landing the men were sent to prison in New York, and the next day their families returned to Long Island. When the troops landed, a line was formed across the island to the North River, to inclose the Americans in New York. 'In vain is the net of the fowler spread in the sight of any bird:' the American rear-guard had escaped."

From a careful consideration of the facts connected with the "Battle of Brooklyn," it is evident,

1. That (as we have already remarked, *ante*, 263), the American *exterior* line of defence was too much extended to admit of its being held against the enemy, except as a mere skirmish-line.

2. That the troops occupying this line should have been re-enforced (which, perhaps, was impracticable and unadvisable, under the circumstances), or else seasonably recalled to the interior fortified lines, which their presence would have considerably strengthened.

3. That, in the absence of any orders of recall, and without re-enforcements, these raw and inexperienced troops, supposing that they were placed there to fight, and knowing nothing of the art of war except to fight right on, committed the serious mistake of making a too prolonged stand against the overwhelming odds which confronted them.

4. That the criminal oversight of the commanding general, or the defection of certain detached troops, or both, which left the Jamaica Pass and road unguarded, and the approach of the British unobserved and unheralded, enabled the latter to flank, surround, and defeat the Americans by detail, with the greatest ease. The "battle," so called, was, in fact, simply a series of unconnected skirmishes —of heroic, but unavailing, efforts on the part of these untrained yeomen to maintain isolated positions which had been hopelessly lost before the fighting began. To the military incapacity of Gen. Putnam, who, although brave and well-meaning, possessed neither

the subordination to obey the orders with whose execution he was intrusted, the skill to carry out the proposed plans of defence, or the ordinary common sense which he might reasonably have been expected to display in the face of an approaching enemy, we may justly attribute the deplorable results of this battle. In this connection we cannot forbear quoting the well-considered and forcible remarks of HENRY B. DAWSON, Esq., our ablest military historical writer, who says[1] in regard to this very point:

"It is unquestionably the duty of the commander of a district to provide, not only the means of securing intelligence of every movement of his enemy, but for the protection of his position; and, especially when any peculiar pass, or hill, or bridge between him and the enemy would secure advantages to that enemy which would be dangerous to him, it is the unquestionable duty of the commander to occupy such position in force; or, in case he neglects it, the disgrace is *his*, and the responsibility for any evil effects arising from such neglect of duty devolves upon *him*. In fact, the commander is a sentinel whom the commander-in-chief or the government has placed to guard the interests of the people, and, like any other sentinel, he cannot sleep on his post without committing one of the highest crimes known to the military law.

"With these axioms before us, let us examine, as far as the evidence goes, who commanded, and who slept on his post. It is said that General Greene commanded on Long Island, that the defences were thrown up under his direction, and that he was taken sick with a fever and left the island.[2] It is said that General Sullivan then assumed the command;[3] that, notwithstanding the enemy was still on Staten Island, he employed mounted patrols, at an expense of fifty dollars per night, to mount guard on roads which he saw the enemy might use in approaching New York;[4] and that, on the 23d of August,—the day after the enemy's army landed on Long Island,—he was superseded by General Putnam.[5] It is said, and has never been contradicted, that General Washington gave General Putnam positive instructions to guard the passes through the hills leading to

[1] Battles of the United States, 148–150.
[2] Gen. Greene to Gen. Washington, Aug. 15.
[3] General Orders, Aug. 20.
[4] His letter to Congress, Oct. 25, 1777.
[5] Sparks' Washington, p. 180.

Brooklyn;[1] it is said, also without contradiction, that General Sullivan, his predecessor and second in command, enforced the same measures on his attention;[2] it is known that, although the enemy, in full force, was encamped within four or five miles, opposite two of those very passes, General Putnam never reconnoitred that enemy's position—in fact, that he never left Brooklyn;[3] and it is equally well known that, although the enemy was then encamped at Flatbush, the mounted patrols which General Sullivan had established,[4] as well as the guards at some of the passes established by General Greene, were withdrawn,[5] leaving the country clear for the enemy's secret movements, and the passes conveniently unguarded for his especial accommodation. It is also a well-established fact, that no general officer was outside the lines at Brooklyn, on the night of the 26th, until the advance of General Grant was made known to General Putnam, at three o'clock, when Generals Sullivan and Lord Stirling were dispatched to Flatbush and the Bay Road, to oppose the movements in those quarters.[6]

"From these facts, it appears conclusively that General Putnam paid no attention to the orders of General Washington, respecting the security of the passes, and that the advice of General Sullivan, on the same subject, was also disregarded, his patrols withdrawn, and the command outside the lines, where his knowledge of the ground rendered him peculiarly useful, taken from him and given to another;[7] that, with an enemy encamped in full force within a few

---

[1] "At the same time, I would have you form a proper line of defence around your encampment and works, on the most advantageous grounds." "*The woods should be secured by abatis, etc., where necessary, to make the enemy's approach as difficult as possible.* Traps and ambuscades should be laid for their parties, if you find they are sent out after cattle," etc.—Orders to Gen. Putnam, Aug. 25.

[2] Gen. Sullivan's letter to Congress, Oct. 25, 1777.

[3] Thompson's Long Island, i. p. 222.

[4] Gen. Sullivan to Cong., Oct. 25, 1777. The "patrol" which Gen. Clinton captured was *a party of officers*, not a regular patrol (*ante*, p. 266, note).

[5] This is shown by Gen. Howe, in his dispatch, where he says: "The General, learning that the rebels *had not occupied the pass*, detached a battalion of light-infantry to secure it," etc.

[6] See Lord Stirling's letter to Gen. Washington, Aug. 29; Gen. Sullivan's letter to Congress, Oct. 25, 1777.

[7] Gen. Sullivan, to Congress, Oct. 25, 1777, says Lord Stirling was ordered to the command outside the lines, while he was ordered to remain *within* the lines, as Gen. Putnam's second in command.

miles of his position, he quietly remained at Brooklyn, without reconnoitring that enemy's position, or sending out a scout; that he withdrew guards and failed to remount them, where they were essential to his safety; and, finally, that to his ignorant, self-conceited inefficiency, the enemy is indebted for one of the greatest victories of the war, and his country for one of the most disastrous defeats, both military and moral, which it ever experienced."

In closing this chapter, it is proper to notice the very limited extent to which the Kings County militia participated in the battle. Previous to its commencement, they were ordered into service within the lines at Brooklyn, under the command of Lieut.-Col. Nicholas Cowenhoven, of Flatbush, and Major Barent Johnson, of Bushwick, the father of the late worthy Gen. Jeremiah Johnson. Many of them, however, embraced the earliest opportunity to join the British army on Staten Island, and others concealed themselves. As a consequence of this universal defection, the regiment was reduced to about two hundred men, and, after the battle, was still further reduced, by desertions, to about one hundred and fifty. This remnant left the island with the rest of the army, under command of Major Johnson,[1] and marched to Harlem, where they dispersed without leave and returned to their homes, where many of them were captured by Tories and incarcerated in the prisons at New York. This was not surprising, when we consider the example set them by their colonel, who left his command within the lines and went privately to Flatbush, where he was seen, shortly after, in company with two British officers. For this he was, upon his return to camp, placed under arrest and sent to Harlem for trial by the Committee of Public Safety. The witnesses were, however, conveniently "spirited away," through the management of friends, and there being no one to appear against him, the colonel was released. After his return to his home in Kings County, he was engaged in certain transactions in the British commissary and barrack departments, and, with many others, was indicted before the Circuit Court, at Albany, at its October term, in 1783, for

---

[1] Major Johnson accompanied the army to Jersey, where he was captured by the British, and returned home on a parole, given by Howe, in January, 1777.

treason against the State, but, by the good management of Alexander Hamilton, he escaped trial. After the adoption of the Constitution of the United States, when the public debt was funded, he was one of the commission which investigated the claims of persons who had suffered loss of cattle and injuries done by American troops in Kings County before they left the island, in 1776. Col. Cowenhoven was afterwards appointed Chief Judge of the Court of Common Pleas of Kings County, and died at New Utrecht on the 6th of March, 1793. In view of his evident sympathy with the British cause, we can only regard his loan of money, in 1782, to Major Wyckoff, as merely a politic concession to the rising fortunes of America.[1]

PART II.

THE BRITISH OCCUPATION OF BROOKLYN.

AUGUST, 1776, TO NOVEMBER, 1783.

The people of Kings County, as we have before remarked, had unwillingly espoused the cause of liberty, and the few who had been persuaded or forced into rebellion, now found themselves abandoned by their countrymen to all its penalties. It was not strange, then, that they should eagerly accept the opportunity of withdrawing from a struggle in which they had no heart, and of throwing themselves upon the mercy and protection of the now dominant power of England.

On the 17th of November, 1776, a large number of the freeholders and inhabitants of Kings County—availing themselves of a proclamation of pardon issued by the British authorities[2]—submitted a very humble and loyal address to Lord Howe, wherein they state that, "reflecting with the tenderest emotions of gratitude on this instance

---

[1] On the back of one of Col. N.'s letters, dated Aug. 23, 1778, and offering Governor Geo. Clinton money for the use of the American prisoners then in the hands of the British, is the following endorsement in the Governor's handwriting: "Letter from N. C. He offers (by way of laying an anchor to windward) to furnish our prisoners on Long Island with as much money as they want."

[2] July 14th, and subsequently Sept. 19th.

of His Majesty's paternal goodness, and encouraged by the affectionate manner in which his Majesty's gracious purpose hath been conveyed to us by your Excellencies, who have thereby evinced that humanity is inseparable from that true magnanimity and those enlarged sentiments which form the most shining characters," they beg leave to represent that they have all signed the Oath of Allegiance, and proceed to say, "that we esteem the constitutional supremacy of Great Britain over these colonies and other depending parts of His Majesty's dominions, as essential to the union, security, and welfare of the whole empire; and sincerely lament the interruption of that harmony which formerly subsisted between the parent State and these her colonies."[1]

The submission of the rank and file was soon followed by that of the leaders, or, at least, the majority of them, who, in December following, presented to Governor Tryon the following "wholesale clearance" of themselves from all complicity with the Rebellion:

"We, the members of the Provincial Congress, the County Committee, and the Committees of the different townships, elected for and by the inhabitants of Kings County, feel the highest satisfaction in having it in our power to dissolve ourselves without danger of the County being desolated, as it was by repeated threats, some short time ago. We do hereby accordingly dissolve ourselves, rejecting and disclaiming all power of Congress and Committees, totally refusing obedience thereto, and revoking all proceedings under them whatsoever, as being repugnant to the laws and constitution of the British Empire, and undutiful to our sovereign, and ruinous to the welfare and prosperity of this County. We beg leave to assure your Excellency we shall be exceeding happy in obeying the legal authority of government, whenever your Excellency shall be pleased to call us forth, being from long experience well assured of your Excellency's mild and upright administration." This was signed by forty persons.[1]

The corps of militia in Kings County, in January, 1777, further testified their "loyalty to their sovereign and zeal to the constitu-

[1] This document, with the names appended, will be found in Onderdonk's Kings Co., sec. 829.

tion," by voluntarily contributing the sum of £310 8s. towards the expense of a new battalion, which was being raised about that time by Col. Fanning.

These evidences of returning loyalty were graciously accepted, and the good people of Kings County no doubt felt themselves amply rewarded by the assurance of Lord Germaine, that "His Majesty has observed with great satisfaction the effusions of loyalty and affection which break forth in the addresses of his faithful subjects upon their deliverance from the tyranny and oppression of the rebel committees; and the proof given by the inhabitants of Kings County of their zeal for the success of His Majesty's measures, by so generously contributing towards the expense of raising Col. Fanning's battalion, cannot fail of recommending them to His Majesty's favor."[1]

At this time, the American prisoners in New York were paroled and billeted on the inhabitants of this county, Congress having agreed to pay two dollars per week for their board. Col. Graydon, who, with the other officers of Col. Shee's and Col. Magraw's regiment, was quartered at Flatbush, gives the following humorous sketch of his accommodations, which will answer, we presume, for a portrait of most of the Dutch families at that day: "Though we were, in general, civilly enough received, it cannot be supposed we were very welcome to our Low Dutch hosts, whose habits were extremely parsimonious, and whose winter provision was barely sufficient for themselves. Had they been sure of receiving two dollars per week, Congress or ourselves being looked on as paymasters, it might have reconciled them. They were, however, a people who seemed thoroughly disposed to submit to any power that might be imposed upon them; and whatever might have been their propensities or demonstrations at an earlier stage of the contest, they were now the dutiful and loyal subjects of His Majesty King George III., and entirely obedient to the behests of their military masters in New York. Their houses and beds we found clean, but their living extremely poor. A sorry wash, made up of a sprinkling of bohea and the darkest sugar, on the verge of fluidity, with half-

---

[1] Onderdonk's Kings Co., sec. 830.

baked bread (fuel being among the scarcest articles at Flatbush) and a little stale butter, constituted our breakfast. At our first coming, a small piece of pickled beef was occasionally boiled for dinner; but to the beef, which was soon consumed, there succeeded *clippers*, or clams; and our unvaried supper was *supon*, or mush, sometimes with skimmed milk, but more generally with buttermilk, blended with molasses, which was kept for weeks in a churn, as swill is saved for hogs. I found it, however, after a little use, very eatable, and supper soon became my best meal. * * * * Their religious, like their other habits, were unostentatious and plain; and a simple, silent grace before meat, prevailed at the table of Jacob Suydam. When we were all seated, he suddenly clapped his hands together, threw his head on one side, closed his eyes, and remained mute and motionless for about a minute. His niece and nephew followed his example; but with such an eager solicitude that the copied attitude should be prompt and simultaneous, as to give an air of absurdity to what might otherwise have been very decent. Although little of the vernacular accent remained on the tongues of these people, they had some peculiarities in their phraseology. Instead of asking you to sit down to table, they invited you to *sit by*."

After the evacuation of Brooklyn, the British, Hessians, Tories, and refugees had unlimited range over Long Island, and were quickly joined by neutrals and "fence gentry." Most of the Whigs were absent with the army; their wives, children, and aged people alone remained at home, and their dwellings became the prey of these wretches, who robbed friend and foe alike. The negroes, also, became their willing aiders and abettors, and frequently guided them in their predatory expeditions. The loyalists were all summoned to attend at headquarters, in Bedford, to be registered; after which, they were ordered to wear a *red* badge in their hats, as a protection and a token of loyalty. They obeyed with ludicrous alacrity, and straightway the loyal badge flamed from every hat and cap in the county. Many ladies wore scarlet ribbons, while all the negroes, of course, were royalists and bedecked their hats with scarlet *rags;* and females even dispensed with their flannel petticoats, in order to supply the unprecedented demand for cloth of the requisite hue. The haughty British officers, however, scarcely deigned to conceal their contempt for the newly-found loyalty of the "red rags," as they were termed, and in less than three months the scarlet emblems were doffed by all except a few negroes who courted distinction.

The protection afforded to the people by the royal authorities, was paternal only in its severity. Long Island, New York city, Staten Island, and Westchester, during their whole subsequent occupation by the British, were kept under the most rigorous military rule. Elections were not allowed; voting, except at annual town meetings, was prohibited; the civil courts were suspended, and their functions arbitrarily dispensed either by a king's justice or a military officer. A sort of police court was, after a while, opened in New York city at the mayor's office; and at length, in 1780, a similar court was established at Jamaica, for the greater convenience of the Long Island people. The old "Fly Market," at the foot of Maiden Lane, New York, was protected by a guard of soldiers, with sentinels on the ferry stairs; and no farmer or other person was permitted to carry any goods or provisions to or from the city without a written pass, obtained either from the mayor's office or from Col. Axtell, at Flatbush, for which a charge of 2s. was exacted. The owner of every market-boat had to obtain a yearly license for the same, wherein the name of each person coming to the city was entered; and these boats and licenses were frequently examined, to prevent the passage of unlicensed travellers. Officers of the British army and navy were alone exempt from this military examination at the ferry stairs. The price of wood, and of all kinds of farm produce, was regulated by proclamation, and the farmers themselves, their horses, wagons, and servants, could be at any time impressed into the king's service, at a stipulated price.[1] Woodland and brushwood was also remorselessly cut down by the British, to be used for fuel

[1] When the British were preparing, in 1777, to enter Pennsylvania and take Philadelphia, the farmers of Kings and Queens counties were required to furnish horses, wagons, and drivers for the use of the army. They were designated by officers, under command of a (refugee) Captain Beman, of the Quartermaster's Department, and were ordered to appear, on specified days, at Bedford, where the value of horse and wagon was appraised and recorded in a book kept for the purpose. After their return from Philadelphia, where many were lost or damaged, a day was set apart for the owners to present their claims; and these claims were paid, it was asserted, from a false record,

and the building of fortifications; and when at length the wood was exhausted, and the inhabitants began to be straitened for want of it, the Hessians dug up the meadows for peat, in spite of the expostulations of the astonished and indignant Dutch farmers.[1] During the summer months, the fields, from Red Hook to the heights of Cripplebush, were white with tents faced with scarlet; and before their removal to New York, nearly all the fences were taken up and burned. The whole district occupied by the troops was a common, and most of the land remained unfenced till the British left the country. In the winter season every village was filled with British soldiers, wagons, etc., billeted in private houses or cantoned in temporary huts. This quartering of officers and billeting of troops among the people, was a serious annoyance. The first notice generally given of such occupation was an abrupt "Well, madam, I've

---

and at about *thirty per cent less than the real valuation.* Protest was futile, the unlucky farmers were told to take what was offered them, or go without. As if to add insult to injury, they were graciously told by the commissioners, "Friends, there is a barrel of rum in the entry—help yourselves!" To which two of the indignant sufferers retorted: "We don't want your rum—give us our own—we can treat ourselves;" an answer which subsequently cost them their woodlands, which were specially designated to the barrack-masters, and cut down for the use of the army. The owners of this wood received only two dollars per cord, while the officials charged and received from the Government ten dollars.

[1] Furman, in his MS. notes, vol. ix., p. 376, preserves this fact relative to the discovery and use of peat in Kings Co.:

"My father, who is now fifty-eight years old, says that previous to the Revolutionary War, the existence of peat in Kings County, and in the town of Newtown, Queens County, was unknown to the inhabitants; and that the same was discovered by the British soldiery who were then and there encamped, in those places where wood had become scarce in consequence of its having been all cut off. They instructed the inhabitants in the art of preparing this valuable article of fuel—which was found on land formerly considered as comparatively worthless—but which is now highly esteemed. It was on the land of my great uncle, William Furman, at the head of the 'Vlie,' in Newtown, that the first turf was thus cut. He remonstrated with the British officers, believing that they would ruin his land, and told them that they might cut all his wood, but should leave his meadow. They replied that all his wood would not serve the British troops about New York for a single month; but that there was turf enough on his land to serve as fuel for the whole British army in America. So they cut it, regardless of his objections, and without paying him for it, as he was known not to be a loyalist, and had relatives in the American army. They also told him that the deeper it was cut, the better it was—which my great-uncle found to be true, and always afterwards used turf for fuel, from preference. It was truly a providential discovery for the Long Island people, who were beginning to be distressed for want of wood, which had nearly all been cut off by the British troops."

come to take a billet in your house." The officers usually appropriated one or more of the best rooms in the house to their own use, and kept a guard constantly parading to and fro before the door. The soldiers made themselves at home in the kitchen. These officers, too, required the utmost condescension from the inhabitants, who were expected, while addressing them, to hold their hats under their arms: and should a farmer, in passing, neglect to doff his hat, he ran a strong risk of a good caning; although if he did it, the Briton rarely deigned to notice him or to return his civility. As a natural consequence, insubordination arose among the slaves, who either ran away from or became less respectful to their masters, whom they saw so humbled before the British officers. When we add to this the carousing, gambling, profanity, and the many other vices of the camp which were introduced into these hitherto quiet and orderly villages by the presence of large bodies of troops, who spread gold and dissipation with equal liberality around them, we cannot envy the condition of the people. It is true that all this afforded a ready market for such of the farmer's produce as had not been previously pilfered by the numerous marauding gangs which prowled around the country, making equal booty from friend and foe. The farmers flourished on British gold; but as there were no banks for its safe-keeping, and few opportunities of investment, they were obliged to keep it by them, and were often robbed. The churches, also, except those of the established faith, were freely occupied as prisons, hospitals, storehouses, and barracks for troops: some were even wantonly destroyed.

In short, between the oppressions of their so-called "protectors," the British, and the depredations of the American whale-boatmen, the good people of Kings County generally were in a most pitiable condition. These whale-boatmen were Americans (many of them refugees from Long Island), who lived along the Connecticut shore, and bore commissions from the governors of that colony and of New York, authorizing them to cruise in the Sound against British vessels. It became, after a while, no unusual thing for them to land, and, under pretence of carrying off British goods, to plunder Whig and Tory alike, until at length the whale-boat warfare degenerated into downright *piracy*. The dwellers along the shore were in constant dread of their visits, and would often climb to the roofs of their houses, where, spy-glass in hand, they anxiously scanned the horizon. If they discerned whale-boats in the bay, the alarm was immediately given by signal-guns or horn-blowing, and all valuables were hastily hid away, leaving only a few articles in the house ; and the robbers, after ransacking the premises, would curse the inmates for their poverty, and depart. In this way, stores were sometimes nearly emptied of their contents in an afternoon, and the goods replaced next morning. If, however, the owners were once caught, they ran a good chance of being tortured until the goods were forthcoming. Another more honorable employment of whale-boats, and one in which they rendered good service, was that of surprising and carrying off distinguished loyalists, in order to exchange them for Whig prisoners.[1]

At this period, and during the war, the whole of the land embraced between the brow of the Heights on the river and the present Fulton and Joralemon streets—now forming one of the most closely-built and beautiful portions of our city—was then under high cultivation. That portion of it nearest to Fulton street was either used for pasturage, with its beautiful crop of grass browsed upon by fat, well-kept cattle, or was kept, at times, in grain. The middle part was almost entirely occupied by fine and thrifty orchards of apple, pear, and other trees ; and the lower portion was used for excellent gardens, which furnished an abundant supply of small fruit and vegetables to the New York markets. This tract of land belonged to several owners, among whom were the Middaghs, Bamper, Colden, Debevoise, Remsens. On the Heights (*ante*, p. 73) stood the mansion of Philip Livingston, Esq.,[2] afterwards known as the "Joralemon House," a large double frame-house, the more modern por-

---

[1] The whale-boats were made sharp at each end, the sheathing not over half an inch thick, and so light as to be easily carried on men's shoulders, either to be hid in the bushes or relaunched in the South Bay. Some were thirty-two feet long, and impelled by from eight to twenty oars, and would shoot ahead of an ordinary boat with great velocity, and leave their pursuers far behind. They were always on the lookout, and, in a calm, would row out of their lurking-places and board market-boats, or even cut off the detached vessels of a convoy.

[2] Philip Livingston and his brother owned the land comprising the farms subsequently belonging to Joralemon and Hicks, which adjoined that of Whitehead Cornell. These farms were divided by a road leading from Red Hook Lane to a public landing

tion of which was built by Mr. Livingston, just previously to the war, for his only son, who was then making the tour of Europe, and was to be married on his return, which, however, was prevented by his death abroad. The house was constructed in the very best manner, having costly carved marble mantels imported from Italy, and other furniture at that day unusual to American houses. During the occupation of the island it was used as an hospital for the British navy,[1] probably as a justifiable retaliation upon its owner, who was a prominent member of the Continental Congress. Attached to the house was an extensive garden, which the well-known taste and abundant means of Mr. Livingston had made the finest in this part of America, and which—to their credit be it said—was kept in good repair by the physicians and officers of the hospital, who appropriated the mansion-house to their own use, sheds and huts being erected for the sick on the farm (formerly known as the Ralph Patchen property) on the southerly side of the present Atlantic street. Things remained thus until 1780–81, when Admiral Arbuthnot[2] assumed the command of this station. He instituted various reforms, among which was the turning out of the surgeons and physicians from their comfortable quarters in the mansion-house, which was forthwith appropriated to

---

at "The Fishing Place." This spot, famous in the memories of old Brooklynites, lay opposite the Livingston farms, between Cornell's Mills and the Remsen Farm, and was called "Livingston Beach."

[1] Furman, MSS., vol. ix. pp. 184, 185: "Dec. 9, 1839. My father tells me that at one period during the Revolutionary War he saw lying in the harbor of New York, when that city and Long Island were in the possession of the British army, eighteen line-of-battle ships and a great number of frigates and smaller vessels of war, with between eighty and ninety transports, belonging to the British navy."

[2] Admiral Arbuthnot was accompanied by Prince William, afterwards King William the Fourth, but then a midshipman in the Royal Navy. "The prince," says Furman, MSS., "was very fond of playing a game of ball called 'rackets,' and used to go very frequently with officers of the British army and navy; and when they came to the 'alley,' which was in John street, New York, and found the young men and apprentices of the city playing, they, without any ceremony, would order them to discontinue and to leave the alley. This, of course, caused bad feeling on the part of the citizens towards the officers, which the former sought every opportunity of manifesting when they could do so with impunity. Thus James West, an apprentice of my father's uncle, James Hallett, a coachmaker in the city of New York (who established the first carriages for hire in that city, afterwards known as 'hacks'), considering himself insulted or wronged by Prince William in some matter about that ball-play, one night gave the prince a good knock-down in the street, and a friend with him did the same

the use of the sick sailors. After that the garden began to go to decay, until, at the close of the Revolution, when the British left Brooklyn, little of it remained but the name. The principal disease among the sick was the scurvy, and they were buried from these hospitals, in the neighboring ground, and that, afterwards, of Hezekiah B. Pierrepont, to the number of twelve and fifteen a day.[1] For many years afterwards, the remains of these poor fellows were from time to time, disinterred by the caving down of the brow of the hill all along this portion of the shore. On the banks of the river, a little east of the easterly line of the continuation of Furman street, and between Pacific and Warren streets, as now laid out, was a knoll of land, where several hundred British sailors and soldiers were buried in regular rows. The heads of the westernmost row were exposed to the lashing of the waves of the East River, by which they were beaten off from the trunks. On this knoll, thus enriched, a superior quality of asparagrus was afterwards raised for the New York markets.

Furman, from whose manuscripts we gain many of these facts, states that the old house, afterwards occupied by Selah Strong, Esq., and which stood in what is now known as Strong Place, just behind Christ Church, was built and inhabited by an English Colonel Thornely, at the desire of the Cornells, with whom he had become quite intimate during the Revolution, and who sold him the land on which it was erected. These Cornells were among the most respectable citizens of old Brooklyn, and, as Furman says, "all staunch King and Church men." Whitehead Cornell, a native of Queens County, came to Brooklyn about the middle of the last century, and married into the old Seabring family, who occupied a portion of the Lubbertson property, near Red Hook, as described on pages 63–67. By this marriage and probably, also, by purchase,[2] he be-

---

[1] Mr. William Furman used to relate that he saw ten or twelve bodies buried in one grave, from the British hospitals, on the Livingston place. His son, the historian of Brooklyn, also states, in his MSS., that by their teeth they appear all to have been young or middle-aged men; and that a negro man belonging to Mr. William Cornell, the subsequent owner of the place, made considerable money by disposing of the teeth, which he found on these burial spots, to the dentists in New York city. Artificial teeth, it must be remembered, were not then known.

[2] The Seabrings, who were Whigs, left the Island with, or shortly after the depart-

THE CORNELL-PIERREPONT MANSION.

(River Front.)

Page 307.

THE CORNELL-PIERREPONT MANSION.

(Rear View.)

Page 307

came the owner of nearly, if not quite, all the Seabring estates in that vicinity. He, also, realized a handsome fortune by contracting to supply the British fleet on this station with meat; the final settlement for which was effected after the war by his son John, who visited England for that purpose. The social and personal standing of the family, however, was in nowise affected by their loyalty to King and Church; and their neighbors showed no disposition to molest them, after the close of the war. Whitehead Cornell divided his estate between his three sons—John,[1] Isaac, and William. The former received sixty acres, including the old Seabring, or "Red Mills," where he pursued the milling business; the flour of his make enjoying a high reputation even in the English market. He was a high-toned, enterprising gentleman, and for many years a vestryman and influential member of St. Anne's Episcopal Church. His brother, William, received a tract of a hundred and fifty acres along the river, which he afterwards sold to Ralph Patchen, while Isaac received ninety acres, adjoining John's farm, upon which he erected a distillery.

The fine old house known as the "Four Chimnies," and afterwards as the Pierrepont mansion, and which has been described (page 284, *note* 3), was erected, as is supposed, by a John Cornell, who may have been a brother of Whitehead.[2] On the wharf, at foot of present Joralemon street, was situated a brewery, belonging to Livingston, and which, during the war, was employed by the British as a "King's Brewery," where they made spruce-beer for the use of the hospitals and fleet on this station.[3] The old people used to say

ture of, the American troops in August, 1776. The Cornelius Seabring house and mill were burned, or partially destroyed, by the British, and owing to this and the length of the war, they found themselves, on their return, much impoverished, and were obliged to dispose of their property, which was purchased, as we have stated, by their neighbors and relatives, the Cornells.

[1] *Not*, as near as we can ascertain, the John who kept the "St. George's Tavern," on the Heights, mentioned on page 220; and who was probably of another Queens County family.

[2] For genealogy of the Cornell family, see Bolton's Hist. of Westchester County, New York, ii., pp. 552–557.

[3] This Distillery Dock, and a molasses distillery on the same, was built about 1766, by a Mr. Jones, a relative of the Livingstons; and the distillery, together with the ferry-house, was burned in 1787. Here, subsequently, was located Mr. Hez. B. Pierrepont's celebrated "Anchor-Gin" distillery.

the best beer that they ever tasted, and that the hospitals used at the rate of twenty barrels a day for their sick. These patients also had the best of medical attention, with abundant supplies of vegetables and excellent soups, and, when they became convalescent, were allowed to roam about the country, in order to breathe the fresh, pure air, and obtain exercise.

On the edge of the hill (or Heights) between the present Orange and Clark streets, was a half-moon fort, garrisoned by Hessian troops, and having a battery of cannon overlooking the harbor.[1] There were then no houses on the Heights, between present Doughty and Clark streets. The first house, a two-story frame edifice south of Clark street, was the residence of Mr. Lodewyck Bamper,[2] an elderly gentleman of fortune, who was supposed to

---

[1] *Ante*, 247. On its site was subsequently placed a large hotel, brought from Flatbush. It stood about the junction of the present Clarke and Columbia streets, where Mr. Henry C. Bowen's house now is; was chiefly patronized by Southerners, and was kept by Edward Macomber, from Providence, R. I., the father of Edward Macomber who built the block corner of Fulton and De Kalb avenues, known as "Macomber's Block." The building was pulled down by David Leavitt, who sold the ground to Mr. Bowen.

[2] The family records say that this Lodewyck Bamper, a son-in-law of the Governor of the Dutch colony of Surinam, came to America at some period between 1720 and '30, in a vessel which was owned by himself, as was also the cargo, which consisted of drygoods and horses. The crew of this vessel were African slaves, belonging to Mr. B., who brought with him, as household servants, four females of the same race, named respectively Europe, Asia, Africa, and America. He seems to have been a man of great wealth, even for that day, as he brought with him 60,000 guineas, an immense amount of silver-plate for daily family use, including two complete tea-services, two large urns, one for coffee and the other for chocolate, tureens, mugs, tumblers, goblets, porringers, chafing-dish, ladles, forks and knives with solid silver handles; also, the richest dress fabrics, such as silks, satins, and costly laces, piles of finest Holland linen, and jewelry of every sort. Among the elegant furniture which they owned was a house-organ, which was always played when the family were at meals, by a person who acted as valet and musician. This organ (in 1842) was in use at the Lutheran church, corner of William and Frankfort streets, New York. Soon after his arrival here, Mr. Bamper purchased ground on the northwest corner of Beekman and Gold streets, upon which he erected a dwelling, after the fashion of the day, fifty feet front and a story and a half high, and which remained, with its exterior unchanged, until 1834 or '35. A garden extended, in the rear of the house, to Ferry street; and, under the care of an imported professional gardener, was cultivated and filled with all kinds of fruits and flowers to which the climate was congenial. In the large walks of this garden were placed, in the summer-time, painted wooden statues, life-size, representing grenadiers in full dress and equipments complete, also female figures representing soldiers' wives and children. Mr. Bamper became a large purchaser in lands of the northern and western parts of New York State; and also on Brooklyn Heights, where he established

have retired from the Holland trade. He had a beautiful garden, and a choice collection of fruit, seldom left his house, and in pleasant weather passed most of his time upon his piazza, which fronted the harbor, or in his garden. He usually dressed with silk breeches, a silk loose-gown, a silk cap upon his head, and carried a gold-headed cane. His residence was then a most retired spot, having no immediate neighbors, except the "Old Stone House," at that time belonging to Gov. Cadwallader Colden, and afterwards owned and occupied by Samuel Jackson, Esq.[1] This house, on Doughty street, fronting on Elizabeth street, was occupied by the Hessian troops as a guard-house and prison, and was the place where all persons arrested in this vicinity were detained—the whole island being at that time under a strict military police. It was a long, one-and-a-half story building, of stone and brick, with a fine large garden in the rear, and was afterwards the residence of Mr. Geo. Hicks. Past this old stone house ran a private lane or footpath, from Love Lane (which then led from Fulton street to the edge of the hill) along the brow of the hill, and descending its side to a landing on present Furman, near Clark street.

---

his country-house, above referred to, on the corner of Clark and Willow streets. It had within it, when taken down, some curious carvings done for the Bampers. The property was bought by Henry Waring from Gideon Kimberly, who bought it from John Barbarin. Mr. Bamper was largely interested in the establishment of a glass factory, on almost the identical spot lately occupied by the glass-works, on State street. The first bottle ever made at this factory, having blown on it a seal bearing the name of Mr. Bamper and the date 1754, is still preserved among the curiosities of the Long Island Historical Society. The factory, however, did not have a long career, on account of an insufficient supply of the necessary kind of sand. Mr. and Mrs. Bamper were members of the Moravian church, New York. They had two daughters, one of whom, during the Revolutionary War, was married to Dr. John Noel Barbarin, from Nantes, in France—then a physician in the British service, and attached to the naval hospital at the Livingston mansion. Subsequently, towards the conclusion of the war, he resigned his position and settled at Brooklyn, in the practice of his profession. Nov. 22, 1784, in Assembly, a petition of *Noel Jean Barbarin*, praying by law the privilege of being naturalized and becoming a citizen, was read and referred to Mr. Ford, Mr. Cooper, and Mr. Joseph Laurence. (Furman MSS.) He was *the first* settled physician in this town, where he was very much respected and esteemed. A curious MS. record, in the French language, of *accouchement* cases, from 1791 to 1796, kept by Dr. Barbarin, is still in existence, and might prove interesting to some descendants of the "old families" of Brooklyn. His son, Aime J. Barbarin, was a resident of Brooklyn within the recollection of many old Brooklynites.

[1] Jackson leased it to John Wells, a distinguished lawyer of that day, who died of yellow fever in 1823.

During the war, the British Wagon Department for the army on this station, was located in Brooklyn, occupying an immense yard, with sheds, stables, blacksmith's forges, etc., and extending from the present Main to Jay streets, and west of Prospect street, which was fenced in, the main gateway being near the present junction of Main and Fulton streets.[1] Joseph Fox, an Englishman, and an old and respected citizen of Brooklyn, was for many years one of the principals of this wagon department. These wagons were, of course, used for the transportation of stores, baggage, and tents of the troops, but more especially for bringing in forage. Every few months, the British commandants in New York would issue general orders, imposing upon the unfortunate farmers of Kings and Queens, and a part of Suffolk County, heavy assessments of grain, hay, straw, etc., and specifying the times at which it was expected to be in readiness for delivery to the forage-masters, at certain prices fixed by the order. At the time specified, the wagons would be sent out into the country, accompanied by military guards, and the grain was duly collected, the owners receiving from the forage-masters written receipts, payable on presentation at the office of the Quartermaster-General. If, however, that officer or his subordinates took it into their heads that the farmer was secretly attached to the American cause, he was certain to be refused payment, and might esteem himself lucky if he got off as easily as that. In the same manner, also, in the fall of every year, the Long Island counties would be assessed for many thousand cords of wood, to be cut down and delivered at certain points, for the use of the British garrisons in New York and vicinity. In this manner both Queens and Kings counties were utterly despoiled of the abundant forests which had been their pride; and when the British finally left the island, scarcely a stick, except a small piece of oak woods, a few miles beyond Jamaica, which belonged to a strong Tory, had escaped the axe. All

---

[1] Gen. Johnson says that this was on John Rapelje's land, ten acres of which was taken in October, 1783, by the British Quartermaster, as a Forage and Wood Depot, enclosed with a high fence, and occupied until the evacuation.

The conductors of British wagon department opened roads wherever they saw fit. One of these roads was opened nearly in a straight line from the Jamaica road, about one-half a mile beyond Bedford, to present entrance of Sands street, which shortened the distance to Jamaica considerably.

REFERENCES

TO

MAP OF BROOKLAND FERRY, IN 1766-67, AND 1867.

THE ancient portion (printed in black) of this map is from RATZER'S (larger) "Map of New York and a part of Long Island"—drawn on a scale of 400 feet to the inch—in the years 1766 and '67.

Over this, the street lines of the modern city (printed in red) have been drawn by Mr. SILAS LUDLAM, City Surveyor.

1. The "Corporation House," or "Ferry Tavern," known during the Revolutionary War as Messrs. Looseley and Elms' "King's Head Tavern." (See page 311.)

2. John Rapalje's house, with garden extending to the river.

3. The "Old Stone Tavern," kept by Benjamin Smith.

4. Mr. Cary Ludlow's house.

5. The Hicks mansion.

6. The Middagh mansion.

7. The Middagh barn.

8. The "Whalebone Gate," so called from its being arched over with the rib-bones of a whale. It opened, at the side of Mr. Thomas Everit's house, into a lane leading up to Mr. Cary Ludlow's house.

the woodlands now in these counties has grown since the year 1783.

At the foot of and on the northerly side of the old road (now Fulton street, near the corner of Front), was situated the "ferry tavern." It was a large and gloomy stone building, about sixty feet square and two stories high, which stood in such a way cornerwise, as to leave only thirty-five and a half feet for the entire width of the street between it and the houses opposite. From the circumstance of its being owned by the corporation of the city of New York, it was known as the "Corporation House,"[1] and had been noted as a tavern for thirty years previous to the Revolution. Its last incumbent, before the Battle of Brooklyn, was Captain Adolph Waldron, who was also "the ferrymaster." Espousing the cause of the Rebellion, and being active as the commandant of a company of light-horse raised in Brooklyn, he was, of course, compelled to absent himself from Long Island during its occupation by the British.[2] He was succeeded by Charles Loosely and Thomas Elms, thorough loyalists, who named the old tavern "The King's Head," fitted it up in the most complete manner,[3] and catered to the tastes of their mil-

[1] Also, from some circumstance connected with hoisting a coffin on the flagstaff of the building, known as "The Coffin House." It was the successor of the ferry-house, erected in 1746, by the corporation of the city of New York, on land purchased of Jacob Morris, in 1694; and which was burned down in 1748, as it was supposed, by the Brooklynites, who were then carrying on a long and bitter litigation with the corporation concerning ferry rights (see Chapter on Ferries). Its site is now (1866) partially occupied by Nos. 19, 21, and 23 Fulton street. At the time of the Revolution, the East River, at high-water mark, came nearly up to Front street, as shown in the accompanying plan. Subsequently to the war, this tavern was kept by Benjamin Smith for many years. It was burned down in 1812 (its walls remaining for many years thereafter), and Mr. Smith removed his stand to a stone building on the opposite side of Fulton street.

[2] *Ante*, p. 247.

[3] It is probable that these gentlemen kept hotel "not wisely, but too well" for their own pockets, at least; for, soon after the signing of the provisional Treaty of Peace, in November, 1782, we find a notice of a "Public Auction of Brooklyn Hall," for "*the benefit of the creditors* of Charles Loosely," of "all the genuine household furniture, consisting of mahogany and other bedsteads, feather beds and mattresses, chintz and other curtains, blankets, sheets, etc.; mahogany drawers, dining, tea, and card tables; an elegant clock in mahogany case; *a curious collection of well-chosen paintings and pictures;* large pier and other looking-glasses, in gilt and plain frames; table and tea sets of china, plate, etc.; *a capital, well-toned organ,* made by one of the first hands in London; a *billiard table* in thorough repair; near twenty globe lamps, fit for hall or passage, etc.;

itary friends and patrons with such shrewd energy and tact, that it became extensively resorted to, during the war, by the officers of the British army and the fashionables of the day, as a place of amusement. Lieutenant Anbury, in a letter to a friend in England, dated New York, Oct. 30th, 1781, refers to it thus: "On crossing the East River from New York, you land at Brooklyn, which is a scattered village, consisting of a few houses. At this place is an excellent tavern, where parties are made to go and eat fish; the landlord of which has saved an immense fortune during this war."[1] We shall have frequent occasion to refer to this headquarters of royalists and Tories, which subsequently seems to have been known by the name of "Brooklyn Hall."

Just off from this old road, on what is now the westerly side of Front street, at its junction with Fulton, was the large stone house owned by John Rapalje, the Tory, which was confiscated after the Revolution, and afterwards sold by the Commissioners to Comfort and Joshua Sands, and by them to Abm. Remsen (*ante*, 78, 79).

1777, September 26th. The loyalists had the pleasure of welcoming Rivington, the printer, on his return from England, whither he had been obliged to flee to escape the wrath of the Americans. On this occasion Loosely and Elms' "King's Head Tavern" was "elegantly illuminated, to testify the joy of the true 'Sons of Freedom.'"

1778. During this year, or at least from July to November, and probably through the winter, the following regiments were encamped at or near Bedford, the 37th, 42d, 44th, 46th, and 17th light infantry; between Bedford and Bushwick, the 1st battalion light infantry; and at Brooklyn ferry, the New York volunteers.

A correspondent of *Rivington's Gazette*, of January 24th, 1778, gives the following account of the manner in which the queen's birthday was observed, by the New York loyalists, at their favorite resort in Brooklyn: "As the loyalty even of individuals ought, at this time, to be properly encouraged, you will infinitely oblige the

---

wagons, horses, cows, etc.; two tenements adjoining the house; a flagstaff, with ensigns, pendants; and several hundred transparent and tin lamps, *fit for an illumination.*" As will be seen in the following pages, landlord Loosely was profuse of illuminations on every possible occasion.

[1] Anbury's Travels, ii. 540.

public and a number of your readers, by inserting a description of the grand and elegant illumination at the King's Head Tavern, on last evening, in honor of her Majesty's birthday; and it is the desire of the public, as Messrs. Loosely and Elms have ever shown their attachment to the British Government, and a detestation of the present rebellion, that, through the channel of your much-esteemed paper, their conduct may be known and approved of in Europe, as well as by the loyalists in New York. The tavern was illuminated with upwards of two hundred wax-lights. In the centre were the royal arms of Great Britain, and above it, statues of the present king and queen, under a canopy of state elegantly decorated, which shone, like their majesties' virtues, conspicuous to the world. The view of the reduction of Mud Fort (on one side) by his majesty's ships, Roebuck and Vigilant, gave that joy which Britons always feel on the success and honor of their country. On the other side, their generous indignation was roused by a view of those men (the Congress) whose ambition has almost ruined this unhappy country, and reduced its inhabitants to the greatest distress. It was very *apropos* of the painter to place the devil at the President's elbow, who tells him to persevere, with so significant a grin as seems to indicate his having no manner of doubt of their making his house their home in the infernal regions. The statue of Mr. Pitt, without its head, was placed near the Congress, as being one of their kidney, and gave a hint of what ought, long ago, to have been done. The verses over the tavern door were very proper on the occasion, and well illuminated. In short, every thing was well conducted, and the *tout ensemble* had really a fine effect. Much is due to Messrs. Loosely and Elms for their patriotic spirit, which meets the approbation of every man who is a friend to his king and country."

1779. In February of this year, the 33d Regiment light infantry (300), and 2d battalion Highlanders (750), were encamped at Bedford, and the 3d Prince Hereditary (350), and 4th Charles (300), at Brooklyn.

Gaine's Mercury, Sept. 27th, advertises "a cricket-match for fifty guineas, between Brooklyn and Greenwich clubs, to be played this day at Loosely and Elms, 10 A. M."

1780. In May, the newly-appointed Governor Robertson writes

to the Home Government that "a large square fort is built on Brooklyn Heights: the season is late; not a blade of grass. The people within the lines begin to repair and rebuild houses, and manure and inclose lands." The fort here referred to was probably the one erected at the junction of Pierrepont and Henry streets, and was by far the most thoroughly constructed and complete fortification erected by the British during their stay on Long Island. The land on which it was built, was, at the time, occupied by several fine orchards, which, of course, were ruthlessly levelled by the engineers of the army. The position was a very commanding one,[1] and the extremely level nature of the ground rendered the work one of great labor. Old inhabitants used to speak of having seen from two to three thousand British soldiers engaged upon these works at the same time, in digging trenches, and wheeling earth in barrows, to form the walls; in addition to which, all the inhabitants on the island were assessed according to their respective counties for a certain number of days' work.[2]

---

[1] We learn from Mr. Henry E. Pierrepont, of Brooklyn, that, according to careful survey made for him in 1838, by Alfred Craven, the well-known engineer of the Erie railroad, and latterly the head of the Croton Water Board, the site of this fort was found to be three feet one inch higher than the level of the land in Washington, near Concord streets, making it the highest, and therefore the most suitable position for such a fortification in that part of the town.

We also learn from Furman's MSS., that when the British army evacuated New York, Messrs. Middagh, Bamper, Golden, and Debevoise, owners of the lands whereon the fort was built, commenced to dismantle the fortification, tearing down its gates, barracks, etc.; quite forgetful of the fact that the property really belonged to the Government, although located on their premises. They at last quarrelled among themselves as to the disposition of the wreck; and the affair coming to the knowledge of Gov. Clinton, he issued an order, through the sheriff of Kings County, commanding them to desist from further dismantling the fort, and to render an account of all property taken away. Although extremely alarmed at this proceeding, the matter was afterwards amicably arranged between the Government and the proprietors, who finally obtained permission to complete the work of demolition. The ramparts, however, remained until about 1836, since which time the ground has been fully occupied by one of the most elegant portions of our city.

[2] All the brushwood in the neighborhood of Newtown was cut down and made up into fascines, about twelve feet long and the size of a man's body, which the farmers were compelled to cart into Brooklyn, where they were to be used in supporting the earth walls of the fort. A man with two horses, or oxen, and a wagon, was obliged to labor for a week or ten days in cutting and transporting these fascines, or timber and other material for barracks. A large number of mechanics were also employed in the construction of a gate and drawbridge—a most substantial and costly work of great

It is said to have been an exciting and exceedingly interesting sight to witness several thousand men, soldiers, mechanics, farmers, and laborers, all busily engaged in erecting this extensive fortification, on lands which, a few months previous, had been covered only with thrifty orchards, under whose grateful shades cattle quietly grazed or reposed. Nature had yielded to the rude hand of war; but years have again passed, and the same locality, under the inspiration of modern civilization, has experienced a still more marvellous change; so that the stranger who walks our thickly populated streets, can scarcely realize that he treads upon "Revolutionary ground."

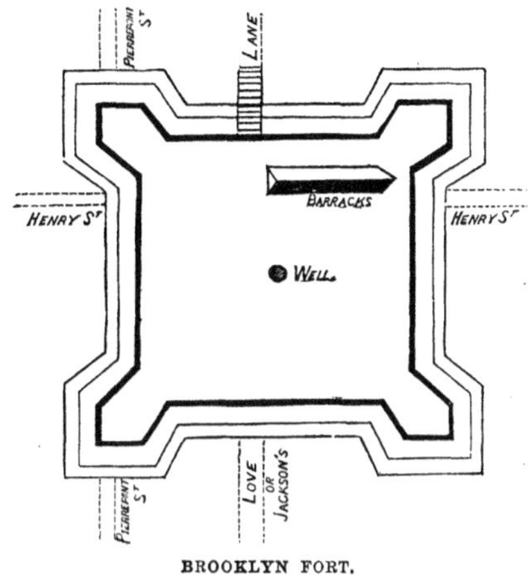

BROOKLYN FORT.

This fort was 450 feet square, with ramparts rising about forty or fifty feet above the bottom of the surrounding ditch, itself twenty feet in depth.[1] At the angles of the fort were bastions, on each of which

weight, having a quantity of iron work about it, yet so admirably constructed as to be easily raised and lowered by one person. Besides these, some forty workmen were employed in digging a well, in the exact centre of the fort—an undertaking of great labor and expense. Furman's MSS. says: "So deep were they obliged to go for water, that they almost despaired of ever finding it, but reached it finally. It is stoned with freestone, regularly cut, and is probably the best constructed and most expensive well on the island, if not in the State, and is now used as a public well, a pump having been put in it for the upper part of Henry street. It was built by a man named Schofield, who received a guinea a day for superintending it. Schofield commenced the job a poor laboring man, working himself; but before long he wore ruffles to his shirt, and hired laborers to carry on the work, which, however, was well done." Under date of August 23, 1823, Furman's MSS. "record the frame of the first building erected on the site of the old British fort, through which Jackson's, *alias* Love Lane, passes, put up this day on Henry street. It is to be a two-story wooden dwelling-house, about thirty feet broad and fifty feet deep, owned by Samuel Jackson, Esq. At this time there are no houses south of Cranberry street." The well in said fort "has not been used since the evacuation, in 1783. It is now cleaned out, and a well-house built over it, for the purpose of supplying the above-mentioned house with water. Considerable part of the remains of the fort has been levelled within a year or two."

[1] In the earlier village days, these ditches of the old fort furnished an excellent place for target-firing, which was frequently practised there by the citizen soldiery.

was planted a buttonwood-tree, which afterwards attained a very large size. The barracks were very substantially constructed. In front of the fort, on the line of the present Fulton street, between Pierrepont and Clark streets, stood a row of small mud huts, erected by the British army sutlers.[1] The fortification was not completed in July, 1781, at which time it had only eighteen cannon mounted.[2]

On June 14, 1780, citizens of Brooklyn thanked the 76th Regiment, commanded by the Earl of Caithness, and afterwards by Capt. Bruce, for their constant good order and decorum during their residence at Brooklyn.[3]

Gaine's Mercury, of July 2d, 1780, contains the following advertisement, issued by Loosely and Elms: "*Pro bono publico.* Thursday next, bull-baiting at Brooklyn ferry. The bull is remarkably strong and active; the best dogs in the country expected, and they that afford the best diversion will be rewarded with silver collars." Such were the elegant and refined amusements with which the aristocracy of the British army whiled away their leisure!

A few days later, July 17th, an address was presented to Gov. Robertson, on the occasion of his accession, in behalf and at the request of the inhabitants of Kings County, signed by Wm. Axtell, Rutgert Van Brunt, Richard Stillwell, Jeromus Lott, Ab. Luquere, M. Cowenhoven, Rem Cowenhoven, Maj. Jeromus V. D. Belt, Adrian Van Brunt, Leffert Lefferts, and Johannes Bergen, who "concur with His Excellency in ascribing to the ambitious and self-interested views of a few who conceal from the multitude the offers of Great Britain, that our countrymen, once so happy, are brought to feel the miseries held up to their fears, to seduce them from the felicity they once enjoyed, subjected, as they now are, to a usurpation that has annihilated their commerce, shed their blood, and wasted their property, and is now dragging the laborious husbandman from the plough to the field of battle, to support their unauthorized combinations with designing popish and arbitrary powers. They cannot sufficiently applaud His Excellency for affording them the means of

---

[1] Furman's MS. Mem., ix., 376, on authority of Mr. Jacob Hicks, an old resident of Brooklyn.

[2] Onderdonk, Rev. Incid., 101.

[3] Onderdonk, Kings Co., p. 187.

extricating themselves, and assure him of their loyal endeavors for His Majesty's service."

About this time the 43d Regiment were encamped near Brooklyn.

This year was a lively one for the troops quartered here, if we may judge from the following advertisements:

"PRO BONO PUBLICO.—Saturday next being the birthday of His Royal Highness the Prince of Wales, Loosely, agreeable to an honest old custom, wishes to see his royal and constitutional friends—dinner at 3. The evening to conclude with fireworks and illuminations. A good band of music. REBELS approach no nearer than the heights of Brooklyn."—*Rivington*, Aug. 9, '80.

"Anniversary of the Coronation of our ever good and gracious King, will be celebrated at Loosely's, 22d inst. It is expected that no rebel will approach nearer than Flatbush wood."—*Rivington*, Sept. 20, 1780.

"BY PERMISSION—THREE DAYS' SPORT ON ASCOT HEATH, FORMERLY FLATLANDS PLAIN.—*Monday*, 1. The Nobleman's and Gentleman's Purse of £60, free for any horse except Mr. Wortman's and Mr. Allen's Dulcimore, who won the plate at Beaver Pond last season. 2. A saddle, bridle and whip, worth £15, by ponies not exceeding 13½ hands: *Tuesday*, 1. Ladies' subscription purse of £50. 2. To be run for by women, a Holland smock and chintz gown, full-trimmed, to run the best two in 3, quarter-mile heats; the first to have the smock and gown of 4 guineas value, the second a guinea, the third a half-guinea: *Wednesday*. County subscription purse, £50. No person will erect a booth or sell liquor, without subscribing two guineas towards the expense of the race. Gentlemen fond of fox-hunting will meet at Loosely's King's Head Tavern at daybreak during the races.

"*God Save the King* played every hour."—*Rivington*, Nov. 4, 1780.

In the early autumn of this year, Lieutenant-General Riedesel was appointed by Gen. Clinton to the command of Brooklyn, a mark of especial confidence, as Long Island was then the great *depot* of supplies for the British army in New York, and was occupied by the best English troops; but few of the German mercenaries being garrisoned there. And, although the British were usually averse to the authority of any of the foreign generals, yet so great was the reputation which this amiable and talented soldier had won for himself, that all, and especially the officers, vied with each other in manifesting their own good-will, as well as their appreciation of his merits. The general's headquarters were in a small house on the shore, where, early in the spring of 1781, he was joined by his wife and family. His domestic comfort, however, was much disturbed by his apprehensions of capture by the Americans, who were always on the alert, and to whom the peculiar nature of the country, with its bays, creeks, and inlets, afforded many chances of success. That his fears were not unfounded, was proved by the fate of one of his officers, Major Maibom, who, having just been exchanged, was one night surprised in his bed and hurried into a second captivity.[1] Riedesel knew that he was a prize much coveted by the Americans, and having recently suffered from the inconveniences and hardships of captivity, took especial pains not to be caught "napping." So careful was he, "that he slept only while his wife was awake; the least noise brought him out of his bed." He had sentinels in and about his house, but never trusted entirely to their watchfulness.[2] The detail of guard-service had been much neglected by the English officers previously in command, but Riedesel instituted very thorough and wholesome reforms in this respect. At a quarter to nine o'clock every morning the guards assembled at the rendezvous, where the parade was formed in four sections. The pickets who had been on duty during the previous night were also obliged to be present at this parade, but were allowed to return to their barracks at its conclusion. At half-past six o'clock in the evening was the

---

[1] Probably the one mentioned by Onderdonk, Kings Co., sec. 189; "On Sunday night April 15th, Capt. Huyler, of Brunswick, made a descent on Michael Bergen's house, at Gowanus, and captured a Hessian major and ensign, with their waiters. *They were in the centre of two picket guards,* yet the address of Huyler was such that the guards were not alarmed until he was fairly out of reach."

[2] There were at this time (1781) quartered at Flatbush a battalion composed of German troops, with German officers, and commanded by Major Lucke. The exchanged Brunswick dragoons, who had been made prisoners at Bennington, were also stationed there, under Captain von Schlagenteuffel, sen., to whom, in general orders of April 29th, General Riedesel says, "Captain von Schlagenteuffel, sen., in locating (*i. e.* quartering) the officers of the regiment of dragoons, will make such arrangements that no officer runs the risk of being captured." And, on the 6th of May, he issued "special instructions regulative for the different guards in and around Brooklyn."

"appell," at which the troops were present with their muskets and full equipments. The general was always present at these morning and evening parades. During the night, three "officers' rounds" were made, and between each of them two patrols, commanded by subaltern officers, visited all the guards and posts in Brooklyn, the fort and the pickets. They also gave their particular attention to the sailors of the British navy, who were apt, when ashore, to get into pot-house broils.

On the 22d of July, 1781, the general, with his family and attendants embarked for Canada, bearing with them the good wishes of the numerous warm friends whose courteous attentions had made their stay in New York and Brooklyn so pleasant.[1]

During the winter of 1780–81, the East River was frozen solid from the Brooklyn shore half-way across, and on the edge of the ice, near the centre of the river, hundreds of cords of wood were piled for the use of the English army. The Long Island farmers, bringing produce to the city, drove on the ice to the middle of the river, where they placed their loads on board the ferry-boats. The English feared lest the Americans should take advantage of the ice to attack New York. The Americans, however, transported some troops and cannon on the ice from New Jersey to Staten Island.—Furman MSS.

1781. "*Pro Bono Publico.*—By permission, four days sport, on Easter Monday, on Ascot Heath. Purses of £50, £50, £100, £100." —*Rivington*, Feb. 12.

"*Grand Races at Ascot Heath* postponed till June 6, on account of the King's birthday; on which occasion it is expected every true subject will so strain his nerves in rejoicing, as to prevent this amusement being agreeable before that time. A hurling match on the ground, June 5, when those who have a curiosity to play (or see) that ancient diversion, will get hurls and bats at the Irish Flag."—*Gaine*, May 30, '81.

"To all who know it not, be it understood,
Pro bono publico means mankind's good.

"This day, being Wednesday, the 20th of June, will be exhibited,

[1] Max von Elkin's Life and Acts of Gen. Riedesel, published at Leipsic, 1856, ii. 321, 333, 337, 340, 346, 359; for translations of which we are indebted to Dr. R. Barthelmess, of Brooklyn. Also Mad. de Riedesel's Mem., pp. 249–252.

at Brooklyn Ferry, A BULL-BAITING after the true English manner. Taurus will be brought to the ring at half-past three o'clock; some good dogs are already provided, but every assistance of that sort will be esteemed a favor. A dinner exactly British will be upon Loosely's table at eleven o'clock, after which there is no doubt but that the song of 'Oh! the Roast Beef of Old England!' will be sung with harmony and glee.

"This notice gives to all who covet
Baiting the bull and dearly love it,
To-morrow's very afternoon,
At three—or rather not so soon—
A bull of magnitude and spirit
Will dare the dog's presuming merit.
Taurus is steel to the back-bone,
And canine cunning does disown;
True British blood runs thro' his veins,
And barking numbers he disdains.
Sooner than knavish dogs shall rule,
He'll prove himself a true JOHN BULL."[1]

At this time (July 8) Brooklyn Fort, although yet imperfect, having but eighteen cannon mounted, had two bomb-proof magazines and a garrison of two hundred Brunswickers. "Cobble Hill," also in process of repair, was occupied by two companies.[2] The Fifty-fourth Regiment were encamped at "Ferry Hill," two miles from Brooklyn, and at Bedford were two hundred grenadiers.

The stationary camp at Bedford was located on broken ground, then on the farm of Barent Lefferts, now crossed by Franklin and Classon avenues, Bergen, Wyckoff, Warren, Baltic, and Butler streets. The huts or barracks were built by throwing out the earth from a trench thirty to fifty feet long and about twelve or fifteen feet wide, with a board roof resting on the bank formed by the excavated earth. A large stone fireplace or two were arranged in

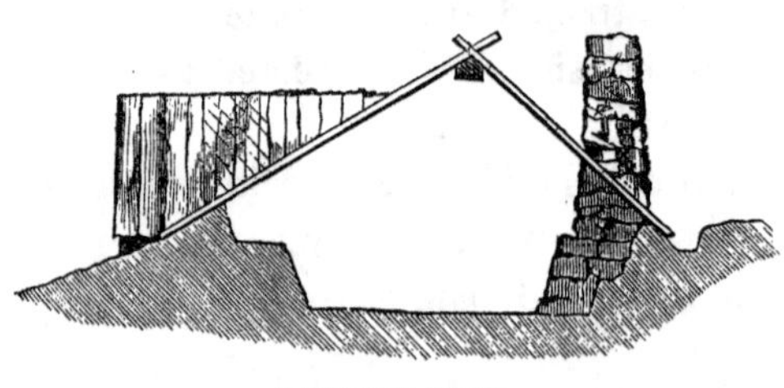

SECTIONAL VIEW.

[1] *Rivington*, June 20, 1781.

[2] "Cobble Hill commanded Brooklyn Fort, but was made lower, for fear it might fall into the hands of the Continentals."—*Onderdonk*, p. 191.

each one. These huts were irregularly scattered, according to the slope of the ground, so as to have the entrance at the middle of the lower side. A small mound on Bergen street, just west of Franklin avenue, designated, until the ground was levelled in 1852, the position of the flag-staff and the entrance of the Bedford camp. Many relics have been dug up on this camping-ground, and human skeletons are often discovered during the progress of grading the land. The site of every hut could still be distinguished in 1852. The officers were located outside of this camp, in the adjacent woods, and wherever convenient and pleasant spots tempted them to pitch their tents. Headquarters were at the Leffert Lefferts house, yet standing on the corner of Fulton avenue and Clove Road, and family tradition states that the lamented Major John André was quartered at this house when he was called to New York on the interview with Gen. Clinton, which resulted in his being sent up the North River on the mission which terminated in his capture and execution as a spy. His personal effects were mostly taken in charge by his fellow-officers; but a camp folding-chair belonging to him was for many years preserved in the Lefferts family, until recently presented to the Long Island Historical Society.

VIEW ON LOWER SIDE.

In the *Royal Gazette* of August 8th, 1781, published at New York, Charles Loosely advertises a lottery of $12,500 to be drawn at "Brooklyn Hall." The same paper contains the following advertisement: "PRO BONO PUBLICO.—Gentlemen that are fond of fox-hunting are requested to meet at Loosely's Tavern, on Ascot Heath, on Friday morning next, between the hours of five and six, as a pack of hounds will be there purposely for a trial of their abilities. Breakfasting and Relishes until the Races commence. At eleven o'clock will be run for, an elegant saddle, etc., value at least twenty pounds, for which upwards of twelve gentlemen will ride their own horses. At twelve a match will be rode by two gentlemen, Horse for Horse. At one, a match for thirty guineas, by two gentlemen, who will also ride their own horses. Dinner will be ready at two o'clock, after which and suitable regalements, racing and other diversions will be calculated to conclude the day with pleasure and harmony. Brooklyn Hall, 6th August, 1781."

"B. Creed's Jamaica and Brooklyn Hall Stage Machine, 6s. a passage; not answerable for money, plate, and jewels, unless entered and paid for."—*Rivington*, March, 1781.

And again: "Brooklyn Hunt.—The hounds will throw off at Denyse Ferry at 9, Thursday morning. A guinea or more will be given for a good strong bag fox by Charles Loosely."—*Riv.*, Nov. 14, '81.

1782. In March of this year we find, in the Tory prints, some bitter complaining, on the part of the inhabitants of the county, against the rebel leaders, on account of heavy debts contracted by their prisoners, from May, '79, to Feb., '81, for board and washing, which, at $2 per week, had accumulated to nearly £20,000, for which their commissary had given notes of hand. Congress, however, afterwards appropriated $30,000 to liquidate these debts.

The Anhault Zerbet Regiment were at this time stationed at Brooklyn.

"A sweepstakes of 300 guineas was won by Jacob Jackson's mare, Slow and Easy, over Mercury and Goldfinder, on Ascot Heath. The two beaten horses are to run for 100 guineas a side, on Wednesday next, on the same ground."—*Rivington*, April 27, '82.

"May 3, on Monday se'nnight the enemy (British) began to break ground to cut a canal on L. I., to run from the Wallabout to the Pond, taking in Cobble Hill Fort. The length of the trench is 2¼ miles. The militia are called out in rotation one day in a week, none above 15 being excused from labor."—*Conn. Courant*, May 7, '82.

This "canal" is more accurately described by General Jeremiah Johnson as a strong line of intrenchment, extending from the hill of Rem. A. Remsen along the high lands of John Rapelje, crossing Sands street near Jay street, and thence over the highest land in Washington street, between Concord and Nassau streets, across the Jamaica Road (Fulton street) to the large fort, already described, on the corner of Henry and Pierrepont streets.

"*Ascot Heath Races.*—Monday next a match for 60 guineas between Mr. Van Mater's Juniper and Mr. Ryerson's Calf-Skin. To run the best of 3 two-mile heats."—*Rivington*, May 25, '82.

June 3d. "The lines drawn between Brooklyn Church and the Ferry, by Clinton, are not likely to be completed by Carlton. They are carting fascines now. On Long Island are now about 3,500 men."[1]

As we have already seen, the enterprising landlord of "The King's Head" tavern was not insensible to the advantages of advertising; and this summer, by way of tickling the humors of his patrons, and, perhaps, of aiding a lottery enterprise which he had in hand, he issued *a newspaper*. This, the first paper ever issued in Brooklyn, was printed upon a dingy sheet of about the ordinary "letter size" now in use, and contained three columns of "close matter," printed on one side of the sheet only. It was named (with Loosely's usual preface, "*Pro bono Publico*)," "THE BROOKLYN-HALL SUPER-EXTRA GAZETTE," dated Saturday, June 8th, 1782, and its contents may be characterized as displaying more loyalty and "heavy wit" than literary merit. A copy of this sheet, the only one known to be in existence, can be seen among the curiosities of the Naval Lyceum, in the U. S. Navy Yard, in this city.[2]

"Baron de Walzogen, Capt. Commandant of the combined detachment of Brunswick and Hessian Hanau troops, *now at Brooklyn camp*, received an address from the inhabitants of New Utrecht, thanking him for the vigilant care, good order, and discipline prevailing among the officers and soldiers under his command at the Narrows, etc."—*Gaine*, Aug. 6, '82.

The crops, at this time, were indifferent in many parts of the country. It was a very dry summer on Long Island.

In December of this year there were stationed at Brooklyn, Hackenbergh's regiment of Hessians, in the large fort back of the Ferry, and in the redoubts a number. At Bedford, also, the garrison battalion of invalids, about one hundred in number, of whom a half were officers, was quartered at the houses of the different inhabitants.[3]

---

[1] Onderdonk, Kings Co., 191.

[2] See Appendix, No. 9.

[3] Onderdonk, Rev. Rem. Kings Co., 261.

1783. In January of this year General Carlton appointed Mr. Ernest de Diemar major of the fort at Brooklyn.

"Subscription assembly at Loosely's, Brooklyn Hall, every other Thursday, during the season, for the gentlemen of the army and navy, public departments, and citizens. Half a guinea each night, to provide music, tea, coffee, chocolate, negus, sangaree, lemonade, etc."—*Gaine*, Feb. 24, '83.

"Race at Ascot Heath. A purse of 100 guineas, on April 9, between Calfskin and Fearnought, the best of 3 one-mile heats."—*Rivington*, April 5, '83.

But the state of things had changed. No longer did the newspapers teem with festive advertisements and loyalist literature. The war was virtually ended by the provisional treaty of peace, signed November 30, 1782, and the British were about to leave the land where, for nearly seven years, their presence had rested like a hideous nightmare upon the people whom they sought to subdue. The "King's Head Tavern" blazed no more with festive illuminations, nor echoed to the sound of revelry. The raps of the auctioneer's hammer resounded through the halls where once the gay officers of the British army and their "toady" loyalist friends of Kings County had feasted, and sung, in harmonious revelry, loyal ballads to their sovereign. The sound of preparation for departure was everywhere heard, and the papers (significant indices of every passing breeze of popular events) were now occupied with advertisements such as the following:

"At auction at the King's Naval Brewery, L. I., 60 or 70 tons of iron-hoops, and 70,000 dry and provision-casks, staves, and heading, in lots of 10,000."—*Rivington*, May 26, '83.

"Auction at Flatbush.—The WALDECK STORES, viz.: soldiers' shirts; blue, white, and yellow cloth; thread-stockings, shoe-soles, heel-taps, etc., etc."—*Rivington*, July 2, '83.

"Saddle-horses, wagons, carts, harness, etc., at auction every Wednesday, at the wagon-yard, Brooklyn."—*Gaine*, Sept. 8, '83.

"King's draft and saddle horses, wagons, carts, and harness for sale at the wagon-yard, Brooklyn."—*Rivington*, August 27, '83.

Desertions also became frequent among the Hessians, who preferred to remain in this country. Tunis Bennet of Brooklyn was imprisoned in the Provost for carrying Hessian deserters over to the Jersey shore.[1]

At length, after protracted negotiations, a definitive treaty of peace was signed at Paris, between the American and British commissioners, on the 3d of September, 1783. And on the 25th of November following, Brooklyn and the city of New York were formally evacuated by the British troops and refugees,[2] whose requiem was sung by ballad-singers in strains like these :

> " When Lord Cornwallis first came o'er
> The cannon roared like thunder ;
> If he should return once more,
> It will surely be a wonder.
> The refugees and Tories all,
> Asking mercy at our hands,
> Upon their bending knees do fall,
> To let them stay and enjoy their lands," etc.

As soon as the armies of Britain had left these shores, and Liberty dawned again upon the land, so long deprived of hope and peace, numerous exiles returned to look after their property and interests. Brooklyn, which, during the war, had been wholly military ground, presented a sadder scene of desolation than any other town in Kings County. In 1776, after its occupation by the British, free range had been given to the pillaging propensities of the soldiery. Farms had been laid waste, and those belonging to exiled Whigs given to the Tory favorites of Governor Tryon. Woodlands were ruthlessly cut down for fuel, buildings were injured, fences removed, and boundaries effaced. Farmers were despoiled of their cattle, horses, swine, poultry, vegetables, and of almost every necessary article of subsistence, except their grain, which fortunately had been housed before the invasion. Their houses were also plundered of every article which the cupidity of a lawless soldiery deemed worthy of possession, and much furniture was wantonly destroyed.[3] At the

---

[1] Rivington, Aug. 1, '83.

[2] On this memorable occasion the American flag was displayed from the same flag-staff, on the Pierrepont mansion, from which signals had been made during the battle of Long Island, in 1776.

[3] More serious outrages by the British soldiery were not infrequent, but redress was not easily obtained by the sufferers. "A Mrs. Lott, of Flatlands, was wantonly shot by

close of this year's campaign, De Heister, the Hessian general, returned to Europe with a ship-load of plundered property. During the next year (1777), the farmers had cultivated but little more than a bare sufficiency for their own subsistence, and even that was frequently stolen or destroyed. Stock became very scarce and dear, and the farmer of Brooklyn who owned a pair of horses and two or three cows, was "*well off.*" The scarcity prevailing in the markets, however, soon rendered it necessary for the British commanders to restrain this system of indiscriminate marauding, and to encourage agriculture. After the capture of General Burgoyne's army, rebel prisoners were treated with more lenity; and in 1778, the towns of Flatbush, Flatlands, Gravesend, and New Utrecht were set apart as a parole-ground, for the purpose of quartering American officers whom the fortunes of war had thrown upon their hands. In these towns, therefore, a greater degree of peace and order prevailed, and the farmers had the twofold advantage of receiving high prices for their produce and pay for boarding the prisoners. Brooklyn, however, remained a garrison town until the peace, and many farms were not inclosed until after the evacuation, in 1783.

When, therefore, the inhabitants returned to their desolated and long-deserted homes, their first efforts were directed to the cultivation of their lands, the re-establishment of their farm boundaries, and the restoration of their private affairs. This being accomplished, their attention was next turned to the reorganization of the town—whose records had been removed, and whose functions and privileges had been totally suspended during the seven years' military occupation by the British. On the first Tuesday of April, 1784, was held the first town-meeting since April, 1776. Jacob Sharpe, Esq., was chosen Town Clerk, and applied to Leffert Lefferts, Esq., the previous clerk, for the town records. Lefferts deposed, on oath, that they had been removed from his custody, during the war, by a person or persons to him unknown; and although that person has since been identified,

---

a soldier while sitting in her window; three men of the 33d Regiment (under Colonel Webster, quartered at Lambert Suydam's) had killed one of his cattle and were skinning it, when he shot the three with one discharge of buckshot; two were killed in Bushwick; three in Newtown; one killed at a shanty, by a man named Cypher, near the Half-way House."—Jeremiah Johnson.

the subsequent fate of the records themselves is, to this day, unknown.[1]

Gradually, under the benign influences of Liberty and Law, order emerged from chaos. The few lawless miscreants who remained were speedily restrained from their mischievous propensities by the whipping-post and imprisonment, angry passions subsided, and those citizens who had hitherto viewed each other as enemies, became united.

INCIDENTS.

From the MSS. of the late General Jeremiah Johnson, we have selected the following incidents illustrative of the British occupation of Brooklyn:

A REBEL-SHOT.—"In the summer of the year 1780, four British officers, who were in quarters in the Wallabout, were engaged in target-shooting in my father's orchard. They were provided with a chair to sit on, and a rest for their guns; their target was placed against a large chestnut-tree, on the margin of a hill, some eighty yards off, and a servant was stationed below the ridge, with a staff, to designate the place on the target where their balls struck. They

---

1 "This was John Rapalje, mentioned (on pp. 78, 79, and 312) as a prominent citizen and Tory, who had been employed by Mr. Lefferts as a clerk, and therefore knew which of the records were most valuable. He came to the house one day, and telling Mrs. Lefferts that he intended removing the papers to a safe place, went into the room used as an office, and there busied himself for some time, selecting what he pleased, packing the whole in a sack, and taking them away.—(J. C. Brevoort, Esq., on authority of Leffert Lefferts, son of Leffert Lefferts, the clerk in question.) These records and papers were taken to England by Rapalje, in October, 1776; and his lands were confiscated, and afterwards became the property of J. & C. Sands. After his death, the papers fell into the possession of his grand-daughter, who married William Weldon, of Norwich, County of Norfolk, England. William Weldon and his wife came to New York about the year 1810, to recover the estates of John Rapalje, and employed D. B. Ogden and Aaron Burr as counsel, who advised them that the Act of Attainder, passed by the Legislature against Rapalje and others, barred their claim. Weldon and his wife brought over with them the lost records of the town of Brooklyn, and offered them to the town for a large sum (according to some, $10,000), but would not even allow them to be examined before delivery. Although a *writ of replevin* might easily have secured them to the town again, the apathetic Dutchmen of that day were too indifferent to the value of these records, and they were allowed to return to England."—(MS. Note of Jeremiah Johnson.)

shot poorly. The writer was looking on, when one of the officers, after loading his gun, asked me whether I would try a shot. I replied in the affirmative, and, presenting the piece at arms' length, fired. The servant signalled the ball as having struck the *bull's-eye*. The party looked at me with surprise and indignation, and exclaimed: ''Tis no wonder the d—d rebels kill our men as they do—here is a *boy* who beats us!' I told them I could do it again, and left them to cogitate on the subject."

HORSE RACING.—A jockey or racing club was formed in the year 1780, within the British lines. Bryant Connor, of New York, was Chief Jockey. Flatland Plain, then called "Ascot Heath," was the race-course; it was then a beautiful open plain, well adapted for racing or parades. Public races were held here until October, 1783. The British officers, with the refugees and Tories, ruled the course. The American officers, then prisoners in Kings County, attended these races, and were frequently insulted by the loyalists, which gave rise to frequent fracases. Wherever a fine horse was known to be owned by any American farmer in the county, the refugee horse-thieves would soon put him into the hands of the jockeys, and the course was thus kept well supplied. General Johnson saw a New Jersey farmer claim a horse on Ascot Heath, in October, 1783, which had been purchased by Mr. John Cornell, of Brooklyn, from a refugee, and entered for the race. The owner permitted the horse to run the race; after which, Mr. Cornell surrendered the animal to the owner in a gentlemanly manner. Whether he ever found the thief afterwards is uncertain.[1]

A MILITARY EXECUTION AT BROOKLYN.—In the summer of 1782, three men, named Porter, Tench, and Parrot, members of the 54th Regiment, then encamped on the farm of Martin Schenck, at the Wallabout, were arrested and tried for their complicity in a foul murder committed on Bennet's Point, in Newtown, three years before. They were sentenced to be hung, but Parrot was pardoned

[1] In 1784, public races were run at New York, on the level of Division street. In the same year, Governor George Clinton (who assumed, though erroneously, that "it belonged to him as an official franchise") leased Governor's Island to a Dr. Price, who built a hotel there and graded a handsome course on the same, on which races were run in 1785 and '86. Afterwards they were held at Harlem, Newmarket, Beaver Pond, New Utrecht, and on the Union Course.

and sent on board a man-of-war. The execution of Porter and Tench, notable as the only case of capital punishment for injuries done to citizens, was witnessed by the late General Jeremiah Johnson, who thus describes the scene: "The gallows was the limb of a large chestnut-tree, on the farm of Martin Schenck. About 10 A. M., a brigade formed a hollow square around the tree; the culprits, dressed in white jackets and pantaloons, and firmly pinioned, were brought into the square, and halters, about eight feet long, were fastened to the limb about four feet apart. Tench ascended the ladder first, followed by Cunningham's yellow hangman, who adjusted the halter, drew a cap over the culprit's face, and then descending, turned him off the ladder. The like was done to Porter, who ascended the ladder by the side of his hanging companion, in an undaunted manner, and was turned towards him and struck against him. They boxed together thus several times, hanging in mid-air about ten feet from the ground, until they were dead. The field and staff officers were inside the square, and after the execution Cunningham reported to the commanding officer (said to be General Gray), who also appeared to treat him with contempt. The troops then left the ground, and the bodies were buried under the tree."

MILITARY PUNISHMENTS.—The British soldiers were punished by whipping or flogging with the "cat-o'-nine-tails," executed by the drummers. The regimental surgeons were obliged to attend the punishments, which were usually very severe—sometimes as many as five hundred lashes being given. Citizens were allowed to be present at these floggings, except at punishments of the 42d Highland Regiment, when only the other regiments were allowed to be witnesses. Punishments in this regiment were, however, infrequent. The dragoons were punished by picketing; the Germans by being made to run the gauntlet. On these occasions the regiment formed in two parallel lines, facing inwards; the culprit passed down between these lines, having an officer before and behind him, and was struck by each soldier with rods. An officer also passed down on the outside of each line, administering a heavy blow to any soldier who did not give the culprit a fair and good stroke. Hessians were also punished by the gauntlet, while the band played a tune set to the following words:

"Father and mother, do not mourn
Over your only son;
He never did you any good,
And now he gets his doom—doom—doom—doom."

The officers often treated their men cruelly. General Johnson remembered to have seen Captain Westerhauge and Lieutenant Conrady beat a corporal with their swords on his back, over his waistcoat, so that he died the next day. They beat the man about two in the afternoon. He was standing: the captain first gave him a number of blows, and then the lieutenant commenced; but before he had finished, the man was too feeble to stand, and the captain stood before him and held him up. The man then laid down on the grass, while the surgeon's mate examined his body, which was a mass of bruised and blistered flesh. His back was roughly scarified by the surgeon's mate, and he was then removed to a barn, where he died the next day—never having uttered a word from the moment of the first blow.[1]

Among the patriotic deeds of the adherents of the American cause in Kings County, we must not fail to record the loans of money furnished to the State Government by them. It was effected in the following manner. Lieutenant Samuel Dodge and Captains Gilleland and Mott, of the American army, had been captured at Fort Montgomery, and were confined as prisoners, under a British guard, at the residence of Barent Johnson, in the Wallabout. Dodge was exchanged in the course of a month, and reported the practicability of borrowing specie from Whigs in Kings County, mentioning Johnson as one who would risk all in the undertaking. It was therefore agreed that *confidential* officers should be exchanged, who were to act as agents in these transactions. Colonel William Ellison was fixed upon to receive the loan. He was exchanged in November, 1777,

[1] It may be worthy of note that Mrs. Peter Wyckoff, mother of Mr. Nicholas Wyckoff, President of the City Bank of Brooklyn, and a daughter of Lambert Suydam, a brave officer in the Continental Army, informed the author, in 1861, that she distinctly remembers, when a school-girl at Bedford, having seen British soldiers tied up to a tree, in front of the house of Judge Lefferts, and flogged. She also remembers to have seen the troops encamped in shanties and tents, between Rem Lefferts' and Peter Vandervoort's, now the house of James Debevoise, on Bedford, near Gates avenue. The officers were billeted on those families.

and conveyed $2,000 in gold to Governor Clinton, a simple receipt being given. In this manner, before 1782, large sums had been loaned to the State. In 1780, Major H. Wyckoff was hid for two days in the upper room of Rem A. Remsen's house, in the Wallabout, while the lieutenant of the guard of the "Old Jersey" British prison-ship was quartered in the house. Remsen loaned him as much as he could carry, and conveyed him in a sleigh, at night, to Cow Neck, from whence he crossed to Poughkeepsie.[1]

The patriotism of many of New York's bravest soldiers was poorly rewarded by the passage of a legislative act, May 6th, 1784, levying a tax of £100,000 upon the Southern District of the State. This odious and well-named "partial" tax, or a moiety of it, could be paid in State scrip, which the soldier had received for his services, and had sold to speculators for from two to six pence per pound. The scrip, it is almost needless to say, immediately rose to the value of ten shillings on the pound, leaving a very handsome profit to the speculators, who had invested it largely in the purchase of confiscated estates.

PART III.

THE BRITISH PRISON-SHIPS.*

THE Battle of Brooklyn, in August, and the capture of Fort Washington, in November, 1776, placed in possession of the British nearly four thousand prisoners; and this number was increased, by the

---

[1] See General Johnson's MSS., and Onderdonk's Queens County, p. 316.

* In the preparation of this chapter, we have drawn freely upon the narratives of Captain THOMAS DRING (of which two editions were published, in 1829 and '31, and a privately printed edition, with annotations, by H. B. Dawson, in 1865); of the Rev. THOMAS ANDROS, published in 1833; of Captain ALEXANDER COFFIN, jr., in his letter to Dr. Samuel Mitchell, in Hist. Account of Am. Martyrs, published in 1808; The Adventures of CHRISTOPHER HAWKINS, privately printed, with copious notes, by Charles I. Bushnell, Esq., in 1864; the Reminiscences, in print and MS., of General JEREMIAH JOHNSON, of Brooklyn; and the incidental descriptions in Memoirs of Rev. ANDREW SHERBURNE, of EBENEZER FOX, Com. SILAS TALBOT, etc., all of which have become scarce books, and, to some extent, inaccessible to the general reader.

arrest of private citizens suspected of complicity with the rebellion, to over five thousand, before the end of the year. The only prisons then existing in the city of New York were: the "New Jail," which still remains, in an entirely altered form, as the "Hall of Records," and the "Bridewell," which was located between the present City Hall and Broadway. These edifices proving entirely inadequate for the accommodation of this large number of captives—to whom they were unwilling to extend the privileges of parole—the British were compelled to turn three large sugar-houses, several of the Dissenting churches, the Hospital, and Columbia College, into prisons for their reception.[1] These buildings, also, were soon crowded to overflowing by daily accessions of captive patriots, who, in many instances, found not even space to lie down and rest upon the hard and filthy floors. Here, in these loathsome dungeons, denied the light and air of heaven; scantily fed on poor, putrid, and sometimes even uncooked food; obliged to endure the companionship of the most abandoned criminals, and those sick with small-pox and other infectious diseases; worn out by the groans and complaints of their suffering fellows, and subjected to every conceivable insult and indignity by their inhuman keepers, thousands of Americans sickened and died. Almost preferable, by comparison, was the fate of those who, without a moment's warning, and at midnight, were hurried by the Provost[2] to the gallows and an unknown grave.

---

[1] These sugar-houses were Van Cortlandt's, which stood on the corner of Thames and Lumber streets, at the northwest corner of Trinity churchyard; Rhinelander's, on the corner of William and Duane streets; and one on Liberty street (Nos. 34 and 36) a little east of the Middle Dutch church, now occupied as the United States Post-office. The churches were the Middle Dutch church, above referred to, which was used as a prison for about two months, and afterwards converted into a riding-school for the British cavalry; the North Dutch church, yet standing on William street, between Fulton and Ann; and the "Brick Church," which, until within a few years, stood in the triangle between Park Row, Beekman, and Nassau streets. Subsequently, this last-mentioned, together with the Presbyterian church in Wall street, the Scotch church in Cedar street, and the Friends' Meeting House in Liberty street, were converted into hospitals. The French church, in Pine street, was used as a magazine for ordnance and stores.

[2] Captain William Cunningham, an Irishman by birth, and a brute by nature, who, during the occupation of New York by the British, held the post of Provost-Marshal of the city. He subsequently suffered the same fate to which he had consigned so many victims—being hung for forgery in London, England, in 1791. In his dying confession, which appeared in the English papers in 1794, and which has always been

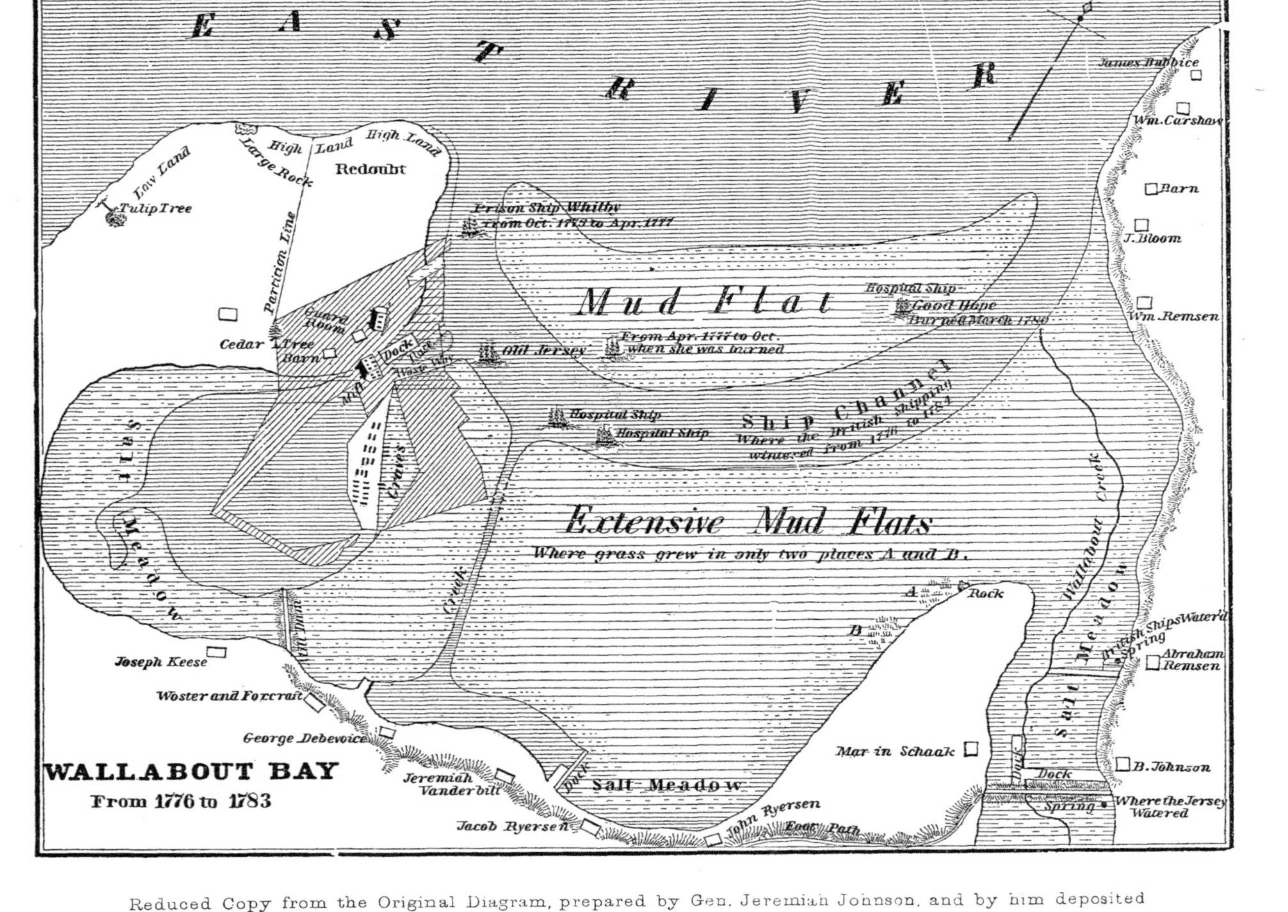

Reduced Copy from the Original Diagram, prepared by Gen. Jeremiah Johnson, and by him deposited in the Lyceum at the United States Navy Yard, Brooklyn, N. Y.

Great, however, as were the sufferings of those incarcerated within the prisons of the city, they were exceeded, if possible, by those of the unfortunate *naval* prisoners who languished in the "prison-ships" of the "Walleboght." These were originally the transport-vessels in which the cattle and other supplies of the British army had been brought to America, in 1776, and which had been anchored in Gravesend Bay, and occupied by the prisoners taken in the Battle of Brooklyn. Upon the occupation of the city by the British forces, these soldiers were transferred to the prisons on shore, and the transports, anchored in the Hudson and East rivers, were devoted more especially to the *marine* prisoners, whose numbers were rapidly increasing, owing to the frequent capture of American privateers by the king's cruisers.

"A large transport, named the *Whitby*," says General Jeremiah Johnson,[1] "was the first prison-ship anchored in the Wallabout. She was moored near 'Remsen's mill,' about the twentieth of October, 1776, and was then crowded with prisoners. Many landsmen were prisoners on board this vessel; she was said to be the most sickly of *all* the prison-ships. Bad provisions, bad water, and

---

held as authentic, he made the following statements in regard to his treatment of the American prisoners: "I shudder to think of the murders I have been accessary to, both with and without orders from Government, especially while in New York; during which time there were more than two thousand prisoners starved in the different churches, by stopping their rations, which I sold. There were also two hundred and seventy-five American prisoners and obnoxious persons executed, out of all which number there were only about one dozen public executions, which chiefly consisted of British and Hessian deserters. The mode for private executions was thus conducted: a guard was dispatched from the Provost, about half-past twelve at night, to the Barrack street, and the neighborhood of the upper barracks, to order the people to shut their window-shutters, and put out their lights, forbidding them at the same time to presume to look out of their windows and doors on pain of death, after which the unfortunate prisoners were conducted, gagged, just behind the upper barracks, and hung without ceremony, and there buried by the black pioneer of the Provost." Watson, in his Annals of New York, states that Cunningham hung five or six of a night, until the women of the neighborhood, distressed by the cries and pleadings of the prisoners for mercy, petitioned Howe to have the practice discontinued. Common fame charged Cunningham with selling, and even poisoning, the prisoners' food, exchanging good for bad provisions, and continuing to draw their rations after their death, or, as they worded it, "he fed the dead, and starved the living." It was not till the spring of 1783, towards the close of the war, that a monthly list of prisoners was printed in Rivington's Gazette.

[1] Naval Magazine, 467, 469

scanted rations, were dealt to the prisoners. No medical men attended the sick, disease reigned unrelieved, and hundreds died from pestilence, or were starved, on board this floating prison.[1] I saw the sand-beach, between the ravine[2] in the hill and Mr. Remsen's dock, become filled with graves in the course of two months; and before the first of May, 1777, the ravine alluded to was itself occupied in the same way. In the month of May, 1777, two large ships were anchored in the Wallabout, when the prisoners were transferred from the *Whitby* to them; these vessels were also very sickly, from the causes before stated. Although many prisoners were sent on board of them, and none exchanged, *death* made room for all. On a Sunday afternoon, about the middle of October, 1777, one of the prison-ships was burnt; the prisoners, except a few, who, it was said, were burnt in the vessel, were removed to the remaining ship. It was reported, at the time, that the prisoners had fired their prison, which, if true, proves that they preferred death, even by fire, to the lingering sufferings of pestilence and starvation. In the month of February, 1778, the remaining prison-ship was burnt at night, when the prisoners were removed from her to the ships then wintering in the Wallabout."

"Better the greedy wave should swallow all,
Better to meet the death-conducting ball,
Better to sleep on ocean's oozy bed,
At once destroyed and numbered with the dead,
Than thus to perish in the face of day,
Where twice ten thousand deaths one death delay."

In 1779, the "Prince of Wales" and the "Good Hope"[3] were used

---

[1] A prisoner (see the Trumbull Papers, p. 76) thus speaks of the WHITBY, in 1776: "Our present situation is most wretched; more than two hundred and fifty prisoners, some sick, and without the least assistance from physician, drug, or medicine, and fed on two-thirds allowance of salt provisions, and crowded promiscuously, without regard to color, person, or office, in the small room of a ship, between decks, and allowed to walk the main deck only from sunrise to sunset. Only two at a time permitted to come on deck to do what nature requires, and sometimes denied even that, and use tubs and buckets between decks, to the great offence of every delicate, cleanly person, and prejudice of all our healths."

[2] Where Little street now is.

[3] We find the "GOOD HOPE" first mentioned in October, 1778. She then lay in the North River, and in January, '79, was designated, with the "PRINCE OF WALES," as the depot for prisoners of privateers arriving in New York. In August, '79, forty-seven American prisoners were returned, under flag, to New London, who were taken out of

as prison-ships. The latter vessel being destroyed by fire in March, 1780, her place in the Wallabout was supplied, shortly after, by the "Stromboli,"[1] "Scorpion,"[2] and "Hunter," all *nominally* hospital-

---

the "Good Hope," and "it must (for once) be acknowledged, are all very well and healthy—only one hundred and fifty left." About this time, also, she was dismantled, and her sails, spars, etc., advertised to be sold. In September, '79, there were many sick on board. *The New Hampshire Gazette*, of November 2d, '79, says that, at one o'clock on the previous morning, nine captains, and two privates, effected their escape from this vessel, then lying in the North River. They confined the mate, disarmed the sentinels, and hoisted out the boat, which was on deck, and took with them nine stand of arms and ammunition. They had scarce got clear before an alarm was given, which brought upon them a fire from these vessels, which, however, did not harm them. The escaped men spoke in the highest terms of the commander of the prison-ship, Captain Nelson, who used the prisoners with a great deal of humanity. *Rivington's Gazette*, of March 8, '80, thus chronicles the destruction of this vessel: "Last Sunday afternoon, the 'Good Hope' prison-ship, lying in the Wallebocht Bay, was entirely consumed, after having been wilfully set on fire by a Connecticut man, named Woodbury, who confessed the fact. He, with others of the incendiaries, are removed to the Provost. The prisoners let each other down from the port-holes and decks into the water." The English Commissary, Sproat, writing to the American Commissary, Skinner, in February, 1781, says of this vessel: "Carpenters ran a bulkhead across the prison-ship Good Hope; the officers berthed abaft and the men before this partition. Two excellent large stoves were erected, one for the officers, another for the men. The hospital-ship was equipped in the same manner, and every sick or wounded person had a cradle, bedding, surgeons. In this comfortable situation did the prisoners remain till March 5, 1780, when they wilfully burned *the best prison-ship* in the *world* (!) The perpetrators were not hanged, but ordered to the Provost. The ship lay in the Wallabocht, near a number of transports, whose people were so alert in snatching the prisoners from the flames, that but two out of some hundreds were missing. They were put in the nearest ship, the Woodlands, where they remained a short time, till the ships Stromboli and Scorpion were got ready."

[1] The STROMBOLI was originally a fire-ship, and, like the Scorpion, was present at the siege of Quebec, in 1759. She came out here at the commencement of the Revolution, in company with the Jersey, in Commodore Hotham's fleet. She was commanded, when a prison-ship, from August 21st to December 10th, 1780, by Jeremiah Downer, and never had less than one hundred and fifty prisoners, and oftener over two hundred, on board. She was advertised for sale, December 6th, 1780 (in which advertisement she was still mentioned as a fire-ship), but no purchaser appeared.

[2] The SCORPION was originally a sloop-of-war of four guns, and appears in the list of the navy as early as 1756. She was in the fleet, under Admiral Saunders, at the reduction of Quebec, in 1759; came out here again at the commencement of the Revolutionary War, and formed one of Sir George Collier's fleet, which destroyed the towns of Fairfield, Norwalk, and Greenwich, Conn., in 1779. In 1780, she became a prison-hulk, and was anchored in the North River. Philip Freneau, who, with some three hundred others, was confined in her, has preserved, in poetry, an interesting and vivid picture of the sufferings of himself and fellow-prisoners:

"Thou, Scorpion, fatal to thy crowded throng,
Dire theme of horror and Plutonian song,

ships.[1] Many other old hulks—the "Old Jersey," the "John,"[2] the "Falmouth,"[3] the "Chatham," the "Kitty," the "Frederick,"[4] the "Glasgow," the "Woodlands," the "Scheldt," and the "Clyde," were also converted into prison-ships.

Of all these, the "OLD JERSEY," or the "HELL," as she was called, from the large number confined in her—often more than a thousand at a time[5]—and the terrible sufferings which they there endured, has

---

Requir'st my lay—thy sultry decks I know,
And all the torments that exist below!
The briny waves that Hudson's bosom fills
Drain'd through her bottom in a thousand rills;
Rotten and old, replete with sighs and groans,
Scarce on the waters she sustain'd her bones;
Here, doomed to toil, or founder in the tide,
At the moist pumps incessantly we plied;
Here doomed to starve, like famish'd dogs, we tore
The scant allowance that our tyrants bore."

In December, 1780, her hull was advertised for sale by the naval storekeeper at New York, but was not purchased.

[1] The HUNTER was originally a sloop-of-war. She was advertised for sale in December, 1780, but found no purchaser. Captain Dring (see his Narrative, p. 71) thinks she was mainly used as a *store-ship* and medical depot.

[2] Alexander Coffin, who was a prisoner in the JOHN, says (Hist. Martyrs, 32) that the treatment of the prisoners there "was much worse than on board the Jersey. We were subjected to every insult, every injury, and every abuse that the fertile genius of the British officers could invent and inflict. For more than a month, we were obliged to eat our scanty allowance, bad as it was, without cooking, as no fire was allowed."

[3] "I am now a prisoner on board the FALMOUTH, in New York, a place the most dreadful; we are confined so that we have not room even to lie down all at once to sleep. It is the most horrible, cursed hole, that can be thought of. I was sick and longed for some small-beer, while I lay unpitied at death's door with a putrid fever, and, though I had money, I was not permitted to send for it. I offered repeatedly a hard dollar for a pint. The wretch who went forward and backwark would not oblige me. I am just able to creep about. Four prisoners have escaped from this ship. One having, as by accident, thrown his hat overboard, begged leave to go after it in a small boat, which lay alongside. A sentinel, with only his side-arms on, got into the boat. Having reached the hat, they secured the sentinel and made for the Jersey shore, though several armed boats pursued, and shot was fired from the shipping."—*Conn. Gazette, May* 25, '80.

[4] Sherburne, who was a patient on the FREDERICK hospital-ship, in January, 1783, says that it "was very much crowded; so that two men were obliged to lie in one bunk." He and his bunk-mate were "obliged, occasionally, to lay athwart each other, for want of room," and the former finally died, stretched across Sherburne. He says "I have seen seven dead men drawn out and piled together on the lower hatchway, who had died in one night on board the Frederick."

[5] Andros (p. 12) says: "When I first became an inmate of this abode of suffering, despair, and death, there were about four hundred prisoners on board, but in a short

THE "OLD JERSEY" PRISON-SHIP.

(Used, by permission, from DAWSON'S edition of DRING'S "Old Jersey Captive.")

Page 337.

EXTERIOR VIEW OF THE "OLD JERSEY."

1. The Flag-staff, which was seldom used, and only for signals.
2. A canvas awning or tent, used by the guards in warm weather.
3. The Quarter-deck, with its barricade about ten feet high, with a door and loop-holes on each side.
4. The Ship's Officers' Cabin, under the Quarter-deck.
5. Accommodation-ladder, on the starboard side, for the use of the ship's officers.
6. The Steerage, occupied by the sailors belonging to the ship.
7. The Cook-room for the ship's crew and guards.
8. The Sutler's room, where articles were sold to the prisoners, and delivered to them through an opening in the bulkhead.
9. The Upper-deck and Spar-deck, where the prisoners were occasionally allowed to walk.
10. The Gangway ladder, on the larboard side, for the prisoners.
11. The Derrick, on the starboard side, for taking in water, etc., etc.
12. The Galley, or Great Copper, under the forecastle, where the provisions were cooked for the prisoners.
13. The Gun-room, occupied by those prisoners who were officers.

14, 15. Hatchways leading below, where the prisoners were confined.

17, 18. Between-decks, where the prisoners were confined at night.

19. The Bowsprit.
20. Chain cables, by which the ship was moored.

won a terrible pre-eminence in the sad history of the prison-ships, of which, indeed, her name has become the synonym. She was originally a fourth-rate sixty-gun ship of the British navy, was built in 1736, and achieved a long and honorable career;[1] but, in 1776, being unfit for further active service, was ordered to New York, as a hospital-ship. In this capacity she remained, in the East River, nearly opposite "Fly Market," until the winter of 1779–80, when she was converted into a prison-ship. For this purpose she was stripped of all her spars, except the bowsprit, a derrick for taking in supplies, and the flagstaff at her stern; her rudder was unhung, and her figure-head removed to decorate some other vessel. Her portholes were closed and securely fastened, and their places supplied by two tiers of small holes, each about twenty inches square, and guarded by two strong bars of iron, crossing at right angles, cut through her sides, for the admission of air. These, however, while they "admitted the light by day, and served as breathing-holes at night," by no means furnished that free circulation of air between the decks, which was so imperatively necessary to the health and comfort of the prisoners.

Thus stripped of every thing which constitutes the pride and beauty of a ship, this old hulk, whose unsightly exterior seemed almost to foreshadow the scenes of misery, despair, and death which reigned within, was removed to the solitary and unfrequented Wallabout, where she was moored with chain-cables, nearly opposite the mouth of Remsen's mill-race, and about twenty rods from the shore.

The appearance of the OLD JERSEY, as she lay in the Wallabocht, is thus graphically described by Captain Dring.[2] Leaving New York, together with one hundred and thirty prisoners, brought in

---

time they amounted to twelve hundred." This was in 1781. Dring says (p. 69): "During my confinement, in the summer of 1782, the average number of prisoners on board the Jersey was about one thousand." Alexander Coffin (Hist. of Martyrs, p. 29, 32) states that during his first captivity on the Jersey, in 1782, he found about one thousand one hundred American prisoners; and on his second imprisonment, in February, 1783, he found "more prisoners than he left, though but very few of my former fellow-prisoners. Some of them had got away, but the greater part had paid the debt of nature."

[1] The complete history of the JERSEY has been given by H. B. Dawson, in his edition of Dring's Prison-ship Recollections, pp. 196–198; and by Charles I. Bushnell, in his notes to Adventures of Christopher Hawkins, pp. 202–214.

[2] Dring's Narrative, p. 26.

by the British ship Belisarius, he proceeded to the place of their imprisonment, under the charge of the notorious David Sproat, Commissary of Prisoners. "We at length doubled a point," he says, "and came in view of the Wallabout, where lay before us the black hulk of the OLD JERSEY, with her satellites, the three hospital-ships, to which Sproat pointed in an exulting manner, and said, 'There, rebels, *there* is the *cage* for you!' * * As he spoke, my eye was instantly turned from the dreaded hulk; but a single glance had shown us a multitude of human beings moving upon her upper deck. It was then nearly sunset, and before we were alongside, every man, except the sentinels on the gangway, had disappeared. Previous to their being sent below, some of the prisoners, seeing us approaching, waved their hats, as if they would say, approach us not; and we soon found fearful reason for the warning." While waiting alongside for orders, some of the prisoners, whose features they could not see, on account of the increasing darkness, addressed them through the air-holes which we have described. After some questions as to whence they came, and concerning their capture, one of the prisoners remarked "that it was a lamentable thing to see so many young men, in full strength, with the flush of health upon their countenances, about to enter that infernal place of abode. 'Death,' he said, 'had no relish for such skeleton carcases as we are; but he will now have a feast upon you fresh comers.'" The new-comers were registered and sent below; but the intolerable heat and foul air rendered sleep impossible; and, when they sought the air-holes, in order to gain one breath of exterior air, they found them occupied by others, who seemed to be justified, by the law of self-preservation, in keeping possession, and who could not be induced, by any amount of persuasion, to relinquish their places even for a moment. Disappointed in this, and shocked by the curses and imprecations of those who were lying upon the crowded deck, and whom they had disturbed in passing over them, they were obliged to sit down in this stifling and nauseous atmosphere, which almost deprived them of sense and even of life, and wait for the coming morning. But dawn brought to their eyes only the vision of "a crowd of strange and unknown forms, with the lines of death and famine upon their faces"—a "pale and meagre throng," who, at eight o'clock, were

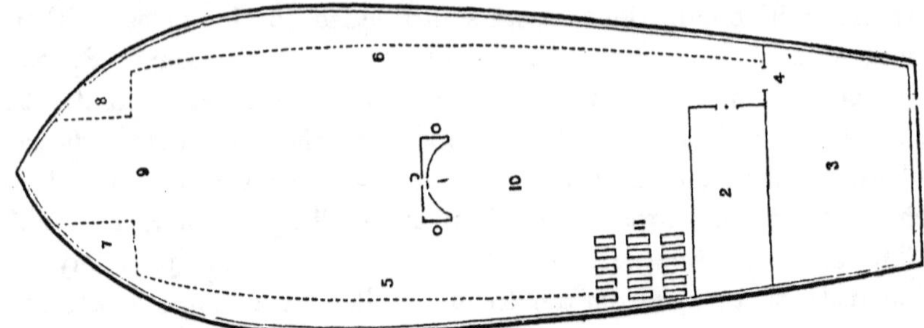

PLAN OF THE UPPER DECK, BETWEEN DECKS.

1. The Hatchway-ladder, leading to the lower deck, railed round on three sides.

2. The Steward's room, from which the prisoners received their daily allowance through an opening in the partition.

3. The Gun-room, occupied by those prisoners who were officers.

4. Door of the Gun-room.

5, 6, 7, 8. The arrangement of the prisoners' chests and boxes, which were ranged along, about ten feet from the sides of the ship, leaving a vacant space, where the messes assembled.

9, 10. The middle of the deck, where many of the prisoners' hammocks were hung at night, but always taken down in the morning, to afford room for walking.

11. Bunks on the larboard side of the deck, for the reception of the sick.

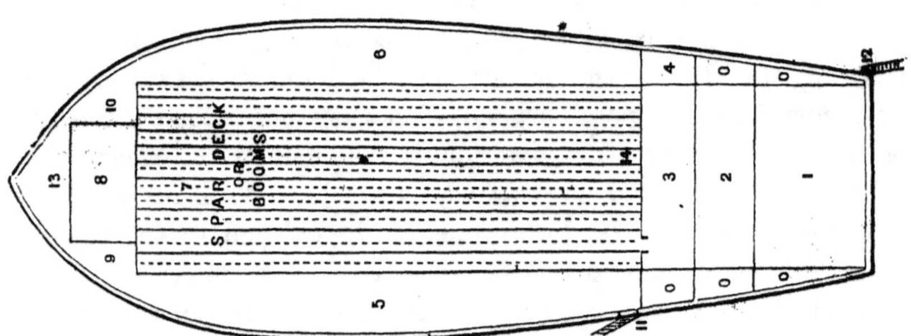

PLAN OF THE GUN-DECK OF THE "JERSEY"

1. Cabin.
2. Steerage.
3. Cook-room.
4. Sutler's room
5, 6. Gangways.
7. The Booms.
8. The Galley.
9, 10. The Cook's quarters.
11. The Gangway-ladder.
12. The Officers' Ladder.
13. Working-party.
14. The Barricade.

000. Store-Rooms.

permitted to go upon deck, "to view for a few moments the morning sun, and then to descend again, to pass another day of misery and wretchedness."

> "On every side, dire objects met the sight,
> And pallid forms, and murders of the night."

Dring gives the following minute description of the interior accommodations of the "Jersey": "The quarter-deck covered about one-fourth part of the upper deck from the stern, and the forecastle extended from the stern about one-eighth part the length of the upper deck. Sentinels were stationed at the gangways on each side of the upper deck, leading from the quarter-deck to the forecastle. These gangways were about five feet wide, and here the prisoners were allowed to pass and repass. The intermediate space from the bulkhead of the quarter-deck to the forecastle was filled with long spars or booms, and called the spar-deck. The temporary covering afforded by the spar-deck was of the greatest benefit to the prisoners, as it served to shield us from the rain and the scorching rays of the sun. The spar-deck was also the only place where we were allowed to walk, and was therefore continually crowded through the day by those of the prisoners who were upon deck. Owing to the great number of the prisoners, and the small space afforded us by the spar-deck, it was our custom to walk in platoons, each facing the same way, and turning at the same time. The derrick, for taking in wood, water, etc., stood on the starboard side of the spar-deck. On the larboard side of the ship was placed the accommodation ladder, leading from the gangway to the water. At the head of this ladder a sentinel was also stationed. The head of the accommodation ladder was near the door of the barricade, which extended across the front of the quarter-deck, and projected a few feet beyond the sides of the ship. The barricade was about ten feet high, and was pierced with loop-holes for musketry, in order that the prisoners might be fired on from behind it, if occasion should require. The regular crew of the ship consisted of a captain, two mates, a steward, a cook, and about twelve sailors. The crew of the ship had no communication whatever with the prisoners. No prisoner was ever permitted to pass through the barricade door, except when it was required that the messes should be examined and regulated; in which case, each man had to pass through, and go down between decks, and there remain until the examination was completed. * * On the two decks below, where we were confined at night, our chests, boxes, and bags were arranged in two lines along the deck, about ten feet distant from the two sides of the ship; thus leaving as wide a space unencumbered in the middle part of each deck, fore and aft, as our crowded situation would admit. Between these tiers of chests, etc., and the sides of the ship, was the place where the different messes assembled; and some of the messes were also separated from their neighbors by a temporary partition of chests, etc. Some individuals of the different messes usually slept on the chests, in order to preserve their contents from being plundered during the night."

At night, the spaces in the middle of the deck were much encumbered with hammocks, but these were always removed in the morning. The extreme after-part of the ship, between decks, which was called "the gun-room," was appropriated by the captive officers to their own use; while the lowest deck was assigned to the French and Spanish prisoners, who were treated with even more cruelty, if possible, than the Americans.[1]

The first care of a prisoner, after arriving upon the Jersey, says Dring, "was to form, or be admitted into, some regular *mess.*[2] On the day of a prisoner's arrival, it was impossible for him to procure any food; and, even on the second day, he could not procure any in time to have it cooked. No matter how long he had fasted, nor how acute might be his sufferings from hunger and privations, his petty tyrants would on no occasion deviate from their rule of delivering the prisoner's morsel at a particular hour, and at no other: and the poor, half-famished wretch must absolutely wait until the coming day, before his pittance of food could be boiled with that of his fellow-captives." The vacancies in the different messes daily provided by *death*, rendered it comparatively easy for the new-comers

---

[1] This seems to have been the reverse of the rule observed in England, where "the American prisoners were treated with less humanity than the French and Spanish, and were allowed only half the quantity of bread per day. Their petitions for relief, offered by Mr. Fox, in the House of Commons, and by the Duke of Richmond, in the House of Lords, were treated with contempt; while the French and Spanish had few or no complaints to make."—British Annual Register, 1781, p. 152.

[2] Sherburne's Mem., 108; Fox's Adv. in Rev., 100.

to associate themselves with some of the older captives, of whose experience they could, in various ways, avail themselves. These messes, consisting generally of six men each, were all numbered; and every morning, when the steward's bell rang, at nine o'clock, an individual belonging to each mess stood ready to answer to its number. As soon as it was called, the person representing it hurried forward to the window in the bulkhead of the steward's room, from which was handed the allowance for the day. This was, for each *six* men, what was equivalent to the *full rations* of *four* men.[1] No vegetables of any description,[2] or butter, was allowed; but, in place of the latter, a scanty portion of so-called sweet-oil, so rancid and often putrid, that the Americans could not eat it, and always gave it to the foreign prisoners in the lower hold, "who took it gratefully, and swallowed it with a little salt and their wormy bread."[3] These rations, insufficient and miserable as they

---

1 That is, each prisoner was furnished in quantity with two-thirds of the allowance of a seaman in the British navy at that time; viz., on *Sundays* and *Thursdays*, a pound of biscuit, one pound of pork, and half a pint of peas; on *Mondays* and *Fridays*, a pound of biscuit, a pint of oatmeal, and two ounces of butter; on *Tuesdays* and *Saturdays*, one pound of biscuit and two pounds of beef; and on *Wednesday*, one and a half pounds of flour and two pounds of suet.

2 Andros (p. 9) says: "Once or twice, by the order of a stranger on the quarter-deck, a bag of apples were hurled promiscuously into the midst of hundreds of prisoners, crowded together as thick as they could stand, and life and limb were endangered by the scramble. This, instead of compassion, was a cruel sport. When I saw it about to commence, I fled to the most distant part of the ship."

3 Sherburne (111) says: "It was supposed that this bread and beef had been condemned in the British navy. The bread had been so eaten by weevils, that one might easily crush it in the hand and blow it away. The beef was exceedingly salt, and scarcely a particle of fat could be seen upon it. * * * Once a week, we had a mess of what is called burgoo, or mush (the Yankees would call it *hasty pudding*), made of oatmeal and water. This oatmeal was scarcely ever sweet; it was generally so musty and bitter, that none but people suffering as we did could eat it." He says, though, that large quantities of provisions were daily brought alongside of the ship, and as long as a prisoner's money lasted, he could get better than the ordinary fare. Andros (p. 17) says of the bread: "I do not recollect seeing any which was not full of living vermin; but eat it, worms and all, we must, or starve."

"In the month of March, 1779, flour and breadstuffs were very nearly exhausted in the British storehouses at New York. There was no good flour; and the Hessians, who were in Brooklyn, drew damaged oatmeal instead of bread. This meal, which was baked in cakes, was unfit for use, and the writer has seen them cast to the swine, which would not eat them. The soldiers were mutinous. All the grain possessed by the farmers was estimated and placed under requisition. The timely arrival of a few victualling ships relieved the scarcity, and saved the British from a surrender to the

were, were frequently not given to the prisoners in time to be boiled on the same day, thus obliging them often to fast for another twenty-four hours, or to consume it raw, as they sometimes did. The cooking was done "under the forecastle, or, as it was usually called, the Galley, in a boiler or 'great copper,' which was enclosed in brick-work, about eight feet square. This copper was large enough to contain two or three hogsheads of water. It was made in a square form, and divided into two separate compartments by a partition. In one side of the copper, the peas and oatmeal for the prisoners were boiled, which was done in fresh water; in the other side, the meat was boiled. This side of the boiler was filled with the salt water from alongside of the ship, by which means the copper became soon corroded, and consequently poisonous, the fatal consequences of which are obvious.[1] After the daily rations had been furnished to the different messes, the portion of each mess was designated by a tally, fastened to it by a string. Being thus prepared, every ear was anxiously waiting for the summons of the *cook's bell.* As soon as this was heard to sound, the persons having charge of the different portions of food thronged to the galley; and in a few minutes after, hundreds of talleys were seen hanging over the sides of the brick-work by their respective strings, each eagerly watched by some individual of the mess, who always waited to receive it." Whether cooked or not, the food must be immediately taken from the boiler when the cook's bell again rang out the warning note, and each mess then received its measured portions of peas and oatmeal.[2] Some, more careful than others, and fearful of

---

Americans, to escape starvation. If the Hessians at this time received bread which the hogs refused, what may be supposed to have been the quality of that given to the prisoners?"—Gen. Jeremiah Johnson, in Star, Dec. 12, 1836.

[1] This is corroborated by Fox, who says: "The inside of the copper had become corroded to such a degree that it was lined with a coat of verdigris," and that the effects of this was evident "in the cadaverous countenances of those emaciated beings who had remained on board for any length of time." He also says: "The Jersey, from her size, and lying near the shore, was embedded in the mud; and I do not recollect seeing her afloat during the whole time I was a prisoner. All the filth which accumulated among upwards of a thousand men, were daily thrown overboard, and would remain there until carried away by the tide. The impurity of the water may be easily conceived, and *in this water our meat was boiled.*"

[2] Sherburne (111) says: "The beef was all put into a large copper, perhaps five feet square and four feet deep. The beef would fill the copper within a few inches of the

the poisonous effects of meat boiled in the "great copper," prepared their own food, by permission, separate from the general mess in that receptacle. For this purpose, a great number of spikes and hooks had been driven into the brick-work by which the boiler was enclosed, on which to suspend their tin kettles. As soon as we were permitted to go on deck in the morning, some one took the tin-kettle belonging to the mess, with as much water and such splinters of wood as we had been able to procure during the previous day,[1] and carried them to the galley; and there, having suspended

---

top; the copper was then filled up with water, and the cover put on. Our fuel was green chestnut. The cook would commence his fire by seven or eight in the morning, and frequently he would not get his copper to boil until twelve o'clock; and sometimes, when it was stormy weather, it would be two or three o'clock. I have known it to be the case that he could not get it to boil in the course of the day. Those circumstances might sometimes be owing to a want of judgment in the cooks, who were frequently exchanged. These misfortunes in the cooks, would occasion many bitter complaints and heavy curses from the half-starved, emaciated, and imperious prisoners. Each mess would take its meat, thus half-cooked and divide it among themselves as it was. A murmur is heard, probably in every mess, and from almost every tongue. The cook is denounced, or perhaps declines any further service; another volunteers his services, and, probably, in a few days, shares the fate of his predecessors." John Van Dyck, a prisoner on board the Jersey in May, 1780, says he went one day to draw the pork for his mess, "and each one of us eat our day's allowance in *one mouthful* of this salt pork, and nothing else." One day, called "pea-day," he went to the galley, with the drawer of a sea-chest for a soup-dish, and "received the allowance of my mess; and, behold! brown water and fifteen floating peas—no peas on the bottom of my drawer—and this for six men's allowance for twenty-four hours. The peas were all on the bottom of the kettle; those left would be taken to New York, and, I suppose, sold. One day in the week, called 'pudding-day,' three pounds of damaged flour; in it would be green lumps, such as the men could not eat; and one pound of very bad raisins, one-third sticks. We would pick out the sticks, mash the lumps of flour, put all, with some water, in our drawer, mix our pudding and put it into a bag, with a tally tied to it, with the number of our mess. This was a day's allowance." He also relates an instance of cruelty on the part of Captain Laird, commander of the Jersey, who one day ordered two half-hogshead tubs, in which the daily allowance of rum for the prisoners had been mixed into grog, to be upset on the main decks, in full view of the famished wretches, whose feelings of disappointment, as they saw it run through the ship's scuppers into the water, may be better imagined than described." Coffin also says that, "on the upper deck of the Jersey, hogs were kept in pens, by those officers who had charge of her, for their own use. They were sometimes fed with bran. The prisoners, whenever they could get an opportunity, undiscovered by the sentries, would, with their tin pots, scoop the bran from the troughs, and eat it (after boiling, when there was fire in the galley, which was not always the case) with seemingly as good an appetite as the hogs themselves."

[1] Dring (p. 98) mentions that this was an article which could not be purchased from the sutler, and the procuring of a sufficient quantity was "a continual source of trouble and anxiety." Sometimes the cooks would steal small quantities, which they sold to

his kettle on one of the hooks or spikes in the brick-work, he stood ready to kindle his little fire as soon as the cook or his mates would permit it to be done. It required but little fuel to boil our food in these kettles; for their bottoms were made in a concave form, and the fire was applied directly in the centre. And let the remaining brands be ever so small, they were all carefully quenched "and kept for future use." "Memory," says a survivor, "still brings before me those emaciated beings, moving from the galley with their wretched pittance of meat; each creeping to the spot where his mess were assembled, to divide it with a group of haggard and sickly creatures, their garments hanging in tatters around their meagre limbs, and the hue of death upon their careworn faces. By these it was consumed with their scanty remnants of bread, which was often mouldy and filled with worms. And, even from this vile fare they would rise up in torments from the cravings of unsatisfied hunger and thirst." The cook was the only one on board who had much flesh upon his bones. He was also a prisoner, who, despairing of ever regaining his liberty, had accepted his situation as one which, at least, would keep him from starvation; and, considering the circumstances by which he was surrounded, displayed a commendable degree of good humor and forbearance; although when, as sometimes happened, his patience became exhausted by the importunities and trickeries of the starving crowd around him, he would "make the hot water fly" among them.

The necessary routine of daily service on board the ship—such as

---

the prisoners; and Dring mentions that once, while assisting at the burial of one of his comrades, he found a hogshead stave floating in the water, which furnished his mess with fuel for a considerable time. At another time he managed to steal a stick of wood from a quantity which was being taken on board for the ship's use, by which his mess "were supplied with a sufficient quantity for a long time, and its members were considered by far the most wealthy persons in all this republic of misery." The mode of preparing the wood for use, was to cut it with a penknife into pieces about four inches long. This labor occupied much of their time, and was performed by the different members of the mess, in rotation; being an employment to them of no little pleasure. The quantity thus prepared for the next day's use was deposited in the chest, while the main stock was jealously guarded, day and night, by its fortunate owners, who even went into mathematical calculations, to ascertain how long it would probably last, if used in certain daily quantities. In a similar manner, by obliging each member of the mess to save a little each day for the common stock, a small supply of *fresh water* was secured and carefully hoarded in the chest.

washing the upper decks and gangways, spreading the awning, hoisting the wood, water, and other supplies which were brought alongside, etc.—was performed by a "working-party" of about twenty of the prisoners, who received, as a compensation, a full allowance of provisions, a half-pint of rum, and, what was more desirable than all else, the privilege of going on deck early in the morning, to breathe the pure air. When the prisoners ascended to the upper deck in the morning, if the day was fair, each carried up his own hammock and bedding, which were placed upon the spar-deck, or booms. The sick and disabled were then brought up by the working party, and placed in bunks prepared upon the centre deck; the corpses of those who had died the night before were next brought up from below and placed upon the booms, and then the decks were washed down. The beds and clothing were kept on deck until about two hours before sunset, when the prisoners were ordered to carry them below. "After this had been done," says Dring, "we were allowed either to retire between decks, or to remain above, until sunset, according to our own pleasure. Every thing which we could do conducive to cleanliness having then been performed, if we ever felt any thing like enjoyment in this wretched abode, it was during this brief interval, when we breathed the cool air of the approaching night, and felt the luxury of our evening pipe. But short, indeed, was this period of repose. The working-party were soon ordered to carry the tubs below, and we prepared to descend to our gloomy and crowded dungeons. This was no sooner done, than the gratings were closed over the hatchways, the sentinels stationed, and we left to sicken and pine beneath our accumulated torments, with our guards above crying aloud, through the long night, "*All's well!*"

What these "accumulated torments" of the night were, may be best understood from Dring's words: "Silence was a stranger to our dark abode. There were continual noises during the night. The groans of the sick and the dying; the curses poured out by the weary and exhausted upon our inhuman keepers; the restlessness caused by the suffocating heat and the confined and poisonous air, mingled with the wild and incoherent ravings of delirium, were the sounds which, every night, were raised around us in all directions."

Frequently the dying, in the last mortal throes of dissolution, would throw themselves across their sick comrades, who, unable to remove the lifeless bodies, were compelled to wait until morning before they could be freed from the horrid burden. Dysentery, small-pox, yellow fever, and the recklessness of despair, soon filled the hulk with filth of the most disgusting character. "The lower hold," says Andros, "and the orlop deck, were such a terror, that no man would venture down into them. Humanity would have dictated a more merciful treatment to a band of pirates, who had been condemned and were only awaiting the gibbet, than to have sent them here."[1] And, again: "Utter derangement was a common symptom of yellow-fever, and to increase the horror of the darkness that shrouded us (for we were allowed no light betwixt decks), the voice of warning would be heard, 'Take heed to yourselves; there is a madman stalking through the ship, with a knife in his hand.' I sometimes found the man a corpse in the morning, by whose side I laid myself down at night. At another time he would become deranged and attempt, in darkness, to rise, and stumble over the bodies that everywhere covered the deck. In this case, I had to hold him in his place by main strength. In spite of my efforts, he would sometimes rise, and then I had to close in with him, trip up his heels, and lay him again upon the deck. While so many were sick with raging fever, there was a loud cry for water; but none could be had, except on the upper deck, and but one allowed to ascend at a time. The suffering then from the rage of thirst during the night, was very great. Nor was it at all times safe to attempt to go up. Provoked by the continual cry for leave to ascend, when there was already one on deck, the sentry would push them back with his bayonet."[2] This guard, which usually numbered about thirty, was

---

[1] Old Jersey Captive, p. 16.

[2] William Burke, a prisoner on board the Jersey for about fourteen months during the Revolution, says: "During that time, among other cruelties which were committed, I have known many of the American prisoners put to death by the bayonet: in particular, I well recollect, that it was the custom on board the ship for but one prisoner at a time to be admitted on deck at night, besides the guards or sentinels. One night, while the prisoners were many of them assembled at the grate at the hatchway, for the purpose of obtaining fresh air, and waiting their turn to go on deck, one of the sentinels thrust his bayonet down among them, and in the morning twenty-five of them were found wounded, and stuck in the head, and dead of the

relieved each week by a fresh party; sometimes English—at others, Hessians or refugees. The latter were, as might have naturally been expected, most obnoxious to the prisoners, who could not bear the presence of those whom they considered as *traitors*. The English soldiers they viewed as simply performing their legitimate duty; and the Hessians they preferred, because they received from them better treatment than from the others.

A very serious conflict with the guard occurred on the 4th of July, 1782, in consequence of the prisoners attempting to celebrate the day with such observances and amusements as their condition permitted. Upon going on deck in the morning, they displayed thirteen little national flags in a row upon the booms, which were immediately torn down and trampled under the feet of the guard, which on that day happened to consist of Scotchmen. Deigning no notice of this, the prisoners proceeded to amuse themselves with patriotic songs, speeches, and cheers, all the while avoiding whatever could be construed into an intentional insult to the guard; which, however, at an unusually early hour in the afternoon, drove them below at the point of the bayonet, and closed the hatches. Between decks, the prisoners now continued their singing, etc., until about nine o'clock in the evening. An order to desist not having been promptly complied with, the hatches were suddenly removed, and the guards descended among them, with lanterns and cutlasses in their hands. Then ensued a scene of terror. The helpless prisoners, retreating from the hatchways as far as their crowded condition would permit, were followed by the guards, who mercilessly hacked, cut, and wounded every one within their reach; and then ascending again to the upper deck, fastened down the hatches upon the poor victims of their cruel rage, leaving them to languish through the long, sultry, summer night, without water to cool their parched throats, and without lights by which they might have dressed their wounds. And, to add to their torment, it was not until the middle of the next forenoon that the prisoners were allowed to go on deck and slake their thirst, or to

---

wounds they had thus received. I further recollect that this was the case several mornings, when sometimes five, sometimes six, and sometimes eight or ten, were found dead by the same means."—Hist. Martyrs, 96.

receive their rations of food, which, that day, they were obliged to eat uncooked. *Ten corpses* were found below on the morning which succeeded that memorable 4th of July, and many others were badly wounded.

Equal to this, in fiendish barbarity, is the incident related by Silas Talbot, as occurring on the Stromboli, while he was a prisoner upon that ship. The prisoners, irritated by their ill treatment, rose one night on the guard, "the commander being on shore, and several, in attempting to escape, were either killed or wounded. The captain got on board just as the fray was quelled, when a poor fellow lying on deck, bleeding, and almost exhausted by a mortal wound, called him by name, and begged him, '*for God's sake, a little water, for he was dying!*' The captain applied a light to his face, and directly exclaimed: 'What! *is it you, d—n you? I'm glad you're shot. If I knew the man that shot you, I'd give him a guinea! Take that, you d—d rebel rascal!*' and instantly dashed his foot in the face of the dying man!!"[1] The conduct of the guards, indeed, according to all accounts, seems to have been as brutal as it was possible to be, and was rivalled only by that of the *nurses.* These nurses, numbering about six or eight, were prisoners, and, according to universal testimony, were all thieves, who, callous to every sentiment of duty or humanity, indulged in card-playing and drinking, while their fellows were entreating for water, and dying in their sight for want of those attentions which they refused to give them.

Not less revolting than these scenes of cruelty and distress, was the manner in which the inanimate bodies of these martyred prisoners were hastily and indecorously consigned to the earth—in some

---

[1] "Two young men, brothers, belonging to a rifle-corps, were made prisoners, and sent on board the Jersey. The elder took the fever, and, in a few days, became delirious. One night (his end was fast approaching), he became calm and sensible, and lamenting his hard fate, and the absence of his mother, begged for a little water. His brother, with tears, entreated the guard to give him some, but in vain. The sick youth was soon in his last struggles, when his brother offered the guard a guinea for an inch of candle, only that he might see him die. Even this was denied. 'Now,' said he, drying up his tears, 'if it please God that I ever regain my liberty, I'll be a most bitter enemy!' He regained his liberty, rejoined the army, and, when the war ended, he had *eight* large, and *one hundred and twenty-seven* small notches on his rifle-stock!"—Med. Repos. Hex., ii., vol. iii., p. 72.

cases, almost before they had become cold.[1] Brought up each morning by the working-party and placed upon the gratings of the upper deck; their glazed eyeballs staring upwards towards the heavens; their ghastly and pinched features contorted with the suffering through which they had passed; their bodies stiff, stark, and naked (for their clothes, if they had any, were the perquisites of the so-called nurses), these corpses of the night awaited the only remaining insult which their captors could inflict upon them—the indignity of an unhonored and unknown grave. Soon the *dead-boat* was seen approaching from the Hunter, receiving her ghastly freight from the other vessels, on her way to the Jersey. Upon her arrival alongside, each corpse was laid upon a board, to which it was bound with ropes, a tackle attached to the board, and the whole lowered over the ship's side into the boat, without further ceremony. "The prisoners were always very anxious to be engaged in the duty of interment; not so much from a feeling of humanity, or from a wish of paying respect to the remains of the dead (for to these feelings they had almost become strangers), as from the desire of once more placing their feet upon the land, if but for a few minutes. A sufficient number of the prisoners having received permission to assist in this duty, they entered the boat, accompanied by a guard of soldiers, and put off from the ship." Captain Dring, who assisted on one occasion of this sort, thus describes the burial, which will afford a correct idea of the general method of interment: "After landing at a low wharf, which had been built from the shore, we first went to a small hut, which stood

---

[1] Captain Coffin (Hist. Martyrs, p. 35) mentions "that a man of the name of Gavot, a native of Rhode Island, died, as was supposed, and was sewed up in his hammock, and in the evening carried upon deck to be taken with others who were dead, and those who might die during the night, on shore to be interred (*in their mode of interring*). During the night it rained pretty hard: in the morning, when they were loading the boat with the dead, one hammock was observed by one of the English seamen to move. He spoke to the officer, and told him that he believed the man in that hammock (pointing to it) was not dead. '*In with him*,' said the officer; '*if he is not dead, he soon will be.*' But the honest tar, more humane than his officer, swore he never would bury a man alive, and with his penknife ripped open the hammock, when, behold! the man was really alive. What was the cause of this man's reanimation, is a question for doctors to decide: it was at the time supposed that the rain, during the night, had caused the reaction of the animal functions, which were suspended, but not totally annihilated." This same man, Gavot, went afterwards in the same cartel with Coffin to Rhode Island.

near the wharf, and was used as a place of deposit for the hand-barrows and shovels provided for these occasions. Having placed the corpses on the hand-barrows, and received our hoes and shovels, we proceeded to the side of a bank near the Wallabout.[1] Here a vacant space having been selected, we were directed to dig a trench in the sand, of a proper length for the reception of the bodies. We continued our labor until our guards considered that a sufficient space had been excavated. The corpses were then laid into the trench, without ceremony, and we threw the sand over them. The whole appeared to produce no more effect upon our guards than if we were burying the bodies of dead animals, instead of men. They scarcely allowed us time to look about us; for, no sooner had we heaped the earth above the trench, than the order was given to march. But a single glance was sufficient to show us parts of many bodies which were exposed to view; although they had probably been placed there, with the same mockery of interment, but a few days before.[2] Having thus performed, as well as we were permitted to do it, the

---

[1] Sherburne (p. 109) says this was called the "Volley Bank."

[2] Andros (p. 14) says: "The first object that met our view in the morning, was an appalling spectacle—a boat loaded with dead bodies, conveying them to the Long Island shore, where they were very slightly covered with sand. I sometimes used to stand and count the number of times the shovel was filled with sand to cover a dead body. And certain I am, that a few high tides, or torrents of rain, must have disinterred them."

General Johnson (Recollections of Brooklyn and New York in 1776) says: "It was no uncommon thing to see five or six dead bodies brought on shore in a single morning, when a small excavation would be dug at the foot of the hill, the bodies be cast in, and a man with a shovel would cover them, by shovelling sand down the hill upon them. Many were buried in a ravine of the hill; some on the farm. The whole shore, from Rennie's Point to Mr. Remsen's door-yard, was a place of graves; as were also the slope of the hill, near the house (subsequently dug away by Mr. John Jackson, and whence he obtained the bones for the '*Dry-bone Procession*'); the shore from Mr. Remsen's barn along the mill-pond, to Rapelje's farm, and the sandy island between the floodgates and the mill-dam, while a few were buried on the shore on the east side of the Wallabout. Thus did *Death* reign *here*, from 1776 until the peace. The whole Wallabout was a sickly place during the war. The atmosphere seemed to be charged with foul air from the prison-ships, and with the effluvia of the dead bodies washed out of their graves by the tides. We believe that more than half of the dead buried on the outer side of the mill-pond, were washed out by the waves at high tide, during northeasterly winds. The bones of the dead lay exposed along the beach, drying and bleaching in the sun, and whitening the shore, till reached by the power of a succeeding storm; as the agitated waters receded, the bones receded with them into the deep. * * * We have, ourselves, examined many of the skulls lying on the shore. From the teeth, they appeared to be the remains of men in the prime of life."

last duty to the dead, and the guards having stationed themselves on each side of us, we began reluctantly to retrace our steps to the boat. We had enjoyed the pleasure of breathing for a few moments the air of our native soil, and the thought of returning to the crowded prison-ship was terrible in the extreme. As we passed by the water's side, we implored our guards to allow us to bathe, or even to wash ourselves for a few minutes; but this was refused us. I was the only prisoner of our party who wore a pair of shoes; and well recollect the circumstance, that I took them from my feet, for the pleasure of feeling the earth, or rather the sand, as I went along. It was a high gratification to us to bury our feet in the sand, and to shove them through it, as we passed on our way. We went by a small patch of turf, some pieces of which we tore up from the earth, and obtained permission to carry them on board, for our comrades to smell them. . . . Having arrived at the hut, we there deposited our implements, and walked to the landing-place, where we prevailed on our guards, who were Hessians, to allow us the gratification of remaining nearly half an hour, before we re-entered the boat. Near us stood a house, occupied by a miller; and we had been told that a tide-mill, which he attended, was in its immediate vicinity; as a landing-place for which, the wharf where we stood had been erected. It would have afforded me a high degree of pleasure to have been permitted to enter this dwelling, the probable abode of harmony and peace. It was designated by the prisoners by the appellation of the 'Old Dutchman's;' and its very walls were viewed by us with feelings of veneration, as we had been told that the amiable daughter of its owner had kept a regular account of the number of bodies which had been brought on shore for interment from the Jersey and the hospital-ships. This could easily be done in the house, as its windows commanded a fair view of the landing-place. We were not, however, gratified on this occasion, either by the sight of herself or of any other inmate of the house. Sadly did we approach and re-enter our foul and disgusting place of confinement. The pieces of turf which we carried on board, were sought for by our fellow-prisoners with the greatest avidity; every fragment being passed by them from hand to hand, and its smell inhaled, as if it had been a fragrant rose."

We have already alluded to the poisonous and disgustingly impure nature of the water in which the prisoners' food was cooked. Equally deleterious in its effects was the water with which they were obliged to slake their constant and tormenting thirst. This was contained in a large water-butt, on the upper deck, and guarded by one of the marines, with a drawn cutlass. From the copper ladles, chained to the cask, the prisoners could drink as much as they pleased, but were not allowed to carry away more than a pint at a time. Dring estimates the daily consumption of water on board the Jersey at about seven hundred gallons, and a large gondola was constantly employed in conveying it from the Brooklyn shore.[1] Brackish as it was, when brought on board, the haste and exertions of every one to procure a draught, gave rise to fearful scenes of confusion, which often called for the interposition of the guard.[2] So much of the water as was not required for immediate use, was conveyed, through leathern hose, into butts, placed in the lower hold of the hulk; and to this the prisoners had recourse, when they could procure no other. These butts had never been cleaned since they were first placed there; and the foul sediment which they contained, being disturbed by every new supply which was poured in, rendered their

---

[1] Dring (p. 91) presumes "that this water was brought from Brooklyn." Captain Coffin (Hist. of Martyrs, p. 30) says it was brought from New York city, in a schooner called the Relief—(well-named; "for the execrable water and provisions she carried, *relieved* many of my brave but unfortunate countrymen, *by death*, from the misery and savage treatment they endured")—water which, he affirms, was worse than he had ever seen on a three years' voyage to the East Indies; "water, the scent of which would have discomposed the olfactory nerves of a Hottentot; *while within a cable's length* of the ship, on Long Island, there was running before our eyes, as though intended to tantalize us, as fine, pure, and wholesome water as any man would wish to drink." General Jeremiah Johnson, in his Rev. Recoll., states that the Jersey was supplied *daily from his spring*, referred to above by Coffin. And this was probably the case—the water being brought from New York only when the Wallabout spring was temporarily exhausted, or when the boats were otherwise employed. Johnson says: "The water-boat of the Jersey watered from the spring daily, when it could be done. Four prisoners were usually brought on shore to fill the casks, attended by a guard. The prisoners were frequently permitted to come to the house to get milk and food, and often brought letters privately from the ship. By these the sufferings on board were revealed. Supplies of vegetables were frequently collected by Mr. Remsen (the benevolent proprietor of the mill) for the prisoners; and small sums of money were sent on board by the writer's father to his friends, by means of these watering parties."

[2] Dring (p. 92), and Roswell Palmer, in Dawson's Dring (p. 179), and others.

contents a compound of the most disgusting and poisonous nature,[1] to which is directly attributable the death of hundreds of the prisoners on the Jersey.

Near the Jersey, as before mentioned, lay three *hospital-ships*—the Scorpion, Stromboli, and Hunter—of whose interiors Dring (who, more fortunate than others, managed to maintain his health) says he could only form some idea "from viewing their outward appearance, which was disgusting in the highest degree." Their condition was probably preferable, in many respects, to that of the Jersey, as they were less crowded, and were provided with awnings, and with wind-sails at each hatchway, for the purpose of conducting the fresh air between decks, where the sick were placed; and, what was still better, the hatchways were left open during the night,[2] the keepers having no apprehension of any danger from the feeble wretches under their control. Every day (*when the weather was good*) a visiting surgeon from the Hunter—which was the station of the medical staff, etc.—came over to the Jersey and examined the sick who were able to present themselves at the gangway, on the upper deck. If a sick man was pronounced by the surgeon to be a proper subject for removal to the hospital-ship, he was hurried into the boat in waiting alongside—not being allowed to go below for the purpose of getting his clothes or effects (if he had any), which became the spoils of the nurses. The condition of the hospital-ships, however, was scarcely less crowded, filthy, and uncomfortable than that of the Jersey itself. Insufficient clothing, scarcity of blankets, the want of dry fuel to keep up even the small fires that were allowed, caused great suffering among the patients,[3] whose only provision

---

[1] Mr. Palmer (Dawson's Dring, p. 72) also mentions this water taken from the hold of the vessel, which was "ropy as molasses."

[2] Sherburne's experience (p. 111) on board the Frederick hospital-ship, Freneau's on the Hunter, and that of Coffin on the John, contradicts this.

[3] Sherburne, who was a patient on the Frederick in January, 1783, says (p. 114): "My bunk was directly against the ballast-port: and the port not being caulked, when there came a snow-storm, the snow would blow through the seams on my bed;" which, however, he esteemed an advantage, when he could not otherwise procure water to quench his thirst. The sufferings which he endured from that cause alone, left their effects upon him until his death. He also mentions that a man near him in the ship was taken sick, and, while in that condition, had his feet and legs so badly frozen, that, at length, while they were being dressed, the toes and bottoms of his feet sloughed off

was a gill of ordinary wine, and twelve ounces of musty and poorly-baked bread, per day. The surgeons visited the ships only once in several days, their manner was indifferent and even unfeeling, their stay on board very brief, and their medicines very sparingly bestowed.[1] The greatest neglect was exhibited by the nurses, of whose conduct all our authorities speak in terms of indignant reprobation. These nurses seemed to take more interest in the death of their patients than in relieving their wants, and scarcely waited for the breath to leave their bodies before they despoiled them of their blankets, clothes, and even their hair. By day their duties were most carelessly performed, and with a heartlessness which added additional pangs to the sufferings of those who depended upon their assistance; but at night there was "not the least attention paid to the sick and dying, except what could be done by the convalescent;

---

from the bone and hung only by the heel. Coffin also says, that "many of the prisoners, during the severity of winter, had scarcely clothes sufficient to cover their nakedness, and but very few enough to keep them warm. To remedy those inconveniences, we were obliged to keep below, and either get into our hammocks or keep in constant motion—without which precautions, we must have perished."

[1] Sherburne (p. 116). "Freneau, who, as a patient on the Hunter, had ample means of knowing whereof he spoke, has pictured, in scathing rhyme, the unfeeling conduct of these medical men.

"'From Brooklyn heights a Hessian doctor came,
Not great his skill, nor greater much his fame;
Fair Science never called the wretch her son,
And Art disdained the stupid man to own.
* * * * *
He on his charge the healing work begun
With antimonial mixtures, by the ton;
Ten minutes was the time he deign'd to stay,
The time of grace allotted once a day.—
He drench'd us well with bitter draughts, 'tis true—
Nostrums from hell, and *cortex* from Peru.
Some with his pills he sent to Pluto's reign,
And some he blister'd with his flies of Spain;
His Tartar doses walk'd their deadly round,
Till the lean patient at the potion frown'd,
And swore that hemlock, death, or what you will,
Were nonsense to the drugs that stuff'd his bill.
On those refusing, he bestow'd a kick,
Or menac'd vengeance with his walking-stick.
Here, uncontroll'd, he exercis'd his trade,
And grew experienc'd by the deaths he made.'"

who were so frequently called upon, that in many cases they overdid themselves, relapsed, and died."

Sherburne mentions the sad case of two brothers, John and Abraham Fall, who lay sick upon a cot near his own. One night, when thus left to suffer in the darkness of this foul and miserable ship, Abraham Fall plead with his brother John to get off from him; and the sick around swore at John for his cruelty in lying on his brother; but John made no reply, he was deaf to the cries of his brother, and beyond the curses of the suffering crowd. In the morning he was found dead; and his brother Abraham, whose exhausted strength had given way under the pressure of the corpse, was in a dying state. The sick were unable to relieve them, and the nurses were not there.

Captain Dring also describes the case of a poor boy, only twelve years old, confined with him on the Old Jersey, and who had been inoculated for the small-pox. "He was a member of the same mess with myself," Dring says, "and had always looked upon me as a protector, and particularly so during his sickness. The night of his death was a truly wretched one to me; for I spent almost the whole of it in perfect darkness, holding him during his convulsions; and it was heart-rending to hear the screams of the dying boy, while calling and imploring, in his delirium, for the assistance of his mother and other persons of his family. For a long time, all persuasion or argument was useless to silence his groans and supplications. But exhausted nature at length sunk under its agonies; his screams became less piercing, and his struggles less violent. In the midnight gloom of our dungeon, I could not see him die, but knew, by placing my hand over his mouth, that his breathings were becoming shorter; and thus felt the last breath as it quitted his frame. The first glimmer of morning light through the iron grate fell upon his pallid and lifeless corpse."[1]

The Jersey became, at length, so crowded, and the increase of disease among the prisoners so rapid, that even the hospital-ships were inadequate for their reception. In this emergency, bunks were erected on the larboard side of the upper deck of the Jersey, for the

[1] Dring's Narrative, p. 84.

accommodation of the sick from between decks. The horrors of the old hulk were now increased a hundred-fold. Foul air, confinement, darkness, hunger, thirst, the slow poison of the malarious locality in which the ship was anchored, the torments of vermin, the suffocating heat alternating with cold, and, above all, the *almost total absence of hope*, performed their deadly work unchecked. "The whole ship, from her keel to the taffrail, was equally affected, and contained pestilence sufficient to desolate a world—disease and death were wrought into her very timbers."

Notwithstanding the increasing mortality on board the Jersey, new arrivals more than supplied the vacancies occasioned by death, and the ship became unbearably crowded. In their despair, the prisoners, early in June, 1782, bethought themselves of petitioning General Clinton, then in command at New York, for permission to transmit a memorial to General Washington, describing their pitiable condition, and soliciting his influence in their behalf. The favor was unexpectedly granted by the British general, and three messengers, chosen by the crew from among their own number, were authorized to leave the ship on this embassy. In addition to the written memorial which they bore, they were directed to state, in a manner more explicit than they dared to commit to paper, the peculiar horror of their situation; the miserable food and water on which they were obliged to subsist; and to promise him that if their release could be procured, they would gladly enter the American army, and serve during the remainder of the war as soldiers.

In a few days after, the prisoners were summoned to the spar-deck to listen to the reading of General Washington's reply; in which he expressed his deepest sympathy with their condition, and his determination to mitigate its severities by every means within his power. To the messengers personally, he had fully explained that their long detention in captivity was owing to a combination of circumstances against which it was very difficult, if not impossible, to provide. "That, in the first place, but little exertion was made on the part of our countrymen to secure and detain their British prisoners, for the purpose of exchange; many of the British seamen being captured by privateers, on board which, he understood, it was a common practice for them to enter as seamen; and that, when this was not the case, they were usually set at liberty as soon as the privateer arrived in port; as neither the owners, nor the town or State where they were landed, would be at the expense of their confinement and maintenance; and that the officers of *the General Government only took charge of those seamen who were captured by the vessels in the public service.* All which circumstances combined to render the number of British prisoners at all times by far too small for a regular and equal exchange." Copies of the correspondence on the subject with the British authorities were also submitted[1] by the general, whose interference was soon followed by an improvement in their fare—especially in the quality of the bread, and in the furnishing of butter instead of rancid oil. An awning was also provided, as well as a wind-sail, for the conducting of fresh air between the decks during the day—which, however, was of no advantage during the nights, as the keepers continued to fasten down the hatchways after dark. To their other privations, the prisoners were obliged to submit, hoping—almost against hope—that further favors might possibly be granted, although they saw "but little prospect of escaping from the raging pestilence, except through the interposition of Divine Providence."

There was, indeed, one condition upon which these hapless sufferers might have escaped the torture of this slow but certain death, and that was enlistment in the British service. This chance was daily offered to them by the recruiting officers who visited the ship, but whose persuasions and offers were almost invariably treated with contempt, and that, too, by men who fully expected to die where they were.[2] In spite of untold physical sufferings, which

[1] The whole correspondence between the American and British authorities, relative to the condition of the American prisoners in the hulks, will be found in Dawson's Dring (Appendix I). From these letters, it will be seen that Washington had not been unmindful of the sufferings of his unfortunate countrymen—his first letter to the British authorities being dated in January 25, 1781;—but his authority in the premises was limited, the real power to negotiate for the exchange of naval prisoners being vested not in him, but in the Financier of the American Government. Exchanges between the belligerents were to be made in kind; and owing, as above stated, to the course pursued by those engaged in privateering, in releasing captives without parole, or enlisting them in the American service, our Government had but few *naval* prisoners to offer; while, to accept the enemy's offer to receive soldiers in exchange, would, by furnishing him immediate re-enforcements in the field, have been subversive of the interests of the United States.

[2] Coffin, Dring, and others.

might well have shaken the resolution of the strongest; in spite of the insinuations of the British that they were neglected by their Government—insinuations which seemed to be corroborated by the very facts of their condition; in defiance of threats of even harsher treatment, and regardless of promises of food and clothing—objects most tempting to men in their condition; but few, comparatively, sought relief from their woes by the betrayal of their honor.[1] And these few went forth into liberty followed by the execrations and undisguised contempt of the suffering heroes whom they left behind. It was this calm, unfaltering, unconquerable SPIRIT OF PATRIOTISM—defying torture, starvation, loathsome disease, and the prospect of a neglected and forgotten grave—which sanctifies to every American heart the scene of their suffering in the Wallabout, and which will render the sad story of the "prison-ships" one of ever-increasing interest to all future generations. "*They chose to die, rather than injure the Republic.* And the Republic hath never yet paid them *the tribute of gratitude!*"

At the expiration of the war, the prisoners remaining on board the "Old Jersey" were liberated, and the old hulk, in whose "putrefactive bowels" so many had suffered and died, was abandoned where she lay. "The dread of contagion prevented every one from venturing on board, and even from approaching her polluted frame. But the ministers of destruction were at work. Her planks were soon filled with worms, who, as if sent to remove this disgrace to the name of our common humanity, ceased not from their labor, until they had penetrated through her decaying bottom; through which the water rushed in, and she sunk. With her went down the names of many thousands of our countrymen, with which her inner planks and sheathing were literally covered; for but few of her inmates had ever

---

[1] Coffin (Hist. Martyrs, p. 35) says he never knew of but *one* who so enlisted. Fox, however, admits that *some* did enter the British service, and was himself one of a small party who enlisted thus for garrison duty in Jamaica—a step which they all bitterly repented afterwards. We have also similar testimony from other sources; yet these were but rare exceptions to the pure spirit of patriotic heroism displayed, in so surprising a degree, by the great mass of the sufferers in the prison-ships.

In many cases, *forcible impressment* of our brave sailors was practised by the British (see Fox, pp. 134, 135), and was justly characterized by Washington, in a letter to Lord Howe, in 1777, as "unprecedented."

neglected to add their own names to the almost innumerable catalogue. Could these be counted, some estimate might now be made of the whole number who were there immured; but this record has long since been consigned to eternal oblivion," and the precise number of these unknown martyrs who perished in the prison-ships, and were buried in the loose sands of the lonely Wallabout, will probably never be accurately known. It was estimated, shortly after the close of the war, when the data were more easily attainable than now, that *upwards of eleven thousand* died in the JERSEY alone![1] The statement was never denied, either officially or by those then resident in New York and elsewhere, who, from their connection with the British Commissary department, had full opportunities of knowing the truth. Calculating, as we safely may, the deaths on board the Jersey as *averaging five a day*, during the time (1779–80—April, 1783) she was occupied as a prison-ship,[2] and adding thereto the large number transferred from her to the hospital-ships, where they died, as well as the hundreds exchanged from time to time, and who

---

[1] This estimate of 11,000, or, as elsewhere stated, 11,500, whether correct or not, undoubtedly originated in the following newspaper paragraph:

"FISHKILL, May 8, '83.

"TO ALL PRINTERS OF PUBLIC NEWSPAPERS.

"Tell it to the world, and let it be published in every newspaper throughout America, Europe, Asia, and Africa, to the everlasting disgrace and infamy of the British King's commanders at New York: That during the late war, it is said, 11,644 American prisoners have suffered death by their inhuman, cruel, savage, and barbarous usage on board the filthy and malignant British prison-ship, called the Jersey, lying at New York. Britons, tremble, lest the vengeance of Heaven fall on your isle, for the blood of these unfortunate victims. AN AMERICAN."

[2] Dring (p. 123) says: "The average number who died on board, during the period of twenty-four hours, was about *five*." Freneau, in his stinging rhyme (The British Prison-ship) says:

"Each day, at least six carcases we bore,
And scratch'd them graves along the sandy shore."

Talbot (p. 106) states that while he was on board the Jersey, the number of deaths was *reduced*, by cool and dry nights (it being then October) *to an average of ten*, and this number was considered by the survivors but a small one when compared with the terrible mortality which had prevailed in the ship for three months previously! Johnson says, "it was no uncommon thing to see five or six dead bodies brought on shore in a single morning." A letter from the Jersey, published in the *Penn. Packet*, of Sept. 4th, 1781, says: "We bury six, seven, eight, nine, ten, and eleven men in a day; we have two hundred more sick and falling sick every day." And similar testimony on this point could be adduced *ad infinitum*.

reached home *only in time to die*,[1]—the above estimate does not seem exaggerated if applied to the mortality, not of the Jersey alone, but of *all* the prison-ships.

The *Prison-ships*, as we have already seen, were condemned vessels of war, totally unsuitable for places of confinement; and, while the abstract right of the enemy to use them as such is unquestionable,[2] yet there was not the least necessity of so doing, when, within a stone's throw, were broad acres of unoccupied land, much better suited for the purpose. Neither was there any real or pretended necessity for resort to the extreme measures which were adopted towards the American naval prisoners. It is true that, according to the law of nations, their claims for consideration, as subjects in rebellion, were not as great as those of captives taken in solemn war; yet it is equally true that the main object of the war—the suppression of rebellion—did not justify the severity of treatment which these prisoners received, and which transcended that higher "law of humanity," which every nation is bound to observe and respect. It is evident that the JERSEY, which had once accommodated a crew of over four hundred, with full armament, supplies, etc., might, without

---

[1] At New London, in February, '79, arrived a cartel of one hundred and thirty of these poor victims of the prison-ships. In such condition were these men placed on board the cartel, that, in the short run between New York and New London, sixteen died on board; and sixty, when they landed, were scarcely able to move, while the remainder were much emaciated. In November, 1781, one hundred and thirty-two prisoners arrived from the prison-ships, "mostly sick." In December of the same year, one hundred and thirty prisoners landed from New York, "in most deplorable condition; great part since dead, and the survivors so debilitated that they will drag out a miserable existence. It is enough to melt the most obdurate heart to see these miserable objects landed at our wharves, sick and dying, and the few rags they have on covered with vermin and their own excrements." At New London, in December, '78, nearly one hundred and seventy-two American prisoners arrived from New York, the "greater part sickly and in most deplorable condition, owing chiefly to the ill-usage in their prison-ships, where numbers had their feet and legs froze."

Lieutenant Catlin, who was placed with two hundred and twenty-five men on board the Glasgow, to be sent to Connecticut as an exchange, says they were aboard eleven days, without fire, and with even less food than before; and that twenty-eight died during the passage, from cold and ill-usage. Multitudes of such cases could be quoted.

[2] In evidence that the Americans did not question this right, we may cite the fact that, in 1782, a vessel, fitly named the *Retaliation*, was fitted up as a prison-ship, moored in the Thames river, near New London, Conn., and used as a place of confinement for captured British seamen.

her stores, dismantled, and anchored in a protected situation, have easily been made comfortable for even the thousand prisoners which she is said to have averaged. That she was not so, and that she became a "festering plague-spot," was attributable largely to the conduct of those inferior officers under whose immediate care the prisoners were placed; and who, by their disregard of the policy of their Government, their avaricious and shameful mal-appropriation of the supplies placed at their disposal by that Government for the use of the prisoners, and their frequent and uncalled-for severity, unnecessarily increased the sufferings which they should have mitigated.

There is ample evidence, moreover, in the various narratives extant concerning the prison-ships, that the prisoners themselves—demoralized by the accumulation of suffering to which they were subjected—were accountable, to a considerable extent, for much of their own suffering.[1] The same narratives also, when divested of the vindictiveness and exaggeration to which their writers not unnaturally gave expression, furnish incontestable evidence that prisoners were, in some instances, treated with more consideration than is generally supposed. Friends were permitted to visit them and

---

[1] For example, although the leakage of the Jersey rendered necessary the frequent use of the pumps to keep her from sinking in the soft mud of the Wallabout, yet we have the testimony of Andros (p. 9) that the prisoners were only forced up to the winches, and to keep the pumps in motion, by the intimidation of an armed guard. He also states (p. 16) that "the prisoners were furnished with buckets and brushes to cleanse the ship, and with vinegar to sprinkle her inside; *but their indolence and despair were such that they would not use them, or but rarely.*"

According to Dring, soon after the Jersey began to be used as a place of confinement, the prisoners established a code of by-laws for their own regulation and government—especially as regarded personal cleanliness, the prevention of profanity, drunkenness and theft, the observance of the Sabbath, etc. For a long time these laws were scrupulously observed; but, as numbers constantly increased, and sickness, despair, and harsh treatment began to have their full measure of influence upon the prisoners, they exhibited the demoralization of despair; and though the rules against theft, fighting, tyrannical conduct, etc., were still enforced, it was not so much from principle, as from an instinct of self-preservation. Hawkins (p. 67) mentions a case of punishment inflicted by the prisoners of the Jersey upon one of their number, which was terribly severe.

The prisoners, also, rendered desperate by their sufferings, took no pains to conciliate their keepers; but, according to all accounts, showed an evident disposition to annoy the guard, the cook, and even the old marines who guarded the water-butt, and who always repaid these petty annoyances with interest, thus adding materially to the inconveniences and horrors of their situation. Fox and others give many instances of this.

to furnish them with articles necessary to promote their comfort;[1] correspondence, under proper restrictions, was allowed with their families; in some cases they were allowed to visit their homes, on their simple word of honor to return at a specified time;[2] and even the reading of the funeral-service was not refused when desired.[3] From these well-substantiated facts, it is evident that the cruelties endured by the unfortunate inmates of the prison-ships, were not systematized aggravations practised by a great and civilized Government; but the result, generally, of avarice, indolence, indifference, and unwarrantable abuse of power by hirelings, "clothed with a little brief authority,"—a class proverbially despotic, cruel, and inhuman in their treatment of the helpless.

Time has softened the asperities engendered by the conflict of the Revolution; and our own recent national experiences in the suppression of a similar revolt, have largely tended to dispel the historic glamour which has hitherto veiled the events of that period. Deplorable as some of these events were, and totally inexcusable on the ground either of justice or humanity, we can, at this time, better appreciate their causes, and understand—although we cannot excuse—the motives of the real actors therein. And, although History cannot blot out from her imperishable pages the sad story of the prison-ships, yet Charity forbids that Vengeance should dictate the record against those who—however harshly their actions may be judged by man—have gone to receive their judgment before a Superior Tribunal.

Although not in strict chronological sequence, we deem it appropriate to conclude this chapter with a narrative of the numerous abortive attempts to secure for the remains of these untold and unknown heroes of the prison-ships, a fitting and permanent place of sepulchre.

---

[1] Sherburne (p. 116) mentions that, through the kindness of some of the benevolent citizens of New York, all the sick on board the Frederick were constantly supplied with a pint each of Bohea tea (well-sweetened with molasses) each day. See, also, the Drowne correspondence, in Dawson's Dring, 173, and others.

[2] See Drowne correspondence, 168; also other authorities in manuscript.

[3] Ibid., 171.

For several years after the close of the Revolution, the bones of those who died on board the prison-ships were to be seen, scarce earthed in the falling banks of the Wallabout, or strewn upon its shores, and bleaching beneath the winter's storm and the summer's scorching sun. And though, during this period, several patriotic individuals called the attention of Congress and of the public to these exposed and neglected remains,[1] yet no formal movement seems to have been made towards their proper interment until 1792, when the citizens of the town of Brooklyn, at an annual town meeting, resolved that the bones disinterred and collected by Mr. John Jackson[2] (who had recently become the owner of the "Remsen

---

[1] Among others, Joseph P. Cook, a member (from Connecticut) of Congress then in session in New York, writing under date of June 3d, 1785, from his lodgings in Brooklyn, near the Wallabout, says: "Soon after we came to live on Long Island, several of us took a walk that way, and were struck with horror at beholding a large number of human bones, *some fragments of flesh not quite consumed*, with many pieces of old blankets, lying upon the shore. In consequence of a representation made to Congress, they were soon after taken up and buried. But walking along the same place, not many days ago, we saw a number more which were washed out; and attempting to bury them ourselves, we found the bank full of them."

[2] John Jackson, a native of Jerusalem, Queens County, L. I., removed with his brothers, Samuel and Treadwell, to the village of Brooklyn, shortly after the close of the Revolution. It is probable that the brothers were possessed of some means, for they soon purchased large estates in Brooklyn, which could, at that early period, be had at very low prices. John Jackson, about 1791, purchased the large and valuable farm then known as the "Remsen estate," situated on the Wallabout, and comprising about thirty acres of land and thirty-five acres of pond, together with the old mill and dwelling-house—for which he paid the sum of $17,000. It was in making improvements on this farm that public attention seems first to have been attracted, by the disinterment of the remains of those buried from the prison-ships—large quantities of bones being found in cutting away the high banks, which then formed the shore of the bay. In the year 1801, Mr. Jackson sold to the United States forty acres of this property, which has ever since been occupied by the Government as a navy-yard. In other instances than this, also, Mr. Jackson appears in Brooklyn history mostly in the character of a shrewd speculator—as the originator and President of the Wallabout Bridge Company—as the builder of a saw-mill on the adjoining meadow, to be moved by wind, which failed—as the vendor of a part of the same meadow (to Captain Isaac Chauncey, of the U. S. N.), for the purpose of erecting thereon powder magazines; but the dampness of the place damaged the powder, and, consequently, the reputation of the magazines. Indeed, in his sale of land and water privilege to the United States for a navy-yard, he seems to have granted rather more of the mill-stream than his own title fairly included, and to have covered the excess by an ambiguously worded deed, which ultimately gave rise to some well-founded complaint on the part of the citizens of the town—to which the said water privilege belonged—and to an extensive correspondence between them and the Secretary of the Navy. Mr. Jackson is described,

farm"—on which they were situated) should be removed to and buried in the graveyard of the Reformed Dutch church, and a monument erected over them. A committee, of which General Johnson was chairman,[1] was appointed to carry the resolution into effect; but their application, in 1793, was refused by Mr. Jackson, who, being a prominent politician and a Sachem of the then influential Tammany Society, or Columbian Order, had conceived the idea of turning to a political use, and to his personal aggrandizement, the large deposit of prison-ship remains of which he had accidentally become the possessor. In accordance with this plan, he subsequently offered to the Tammany Society an eligible piece of land upon his property in the Wallabout, for the purpose of erecting thereon a suitable sepulchre. The society accepted his offer; and on the 10th of February, 1803, an eloquent memorial was prepared, and presented by the learned and distinguished Dr. Samuel L. Mitchell to the House of Representatives, then in session in Washington. From Congress, indeed, much was expected, as the subject of the application to them was purely national, and one which deeply interested the public sensibility. No measures were, however, adopted by that honorable body, and the matter rested until 1808.[2] On February 1st of that year it was again revived by the Tammany Society, who appointed a Wallabout Committee, which proceeded to take immediate steps towards effecting the long-talked-of and long-neglected sepulture of the remains, of which upwards of thirteen hogsheads had been collected. They initiated an extensive correspondence, published a stirring appeal in the columns of the public press, invited the cordial co-operation of their patriotic fellow-

---

by those who knew him, as a large man, of coarse features and florid complexion, loud spoken, energetic in his movements, and an ardent politician.

[1] This movement was undoubtedly made at the suggestion of General Johnson himself.

[2] In the interim, however, the patriotism of a private citizen, Mr. Benjamin Aycrigg, reproved the hesitation of the Congress of a great people. As we learn from documents published in the Transactions of the American Institute for 1852, Mr. Aycrigg, shocked at the exposed condition of these remains, during the summer of 1805, made a written contract with an Irishman living in the Wallabout, by which the latter was to "collect all the human bones as far as may be without digging," and deliver the same to Mr. A. at a stipulated price—which was done, and the remains thus collected formed a portion of those which were subsequently interred in the vault erected by the Tammany Society. A biographical sketch of Mr. Aycrigg will be found in Stiles' privately printed edition of the Hist. Account of the Interment of the Martyrs, etc., pp. 218–220.

citizens in every part of the Union, and in various ways strove to arouse a national interest in the sacred trust which had been confided to their care. In this they were eminently successful, and THE NATION, aroused by their appeal, touched by the memories which clustered around those martyr graves amid the sand-hills of the Wallabout, and shamed, it may be, by a consciousness of its own too great neglect, turned at last, with a quickened impulse of generous affection, towards the work of providing for those honored remains a place of final deposit.

Indeed, so unexpected was the zeal manifested by the public, and so effective were the individual exertions made in behalf of this object, that the committee were induced, at a much earlier period than they had originally contemplated, to commence the building of the vault. On Wednesday, April 13, 1808, the corner-stone was laid. The imposing military and civic procession which took place on that occasion formed at the old ferry (now Fulton ferry, Brooklyn), under the directions of Major Aycrigg, Grand Marshal of the day, and marched through Main, Sands, Bridge, York, and Jackson streets, to the vault, on Jackson street, adjoining the Navy-yard.

Arriving at the latter place, the artillery were posted on an adjacent hill: the other parts of the procession took appropriate positions, and Benjamin Romaine, Esq., Grand Sachem of Tammany, assisted by the Wallabout Committee and the master-builders, laid the corner-stone of the vault, upon which was the following inscription:

"*In the name of the Spirits of the Departed Free—Sacred to the Memory of that portion of American Seamen, Soldiers, and Citizens who perished on board the Prison-ships of the British at the Wallabout during the Revolution.*

"This is the corner-stone of the vault erected by the Tammany Society, or Columbian Order, which contains their remains. The ground for which was bestowed by John Jackson.—Nassau Island, season of blossoms. Year of the discovery the 316th, of the institution the 19th, and of American Independence the 32d, *April* 6, 1808."[1]

---

[1] Jacob Vandervoort, John Jackson, Burdett Striker, Issachar Cozzens, Robert Townsend, jr., Benjamin Watson, Samuel Cowdrey, *Wallabout Committee.* David & William Campbell, *builders.*

The completion of this ceremony was followed by national salutes from the Marine Corps and the Artillery, and solemn music by the bands. Then, before the procession and some two thousand citizens gathered in a circle around the door of the vault, JOSEPH D. FAY, Esq., a member of Tammany, pronounced a brilliant and eloquent oration over "the tomb of the Patriots." At the conclusion of his address, the procession returned to the place of rendezvous at the ferry, where they formed a circle around the Liberty-pole,[1] near the market, gave three cheers, and dispersed to their homes.

Upon the completion of the vault, the remains were removed thereto on the 26th day of May following, with a civic and military pageant unprecedented for splendor and impressiveness, and which was witnessed, as then estimated, by upwards of thirty thousand persons.[2] At the head of this procession rode a trumpeter, mounted on a black horse, and dressed in black relieved with red, wearing a helmet ornamented with flowing black and red feathers, and bearing in his right hand a trumpet, from which was suspended a black silk flag, edged with red and black crape, bearing the following motto, in letters of gold:

MORTALS AVAUNT!
11,500
SPIRITS OF THE MARTYRED BRAVE
APPROACH THE TOMB OF HONOUR, OF GLORY, OF
VIRTUOUS PATRIOTISM!

He was followed by the Chief Herald, in full military dress, and

---

[1] This Liberty-pole stood at the foot of Fulton street, Brooklyn, near the old market, which finally came to be regarded as a nuisance, and was torn down one night, in 1814, by a party of young men. The site of the market is now marked by the flag-staff which stands in the middle of Fulton street, near the Ferry-house.

[1] A full account of these ceremonies is given in a now rare volume, entitled, "An Account of the Interment of the Remains of 11,500 American Seamen, Soldiers, and Citizens, who fell victims to the cruelties of the British, on board their prison-ships at the Wallabout, during the American Revolution, with a description of the grand and solemn funeral procession, which took place on the 26th May, 1808, and an oration delivered at the Tomb of the Patriots by Benjamin DeWitt, M. D., a member of the Tammany Society, or Columbian Order; compiled by the Wallabout Committee. New York: Printed by Frank, White & Co. 1808: 96 pages, 12mo." A very elegant edition, limited to one hundred and fifteen copies, was issued from the "Bradstreet Press," New York, in 1865, with notes and historical appendix, by the author of this history.

mounted on an elegant white horse, richly caparisoned, bearing the staff and cap of liberty, from which was suspended an elegant blue silk shield, edged with red and black crape, the field covered with thirteen stars in gold, emblematic of the original American constellation. Major Aycrigg, the son of a sufferer in the sugar-house, and Captain Alexander Coffin, himself twice a sufferer in the prison-ships, acted as his aids. The long line which followed was composed of cavalry, artillery, infantry, the members of the Cincinnati; the clergy, the Tammany Society, in the full and imposing regalia of their order, surrounding the *thirteen coffins filled with the remains of the prison-ship dead*, to which one hundred and four Revolutionary veterans, headed by the Hon. Samuel Osgood and the Hon. Henry Rutgers, acted as pall-bearers; the sailors, members of the Municipal, State, and General Governments, foreign diplomatists, societies, trades, Masons, etc. The central feature of the procession, however, was the "*Grand National Pedestal*," as it was called, consisting of an oblong square stage, erected on a large truck-carriage, the margin of which represented an iron railing; below this dropped a deep festoon, which covered the wheels; on the stage was a pedestal representing black marble, eight feet long, six feet high, and four wide, the four panels of which bore the following inscriptions:

(Front.)

AMERICANS! REMEMBER THE BRITISH.

(Right side.)

YOUTH OF MY COUNTRY! MARTYRDOM PREFER TO SLAVERY.

(Left side.)

SIRES OF COLUMBIA! TRANSMIT TO POSTERITY THE CRUELTIES PRACTISED ON BOARD THE BRITISH PRISON-SHIPS.

(Rear.)

TYRANTS DREAD THE GATHERING STORM,—
WHILE FREEMEN, FREEMEN'S OBSEQUIES PERFORM.

From a staff on the top of the pedestal was displayed a superb blue silk flag, eighteen feet by twelve, emblazoned with the arms of the United States; the staff itself, eighteen feet high, being crowned by a globe, on which sat the American Bald Eagle, enveloped in a cloud of crape.

The "Genius of America" was represented by Josiah Falconer, a member of the Tammany Society, and the son of a Revolutionary patriot. His dress was a loose under-dress of light-blue silk, which reached to his knees, over which was a long flowing white robe, relieved by a crimson scarf and crape. He wore sandals on his feet, and on his head a magnificent cap, adorned with the most elegant feathers which could be obtained, all in the Mexican style. On the stage and around the pedestal, stood nine young men, each holding by a tassel the end of a cord connected with the flag. These represented Patriotism, Honor, Virtue, Patience, Fortitude, Merit, Courage, Perseverance, and Science, and were styled the "Attributes of the Genius of America." They were all dressed in character, with a plume of feathers in their hats, a white silk scarf, relieved with crape; and each wore a scarlet badge, edged with elegant dark-blue silk fringe, in the shape of a crescent, inscribed in gold with the name of the attribute which he represented; and each held also in his hand a blue silk banner, emblematic of the institution to which he belonged. This beautiful structure was drawn by four horses, dressed in ribbons and crape, and under the charge of two postilions.

The procession, after passing through various streets, reached the East River, where, at different places, boats had been provided for crossing to Brooklyn. Thirteen large open boats transported the thirteen tribes of the Tammany Society, each containing one tribe, one coffin, and the pall-bearers. The Grand Sachem, Father of the Council, and other officers not attached to tribes, accompanied by the Chief Herald, his aids, and the Trumpeter, led the van, the boats following in order. The car was embarked on board a vessel specially constructed for the purpose, and transported under the management of several masters of vessels, who volunteered their services, the Genius and supporters retaining their positions. "This beautiful structure," says the account, "in its passage attracted the notice of every eye. From the current, it received a direction down the river, which made its course circuitous, describing a line of perfect beauty; the elegant standard floating in the wind, on which were seen the badges of each society, the white robes loosely flowing around the tall and graceful figure of the Genius, and the cloud-colored pedestal which supported them, presented to the imagination of every beholder an object of the most pleasing admiration." * * * "Fleets of small craft were seen industriously plying to and from the city, extending from the southerly point of the city to Corlaer's Hook.[1] Pleasure-boats, with their colors waving half-mast high, and streaming far out in the wind, were sailing swiftly up and down the stream. Minute-guns were fired from all quarters. At a distance were seen volumes of smoke wheeling up the sky, succeeded in short intervals by the roaring of the cannon. The arms of the military glistened in the sun from the heights of Corlaer's Hook; and on the hills of Brooklyn crowds of ladies eyed with serious contemplation the vast grandeur of the scene. The waters of the East River foamed beneath the oars of a thousand boats, the sails of a hundred vessels swelled to the breeze, and a mild sun seemed to smile benignantly on the interesting scene."

At Brooklyn ferry the procession formed again, and being joined by many citizens and ladies[2] of Brooklyn, marched to the tomb of the valiant. "It is impossible to describe the interesting effect of the procession marching over the green hills of Brooklyn.[3] The colors of the military waved in the wind, changing and turning to the sound of slow and most impressive music. High floated the flag of America, as if triumphant that the stain of ingratitude was this day to be wiped away. The procession streamed along the valley and over the hill, and arrived at the tomb of the martyrs amidst a vast and mighty assemblage. A stage had been here erected for the orator, trimmed with black crape. The coffins were placed in front, and the pall-bearers took their seats beneath the eye of the orator. The Genius of America, 'high upon the car,' stood on his right. The Tammany Society arranged itself before him, and citi-

---

[1] Foot of Grand street, East River.

[2] "There, however, was displayed a lively mark of female patriotism ana affection, as well as ingenious portray of fancy in the circumstance of arranging a beautiful group of ladies in the train of the *Genius of Liberty*. These fair daughters of Columbia gave the tear of sensibility to the memory of the brave, and exhibited the undissembling testimonial of virtuous hearts."—N. Y. Public Adv., May 27.

[3] The ground around the present Navy-yard was, at the time of these ceremonies, quite high; and there were several eminences in the neighborhood, such as "Vinegar Hill" and "McKenzie's One Tree Hill," any one of which would have formed advantageous positions both for the artillery and the spectators.

zen behind citizen covered the plain and the hill as far as the prospect extended. A detachment of the military marched to the southeast bank of the East River with the cannon, from whence they fired minute-guns for some time; and were answered by the thunder of artillery from Corlaer's Hook, Fort Jay, and other military posts. As soon as the firing ceased, a solemn silence pervaded the multitude, and expectation sat on every countenance—the tomb was open to receive them—the remains of American Martyrs were about to be honored with the rites of sepulture." Amid the impressive silence which reigned, the Rev. RALPH WILLISTON addressed "the God of Battles" in "a most solemn, eloquent, and pious supplication." Dr. BENJAMIN DEWITT then delivered the funeral oration, which he had prepared at the request of the Tammany Society, in a style and manner dignified, pathetic, and eloquent. "He described the heroic fortitude with which the martyrs endured indescribable misery, and while the audience listened to catch the relation, tears of sympathy bedimmed their eyes. It was a solemn and sublime hour."

At the close of the oration, the coffins were deposited in the tomb, the ceremonies were closed with the solemn benediction, "To the King Immortal, Invisible, the All-wise God, be glory everlasting. Amen!" and the procession returned to Brooklyn ferry, from whence its passage to the city was pleasant and expeditious. It was formed there again and proceeded to the Park, where a circle was formed, the Car of Liberty and the standards of the different societies were placed in the centre, and an air from the band was performed; after which, by a signal from the Grand Marshal, the procession was dismissed.

Thus ended the solemnities of a funeral procession which had excited more interest than any other that had ever taken place in America; and which was, as the event proved, as grand in promise as it was empty in result.

For awhile, after the temporary interment of the bones of the martyrs, there seemed to be no doubt that a nation's gratitude would be converted into the gold which should build their monument. Tammany Hall flamed with excitement. Committees were appointed to collect money, individuals proffered donations, the State itself contributed one thousand dollars. But all this fervid excitement soon collapsed. Tammany Hall, good at the beginning, did not keep up the stimulus. Some money was collected, but scattered—no one knew or cared where—private donations were not called for, and the sum appropriated by the State was finally returned to its treasury, to be realized, it is hoped, with increase, at some future day, when the patriotism of our people shall finally make amends for the long delay of the past.

So the bubble burst—the tide of population so surged in upon this favored region of Brooklyn, that the old elements were dissolved in the current of new-comers, and the very purpose of this vault and its wooden covering was well-nigh forgotten. In course of time, by an alteration of the grade of Jackson street, the walls of the vault were infringed upon; and finally, the very lot on which it stood was *sold for taxes!* Then Benjamin Romaine, the treasurer of the fund of 1808—a true patriot, and fully earnest in his efforts to secure a monument—came forward and bought it. He had been himself a sufferer by imprisonment in the old sugar-house prison at New York, and he now took pleasure in rescuing from desecration the remains of those whose sufferings he had shared, and whose memory he revered. He erected an ante-chamber over the vault, and other appropriate adornments and inscriptions.[1]

---

[1] These improvements, etc., are thus fully described in a little pamphlet published by him on the 4th of July, 1839:

The following inscriptions are now displayed in and about the sacred premises:

"*First.* The portal to the Tomb of 11,500 patriot prisoners of war, who died in dungeons and pestilential prison-ships, in and about the city of New York, during the War of our Revolution. The top is capped with two large urns, in black, and a white globe in the centre.

"*Second.* The interior of the tomb contains thirteen coffins, arranged in the order as observed in the Declaration of Independence, and inserted thus—New Hampshire, Massachusetts, Rhode Island, Connecticut, New York, New Jersey, Pennsylvania, Delaware, Maryland, Virginia, North Carolina, South Carolina, and Georgia.

"*Third.* Thirteen beautifully turned posts, painted white, each capped with a small urn, in black; and between the posts, the above-named States are fully lettered.

"*Fourth.* In 1778, the Colonial Congress promulgated the Federal League Compact, though it was not finally ratified until 1781, only two years before the Peace of 1783.

"*Fifth.* In 1789, our grand National Convention, 'to form a more perfect union,' did ordain 'the present Constitution for the United States of America,' to be one entire sovereignty, and in strict adhesion to the equally necessary and sacred State rights. Such a republic must endure forever!'

The better to prevent any further desecration of this, to him, hallowed spot, Mr. Romaine appropriated the tomb as a burial-place for himself and his family, and with that intent, placed there, many years before his death, the coffin in which he should be interred.

The interior of the tomb, at this time, has thus been well described by an old resident of Brooklyn:[1]

"One Saturday of school-boy leisure for that 'mischief' which Satan finds for 'idle hands to do,' I determined to penetrate the depth of this tomb, and sought the building, fully bent on gaining the interior, and knowing all that could be revealed to the astonished eye. This was not very difficult—the fastenings were loose—and after some little toil, the exterior door swung open and revealed a sort of vestibule, in which were a few plaster busts of distinguished heroes, covered with the incrustations of dampness and neglect. There were steps leading below into a vault. These I fearlessly

---

"*Sixth.* In the same year, 1789, in the city of New York, Washington began the first Presidential career. The wide-spread Eagle of Union, with a gilded sun and star in his beak, and standing erect on a globe, is now represented as waiting on Washington's command, and then as instantly raising his flight in the heavens, and, like the orb of day, speedily became visible to half the globe. Washington had appeared, uncovered, before the majesty of the people, under the canopy, in front of our City Hall, when Chancellor Livingston administered to him the oath of office, and then proclaimed, *Long live George Washington!* The air was rent with shouts of acclamation, and our goodly ship Union moved on our ways, a model for the Universe! A witness to this scene declared that it appeared to him that the hosts of heaven, at that moment, were looking down with approbation on the act; that he was deprived of utterance, and could only wave his hat among the multitude. I was also a witness to the scene. Then it was, at that moment, when our State sovereignty, not our equally sacred State rights, ceased to exist, and the sovereign power was proclaimed to be invested in the whole people of the United States, one and indivisible!

"*Seventh.* The Constitution of the United States consists of two parts—the supreme sovereignty, and the unadulterated State rights, one and inseparable. It has no parallel except the sacred Decalogue of Moses, which proclaimed our duties to God and man, one and indivisible, six thousand years ago.

"*Eighth.* In the ante-chamber of the tomb will be arranged the busts, or other insignia, of the most distinguished deceased military men and civilians of the Revolution. The Governors and Legislatures of the old thirteen States, will confer a great favor by sending them to Benjamin Romaine, No. 21 Hudson street, city of New York."—Review.

The Tomb of the Martyrs, adjoining the United States Navy-yard, Brooklyn city, in Jackson street, who died in dungeons and prison-ships, in and about the city of New York, during the seven years of our Revolutionary War. By Benjamin Romaine, an old native citizen of New York. New York: Printed by C. C. & E. Childs, jr., 80 Vesey street, 4th July, 1839. 8vo, pp. 7, and lithographic view of tomb, from which our engraving is copied.

[1] A. J. Spooner, Esq., in "Once-a-Week," Feb. 6, 1864.

THE TOMB OF THE MARTYRS.

(As restored by Mr ROMAINE, in 1839.)

Page 376.

descended, and then stood entranced and nearly paralyzed by a sense of awe which has not left me to this day. Standing, chiefly in perpendicular positions, around the vault, were thirteen immense coffins, each having thereon the name of one of the thirteen original States. I could see enough through interstices to show me that these were filled with bones, and I knew I was standing in the midst of that noble army of martyrs whose blood had gone up as a holy and acceptable sacrifice on the altar of American freedom. I have felt the thrill of other altar-places; have felt deep emotions at the grave, and sublime sensations upon the mountain-tops; but I am very sure that on no other occasion did I ever feel my whole nature so elevated to a sense of majestic reverence, as in the presence of that sublime and silent company. Resting on one or two of the coffins which were laid horizontally, was one smaller coffin of the ordinary size of one individual. This was vacant, but had upon its lid the name of 'Benjamin Romaine,' as if it was intended that some person of this name yet walking among the liliputians of the earth should, in his dust, be placed here to lie among these giant patriots, secure, if with them forgotten upon earth, to rise with them hereafter."

And there, in that vault, and in the coffin so long and so reverently prepared, was buried Benjamin Romaine (at his death in 1844, at the advanced age of eighty-two)—fit sentinel of that group, who performed deeds of heroic sacrifice, the worthiest which pen, pencil, and monument can celebrate.[1]

---

[1] Benjamin Romaine (or, as the name should be more properly spelled, *Romeyn*) was of French extraction, and a native of New York. At the commencement of the Revolutionary War he was a mere lad at school, preparing for admission to King's (now Columbia) College, but upon the occupation of the city by the British army, his father's family retired to the neighborhood of Hackensack, in New Jersey. His studies being thus interrupted by "war's rude alarms," he enlisted in the American army, and served several terms of six months each, finally attaining the rank of sergeant, and was engaged in several hotly-contested skirmishes. He was finally taken prisoner, and immured in two of the prisons in New York; from which, after a confinement of seven weeks, he was released, by exchange, in October, 1781. After the close of the war, his family having suffered considerably in the loss of their property, young Romaine opened a school for both sexes in New York, where he soon established a very good reputation as a teacher—numbering among his pupils Washington Irving, Professor John Anthon, the late Judge J. T. Irving, and others since distinguished in the literary professional, and social circles of the city.

Two years before his death, however, in the year 1842, the citizens of Brooklyn, through a highly respectable committee, petitioned the Legislature for leave to remove the bones, for the purpose of ap-

---

In the spring of 1797, being then about thirty years of age, the condition of his health obliged him to relinquish teaching; and as he had, by his economical habits and natural thrift, accumulated a competency sufficiently ample for his wants, he never afterwards engaged in any regular business.

In politics he was a Democrat, and in 1808 was Grand Sachem of Tammany Society. He also held the office of Comptroller during the mayoralty of De Witt Clinton, to which he formed an antipathy which made him a violent "bucktail," as the members of the anti-Clinton wing of "Old Tammany" were called. In the War of 1812 he was a strong Jeffersonian, and sustained the vigorous prosecution of the war, during which he held an important departmental position, with the rank of major.

During the latter portion of his life, Mr. Romaine employed himself in the care of his extensive property in several parts of the city, and in literary pursuits. His reading was chiefly confined to history, politics, and the science of government, and his pen was constantly employed in contributing to the press (under the *nom de plume* of "An Old Citizen") articles upon the passing and important topics of the day. In 1832 he published a pamphlet (State Sovereignty, and a Certain Dissolution of the Union. By Benjamin Romaine, An Old Citizen of New York. To the Hon. John C. Calhoun, now Vice-President of the United States. New York: J. Kennaday, Printer, No. 2 Dey street. 1832. 8vo, 54 pages.), in which he vigorously assailed the doctrine of State rights as then advocated by the nullifiers of South Carolina, and with a prescience which, in the light of recent events, seems most remarkable, foretells the consequences of such principles.

In literary, as well as personal character, Mr. Romaine may be said to have been distinguished, not so much for any personal range or brilliancy of intellect, as for soundness of understanding, elevated views, and high moral integrity. Although Mr. Romaine was not a professing Christian, but rather a moralist; and although "Pope's Essay on Man" (which he knew by heart) was probably a greater favorite with him than the Bible, yet he respected and valued the ordinances of Christianity, and, in his own life, was a bright exemplar of all its virtues. In his personal habits he was remarkably cleanly and orderly; liquor and tobacco, in any form, were very obnoxious to him, and his manner of life was extremely simple, frugal, and temperate. Possessing great pride of character, with very little vanity, he passed through life unostentatiously, but with comfort to himself, and with the respect of others. His personal appearance has been described as tall, slim, and commanding in figure, with great vigor of body and motion, and with a countenance displaying seriousness mingled with kindness and affability.

Indeed, this kindness of heart was always manifested, except when he came in contact with Englishmen. Then his prejudices quickly and unmistakably manifested themselves, and amusing stories are yet related of the rough manner in which he would absolutely refuse to treat with any Englishman who applied to become a tenant of any of his houses. In fact, the recollection of what he had suffered, and of the horrors which he had witnessed in the British prisons, filled his mind with an intense hatred of British rule, and of anything pertaining to it, which he could never banish from his mind.

It was this, also, in great measure, which influenced him in 1839, when the lot in Brooklyn, on which the bones of the martyrs of the prison-ships had been buried, were

propriate sepulture. Against this Mr. Romaine remonstrated. He said: "I have guarded these sacred remains with a reverence which, perhaps, at this day, all may not appreciate or feel, for more than thirty years. They are now in their right place, near the Wallabout, and adjoining the Navy-yard. They are my property. I have expended more than nine hundred dollars in and about their protection and preservation. *I commend them to the protection of the General Government. I bequeath them to my country.* This concern is very sacred to me. It lies near my heart. I suffered with those whose bones I venerate. I fought beside them—I bled with them." In consequence of this remonstrance, nothing was then done. But after the old man had passed away, in the year 1845, public attention was again called to the neglected condition of these remains, and the matter was also brought to the attention of the National Congress, by a report introduced by the Military Committee to the House of Representatives,[1] recommending an appropriation of $20,000 for the purpose of affording a secure tomb and fitting monument to the Martyrs. This also failed of its object, and the matter slept for ten years. At the expiration of that period, in 1855, a large and influential meeting of the citizens of Brooklyn was held, at which it was resolved, "that the time has arrived when the cities of New York and Brooklyn cannot, without criminality, longer delay the necessary efforts for rearing the monument to the martyrs of the prison-ships," and an organization was formed for the purpose, entitled "The Martyrs' Monument Association," in which each Senatorial District in the State of New York, and each State and Territory, is represented. They set to work with commendable activity, selecting a fitting site—the lofty summit of Fort Greene—secured plans for the proposed monument, agitated the subject publicly and privately, solicited donations, etc., and "yet there is no

---

sold for taxes, to become its purchaser; and it was this which, through all his subsequent life, made him cling with jealous care to the custody of these remains—constantly protesting against any disposal being made of them, *except* by the *General Government,* which he rightly considered as the *only proper custodian.* It has been a sincere pleasure thus to collect these facts concerning this patriotic and useful citizen; and we can only regret that the diligent inquiries which we have made have resulted in eliciting so little information concerning him.

[1] This report, drawn up by the Hon. Henry C. Murphy, of Brooklyn, forms Document No. 177, Rep. of Ho. of Reps., 1844–45.

monument—no stone bearing the record of their patriotic devotion to principle, and their more than heroic death!"

We understand that the "Martyrs' Association" still entertain hopes of ultimately securing their object, and that they have made progress in their endeavors; that an appropriate lot of land on Fort Greene, or Washington Park, has been granted by the Common Council of the city of Brooklyn; and, surely, we may hope that this attempt to honor the memory of the dead heroes will not prove abortive, as its predecessors have done.

To the citizens of New York and Brooklyn are peculiarly appropriate those solemn words of an ancient patriot, under circumstances not unlike our own—"Oh, my countrymen! these dead bodies ask no monument. Their monument arose when they fell, and as long as liberty shall have defenders, their names will be imperishable. But, oh, my countrymen, it is *we* who need a monument to their honor; *we*, who survive, not having yet proved that we, too, could die for our country and be immortal. *We* need a monument, that the widows and children of the dead, and the whole country, and the shades of the departed, and all future ages, may see and know that we honor patriotism, and virtue, and liberty, and truth; for next to performing a great deed, and achieving a noble character, is to honor such characters and deeds!"

THE PRESENT CONDITION OF THE "MARTYRS' MONUMENT."

CHAPTER X.

FROM THE CLOSE OF THE REVOLUTION TO THE WAR OF 1819.

For the first few years succeeding the war, but little of interest can be gleaned concerning the progress of the town, or the doings of its inhabitants. They doubtless found plenty of work for their hands to do in repairing the ravages which their property had suffered during a seven years' hostile occupation. Yet the spirit of improvement was astir; and, in 1785, the staid old Dutchmen who worshipped in the ancient edifice in the middle of the road at "Brooklyn Church," as well as the few but loyal Episcopalians, who had set up their Ebenezer in John Middagh's barn, on the corner of present Henry and Poplar streets, found a denominational rival in the little handful of stout-hearted "Independents," who erected a small place of worship on the ground now occupied by "St. Anne's Buildings," on Fulton street.[1] In this year, also, were the beginnings of the "Brooklyn Fire Department."[2] In the fall of 1786, advertisements of races and fox-hunts on Ascot Heath, Flatbush, and a fox-chase "from Mr. Dawson's, at Brooklyn Ferry," give evidence that there was still in the county a lingering taste for the gay sports with which, in days bygone, the British officers had so often whiled away their hours of leisure. The erection of that excellent institution, "Erasmus Hall," at Flatbush, in 1787, proved that the higher interests of education and morality were properly appreciated by the inhabitants of Kings County; while the celebration of the Fourth of July, in the same year, by a number of gentlemen, at Dawson's, in Brooklyn—with toasts and the firing of rockets—may be accepted as gratifying testimony to their patriotism.

---

[1] See Hist. of Churches, in second volume.

[2] The history of the Department will be found in the second volume.

1788. On the 7th of March of this year, Brooklyn was recognized as a town under the State Government.

1794. It may amuse our readers to learn, that at a regular town-meeting, held in April of this year, it was "*Resolved*, That the Supervisors raise the sum of £19, 13s., 6d., which money has been expended for the purpose of building a *cage and stocks*."[1]

1795. In the summer of this year the "New," or Catherine street ferry, was established by William Furman and Theodosius Hunt—the former of whom was interested in a rope-walk, the head of which was in Main street, near the ferry, and extended northeasterly, over the shoals and water.

1796. In the library of the Long Island Historical Society is a curious little duodecimo volume, entitled "The New York and Brooklyn Directory and Register, for the Year 1796," printed at New York, "by John Buel, corner of Water street and Fly Market, and John Bull, 115 Cherry st." This work, compiled by John Low, comprises within the last three pages a "*Brooklyn Directory, containing the names of the inhabitants, alphabetically arranged, never before published*," for that year, which our readers will find reproduced in Appendix, No. 10.[2] It is, apparently, the work of a canvasser, who went *up* the "Old Road" (Fulton street) and *down* "New Ferry street" (Main street), gathering the names only of those persons living on or between the two streets, and does not seem to contain the names of any persons who lived further back from the ferry. It possesses peculiar interest, from the fact that it antedates, by twenty-five years, the earliest village directory—that published by Alden Spooner, in 1822.

The sum of £49 4s. was this year raised by subscription for purchasing "a suitable bell for the use of the town of Brooklyn." This bell was hung in a small cupola on the top of Buckbee's Hay Scales, which stood on the southerly side of Fulton street, close by "Buckbee's Alley."[3]

---

[1] Town Records. See, also, page 387.

[2] This Directory, with notes by the author of this history, was published in the Brooklyn Corporation Manual for 1864, pp. 139–143.

[3] Now "Poplar Place," a crooked alley running from Poplar to Fulton street, between Henry and Hicks streets. Its original name was derived from one Buckbee, who, with his son Palmer, kept a small grocery on the corner of the alley and Fulton street.

In the spring of this year, the Rev. Dr. John Henry Livingston, a distinguished scholar and member of the Reformed Dutch Church, established a theological school at the then village of Bedford, now embraced with the limits of Brooklyn. A Mr. Freligh, the first student licensed in Kings County, studied under him at the Cowenhoven house, west of Mr. Brevoort's present dwelling, and boarded around among the neighbors. The school, however, was broken up in 1797.

1798. Rev. Dr. Jedediah Morse's "American Gazetteer," issued this year, thus briefly disposes of Brooklyn: "A township in Kings County, N. Y., on the west end of Long Island, having 1,603 inhabitants, and 224 are electors, by the State census of 1796. There are a Presbyterian church, a Dutch Reformed church, a powder magazine, and some elegant houses, which lie chiefly on one street. East River, near a mile broad, separates the town from New York."

VIEW OF BROOKLYN IN 1798—(As seen from the North).

We take pleasure in presenting our readers with an interesting view, never before published, of the village of Brooklyn, as seen from a northerly point on New York Island, copied from a remarkably careful and evidently accurate sketch of New York City and Bay,

---

The family was a very disreputable one—the old man finally dying of wounds received in attempting, with his son Palmer, to commit a burglary upon the house of James W. Smith. Palmer, a giant in stature, and possessing great courage and strength, was the terror of the slender police force of the village at that day, and many anecdotes are told of his exploits. He was subsequently hung, in San Francisco, by the Vigilance Committee.

made by Mons. Jules Févret de Saint Memin, a French artist, of some celebrity, who resided in this country between the years 1796 and 1810.

1799. On the 6th of June, 1799, the "*Courier and New York and Long Island Advertiser,*" the second paper ever published on Long Island, was commenced at Brooklyn, by Thomas Kirk. A stray "No. 87, vol. 2," dated Feb. 25, 1801, has come to our notice. It is a small, dingy sheet, purporting to be published "every Wednesday morning," and possesses little or nothing of interest to us of the present day. Its columns are mostly filled with New York advertisements. A few Brooklynites, however, seem to have possessed a spirit of enterprise, inasmuch as John Van Brunt advertises his house, situated about one hundred yards from the old (Fulton) ferry, as being an excellent stand for a tavern. John Harmer, painter and glazier, advertises his patent floor-cloth manufactory; William Carpenter, his tobacco and snuff factory; Furman and Sands, their store at New (Catherine street) Ferry; and Derick Amerman, his groceries.

During this year, land, not exceeding an acre, was appropriated by the town for a public burial-place; but the records bear evidence that, in 1800, the object had not been effected.

1800. In an old scrap-book of this date, in the possession of the family of General JEREMIAH JOHNSON, is preserved what may properly be called *the first written history* of Brooklyn. It consists of newspaper slips, undoubtedly cut from the columns of Thomas Kirk's paper, "The Long Island Courier," to which are added numerous manuscript corrections, notes, and even whole pages of new matter, in the well-known handwriting of General Johnson, to whom we probably do not err in attributing their authorship. That this careful arrangement and revision of these papers was made with a view to their republication in pamphlet form, is apparent from the fact that they are preceded by a title-page in MS., "*A Topographical View of the Township of Brooklyn in Kings County, State of New York* (motto), *Brooklyn: Printed by Thomas Kirk.* 1800." The series consist of about six papers, which form an interesting, though diffuse, *pot-pourri* of historical facts, speculations, etc., from which we select a few samples for the amusement of our readers.

"Kings County," says the author, "contains 4,495 inhabitants, including 621 electors: 930 of these are free white males, of ten and upwards; 700 free white male under that age; 1,449 free white females; 1,432 slaves, and 46 free persons not enumerated. The inhabitants are chiefly of Dutch extraction. Some are attached to their old prejudices; but, within a few years past, liberality and a taste for the fine arts have made considerable progress. The slaves are treated well, but the opinion relative to their freedom is yet too much influenced by pecuniary motives. It would certainly redound to the honor of humanity, could that blessing be effected here."

After defining the boundaries of the township of Brooklyn, and enumerating the different settlements therein,[1] he mentions "OLYMPIA," a tract of land which, he says, "was surveyed and laid out in streets as long ago as the year 1787, and then intended as a city; its progress has been arranged according to the plan, and begins to

---

[1] The town of Brooklyn at this period—and, indeed, until the incorporation of the *village* of Brooklyn—was divided, for ecclesiastical, school, and other purposes, into *seven* districts, retaining the same names which had descended from the "neighborhoods" or hamlets of the earlier settlements, viz.: "The Ferry" (*het Veer*); the "Red Hook" (*de Roede Hoek*); "Brooklyn" (*Breuckelen*); "Bedford" (*Betfort*); "Gowanus" (*Goujanes* or *Gouanes*); "Cripplebush" (*het Creupelbosch*); and "the Wallabout" (*de Waal-boght*). (1) *The Ferry District* included all the lands and dwellings between the Wallabout Mill-pond and Joralemon street; and, afterwards, along Red Hook lane to District street, crossing from Brouwer's (afterwards Freeke's) mill-pond to Red Hook lane; comprising the first five of the subsequent city wards. (2) *The Red Hook District* included the lands lying west of District street, and a line extending from the head of Brouwer's mill-pond to the corner of Red Hook road, and including Red Hook Point. (3) *Brooklyn District* comprised the land south of the Ferry to Flatbush, between the estate formerly of N. R. Cowenhoven and the Post Road. (4) *Bedford District* included all the land east of Brooklyn line, including the north farm of Rem Lefferts, to the third division of woodlands, and along the line of Lot. No. 1 to the town of Bushwick. (5) *The Gowanus District* comprised that part of Brooklyn lying west of Brooklyn, Bedford, and Red Hook, and bounded southerly by the town of Flatbush and westerly by the town of New Utrecht. (6) *Cripplebush District* was bounded southerly by Bedford, easterly by the town of Bushwick, northerly by Wallabout Creek, and westerly by the easterly line of Garret Nostrand. (7) *The Wallabout District* was bounded westerly by the District of Brooklyn, easterly and southerly by Bedford, easterly and northerly by the town of Bushwick, and southwesterly, northerly, and westerly by the Wallabout Bay and the Ferry District.*

---

* Gowanus, Red Hook, The Ferry, and Wallabout Districts are bounded northerly by the North and East rivers.

have the appearance of regularity. It lies to the east of Brooklyn Ferry, and is bounded by the Wallabout and the East River."

This was evidently the Comfort and Joshua Sands estate, purchased by them, in 1784, from the Commissioners of Forfeiture—it having been the property of John Rapalje, the loyalist.[1] The survey, to which reference is made, was by Casimer Theodore Goerck, in 1788, and a copy of his map is still in existence.[2] John Jackson's Remsen estate was also included within the bounds of the prospective village. Our author then proceeds to say that

"The holders of this tract (*i. e.*, Messrs. Sands and John Jackson—Ed.) appear to be desirous to encourage the undertaking, by their willingness to dispose of lots at a reasonable price. * * * This village, contemplatively a city, comprehends at present an extent of land within the following boundaries, viz.: Beginning at two rocks called 'The Brothers,' situated in the East River, from those to Brooklyn Square,[3] through James street to Main and Road streets, to the seat formerly the residence of the Rev. Mr. Johnson, now Red Hook road,[4] from thence across the Wallabout, then to the East River to the place of beginning. This tract of land is better situated than any other near New York for the counterpart of that city. It is certain that, on the southern side of Brooklyn Ferry ("the Heights."—Ed.), the hills are so high, and such astonishing exertion is necessary to remove them, that Brooklyn Ferry can never extend any great distance upon that quarter, and all improvements must necessarily be made in Olympia. Add to this the want of disposition in the proprietors of that soil to sell any part of it.[5] And, moreover, Olympia and Brooklyn Ferry must always continue to increase in a ratio with New York, unless some exertion of their own is made. But as that city can never extend further southward, but is continually progressing a contrary way, it is evident, if the former position be true, that Olympia must receive the whole progress which otherwise would be given to Brooklyn Ferry.

"Olympia is extremely well calculated for a city, on a point of land

---

1 *Ante*, pp. 78, 79, 312.

2 *Ante*, p. 79, note 2.

3 The neighborhood of the old Dutch village of Breuckelen, *ante*, pp. 45, 96, etc.

4 Corner of Fulton avenue and Red Hook lane.

5 The owners of these lands on the Heights were mostly of old Dutch stock, the Hicks, Middaghs, Joralemon, Patchen, Bamper, Golden, and others, and were averse to change or improvement. The Hicks and Middagh estates were the first to follow the example of their Yankee neighbors on the other side of the Old Ferry road.

which presents its front up the East River, surrounded almost with water; the conveniences are almost manifest. A considerable country in the rear affords the easy attainment of produce. A pure and salubrious atmosphere, excellent spring water, and good society, are among a host of other desirable advantages. As regards health in particular, it is situated on the natural soil—no noxious vapors, generated by exhalations, from dock-logs, water, and filth sunk a century under its foundation, are raised here. Sand and clay for building are in the village. Stone is brought from a short distance. Timber, lath, and boards are to be had on the spot. In fact, almost every article for building is afforded here as cheap as in New York. Could the inhabitants once divest themselves of their dependence upon that city, and with unanimous consent resolve that their own village should prosper, there requires no supernatural agent to inform us of the consequence.

"Want of good title has been alleged by some against building here; but it is ascertained, and from undoubted authority, that none was ever clearer or less entangled, and that reports here circulated what truth is obliged to deny.[1]

"The principal streets in this village are sixty feet, but the cross-streets are not so wide. They are not yet paved, though a vast number of pebbles may be had here. Latterly, it appears to have had the appearance of a regular town. Edifices are erecting, and other improvements constantly making. When we observe the elevated situations, the agreeable prospects, the salubrity of the atmosphere, and the contiguousness to New York, with many other interesting advantages, it may claim, perhaps, more consideration than any part of the township."

The following remarks cannot fail to give comfort to the would-be *bridge-builders* of the present day:

"It has been suggested that a bridge should be constructed from this village across the East River to New York. This idea has been treated as chimerical, from the magnitude of the design; but whosoever takes it into their serious consideration, will find more weight in the practicability of the scheme than at first view is imagined. This would be the means of raising the value of the lands on the east side of the river. It has been

[1] The allusion to doubtful titles evidently refers to the Rapalje estate.

observed that every objection to the building of this bridge could be refuted, and that it only wanted a combination of opinion to favor the attempt. A plan has already been laid down on paper, and a gentleman of acknowledged abilities and good sense has observed that he would engage to erect it in two years' time."

"It has also been observed that the Wallabout would form an excellent navy-yard.[1] Should such a plan be carried into execution, it would considerably increase the importance of this place. As a retreat from New York in summer, Olympia would furnish many superior excellences over other places—such as its vicinity to that city, the opportunity of freighting and unloading vessels during the period of fever, the sale of goods to the yeomanry who are fearful of entering the city, etc. (Here a mutilation breaks the narrative.) * * * often the resort of the inhabitants of New York in their pedestrian excursions. This village has no peculiar privileges of its own. Joined with the several townships, it supports two ministers." * * *

In speaking of *manufactures*, he says: "With respect to 'Olympia' and Brooklyn Ferry, which are the principal villages in this township, they produce scarcely any thing of the manufacturing kind but what is useful in common life. There are eight grist-mills in this township, which grind by means of the tide of the East River. Some of these mills are employed to grind grain for exportation, others to supply the neighboring farmers. Cables, cordage, lines, and twine are spun and laid to considerable profit. A new patent floor-cloth manufactory is about to be introduced. * * * Brewing and distilling, with a capital, might be carried on to advantage. Nails are afforded very cheap. Chair-making, too, answers extremely well. Besides these, there are all the different mechanical trades peculiar to settlements of this kind."

In regard to *literature* and *education*, he says, "There are three schools in this township—one at Bedford, one at Gowanus, and the other at the Brooklyn Ferry. This last claims the preference, having been established a considerable length of time, under the super-

---

[1] It is probable that negotiations were already in progress for the realization of this plan, as the purchase, by the United States Government, of a portion of the Wallabout was concluded in the following year.

intendence of trustees. There are about sixty scholars, who are taught the common rudiments of education, with English grammar, geography, and astronomy. Two preceptors have the immediate direction. A beautiful eminence to the east of Brooklyn Ferry will afford an eligible situation for an academy." Thomas Kirk's newspaper, *The Courier*, then in its first year, is favorably mentioned, and the fact is furthermore stated that there are "no libraries, or places for the sale of books in the town." "There is but one society, properly speaking, in this township, and that is the Masonic. This, which is the first and only Lodge in the county, was erected in 1798 in Olympia, at the corner of Main and James streets."

A brief outline of some of the main points of early Brooklyn history is given, and reference is made to two volunteer companies, "whose uniform is as handsome as their conduct is patriotic."[1] A powder-house and arsenal are said to be "already established." In the Appendix to this compilation, General Johnson strongly advocates the establishment of a *village corporation*, concerning the advantages of which he discusses fully and eloquently, considering it "now proper time that a corporation for Olympia should commence its operations, and particular appropriations be made for extensive market-places, a square for an academy, another for a promenade, others for public buildings of different sorts, as churches, court-houses, alms-houses, etc., and not to sleep on an ideal prospect." And long before the venerable author was gathered to his fathers, he had seen the more than realization of his "ideal prospect."

The spirit of speculation, as will be seen from the above glowing account of "Olympia," had begun to agitate the minds of the Brooklynites, and it received no inconsiderable impulse, in 1801, from Mr. John Jackson's sale to the United States (through Francis Child, a middle-man) of forty acres of the Wallabout, including the old mill-pond, for the handsome sum of $40,000. Shortly after this, a portion of the estate of Comfort Sands, contiguous to the lands of Mr.

[1] These were the "Washington Fusileers," a very handsome uniformed company, commanded by Mr. William Furman, father of the historian of Brooklyn, Hon. Gabriel Furman, and the "Republican Rifles," dressed in green hunting-shirts and pants, and commanded by Captain Burdett Stryker. These latter, from the color of their uniform, were sometimes called "The Katydids."

Jackson, was sold, and Jackson street was opened to Jackson Ferry. About this time, also, the suppression of the rebellion in Ireland caused the emigration to this country of many persons who had been engaged in that unfortunate struggle, some of whom came to New York. A portion of these refugees, who had a little property, were induced to purchase lots on Jackson's land, at a spot to which—cleverly appealing to their patriotism—he had given the name of "Vinegar Hill,"[1] in honor of the scene of the last conflict of that memorable rebellion.

On the 2d of April, 1801, the village of Brooklyn was incorporated as a fire district, by an act entitled "An Act to vest certain powers in the Freeholders and Inhabitants of part of the Town of Brooklyn, in Kings County," etc., the 6th section of which is of much importance, inasmuch as it authenticated the copies of Old Road Records, then recently transferred from the County Clerk's office to the office of the Clerk of the Town.

> "And be it further enacted, that all copies and abstracts of records in the said County relative to roads and highways in the said Town of Brooklyn, examined and certified to be true copies by the Clerk of the said County, and registered by the Clerk of the said Town, in a book to be provided by him for that purpose, shall be deemed to be the records of the said Town, and of the same validity as the original records remaining in the office of the Clerk of the said County."[2]

Crime and vice seem to have made fresh and increasing inroads upon the primitive simplicity of this old Dutch town; for, in 1802, the town took measures to determine the location and ascertain the expense of erecting a "cage, or watch-house." Whether this was a rebuilding of the old one, or an additional one, is somewhat uncertain.[3] At the same meeting, the foremen of the fire-engines were

---

[1] Near the Navy Yard.

[2] A similar act had been passed, Feb. 9th, 1798, whereby, in consideration of the loss or destruction of the original records of the Town, during the Revolutionary War, such copies and abstracts of the County Records as related to the Town of Brooklyn, were considered as records of the said Town.

[3] This was a movable structure, made of joists strongly put together, and capable of holding four persons, one only of whom could sit down. When it was deemed desira-

authorized to establish and regulate a "Guard, or Night-Watch within the Fire District, by and with the consent of the majority of the inhabitants."

Previous to this time the stages from Flushing came to Brooklyn, *via* Jamaica, a distance of seventeen miles, and the people of Newtown and Bushwick came here by the roundabout way of Bedford. About 1802, a Mr. William Prince, of Flushing, procured the incorporation of the "Flushing Bridge and Road Company," by which route the distance from that town to Brooklyn was shortened about four miles. Seeing the practicability of lessening the distance to Brooklyn Ferry about three miles more, Mr. Prince, in the year 1805, procured the incorporation of the "Wallabout and Brooklyn Toll-bridge Company." The road was laid out from the Cripplebush road to the easterly side of the Wallabout Mill-Pond, over which a bridge was built to Sands street in Brooklyn.[1] Through Mr. Prince's exertions, therefore, the travelling distance between the two towns was lessened by seven miles; an improvement, in those days of hard roads and rough travelling, fully entitling him to the gratitude of Kings and Queens Counties, and undoubtedly contributing in many respects to the material interests of Brooklyn.

1806. In the columns of *The Long Island Weekly Intelligencer*, published by Robinson & Little, Booksellers and Stationers, corner of Old Ferry and Front streets, October 9th, vol. i., No. 15, we find the advertisements of Thomas Langdon, dealer in boots and shoes; Henry Hewlet, general merchandise, near the Old Ferry; John Cole,

---

ble, for the "moral effect" of the thing, to expose the prisoners, the cage was moved to the corner of Fulton and Front street, where it undoubtedly attracted the attention of those passing to and from the ferries, very much as the bulletin-board of the "*Union*" office now does. Its usual stand, however, was on the shore (now Water street) near Birbeck's foundry, and its most frequent use latterly—for it existed within the recollection of some now living—was to confine Sabbath-breaking sailors. It was finally tumbled off into the river.

[1] Act of Incorporation dated April 6, 1805. The following gentlemen composed the first Board of Directors, viz.: John Jackson, *Pres.;* John Hicks, *Treas.;* Peter Sharpe, *Sec.;* Jeremiah Johnson, William Prince, Richard M. Malcolm, and Samuel Sackett. The bridge was originally designed to be 1,400 feet long and 24 feet broad; but Furman says, in 1823 (MSS., iii. 41), that it was only 768 feet in length, the remaining part being made into solid causeway. The causeway at the easterly end of the bridge was about 340 feet long; in addition to which there was another at the westerly end, of considerable length.

coach-maker; Doctor Lowe "at the Rev. Mr. Lowe's, corner of Red Hook Road" (present corner of Fulton street and Red Hook Lane); and William Cornwall, merchant tailor, corner of Front and Main streets, near the New Ferry. Five apprentices are wanted at Amos Cheney's Ship-yard; William Milward, Block and Pump Maker, is located "at the Yellow Store, on Joshua Sands', Esq., wharf, between the Old and New Ferries;" while Benjamin Hilton sells China, glass, and earthenware, "at New York prices," in Old Ferry street, in the house formerly occupied by Mr. Derick Amerman. Land and property is advertised by Henry Stanton, corner of Front and Main streets; by Robert M. Malcolm, corner of Washington and Sands streets, and by Thomas Lalliet. Joel Bunce, Postmaster, advertises the address of 53 letters uncalled for in his office.

In the next issue of the Intelligencer (October 16th), we learn that a fire occurred on the Saturday previous, in a stable owned by Mr. Campbell, and used by John Wilson, baker—one horse was burned to death, and another injured. John Doughty returns thanks to his friends and neighbors for their successful exertions in saving his premises. The inhabitants "felt themselves obligated to the members of the New York *floating* engine," for their efforts in bringing over their machine, although the fire was subdued before their arrival.

"We have been requested," says the editor, "to suggest the propriety of each family placing lights in the front of their houses, not having the advantage of lamps, as great inconvenience and loss of time arises from the neglect, particularly on dark nights."

William Vander Veen, Apothecary, "takes the liberty of mentioning that he has been regularly educated to the Surgery and Apothecary business, in Amsterdam." His drug store was in the house of Dr. George A. Clussman, who, together with Dr. Samuel Osborn, guaranteed that they would "so far attend to Mr. Vander Veen's preparations of Medicines, that purchasers may rest satisfied that they will obtain genuine articles," etc. Possibly, the Brooklynites of the present day would not object to a similar assurance from their medical advisers.

Also the advertisements of Dr. Charles Ball, in Mr. Cooper's old house, near the junction of Old and New Ferry streets, and of

Thomas Crouchley, boat-builder, adjacent to Barbarin's Lumber Yard, between Old and New Ferries.

In the issue of October 23d, we notice the advertisement of Augustine Elliott, "Taylor and Lady's Dress-Maker," in old Ferry street; and five verses of *original poetry*, "after the manner of Burns," extolling the beauties of, and the splendid prospect to be obtained from "Brooklyn, or McKenzie's One Tree Hill." This hill was located on Pearl street, between York and Prospect streets. All around that portion of Brooklyn, north of Washington and west of Sands street, was a series of hills, some of which were covered with grass and had a few trees; others were of sandy soil, with here and there a slight covering of grass, and with some buttonwood trees, while others still were nothing but sand-hills. McKenzie's Hill, the most noted of these, was a fine green elevation, crowned with a single gigantic buttonwood tree, and afforded a beautiful view of the city and harbor of New York. It was marked, as was many of the surrounding hills, by the traces of intrenchments and fortifications thrown up by the British during their occupation of the Island; and was finally levelled about 1807–9, in order to fill in the wharves built out over the flats in the river, to the northwest of Main street. Another rather noted hill was located some distance farther west (bounded by Front, Adams, and Bridge streets, near the water-line of the East River), and was a barren, sandy eminence, on which every pebble or stone seemed to have been calcined by some extreme heat, while three or four feet below the surface were found regular layers of ashes, mingled with bits of charcoal, and vitrified stones and sand.[1] All of these hills have now disappeared—that known as "Fort Greene, or Washington Park," being the only one which remains. On the lower slope of the hills, near the East River, there stood, at the time of which we write, the celebrated "Tulip Tree," well known to the oldest Brooklynites. It was an immense Magnolia, which, when in blossom, perfumed the air for a great distance around; and was a favorite resort for pic-nic parties from New York, who, on warm afternoons, were wont to cross

---

[1] There was at this time, also, another hill on the site of present Gothic Hall, in Adams street, between Concord and Nassau, which was used as a negro burying-ground.

the river in row-boats, build their little fires under its generous shade, when the women would boil the kettle and make tea—and so, after a pleasant repast, would return home about sunset. The people of Brooklyn used frequently to meet and join with them in these out-of-door tea-parties, and the oldest inhabitants even now describe with zest their enjoyment of those simple pleasures. Then, in addition, there was the delight of the leisurely homeward sail or row across the river, on a calm summer's eve, untroubled by fear of accident, for, in those days, there was but little shipping in the river, and steamboats had not been heard of. Sometimes, after an unusually warm day, the clouds rolling up in the west, about sunset, presented a most gorgeous appearance, and the voyagers would be lost in admiration of the scene, until, admonished by a warning flash of lightning and the deep-toned but distant thunder, to hasten their progress, if they would avoid the coming shower.

So, for many years, it was the trysting-place of Youth, and the delight of Old Age—but, one still summer Sabbath morning, the good people of Brooklyn were startled by an alarm of fire. After some time, it was discovered that the old Tulip Tree was burning; being hollow from age, it was supposed to have been accidentally set on fire by some fishermen who had made a fire within the cavity to cook their breakfast. While it was burning, the people were afraid to go near it, on account of its proximity to a powder magazine. In spite of this accident, however, it continued to put out leaves for several years longer, and when, at last, it died, its loss was much deplored by the people of New York and Brooklyn, many of whom continued to visit it until its total destruction.

1808, April 13th. On this day the corner-stone of a monument to the Martyrs of the Prison Ships was laid, as described on pages 365 and 366.

In August following, the town was one day startled by the explosion of Sands' Powder Mill, which was situated in the vicinity of the present Jay and Tillary streets. Fortunately, it happened between twelve and one o'clock in the day, when the people were all at dinner,—consequently no lives were lost, although forty kegs of powder were lost. The recently erected stone church, belonging to St. Anne's Episcopal Society, was considerably damaged, its walls being somewhat weakened, and the windows badly broken. An adjoining rope-walk was also levelled to the ground.

This year the sum of $1500 was appropriated by the town for the erection of a new "Poor-house."

1809, March 17th. "The Brooklyn, Jamaica, and Flatbush Turnpike Company," was incorporated. Its first officers were William Furman, *Pres.;* John Lefferts, *Sec.;* James Foster, *Treas.* The Company, during the year, paved Main and Old Ferry streets in the village.

In June of this year, the *Long Island Star* was established by Thomas Kirk. The number for June 22, contains the following advertisements: Joseph B. Pirsson (removed from New York), circulating library, in Main st., two doors from Sands street; Joel Bunce, corner of Old Ferry and Front streets, hardware and groceries; Joseph Herbert, boot and shoe maker, in Sands street, between Main street and the Bridge; and George Hamilton, who kept a Select School, where "students were taught to make their own pens."

The number for June 29th, contains proposals for constructing a turnpike road from Brooklyn to Jamaica—and an advertisement for two *Postriders,* "immediately, at this office;" also Hot and Cold Baths by one Peter Van Rooten.

September 7th, John Gibbons announces that he has opened an Academy for both sexes, at the place lately occupied by Geo. Hamilton, where the various branches of education are "taught on unerring principles." Also "Mrs. Gibbons will instruct little Girls in Spelling, Reading, Sewing, and Marking." An evening school for young men is proposed, and "N. B. Good Pronunciation:"

During the months of July, August, and September, of this year, the yellow fever prevailed in Brooklyn, which gave rise to a long and wordy newspaper war between the physicians of the village, Drs. Osborn, Ball, and Wendell. On the 27th of September, De Witt Clinton, Mayor of New York, issued a Proclamation, announcing the disappearance of the disease, and the resumption of the ordinary intercourse between that city and Brooklyn, which had been interdicted by his previous proclamation of 2d of August. Twenty-eight persons had died of the fever in Brooklyn, all of whom were under twenty-eight years of age. It was at first thought that the contagion was brought in the ship Concordia, Captain Coffin, on board of which vessel the first case and death occurred. But in the long and very able report of Dr. Rogers, the Health officer of the Board of Health of New York, which was published in December, after the subsidence of the disease, the epidemic in Brooklyn was clearly traced to purely local causes.[1]

1810. October 11, about 10 o'clock, P. M., a fire broke out in a building occupied by a Mr. Lacour, for the manufacture of crucibles, and extended to some stores belonging to Joshua Sands, between Old and New Ferries, which were filled with cotton and hides. A *floating* engine was brought into service at this fire.

Brooklyn, at this time, was well supplied with private schools. One Whitney kept school opposite the Post-office; there was also the Brooklyn Select Academy, taught by Mr. John Mabon, and having as trustees, Messrs. Joshua Sands, S. Sackett, and H. I. Feltus. Platt Kennedy's scholars were advertised to hold an exhibition on Christmas Eve, at the Inn of Benjamin Smith, a large stone building on the east side of the road, opposite the old "Corporation House."

Recreation and refreshments were provided for the public, by the proprietor of "Columbian Garden," and Mr. Green at the "Military Garden."[2]

The industrial interests of Brooklyn were at this time represented by I. Harmer's Floor Cloth Manufactory, Chricton's Cotton Good Manufactory, employing eight to ten looms, and three or four extensive ropewalks furnishing work to over one hundred persons.

The Long Island Star, of February 14th, 1811, contains a petition to the Legislature for the establishment of a *Bank* in Brooklyn. The great inconvenience of crossing the ferry in bad weather, on days when notes fall due, is particularly dwelt on by the petitioners. There was at this time only one dry goods store in town, which was kept by Abraham Remsen, on the corner of Old Ferry (now Fulton)

---

[1] See *Star*, for Dec. 14 and 21st, 1809. Furman's Hist., Notes in the first Brooklyn Directory, of 1822, gives the number who died in Brooklyn from the fever as "twenty-*nine*, between the 12th of July and the 10th of September."

[2] This Garden stood on the site now occupied by the Kings County Court House, at the junction of Joralemon and Fulton streets. It was pulled down in 1862.

and Front streets;[1] and the mails passed through Long Island only once a week. The publication of the Long Island Star was relinquished by Mr. Kirk, on June 1st, to Alden Spooner.

In July, 1811, the census of Long Island estimates the population of Brooklyn as being 4,402.

Proposals were issued, during the fall of this year, by Messrs. B. F. Cowdrey & Co., job printers, for the publication of a new weekly paper, to be entitled *The Long Island Journal and American Freeman.* The design, however, was never carried into effect.[2]

1812, June 11. News was received in Brooklyn of the Declaration of War between the United States and Great Britain.

One of the most remarkable characters in Brooklyn, at this time (1811–'12), was "the Rain-Water Doctor." He was a German who landed in Philadelphia, in the early part of the year 1811, and came, shortly after, to Brooklyn, where he remained for about a year, occupying a small house above the "Black-Horse Tavern." In 1812, he removed to Providence, Rhode Island, where he had a large practice; then went, in 1813, to East Hartford, Connecticut, where he enjoyed an extraordinary success, but again returned to Providence, and died there in 1814–15. He was an educated physician, honest, skilful, extremely eccentric, and noted for his many deeds of charity. While he resided in the village of Brooklyn, he was consulted by thousands from the city of New York, and from Long Island, seeking relief from all the ills that flesh is heir to. The medicines which he prescribed were mostly herbs and simples, and his recommendation, to all his patients, to use *rain-water* as a drink, won for him the cognomen of "the Rain-Water Doctor." Although he gave himself no distinct name, he sometimes signed himself, "*Sylvan, Enemy of human diseases.*"[3] He pretended to sell his remedies at

---

[1] Remsen occupied a brick store and dwelling, which he had erected on the site of, and partly with the stone of the old Rapalje house. After his failure (*ante*, 82) it was replaced with the present building.

[2] The more particular history of these early newspapers will be found in that portion of the second volume devoted to the record of the Brooklyn Press.

[3] He must not be confounded with his evident imitators, the "Rain-Water Doctor," *alias* Sylvan Gardener, who flourished awhile, about 1817, at Roxbury, Massachusetts, and elsewhere (see Hist. Mag., Feb., 1862); or Octavius Plinth, the Rain-Water Doctor;

cost, and—affecting a contempt for money—he frequently refused the liberal pecuniary offers of his gratified patients. Among the many who came to him here for relief, was one Apollos Nicolls, who died soon after he had placed himself under the doctor's care. The circumstances of the case seem to have so deeply affected the physician's feelings, that he erected over his patient's grave[1] a handsome marble slab, with the following

INSCRIPTION.

"In the mournful instances of human frailty, concording to demonstrate the destiny; also, as a baneful occurrence of both, and of an unshaken resolution and usual disappointment, here lies the no more animated and wasting remains of APOLOS NICOLL, born in Smithtown, Ap. 11, 1776: 14th of the same month, 1811, departed and delivered up to the elementary menstrum of dissolution, nought, Resurrection, and Ascension; Conspicuous example of an unavoidable fate, who after his having been tired of experiencing for eight months of various diseases, in expectation to find alleviation to his painful existence, started in quest of relief, and firm in his resolution, notwithstanding an inconsiderable distance, contended three weeks in battling against the progressive obstacles of his perilous situation, opposing his design, to reach a dwelling which his delusive confidence had flattered himself to find alleviance, the end of his distress and complicated misery, but unfortunately found the one of his days accelerated by his bold attempt, and both his stranguary dropsical state and the strenuous motion of the last vehicle which conveyed him to the one by whom he eagerly expected to be alleviated and receive his existence prolongation: but vain hope! soon aborted! subject likewise to asthmatical affection by a sudden violent paroxism, effect of the combusted system stimulating the accumulated mass out of its recess, and which completed by obstructing the airy passage speedily produced suffocation, and that fatally; this incident ter-

---

or Dr. C. Humbert, *alias* Sylvan Gardner, who died in the vicinity of Philadelphia, in June, 1825, at "the supposed age of one hundred years" (see L. I. Star, June 9, 1839). This little piece of eccentric medical biography has engaged the attention of Dr. S. B. Barlow, of New York city, to whom we are indebted for some of the facts above stated.

[1] In the old public burying-ground or Potter's field of Brooklyn, situated on Livingston street, in the rear of the Military Garden; this ground has been quite swept away by modern improvements. The last monument was exhumed by the workmen engaged in digging the foundation for the new County building, erected in 1862, and bore the name of "Peter Taylor, 183–."

minated the earthly career, in putting an end to the suffering venturing afflicted; sorrowful consequences which inseparably has condemned the one he so considerately intrusted with his corporal repair, to become of his disaster passive spectator, instead of a desirous benefactor: predetermined in the witness which initially and peremptorily was to sustain the view of such sinister catastrophe, the inexorable po . t . . ces manifested to only have afforded to their destined victim enough of vital faculty, for reaching the spot whereupon the minutes residue of the last hour was to be exhausted, and for implacably having after the fatal final thread cut off; To memorize such a dismal event, the concern it has caused to the unaccustomed beholder, may this cold stone, relating the particulars, be of a consolatory nature, for the surviving consort and relatives of the deceased, and help them to be in their privation resigned to the unalterable Supreme Will, and with fortitude submit to the execution of its irrevocable decree"

CHAPTER XI.

BROOKLYN'S SHARE IN THE WAR OF 1812.

THE difficulties which had been for some time pending between this country and Great Britain, ripened at length into open hostilities. The Embargo of April, 1812, was followed, on June 18th, by a formal declaration of war, on the part of the United States, against her ancient antagonist, and ere long the papers began to abound with war news, political diatribes and patriotic poetry, all of which served to inflame the already excited popular mind, and to raise the martial ardor of the nation to a "white heat."

Brooklyn, both from its position, and intimate connection with New York—then, as now, the Metropolis of the Union—could scarcely fail to share the interest, and to catch the enthusiasm which ruled the hour, and filled every heart. *The Star*, of July 8th, contains the following notice:

"A new company of Horse or Flying Artillery is lately raised in this vicinity, under the command of Captain John Wilson. This company promises, under the able management of Captain Wilson, to equal if not excel any company in the State. The Artillerists of Captain Barbarin are fast progressing in a system of discipline and improvement which can alone, in the hour of trial, render courage effectual. We understand this company have volunteered their services to Government, and are accepted. The Riflemen of Captain Stryker and the Fusileers of Captain Herbert are respectable in number and discipline. The County of Kings is in no respect behind her neighbors in military patriotism."[1]

---

[1] The *Fusileers* were uniformed in short green coatees, and Roman leather caps, numbered only about twenty members, and were, at this time, commanded by Captain Joseph Herbert. The *Rifles*, commanded by Captain Burdett Stryker, were a large company, comprising some fifty or sixty members, and wore green frocks trimmed with yellow fringe, in which originated their their familiar appellation of "Katy dids."

Aug. 5th, 1812. "On Thursday last, the Artillery of Brooklyn, under the command of Captain Barbarin, took an excursion to the Narrows for the purpose of firing at a target. The guns were 3-pounders; the target was ten feet square; and placed at the distance of four hundred and fifty yards. Forty shots were fired, twenty of which pierced the target. The medal was awarded to Mr. John S. King."

Although her citizen soldiery were thus prompt in preparing for the war, it was not until the year 1814 that Brooklyn became the theatre of warlike operations. In the summer of that year, it became evident that the large British fleet, which for months past had been quietly concentrating upon the Bermuda Station, was intended to make a formidable descent upon some point upon our coast. Whether the blow was about to fall on New Orleans, Norfolk, Washington, Baltimore, New York, or Newport—all of which places were much exposed—was a matter of conjecture, and in consequence much alarm was felt at all those points. The commercial value of New York, and the importance of its position with reference to ulterior measures of offence, gave to its citizens considerable ground for anxious fears, which were in no degree lessened by the remembrance of a similar attack and occupation by the British during the Revolutionary War. That these fears were not altogether groundless, was sufficiently proved by the secret report of the Committee of Defence, appointed by the Common Council of the City of New York, made and approved July 17th, 1814.

From this document it appeared that the city was open to an enemy's approach, in two ways by water, and in two ways by land. He might come up by Sandy Hook, which route was protected, although not completely, by several strong and important works; or, approaching through the Sound, he might pass the unprotected Hell Gate with safety. He might land at Gravesend, as in the Revolutionary War, and arrive at Brooklyn in the rear of the fortifications; or landing on the main-land above Hell Gate, he might at once command the city, and cut off all communication with the upper counties. These two latter approaches—which in themselves presented the most feasible route of attack—were quite unprotected, and therefore called for the prompt attention and most energetic action of the authorities. With regard to troops and munitions of war, the city was equally unprepared to repulse the attack of a powerful and determined foe. The various United States forts in the harbor contained guns which required the services of at least 4,000 men, whereas the regular force in the vicinity did not exceed 1,600, mostly raw recruits, of whom probably not one hundred were acquainted with the use of great guns. And even this force, being distributed among the various forts from Sandy Hook to Greenbush, could never be concentrated at any given point to meet the advancing enemy without a total abandonment of the works. Nor could the inadequacy of the regular force be supplied by the local militia, for the brigade of artillery contained barely 1,000 effective men, a considerable portion of whom were principally conversant with infantry tactics; while fifty of the corps were even then stationed at Sag Harbor, for the defence of that place. The 13,500 militia of the State, ordered to be held in readiness for its defence, by the General Government, were only undisciplined raw troops, whom it would be almost impossible to concentrate at any point in time to defeat the objects of an enemy. In addition to this, the supply of munitions and equipments of war, both those belonging to the General Government and State, were entirely inadequate to the crisis. Such was the perilous situation in which the citizens of New York found their goodly city—on awakening from the "sweet dream of peace," into which they had been lulled by then pending negotiations, which promised a speedy termination to the war. But, shaking off the lethargy into which they had been well-nigh fatally betrayed, they bestirred themselves energetically in the work of preparation and defence. The principal measures recommended by the Committee of Defence, for the protection of the city against attacks by land, were as follows:

1. The immediate erection of two fortified camps, one on the heights of Brooklyn, and the other on the heights of Harlem, which it was presumed could soon be constructed by the voluntary labor of the citizens, and the militia who were ordered to occupy them.

2. That the General Government should be requested to direct the completion of unfinished works, and the construction of new fortifications in the vicinity of the city; as also the augmentation

of regular forces, ammunition, and provisions of war; and the authorization of the immediate enrollment of a portion of the militia, or their payment by the United States, after being ordered out by the State.

3. That the Governor of the State should be requested to call out, for the defence of the city, a competent number of militia to occupy the proposed camps, for which purpose the Corporation offered to loan the necessary funds, to an amount not exceeding the sum of $300,000, to be reimbursed by the State. And furthermore, that the Governor be requested to increase the munitions of war in this part of the State, and to cause the field artillery and arms to be put in complete order.

4. That immediate measures be taken for the removal of the shipping from the harbor to some place of safety; for the organization and enrollment of exempts; and for securing the voluntary labor of citizens on the proposed encampments.

These measures having been fully agreed upon, and assurances of ample assistance having been received from the State and General Governments, the Committee of Defence requested Brigadier-General Joseph G. Swift, of the Corps of Engineers, to furnish them as soon as possible with the plans of such additional works of defence as might be deemed necessary by him, to place the city in a state of complete defence. To this request that energetic and talented officer gave prompt attention; and shortly after, being furnished by him with the required plans, the Committee, on the 1st of August, issued a patriotic and eloquent address, calling upon their fellow-citizens to enroll themselves into effective corps, in order that by suitable preparation and discipline they might be able effectually to assist in repelling any hostile attacks; and also calling upon all, without distinction of rank or color, to aid by voluntary labor in the construction of the proposed lines of defence, both on Long Island and at Harlem.

This appeal was answered as with one heart and one mind. Every one seemed most anxious to offer his services on the interesting occasion. Volunteer associations pressed forward, all solicitous to be engaged on the earliest day that could be appointed, in the honorable employment of defence. In these overtures, there seemed to be no distinction of party or situation in life. Citizens of every political party vied with each other only in their efforts to protect the city from invasion by the common enemy, and met on the ground of self-defence, as on a common platform. That the city must be gallantly defended was the universal opinion, and every individual felt it necessary to spare no pains, or no means within his power, to defeat any hostile attempt. The rich and the poor proffered their services and mingled their labors on the same works in the purest spirit of patriotic emulation. Those who, from any cause, were unable to give their personal labor to the common cause, voluntarily and liberally contributed of their means for the employment of substitutes, while many both gave and worked. Even women and schoolboys[1] caught the inspiration of the hour, and con-

---

[1] Furman's MS. contains the following reminiscence of "The jaunt of the Students of 'Columbia Academy' in Bergen, New Jersey, to work in the fortifications in the town of Brooklyn, on Long Island."

1814. "During this summer, actuated by the spirit of patriotism and a desire to serve our country at this critical juncture of the war between the United States and Great Britain, several of us students signed a paper tendering our services to the Committee of Defence, in the city of New York, and asked permission to contribute our small assistance to raise the fortifications on the Heights of Brooklyn, in order to repel the enemy, should he attempt to land. We then painted a flag with the following inscription, 'Volunteers of Columbia Academy.' The next morning we arose, and while the stars were in the sky, took up our line of march for Brooklyn Heights, the Academy bell ringing to a merry tune. In passing through Paulus Hook (Jersey City), we were saluted by the women with 'God bless you, boys!'—the spirit of our Revolutionary sires seems to have pervaded the bosoms of all. We crossed the Paulus Hook ferry free of ferriage; when we got to the Fulton ferry, we each received a ticket, valued at two cents, from an agent of the Corporation of the City of New York, to recross the ferry with. We reached the Brooklyn shore quite early in the morning, and marched along directly through the town, in company with a large body of brewers from New York, to Fort Greene, where we were detached by the Superintendent, Mr. (Robert) Nicholls, to clear the easterly part of the fort of small round stones, and to carry dirt in small wheelbarrows to raise a step to enable the infantry to fire over the top of the wall. We worked till dinner-time, when we broke off; ate our dinner and commenced work again, and continued until four o'clock in the afternoon, when we stopped and commenced our return march to Bergen. When we reached Paulus Hook it was almost dusk. In travelling up the road to our place of destination, we met a gentleman in his horse and chair going to Paulus Hook; his horse appeared frightened at our flag. We offered to lower it; but he said, 'Never mind, boys; here (throwing some money to our standard-bearer), treat your company.' When we arrived at Coulters, we laid out our new friend's donation in refreshments—some cakes—and continued on to the Academy. We formed a ring on the square formed by the meeting of the streets at the side of the Academy, gave three cheers for our safe return home, dismissed, got our supper, went to bed, and soon were lulled to sleep without rocking. I feel a pride, which every free

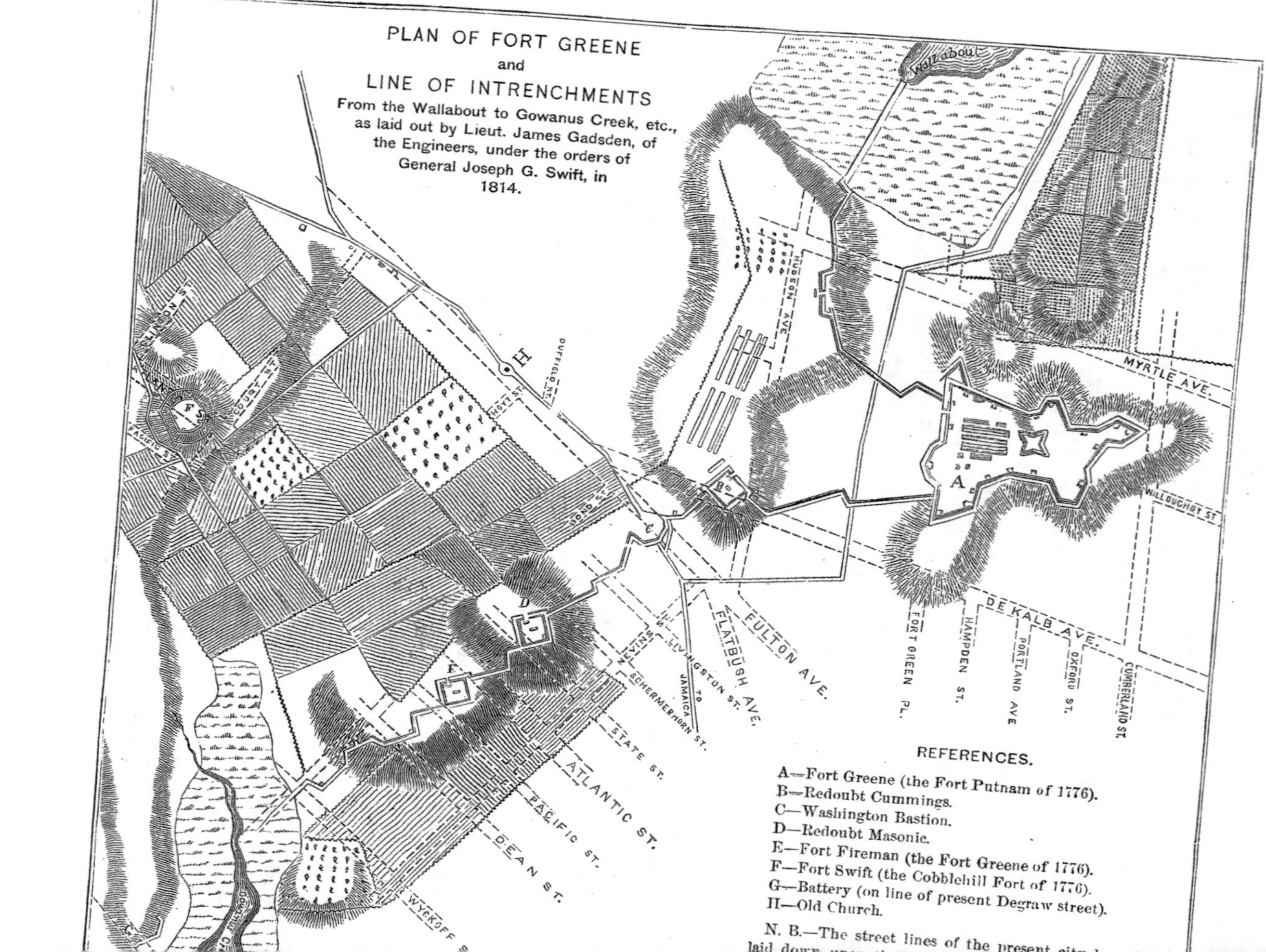
PLAN OF FORT GREENE
and
LINE OF INTRENCHMENTS
From the Wallabout to Gowanus Creek, etc., as laid out by Lieut. James Gadsden, of the Engineers, under the orders of General Joseph G. Swift, in 1814.
Wallabout
HUDSON AVE
MYRTLE AVE.
WILLOUGHBY ST
DE KALB AVE.
CUMBERLAND ST.
OXFORD ST.
PORTLAND AVE
HAMPDEN ST.
FORT GREEN PL.
FULTON AVE.
FLATBUSH AVE.
LIVINGSTON ST.
TO JAMAICA
SCHERMERHORN ST.
NEVINS
STATE ST.
ATLANTIC ST.
PACIFIC ST.
DEAN ST.
WYCKOFF
DUFFIELD ST.
HOYT ST.
BOND
COURT ST.
PACIFIC
A
B
C
D
E
F
H
REFERENCES.
A—Fort Greene (the Fort Putnam of 1776).
B—Redoubt Cummings.
C—Washington Bastion.
D—Redoubt Masonic.
E—Fort Fireman (the Fort Greene of 1776).
F—Fort Swift (the Cobblehill Fort of 1776).
G—Battery (on line of present Degraw street).
H—Old Church.
N. B.—The street lines of the present city

tributed their quota of labor upon the works, and the people of the interior towns in the neighboring States of Connecticut and New Jersey hastened to proffer their assistance in averting what was felt to be a common national danger.

The lines of defence on Long Island, as planned by General Swift, commenced at Mount Alto on the Hudson; thence, by McGowan's Pass, a line of redoubts and block-houses ran along the Heights of Harlem to, and across Hell Gate, including a block-house on Mill Rock, and a castle on the high ground of Long Island. On Long Island, the defences began at the Wallabout, covered by Fort Greene, and extended across to Bergen's Heights,[1] to Fort Lawrence, including several redoubts, which were overlooked by Forts Greene and Lawrence.[2]

These lines were commenced upon, at 8 A. M. of Tuesday, the 9th of August, 1814, by Captain Andrew Bremner's Artillery company, the officers of the Third Brigade of Infantry, under command of General Mapes, and a body of volunteers from the Seventh Ward of New York, who broke ground for the intrenchments on Fort Greene, under a salute from six-pounders. By the aid of the papers of that day, we are able to trace the progress of the works to their completion.

On Wednesday, August 10th, the labor of the day at Fort Greene was performed by the Tanners and Curriers, the Veteran Corps of Artillery, a Society of Plumbers, a large force of Exempts from the Second Ward of New York, Major Dunscombe's battalion of Governor's Guards, and Captain Swaime's company of Artillery.

Friday, August 12. The labor was continued by the officers of the Tenth Brigade of Infantry, the officers, non-commissioned officers, and matrosses of the Thirteenth Regiment of Artillery, under command of Lieutenant-Colonel M. Boerum, a military association of young men, the Hamilton Society, Students of Medicine, sixty

---

born American ought to feel, in saying, this is the second day I have worked to raise fortifications, during this contest, to protect my country from an invading foe."

Furman mentions, also, that between Nassau street and Fort Greene, all was open fields, covered with buildings, erected for the use of the quartermasters and sutlers

[1] So called from its owner, Jacob Bergen. Smith street now runs through it.

[2] There, was, also an earthwork bastion on Red Hook.

hands from the Wire Factory at Greenwich, and forty hands from the Eagle Foundry.

Saturday, August 13th. The intrenchments were manned by a party of citizens raised by Mr. A. Stagg, a number of volunteers from Division street and vicinity, and the journeymen Cabinet-Makers of New York.

The appearance of these latter gave rise to the following impromptu lines:

"Their hearts with the love of their country *inlaid,*
They fling by the *chisel* to handle the *spade;*
Leave *mahogany shavings* the rough earth to *shave,*
And prepare for invaders a *coffin* and *grave.*"

Monday, August 15th. The infantry companies, under command of Captains Skillman, Schenck, and Dean, together with the artillery company of Captain Brouwer,[1] broke ground on the old Revolutionary works at Cobble-Hill, on which occasion a salute was fired, and the fort named "Fort Swift,"[2] in honor of Brigadier General Joseph G. Swift.

Tuesday, August 16th. The workmen this day were military companies, under command of Captains Stryker, Cowenhoven, and Herbert, the Exempts of Bedford and the Wallabout, and the Fire Company No. 2, of Brooklyn.

Wednesday, August 17th. The people of the Town of Bushwick, under the lead of their pastor, Rev. Mr. Bassett, repaired to Fort Swift, to labor on that fortification. "Their operations were commenced by a prayer from that venerable patriot, and an exhortation to zeal and unanimity in their country's cause, in defence of which, they were then to be employed on the works, which he had in person, nearly forty years ago, assisted in erecting. He continued encouraging them, and distributing refreshments through the day; and at evening, returned home with his flock, satisfied with having set an example, impressive, admirable, and commanding the

[1] The Artillery corps, under Captain Laurence Brouwer, belonged to Brooklyn, but did duty in New York, at Castle Garden, where they were attached to the Thirteenth Regiment of Artillery, Lieutenant-Colonel Boerum.

[2] See page 252, *note*. We learn from the next paper, that this was originally called Fort Pitt.

plaudits of an approving conscience and a grateful country."—*N. Y. Columbian*."[1]

Among the many interesting incidents of the day, the following is related by the *New York Gazette*: "An aged and respectable stranger and his four sons passed over the Brooklyn Ferry on Wednesday morning, and walked to Fort Greene, where about two hundred of our citizens were at work. After they had taken a view of the Heights and the adjacent country, the old gentleman observed that he never passed through the city of New York, without coming over to visit the ground. 'Nearly forty years ago,' added he, 'these hands assisted to erect a fort on this spot, and, as old as they are now grown, they shall again contribute their mite to the same important object.' He then threw off his coat, seized a shovel, and

---

[1] During the day, they held a meeting in Fort Swift, the proceedings of which are thus detailed in the *Star*:

"At a meeting of a number of the inhabitants of Bushwick, exempt from military duty, held at Fort Swift, on Wednesday, August 17th, 1814, the Reverend Dr. Basset, Chairman; Tunis Wortman, Secretary; the following preamble and resolutions were read and adopted:

"Next to the duties which we owe to Heaven, those which belong to our Country demand our chief attention. As a people, we are pre-eminently blessed. Divine Providence has favored us with a free and excellent constitution, and commands us to preserve it. In defence of our liberties, property, and lives, for the protection of our native land, or the land of our choice, we this day solemnly step forward—we take up arms for general preservation, and will not lay them down while danger exists. In a crisis like the present, no good and faithful citizen should consider himself exempt. The spirit of party should be lost in the generous ardor of universal patriotism. All who feel that they possess a country to defend and love, should step forward with a degree of zeal and alacrity, which shall teach the enemy, and convince the world that America is a virtuous, great, and united nation.

"*Resolved*, That the citizens and inhabitants of the Town of Bushwick, exempt from ordinary military duties, embody themselves into a volunteer company for the protection and defence of Nassau and Manhattan Islands, under such officers as they shall select.

"*Resolved*, That a committee of eleven citizens be appointed to request the assistance and co-operation of our fellow-citizens of Long Island, to prepare and publish a suitable address for that purpose.

"*Resolved*, That such committee be authorized and instructed to enter into such arrangements, and to form such correspondence as may be necessary and proper to carry the objects of this meeting into effect; and that the committee consist of Major Francis Titus, Dr. Cornelius Lowe, John Skillman, senior; Alexander Whaley, senior; Peter Wyckoff, William Conselyea, senior; Peter Meserole, Gysbert Bogert, Abraham Meserole, John Van Alst, and Tunis Wortman.

"*Resolved*, That our thanks be tendered to the Corporation of New York, and to citizens of Patterson, New Jersey, for their aid and labor in the works," etc., etc.

calling on his sons to follow his example, descended into the ditch, where he continued to labor with great zeal during the day. Two of his sons continued at labor until night,—the other two, having thoroughly fatigued themselves, gave up their labor at an earlier hour. The old gentleman dryly observed that the latter, for their want of courage, should be court-martialled, while the former, who had bravely persevered to the end, should be promoted."

Thursday, August 18th. The people of Flatbush were employed on the works.

Friday, August 19th. The people of Flatlands took their turn upon the fortifications. Also about five hundred carpenters from New York repaired to Fort Greene, with their tools, and there laid seven gun-platforms, "in different angles of that extensive work, on one of which a salute was fired in the afternoon, it being only the tenth working day since the repair of the fort was commenced."

Saturday, August 20th. The people of Gravesend contributed their quota of labor. A party of about seventy volunteers from Paterson, New Jersey, commanded by Colonel Abraham Godwin (a Revolutionary officer, who had been on the same grounds in 1776), arrived at the Brooklyn Ferry, about six or seven o'clock A. M. *en route* for Fort Greene.

This day, also, some 1,200 patriotic Irishmen volunteered their labors on Fort Greene, and were "distinguished by uncommon and well-directed industry."[1] On the evening of the same day, several uniformed companies of militia from the interior of the State, arrived at Brooklyn to go into camp. As they landed, they met and were enthusiastically received by the Irishmen, who had returned from their day's labor, and, with banners, flags, and two bands of music, were awaiting the arrival of the ferry boat, in a line which extended from the wharf to the end of Ferry street. "On coming ashore, the patriotic cavalcade opened their lines, faced them inwards, and saluted the troops with flourishes of their music and colors, and a continued roar of applause from two thousand cheering voices, till

---

[1] The peculiar nature of their labor appears from the following advertisement in the papers of the day: "THE PATRIOTIC SONS OF ERIN are requested by the Committee of Defence, to lend their assistance, particularly in SODDING; and the Ward Commanders are desired to make known this invitation as far as the time will permit. By order," etc

they had passed, with their baggage, between the ranks, through the whole length of the jolly-hearted procession."

Monday, August 22d. The people of New Utrecht, and one thousand citizens of color from the city of New York, worked on the fortifications.

Tuesday, August 23d. Labor was performed by the Mechanics' Society of Kings County, the Military Exempts, and Fire Companies Nos. 1 and 2 of Brooklyn.

The unbounded popular enthusiasm of the times found expression in the following song, which was sung, played, and whistled everywhere on the streets and in the trenches.[1] It was the production of Samuel Woodworth, well known as the author of "The Old Oaken Bucket;" and was entitled—

THE PATRIOTIC DIGGERS.

JOHNNY BULL beware,
Keep at proper distance,
Else we'll make you stare
At our firm resistance;
Let alone the lads
Who are freedom tasting,
Recollect our dads
Gave you once a basting.
Pickaxe, shovel, spade,
Crowbar, hoe, and barrow,
Better not invade,
Yankees have the marrow.

To protect our rights
'Gainst your flints and triggers,
See on Brooklyn Heights
Our patriotic diggers;
Men of every age,
Color, rank, profession,
Ardently engage
Labor in succession.
Pickaxe, shovel, spade,
Crowbar, hoe, and barrow,
Better not invade,
Yankees have the marrow.

Grandeur leaves her towers,
Poverty her hovel,
Here to join their powers
With the hoe and shovel.
Here the merchant toils
With the patriot sawyer,
There the laborer smiles,
Near him sweats the lawyer.
Pickaxe, shovel, spade,
Crowbar, hoe, and barrow
Better not invade,
Yankees have the marrow.

Here the mason builds
Freedom's shrine of glory,
While the painter gilds
The immortal story.
Blacksmiths catch the flame,
Grocers feel the spirit,
Printers share the fame,
And record their merit.
Pickaxe, shovel, spade,
Crowbar, hoe, and barrow,
Better not invade,
Yankees have the marrow

[1] [Copy of Advertisement in Long Island Star.] BROOKLYN HEIGHTS.—Just published, price six cents, and for sale at this office, a Song called the PATRIOTIC DIGGERS. *Tune,* "Great way off at Sea, or Rob and Joan." Copyright secured. Brooklyn, August 23, 1814.

Scholars leave their schools
  With their patriot teachers;
Farmers seize their tools,
  Headed by their preachers.
How they break the soil!
  Brewers, butchers, bakers,
Here the doctors toil,
  There the undertakers.
    Pickaxe, shovel, spade,
      Crowbar, hoe, and barrow,
    Better not invade,
      Yankees have the marrow.

Plumbers, founders, dyers,
  Tinmen, turners, shavers,
Sweepers, clerks, and criers,
  Jewellers, engravers,
Clothiers, drapers, players,
  Cartmen, hatters, tailors,
Guagers, sealers, weighers,
  Carpenters, and sailors.
    Pickaxe, shovel, spade,
      Crowbar, hoe, and barrow,
    Better not invade,
      Yankees have the marrow.

Bright Apollo's sons
  Leave their pipe and tabor,
'Mid the roar of guns
  Join the martial labor;
Round the embattled plain
  In sweet concord rally,
And in freedom's strain
  Sing the foe's finale!
    Pickaxe, shovel, spade,
      Crowbar, hoe, and barrow,
    Better not invade,
      Yankees have the marrow.

Better not invade;
  Recollect the spirit
Which our dads displayed,
  And their sons inherit;
If you still advance,
  Friendly caution slighting,
You may get, by chance,
  A bellyful of fighting.
    Pickaxe, shovel, spade,
      Crowbar, hoe, and barrow,
    Better not invade,
      Yankees have the marrow.

Wednesday, August 24th. The free people of color of Kings County, labored faithfully in the common work of defence. The Committee of Defence for the Town of Brooklyn, publish a card acknowledging the patriotic services of the inhabitants of Kings County, and stating that "the promptitude with which those services had been rendered, emboldened them to ask of their fellow-citizens a *second tour of duty*," which they had ascertained was necessary on Fort Swift. This request was accompanied by a programme of the corporations, bodies, and associations assigned to each day, etc., as follows:

Thursday, August 25th. The military companies commanded by Captains Skillman, Dean, Schenck, and Brouwer.

Friday, August 26th. The military companies of Captains Stryker, Cowenhoven, and Herbert; Fire Company No. 3, of Brooklyn, and the Exempts of Bedford and the Wallabout.

Saturday, August 27th. The people of Bushwick.

Monday, August 29th. The people of Flatbush. This day was also signalized by the arrival at Fort Greene of the finely equipped and elegantly uniformed Albany Riflemen, Trojan Greens, and Montgomery Rangers.

Tuesday, August 30th. The people of Flatlands and Gravesend united in laboring on the works.

The papers state that "the labor on the forts is continued with unremitting assiduity. The new fort on the right of the line of defence is called Fort Lawrence. This evening a large party were at work by *moonlight!*" A card from the General Committee of Defence, signed by Nicholas Fish, Chairman, states that contributions, especially vegetables, will be received by Major Ingraham, Brigade Quartermaster at Brooklyn,—requests further labor on the works both at Harlem and Brooklyn, and acknowledges the receipt of one hundred and twenty loads of fascines (averaging twenty-five bundles to a load) from the town of Jamaica, brought to Fort Greene by citizens of that place, headed by the Rev. Mr. Schoonmaker. Mr. Egenbrodt, the Principal of the Academy at Jamaica, with his pupils, aided in cutting these fascines.

Wednesday, August 31st. The Grand Lodge of Free and Accepted Masons, to the number of seven hundred and fifty, headed by its Grand Master, De Witt Clinton, repaired to the Heights, where they broke ground in a field south of Flatbush Road, and constructed a fort, called "Fort Masonic." The parole of the day was, "The Grand Master expects every Mason to do his duty."

Fort Greene was enlivened by the presence of a company of ladies, who came over from New York and formed in procession at the Ferry, whence they proceeded, with music—their numbers increasing, as they went, to between two and three hundred—to Fort Greene, where they performed a few hours' labor. The Tammany and Columbian Orders, to the number of 1,150, also turned out for duty.

Thursday, September 1st. The Mechanics Society of Kings County, Fire Companies Nos 1 and 2, the residue of Brooklyn Exempts, and Fortitude Lodge of Masons, with other members of the Fraternity, performed this day's labor.

Saturday, September 3d. The *Columbian* of this date, says, "Nearly eight hundred (probably increased since much beyond the number) citizens of Newark, transported in a line of wagons nearly covering the causeway on the road, reached Paulus Hook [Jersey City]

Ferry, crossed the North River, and passed through this city to Brooklyn Ferry, before one o'clock this morning. They had several bands of wind and military music, with flags, and a label on each hat, 'Don't give up the soil,' and proceeded to work on the fortifications at Brooklyn with an alacrity truly admirable and commendable. Such an instance of patriotic enthusiasm in the inhabitants of a neighboring State, from a distance of seven miles, cannot be too highly appreciated or recorded in terms too honorable to the zeal and disinterestedness of our fellow-citizens of New Jersey. Newark will forever live in the grateful remembrance of the people of New York."

Wednesday, September 7th. One hundred and eighty-four inhabitants of Hanover Township, Morris County, New Jersey, principally, however, from the village of Parsippany, headed by their pastor, Rev. Mr. Phelps, came over to Brooklyn and labored upon the defenses there.

September 23d. The members of the Baptist Church in Mulberry street, New York, under the lead of their eloquent pastor, the Rev. Archibald McClay, rendered an efficient day's work.

By the early part of September, the fortifications whose construction we have thus traced from day to day, were nearly completed, and mounted with heavy artillery. Within the lines was stationed the Twenty-Second Brigade of Infantry, 1,750 strong, composed of the militia of Kings and Queens Counties (the Sixty-Fourth, Ninety-Third, One Hundredth, and One Hundredth and Seventeenth), under command of Brigadier-General Jeremiah Johnson of Brooklyn. They were encamped in front of Fort Greene, along the present line of Hudson street. Kings County furnished the Sixty-Fourth Regiment, composed of five companies, of one hundred men each, officered as follows:

Major, Francis Titus, Commanding.

Second Major, Albert C. Van Brunt.

Adjutant, Daniel Barre.

Quartermaster, Albert Van Brunt.

Surgeon, Schoonmaker.

New Utrecht Company.—Captain, William Denyse; Lieutenants, Barcalo, Vanhise; Ensign Suydam.

BROOKLYN COMPANY.[1]—Captain, Joseph Dean;[2] Lieutenants, Chas. J. Doughty and John Spader; Ensign, William A. Mercein.

WALLABOUT AND BUSHWICK COMPANY.[3]—Captain, Francis Skillman;[4] Lieutenants, Joseph Conselyea and Daniel Lott.

GOWANUS COMPANY.—Captain, Peter Cowenhoven, afterward John T. Bergen; Lieutenants, John Lott and Adrian Van Brunt.[5]

GRAVESEND AND FLATBUSH COMPANIES.—Captain, Jeremiah Lott; Lieutenants, Robert Nicholls[6] and Charles Rapelye; Ensign, Jeremiah Johnson.

This regiment was mustered into the service of the United States, at Bedford, on the 2d of September, 1814, and the men were dismissed to their homes on the 13th of November ensuing.[7]

The *Star*, of 28th, remarks: "We take a great satisfaction in mentioning the very orderly deportment of the large body of citizen-soldiers now quartered in Brooklyn, towards the inhabitants of the village. The perfect quiet of the village, both of day and night, and even in those parts contiguous to the camp, is honorable to the soldiers and officers. We hope our citizens are not unmindful of this, and will do all in their power to render the situation of the soldiers comfortable. Many of them have come two hundred miles, leaving all the endearments of domestic and social life, and cheerfully put

---

[1] By order of September 14th, Captain Dean, in addition to his own company, received command of those of Captains Stryker and Herbert, to which were attached Lieutenants Doughty, Spader, and Ensign Mercein. A Muster-Roll of this company will be found in Appendix 11.

[2] Captain Dean, who is now living, and to whom we are greatly indebted for valuable information relative to the War of 1812, was commissioned Ensign in the Sixty-Fourth Regiment of Kings County Militia, March 18, 1809; Captain in same regiment, February 29, 1812; Brigade Major and Inspector of Twenty-Second Brigade, June 21, 1815; commissioned as same Inspector of the Forty-Fourth Brigade, to take rank from former date, July 8, 1816; as Colonel (the first ever commissioned in Kings County, in place of Lieutenant-Colonel) of the Sixty-Fourth Regiment, March 4, 1817.

[3] The Bushwick Company, Captain Van Cott, and Joseph Conselyea, Lieutenant, was consolidated with Captain Skillman's company.

[4] Francis Skillman, appointed Ensign, March 23, 1796; Captain, April 7, 1807; Major, May 10, 1815.

[5] Adrian Van Brunt was first Ensign, then Lieutenant, then Adjutant.

[6] Robert Nicholls, the late worthy President of the Brooklyn Gas Company, was made Captain and placed in command of Fort Swift—relieving Captain Spader, then in command.

[7] The house of John R. Duryea was designated as the *alarm-post* of the Sixty-Fourth Regiment.

up with all the privations connected with the life of a soldier. Let those who are exulting in their fortunate exemption be not unmindful of our brave defenders."

In addition to these, there was also stationed at Brooklyn a brigade under command of Brigadier-General Samuel Haight, consisting of some 1,800 men, mostly from the northern part of the State. They were discharged from service about the same time as Johnson's brigade, and their place at Fort Greene was supplied by Colonel Bogardus' regiment, Forty-First United States Regulars, together with the Albany Rifles and Trojan Greens, who were ordered up from Camp Lewis, at New Utrecht.[1] Fortunately, however, the storm of war was averted, and Brooklyn was saved from again becoming the scene of warlike strife. On Saturday evening, February 11th, 1815, the glorious news of an honorable peace was received, amid general rejoicings, which was testified by illuminations, bonfires, etc. On the 20th of that month New York city was illuminated in honor of the event, and Brooklyn followed the example in handsome style on the evening of the 21st, when, among other demonstrations, the fine band of the Forty-First United States Regiment, then stationed here, serenaded the inhabitants, and "all went merry as a marriage bell."

---

[1] See Annual Message (Sept. 30, 1814) of Gov. D. D. Tompkins. There were also in camp, Captain J. T. Bergen's New Utrecht Company; Captain John Lott's, Jr., Flatlands Company; Captain Areson's Flushing Company; Captain Van Wyck's Jamaica Company; Captain Leverich's Newtown Company; and another under Captain Skidmore.

APPENDICES.

APPENDICES.

APPENDIX I.—(PAGE 16.)

DEED BOOK VII.—(Doc. Hist. N. Y., p. 49.)

NEW YORK, february 14; 1684–5.

The Deposicon of Catelina Trico aged fouer score yeares or thereabouts taken before the right honora^{ble} Coll^{o} Thomas Dongan Leu^{t} and Governour under his Roy^{ll} high^{ss} James Duke of Yorke and Albany etc. of N. York and its Dependcyes in America who saith and Declares in the p^{r}sens of God as followeth

That she Came to this Province either in the yeare one thousand six hundred and twenty three or twenty fouer to the best of her remembrance, and that fouer Women Came along with her in the same Shipp, in which ship the Governo^{r} Arian Jorissen Came also over, which fouer Women were married at Sea and that they and their husbands stayed about three Weekes at this place and then they with eight seamen more went in a vessell by ord^{r} of the Dutch Governo^{r}, to Dellaware River and there settled. This I certify under my hand and ye seale of this provine.

THO. DONGAN.

(N. Y. Col. MSS. XXV.—Doc. Hist. N. Y., pp. 50, 51.)

Catelyn Trico aged about 83 years born in Paris doth Testify and Declare that in ye year 1623 she came into this Country wth a Ship called ye Unity whereof was Commander Arien Jorise belonging to ye West India Company being ye first Ship y^{t} came here for ye s^{d} Company; as soon as they came to Mannatans now called N: York they sent Two families & six men to harford River & Two families & 8 men to Delaware River and 8 men they left att N: Yorke to take Possession and ye Rest of ye Passengers went wth ye Ship up as farr as Albany which they then Called fort Orangie When as ye Ship came as farr as Sopus which is ½ way to Albanie; they lightned ye Ship wth some boats ye were left there by ye Dutch that had been there ye year before a tradeing wth ye Indians upont there oune accompts & gone back again to Holland & so brought ye vessel up; there were about 18 families abroad who settled themselves att Albany & made a small fort; and as soon as they had built themselves some hutts of Bark: ye Mahikanders or River Indians. ye Maquase: Oneydes: Onnondages Cayougas. & Sinnekes, wth ye Mahawawa or Ottawawaes Indians came & made Covenants of friendship wth ye s^{d} Arien Jorise there Commander Bringing him great Presents of Bever o^{r} oy^{r} Peltry & desyred that they might come & have a Constant free Trade with them wch was concluded upon & ye s^{d} nations came dayly with great multidus of Bever & traded them wth ye Christians, there s^{d} Comman^{r} Arien Jorise staid with them all winter and sent his sonne home with ye s^{d} Deponent lived in Albany three years all which time ye s^{d} Indians were all quiet as Lambs & came & Traded with all ye freedom Imaginable, in ye year 1626 ye Deponent came from Albany & settled at N: Yorke where she afterwards for many years and then came to Long Island where she now lives

The s^{d} Catelyn Trico made oath of ye s^{d} Deposition before me at her house on Long Island in ye Wale Bought this 17th day of October 1688.

William Morris
Justice of ye pece

It will be seen that these depositions of Catalina Trico do not substantiate the statement hitherto made by our historians concerning the early settlement, at the "Waal-Boght," of the Walloons. (See Note 2, p. 25, of this volume.) One of these historians, Dr. E. B. O'Callaghan, of Albany, corrects his earlier error by very kindly placing at our disposal the following translation of a Minute of the Dutch Council, which establishes the date of the first settlement on the West end of Long Island.

(N. Y. Col. MSS. X., Part iii., p. 93.)

The Director General & Council of New Netherlands hereby certify and declare at the request of John Cooper an inhabitant of Southampton on Long Island, that it is true and truthful that the six or seven Englishmen who attempted to settle in the year 1640 on Long Island in Schout's bay were removed from there by order of the Director General and Council then in office, as appears by the extract annexed, and about the middle of May of the aforesaid year 1640, after they had by their own declaration, pulled down the Arms of their High Mightinesses long before set up there, and put a Fool's head instead, after this *westerly part of Long Island had*, about eight years before, *to wit in the year* 1632, *begun to be settled* and populated by their High Mightinesses' subjects; 8 or 9 years before any other nation had settled themselves on any part of Long Island. Dated 10 March 1664.

In regard to the derivation and meaning of the name "Waal-Boght," we take this opportunity of giving the opinion of that excellent scholar, Mr. SAMUEL ALOFSEN, of Jersey City, who (in the Literary World, No. 68, May 20, 1848) maintains that the locality was named by the early Dutch settlers *prior* to the arrival of the Walloons; and, of course, without reference to their settlement there. The *name*, he thinks,—like that portion of the City of Amsterdam which bears the same appellation,—is derived from "EEN WAAL"—a basin of a harbor, or an inner harbor—and "EEN BOGT," a bend; and, like its European namesake, signifies "*The Bend of the Inner Harbor.*"

APPENDIX II.—(PAGE 26.)

INDIAN DEED OF BUSHWICK.—(N. Y. Col. MSS. G. G., 27.)

WE, THE DIRECTOR GENERAL AND COUNCIL OF NEW NETHERLANDS, *residing on the Island Manhates in Fort Amsterdam, under the jurisdiction of their High Mightinesses the Lords States General of the United Netherlands, and the Incorporated West India Company, Chamber at Amsterdam*, acknowledge and declare that on this day, the date underwritten, before us in their proper persons appeared and came forward Kakapoteyno, Menqueuw & Suwirau, Chiefs of Keskaechquerem, in the presence of the subscribing witnesses and voluntarily and most deliberately declare with consent of the Tribe (*gemeente*), for and in consideration of Eight fathoms of Duffels, Eight fathoms of Wampum, Twelve Kettles, Eight Adzes and Eight axes, with some Knives, Beads, Awl blades, (which they acknowledge to have received into their hands and power to their full satisfaction and contentment before the execution hereof,) to have ceded, transported, conveyed and transferred as they do hereby transport, cede, convey and transfer in a true, right and free property, to and for the behoof of the Hon[ble] Directors of the General Incorporated West India Company, Chamber at Amsterdam, a certain parcel of land situate on Long Island, south of the Island Manhates extending in the length from George Rapaelje's plantation called Rinnegackonck eastward one mile and a half to Mespaechtes and in breadth from the East river about one mile unto the Cripplebush of said Mespaechtes, and that with all the action and right to them belonging &c. In Witness these presents are confirmed with our usual signature and seal, depending herefrom. Done on the Island Manhates, Fort Amsterdam this 1st August a° 1638

Maurits Jansen }
Claes van Elstant } Witnesses

To my Knowledge
Cornelis van Tienhoven
Secretary.

APPENDIX III.—(Page 36.)

PETITION OF THE INHABITANTS OF LONG ISLAND.—(Col. MSS., pp. 416, 417.)

We, the undersigned, inhabitants and subjects residing on Long Island, under the jurisdiction of the Hon[ble] Lords, the Mighty Lords States General of the United Netherlands, the Serene Prince, his Highness, and the General Incorporated West India Company, and under your Hon[ble] Government.

Request with all humble submission—whereas, a short time ago the scum of this place, which is justly called our fatherland, hath revolted against the righteous side, our common friends; and whereas, we see their preparation for hostilities tending to the ruin and destruction of the inhabitants who are under the necessity of earning by steady labor, in fields and wood, food and support for their wives and children, each for himself, and conjointly for us all, regarding the inconveniences which must spring therefrom, do request as above, and humbly pray, in all respectful obedience—that we, in general, may be granted and allowed such public enemy to ruin and conquer, and, further, from time to time, unto the establishment of our common peace and welfare, so that at once the previous and much wished for peace of this place may be and remain permanent. This day in the name of us all.

(Signed) GERRIT WOLFFERSEN, JACOB WOLFERSEN, DIRCK WOLFMAN, HANS HANSEN [Bergen], LAMBERT HUYBERTSEN MOL.

POSTEL.

We cannot, at present, resolve to attack the Indians at Mareckkawick, as they have not given us hitherto any provocation, and as it would draw down an unrighteous war upon our heads, especially as we are well assured that they would be on their guard and hard to beat, and apparently excite more enemies, and be productive of much injury to us, whilst we trust that it will, through God's mercy, now result in a good issue.

But in case they evince a hostile disposition, every man must do his best to defend himself.

Meanwhile each must be on his guard and arm himself, as is done here, according as time and circumstances shall best determine.

In presence of the Hon[ble] Director, the Fiscal, Everardus Bogardus, preacher, Hendrick van Dyck, Ghysbert Op Dyck, and Oloff Stevenson. Done the 27th of February, A° 1643 in Fort Amsterdam. New Netherlands.

It may, perhaps, seem strange to our readers that we have not, in the earlier part of this history, given some extended notice of the Indians who inhabited the territory now occupied by the City of Brooklyn. We omitted to do so, because the subject was obscure at the best; because the Indians of Brooklyn resembled Indians elsewhere in every respect; and because the very little that is known of their political divisions, their habits, etc., etc., has already been sufficiently stated in our State and Island Histories—of which we refer our reader to O'Callaghan's Hist. of New Neth., i., p. 49; Brodhead's Hist. N. Y., i., p. 73; Thompson's Hist. L. I., i., pp. 93–95; Furman's Notes on Brooklyn, pp. 5, 6; and Prime's Hist. L. I., pp. 90–120. It will suffice to say here, in addition to what has already been stated in our text, that the Marechawiecks, who inhabited Brooklyn, were of the

Canarsee tribe, which occupied Kings County and a part of Jamaica, and which held its council fires probably at Flatlands, at the place yet known as Canarsee.

APPENDIX IV.—(Page 45.)

A VISIT TO BROOKLYN, IN HOLLAND.—(From the Brooklyn Eagle, Sept. 12, 1859.)

"The village lies for the most part between the main road and the stream, and consists of three or four hundred houses, accommodating about 1,500 inhabitants. It is a very old place; the houses are small and dull with age, the few streets which intersect it are very irregular, and the people apparently without enterprise or thrift. There were a few large houses, especially three or four, intended for refreshments or resorts for the village topers. The Reformed Church is rather a commodious building with a handsome spire. But upon the whole the impression of the interior of the town was not pleasing. We went through the main road in both directions; for as we were probably the first natives of Brooklyn who had ever visited it,—as least so far as any known record goes,—we determined to see it thoroughly. We found, when we got out to the fields, snug residences surrounded with flowers and duck ponds, and every thing around them in perfect neatness and order. On one side of the village we entered a little covert of shrubbery laid out in walks, and containing perhaps half an acre of ground. This was the village park,—a sign of living taste, and we began to have a better feeling about the place. We at length crossed the bridge which spans the Vecht and connects the two communities of Breukelen Nijenrodes and Breukelen St. Pieters. It is in the former that the village of Breukelen is situated; the latter is entirely a rural district.

"The view from the point we had now reached was charming. Nothing can exceed the quiet beauty of the scene. The Vecht is about an hundred yards wide, and its waters flow sluggishly along on an unchanged level from one end of the year to the other, meandering through green meadows and in front of plain but substantial country houses, which show every sign of comfort as well as antiquity. The village reposes upon it a picture of perfect indolence. All along the margin of the river are *koepels* or tea houses belonging to the dwellings of the town; though these summer-houses are the least ornamental, as a whole, that we have seen any where, being, without exception, plain square buildings, ten or twelve feet either way. A little garden connects them with the houses, which are not much larger, and in the midst of which, towering high over all, rises the church spire. I have before alluded to the practice of giving a name to every residence which can raise a koepel. It prevails here as elsewhere, and each one has its designation accordingly painted upon it, such as *Vrede Vecht*, *Vechten dorp*, *Vecht en hof*, *Boom en bosh*, and the like. Some have names of a Greek origin apparently, as *Hodorama* and *Potorama.* On the side of the river—the east side, which we had now reached—and directly opposite the village, stands the ancient Castle of Gunsterstein—the abode formerly of Oldenbarneveld—venerable martyr to party vengeance. It has been modernized, the towers and turrets have been removed, and it now presents a perfect pattern of one of that class of buildings in our country which delights in white paint and a cupola in the middle of the roof. It is, however, surrounded still by a moat, and has fine large trees in the park behind it.

"Breukelen cannot be considered a celebrity, unless it may acquire a reflected lustre from its greater namesake. It has given birth to no genius whose name is great even within the circumscribed limits of these provinces. It is, however, famous for its antiquity, if we may credit the marvellous, but still well authenticated fact that, in rebuilding the tower of the church, one hundred and fifty years ago, they discovered, under the foundation, coffins of stone, eight, ten, and twelve feet long, containing the bones of a gigantic race of men, whose existence is more ancient than tradition. The town lies in the midst of a marshy district, and hence its name; for Breukelen—pronounced *Brurkeler*—means *marsh land.* And on this point I may quote a writer, with whom all the Dutch authorities on the subject concur, inasmuch as our home chroniclers have labored under a misapprehension upon the subject. 'In all probability,' says the author of the *Kabinet van Nederlandsche en Kleefsche Outheden*, 'the name has the same origin as Maarssen, namely, from its marshy and watery turf lands—(van de drassige en broeckactige veen landen); and, although the name is spelled in ancient documents and letters Bracola, Broecke, Broeckede, Broicklede, and Brocklandia, they all indicate one and the same origin.'

"There are some curious points of coincidence both as regards the name and situation of the Dutch Breukelen and our Brooklyn. The name with us was originally applied exclusively to the hamlet which grew up along the main road now embraced within Fulton Avenue, and between Smith street and Jackson street, and we must, therefore, not confound it with the settlements at the Waaleboght, Gowanus, and the Ferry,—now Fulton Ferry,—which were entirely distinct, and were not embraced within the general name of Brooklyn, until after the organization of the township of that name by the British Colonial Government. Those of our citizens who remember the lands on Fulton avenue near Nevins street and De Kalb Avenue before the changes which were produced by the filling in of those streets, will recollect that their original character was marshy and springy, being in fact the bed of the valley which received the drain of the hills extending on either side of it from the Waaleboght to Gowanus Bay. This would lead almost to the conclusion that the name was given on account of the locality; but though we have very imperfect accounts as to who were the first settlers of Brooklyn proper, still reasoning from analogy in the cases of New Utrecht and New Amersfoort, we cannot probably err in supposing that Brooklyn owes its name to the circumstance that its first settlers wished to preserve in it a memento of their homes in Fatherland. After the English conquest, there was a continual struggle between the Dutch and English orthography. Any one who will take the trouble to consult the colonial laws and our County records, will find quite as great a variety of spelling of the name in them as in the Dutch Chronicles of Breukelen. Thus it is spelled Breucklyn, Breuckland, Brucklyn, Broucklyn, Brookland, Brookline, and several other ways. At the end of the last century it settled down into the present Brooklyn. In this form it still retains sufficiently its original signification of the *marsh* or *brook land*."

APPENDIX V.—(PAGE 62.)

COPY OF AN ORIGINAL PAPER IN THE ARCHIVES OF THE NEW YORK HISTORICAL SOCIETY.

This paper, presented to the Society by Peter A. Jay, gives some curious information in relation to the localities occupied by Jacob Hanse and Jores Hanse (two sons of Hans Hansen Bergen), and by their descendants. The paper is endorsed:

"ISRAEL HORSEFIELD,
ads.
ON D. OF HANS BERGEN. } *Copy of what witnesses can say.*"

Also endorsed in handwriting of Governor John Jay, "see Remsen's Evid. respecting Nutten's Island." Underneath is the following endorsement by Peter A. Jay: "The first two pages of these notes are, I believe, in the handwriting of John Chambers, an eminent counsel, afterwards Judge of the Supreme Court of the Colony—the note on the margin is in the writing of John Jay, his nephew and executor of his widow.

"P. A. JAY."

The trial appears to have taken place in 1741, but no records have been seen throwing light upon its results.

"Gerrit Dortland says he is 86 years of age. Was born at the ferry, and lived after at Brookland; knew Frederick Lubbert's land since a boy, says that he knew where Frederick Lubbertse lived, which is S. Westward of Sebring's mill,[1] and it was commonly esteemed that Frederick Lubbertse's line was near to his house. Remember Joost Francey in possession of land that George Bergen and Israel now have; fences went to the creek, about sixty years since he knew them; has now seen the fences and think they stand as then. Remembers Jane Evertse Bout in possession of Bevois land, was a man of 75, and married a girl of 16. Says he help't him to make his fences; work't there two years and fences stood as now, was then about 23 years old; never then heard that Frederick Lubbertse made any pretension to these lands nor any for his right till now.

"Maritie Bevois says is aged 84 years, near 85, was born in New York; it's last May 63 years since she came to live at Brookland; knew Frederick Lubbertse lived where Hans Bergen now lives. Remembers was going to the place where Brewer's mill[2] is now from Brookland by the house of Lubbertse and saw many little hills in the way from the house to the mill along the neck and enquired what the hills were, and was answered by them with her that it was the Indian corn land; knows where Mauchonell lived a little below Tommeties; knew the land of George Bergen to have belonged to Maritie Gerritse, or Ex. She let it to Israel Francey (Maratie Ex.) lived at New York. She remembers Francey on it about 60 years ago, that Francey lived on it till Maratie sold it to George Hanse, father of George Bergen. Remembers it to be always in fence, and that the fences stood as they now stand and the same of the other lotts; has lived at Brookland ever since she removed from York as before.

---

[1] This is evidently an error, Lubbertse's house being southeastward from Sebring's mill, and north northwest of Freek's mill pond, formerly Brower's, at the head of a small creek, and near the junction of the present Hoyt and Warren streets.

[2] Brower's Mill.

"Heard Jeromus Remsen's mother say, that there was only a small creek between Nutton Island and the shoar, and that a squah carried her sister over it in a tub; that that sister was the first born in this country.[1]

"Says that George Bergen's half-sister[2] lived at Bevois place on rent, and had a mind to buy Maratie's Ex. place but was disappointed, and complaining of it with tears said it was her brother Jacob Hanse Bergen and brother Michael that were the cause of Jorey's buying it and disappointing her.

"Joost Van Brunt, aged 77 years and upwards, born and lived at New Utrecht, says when he was about nine years old, when the Dutch came to take New York, he came with his father, mother and brothers in a wagon down the hollow near Tommeties, and they said that the other side of the hollow was Fred Lubbertse's land. Says that a great deal of the land is wash't away against Nutten Island, and it went farther out than now, but can't say how mutch. Remember to have seen meadow before Sebring's house, but how far out he knows not; has seen the fences at Bergen's and does not remember to have seen them otherwise than as now. That he was an arbitrator about dividing the land between Sebring and Bergen about 14 or 15 years ago, and that there was no pretence that lands in question were part or that they claimed any right there.

"Jerome Remsen, aged 77 years, was born about Brookland, and lived all his days there. Knew Frederick Lubbertse lived where Hans Bergen now—but had little acquaintance with him—remembers about 55 years ago, that Jacob Hans Bergen, father of Lessor, lived at Lubbertse's place, that he came to this depon't to get a pr. of shoes made, that then he told the depon't he had been at York with Maratie Gerretse to ask if she would sell her place, and that she had said she would, and said that he was going to his brother George Hansen, at Flatbush, to get him to buy it; that George Hansen bought it soon after and lived there; that he was there a long time before the date of the deed; that deed was only given at last paym't;[3] that the year depon't was married, which was 1688, the said Joris

---

[1] Jeromus Remsen's mother was Jannetie, dau. of Joris Jansen de Rapalie; her sister Sarah, who m. successively, Hans Hansen Bergen and Tunis Gysbert Bogaert, was the eldest child of Joris Jansen de Rapalie, and reputed to be the first born of Europeans in the country, in which respect the testimony of the witness agrees with what is generally admitted. According to this witness, Sarah was the one carried over in a tub.

[2] This half-sister, was one of Sarah de Rapalie's children, by Bogaart, her second husband.

[3] The deed is dated Sept. 13th, 1698.

Hanse, being a carpenter, agreed to do a job of work for depon't, if depon't would plow for him, and that depon't did plow for him the very land now in question, close up to the meadows, that it was then in fence and fences stand now in the very place they were then. Never heard of any pretence, and says that if he had any he would not have gone to advise his brother; says that he turned his plow ag't the fence of the land of Bevois, and that fences stood then as now so far as he thinks. Says that he has heard his mother say she was carried off Nutten Island by a Squah, and that it was all sedge and meadow, only a creek between Nutten Island and Long Island; his mother's sister was first born in this country; its now 116 or 117 years since she was born;[1] his mother was four years younger; he heard often from other people that there was but a small creek between Nutten and Long Island.[2]

"Abraham Lott, aged 57, remembers between 30 and 40 years that fences stand at George Bergen's as now; says he was an arbitrator; was shown then the will of Fred. Lubbertse, who devised to his own two daughters each one plantation as then in fence, and to his wife's two sons[3]

---

[1] From this testimony it appears that Jannatie, dau, of Joris Jansen de Rapalie, who m. Rem Vanderbeek, the common ancestor of the Remsens and the mother of Jeromus, was also carried from Nutten (now Governor's) Island to Long Island, by a squaw; that her sister (Sarah) was born about 1625, which agrees with the recorded date of her birth. *Quære:* from the witness's reference to his mother's sister Sarah, might it not be inferred that he intended to be understood that Sarah, and not his mother Jannatie, was the one carried over, as previously testified to by Maratie Bevoise, and that the tradition referred to the same person?

[2] On the margin against this paragraph is the following, in the handwriting of John Jay: "His mother carr'd from Nutten to Long Island by a squaw. Sworn 1711, at ye Tryal." (A reference to Ratzer's Map will show that "Red Hook," or "Lubbertse's Neck," or "the Neck of Brookland," as it was indifferently called, was almost completely isolated from the main-land, in its rear, by extensive salt meadows and creeks. At certain seasons and in certain conditions of the tide—as corroborated by the memory of those even now living—Red Hook became, in fact, *an island.* Moreover, being comparatively high ground, when viewed from the main-land, it concealed Nutten (or Governor's) Island in some measure. It is probable, therefore, that Red Hook Point became confounded, in Jannatie de Rapalie's subsequent recollections, with Nutten Island; and that the "creek between that Island and Long Island," as it seemed to her childish apprehension, and over which she was ferried in a tub, was in fact only the overflowed meadow between Red Hook and the main-land. This is our theory concerning the origin of the tradition relative to the former connection between Red Hook and Governor's Island, which certainly is disproved by the earliest known surveys and soundings, and which is unsupported by any philosophical explanation of the physical changes, etc., which that locality may have undergone since the early settlement of the country.—*Stiles.*)

[3] These were Cornelius Corssen and Peter Corssen, children of Tryntje Hendricks, the wife of Frederick Lubbertse, by Cornelius Petersen Vroom, her first husband.

other lotts; seems pretty sure the words were as then in fence; heard no discourse of any claim of neighbor's land out of fence.

"Peter Stryker, aged 44, says that being on a jury of view about 6 or 7 years ago, Jacob Hanse, father of Hanse Bergen, said at his house on talking of Worpus, there's Worpus,[1] pointing with his finger thro' his window to the head of the creek by his garden; remembers about 30 years the land in fence as now and no claim till within this year or two.

"Peter Winans, aged 79, born at Bedford, and about 8 or ten years old when he came to live at Brookland; knows the land in dispute upwards of sixty years ago, and believes the fences stand now much as they did then; ab't 40 or 45 years ago he went to live at Staten Island; he remembers Nicholas Baker,[2] who was husband of Maritie Gerretsen, first lived upon the land of George Bergen, and the witness's father and Joost France hired it of Maritie Gerretsen, or her husband, and his father left it to Joost France. He remembers Jan Evertse Bout, who lived upon the land sold by Carel De Bevoise to Israel, above 60 years ago; he knew Fred. Lubbertse, and never heard he made any pretense on any of their lotts. Knew old George Hanse Bergen, father of the present George, in possession of the premises above 40 or 45 years agoe, when France's time was out, and he was often in the house.

"Benjamin Van Dewater, aged 71 years, said he knew Jan Evertse Bout, the son of the patentee; that he had heard and understood that the father was owner of both the place of Bergen[3] and Debevois, that he made a will and died before his son was born; that 63 years ago he remembers Annetje Pieterson, widow of Jan Evertse Bout the elder, in possession of the land of Carel Debevoise; they lived on it about 12 years and then let it out."

In the *Bergen Genealogy*, p. 229, and also in *Brooklyn Corporation Manual* for 1864, is a fac-simile of an ancient map of this property in possession of a descendant of Hans Hansen Bergen.[4]

---

[1] See *ante*, p. 64, *note*. The "Worpus" pointed out by Jacob Hanse may also have been the site of an Indian village, a large Indian burying-ground being located in the vicinity, where remains were exhumed a few years ago in levelling the ground for city purposes; Indian maize lands being also, in that region, referred to in the early patents.

[2] Maritie's husband was Nicholas Janse, baker.

[3] The deed from Maritie Gerretse to Jores Bergen, in addition to the plantation patented by Kieft to Garret Wolpherste Couwenhoven, covers the one-half of the neck of land butting against Gowanus Creek, patented to Jan Evertse Bout.

[4] The annotations to this Appendix are by Hon. Teunis G. Bergen.

APPENDIX VII.—(PAGE 141.)

EXTRACTS FROM ANCIENT RECORDS OF THE FIRST PROTESTANT REFORMED DUTCH CHURCH IN BROOKLYN.

(Copied by Hon. Teunis G. Bergen.)

List of Church Members March 12th, 1660, when the Church was first organized.

Joris Dirckson.
Susanna Dubbels.
Albert Cornelissen (Wantenear, *i. e.* "the glove maker").
Tryntie Hadders (Hudden ?).
Willem Gerritse van Couwenhoven.
Aeltje Joris (Brinckerhoff).
Pieter Montfoort.
Sara de Plancke.
Jan Evertse (Bout).
Tryntje Symons.
Willem Bredenbent.
Aeltje Brackunee.
Jan Pietersen.
Grietje Jans.
Teunis Nyssen (Denyse).
Femmetie Jans.
Adam Brouwer.
Magdalena Jacobs.
Johannes Marcus.
Elsje Hendricks.
Teunis Janse.
Barber Lucas.
Jan Jorisse (Rapalie).
Jan Hibon (under censure).
Gertruyt Barents.
1660, Oct. 17th. Maria Fredericks, of the Haag.
Pieter Jansen, of the Manhattens.
Annetje Jans, of Amsterdam.
Dec. 29. Wiggert Reyniersen, of Oosturieslant.
Swantie Jans, wid. of Cornelis Potter.
Jan Martyn van Campen.
1661, April 10th. Sara Joris Rapalje (wife of Hans Hansen Bergen), taken on certificate from the Manhattans, as a member.
Dirck Jansen, of Amsterdam.
Marritien Teunis, of Nieuw Netherland.
Thomas Jansen (van Dyck), of Nieuw Utrecht.
Fytie Dircks, of Amsterdam.
Pieter Prae, of Diepe.
Catharine Lethie.
Marcus Soison.
Lysbeth Rossillou, of Leyden.
May 29th. Symon Joosten, of Marrelbeeck.
Auneken Barents, of Amsterdam.
Teunis Gysbertse (Bogaart), of Heykoop.
Aris Willemzen (Bennet), of Nieuw Netherland.
Garrit Dirckzen Crousen, of Wynschoot.
Jannekin Pieters, wife of Jan Cornelissen de Zeen.
Oct. 2d. Jan Clerk, of Brazil, admitted to membership.
Dec. 25. Willem Willemse (Bennet).
Gertruyt van Mullen.
Thomas Verdon.
Janneken Claese.
1662, April 2d. Brecktje Hans (Bergen), of Nieuw Netherland.
May 22. Fytie Martens, of Hamburg.
September 27th. Mechtelina Specht, of Utrecht.
Marritie (Baddia, *née*, Bennett, *née*) Thomas, wife of Mr. Paulus (Vanderbeeck).
Anneken Hans (Bergen), of Nieuw Netherland.
Agnietie Jans, of Amsterdam.
Dec. 25th. Joris Jansen Rappalje
Catherine Jeronymus (Rappalje).
Catharine Joris Rapalje, of Nieuw Netherland.
Frederick Lubbertsen.

Tryntje Hendricks.

Paulus Derckse, with attestation of Fort Orange.

Jan Pietersze.

Maria Hoogeboom, of Bunninck.

1663, Feb. 21st. Wilhelmus Bredenbent, of Cujanus (Gowanus), chosen Elder in place of Jan Jorise, who died on the 28th of January, 1663.

March 25th. Marten Reyerszen, of Amsterdam, admitted to membership with attestation of Flatbush.

Anneken Dourcoop, wife of Michael Syperus, with attestation of certificate of the Manhattans.

Sept. 23d. Pierre Parmentier, of Manhiem.

Thonnet Terrin, of Manhiem.

Roelof Willemszen, of Beverwyck.

Willemken Tyssen, from Beverwyck.

Dec. 23d. Cornelis van Bossum (Borsum).

Geertje Gysbert.

Jean Messural.

Jenne Carton.

1664, April 9th. Meynert Jorney, of Manheim.

Jacob Leendertsen, of Middlewout.

Rebecca Fredericks, of Middlewout.

Albert Coninck, of Middlewout.

Tryntje Jans, of Middlewout.

Aert Teunissen Middagh, of Heykoop.

Janneken Jans, of Almeloo.

Judith Joris (Rapalie), of Nieuw Netherland.

Janneken Montfoort, of Nieuw Netherland.

Anneken Rems, of Nieuw Netherland.

Nieltje Jans, of Nieuw Netherland.

1670, May 13th. Dirck Storm.

Jan Pietersen Mackelyck.

Styntien Janssen, his wife.

1684, Oct. 3d. Maria Baddia presented the Church with a silver "beecker," or communion-cup. (This Maria Baddia, sometimes called Mary Thomas, mar. 1. Jacob Vardon or Verden; 2. Willem Adriaense Bennet, and 3. Mr. Paulus Vanderbeeck.

OLD AND NEW COMMUNICANTS OF BROOKLYN.

Extracted from a list of communicants in the Protestant Reformed churches of Brooklyn, Flatbush, Flatlands, and New Utrecht, from September 6th, 1677 to 1685, copied, by Hon. Teunis G. Bergen, from the church records of Flatbush, in the handwriting of Rev. Casparus Van Zuuren, who, during said period, was Pastor of the churches in the above-mentioned towns. The original spelling of the record has been followed as nearly as possible.

RESIDING AT "BETHFORT" (BEDFORD).

Thomas Lambertsz and Jannetje Jurriaans his wife.

Jans Hansz Bergen and Jannetje Teunis his wife (moved to Jamaica).

Dirk Paulus and Aagje Teunis his wife.

Paulus Dirksz and Jannetje his wife (moved to Jamaica).

Lysbeth Thomas.

Maria Storm (moved).

Hendrikje Johannis (moved to Staten Island).

Hendrik Claaz.

Jacob Joris and Lysbeth Thomas his wife.

Willem Jorisz and Hendrikje Johannes his wife.

Hendrik Timonsz.

Jan Gerritz and Anna Rems his wife.

Teunis Janz and Barbara Lucas his wife.

Styntje Gerrits (moved to New Lotts).

Hans Teunisz and Marritje Teunis his wife (Bushwick).

Lucas Teunisz.

Marriy Teunisz.

Paulus and Lysbeth Paulus his wife.

Matthys.

Bourgon Broucard and Catharina his wife (moved to Flatbush).

RESIDING AT THE "WALE-BOCHT."

Rem Jansz and Jannetje Joris Rapailie his wife.

Teunis Gysbertsz Boogaart and Sara Joris Rapailie his wife.

Jan Teunis and Catalina Teunis Bogaart his wife.

Frederik Lubbertsz (dead) and Tryntje his wife.

Jacob Hansz Bergen and Elsje Frederiks his wife.

Daniel Joris Rapailie and Sara Abrahams Clock his wife.

Cataline Rapailie.

Pieter Van Neste and Judith Joris Rapailie his wife.

Pieter Pietersz Van Neste, Jun'r.

Marten Reyersz and Annetje Joris Boogart his wife.

Joris Remsz.

Femmetje Remsz, Jannetje Remsz, sisters of Joris.

Aaltje Teunis Begaart (moved to Flatbush, and then to Jamaica).

Cataline Boogart.

Jan Damen and Sophia Martens his wife.

Michiel Hainelle and Hendrika Strokels his wife.

Michiel Hansz Bergen and Femmetje Teunis his wife.

Hendrik Corsen and Josina Pietersz Van Neste his wife (moved to the Raritans).

Cornelis Corszen and Marritje Vander Grist his wife (moved to Staten Island).

Pieter Corzen.

Juriaan Hendriksz and Corneliae Beauvois his wife.

Sander Egbertsz (died Oct. 7, 1681, at Staten Island).

Gerrit Gerritsz Dorland and Geertrud Aukes his wife.

Jan Buys and Willemje Thyssen his wife.

Machild Roelofs (moved to Bergen).

RESIDING IN QUARTERS OF BROOKLYN NOT SPECIFIED.

Jacques Couzard (dead) and Lydia Willemsz his wife (of Bushwick).

Hendrik Matthysz.

Abraham de Rivier.

Volkherd Dirksz and Annetje Philips.

Cornelis Nevius and Agatje Joris.

Annetje Teunis Boogaart.

Neltje Teunis Boogaart.

Femmetje Dirks.

Sara Catharina Nevius.

Aert Anthonisz Middag.

Mauritsz Teunisz.

Aeltje Akkermans.

Annetje Teunis Couvers.

Marritje Martens.

Aeltje Dratz.

Lysbeth Van Neste.

Harmtje Dirks (moved).

Maria Bennet.

Sara Schouten.

Jacob Remsz.

Hieronymus Remsz and sister Jannetje Remsz.

Hieronymus Van Neste.

Jacomyntje Van Neste, sister of Hieronymus.

Cornelia Jans Damen.

RESIDING AT THE "KREUPEL-BOSCH."

Bourgon Brougard and Catharina his wife.
Abraham de Rivier.
} All, in 1680, removed to Staten Island.

RESIDING AT THE "VEER VAN BREUKELEN" (FERRY).

Dirk Jansz (the ferryman) and Marritje Teunis his wife.

Jan Gerritsz Van Couwenhoven and Gerdientje de Sille his wife.

Jan Aartsz and Adriantje his wife.

Hieronymus Jorisz de Rapailie and Annetje Teunis his wife.

Pieter Corsz and Catarine Vander Beek his wife (removed to New York).

Cornelis Teunis and Hermtje Dirks his wife.

Joris Jacobsz and Tryntje Claassen his wife.

Matthys Brouwer and Marritje Pieters his wife.

Jan Teunisz and Zwaantje Potters his [wife.]

Denys Teunisz.

RESIDING IN THE "DORP" (VILLAGE).

Jan Damen Buys and Willemtje Tyssen his wife.

Wouter Gysbrechtsz and Lysbeth Jans his wife (removed to Flushing).

Sophia van Lodenstien.

Jacobus Beauvois and Maria Joosten his wife.

Gertrude Beauvois.

Catharina Beauvois.

Cornelia Beauvois.

Hendrik Slecht and Elsje Barends Lieveling his wife.

Andries Jurriaaansz and Annetje Pieters his wife (died 19th March, 1680).

Lambert Dorland and Harmtje his wife.

RESIDING AT "GOUWANUS."

Adam Brouwer and Magdalena Verden his wife.

Pieter Adamsz.

Gerrit Croesen (died 7th March, 1680), and Neeltje Jan his wife.

Claas Aaertsz and Lammetje Vechten his wife.

Hendrik Clausz Vechten.

Gerrit Clausz Vechten.

Jan Frederiksz and Aaltje Jans his wife.

Pieter Jansz and Annetje Jans his wife.

Jan Pietersz and Elsje Pieters his wife (moved to Staten Island).

Willem Willemsz Bennet and Gertrude Van Mullen his wife.

Paulis Vander Beek (dead, 1680) and Maria Badye his wife.

Aaltje Bredenbent.

Jurriaan Plank and Hester Vander Beek his wife.

Paulis (Pauli-filius) Vander Beek and Sara Schouten his wife (moved to New York).

Johannes Christoffelsz and Maria Willemsz Bennet his wife.

Thomas Jansz Van Dyk and Marritje his wife.

Haggaus Jansz Van Dyk and Jannetje Lamberts his wife.

Hendrik Matthysz and Annetje Tilemans his wife.

Willem Huykke and Annetje his wife.

Thomas Verdon and Annetje Verdon his wife.

Lambert Hendriksz.

Matthys Pietersz Luyster.

Willem Brouwer and Magdalena Verden his wife.

Jan Jansz.

Conradus Vander Beek and Elsje Vander Beek (moved to New York).

Geertruid Vander Hard.

Annetje Tilemans.

Arien Willemsz Bennet and Agnietje Van Dyck his wife (come from New Utrecht).

Jan Willemsz Bennet.

Tryntje Ariens Bennet.

The Records of the Reformed Dutch Church of Brooklyn commence on the 5th day of Sept. 1660, on which day they petitioned the Governor and Council, in consequence of the great age and infirmities of their Minister, Do. Polhemus, and the difficulties of the road to Flatbush, to aid in providing them with another Minister. An application having been made to the Classis of Amsterdam, Do. Henricus Selyns was sent over. At this time Joris Dirckzen Brinckerhoff was Elder, and Wilhelmus Bredenbent and Pieter Monfoort Deacons of the Church. Selyns was engaged, in addition to Brooklyn, to preach at Governor Stuyvesant's Bouwery (farm), in New Amsterdam.

On his arrival, preparation was made to build for his use a suitable dwelling-house, and also a small church, which matters were placed in the charge of the Elder, Joris Dircksen, and with him was associated Albert Cornelisen, Schepen of Brooklyn. Aucke Jans (Van Nuyse) and Frans Blootgoet were the mechanics employed in the erection of the dwelling-house.

The Elder, Joris Dircksen and Deacon Pieter Montfoort having died, on the 9th of Feb., 1661, an election took place, when Willem Bredenbent was chosen Elder, and Teunis Jansen Coevers and Jan Jorizen (Rapalie) Deacons.

On an accounting by the Deacons, it appears that there was			
received in 1660	gl.	255	5 st.
To the 2d of March, 1661		62	28
		317	33

Paid out in 1660, from 2d Oct.	gl.	66	15
In 1661, to 2d March		50	
		116	15

On hand, in specie, prior to the date of the account	gl.	152
Legacy from Barent Balde, for aid to the poor		50
		202

Joris Dirckzen having, prior to his death, acted as chorister, and since that period Do. Selyns having performed the same service, it was now, May 29th, determined to procure the services of a regular chorister, precentor, and schoolmaster. On this determination, on the 6th of July, the services of Mr. Carel d' Beauvois, schoolmaster ot New Amsterdam, was employed, under the following regulations:

1. Said Precentor to cause the Psalms sung before the sermon to be properly set forth or noted on the Psalm board.
2. After the first ringing of the bell, he shall place the stools and benches in the church or meeting-place in order, and read a chapter out of the Holy Scriptures, and the twelve articles of the Christian belief.
3. He shall in particular read in the books of the Old and New Testament, out of the Psalms and Prophets, during the administration of the Lord's Sacrament, from the 22d, 23d, 31st, 40th, 42d, 51st, 69th, 111th, 112th, or 113th Psalms; from the 53d chap. of Isaiah, the 6th and 13th chap. of John to the end of his Gospel, and the 27th chap. of Matthew. Also 10th and 11th chap. of 1st Corinthians; 7th, 8th, 9th, and 10th chap. of the Epistle to the Hebrews, and the 2d and 3d chapters of the Revelations.
4. He shall, immediately on the third ringing of the bell, begin to sing the designated Psalm.
5. During sickness or necessary absence, he shall allow no one to act in his place, unless known to be of good character, nor without notice to the Consistory.
6. He shall properly, diligently, and industriously attend to the school, instil in the minds of the young the fear of the Lord, and set them a good example: to open the school with prayer and close with a Psalm, also to exercise the scholars in the questions in the "groat regulen" of the Rev. pious and learned father, Do. Johannes Megapolensis, Minister of the Gospel in Amsterdam, in N. Netherland.

Lastly. That the said Precentor, in addition to the salary allowed by the Governor and Council of N. Netherland, and the magistrates of Brooklyn, will be furnished by the Consistory with house-rent and entertainment or provisions.

On the 21st Feb., 1663, Jan Jorise (Rapalie) having died, at an election for church officers, Willem Bredenbent was continued as Elder for one year, Teunis Jansen Coevers, elected Elder, Willem Gerritsen Van Couwenhoven and Teunis Gysbertse Bogaert, Deacons.

On the 27th of Feb., 1664, Teunis Janssen Coevers and Teunis Gysbertse Bogaert were elected Elders, and Willem Gerritse Van Couwenhoven and Willem Willemsen (Bennet), Deacons, who were in office when Selyns resigned his charge.

List of "Catechumenen" (students of the Catechism) in the Church at Brooklyn, Nov. 26th, 1662.

Catalyntie Teunis.
Aeltie Teunis Gysbertsen (Bogaert).
Saertie Pieters.
Catharyn, Getruyd, } d'Beauvois.
Hendrickie Jans.
Catharyn, Marritie, } Joosten.
Saertie Teunis (Covert).
Jenrie Probasco.
Hendrick Obee.
Daniel Jorissen.
Pieter Pietersen.
Jan Pietersen.
Laurens Haf.
Cornelis Jansen.
Jan Teunissen (Denyse).
Nys Teunis (Denyse).
Anna Tielemans.
Jacob, Willem, } Jorissen.
Joost Symonsen.
Hendrick Janssen.
Jan Teunissen.
Stoffel Probasco.
Cornelis Abramsen.
Lucas Teunissen (Covert).
Joris Hansen (Bergen).
Marie Hansen (Bergen).
Annetie Teunis (Denyse).
Janneken Montfoort.
Aecht Teunis.
Janneken Teunis.
Anneken Rems.
Aeltie Teunis Jansen.
David de Potter.
Marten Reyersen.
Pieter Lambertsen.

APPENDIX VII.—(PAGE 198.)

BROOKLYN TAX LISTS, OF THE OLDEN TIME.

ASSESSMENT OF THE REAL AND PERSONAL PROPERTY OF THE INHABITANTS OF BREUCKELEN, MADE UP ON THE 20TH AUGUST, ANNO. 1675.

(N. Y. Doc. Hist., iv., pp. 144–150.)

Theunis Jansen—3 polls, 4 horses, 1 ditto of 1 yr.; 2 oxen, 4 cows, 4 ditto of 3 yrs.; 2 ditto of 2 yrs.; 4 ditto of 1 yr.; 5 hogs, £169; 23 morgens of land and valley, £46: Total, £215.

Claes Arense—3 polls, 1 horse, 4 cows, 1 ditto of 3 yrs.; 1 ditto of 2 yrs.; 1 ditto of 1 yr., £94; 14 morgens of land and valley, 28: Total, £122.

Mattheis Brouwer—1 poll, 2 cows, £28; 1½ morgen valley, £3: Total, £31.

Paulus Vander Beecke—2 polls, 2 horses, 4 cows, 3 ditto of 3 yrs.; 1 ditto of 1 yr., £93.10; 20 morgens of land and valley, £40: Total, £133.10.

Jan Pieterse, the Elder—1 poll, 4 oxen, 3 ditto of 2 yrs.; 4 ditto of 1 yr., £45.10; 16 morgens of land and valley, £32: Total, 117.10.

Jan Cornelise Buys—1 poll, 2 horses, 2 cows, 1 ditto of 2 yrs.; 1 ditto of 1 yr.; 12 sheep, £59.

Dierck Stoorm—1 poll, 2 cows, 1 ditto of 3 yrs.; 1 hog, £33.

Nicklaes Backer—1 poll, 1 horse, 3 cows, 3 ditto of 2 yrs.; 2 ditto ot 1 yr.; 6 hogs, £61.10; 18 morgens of land and valley, £36: Total, £97.10.

Joost Fransen—1 poll, 2 horses, 4 cows, 1 ditto of 3 yrs.; 3 ditto of 2 yrs.; 2 ditto of 1 yr., £76.10; 10½ morgens of land and valley, 21: Total, £97.10.

Cornelis Corse(n) Vroom—1 poll, 2 horses, 1 ditto of 1 yr.; 3 cows, 2 ditto of 2 yrs.; 1 ditto of 1 year; 4 sheep, 2 hogs, £70; 22 morgens of land and valley, 44; Total, £114.

Jan Pieterse Mackelyck—1 poll, 4 oxen, 4 cows, 1 ditto of 1 yr.; 2 hogs, £65.10; 12 morgens land and valley, 24: Total, £89.10.

Dierck Cornelise Hooglant—3 polls, 2 horses, 6 cows, 2 ditto of 2 yrs.; 3 ditto of 1 yr.; 2 hogs, £119.10; 8 morgens of land and valley, £16: Total, £135.10.

Paulus Mickielse Van der Voort—1 poll, 1 horse of 3 yrs., 2 oxen, 3 cows, 1 ditto of 3 yrs.; 1 ditto of 1 yr., £58.10; 10 morgens of land and valley, £20: Total, £78.10.

Willem Willemse—1 poll, 2 horses, 2 oxen, 6 cows, 2 ditto of 2 yrs.; 4 ditto of 1 yr.; 1 hog, £96; 13½ morgens of land and valley, 27: Total, £123.

Dierck Hattum—1 poll, 2 oxen, 1 cow, 1 ditto of 2 yrs., £37.10; 1½ morgen of land, £3: Total, £40.10.

Rem Jansen—3 polls, 5 horses, 8 cows, 4 ditto of 3 yrs.; 4 ditto of 1 yr.; 2 hogs, £188; 19 morgens of land and valley, £38: Total, £226.

Frederick Lubbertse—1 poll, 6 cows, 1 ditto of 2 yrs.; 2 ditto of 1 yr.; 7 sheep, £56.10; 15 morgens of land and valley, £80: Total, £86.10.

Pieter van Neest—1 poll, 5 cows, 2 hogs, £45; 5½ morgens of land and valley, £11: Total, £56.

Pieter Jansen—1 poll, 2 horses, 5 cows, 3 ditto of 2 yrs.; 4 ditto of 1 yr., £80.10; 8 morgens of land, £16: Total, £96.10.

Big Jan—2 polls, 2 oxen, 2 cows, 1 ditto of 2 yrs.; 1 ditto of 1 yr., £44; 2 morgens of valley, £4: Total, £48.

Johannes Christoffel—1 poll, 2 oxen, 2 cows, £40; 6 morgens of land and valley, £12: Total, 52.

Thomes Jansen—1 poll, 2 horses, 2 cows, £52.

Conradus vander Beek—1 poll, 2 oxen, 3 cows, £45; 14 morgens of land and valley, £28: Total, £73.

Ackeys Jansen—1 poll, 1 cow, £23.

Paulus Dierckse—2 polls, 2 horses, 2 oxen, 7 cows, 2 ditto of 2 yrs.; 5 ditto 1 yr.; 3 hogs, £122.10; 12 morgens of land and valley, £24: Total, £146.10.

Dierck Pauluse—1 poll, 1 horse of 3 yrs., 3 cows, 4 ditto of 2 yrs.; 3 ditto of 1 yr.; 1 hog, £56.10; 2 morgens of land and valley, £24: Total, £80.10.

Weynant Pieterse—1 poll, 2 horses, 3 cows, 1 ditto of 2 yrs.; 2 ditto of 1 yr., £62.10; 5 morgen of land, 10: Total, £72.10.

Adam Brouwer—2 polls, 2 cows, 3 ditto of 3 yrs.; 3 sheep, 1 hog, £60; 1½ morgen of valley, £3: Total, £63.

Johannes Marcuse—1 poll, £18.

Evert Hendrickse—1 poll, £18.

Gerrit Croesen—1 poll, 2 oxen, 4 cows, 2 ditto of 3 yrs.; 3 ditto of 2 yrs.; 2 ditto of 1 yr.; 3 hogs, £27.10; 14 morgens land and valley, £28: Total, £99.10.

Egbert Steuense—1 poll, £18.

Simon Aersen—1 poll, 2 oxen, 3 cows, 2 ditto of 1 yr.; 3 hogs, £51; 10 morgens of land and valley, £20: Total, £71.

Pieter Pieterse—1 poll, 1 horse, £30.

Lambert Jansen Dorlant—1 poll, 4 cows, £38; 8 morgens of land and valley, £16· Total, £54.

Jerom. de Rappallie—3 polls, 3 cows, 1 ditto of 1 yr.; 1 horse, £82.10; 8 morgens of land and valley, £16: Total, £98.

Daniel de Rappallie—1 poll, 1 horse, 1 cow, £35.

Simon Claessen—1 poll, 1 horse, 1 cow, 1 ditto of 3 yrs.; 2 hogs, £41; 6 morgens of land, £12: Total, £53.

Theunes Gisbertse Bogaert—3 polls, 4 horses, 1 ditto of 1 yr.; 2 oxen, 14 cows, 6 ditto of 3 yrs.; 6 ditto of 2 yrs.; 10 ditto of 1 yr.; 6 hogs, £247; 40 morgens of land and valley, £80: Total, £327.

Susanne Dubbels—2 oxen, 5 cows, 3 ditto of 2 yrs.; 3 ditto of 1 yr., £49; 8 morgens of land and valley, £16: Total, £65.

Pieter Corse(n)—1 poll, £18.

Hendrick Corse(n)—2 polls, 2 horses, 2 sheep, £61; 10 morgens of land and valley, £20: Total, £81.

Hendrick Theymese—1 poll, 1 horse, 3 cows, £45; 3 morgens of land, £6: Total, £51.

Thomes Lambertse—2 polls, 3 horses, 1 ditto of 1 yr.; 6 cows, 2 ditto of 3 yrs.; 4 ditto of 2 yrs.; 2 ditto of 1 yr.; 6 sheep, 1 hog, £129.10; 23 morgens of land and valley, £46: Total, £175.10.

Jan Gerritse—1 poll, 2 horses, 1 ditto of 2 yrs.; 3 cows, 1 ditto of 2 yrs.; 3 ditto of 1 yr.; 2 sheep, 1 hog, £71; 11½ morgens of land and valley, £23: Total, £95.

Jean Aersen—1 poll, 4 horses, 3 cows, 1 ditto of 2 yrs.; 2 ditto of 1 yr.; 1 hog, £87.10.

Juff'w Potters—1 horse, 1 ditto of 2 yrs.; 4 cows, 1 ditto of 2 yrs.; 2 ditto of 1 yr.; 2 hogs, £44.10; 18 morgens of land and valley, £36: Total, £80.10.

Dierck Janse Woertman—1 poll, 2 horses, 3 cows, £57; 9 morgens of land and valley, £18: Total, £75.

Maerten Ryerse—1 poll, 4 horses, 1 ditto of 3 yrs.; 6 cows, 1 ditto of 3 yrs.; 2 ditto of 2 yrs.; 1 ditto of 1 yr.; 1 hog, £115.10; 31½ morgens of land and valley, £63: Total, £178.10.

Catherine Jeronimus—1 ox, 1 cow, £11.

Jabeck Gisbertse—1 poll, 2 horses, 3 cows, 1 ditto of 3 yrs.; 3 ditto of 2 yrs.; 1 ditto of 1 yr.; 2 hogs, £67; 8 morgens of land and valley, £16: Total, £83.

Jan Frederickse—1 poll, 2 cows, 1 morgen of valley, £30.

Baerent Hegbertse—1 poll, 1 cow, 3 ditto of 3 yrs.; 1 ditto of 2 yrs.; 2 ditto of 1 yr., £40.10; 4 morgens of land and valley, £8: Total, £48.10.

Jan Hansen—1 poll, 2 horses, 4 cows, 2 ditto of 3 yrs.; 2 ditto of 2 yrs.; 1 ditto of 1 yr.; 4 hogs, £80.10; 10 morgens of land and valley, £20: Total, £100.10.

Pieter Jansen—1 poll, 1 horse, 3 cows, £45; 8 morgens of land and valley, £16: Total, £61.

Michil Hansen—1 poll, 2 horses, 4 cows, 2 ditto of 3 yrs.; 2 ditto of 2 yrs., £75; 20 morgens of land and valley, £40: Total, £115.

Wouter Geisse—1 poll, £18.

Andries Jurianse—2 polls, 4 horses, 6 cows, 3 ditto of 2 yrs.; 1 ditto of 1 yr.; 4 sheep, £124.10; 28 morgens of land and valley, £56: Total, £180.10.

Jan Gillese—1 poll, 1 hog, £19.

Joores Jacobse—3 polls, 5 horses, 1 ditto of 1 yr.; 5 cows, 3 ditto of 3 yrs.; 2 ditto of 2 yrs.; 4 ditto of 1 yr.; 2 hogs, £167; 40 morgens of land and valley, £80: Total, £247.

Total amount of the valuation of the jurisdiction of Breuckelen, £5,204.

ASSESSMENT ROLL OF BREUCKELEN, MADE UP SEPTEMBER, 1676.

(N. Y. Doc. Hist., ii., p. 475.)

Claes Aerense—3 polls, 1 horse, 5 cows, 2 ditto of 2 yrs.; 2 ditto of 1 yr., £96.10; 10 morgens of land and valley, £28: Total, £124.10.

Jan De Swede—1 poll, 1 horse, 1 ditto of 1 yr.; 4 cows, 1 ditto of 1 yr.; 1 hog, £55.10; 2 morgens of land, £4: Total, £59.10.

Baerent Hegbertse—1 poll, 1 cow, £62; 3 morgens of land, £6: Total, £68.

Joost Fransen—1 poll, 2 horses, 1 ditto of 1 yr.; 5 cows, 1 ditto of 2 yrs.; 3 ditto of 1 yr.; 2 hogs, £79; 19 morgens of land and valley, £38: Total, £117.

Andries Juriaense—1 poll, 2 horses, 2 ditto of 3 yrs.; 8 cows, 1 ditto of 2 yrs.; 2 ditto of 1 yr., £103.10; 28 morgens of land and valley, £56: Total, £159.10.

Lambert Jansen Dortlant—1 poll, 3 cows, £33; 8 morgens of land and valley, £16: Total, £49.

(Evert) Hendrickse—1 poll, £18.

Wouter Geisse [?]—1 poll, £18.

Simon Aersen—1 poll, 2 oxen, 4 cows, 1 ditto of 2 yrs.; 1 hog, £56; 8 morgens of land and valley, £16: Total, £72.

Jean Pietersen Mackelyck—1 poll, 4 cows, £38; 8 morgens of land, £16: Total, £54.

Jean Frederickse—1 poll, 2 horses, 2 cows, £52; 7 morgens of land, £14: Total, £66.

Johannes Christoffel—1 poll, 2 oxen, 2 cows, 1 ditto of 2 yrs., £42.10; 7 morgens of land, £14: Total, £56.10.

Mr. Paulus van der Beeck—2 polls, 3 horses, 4 cows, 2 ditto of 2 yrs.; 2 ditto of 1 yr., £100; 20 morgens of land and valley, £40: Total, £140.

Theunes Gisbertse (Bogaert)—3 polls, 4 horses, 1 ditto of 2 yrs.; 5 oxen, 2 cows, 5 ditto of 3 yrs.; 10 ditto of 2 yrs.; 8 ditto of 1 yr.; 9 hogs, £251; 40 morgens of land and valley, £80: Total, £331.

Simon Claes—1 poll, 1 horse, 2 cows, 1 ditto of 2 yrs.; 2 do of 1 yr.; 1 hog, £46.10; 7 morgens of land and valley, £14: Total, £60.10.

Juffrouw Potters—1 horse, 1 ditto of 3 yrs.; 4 cows, 1 ditto of 2 yrs.; 3 hogs, £45.

Jean Aersen—1 poll, 3 horses, 2 cows, 1 ditto of 3 yrs.; 2 ditto of 2 yrs.; 1 ditto of 1 yr., £74.10; 18 morgens of land and valley, £36: Total, £110.10.

Thomas Jansen Van d(uyn?)—1 poll, 2 horses, 3 cows, £57; 1 morgen of land, £2: Total, £59.

Acheys Jansen van deick—1 poll, 2 oxen, 2 cows, 1 ditto of 1 yr., £41.10; 1 morgen of land, £2: Total, £43.10.

Dierck Hattum—1 poll, 2 oxen, 2 cows, 1 ditto of 3 yrs.; 1 ditto of 2 yrs., £50.10; 1 morgen of land, £4: Total, £54.10.

Jurian Blancke—2 horses, 1 cow, 2 ditto of 1 yr., £32; 6 morgens of land, £12: Total, £44.

Daniel de Rappallie—1 poll, 1 horse, 2 cows (valuation destroyed).

Jerm. de Rappallie—2 polls, 2 horses, 2 cows; 8 morgens of land (valuation destroyed).

Pieter Jansen—1 poll, 2 horses, 2 oxen, 6 cows, 4 ditto of 2 yrs.; 3 ditto of 1 yr., £98.10; 25 morgens of land and valley, £50: Total, £148.10.

Jan Jansen—1 poll, 2 oxen, 2 cows, 1 ditto of 2 yrs.; 3 ditto of 1 yr., £45.10; 2 morgens of land, £4: Total, £49.10.

Hendrick Corsen—1 poll, 3 horses, 2 cows, 1 ditto of 2 yrs., £66.10; 12 morgens of land and valley, £24: Total, £90.10.

Pieter Corsen—1 poll, £18.

Casper Cornelise—1 poll, £18.

Willem Willemse Bennett—1 poll, 2 horses, 2 ditto of 1 yr.; 2 oxen, 5 cows, 4 ditto of 2 yrs.; 3 ditto of 1 yr., £99.10; 13½ morgens of land and valley, £27: Total, £126.10.

Rem Jansen—3 polls, 4 horses, 2 cows, 5 ditto of 3 yrs.; 2 ditto of 2 yrs.; 1 ditto of 1 yr.; 2 hogs, £184.10; 19 morgens of land and valley, £38: Total, £222.10.

Dierck Stoorm—1 poll, 1 horse, £30; 11 morgens of land and valley, £22: Total, £52.

Maerten Ryerse—1 poll, 4 horses, 8 cows, 1 ditto of 2 yrs.; 3 ditto of 1 yr.; 2 hogs, £117.10; 31½ morgens of land and valley, £63: Total, £180.10.

Aerent Isaack—1 poll, £18.

Susanne Dubels—2 oxen, 6 cows, 3 ditto of 2 yrs.; 3 ditto of 1 yr., £62.10, 18 morgens of land, £36: Total, £98.10.

Theunis Jansen—3 polls, 3 horses, 1 ditto of 2 yrs.; 2 oxen, 4 cows, 4 ditto of 9 yrs.; 4 ditto of 1 yr.; 2 hogs, £151; 23 morgens of land and valley, £46: Total, £197.

Jan Hansen—1 poll, 2 horses, 4 cows, 1 ditto of 3 yrs.; 1 ditto of 2 yrs.; 1 hog, £69.10; 18 morgens of land and valley, £36: Total, £105.10.

Dierck Pauluse—1 poll, 2 horses, 4 cows, 4 ditto of 2 yrs.; 3 ditto of 1 yr., £76.10; 12 morgens of land and valley, £24: Total, £100.10.

Thomas Lambertse—1 poll, 2 horses, 1 ditto of 3 yrs.; 4 oxen, 8 cows, 2 ditto of 1 yr.; 4 sheep (MS. destroyed), £147.04; 23 morgens of land and valley, £46: Total, £193.04.

(Name destroyed)—1 poll, 1 horse of 1 yr., 1 ox, 4 cows, 1 ditto of 2 yrs.; 2 sheep, £51; 15 morgens of land and valley, £30: Total, £81.

Paulus Dierckse—2 polls, 2 horses, 2 oxen, 5 cows, 2 ditto of 3 yrs.; 5 ditto of 2 yrs.; 3 ditto of 1 yr.; 5 hogs, £127; 12 morgens of land and valley, 24: Total, £151.

Jean Gerritse—1 poll, 2 horses, 2 cows, 2 ditto of 3 yrs.; 2 ditto of 2 yrs.; 2 ditto of 1 yr.; 2 sheep, 1 hog, £70; 11½ morgens of land and valley, £23: Total, £93.

Bourgon Brouchaert—1 poll, 2 cows, £28; 11½ morgens of land and valley, £23: Total, £51.

Adam Brouwer—1 poll, 3 cows, 4 sheep, and 1½ morgens of valley, £37.14.

Willem Brouwer—1 poll, £18.

Jabecq Brouwer—1 poll, £18.

Conradus Vander (Beek)—1 poll, 2 oxen, 2 cows, 1 ditto of 1 yr., £43; 14 morgens of land, £28: Total, £71.

Capt'n Cornelis—1 poll, 3 horses, 2 cows, 2 ditto of 3 yrs.; 1 ditto of 2 yrs.; 1 ditto of 1 yr., £84; 22 morgens of land and valley, £44: Total, £128.

Weynant Pieterse—1 poll, 2 horses, 3 cows, £57; 5 morgens of land, £10: Total, £67.

Paulus Michilse Vander Voort—1 poll, 2 oxen, 3 cows, 1 ditto of 2 yrs.; 1 ditto of 1 yr., £49; 12 morgens of land and valley, £24: Total, £73.

Pieter Van Nest—3 polls, 4 cows, 1 ditto of 1 yr.; 1 hog, £80; 5½ morgens of land and valley, £11: Total, £91.

Michil Hansen—1 poll, 2 horses, 5 cows, 1 ditto of 3 yrs.; 2 ditto of 1 yr., £74; 20 morgens of land and valley, 40: Total, £114.

Hendrick Theunese—1 poll, 1 horse, 2 cows, 1 ditto of 2 yrs., £42.10; 4 morgens of land, £8: Total, £50.10.

Jores Jacobse—3 polls, 4 horses, 3 ditto of 2 yrs.; 2 oxen, 3 cows, 2 ditto of 3 yrs.; 4 ditto of 2 yrs.; 4 ditto of 1 yr.; 2 hogs, 3 sheep, £6; 30 morgens of land, £60: Total, £66.

Dierck Cornelisse—1 poll, 2 horses, 3 cows (MS. destroyed); 15 morgens of land (MS. destroyed).

Jan Cornelise Buys—1 poll, 2 horses, 3 cows, 1 ditto of ——, 2 hogs, 12 sheep (MS. destroyed); 8 morgens of land and valley (MS. destroyed).

Gerrit Croes(en)—1 poll, 2 oxen, 2 cows, 1 ditto of 3 yrs.; 2 ditto of 2 yrs.; 3 do of 1 yr., £76.10; 14 morgens of land and valley, £28: £104.10.

The whole property of Breuckelen amounts to £5,067.18.

Taxed at 1*d.* in the pound sterling, should amount to £21. 2*s.* 4*d.*

Your obedient servant,

MICHIL HAINELLE.

VALUATION OF BREUCKELEN, TAKEN 26 SEPTEMBER, 1683.

(N. Y. Doc. Hist., ii., pp. 498–503.)

Jeronimus Jorisen—1 poll, 1 horse, 6 cows, 2 ditto of 2 yrs.; 1 ditto of 1 yr.; 2 hogs, £68.10; 8 morgens of land, £16: Total, £84.10.

Jan Cornelis Damen—2 horses, 5 cows, 4 ditto of 2 yrs.; 3 ditto of 1 yr., £63.10; 10 morgens of land, £20: Total, £83.10.

Teunis Jansen—2 horses, 5 cows, 6 ditto of 2 yrs.; 3 ditto of 1 yr.; 4 sheep, 1 poll, £90.10; 20 morgens of land, £40: Total, £130.10.

Willm Huicke—2 horses, 1 ditto of 1 yr.; 3 cows, 3 ditto of 2 yrs.; 2 ditto of 1 yr., £53.20; 8 morgens of land, £16: Total, £69.20.

Daniel Rapelie—5 horses, 6 cows, 4 ditto of 2 and 3 yrs.; 3 ditto of 2 yrs.; 2 ditto of 1 yr., £110.10; 24 morgens of land, £48: Total, £158.10.

Jan Aersen (Middagh)—3 horses, 5 cows, 2 ditto of 2 yrs.; 4 sheep, £70; 27 morgens of land, £54: Total, £124.

Thomas Vardon—2 horses, 3 cows, 1 ditto of 2 and 3 yrs.; 4 ditto of 1 yr.; 1 poll, £65.10; 8 morgens of land, £16: £81.10.

Jacob Jansen Bergen—2 horses, 1 poll, 3 cows, 1 ditto of 1 yr.; 3 ditto of 3 yrs.; 1 ditto of 1 yr., £67.30; 24 morgens of land and valley, £48: Total, £115.30.

Joris Hansen—1 poll, 2 horses, 3 cows, 2 ditto of 3 yrs.; 1 ditto of 2 yrs.; 2 ditto of 1 yr., £86.10; 12 morgens of land, 24: £110.10.

Cornelis Sebrings—1 poll, 2 horses, 2 cows, 3 ditto of 3 yrs., £64; 17 morgens of land and valley, £34: Total, £88.

Tryntie Korssen—3 cows, 2 ditto of 2 yrs.; 2 ditto of 3 yrs., £28; 2 morgens of land and valley, £4: Total, £32.

Pieter Korssen—1 poll, 2 horses, 4 cows, £62; 10 morgens of land and valley, £20: Total, £82.

Hendrick Korssen—10 morgens of land, £20.

Jacob Brouwer—2 cows, 1 ditto of 2 yrs., £30.10; 6 morgens of land and valley, £12: Total, £42.10.

Pieter Jansen—1 poll, 3 horses, 6 cows, 2 ditto of 3 yrs.; 1 ditto of 2 yrs.; 3 ditto of 1 yr., £99.20; 18 morgens of land and valley, £36: Total, £135.20.

Klaes Arentse—2 polls, 4 cows, 2 ditto of 2 yrs.; 2 ditto of 1 yr., £64; 12 morgens of land, £24: Total, £88.

Paulus Dirckse—1 poll, 3 horses, 5 cows, 2 ditto of 3 yrs.; 4 ditto of 2 yrs.; 2 ditto of 1 yr.; 1 ditto of 6 yrs., £106; 25 morgens of land, £50: Total, £156.

Liesbet Pouluse—1 cow, 1 ditto of 3 yrs.; 1 ditto of 5 yrs.; 1 ditto of 2 yrs.; 1 ditto of 1 yr., £19.

Mattys Brouwer—1 poll, 1 cow, 1 ditto of 3 yrs., £27.

Jan Frederickse—1 poll, 3 horses, 6 cows, 2 ditto of 2 yrs.; 1 ditto of 1 yr., £90.10; 14 morgens of land, £28: Total, £118.10.

Joost Franse—1 poll, 2 horses, 3 cows, 1 ditto of 3 yrs.; 2 ditto of 2 yrs.; 1 ditto of 1 yr., £67; 16 morgens of land and valley, £32.10: Total, £99.10.

Ariaen van Laer—1 poll, 2 cows, 1 horse, 1 yearling, £41.10; 1 morgen of land, £2: Total, £43.10.

Abraham Ackerman—1 poll, 1 cow, £23.

Thomas Lammerse (Lambertse?)—2 polls, 3 horses, 1 ditto of 2 yrs.; 7 cows, 1 ditto of 3 yrs.; 4 ditto of 2 yrs.; 4 ditto of 1 yr.; 4 sheep, £136; 18 morgens of land, £36: Total, £172.

Willem Joresen—1 poll, 5 cows, 2 ditto of 2 yrs.; 2 horses, £82; 12 morgens of land, £24: Total, £96.

Folckert Hendrickse—1 poll, 2 horses, 6 cows, 2 ditto of 2 yrs.; 2 ditto of 1 yr., £80; 14 morgens of land, £28: Total, £108.

Jacob Joreson—1 poll, 3 horses, 5 cows, 2 ditto of 2 yrs.; 1 ditto of 1 yr.; 2 sheep, £87.10; 12 morgens of land, £24: Total, £111.10.

Joris Jacobsen—3 horses, 6 cows, 2 ditto of 2 yrs., £71; 16 morgens of land, £32: Total, £103.

Cornelis Nevius—1 poll, 3 cows, 1 ditto of 2 yrs.; 1 ditto of 1 yr., £37.

Adam Brouwer—1 poll, 1 mill, 3 cows, 1 ditto of 2 yrs.; 2 ditto of 1 yr.; 3 sheep, £143.10; 3 morgens of land, £6: Total, £149.10.

Hendrickse Sleght—2 horses, 4 cows, £44; 21 morgens of land, £42: Total, £86.

Rendel Evans—2 horses, 1 poll, £42.

Jacobus vande Water—1 poll, 1 horse, 4 cows, 1 ditto of 2 yrs.; 2 ditto of 1 yr.; 4 sheep, £59.10; 12 morgens of land, £24: Total, £83.10.

Machiel Hansen—1 poll, 2 horses, 6 cows, 4 ditto of 3 yrs.; 5 ditto of 2 yrs.; 5 ditto of 1 yr., £108; 20 morgens of land, £40: Total, £148.

Thomas Jansen—1 poll, 2 oxen, 1 horse, 2 cows, 2 ditto of 3 yrs.; 3 ditto of 2 yrs., £67.10; 11 morgens of land, £22: Total, £89.10.

Hendrick Tysen—1 poll, 2 oxen, 2 cows, 3 ditto of 2 yrs.; 1 horse of 1 yr., £50.10; 12 morgens of land, 24: Total, £74.10.

Josies Dregz—1 poll, 1 horse, £30.

Evert Hendrickse—1 poll, 1 cow, 1 ditto yearling, £24.10.

Akus Jansen—1 poll, 2 oxen, 3 cows, 1 ditto of 2 yrs.; 2 ditto of 1 yr., £50.10; 8 morgens of land, £16: £66.10.

Ariaen Willemse—1 poll, 3 horses, 6 cows, 1 ox of 4 yrs; 4 ditto of 4 yrs.; 3 ditto of 1 yr., £109; 25 morgens of land, £50: Total, £159.

Jan Gerritse Dorlant—1 poll, 2 horses, 1 ditto of 2 yrs.; 1 ditto of 1 yr.; 5 cows, 2 ditto of 2 yrs.; 2 ditto of 1 yr., £83; 20 morgens of land, £40: Total, £123.

Simon Aersen—1 poll, 4 oxen, 4 cows, 4 ditto of 2 yrs.; 1 ditto of 1 yr.; 1 horse, £81.10; 24 morgens of land, £48: Total, £129.10.

Jan Teunisen—1 poll, 2 horses, 4 cows, 2 ditto of 2 yrs., £67; 21 morgens of land, £42: Total, £109.

Jan Jansen—1 poll, 2 horses, 2 oxen, 7 cows, 2 ditto of 3 yrs.; 5 ditto of 1 yr., £104.10; 21 morgens of land, £42: Total, £146.10.

Luickes Teunise—1 poll, 3 horses, 1 ditto of 1 yr.; 2 cows, £67; 10 morgens of land, £20: Total, £87.

Frans Abrahamse—1 poll, 2 horses, 1 cow, £47; 8 morgens of land, £8: Total, £55.

Hendrick Jansen—1 poll, 2 horses, 2 cows, 1 ditto of 4 yrs., £56.

Johannes Kasperse—1 poll, 2 horses, 4 cows, 2 ditto of 2 yrs., £67; 5 morgens of land, £10: Total, £77.

Casper Jansen—2 polls, 3 horses, 1 ditto of 2 yrs.; 2 cows, 2 ditto of 2 yrs., £92; 11 morgens of land, £22: Total, £114.

Juraen Blanck—1 poll, 1 horse, 2 cows, £40.

Winant Pietersen—2 polls, 1 cow, 1 ditto of 3 yrs.; 1 ditto of 2 yrs.; 1 ditto of 1 yr., £49.

Hendricka Sprokels—1 horse of 4 yrs.; 1 ditto of 2 yrs.; 4 cows, 2 ditto of 3 yrs.; 3 ditto of 2 yrs.; 4 sheep, £52.10; 10 morgens of land, £20: Total, £72.10.

Jan Smit—1 poll, 1 horse, £30.

Tuenes Giesbertse Bogert—4 horses, 1 ditto of 3 yrs.; 10 cows, 6 ditto of 2 yrs.; 6 ditto of 1 yr.; 2 polls, £166; 40 morgens of land, £80: Total, £246.

Marten Reisen—1 poll, 2 horses, 2 ditto of 1 yr.; 5 cows, 3 ditto of 2 yrs.; 1 ditto of 1 yr., £84.10; 19 morgens of land, £38: Total, £122.10.

The widow of Rem Jansen—3 polls, 6 horses, 12 cows, 1 ditto of 4 yrs.; 4 ditto of 3 yrs.; 6 ditto of 2 yrs.; 6 ditto of 1 yr., £228.10; 22 morgens of land and valley, £44: Total, £272.10.

Johanes Cristoffelse—1 poll, 3 horses, 2 cows, 2 ditto of 2 yrs., £69; 9 morgens of land, £18: Total, £87.

Willem Bennings—1 poll, 2 horses, 1 ditto of 3 yrs.; 1 ditto of 2 yrs.: 6 cows, 3 oxen, 1 ditto of 2 yrs.; 1 ditto of 1 yr., £107; 21 morgens of land, £42: Total, £149.

Rissiert Gibs—1 poll, 1 horse, £30.

Thomas Jansen op Brackelen—1 poll, 2 horses, £42.

Pieter Van Nest—2 polls, 3 cows, 1 yearling, £52.10.

Jan Buys—1 poll, 2 horses, 2 cows, £52.

Dirck Jansen—1 poll, 3 cows, 1 ditto of 3 yrs.; 1 ditto of 1 yr.; 2 horses, 1 ditto of 3 yrs., £70.10; 30 morgens of land, £60: Total, £130.10.

+ Jan Cornelise Damen,
Jan Gerritse van Couwenhoven, } *Clerks.*

A LIST OF ALL THE FREEHOLDERS, THEIR WIVES, CHILDREN, APPRENTICES, AND SLAVES, IN THE TOWN OF BROOKLAND, ABOUT 1698.

[NOTE.—*E* affixed to the name, means *English*; *F*, *French*.]

	Men.	*Wo.*	*Ch.*	*App.*	*Sla.*
Adriaen Bennet	1	2	4	–	–
Jacob Bennet	1	1	–	–	–
Jan Bennet	1	1	2	1	–
Simon Aerson	1	1	12	–	2
Wouter van Pelt	1	1	4	2	1
Christopher Schaers	1	–	–	–	–
Claes van Dyck	1	2	5	–	1
Maria Van Dyck	–	1	–	–	–
Achias Van Dyck	1	1	7	1	–
Jan Pieterse	1	2	2	–	–
Volkert Bries	1	2	2	–	–
Geertie Bries	–	1	–	–	–
Jacobus Van DeWater	1	1	3	–	–
Jan Buys	1	2	1	–	–
Cornelis Poulisse	1	1	1	–	–
Cornelis Slegt	1	1	–	3	–
Joannes Slegt	1	–	–	–	–
Cornelis Van Duyn	1	2	3	–	–
Thomas Vardon	1	2	–	–	–
Jan Bennet	1	1	5	–	2
Willem Bennet	1	1	5	2	–
Willem Brouwer	1	1	2	2	–
Jacob Hansen Bergen	1	1	6	–	2
Cornelis Suebring	1	1	8	–	2
Catharina Hendrikse	–	1	–	–	–
Dirck Woertman	1	1	2	–	4
Jan Gerritz Couwenhoven	1	1	3	–	–
Robert Everden (*E*)	1	1	–	1	1
Jan Arison	1	1	8	–	7

	Men.	*Wo.*	*Ch.*	*App.*	*Sla.*
Latitie Smith (*E*)	–	2	–	–	–
Stoffel Hooghlandt	1	1	–	–	–
Joris Jacobse	1	1	–	–	4
Harmen Jorisse	1	1	2	1	–
Jan Woertman	1	1	4	–	1
Juriaen Andriesse	1	–	–	–	–
Jurian Bries	1	1	4	–	–
Joannes Janse	1	3	3	–	–
Barent Sleght	1	1	2	1	–
Margaret Dolstan (*E*)	–	1	2	–	2
Elsie Sleght	–	1	2	–	–
Jacobus Beauvois	1	1	5	–	–
Thomas Knight (*E*)	1	1	1	–	–
Magdalena Farden	–	1	–	–	–
Joris Hansen Bergen	1	1	11	–	2
Jan Fredrickse	1	1	7	–	–
Gerret Middag	1	1	3	–	2
Jan Janse Staats	1	1	8	–	–
Pieter Gerbrantse	1	1	–	1	–
Pieter Janse Staats	1	1	4	–	–
Cornelis Jorisse Bouman	1	1	1	–	–
Mighiel Hanse Bergen	1	1	3	–	2
Jacob Brouwer	1	1	6	–	–
Adam Brouwer	1	1	4	–	–
Claes Vechten	1	1	–	–	–
Hendrick Vechten	1	1	4	–	3
Jan Cornelisse Damen	1	1	4	–	1
Gerret Middag	1	1	3	–	2
Samuel Berry	1	1	3	–	1
Gerrit Couwenhoven	1	1	3	1	–
Abraham Van Duyn	1	2	2	–	–
Judith Van Este	–	1	3	2	1
Annetie Rapaille	–	1	–	–	–
Jeronimus Rapaille	1	1	6	–	2
Teunis Rapaille	1	1	1	–	–
Daniel Rapaille	1	1	5	–	3
Jannetie Remsen	–	2	2	–	–
Abraham Remsen	1	1	2	–	1
Gysbert Bogaert	1	2	5	–	1
Teunis Bogaert	1	–	–	–	–
Neeltie Rapallie	–	2	1	–	1
Jacob Cousseau (*F*)	1	1	1	–	–
Jacob Buys	1	2	4	–	–
Matthys Cornelisse	1	1	5	–	–
Anthony Coesaer	1	1	1	1	–
Tys Lubbertz	1	1	4	–	–
Lysbeth Tysen	–	1	3	–	–
Frans Abrahamse	1	–	2	1	–
Lambert Andriesse	1	2	1	–	–
Cornelis Vanderhoef	1	1	3	–	2

	Men.	Wo.	Ch.	App.	Sla.
Thomas Lamberts	1	–	–	–	1
Dirck Tyssen	1	1	–	1	–
Isaac Mennist	1	1	1	–	–
Hend'k Hendrickse	1	1	1	–	–
Jeronimus Remsen	1	1	–	2	3
Jan Gerritz Dorlant	1	1	3	1	–
Gerret Sprong	1	1	5	–	–
Barbara Luycas	–	1	–	–	3
Clars Barents Blom	1	2	4	–	–
Jan Bibon	1	1	6	1	–
Benj'n Van De Waeter	1	2	3	1	–
[Ought to be 78 Men and 102 Women.]	77	101	240	26	65

A LIST OF ALL THE INHABITANTS OFF THE TOWNSHIP OFF BROOKLAND, BOTH OFF WHITES AND BLACKS, MALES AND FEMALES, ETC., IN THE YEAR 1738.

(N. Y. Doc. Hist., iv., pp. 195–198.)

The names of ye masters of the house or mistresses, etc.	White males above 10 years.	White males under 10 years.	White females above 10 years.	White females under 10 years.	Black males above 10 years.	Under 10 years.	Black females above 10 years.	Under 10 years.
Jeronymus Rapalje	1	1	3	–	1	–	2	3
George Rapalje	2	1	2	1	2	–	2	–
Isaac Johnson	3	2	3	1	–	–	–	–
Jacob Ryerson	4	1	–	2	–	–	1	–
Hans Bergen	2	2	3	–	–	–	–	–
Jacob Bergen	2	–	2	1	1	–	1	–
Jeremias Remsen	1	–	2	4	–	1	–	1
Gizbart Bogaert	2	–	2	–	–	–	–	–
Gizbart Bogaert Junr.	2	2	1	2	–	–	–	–
Cornelius Bogard	1	1	2	1	1	1	–	1
Nicasius Couwenhoven	3	–	1	–	1	1	–	1
Marten Vanderhoeven	4	1	2	1	–	–	–	–
Gerrit Adriaanse	2	1	2	1	1	–	–	–
Nicholas Vechten	1	–	2	2	1	–	–	–
Fredrick Blaeuw	2	1	1	–	–	–	–	–
John Blaeuw	1	–	1	1	–	–	–	–
Juryen Blaeuw	1	–	1	1	–	–	–	–
Peter Staets	4	–	3	2	–	–	1	–
Adrian Bennet	3	–	1	–	–	–	–	1
Cornelius Van Duyn	2	–	2	1	1	–	1	–
Johannes Holst	2	2	3	–	–	–	–	–
John Bennet	3	–	3	1	1	–	–	–
Jacob Bennet	2	–	2	–	–	–	–	–

The names of ye masters of the house or mistresses, etc.	White males above 10 years.	White males under 10 years.	White females above 10 years.	White females under 10 years.	Black males above 10 years.	Under 10 years.	Black females above 10 years.	Under 10 years.
Thomas Van Dyck	2	-	1	1	1	-		-
Samuel Stellingwerg	1	-	2	1	2	-	-	-
Simon D' Hart	2	-	3	2	6	2	3	2
Wouter Van Pelt	4	-	3	-	3	-	1	-
Joseph Hegeman	1	3	3	2	-	-	1	1
Hendrick Van Dyck	1	1	2	-	1	-	3	1
Elizabeth Garner	0	1	1	-	-	-	-	-
George Remsen	1	1	1	-	1	-	1	-
Rem Remsen	2	-	2	1	-	1	1	-
Isaac Sebering	4	2	2	1	1	2	1	2
Aeltje Sebering	2	-	2	-	2	-	1	1
Israel Horsfield	3	1	1	2	3	-	-	-
John Thompson	1	1	1	-	-	-	-	-
Mally Burwouter	-	2	1	-	-	-	-	-
Theophilus Elsworth	4	1	4	1	5	3	2	1
Petrus Ewetse	1	1	1	2	2	-	-	-
John Rhyn	2	1	2	1	-	-	-	1
Gabriall Cox	3	4	2	4	-	-	1	-
John Rapalje	2	-	1	-	2	1	2	-
Thomas Browne	1	1	1	3	-	-	-	-
Billy Nicbin	1	1	1	1	-	-	-	-
Daniell Bontecoue	1	-	2	2	1	1	-	-
Aert Middagh	1	-	1	-	-	1	-	-
Breghje Glieiff	-	1	1	-	-	-	1	-
Hendrick Stryker	2	-	1	3	1	-	1	-
Cornelius Filkin	1	1	2	-	-	-	-	-
Aeltje Provoost	1	-	2	1	1	-	-	-
John Middagh	1	1	1	1	1	-	1	-
Christopher Codwise	12	2	5	2	2	-	2	-
Cornelius Ewetse	7	-	1	2	-	-	1	-
John Ewetse	2	2	2	1	-	-	-	-
James Harding	1	1	5	-	1	-	-	-
Jacob Deklyn	1	-	2	1	-	-	-	-
Rem Remsen	7	-	4	2	2	1	1	1
Everardus Brouwer	2	2	2	2	-	-	-	-
Johannes Johnson	3	-	-	-	-	-	1	1
Albertje Johnson	-	-	1	-	-	-	-	-
George Bergen	1	2	2	2	-	1	-	-
Jacob Hanse Bergen	1	-	1	-	1	-	-	-
Cornelius Webbers	1	2	2	-	-	-	-	-
Isaac D'Graw	2	2	2	1	-	-	1	-
Joost D'Beavois	2	-	5	1	-	-	-	-
Jacobus Beavois	3	-	1	-	1	-	-	-

The names of ye masters of the house or mistresses, etc.	White males above 10 years.	White males under 10 years.	White females above 10 years.	White females under 10 years.	Black males above 10 years.	Under 10 years.	Black females above 10 years.	Under 10 years.
John Ellen	1	–	–	–	–	–	–	–
Hans Bergen	4	1	6	–	1	–	1	–
Jacobus Vandewater	3	1	1	2	–	–	–	–
Benjamin V. D. Water	3	–	3	–	–	–	–	–
Styntje Vander Voort	–	–	1	–	–	–	–	–
Lambert Andriesen	3	–	2	–	–	–	–	–
Jacobus Leffertze	2	1	3	–	1	2	1	–
George Rapalje	2	3	2	–	–	1	1	–
Barent Blom	2	2	4	3	1	–	–	–
Rem V. D. Beek	2	2	1	1	–	1	–	–
John Dorland	1	1	1	2	1	–	–	–
Hendrick Suydam	3	–	2	–	1	–	–	–
Cornelius V. D. Hoven	1	–	1	–	1	–	1	1
Cornelius V. D. Hoeven, jr.	2	2	1	2	1	–	–	–
Peter V. D. Voort	1	2	1	2	1	–	–	–
Paulus V. D. Voort	1	–	1	2	–	–	–	–
John V. D. Voort	5	1	1	–	–	–	–	–
John Van Noortstrant	2	1	2	2	2	1	1	2
Dirck Rapalje	1	–	1	–	1	–	–	–
Sara Rapalje	–	–	1	–	1	–	1	–
Jacob Cossauw	5	3	–	1	–	–	–	–
Isaac Remsen	7	1	2	2	2	–	1	–
Jacob Durrie	3	3	2	–	1	1	1	–
Mathys Van Dyck	2	2	2	2	2	1	1	1
Abraham Brewer	1	1	2	2	2	–	–	–
Juryen Brewer	1	2	2	2	–	–	–	–
	199	81	175	92	69	23	43	23

APPENDIX VIII.—(PAGE 206.)

THE BROOKLYN WOODLANDS.

[We are indebted for the following to Mr. J. Carson Brevoort, of this city.]

At an early date, the woodlands covering the range of hills bounding the town north and east of the Flatbush road were apportioned in parcels of about ten acres each among the freeholders of the town of Brooklyn, excepting the Gowanus owners, whose woodlands were attached to their respective farms.

Some eight or nine hundred acres were thus allotted, in three larger divisions of about three hundred acres each. The first division was comprised between the Flatbush and Clove roads; the second between the Clove and Hunterfly roads; and the third between the last-named road (which is probably a corruption of *Aan der fly*, that is, "the road to the creek," or bay) and that leading to Jamaica. There appears to have been another division north of this last road; but, if so, it was cleared and cultivated shortly after its allotment.

The first division was composed of irregular-shaped lots, and was covered until the year 1855 with fine woods. The second division was divided more regularly into long, narrow lots, of ten acres each, and of nearly equal length, running north and south. The greater part of these woods has been but recently felled. The third division was composed of very long, narrow lots running east and west, of various lengths. A record of this last division has been preserved, and is authenticated by the town clerk. The records of the others may, perhaps, be among some of the few papers preserved of the town records.

THE BROOKLYN SALT MEADOWS.

The freeholders of the town, having no salt meadow attached to their farms, it was at an early date arranged that a part of the salt meadows or Jamaica Bay, in the town of New Lots, west of Spring Creek, and in the County of Queens, just adjoining on the east side of the same creek, should be allotted to them. This last portion is known as the Brooklyn meadows, and many lots in both of them are still owned by residents of Brooklyn. The regular price of these lots was until recently but ten dollars per acre. The division lines were marked by short stakes or corner-stones lying loose on the meadow; but no one encroached on his neighbor, the lines being known to all the owners. This salt hay was cut in September, and used as a winter forage for cows and horses, though never held in very high estimation for this purpose.

Sedge-grass, from the detached meadows and islands in the bay, was free to all, and was often cut to be used as a thatch for sheds or for manure. Sea-weed, principally eel-grass (*Zostera marina*), was also collected for manure. Recently, this last grass, dried and washed by rain, has been much used for stuffing mattresses.

APPENDIX IX.—(Page 323.)

EXTRACTS FROM THE FIRST NEWSPAPER ISSUED IN BROOKLYN.

This is reprinted from the only copy known to be in existence, and which Mr. Edwin B. Spooner, of the *Brooklyn Star*, found a number of years ago at the Long Island Hotel, in Fulton street, near the Ferry, where it had been left some time before by a countryman, who requested the proprietor, Mr. Carman, to preserve it for him until his return. Several years having elapsed without any demand having been made for it, Mr. Spooner became its owner; and, subsequently, presented it to the Lyceum at the United States Navy Yard, where it may now be seen.

The usual channels afford no information whatever concerning this paper; and it is not even mentioned in any of the histories, local or national.

From certain remarks in the *Super-Extra Gazette*, we might, perhaps, infer that a paper of this name was published regularly at the Brooklyne-Hall, or Looseley's. If such was the case, it is singular that it has not been recognized and perpetuated by history; and that but one copy—and that evidently an "extra"—should have been preserved. It has been suggested that the *Super-Extra Gazette* was a Brooklyn extra of the *New York Royal Gazette*, issued on some special occasion; our own impression, however, is that it was merely a handbill, published by the enterprising Looseley to advertise the lottery which was then drawing at his tavern.

The "original" is printed on a dirty sheet, in three columns, and on one side only: its spelling and punctuation is here faithfully preserved.

PRO BONO PUBLICO

BROOKLYNE HALL SUPER-EXTRA GAZETTE.

SATURDAY. June 8, 1782.

Brooklyne.

ON Thursday evening last, we were blessed with many refreshing showers attended with hard thunder, &c.—The distance from our friends in New York, prevented us from giving them more early intelli gence.

* * * * * * *

It is with particular satisfaction we inform the public, that the people here begin to be more civilized since they have indulged their loyal sensations for the immortal victory obtained over the French fleet.[1] Bull-baitings here are absolutely forbidden.

FLAT-BUSH. *June* 6.

To the EDITORS of the BROOKLYNE HALL SUPER-EXTRA GAZETTE.

GENTLEMEN.

THE Songs that generally appear in the New York papers are in too high a stile for our conception, and with the tunes we are not acquainted; therefore, accept from a Loyal Society, among us, composed for our amusement.

TUNE. *Babes of the Wood, or Chevy Chace.*

I.

Unhappy times of late we've seen,
Unhappy days indeed,
For such the rueful hours have been,
Did make our hearts to bleed.

II.

Rebellion did with all its force,
Pour down upon our heads,
The stream took such a rapid course,
It drove us from our beds.

III.

But now those times are blowing o'er,
And we with heart and voice,
That such disasters be no more,
With one accord rejoice.

---

[1] The defeat of De Grasse's French fleet in the West Indies, April 12th, 1782, by the British fleet under Rodney.

IV.

For glorious news, surround our King,
And England's noble cause,
So all true souls and faithful men,
Will shout with one applause.

V.

For now with safety we may keep,
Our hard begotten store,
For in security we sleep,
And bury gold no more.

VI.

No more our flocks and herds will stray,
Our Nymphs and Swains shall sing,
And ever bless the welcome day,
That binds us to our King.

N. B. We are extremely fond of tunes of such soft melodious sounds, because they approach so near to our Church music, besides these were the sort of tunes which were brought over by the first European settlers.

Religion and morality gain much ground; for to be sure, a Tavern-keeper, a few days since, gave away his old black coat to enable a Minister of the Gospel (just then come in from the Rebels) to mount the rostrum with dignity.

The nativity of our Sovereign was so acknowledged amongst us, that we outdid all our former doings: The man that was so stigmatized sometime since by the name of BONIFACE,[1] behaved beyond description, and the Commander of our civil guns had a remarkable share in the splendour and glory of the day.

The prospect of such plenty of fruit on this island, must make the Lovers of cherries, peaches, &c., smile—and no doubt will produce a large effusion of mouth-water.

Butter-milk will fall in price next week, at least one hundred per cent.

---

[1] An allusion, undoubtedly, to Loosley, the host of the "Brooklyne-Hall" Tavern.

New Milk, Ditto. Fresh Butter, Ditto. Vegitables, Ditto. And most articles which are the products of a farm, will share the same fate. RAM MUTTON and BULL BEEF excepted.

Some few days since a Scrivener, who sometime resides amongst us, indulged himself with a walk to ASCOT-HEATH RACES, he walked around the course, refreshed himself at Loosley's Barn;—He then walked down to the Ferry, and very deliberately walked into the river and had it not been for the friendly assistance of some gentlemen belonging to the army, in all probability he would have then stepped into eternity.

So great a number of Satires in Verse have, and do daily appear here, that one would imagine all the people of Brooklyne were turned Poets.

* * * * * * *

The State of Massachusetts Bay, being now convinced of the necessity of fitting a fleet to support their fishery, have sent two schooners of 6 carriage guns, and a sloop of 4 guns and well manned, to cruise off Halifax, with strict orders to bring all the British frigates into Marblehead.

Extract from a Philadelphia Paper.

When the account of the defeat of the British fleet, off Dominica, on the 12th of April, arrived here, the Congress, by the desire of Mr. Luzerne, immediately assembled and passed the following resolves:

" 1st. *Resolved nem. con.* That the exigencies of our public affairs were such, that the British fleet ought to have been defeated.

2d. *Resolved nem. con.* That as Mons. Luzerne has assured us the fleet of his Most Christian Majesty had totally defeated the fleet of the British King on the 12th of April, off Dominica, the British fleet certainly was defeated.

3d. *Resolved nem. con.* That the thanks of this House be presented to Mons. Luzerne, for this early and important intelligence.

By Order of Congress,

CHARLES THOMSON, *Sec'ry.*

In Congress, May 27, 1782.

After which *Te Deum* was sung in Congress, *nemine contradicente*, high Mass performed, a *Feu-de-Joie* fired in the evening, and the city of Philadelphia grandly illuminated.

His Excellency Benjamin Franklin, Esq., Minister Plenipotentiary for the United States of America, having introduced the use of Electrical Rods in the French navy, was the occasion of drawing the British thunder upon them in the West Indies. *Probatum est.*

By a letter from Maryland we are informed, the Assembly of that province are determined to shake off the fetters of Congress and throw themselves into the arms of their old friend and parent.

Now selling off at prime cost, at No. 9, the remaining stock in trade of an eminent Clergyman leaving off business for the good of his health, which has been much impaired by nocturnal lucubrations, consisting of a complete set of manuscript sermons, for the year round, with national and synodical fasts; also a variety of sermons against the 30th of January, Mons Meg charged and primed for the 5th of November, a rod for the Whore of Babylon, the Sins of the Nation described, Tracts upon the Crook of the Lot, or the afflicted man's Companion, Ten Steps of Jacob's Ladder, Boston's fourfold State, the Cloud of Witnesses, Bunyan's Hitch for a heavy ars'd Christian, ditto, Pilgrim's Progress, ditto Holy War, a Rod for Billy's Breach, Gospel Sonnets, &c, &c, &c. Inventory of which may be seen at any time.

The Rev. Doctor Witherspoon, President of the College of Prince-Town, has invented a new creed, and is now writing a paraphrase upon the 5th Commandment, by which he intends fully to prove, that there is no duty due from a child to a parent, from an inferior to a superior, from a subject to a Sovereign, unless a Congress, which is to be published as an appendix to an essay, ready for the press, entitled "A Treatise against Moral Obligations."

Friend Loosley suffered much on Tuesday evening last,—To grace the ceremony and assist the joys of the people, a large piece of ordnance was discharged so close to his house, the explosion of which shattered his windows in a most terrible manner. No doubt but Loosley's glazier rejoices at the accident.

With sorrow we inform our neighbors and our distant friends, that many depredations have lately been made in the face of open day, on this island, but more particularly in the city of New York.—The initials of the culprits names are G E— —. A parole is appointed to traverse the streets of Brooklyne every hour day and night, to prevent street robberies.

A melancholy event had liked to have happened here a few days ago. A person belonging to Mr. Elms of this place, was driving a horse and chair into the river, the horse proving unruly, was taken into the stream, and it was with great difficulty they were got out again; unhappily the horse was sadly wet, but the man received no other hurt than catching a slight cold and damaging his watch.

Our passage boats have had a middling good time in crossing the ferry lately, not a single fee has been lost.

Whether or no we meet esteem,
Regardless as a praw;
No real injury we mean
In our Gazette extra.
Critics may snarl, but should they bite,
Then we'd our pow'r exert;
For we're assured, the more we write
Will make us more expert.

A Generous Price will be given by the Editors for the latest Rebel Papers.

BROOKLYNE-HALL LOTTERY

COMMENCED drawing on the 4th of June, when only TEN TICKETS were drawn, the numbers taken from the Check Book are the following; No. 598—906—1702—1827—1861—1912—2547—2582—2808—2968.

This Lottery being for charitable purposes, every means will be adopted to promote the interest thereof.

A few Tickets remain unsold, which may be had at the usual places.

The LOTTERY re-commenced drawing on Wednesday the 12th instant, and will Continue drawing till all is finished. N. B. There were two Ten Dollar Prizes, three of Five Dollars, and Five Blanks drawn.

CHARLES LOOSLEY.[1]

CONTINUES to provide every accommodation for the reception of his friends; and they may depend the greatest care will be taken to give universal satisfaction.

THOMAS ELMS

TAKES the liberty of informing the public, that he has a most capital CARRIAGE, and excellent HORSES for their accommodation. Likewise, his commodious STAGE WAGGON,[2] as usual for select parties.

THOMAS SMITH,

WATCH MAKER, from NEW YORK, acquaints the public, he has moved into the house formerly occupied by Mr. Ross, at Brooklyn-Ferry, where he carries on the business in its different branches.

JOHN ROSS

BEGS leave to inform the public in general, and his friends in particular, he has removed from where he formerly lived to two doors higher up, next to Mr. Loosley's, where he has opened TAVERN, and laid in an assortment of the best LIQUORS.

N. B. He carries on his business as usual, at the above place.

MACKINTOSH

CARRIES on the Business of a TAYLOR, with the greatest propriety, at his Shop, situated between Mr. Smith's, Watch-maker, and Mr. Ross's Tavern.

Vivant Rex & Regina.

BROOKLYNE-HALL: Printed in the YEAR, 1782.

---

[1] Loosley, after the war (1784), kept hotel at Port Roseway, Nova Scotia, where, with other loyalists, he suffered great privations.

[2] In Rivington's paper, May 26th, 1779, we find that "Loosley and Elms propose to run a CARAVAN to Jamaica and back to Brooklyn Ferry, on Fridays, Thursdays, and Sundays."

1782, Oct. 3d. "New flying machine, on steel springs, Thursday, Sunday, and Tuesday, from Brooklyn, at 8 o'clock, to Jamaica, and return the same evening. Breakfasting at Brooklyn-Hall, stage mornings." There were also other stages running on the same route.

APPENDIX X.—(Page 378.)

"BROOKLYN DIRECTORY FOR 1796—CONTAINING THE NAMES OF THE INHABITANTS—ALPHABETICALLY ARRANGED. NEVER BEFORE PUBLISHED."

Alexander, John, rope maker.
Armstrong, John, tavern keeper.
Barbarin, John N., physician, Main Road.
Beezely, William, laborer.
Beezely, Thomas, blacksmith, Sand's Dock.
Bennet, John, livery stable, Main Road.
Bennet, widow, washer, Main Road.
Berry, ———, farmer, near the Episcopal Church.
Blackslee, Archibald, near the Episcopal Church.
Boerum, Martin.
Brown, widow Hannah, facing Capt. Dawson's, Old Ferry.
Brower and Beezely, blacksmiths, Main Road.
Burlock, Thomas, livery stable, Main Road.
Burns, widow.
Cannon, Peter, cooper, near Sand's Dock.
Carpenter, William, lumber merchant, near the Old Ferry.
Carpenter, widow, near the Old Ferry.
Carstand, John, rope maker.
Clows and Rhodes, store keepers, Main Road.
Coe, Thomas, blacksmith.
Cole, John, coach and chair maker.
Coop, Edward, blacksmith.
Cornelison, John, rope maker.
Cornell, Smith, cartman.
Cornell, William, boarding-house.
Cornell, Whitehead.
Davis, widow Elizabeth, Main Road.
Dawson, Henry, near the Old Ferry.
Deane, John, shoemaker.
Denton, George, house carpenter.
Dougherty, William, house carpenter.
Doughty, John, butcher.
Doughty, Charles.
Douglas, ———, butcher.
Eagles, Jacob, grocer, Main Road.
Field, Joseph, grocer, Main Road.
Fisher, John.
Foster, teacher, near the Episcopal Church.
Fox, Joseph, store keeper, Main Road.
Fuller, Benjamin, painter and glazier, Main Road.
Furman, William, one of the proprietors of the New Ferry, Main Road.
Garrison, John, butcher.
Gilbert, Robert, blacksmith.
Grant, William, Jayler.
Guy and Harmer, dyers, near the New Ferry.
Guy, Francis, dyer, near the New Ferry.
Hampstead, ———, rope maker, near the New Ferry.
Hargrave, Robert, tinsmith, Main Road, near the Methodist Church.
Harris, widow Grace, Main Road.
Hastings, John, gardener, opposite the Methodist Church.
Havens, Thcmas tavern keeper, near the Old Ferry.
Herbert, James, shoemaker, New Ferry Street.
Hicks, Jacob, tavern keeper, Old Ferry Dock.
Hicks, Jacob M., Main Road.
Hicks, John M., Main Road.
Hicks, John, one of the proprietors of the Old Ferry.
Hicks, George, one of the proprietors of the Old Ferry.
Hicks, Isaac, merchant; store, Pearl Street, New York.
Higby, Aaron, tavern keeper, Main Road.
Higby, Edward, tavern keeper, New Ferry Dock.
Hodge, Robert, bookseller, opposite the Methodist Church; store, Water Street, New York.

Hunt, Theodosius, one of the proprietors of the New Ferry, Main Road.
Ingles, Jacob, cooper.
Jackson, ———, house carpenter.
Jarvis, Isaiah, tavern keeper, Main Road.
Johnston, John.
Kitchum, Pelick, tavern keeper.
Kyd and Jedlye, grocers, corner of the Main and New Ferry Roads.
Lambertson, ———, grocer.
Layhat, the Rev. Charles, Minister of the Second Baptist Church of New York, Main Road.
Lovett, James, saddler, Main Road.
Lynch, ———, rope maker.
M'Combs, John, miller.
M'Lachlan, Robert, rope maker.
M'Moneygil, widow, school mistress, Main Road.
Maddock, Roger Whitington, brewer, near the Brewery.
Martin, John, dock builder.
Middagh, John, hatter, Main Road.
Mitchel, Samuel, rope maker.
Montany, John, house carpenter.
Moore, Lambert.
Moore, widow.
Morris, William, land broker, Main Road.
Mosier, John, house carpenter, near the Brewery.
Mott, Ridgeble, tavern keeper, near the Old Ferry.
Nicholas, Isaac, cabinet maker.
Nostrand, Timothy, tavern keeper, near the Old Ferry.
Parsons, Nap, rope maker.
Patchin, Jacob, butcher.
Patchin, Ralph, dairy man.
Phist, John, rope maker.
Price, Nathaniel, copper plate printer, near the Methodist Church.
Rapley, Abraham, coach and chair maker, Main Road.
Rattoone, John, laborer, Sand's Dock.
Remsen, Isaac, tavern keeper.
Sands, Joshua, between the Old and New Ferries.
Sharp, Jacob, Judge of the County Court, Main Road.
Sharp, Jacob, jun., Clerk of ditto, Main Road.
Shotts, Nicholas, laborer, Main Road.
Shrader, Christopher, rope maker, New Ferry Road.
Sing, William, merchant, store Pearl Street, New York.
Smith, Hassel, house carpenter, New Ferry Road.
Smith, Joseph, tavern keeper, New Ferry Road.
Snedecor, Lewis, tavern keeper, Old Ferry Dock.
Somendyke, Nicholas, house carpenter.
Strytser, Bourdet (Burdett Stryker), tallow chandler and butcher.
Swartcoop (John V.), gunsmith.
Taylor, Solomon, blacksmith, Main Road.
Tilford, ———, weaver, Main Road.
Thome, Samuel, baster, New Ferry Road.
Tillotson, Jeffrey, hatter, Old Ferry Dock.
Titus, Abiel, tavern keeper, Main Road.
Townsend, Nathaniel, hatter, Main Road.
Troutman, Andrew, laborer, New Ferry Road.
Tuttle, Barzillai, house carpenter, near the Brewery.
Underhill, Peter, jun., taylor, near the Old Ferry.
Van Aulen, Cornelius, laborer, Sand's Dock.
Van Aulen, Peter, tavern keeper, Main Road.
Van De Water, John, livery stable, New Ferry.
Van Mater, Gilbert, grocer, Old Ferry Dock.
Van Pelt; Thomas, mason and master builder, New Ferry Dock.
Walling, Philip, mason.
Ward, Barnabas, chair maker, Main Road.
Ward, John, rope maker, near the New Ferry.
Walters, John, tavern keeper.

APPENDIX XI.—(PAGE 409.)

BROOKLYN VETERANS OF 1812.

Muster Roll of a Company of Infantry, under the command of Captain Joseph Dean, in the Consolidated Regiment of Militia, commanded by Lieut.-Col. John A. Ditmars, from Sept. 2, 1814, when last mustered, to the 13th of Nov. 1814, in the service of the United States.

[The letters R. and F., affixed to some of these names, are to designate them as members of the *Rifles* or of the *Fusileers*, two uniform companies at that time belonging to Brooklyn. These are affixed on the memory of Capt. Dean, and although generally correct, it is possible that one or two may be wrong. Those with this † mark were part of a detachment of substitutes sent to relieve Lt. Spader, at Ft. Swift, Oct. 5, 1814.]

Joseph Dean, Captain, Sept. 2, 1814.
John Spader, Lieutenant, Sept. 2, 1814.
Charles J. Doughty, Lieutenant, Sept. 1, 1814.
Wm. A. Mercein, Ensign, Sept. 2, 1814.
Garret Duryea, Orderly Sergeant, Sept. 2, 1814.
Michael Vanderhoof, Orderly Sergeant, Sept. 2, 1814.
David Storms, Orderly Sergeant, Sept. 2, 1814. On Furlough by permission of General.
Thomas Chadwick, Orderly Sergeant, Sept. 2, 1814.
Wm. R. Dean, Orderly Sergeant, Oct. 31, 1814.
James Gildersleeve, Corporal, Sept. 2, 1814.
Joseph Pettit, Corporal, Sept. 2, 1814.
Wm. Kirkpatrick, Corporal, Sept. 2, 1814.
Wm. Bennet, Corporal, Sept. 2, 1814. Sick at home with typhus fever.

PRIVATES.

John Smith, R., Gowanus.
Jas. C. Provost, R., Bushwick.
Uriah Ryder, F.
Joseph Butler. †Substitute for Isaac Selover.
Michael Mapes, F.
Benj. J. Waldron, R.
Luke Covert. †Substitute for John Selover.
Samuel Vail.
Carman Seaman. Deserted.
Thomas Lain.
David Hillyard. †An Irish deserter from the British army in Canada, a drummer, and acting as substitute for Winant P. Bennet.
John Sharpe.
Wm. Thomas.
Jacob Coope.
Samuel Hart. On furlough, by permission of General.
Nathan Furman.
Jas. McFarlan.
Samuel McGrady.
Joseph Stringham.
Joseph Robinson.
Gilbert Reid.
Elijah Raynor.
John Swinburn (English).
John Thurston.
John Ward.
John Rogers.
Nicholas Covert.
Stephen Austin. Substitute for William C. Bright.
Thomas Furman.
Zachariah Clevenger, R., Bushwick.
David Craven, R.
Josiah Applegate, F.
Francis Meserole, R., Bushwick.
Jacob Nostrand. Not on list of *present*.
Peter Colyer, R., Bushwick.
Jas. McDonough, R.
Stephen R. Boerum, Wallabout.

Philetus Fleet. Substitute for (Ex-Mayor) Samuel Smith.
Henry Dezendorf. †Substitute for Bernard Dezendorf.
John Applegate, F.
Cornelius Van Horne.
Abraham Bennet, jr.
John Hulst, R.
Michael Gillen, R.
Jacob W. Bennett, R., Bushwick.
Enoch Elbertson. †Substitute for Wm. Stoothoff, jr.
James Webb. (Name not on list of *present.*)
Francis Blaise. Substitute for Wm. Hills.
John Kaler, R.
Jesse Waterbury. †Substitute for Levi Hart.
Richard M. Bouton, F.
Abm. Blauvell. †Substitute for Jno. Burtis.
Samuel Goldsmith. Substitute for Jno. Murphy.
Isaac Devoe, F.
Henry Wiggins.
Abraham Bennett, F.
Peter Snyder.
John Hagerty.
Jas. Strain (Irish).
Richard Hunter.
Jesse Coope.
Jacob Furman.
Aaron Swain Robbins.
Jas. Lynch. Substitute for Stephen Schinck.
Peter Chatterlon. †Substitute for John Burtis.
Israel Rummels.
Samuel Pettit.
Samuel Nostrand.
Abraham Bogert.
Michael Harvey (Irish cook).
Peter Bennet. Enlisted Sept. 29, 1814.
Samuel Mott. (Name not on the list of *present.*)
William Jackson (mulatto servant).
John Fitch (colored servant).
Abm. Thompson (colored servant).
Edward Higbie, Drummer.

PIONEER CORPS.

William N. Kettletas, Sergeant of Pioneers.
Jaques W. Cropsy, R., Corporal of Pioneers.

PRIVATES.

Henry Van Dyke,
Wm. G. Verity,
Jacob Denyse,
John Van Brunt,
William Johnson,
Henry Cropsy,
Joseph Wardle,
David Denyse,
James Wallace.

The Bushwick and Wallabout Companies, in the 64th Regiment, were consolidated under Capt. Skillman, of the latter company. We have been unable to obtain a full Muster Roll of these companies, but are able to furnish a partial list of members, compiled from Capt. Dean's papers.

By order of Gen. Johnson, October 5, 1814, Lieutenants Doughty and Nichols, and Ensign Johnson, proceeded to Fort Swift, with substitutes from Major Ditmar's Regiment, to relieve Lieut. Spader. The names of substitutes and principals in Captain Skillman's command, composed as we have seen mostly of Wallabout and Bushwick men, were as follows:

[*a* Reported sick in camp. *b* Appeared when men were mustered, marched to Fort Swift, then was missing. Those to whose names an * is affixed did not appear when the substitutes were mustered in.]

Thomas Gardner.*a* Substitute for Ely Elmore.
David Capron.* Substitute for Henry Lane.
John Thursby. Substitute for Jas. Fletcher.
Joseph Goldsmith. Substitute for Mr. Tinney.

Joseph Russell. Substitute for Thos. Parsall.

William Boerum. Substitute for Thos. Arnold.

Daniel Bevoise. Substitute for Peter Sandford.

John Wheaton. Substitute for Moses Suydam.

Simon Denyse. Substitute for Gabriel Debevoise.

Joseph Deshay. Substitute for Joseph Goldsmith.

Jas. Van Loo. Substitute for Isaac Coovert.

David Weed. Substitute for Jacobus Lott.

Charles Debevoise.* Substitute for Abraham Boerum.

Wm. Turner. Substitute for Henry Read.

Jos. Miller. Substitute for Jacob Bennett.

Jas. Redding. Substitute for Hendrick Suydam.

Jas. Furman.* Substitute for David W. Van Cott.

Samuel Conklin. Substitute for Joseph S. Allen.

Jas. Wallis. Substitute for Abraham Hoothoof.

Godfrey ———. Substitute for Enoch Sopher.

Jas. Kellahan. Substitute for Horace D. Smith.

John Van Pelt. Substitute for John Bennet.

Zebulon Whitman. Substitute for Patrick Cator.

John Simpson. Substitute for Daniel Cortelyou.

Isaac Collins.* Substitute for Jacob Van Pelt.

William Bache.*b* Substitute for John Wardell.

John H. Curtis. Substitute for Wm. Van Pelt.

Francis Morgan. Substitute for Ruliff Van Brunt.

Hugh Smith. Substitute for Stephen Covert.

Henry Cutter.* Substitute for Timothy Cortelyou.

Oliver Place. Substitute for Winant J. Bennett.

David Stewart. Substitute for Chas. Lott.

Daniel Everitt. Substitute for John Van Sicklen.

James Smith. Substitute for Court Lake.

Wm. Conklin. Substitute for Court Johnson.

Hamilton Carr. Substitute for Cornelius Stryker.

John Van Tassel. Substitute for Daniel Stillwell.

Rich. Goldsburgh. **a* Substitute for Richard J. Stillwell.

Moses Griffing. Substitute for Stephen Stryker.

George Sagors. Substitute for Cornelius Emmans.

Jonah Raymond. Substitute for Steph. J. Vorhees.

John Torrey. Substitute for Samuel Emmans.

INDEX TO VOLUME I.

NOTE.—The names contained in the Appendices VI., VII., X., and XI., are not included in this Index.

C.

D.

E.

F.

G.

H.

M.

W.

Y.

Z.

www.ingramcontent.com/pod-product-compliance
Lightning Source LLC
LaVergne TN
LVHW020922110826
845150LV00004B/741

* 9 7 8 1 4 2 5 5 5 6 0 2 0 *